Administrative Law in Ireland

Administrative Law in Ireland

Ronald M. Stout

Institute of Public Administration

First published in 1985

by the Institute of Public Administration
57-61 Lansdowne Road, Dublin 4, Ireland

British Library Cataloguing in Publication Data

Stout, Ronald M.
Administrative law in Ireland.
1. Administrative law—Ireland
I. Title
344.1702'6   [LAW]

ISBN 0-906980-40-2

Design by Della Varilly
Typeset in 11/13 Baskerville and printed by Cahill Printers Limited, Dublin 3

To Elizabeth

Contents

10 Availability and Scope of Judicial Review   420

11 Further Modes of Oversight   476

Appendix 1   496

Preface

Since administrative law is concerned with the constitutionality and legality of determinations and actions of administrative bodies, it is of interest to legislators, jurists, lawyers, administrators and private individuals or organisations interacting in the myriad of citizen-to-government relationships characteristic of the modern administrative state. In view of these multiple interests, this book is intended for use by not only lawyers and law students, but also administrators and others outside the legal profession who deal frequently with regulatory agencies of government. The principal topics in administrative law texts which are oriented to law students and lawyers are covered, such as the constitutionality of delegation of discretionary administrative powers, liability of the state and administrators to suit, requirements of natural and constitutional justice in administrative actions and decision-making, and the nature and availability of judicial remedies and scope of judicial review. In addition, the scope and nature of the administrative discretionary rule-making, investigating, licensing and directing or ordering powers over persons and property and the extent to which their exercise is subject to the requirements of natural justice are dealt with as separate, albeit interrelated topics. The objective is to provide a perspective on administrative law pertinent to the multiple interests indicated above, despite an overlapping of subject at certain points. More detail is provided concerning the facts and the content of related judgments in the discussion of certain cases than is usual in a text or treatise, to give readers an appreciation of how and why a decision-making process or an action generated legal issues, and the reasoning of the court in resolving them. Comparative reference is made on occasion to English and American administrative law, and in a few instances, to the administrative court system of France, where such reference might enhance understanding of Irish administrative law and of alternative approaches to administrative law.

This approach reflects my experience of teaching undergraduate and graduate-level courses in administrative law and conducting sessions on the subject in training programmes for public administrators since 1946. The original impetus for a book on administrative law in Ireland came from my developing Irish case materials and legal concepts to parallel American cases and concepts already in hand for a course on administrative law given as a visiting lecturer at the School of Public Administration, of the Institute of Public Administration. The co-operation of Colum Gavan Duffy, then librarian of the Incorporated Law Society, in facilitating my search for Irish cases, and of Desmond Roche, then Principal, School of Public Administration, Institute of Public Administration in arranging for reproduction of case materials by his staff was most helpful in this regard. Irish administrative law came to be of increasing interest to me, especially since Ireland's constitutional-legal and governmental system within which its administrative law has developed, contains important elements of both the British and American systems of government. A sabbatical leave some years later enabled more extensive research on the subject, which was supplemented in subsequent trips to Ireland.

This book could not have been produced without the support of the Institute of Public Administration as provided by certain of its members, to whom I am most grateful. That support took the form of T. J. Barrington's active encouragement of the initiation and continuation of the project when he was Director of the Institute; James O'Donnell's arrangements for editorial assistance, and prodding to keep the project moving combined with forbearance when deadlines he set as Head of Publishing were not met; Sarah O'Hara's work in co-ordinating the editorial process from manuscript to proofs to book, complicated by the author's being on the other side of the Atlantic; and Mary Prendergast's help as librarian of the Institute in identifying and generously loaning library materials and arranging the purchase of books.

Brendan Kiernan, barrister-at-law and member of the European Commission on Human Rights, brought his breadth of experience and knowledge of law and administration in Ireland to bear in reading the original and revised manuscripts on behalf of the Institute, which I much appreciated. I am indebted to him for his cogent, valuable suggestions on technical legal and editorial matters, and his effort to prevent the gaffes and errors a person with an American administrative law perspective can make in writing about Irish administrative law. I also am grateful that the Institute obtained the services of Helen Litton to undertake preparation of the index.

The reviews made of the original manuscript by the Institute's readers were appreciated; their comments influenced the revision of the manuscript. I wish to thank Margaret Byrne, who succeeded Colum Gavan Duffy as librarian of the Incorporated Law Society of Ireland, for the courtesies extended and help given to facilitate use of the resources of the Society's law library. I also wish to state my appreciation to Maxine Mormon for her many hours of typing manuscript despite competing demands for her stenographic work at the Graduate School of Public Affairs, State University of New York at Albany.

Finally, I thank my wife, Elizabeth, who not only endured working 'vacations' at Cape Cod accompanied by typewriter and boxes of case materials, but also acted as editorial critic and proof reader at all stages, while providing supportive encouragement throughout the long process leading to completion of the project.

Table of Statutes

Table of Cases

1 The Nature of Administrative Law

The issue central to this study of administrative law in Ireland is how a balance may be maintained between securing administrative effectiveness in achieving the public interest while at the same time protecting the constitutional and legal rights of the individual.

With regard to this issue, three systems for providing administrative justice were identified in a report made by a working committee under the chairmanship of the then Chief Justice, Cearbhall Ó Dálaigh. In their 'Note on Administrative Law and Procedure', published as the first appendix of the *Report of Public Services Organisation Review Group, 1966-1969* (the 'Devlin Report', a major enquiry into public administration in Ireland), it was stated:

> Administrative legality is placed in the care of . . . a distinct system of administrative courts, independent of the ordinary courts . . . . France, Greece and Turkey are examples.
>
> Administrative institutions are established for specific cases but are not standardised. Examples are Ireland, United Kingdom, Finland, Sweden, West Germany and Portugal.
>
> Institutions and procedures are standardised under an Administrative Procedure Act. Examples are U.S., Spain, Norway, Austria and some east European countries. (page 450)

The analysis of the nature and development of administrative law in Ireland by the working committee emphasised the central issue by converting it into a broad objective of their proposals for reform:

> for some time to come, the course of advantage and convenience is to remain in the second of these three groups . . . . The main thrust of reform of our administration will, we assume, continue to be directed towards making it more effective . . . . The emphasis must be on speed of decision and response and on the promotion of the greatest good of the greatest number. But we believe that these aims can be, and should be, reconciled with the principle of fairness. We proceed therefore in what follows to indicate desirable standards of fairness and the

1

> means of attaining them. We draw on what is best in our present system as well as on developed systems elsewhere. (page 450)

The identification of different approaches to administrative justice, and reference to drawing on other developed systems as well as that of Ireland for reform, suggests that comparison of certain aspects of Irish administrative law with those of English and American administrative law in this study would enhance an understanding of the subject. Irish administrative law has developed within a system of government which has significant elements of the British, and some features of the American, governmental systems. For example, Ireland's bicameral parliament, cabinet government, civil service and legal system show strong British influences. However, Ireland also has governmental aspects typical of the United States such as a written constitution which asserts the sovereignty of the people, divides powers among three branches of government and enumerates personal and property rights. The power of the judiciary to declare legislative acts unconstitutional, which in the United States was established by the decision of the US Supreme Court in *Marbury v. Madison* 1 Cranch 137 (1803), is explicitly granted to the High and Supreme Courts by Ireland's Constitution. The effect of these dual influences can be seen in judgments of Irish courts on issues in administrative law which in many instances reflect English jurisprudence, but at times are more typical of those made in American administrative law. And while French administrative law does not have this type of influence, in Ireland some reference to its contrasting system may provide insights. In recent years, moreover, Irish courts have been referring cases to the European Court of Justice, the judgments of which have been influenced by the model of the higher French courts.[1]

Definition and Scope of Administrative Law

The difficulty of defining administrative law and determining its scope has been indicated by the English authority, Garner, when he stated in 1974:

> At the outset of the study of any branch of law, it is desirable

to endeavour to define and delimit the field of study; administrative law, or the law relating to the administration, however, defies almost any precise definition or limitation.[2]

This may explain why administrative law was still not recognised as a category of law in the *Irish Digest* for 1959/60 despite the publication in *The Irish Jurist* as early as 1935 of an article by George Gavan Duffy entitled 'Administrative Law: The Urgent Need for Systematisation and Publicity'.[3]

Garner's caveat is well taken since authorities on administrative law do present varied definitions and perspectives of its subject matter, and how it is to be organised, described and analysed in their publications. However, a review of publications dealing in whole or part with Irish, English, American and French administrative law (particularly those making some comparative analysis) also reveals that underlying the individual variations, the authors' definitions contain common elements. There is also a basic similarity in the choice of certain major topics of administrative law, and in the issues identified as pertaining to those topics.[4]

The common elements in the definitions of administrative law by the authorities reviewed may be expressed as a general or composite definition:

> Administrative law is the law found in constitutions, statutes and judicial decisions concerning the organisation, functions, and discretionary powers of administrative agencies, and the modes of legislative and judicial controls over the exercise of those discretionary powers. It also may be found in administrative rules, orders or directives, and in adjudicatory decisions of administrative agencies.

This definition both reflects and is conditioned by certain factors: (1) constitutional law and administrative law overlap in respect of certain basic issues and their resolution; (2) administrative law also involves certain issues and concepts contained in civil and criminal law; and (3) much of administrative law is judge-made law, even in France, where other major branches of law have been codified. The basic topics of administrative law, and the issues which are raised within these topics, as perceived by the authorities reviewed include:

B

1. The delegation of discretionary powers to administrative agencies. This leads to issues of the constitutionality of such delegation, particularly in respect of rule-making and adjudicatory powers.

2. The legal position of the state as sovereign, and of its agents (e.g. ministers, departments, state-sponsored bodies, local authorities) when they are sued by or are suing private individuals or organisations. This raises issues concerning the respective legal rights of the state and of the private parties in regard to such matters as contracts, torts, debts and executive privilege.

3. The scope and nature of adjudicatory power and procedures through which decisions are reached in the exercise of discretionary rule-making, investigating, licensing and directing powers and in the resolution of conflict between private parties. This leads to issues regarding compliance with the rights to fair notice and hearing; to be represented by a lawyer, to submit evidence on one's own behalf and to cross-examine witnesses; to discovery of documents and to a hearing officer free from bias and from performing conflicting roles. In addition the adjudicatory personnel must make findings of fact, draw conclusions according to legal principles, and give reasons for the determination made while being independent in function of the parties to the dispute.

4. The scope and nature of administrative rule-making power. This raises issues as to both the substance of regulations (e.g. are they *intra* or *ultra vires* the statute, reasonable or unreasonable) and the procedures by which regulations are made. A further question is that of the extent and means of the legislature's control over rule-making.

5. The scope and nature of the discretionary investigating, licensing and directing regulatory powers delegated by the legislature to administrative agencies so that they may implement and enforce compliance with standards established in statutes and in administrative regulations. The issues raised include those as to whether the action or determination taken is contrary to a constitutional right or to legislative intent, or

ultra vires the statute, i.e. in excess of jurisdiction, and whether requirements of natural and constitutional justice have been met in the process of applying those powers to individuals and organisations.

6. The scope and nature of the role and powers of the courts in reviewing administrative actions and determinations. The related issues involve the appropriate forms of judicial remedies and the grounds for granting them under judicial doctrines concerning the availability of judicial review, namely: *locus standi*, exhaustion of administrative remedies, timeliness for review and finality of administrative determinations. Assuming that the parties in litigation have met these conditions for judicial review, the remaining issues concern the scope and nature of judicial review of facts and law by the courts, particularly in respect of substitution of the court's judgment for that of the administrative agency regarding facts and law contained in the administrative determination.

It should be noted that among the authorities reviewed, some refer to additional topics but give them relatively limited treatment compared to the extensive attention given by others. For example, the informal administrative process in administrative law is noted in publications on English administrative law, but treated in detail primarily in American publications. English and French authorities tend to provide descriptive analyses at some length on the organisation, powers, and processes of governmental bodies (e.g. the legislature, prime minister, Conseil d'État, administrative tribunals, civil service, state-sponsored bodies and local authorities) as they relate to administrative law. American authors, on the other hand, tend to summarise the descriptive analyses of governmental or structural-functional aspects as introductory background in one chapter. They then concentrate on the conceptual aspects of legal issues in the exercise of administrative discretionary powers and their resolution by the judiciary, without emphasis upon whether a department of central government or an independent body or a state or local authority is involved unless the unique characteristics of the authority are critical to an understanding of the issue.

The Growth of Administrative Law

A characteristic of administrative law has been its rapid growth as a field of law and its tendency to pervade the interests of persons and organisations. This growth is manifested by the proliferation of governmental schemes in legislative Acts which give powers (frequently of a discretionary character) to administrative bodies to make rules establishing explicit details of the schemes and to apply Acts and rules in granting benefits to or controlling the activities of persons so as to achieve the purposes specified in the authorising statutes. Other indicators of growth are the constantly increasing number of administrative rules and determinations through which grants are made, or controls are exercised through licensing and directing systems, the numbers of appeals to higher administrative authorities from lower-level determinations, and the increase in the number of judicial decisions reviewing administrative determinations. An idea of the extent of this growth may be obtained from the account given in Appendix I of examples of administrative law functions of ministers and their departments, administrative tribunals and licensing boards and of statistics of appeals to administrative appellate bodies.

Reasons for Growth of Administrative Law

The reasons for the growth of administrative law may be found in social, economic and technological developments and trends typical of modern societies. These demand responses from government exceeding the capacity of traditional institutions, and lead to what has been termed the 'administrative state'. This is typified by an early statement made in 1935 by George Gavan Duffy (later Judge Gavan Duffy):

> The modern theory of government in the Irish Free State means the definite and, no doubt, permanent rejection of the British Victorian principle of *laissez-faire*. The recognised duty of the State is now to watch over the well-being of its citizens and the duty involves considerable interference in the day to day affairs of life. Hence we have, side by side with the statutes, a growing mass of departmental law. . . Paternal government has come to stay, and to be effective it must mean the devolution

of very wide powers of control to be exercised in practice by the expert chiefs of the principal Government services.[5]

The urbanisation, industrialisation, and technological developments present in modern societies have created socio-economic problems to which government must respond. These problems grow out of the inability of individuals and of organisations to protect themselves from the adverse social, economic and physical effects of such developments which may occur when a society's economic resources are allocated through competition in the market place free from any restraint and when individuals in entrepreneurial, professional and other private occupational groups are subject only to the types of controls traditionally exercised by the legislature, executive and courts. Individuals injured in industrial accidents or made ill by food and drugs sold in the absence of governmental requirements, or persons made redundant owing to a change in technology often are unable to safeguard themselves through personal preventive action. Nor can they obtain meaningful remedies in most instances through civil law suits for damages or criminal law punishment as retribution for injuries suffered. A labour strike can have disastrous effects on a wide range of individuals and organisations with little relief in existing civil law remedies. Unrestrained land use and development can result in permanent adverse effects upon large numbers of individuals, groups and even local authorities, for which monetary awards in civil suit or criminal law penalties cannot compensate adequately, since the most effective response is to prevent the initiation or stop the continuation of land use contrary to larger public interests.

The difficulties which traditional governmental institutions and processes have in meeting these problems arise from various factors. The legislature's capacity to enact specific standards in its Acts is limited by: (1) lack of technical knowledge in certain areas necessary to specify detailed standards; (2) inability to adjust existing Acts quickly enough to the frequent changes in various areas constituting the subject of legislation to avoid inadequacy or obsolescence; and (3) political considerations involved in adopting detailed statutes which generate adverse pressures from interest groups and unfavourable reaction from constituents in elections. The long-established executive branch law enforcement processes of police and prosecutors tend to follow a punitive rather than preventive approach by investigation after complaint, arrest and prosecution following the violation of law. The courts are essentially waiting tribunals with expertise in the interpretation and application of law to facts in the resolution of conflict situations, but they are not responsible for initiating action to achieve statutory purposes. They also are limited in terms of the volume of business they can deal with and the rapidity with which they can transact it through their formal processes, and court actions also can be costly.

Such factors leading to the growth of administrative law have been recognised and documented in governmental enquiries and studies, as well as by the authorities on administrative law. In the 'Note on Administrative Law and Procedure' of the Devlin Report, it was stated that the reasons for the growth of administrative tribunals in Ireland may be attributed to the formal processes and expense of litigation in court which may be out of proportion to issues such as a small pension increase. Certain types of issue can be understood more quickly with greater understanding by expert administrative adjudicators. Moreover, in some situations, the issue involved goes beyond an individual grievance and entails a clash between public and private interests, which raises questions of policy as well as of fact, as in compulsory land acquisition.[6] The report of the United States Attorney General's Committee on Administrative Procedure in Government Agencies (1941) advanced the following reasons for the growth of administrative law: the advantages of administrative over political executive action; constitutional limits on the powers of courts; the trend towards preventive legislation; the limitations on effective legislative action and on exclusively judicial enforcement; the advantage of continuity of attention and clear responsibility and the need for organisation to handle the volume of business.[7]

The Rule of Law and Administrative Law

As noted above, there are common elements in publications of authorities on administrative law regarding its definition, major topics, related issues and reasons for its growth. Consequently, an underlying accord might be expected as to the overall issue of administrative law stated at the outset of this chapter. This is illustrated by the 'Note on Administrative Law' of the Devlin Report quoting a corroborating statement from the British Franks Committee Report on Administrative Tribunals and Enquiries:

It is recognised that the main difficulty in prescribing rules of procedure in adjudicatory proceedings is to maintain a balance between ease and efficiency of administration on one side and, on the other, the protection of individual rights. As the Franks Report puts it: "Administration must be not only efficient in the sense that the objectives of policy are securely attained without delay. It must also satisfy the general body of citizens that it is proceeding with reasonable regard to the balance between the public interest which it promotes and the private interest which it disturbs." (page 454)[8]

The literature on administrative law frequently associates a major concern of the objectives delineated in the above statement with a more general concept, namely, the need to maintain what is called 'the rule of law' in the face of the nature and growth of administrative law. The term has its complexities, as Griffith and Street indicate, and describe five different meanings.[9] Wade discusses four meanings of the rule of law which include the concepts that every act of government must be authorised by law; that government must be carried out under rules and principles restricting discretionary power; that conflicts over legality of governmental acts be decided by an independent judiciary; and that while government must have a range of powers unique or special to government, it does not have exemptions from the law which are unnecessary.[10]

Wade's fourth meaning in particular would seem to relate to Davis's criticism of an 'extravagant version' of the rule of law which would oppose, and try to protect against, all discretionary power. In his view, the rule of law should mean not to 'try to eliminate *all* discretion; we should try to eliminate *unnecessary* discretion'. Given the need for discretionary administrative powers, and the fact that they will continue to grow in the twentieth century:

We should adopt a sound meaning of the rule of law — that discretionary power should be eliminated or controlled to whatever extent it can be eliminated or controlled without undue sacrifice of other values that we may deem more important.[11]

It should be recognised that the concern with balancing administrative efficiency and legal rights and, more generally, maintaining the rule of law has appeared not only in publications by academic authorities but also in government-sponsored enquiries and studies, such as Ireland's Devlin Report, Law Reform Commission Working Paper No.8, and Report of the All-Party Informal Committee on Administrative Justice, the British Donoughmore, Franks Committee and Whyatt Reports, and the American President's Committee on Administrative Management, Attorney General's Committee on Administrative Procedure, Hoover Commission, Landis and Ash Council reports.[12] Although they differ in their particular scope and method, they deal in various ways with those overall concerns. The British studies led to reform such as the Statutory Instruments Act 1946, the Crown Proceedings Act 1947, the Tribunals and Inquiry Act 1958, the Parliamentary Commissoner Act 1967 and the Tribunals and Inquiries Act 1971.

In the United States, the Administrative Procedure Act 1946 as amended, and the Administrative Conference Act 1964, and in Ireland, the Local Government (Planning and Development) Acts 1976-83 amending the original 1963 Act, and the Ombudsman Act 1980, reflect concepts of certain of the reports made in the United States and Ireland.

Given this common concern for combining administrative effectiveness and the protection of legal rights, as an underlying theme, the component elements of Irish administrative law will be analysed in the following manner. First, since the specific issues of administrative law are affected by the nature of the governmental system of a particular country, chapter 2 will delineate briefly the principal constitutional, political and administrative aspects of the Irish governmental system which provide the context in which Irish administrative law operates, noting, where relevant, comparative aspects of the English, American and French governmental systems. This frame of reference constituting the parameters for Irish administrative law and process will be continued in chapter 3, in which leading judicial decisions resolving interrelated issues stemming from the Irish constitutional arrangements will be considered. Such issues include those pertaining to the delegation and control by the Oireachtas of rule-making power to administrative agencies, the nature of executive power and the extent to which executive policy making and execution of policy is subject to limitations imposed by judicial review. Further issues are the independence of the judiciary, the scope and nature of judicial power and the extent to which it may be delegated to administrative agencies, together with the nature of judicial remedies and grounds for granting such remedies, as integral elements of the judicial power. The concluding aspect of this frame of reference is the relationship of the citizen to the sovereign state in litigation, when the state is plaintiff or defendant in actions such as suits in contract, for debts, or torts, which will be dealt with in chapter 4.

Subsequent chapters cover major aspects of administrative law and process in operation, the main concern of this study. Chapter 5 will deal with the legal issues based on the requirements of 'natural justice' and 'constitutional justice' which are raised in challenges to the exercise of administrative discretionary powers. Typically these issues deal with whether an adjudicative trial-type hearing as against a legislative argument-type hearing is required; what constitutes a fair notice and hearing; who may participate in a hearing; the independence of the hearing officer and absence of bias; the right to discovery of documents; the nature of the evidence that may be admitted and its sufficiency to support findings. Also involved are the problems of substitution of hearing officers, official notice of matters not in the record, and the requirements and availability of findings and reasons.

Given this understanding of the statutory and judicial require-ments of natural and constitutional justice applicable to the exercise of discretionary regulatory powers, an analysis is made in chapter 6 of the rule-making power and in chapter 7 of the investigatory power. Chapter 8 discusses the licensing power and chapter 9 the directing power delegated to and exercised by administrative agencies. The emphasis throughout the analysis is upon the distin-guishing characteristics of each of these powers as modes of adminis-trative control for achieving statutory purposes, together with the legal issues raised by the application of these powers and the requirements of natural and constitutional justice imposed by the courts on agencies exercising these powers.

The final issues are those concerned with holding administrative agencies accountable. The availability of judicial review involving questions as to administrative finality, standing of parties to secure review, exhaustion of administrative remedies and ripeness for review as well as the scope of judicial review once it is granted are discussed in chapter 10 while proposals for change and reform are considered in chapter 11.

The approach to administrative law in Ireland summarised above is essentially generic, concentrating on the nature of discretionary administrative powers exercised by administrative agencies, and the constraints placed upon them, regardless of the type of agency or level of government involved. From the perspective of this approach, for example, the power under statutory authority to set standards for a licence, to investigate the degree of compliance by an applicant, and to decide to grant, refuse, or revoke a licence following due notice and hearing, has common characteristics in terms of issues raised and processes involved, whether that power is exercised by a government department, a local authority or a professional association.

These common characteristics of power and process are the critical matters of concern to private parties, administrators, the legal profession and courts, while details of organisation, level of government or category of agency are significant only as they may affect tangentially the exercise of discretionary powers. Consequently, the description of structural-functional aspects of the governmental system, the organisation, functions, powers and process of departments, state-sponsored bodies, local authorities and administrative tribunals (to which some administrative law texts devote several chapters) is limited to a summary exposition, which includes brief comparative aspects of other countries, in chapter 2. This will provide a general overview, together with reference to literature containing descriptive or analytical details concerning structural-functional characteristics of Ireland's government while the remaining chapters will concentrate upon the generic aspects of administrative law in Ireland.

Notes to Chapter I

1. Brown and Jacobs, *The Court of Justice of the European Communities* (1977) 230, and generally 229-36
2. Garner, *Administrative Law* 1 (1974)
3. *Irish Jurist* 34-6 (Vol. 5, August 1935)
4. See as examples of publications on administrative law:

    Irish Law
    Asmal, 'Administrative Law in Ireland' in *Survey of Public Administration and Administrative Law in Ireland* 71-8, Extract from *International Review of Administrative Sciences* (Vol. 34, 1968)
    Donaldson, *Some Comparative Aspects of Irish Law* 183-228 (1957)

Grogan, *Administrative Tribunals in the Public Service* (1961)
Kelly, *Fundamental Rights in the Irish Law and Constitution* 280-349 (1968); 'Administrative Discretion and the Courts' *The Irish Jurist* 209-221 (Vol. 1, Winter 1966); 'Judicial Review of Administrative Action: New Irish Trends' *The Irish Jurist*, 40-49 Vol. 6 (1971
King, 'Administrative Law', *Irish Law Times* Parts 1-4 at 155-6; 161-4; 167-9; 171-4 (1951)
O'Sullivan, *Irish Planning and Acquisition Law* (1978); O'Sullivan and Shepherd, *A Sourcebook on Planning Law in Ireland* (1984)

British Law
de Smith, *Judicial Review of Administrative Action* (1980)
Garner, *Administrative Law* (1979)
Wade, *Administrative Law* (1982)
Schwartz and Wade, *Legal Control of Government* (1972) (comparative British and American administrative law)

American Law
Barry and Whitcomb, *The Legal Foundations of Public Administration* (1981)
Carter, *Administrative Law and Politics: Cases and Comments* (1983)
Cooper, *Public Law and Public Administration* (1983)
Davis, *Administrative Law Treatise*, Vols. 1-4 (1979-1984); *Administrative Law, Cases, Text, Problems* (1977)
Gellhorn, Byse and Strauss *Administrative Law, Cases and Comments* (1979)
Warren, *Administrative Law in the American Political System* (1982)

French Law
Brown and Garner, *French Administrative Law* (1983)
David, *French Law, Its Structure, Sources and Methodology* (1972), especially at 76-92; 93-107; 122-143;
Freedeman, *The Conseil d'État in Modern France* (1961)
Schwartz, *French Administrative Law and the Common Law World* (1954)

5. Gavan Duffy, 'Administrative Law: The Urgent Need for Systematisation and Publicity' *Irish Jurist* 34 (Vol.5, 1935); See also comparable statements on the growth of the 'administrative state' in Wade, *Administrative Law* 4-5 (1982)
6. *Report of Public Services Organisations Review Group* (Devlin Report) 448-49
7. Attorney General's Committee on Administrative Procedure, Final Report, *Administrative Procedure in Government Agencies* Senate Document No. 8, 77th Congress, 1st Session, 11-18 (1941). For statements on socio-economic reasons for the growth of the administrative state including limitations of traditional branches of government, see Wade, *Administrative Law* 3-4, Griffith and Street, *Principles of Administrative Law* 1-2, Gellhorn, Byse and Strauss, *Administrative Law*, 2-18, Jaffe and Nathanson, *Administrative Law* 1-12 (1976)
8. For similar statements, see quotation from Professor Fessler, interview reported in 'Administrative Justice in the USA' *Léargas* 4 (September-October 1974) Brown and Garner, *French Administrative Law*, 1-2
9. Griffith and Street, *Principles* 18-22
10. Wade, *Administrative Law* 22-24
11. Davis, *Administrative Law, Cases* 28
12. *Irish Studies*
Report of Public Service Organisation Review Group, 1966-1969, Appendix 1, 'Note

on Administrative Law and Procedures', 447-58
The Law Reform Commission, Working Paper No. 8, 'Judicial Review of
Administrative Action: The Problem of Remedies' (1979)
Report of the All-Party Informal Committee on Administrative Justice (1977)

British Studies
Report of the Committee on Ministers' Powers, Cmd. 4060 (1932) (Donoughmore
Report)
Report of the Committee on Administrative Tribunals and Enquiries, Cmnd 218 (1957)
(Franks Committee)
The Citizen and the Administration (*Justice*, 1961) (the Whyatt Report, an
unofficial report)

United States Studies
President's Committee on Administrative Management, *Report with Special
Studies* (1937);
Attorney General's Committee on Administrative Procedure, Final Report,
Administrative Procedure in Government Agencies, Senate Document No. 8, 77th
Congress, 1st Session, (1941)
Commission on Organisation of the Executive Branch of the Government,
(1947-1949) (1st Hoover Commission Report) especially its *Task Force Report
on Regulatory Commissions)*
Commission on Organization of the Executive Branch of Government (1953-
55) *Task Force Report on Legal Services and Procedures* (2nd Hoover Commission
Report)
Report on the Regulatory Agencies to the President Elect Senate Committee on the
Judiciary; 86th Congress, 2nd Sess (Comm. Print 1960) (Landis Report)
President's Advisory Council on Executive Organization, *A New Regulatory
Framework: Report on Selected Independent Agencies* (January 1971) Ash Council
Report)

2 The Governmental Context

The constitutional concepts, the institutions and the administrative characteristics of the Irish public sector condition the nature of its administrative law and processes. They also have major elements of the British and certain features of the American systems of government which contribute to the comparative aspects of interest in Ireland's administrative law. In contrast, France's administrative law represents a major alternative to that of the three common-law countries. Consequently, in the following summary description of Ireland's governmental system, reference is made to certain comparative aspects of the governments of Britain, the United States and France. Among such aspects are constitutional provisions as to where sovereignty lies, the definition, allocation and degree of separation of legislative, executive and judicial powers and guarantees of individual rights. These are critical factors in the resolution of such administrative law issues as the right of the citizen to sue the government and its officers, the delegation to and manner in which rule-making and adjudicatory powers are exercised by administrative bodies, and the ways in which the protection of legal rights and interests of individuals are balanced against the public interest.

Constitutional Concepts and Institutions: Ireland

Irish administrative law was developing before and during the periods of the Constitution of Dáil Éireann of 1919 and the Constitution of the Irish Free State of 1922. The Irish Free State government was patterned essentially after that of British cabinet government with collective and individual responsibility of ministers, and the civil service and court system reflected their counterparts in Britain. Although certain provisions for referendum, initiative, and extern ministers were designed to prevent a strong cabinet with majority party support from controlling both the Dáil and Seanad and to increase popular and parliamentary control, they either were removed or became inoperative by 1926.[1] The 1922 Constitution permitted amendment by simple majority of both Houses of the Oireachtas up to 1930, and the Oireachtas by amend-

15

ment extended this eight-year limit indefinitely.[2] However, the 1937 Constitution did involve a revision which, in Chubb's opinion:

> involved first, the removal from the Irish Free State Constitution of all signs and symbols of Commonwealth status, and then, the construction of an entirely new constitution 'unquestionably indigenous in character'. This constitution would stress the republican and popular nature of the state, superseding the Commonwealth concepts entirely.[3]

In respect of the republican and popular nature of the state, the preamble of the 1937 Constitution states that 'We the people of Eire . . . do hereby adopt, enact and give to ourself this constitution', and the sovereignty of the people is reinforced by article 6.1 which provides that the people are the final source of governmental powers:

> All powers of government, legislative, executive and judicial, derive, under God, from the people, whose right it is to designate the rulers of the State, and, in final appeal, to decide all questions of national policy, according to the requirements of the common good.

Fundamental rights of the individual are provided for in articles 40 to 44, including such substantive rights as equality before the law, freedom of expression, assembly and association, private property rights and rights associated with family and religious freedom, and procedural rights implied under personal rights and liberty, habeas corpus and inviolability of the dwelling. A further symbol of republican as against British Commonwealth status noted by Chubb is in the provision in article 12 for the election of a President, who may not be a member of either House of the Oireachtas. In the words of the architect of the 1937 Constitution, Eamon de Valera, the President 'is there to guard the people's rights and mainly to guard the Constitution' through certain powers given to him and 'in exercising these powers he is acting on behalf of the people who have put him there for that special purpose'.[4]

The 1937 Constitution may not be amended by Act of the Oireachtas alone, since every proposal for an amendment under article 46.2 must be initiated in the Dáil as a bill, and upon passage by both Houses, must be submitted on referendum for decision by the electorate in accordance with the law in force relating to the referendum. The bill may not contain any other matter, and must be signed by the President upon his being satisfied that the provisions for amendment have been complied with, and the proposal duly approved by the people through a majority of the votes cast on such referendum, according to articles 46.4-.5 and 47.1.

The 1937 Constitution retained the unitary structure of government in Ireland since the national government is the source of authority for all power exercised or functions performed by local authorities or other sub-systems of government, as may be inferred from articles 1, 2, 3 and 6. It also expresses the concept of the division or (as it is increasingly referred to in Irish publications on government) the separation of powers between branches of government.[5] Article 6 classifies the powers as 'legislative, executive and judicial', and this division or separation of powers is amplified in article 15.2 which states that 'the sole and exclusive power of making laws' is given to the Oireachtas; in article 28.2 which provides that 'the executive power of the State shall . . . be exercised by or on the authority of the government'; and in article 34.1 which states that 'justice shall be administered in courts established by law by judges appointed in the manner provided by this constitution'. After providing for appointment of judges by the President on the advice of the government in articles 35.1 and 13.9, the Constitution protects the independence of judges in article 35 by prohibiting removal of a Supreme or High Court judge by the President save for stated misbehaviour or incapacity, on resolution of the Houses of the Oireachtas and due notice by the Taoiseach (the Prime Minister) to the President of such resolution, and prohibiting the reduction in remuneration of a judge while in office. Original jurisdiction is given to the High Court by article 34.3(2) over questions on the validity of any law in relation to provisions of the Constitution, and article 34.4(4) states that no law shall be enacted which would except cases involving questions of the constitutionality of a law from the appellate jurisdiction of the Supreme Court. This clearly gives the High and Supreme Courts jurisdiction over cases originating under article 15.4(1) which provides that the Oireachtas 'shall not enact any law which is in any respect repugnant to this Constitution or any provision thereof'.

However, the concept of separation of powers (which is emphasised in respect of the independence of the judiciary and its power of judicial review) is qualified and modified in various degrees with regard to the nature of the powers and relationships of the executive and legislative branches. As previously mentioned, although the President is directly elected, and prohibited from membership of the Houses of the Oireachtas, his functions such as appointing the Taoiseach must follow nomination by the Dáil and his appointment of other members of the government are made after the Taoiseach's nomination with prior Dáil approval. Other functions such as signing Oireachtas bills into law, command of the defence forces and granting of pardons and commutations under article 13.1 are conditioned by article 13.9 which provides that his powers may be exercised only on advice of the government unless otherwise specified by the Constitution.

The President does have four discretionary powers. Under article 26.1 he may refer any bill other than a money bill or proposed constitutional amendment to the Supreme Court for a decision on the bill's constitutionality. Article 27 provides that if a majority of the Seanad and one third of the Dáil jointly petition the President not to sign a bill on the ground that it is of such national importance that the people's will should be ascertained, he may refuse to sign the bill until it is approved on popular referendum (or by a newly constituted Dáil after dissolution of the Dáil and a general election). The President may, under article 13.2, convene a meeting of either or both Houses of the Oireachtas. Finally, under article 28.10 a Taoiseach must resign from office when he ceases to retain support of a majority in the Dáil, unless on his advice the President dissolves the Dáil. However, the President under article 13.2 may 'in his absolute discretion refuse' to dissolve the Dáil, which means that the Taoiseach must resign, giving the Dáil the opportunity to nominate a successor. In exercising the first three discretionary powers, the President is obliged to consult (but not necessarily accept the advice of) the Council of State: a body composed of up to seven incumbent and former office holders or others the President chooses to appoint. Thus, in some situations, certain presidential powers, as Chubb states, 'are politically important and their exercise might involve him in controversy, the more so since they are to be exercised precisely at periods of political disagreement or crisis'.[6] However, it is the Taoiseach who is designated as head of the government in article 28.5. The Taoiseach nominates the Tánaiste and other members of the government for approval by the Dáil and the President appoints them. The Taoiseach and other members of the government must be members of the Oireachtas subject to the Taoiseach, Tánaiste and Minister for Finance being members of the Dáil, and no more than two of the maximum fifteen in the government being members of the Seanad. (See article 28.5-7; 13.1.)

The government meets and acts as a collective authority responsible for the departments of state administered by the members of the government, and prepares the budget for presentation to the Dáil, as provided in article 28.4. The Dáil may not enact a revenue appropriation unless its purpose has been recommended by a message from the government signed by the Taoiseach, under article 17.2; money bills may be initiated only in the Dáil and sent to the Seanad for its recommendation according to article 21. As previously noted, under article 28.10 the Taoiseach must resign from office upon ceasing to retain the support of a majority in the Dáil, unless on his advice the President dissolves the Dáil, and then on the reassembly of the Dáil the Taoiseach secures the support of the majority in the new Dáil. The resignation of a Taoiseach also means that the other members of the government have resigned under article 28.11; however, the Taoiseach and other government members continue in their duties until their successors are appointed, as also is the case if the Dáil is dissolved.

The Taoiseach has been characterised as the spokesman for the government on important policy issues and the coordinator of departments, resolving conflicts so as to carry out the plans of the government. He answers questions in the Dáil on key policy matters. His coordinating role is also present in the legislative process, since he develops through his Minister of State a comprehensive parliamentary programme which integrates the proposals originating in the various ministries.[7]

The Houses of the Oireachtas consist of Dáil Éireann, with 166 members called Teachtaí Dála (TDs) elected from 41 constituencies of 20,000 to 30,000 population and Seanad Éireann with 60 members (11 nominated by the Taoiseach, 6 elected by the universities and 43 from five panels of candidates from broad occupational groupings). The Dáil and Seanad have similar powers in respect of representation on the Council of State, removal of the President, the Comptroller and Auditor General and judges of the Supreme or High Court, the declaration and termination of a state of emergency, initiation of bills other than money bills originating in the Dáil, and annulment of statutory instruments.[8] However, the Dáil clearly has greater powers than the Seanad. Article 28.4 of the Constitution states that the government shall be responsible to Dáil Éireann, that the government shall be collectively responsible for the departments of state administered by members of the government and will prepare estimates of receipts and expenditure of the state for each financial year and present them to the Dáil for its consideration. The Dáil's role in the nomination of the Taoiseach, and approval of his nomination of government members was previously mentioned; in addition, the Dáil must approve international agreements causing charges on public funds, or to be part of domestic law and a declaration of war under articles 29.5-6 and 28.3(1). The ultimate power behind these provisions is the withdrawal of support of a majority in the Dáil, leading to resignation by the Taoiseach and a general election.

The Oireachtas has the exclusive power to legislate under the Constitution, including the extraordinary power provided in article 28.3(3) that 'nothing in this constitution shall be invoked to invalidate any law enacted by the Oireachtas . . . for the purpose of securing the public safety and the preservation of the State in time of war or armed rebellion . . .' However, in practice, its role is limited, in regard to initiating, formulating or modifying the content of bills proposed by the government for its consideration and enactment. In this respect Chubb quotes a statement from a 1980 Fine Gael policy document on reform of the Dáil that 'under the Constitution the Oireachtas has the "sole and exclusive power of making laws for the state"'. Nonetheless in practice it plays practically no effective part in either making the laws or significantly changing them. Chubb's own evaluation is that:

> The government has an almost exclusive initiative in proposing measures. With the assured, stable support of the party majority in the Dáil, and almost always in the Seanad too, the government controls the passage of business through the two houses. Its proposals are usually endorsed by the Oireachtas with few changes[9].

O'Donnell characterises the law-making process in similar terms:

> what happens in practice is that the members of the party or coalition of parties that have won the general election leave the

formulation of policy to their leaders, now the government, and by giving them their support in the Oireachtas secure the implementation of these policies . . . . it is the government who decide what measures will be introduced, when and for how long they will be debated, what will be voted upon and what conceded; and it is the members of the government who assume the task of conducting business through the Dáil.[10]

A potentially important part of the policy-making process in legislatures is the role and use made of legislative committees and the parliamentary question. Until recently, committees of the Dáil and Seanad were limited to those dealing with internal organisation and procedures (e.g. Dáil and Seanad Committees on Procedure and Privileges, Joint Services Committee) and a few oversight Committees such as the Seanad Committee on Statutory Instruments, the Dáil Committees on Public Accounts and the Joint Committee on Secondary Legislation of the European Communities. With the appointment of a Joint Committee on Commercial State-Sponsored Bodies in 1978, a more activist role was undertaken, in Chubb's opinion, in terms of the Committee's having a professional staff and engaging in evaluation of and commentary on the performance of such bodies, based on review of the policy briefs of the state-sponsored bodies.[11] A number of ad hoc committees on special topics were established in 1983, such as the Joint Committees on Building Land, on Cooperation with Developing Countries, on Small Businesses, and on Marriage Breakdown and on Women's Rights, as well as a Dáil Committee on Crime, Lawlessness and Vandalism. Ad hoc committees make inquiries and have concluded their remit (and cease to exist) when they have given reports on their particular subject matter to the Oireachtas. They are not permanent committees regularly receiving, evaluating and proposing modifications or alternatives to policy initiatives from the government. The permanent committees established in 1983 include the Dáil Committee on Public Expenditure and the Joint Committee on Legislation.

The parliamentary question involves the right of the member of the Dáil to address questions in writing to members of the government concerning public affairs or administrative matters concerning their departments, usually on three day's notice; these are answered at certain hours on designated days. This again essentially is a form of legislative oversight. On balance, however, despite the dominant powers of the government in the policy-making process, it still must obtain the consent of the Houses of the Oireachtas. This makes the views of the members of the legislature, especially those of the party in power, important to the government, and in addition, the Oireachtas is the major institution for public debate and discussion of public policy.

Constitutional Concepts and Institutions: Britain and United States

The above constitutional provisions for the allocation and separation of powers among the major institutions of Ireland's government are both similar and dissimilar to those of Britain and the United States. An initial major difference lies in the fact that Ireland and the United States have written constitutions adopted by the electorate in Ireland, and in the US by state conventions the voters elected for that one purpose. Britain has an 'unwritten' constitution. Bunreacht na hÉireann is similar to the United States Constitution in providing for the republican and popular nature of the state. This is expressed in both of their preambles which contain the concept of sovereignty resting in the people, and in their constitutional provisions requiring that proposals for amendment made by the legislature be approved on referendum by the electorate in Ireland, and by three quarters of the legislatures, or conventions elected by the voters of the state for that purpose in the United States. In Britain, as Garner has noted, 'because the Constitution is part of the "ordinary law" ', the Constitution can be changed by an Act of Parliament in the same way that any other law may be enacted by Parliament.[12] Thus, fundamental rights of the individual have the protection of being expressed in the Irish Constitution and in the Bill of Rights of the American Constitution and are not subject to repeal by the legislature, while legally, if not politically, the English Habeas Corpus Act 1679, the Bill of Rights 1689, and the Act of Settlement 1700 could be changed simply by an Act of Parliament.[13]

On the other hand, Ireland's unitary system of government is like that of Britain's, in contrast to the American federal system. As in Ireland, Britain's parliament is the ultimate source of legislation which grants powers and functions to not only the national, but also local, governments. This contrasts with the American system in which the Constitution grants explicitly enumerated powers to the national government, and reserved powers (often referred to as 'police powers' over public health, safety, morals and convenience) to the states. Each state has its own constitution, governor, legislature, courts and local governments with consequent divergences in legislation and jurisprudence, including in their administrative law. Local governments are creatures of the state, so that the constitutional relationship is unitary between state and local governments, like that of Ireland's national government to its local authorities.

In comparison with Britain and the United States, Ireland's constitutional allocation and 'separation' of powers between its major institutions of government would appear to be positioned between, or constitute a blend of, the dominant patterns in the other two countries. As indicated previously, the model of the cabinet form of government in Ireland is the British cabinet system of government, typified by the prime minister and cabinet, who are members of Parliament, the concept of ministerial responsibility, the use of the parliamentary question and the ultimate power of Parliament through a vote of no confidence to bring down a government with a subsequent general election. Although the separation of powers between the executive and the legislative branches of government provided for in Ireland's Constitution obviously goes beyond that of Britain, it does not begin to approximate to that of the separation of powers, complete with checks and balances, characteristic of the relations between the legislative and executive branches provided for in articles I and II of the United States Constitution. These include a President elected for four years, whose powers require him to perform the combined roles of prime minister and constitutional head of state, since they encompass his being Commander-in-Chief, making treaties, recommending proposals for legislation and the national budget for consideration by Congress, appointing a considerable number of high-ranking officers of the government and their principal subordinates, appointing ambassadors and the judiciary, vetoing Acts of Congress to which he has policy or constitutional objections and granting pardons. However, neither the President nor members of his cabinet may be members of the Congress which is composed of a House of Representatives elected every second year and a Senate of two members from each state, one third of whom stand for election every second year. Congress can and does override presidential vetoes by extraordinary majorities, revises, modifies or substitutes its own version of budgetary and legislative measures which the President has proposed, and originates its own bills. Presidential appointments and treaties are subject to approval by the Senate. In a constitutional crisis, the House of Representatives has the ultimate power to impeach and the Senate, presided over by the Chief Justice of the Supreme Court, the power to try the President.

Ireland's constitutional provisions pertaining to the judiciary and judicial power are similar to those of the United States rather than those of Britain. Given the fact of sovereignty resting in Parliament and parliamentary supremacy, the British judiciary does not have the power to declare an Act of Parliament unconstitutional. In the United States, the Supreme Court through interpretation of provisions of its written Constitution, asserted the power of the Court to declare Acts of Congress and of state legislatures unconstitutional in the landmark cases of *Marbury v. Madison* 1 Cranch 137, 2 L.Ed 60 (1803) and *McCulloch v. Maryland* 4 Wheat. 316, 4 L. Ed. 579 (1819). In Ireland, in addition to safeguarding the independence of its judiciary, the 1937 Constitution explicitly provides for the power of the High Court, and the Supreme Court on appeal, to declare Acts of the Oireachtas unconstitutional; it also gives power to the President to submit a bill to the Irish Supreme Court for determination as to its constitutionality. This grants a further power of judicial review which the American Supreme Court, despite its activism, would not exercise since it would be perceived as rendering an 'advisory opinion' which the Supreme Court has refused to do.

The above constitutional factors of the three countries are primary influences on the nature and operation of their administrative law. However, their informal political processes and administrative institutions reflect and also contribute to the formal constitutional influences. In Ireland and Britain, there is normally strong party discipline and control by the prime minister and cabinet over formulation, enactment and implementation of policy, supported by the tradition of ministerial responsibility and the non-political professional nature of the civil service. This contrasts with the comparatively weaker party discipline, particularly at the national level in the United States owing to the federal system, separation

of powers and checks and balances in executive to legislative relationships. This has facilitated the capacity of Congress through its
powerful committees and sub-committees, with their ample research
staffs, to compete with the President in policy-making and oversight
of executive agencies' implementation of policy. For example,
although the power of the President to remove heads of departments
at will was upheld in *Myers v the United States* 272 US 52 (1926),
Congress has established independent regulatory commissions with
powers over important sectors of the economy and administrative
law, whose commissioners may not be removed by the President on
the grounds that their policies are in conflict with his policies. The
only grounds for their removal are those provided by statute, namely
incompetence, malfeasance or neglect of duty in office, upheld in
Humphrey's Executor v. the United States 195 US 602 (1935).

Commentary at this point on the influence of Ireland's constitutional concepts and institutions on administrative law would be
redundant in that these aspects are treated in detail in subsequent
chapters. However, since Ireland's administrative law (like its
constitutional aspects) has characteristics of both British and
American administrative law, examples of certain overall effects
which the British and American constitutional concepts have upon
their administrative law is relevant for later comparative reference.
Among those effects is the scope of judicial review of administrative
determinations. Judicial doctrine in both countries requires that
there must be statutory authority for any action of an administrative
agency which adversely affects the rights or interests of individuals,
and the courts may hold a regulation or action taken by an agency
to be *ultra vires* a statute no matter how wise or socially desirable it
may be. However, British courts are conditioned by the fact that,
as Garner states, 'even the House of Lords, the highest Court of
Law in the country, cannot refuse to enforce an act of Parliament,
on the grounds that it is "unconstitutional".'[14] Although English
courts may construe the meaning of a statute and apply its provisions in a particular manner in specific cases, they may not ignore
those provisions.[15] In the United States, judicial review may include
not only construction of statutes as applied to administrative
actions, but also judicial determinations that such statutes and thus
the actions based upon them are unconstitutional and therefore
invalid.

In their comparative study of administrative law in Britain and the United States, Schwartz and Wade point out that American administrative law has reflected a more legalistic emphasis, stressing procedural aspects, in which the American judges have exercised a wider scope of judicial review than have British judges. Based upon the American Constitution's due process of law amendments (fifth and fourteenth), American courts have developed judicial doctrines of procedural requirements which administrative agencies must meet regardless of what statutes or administrative regulations may provide, and the constitutional base of American courts has given them discretion to influence changes in administrative procedures and regulations.[16] However, Schwartz and Wade also state that one should not presume that the seemingly weaker position of the British judiciary vis-a-vis the power of parliament implies a similarly weak posture in its review of administrative process. Rather:

> [British courts] have staked out for themselves a strong and well defined position as the protectors of the citizen against unlawful acts of government. This they maintain without any express constitutional prerogative, by virtue of the respect in which they are held by public opinion and the accepted tradition that it is their primary duty to uphold the rule of law.[17]

It is in the area of administrative law that British courts have been particularly creative regarding such aspects as judicial denial of unlimited administrative discretion and of the royal prerogative to suppress evidence on the claim that it is not in the public interest to admit it. However, on balance, American public opinion approves of 'judicial activism' or encroachment through decisions which involve courts in policy-making, in contrast with what British public opinion perceives to be the proper role of the courts in such matters. Consequently, English judges exercise their 'creativity' more carefully through emphasis on logic, technicalities and precision of analysis.[18]

It also should be recognised that England's unitary system leads to a national body of administrative law, while the American federal system means that there may be differences between specific aspects of administrative law at the national level, and the administrative law of the fifty states, subject to federal supremacy in areas where state judicial decisions conflict with federal law, treaties or regulations. Another contrast stems from the American separation of powers in the form of independent regulatory commissions whose position in relation to the executive and legislative branches, and role in administrative law, is such that it is unlikely to be replicated in a cabinet form of government.

In addition to the above constitutional concepts and institutions, Irish administrative law is influenced by the nature of Ireland's administrative system, which requires consideration of its national administration and civil service, local authorities, state-sponsored bodies, and by its membership in international organisations.

National Administration

Ireland's Ministers and Secretaries Act 1924, implementing the 1922 Constitution, established eleven government departments assigned to ministers and brought under their control a complex mixture of existing departments, boards and commissions and administrative services. It made explicit the minister's legal authority over and responsibility for these departments as follows:

> Each of the Ministers, heads of the respective Departments of State mentioned in Section 1 of this Act, shall be a corporation sole under his style or name aforesaid ... and shall have perpetual succession and an official seal ... and may sue and (subject to the fiat of the Attorney General having been in each case first granted) be sued under his style or name aforesaid, and may acquire, hold and dispose of land for the purposes of the functions, powers or duties of the Department of State of which he is a head or of any branch thereof. (Section 2(1), Ministers and Secretaries Act 1924)

The concept of the minister as corporation sole poses an administrative dilemma summarised by the Devlin Report, which is pertinent to certain processes and issues in administrative law. The acts of a department are considered to be those of its minister, who is responsible to parliament for whatever a department does and who cannot delegate that responsibility. However, the complexity and detail of modern administration makes it impossible for a minister to have direct personal knowledge of all of a department's operations. The extra-legal device adopted to meet this dilemma has been to issue departmental communications (such as regulations and orders) in the name of the minister, although they actually are largely the work of senior departmental officials. In Barrington's view these officials are handling large amounts of detailed business, with less time for consideration of broad policy questions. In addition, a consensus on the need to depoliticise operation of the public business has resulted in 'hiving off' services from departments and giving new functions related to departmental jurisdiction to state-sponsored bodies, raising questions of ministerial responsibility.[19]

A third result of the corporation sole concept of direct consequence to administrative law has been that a typical process for a person in Ireland who has been refused some benefit by a department is to make an informal appeal to the minister directly or through the good offices of the individual's representative in the Dáil or, alternatively, if there is a statutory right of appeal, to make it in accordance with statutory procedure. Exceptions to this pattern are the Appeals Office of the Department of Social Welfare, the Land Commission, the Revenue Commissioners, and more recently, An Bord Pleanála (the Planning Board), which now hears appeals from decisions of local planning authorities previously taken to the Minister for the Environment. Beginning in 1984, complaints concerning administrative action, inaction and delay may be taken to the newly established Office of the Ombudsman, subject to the limits of his jurisdiction under the Act as it now stands.[20]

The operations of the central government are currently carried out by eighteen departments and the commissions, offices and agencies of, or attached to, the departments and some one hundred state-sponsored bodies.[21]

The major categories of employment in the civil service are industrial and non-industrial civil service, and contract employees. There are over 1,000 different grades in the non-industrial civil service divided into general service grades common to departments, and departmental grades of individual departments. The main occupational groups, to which both the terms grades and classes are applied in the literature on administration, include administrative (Secretary, Deputy Secretary, Assistant Secretary, Principal etc.), executive, clerical and professional grades; the inspectorate, supervisory and manipulative occupations and messenger and cleaner posts constitute the other types of employment.[22]

The administrative class advises ministers and conducts top-level work, supported by the executive class and professional staff. The Irish civil service has a strong tradition of professionalism inherited from the British civil service when some 21,000 civil servants were transferred in 1922 to the Irish Free State. This tradition, combined with the concept of the minister as corporation sole, has resulted in continuing the English tradition of anonymity and loyalty to whatever ministers and party are in power, as pointed out by Dooney in his analysis of the civil service.[23] This pattern of the British and Irish civil services operating up to the highest posts excepting the ministers themselves contrasts with the American system in which public officers at the upper levels (e.g. under and assistant secretaries, general counsels) are not recruited by open competition, so that a change of government means a change of personnel in top policy-making positions. The advantage of the professionalism and non-partisan loyalty in the Irish civil service, Barrington notes, is that the civil service can be honest in giving advice which the minister, publicly responsible for success or failure, is free to ignore or accept. However it also makes for secrecy concerning the internal inputs to decision-making with implications for administrative law and processes. This will be seen later in this study regarding such issues as availability to private parties of findings of inspectors, the inputs of departmental staff, and their recommendations to ministers in proceedings which lead to administrative determinations.[24] In contrast is the relative openness of administrative proceedings and availability of findings and recommendations and documents in general in the United States, typified by its Freedom of Information Act. Appendix I summarises the statutory functions of some ministers and agencies, commissions and boards within or attached to their departments and the functions of certain state-sponsored bodies with regulatory powers related to administrative law.

In addition to the ministers of the government and their departments, the role and functions of the Attorney General of Ireland have a special significance in administrative law. The Attorney General under constitutional article 30 may not be a member of the government. He is appointed or removed by the President on the nomination or advice of the Taoiseach, and must resign if the Taoiseach resigns. His primary function is to advise the government in matters of law and legal opinion. In contrast with the Attorney General of the United States, and more like the British system, it is accepted doctrine that the Attorney General is an independent officer. As stated in *McLoughlin v. Minister for Social Welfare* 1958 IR 1, he may have to take a position opposed to the government. He is not subject to the Taoiseach's direction in the exercise of his legal functions.[25] As delineated in Casey's study of the Attorney General, his roles related to administrative law fall into three general categories.

Asserting the public interest: The largest share of litigation in Ireland on issues of constitutionality of statutes (often involving important questions concerning administrative law and processes) take the form of a request for a declaration with the Attorney General as defendant. When there are cases of this nature involving only private parties, representation of the public interest has been provided for by rules of the courts since 1926 which require that the Attorney General be given notice and that he has the right to appear as a party to the proceedings in respect of the issue of constitutionality of law. He is also legal representative of the people to assert public rights, as exemplified by *Attorney General v. Northern Petroleum Tank Co. Ltd* 1936 IR 450 (Attorney General's right to be a plaintiff for the public in suit for damages by defendant's ship to a water main on a sea bed) and in *Attorney General and Minister for Justice v. Dublin United Tramways Company* 1939 IR 590 (Attorney General's right on public behalf to sue for damages for loss of services of injured garda).[26]

Legitimising suits as a relator: Since the Attorney General is the public's representative for forensic purposes, a private party through the relator action may sue in the Attorney General's name after obtaining permission to do so as is the case in England, thus overcoming problems of *locus standi*. A recent example is *Attorney General v. Dublin Corporation* 1983 ILRM 254, where relator sought an injunction to stop the Dublin Corporation from building offices on an early Viking settlement site, overcoming his lack of *locus standi* by obtaining leave from the Attorney General to utilise his name in the proceedings.[27]

Defendant on behalf of the public: The Attorney General has also been made a defendant in claims against the state (as well as in cases asking for a declaration of unconstitutionality of a statute). Casey quotes Walsh J., who stated in *Byrne v. Ireland and Attorney General* 1972 IR 241, that in all cases which involved seeking damages against the state:

the correct procedure would be to sue the state and join the Attorney General in order to effect service on the Attorney General for both parties. In effect the Attorney General would be joined in a representative capacity as the law officer of state designated by the Constitution. If the claim should succeed judgement would be against the state and not against the Attorney General.[28]

In respect of suing the state it should be noted that the provision in the Ministers and Secretaries Act 1924 that the Attorney General's fiat must be obtained before suing a Minister was held unconstitutional in *Macauley v. Minister for Posts and Telegraphs* 1966 IR 345.[29]

In addition, the Attorney General under sections 2 and 4 of the Statutory Instruments Act 1947 may decide whether or not a regulation constitutes a statutory instrument which must be printed and made available to the public. He may exempt a statutory instrument or class of instruments from compliance with the Act when in his opinion they are of merely local or personal application or limited operation 'or for any other reason'.

Local Authorities

Local authorities carry out functions and programmes significant to administrative law and processes. The elected local authorities in 1984 were 27 county councils, 4 county borough corporations, 7 borough corporations, 49 urban district councils, and 25 boards of town commissioners. However, the 27 county councils, and 4 county borough corporations with their county managers are the major units of local government, despite the fact that the 7 boroughs and 49 urban districts are entitled to exercise a considerable range of powers. The principal functions of local authorities include planning and development, in which issues have arisen of major importance in Ireland's administrative law. Under the Local Government (Planning and Development) Acts, 1963 to 1983, county councils, county borough and borough corporations and urban district councils must prepare and implement development plans which are subject to revision every five years, in order to control development and preserve and improve amenities. In this regard, any projected development involving building in, on, or under land, or changing the use of structures or land, must first have permission from the planning authority (in effect, a licence) and any person may appeal within a specified time to An Bord Pleanála, against the planning authority's decision. In addition, local authorities are road authorities for their areas and responsible for all aspects of such roads. They have housing responsibilities including assessing the adequacy of housing and enforcing minimum standards, the provision of housing for those not able to house themselves and granting assistance to persons providing housing. Local authorities are also involved in water supply and sewerage, and environmental protection activities, such as refuse disposal, water safety and pollution controls. They also provide recreation facilities and general amenities. Although regional agencies are not local authorities as such, mention of the eight Health Boards established under the Health Act 1970 (and their local advisory committees) should be made. They perform a range of services involving community care services, general hospital services and special hospital services. Certain aspects of health services may raise issues in administrative law in their administration, as may the activities of Regional Fisheries Boards and the Central Fisheries Board under the Fisheries Act 1980.[30]

The diversity of American municipal subdivisions within the fifty states makes comparison difficult. However, their range of functions generally include those of Ireland's local authorities and additional functions such as police, education, and public assistance or welfare activities, as do the local authorities in Britain. As might be expected, these functions are pertinent to administrative law in the United States and Britain, and the source of issues requiring judicial resolution. Another common ground is that of the extent of supervisory controls exercised over local authorities by the central governments in the case of Ireland and England, and the state governments in the instance of the United States. As O'Donnell notes:

> Another point . . . about local bodies is that their discretion and ability to act is clearly circumscribed by law. The state has delegated a wide range of different powers to them and closely supervises their operations . . . the major role [of local bodies] is to carry out the policies of the Department of the Environment in . . . housing, roads and traffic and environmental services. The Department of Health . . . works through regional health boards. The Department of Education organ-

ises vocational education through local vocational educational committees.[31]

Barrington also comments on 'the subjection of a great part of the day-to-day operations of local authorities to the most intense subordination and control'. He notes the establishment of the Local Appointments Commission to parallel the national Civil Service Commission as a means of controlling recruitment to more important positions in local government, so as to provide a professional corps of officers.[32]

Wade comments that 'local government is subjected to central government in numerous and important ways. The Act of 1972 and other Acts conferring powers are shot through with restrictive provisions giving powers of yea or nay to the Secretary of State and ministers'. He notes that central government exerts the most control through financial administration.[33] In the United States, despite the increasing grant of 'home rule' to local governments, the local governments are subject to a wide range of central influences, such as detailed state statutes mandating performance of functions, regular fiscal audits by state comptrollers and control of their policies by regulations of state agencies, together with the imposition of conditions accompanying grants in aid.

State-Sponsored Bodies

There are some one hundred 'state-sponsored bodies' carrying out functions of direct concern to the national government. As they are characterised by Basil Chubb:

> State-sponsored bodies are autonomous public authorities (other than universities, judicial bodies, or purely advisory bodies) endowed with duties and powers by statute or by ministerial authority. Their staffs are not civil servants; the government or individual ministers appoint some or all of the members of their governing boards or councils. The legal form of most state-sponsored bodies is that of a statutory corporation or of a public or private company incorporated under the Companies Acts with a minister or ministers holding some or all of the shares. Some, however, are 'statutory companies';

others are set up as corporate bodies under general enabling acts; still others are unincorporated. Some state-sponsored bodies are even not wholly publicly owned but are mixed public and private enterprises.

Just as state-sponsored bodies are autonomous in the sense that each has a legal status and personality, so, too, are they free both from the full rigours of control by the Departments of Finance and the Public Service, to which central departments are subject, and from detailed scrutiny by the Oireachtas, to which in principle at least departments must submit. Each state-sponsored body, however, has a sponsor minister who is ultimately responsible for it.[34]

Compared to multiple-purpose departments, Barrington notes that state-sponsored bodies are single-purpose executive bodies, organised on a business-type pattern, directed by a board (often businessmen serving part time) appointed by the shareholder who is usually a minister. Civil servants from the concerned department are often on the boards to facilitate the flow of information, or in some instances board members may be persons representing interest groups affected by the enterprise. The Board appoints a chief executive and other top management, exerts fiscal controls, supervises personnel policy and evaluates performance. In his opinion, the Board's most important role is that of being a focal point of interaction between the objectives of the minister and the recommendations made to the Board by the exeuctive management, tempered by the experience of the Board.[35]

The size, functions, purposes and legal origins of state-sponsored bodies vary considerably as well as do the mechanisms of ministerial control. As the *Devlin Report* noted, they ranged in size from Coras Iompair Éireann (CIE) and the Electricity Supply Board (ESB) which together employed about half of the 60,000 staff in the state-sector to the Hospitals Trust Board with no staff at all at the time of the Report. In respect of functions and purposes, the Devlin Report identified two categories, namely commercial state-sponsored bodies and non-commercial or executive bodies. Commercial bodies sell goods or services to obtain the major part or all their revenues though government may subsidise capital expansion or uneconomic services. There are two groups of commercial bodies.

The first establishes an infrastructural base for the whole economy, of activities in which private enterprise did not, or does not, wish to engage, e.g. Aer Lingus, CIE, ESB. The second group provides employment for types of workers or areas or promotes development of natural resources, e.g. Bord na Móna, Erin Foods, Gaeltarra Éireann, and also engages in 'rescue operations' when the state takes over financially threatened private enterprise such as Irish Steel Holdings.

Non-commercial or executive bodies include marketing bodies (Pigs and Bacon Commission), promotional bodies (Bord Fáilte Éireann), research, advisory and training bodies (AnCO, Medical Research Council), bodies registering and regulating professions (Dental Board, Medical Registration Council), and miscellaneous service bodies (Central Bank, Hospitals Trust Board).[36]

The legal status and nature of the commercial state-sponsored bodies reflect their establishment on an *ad hoc* basis in response to needs as they arose, rather than on a pre-determined juridical form developed in advance for this type of enterprise, according to G.M. Golding. For example, a commercial state-sponsored body or 'statutory corporation' may derive its corporate status from an Act of the legislature, or it may have been a company incorporated by registration under the Companies Act and later taken under state control by an enabling Act.[37] Differences between the 'statutory corporation' and a private company incorporated by registration are that the commercial state-sponsored body may be given compulsory powers to acquire land, is restricted to the statutory purposes of its establishment and cannot apply funds to purposes not authorised by the conditions of incorporation. In addition, there are ministerial controls over appointment of the chairman and directors, over share capital and capital investment programmes and borrowing, examination of audited accounts and reports and approval of super-annuation schemes for staff.[38] Golding notes that state-sponsored bodies may sue and be sued, and are bound by the law of contract as much as private enterprise. However, while private enterprise might risk ignoring or infringing upon orders made under restrictive practices legislation, or hire-purchase laws or labour law, the state enterprises must comply strictly since there are political as well as legal consequences for the state-sponsored body which do not apply to private enterprise. Again, under company law private firms must act in the shareholder's economic interest, but since the minister is

C

the shareholder in state-sponsored bodies, the management must take a politically desirable alternative if it conflicts with an economically desirable one.[39]

In addition to commercial state-sponsored bodies being the objects of various types of administrative regulation, certain non-commercial or executive bodies, such as the Medical Council, the Dental Board, or the Pigs and Bacon Commission are engaged in administrative law as regulatory agencies exercising controls over professions or marketing.

It should be noted that there are parallels to the Irish state-sponsored bodies in both England and the United States. As Wade notes, 'There are corporate bodies which are cogs in the central government machine such as the National Enterprise Board. Regional Health Authorities, the Housing Corporation, (and) many other governmental or quasi-governmental corporations such as the Civil Aviation Authority ... the British Airports Authority, the British Broadcasting Corporation and the Independent Broadcasting Authority.' Other bodies identified by Wade are independent and commercial bodies such as the London Transport Board, and British Petroleum Ltd. As Wade states, 'There is no stereotype'.[40] In the United States there are many bodies at both the national and state levels called 'authorities' or 'corporations'. Examples are the Tennessee Valley Authority, the Reconstruction Finance Corporation, the Federal Deposit Insurance Corporation and the National Mortgage Association at the national level, and in New York State, the Power Authority, the Thruway Authority and the Dormitory Authority among the many authorities in that state. The reasons for their creation are to quite an extent the same as for creation of state-sponsored bodies in Ireland, and the issue of maintenance of controls to provide for responsibility to the government is also common in the three countries.

EEC Membership

A relatively recent development in Ireland's governmental system directly affecting its administrative law and processes is that of Ireland's membership of the European Coal and Steel Community, the European Economic Community and the European Atomic Energy Community (hereafter EEC). Article 29.4(3), amending Bunreacht na hÉireann to authorise membership, states;

> No provision of the Constitution invalidates laws enacted, acts done or measures adopted by the State necessitated by the obligations of membership of the Communities or prevents laws enacted, acts done or measures adopted by the Communities, or institutions thereof, from having the force of the law in the State.

In his analysis of the European Communities Act 1972, Kelly states that section 2 made treaties governing the EEC a part of the domestic law of Ireland and provides in section 3 that Ministers of State may make regulations to implement section 2 of that Act. The regulations may have those supplementary or consequential provisions which the Minister considers necessary for the purpose of the regulations, except that they may not create an indictable offence. The subsequent European Communities (Amendment) Act 1973 provided in section 1(1) that ministerial regulations will have statutory effect. However, if the Oireachtas Joint Committee on Secondary Legislation of the European Communities recommends to the Oireachtas that any such regulations be annulled, an annulment resolution passed by both Houses within one year after the making of the Regulations will nullify their statutory effect, without prejudice to prior action under the regulations.

By the end of 1982, Kelly notes, some 255 sets of regulations, 48 statutory instruments and 13 statutes or sections of statutes designated as 'necessitated' by EEC membership had been adopted in Ireland. This body of law *prima facie* is beyond the jurisdiction of Irish courts on constitutional grounds, although the designation of 'necessity' does not preempt determination of whether in fact it is so 'necessitated'. At the same time, final determination of the legal issue of 'necessity' may not rest solely in the Irish courts since the European Court's jurisdiction may be invoked if the dispute involves Ireland and the EEC or other parties.[41]

Article 16 of the Treaty of Rome provides that when an interpretation of the Treaty, an act of a Community institution or a statute of a body established by an Act of the Council is raised before any member state's court, that court may request the Court of Justice to give a preliminary ruling if it is considered necessary to enable the domestic court to give judgment on the question. Moreover, when any such question is raised in a case pending before a member state court against whose decisions there is no judicial remedy under

national law, that court shall bring the matter before the Court of
Justice. These provisions, as Kelly points out, intrude upon the
exclusive power of the Irish courts in administering justice and the
Supreme Court's finality of decision. Further, regulations of the
EEC and of Eurotom and decisions of the European Coal and
Steel Community apply to member states directly without any
requirement of a member state's domestic legislation to put them
into effect.[42]

Chubb comments on additional implications of EEC membership
on domestic law in Ireland:

> Although the economic and social matters that are the concern
> of the Communities hardly touch upon family law, they do
> subsume such areas as social welfare and such personal rights
> as sex equality, equal pay, the right to work and freedom of
> establishment. It is most obviously matters such as these, as
> also the rights and powers of the Communities' institutions,
> that impinge upon the Constitution and raise questions about
> the need for constitutional amendment.[43]

Among the aspects of Chubb's analysis is the view of some lawyers
that Irish statutes may be open to challenge by reference to Community law, the seeming response to EEC directives in the form of
changes made in Irish labour law in 1977, and the potential effect
of article 173 of the Treaty of Rome which provides that 'any natural
or legal person' has the right to resort to the European Court.
Chubb indicates that not only are Irish courts expanding rights of
Irish citizens through interpretation of the Irish Constitution, but
simultaneously the European Court has expanded rights of individuals to sue their public authorities in the courts of member states
under European law. The European Court is also creating and
defining new economic and social rights such as freedom from
discrimination based on nationality, the equality of sexes in employment and the right to establish a business or engage in a profession.

Both Kelly's and Chubb's commentary on the potential effect of
EEC membership on Irish jurisprudence are reflected in recent
cases in Irish administrative law, such as *Pigs and Bacon Commission
v. McCarran and Company* Court of Justice of the European Communities, unreported, 27 June 1979. The European Court, in response
to issues referred to it by the Irish High Court, held that the Treaty

relating to Free Movement of Goods Regulations No. 2759/75 must be interpreted as meaning that the power of the Irish Pigs and Bacon Commission to charge a levy on all pigs slaughtered in Ireland for bacon to be used to pay export bonuses for bacon intended to be marketed in the EEC countries, or exported to non-member countries, and to inflict financial disadvantage on any producer who sells directly rather than through the Commission, is incompatible with the common organisation of the market in pigmeat. Furthermore such levy may not be required from producers to the degree that it is devoted to purposes incompatible with the Treaty on free movement of goods.

In *Doyle and Others v. Taoiseach and Government of Ireland*, unreported, High Court, per Barrington J., 29 November 1979, the High Court at the request of plaintiffs referred to the European Court the question of whether or not a two per cent excise levy on agricultural products can be reconciled with the provisions of the Treaty of Rome and subordinate legislation. In *Dreher v. Irish Land Commission, Ireland and the Attorney General* case, unreported, The High Court, per Hamilton J., 1 June 1971, it was held that a German national could not claim rights under the Treaty of Rome pertaining to a series of transactions connected with acquisition of his land by the Land Commission because they were commenced before the Treaty became effective in Ireland.

Constitutional Concepts and Institutions: France

The French Constitution of 1958 affirms the sovereignty of the people, provides for a President elected by an electoral college, a government composed of a prime minister and cabinet responsible to a parliament, and emphasises the separation of powers between branches of government. As in the case of Ireland and England, France has a unitary system of government. Despite this seeming constitutional-structural similarity of French and Irish government, a summary review of certain key aspects of French government reveals important differences. The powers and role of the President of France exceed those of the President of Ireland. The French President is responsible for the operation of public services, appoints the prime minister and on the latter's nomination, appoints (and dismisses) other ministers; presides over the Council of Ministers; promulgates statutes; on the proposal of the government may submit proposed laws to referendum; has the power to dissolve the National Assembly under certain circumstances; signs ordinances and decrees adopted by the Council of Ministers; appoints civil and military employees of the state; is commander-in-chief of the armed forces and has virtually unlimited dictatorial power in time of national emergency.[44]

The government, headed by the prime minister, determines and implements policy as in Ireland, but a member of the government may not be a member of Parliament or at least must relinquish his parliamentary seat until the next election (article 23). The National Assembly may adopt a motion of censure or refuse to approve the platform or a general policy statement of the government which requires the prime minister to submit the government's resignation to the President (article 49) but in doing this the National Assembly risks dissolution by the President (article 50). Parliament may initiate legislation and amend it, but bills and amendments originating with a member of Parliament are inadmissible when their adoption would result in diminution of revenues or establish or expand a public charge according to article 40.[45]

A significant contrast with Ireland, England and the United States is that although the French Parliament has the power to enact statutes (*lois*), such power is limited in article 34 to enumerated matters upon which Parliament may legislate, while article 37 provides that all matters not listed in article 34 fall solely within the separate regulatory powers of the executive, which may issue decrees (*décrets*) or regulations having the force and effect of law. The government may also obtain consent by 'ordinance' for a limited period on matters ordinarily reserved for Parliament, under article 38. Should Parliament try to legislate outside of its constitutional domain, the President, prime minister, President of the Senate, or President of the Assembly may refer the law before its promulgation to the Constitutional Council (created by the 1958 Constitution) for a decision as to its constitutionality; the decision is final and binding on all organs of government. On the other hand, a challenge that a regulation issued by the government trespasses on the parliamentary area is subject to review by the Conseil d'État, an integral organ of the Executive Branch.[46]

This division of legislative power between legislature and executive in France is an important contrast with Ireland, England and the United States, since in the common law countries, administrative regulations having the force of law may be adopted and applied only when administrators are authorised to do so by statute, which defines the limits of such regulations. On the other hand in France:

> In a sense, the 'décrets' which the government issues under article 37 of the Constitution are just as much legislation as the 'lois' which parliament enacts under article 34. Moreover . . . prefects and mayors may issue 'arrêtes' under their inherent *pouvoir réglementaire* which are in no sense *delegated* legislation.[47]

The greatest difference in administrative law between France and the common law countries is its system of administrative law courts, which are not a part of the 'judicial branch', headed by the Conseil d'État. The Conseil d'État, composed of an elite corps of the civil service, is organised into four administrative sections, namely finance, home affairs, public works and social (*Section des finances, Section de l'intérieur, Section des travaux publics, Section sociale*) and a fifth section, *Section du contentieux* or the judicial section. All bills (potential *lois*) introduced by the government into Parliament must be submitted first for advice of the Conseil, as must be texts of governmental decrees (*décrets*). The advisory function of the Conseil d'État concludes once a bill is before Parliament, but through its adjudicatory powers the Conseil can annul a government decree not conforming to the original text submitted to the Conseil or not including the modifications it proposed. The Conseil d'État is also legal advisor to the government.[48]

The most important function of the judicial or litigation section of the Conseil d'État in Paris is that of being an appellate court over the Tribunaux Administratifs which act as administrative courts of first instance in their respective regions in France. It also exercises supervisory jurisdiction in *cassation* over other subordinate administrative jurisdictions and has jurisdiction at first and last instance over certain categories of proceedings. The Conseil d'État controls administrative action in response to private citizen petition by either negating administrative action or granting damages or other remedies, in respect of actions by French executive officials at the *commune, arrondissement,* or departmental levels. A citizen thus initiates an action in the local administrative court of first instance, with an appeal to the Conseil d'État.[49]

Given the framework of the constitutional concepts and institutions within which the Conseil d'État and French administrative law have evolved, certain general principles of law have been established. The principle of legality, in addition to requiring that administrative action must be within the Constitution and legislation, has been broadened to include unwritten general principles of law, which involve a balancing of the powers of the administration to protect the public interest and the rights of individuals. The rights include freedom of expression, assembly, personal liberty, equality before the law, economic and social rights, as well as procedural rights of both sides to be heard, impartiality of the decision-maker, non-retroactivity of law and judicial review.[50] Characteristics of the French administrative law system which to Brown and Garner typify its advantages are confidence in the administrative expertise of the Conseil d'État and the Tribunaux Administratifs, and a case-law approach respecting but not bound by prior decisions. A further advantage is the use of only three forms of action, i.e. *recours pour excés de pouvoir* and *recours en cassation* in respect of matters of legality and *recours de pleine juridiction* in cases where damages or greater relief are sought, which provide what remedies are necessary as against the more complex remedies of common law countries. The appellate jurisdiction of the Conseil d'État over the administrative tribunals contributes to uniform application of the law. The Conseil d'État has also developed the concept of *détournement de pouvoir* under which an administrative judge may go beyond the external appearance of legality and examine the administrator's motives, and *violation de la loi*, which permits review of fact as well as of law. French administrative law has also taken an advanced position in the development of jurisprudence regarding actions for damages under the law of public liability and administrative contracts.[51]

Granted the general consensus on the definition of administrative law (see chapter 1), it is also true that the differences and similarities of governmental systems summarised above affect the specific nature and operation of their administrative law and processes. For example, the legislative delegation of rule-making power to administration does not raise the constitutional-legal issues in France, or for that matter in England that it has at times in the

United States and in Ireland. The legal status of the minister as corporation sole in Ireland, and the concept of ministerial responsibility to Parliament in Ireland and England as against the roles of heads of departments and agencies and independent regulatory commissions in relation to the President and Congress in America, has made for differences in certain specific aspects of the operation of their administrative law processes. The contrasts of the common law legal system and role of the general courts in the review of administrative determinations in Ireland, England and the United States, with the French legal system and its unique institution of the Conseil d'État, would indicate that Irish administrative law will probably continue to evolve along lines paralleling those of England and the United States. As will be seen in the following chapters dealing with specific aspects of Irish administrative law, there are strong English influences, but at the same time there is a movement in various areas towards certain characteristics of American administrative law.

Notes to Chapter 2

1. See Chubb, *The Constitution and Constitutional Change [Constitutional Change]* 14-15 (1978) and Chubb, *The Government and Politics of Ireland [Government and Politics]* 42-5 (1982); Kelly, *The Irish Constitution* xxxvi-xxxix (1984)
2. Beth, *The Development of Judicial Review in Ireland, 1936-1966* 4 (1967)
3. Chubb, *Government and Politics* 45
4. Chubb, *Constitutional Change* 26
5. Kelly, *The Irish Constitution* 28-32; Chubb, *Cabinet Government in Ireland [Cabinet Government]* 9-10 (1974)
6. Chubb, *Constitutional Change* 28
7. See Chubb, *Government and Politics* 201-205, including his quotations from Ó Muimhneacháin, 'The Functions of the Department of the Taoiseach' in *Administration* 293, (Vol. 7, No. 4) and an interview, 'Lemass on Government' quoted in *Léargas* (Vol. 3, No. 12, Jan-Feb. 1968). See also Chubb, *Cabinet Government* (1974) for detailed analysis of the role and power of the Taoiseach and the cabinet government in Ireland.
8. McGowan Smyth, *The Houses of the Oireachtas [The Oireachtas]* 20-33 (1979)
9. Chubb, *Government and Politics* 175
10. O'Donnell, *How Ireland is Governed* 29 (1979)
11. Chubb, *Government and Politics* 217
12. Garner, *Administrative Law* 19 (1974)
13. Schwartz and Wade, *Legal Control of Government: Administrative Law in Britain and the United States [Legal Control of Government]* 111 (1972); Wade, *Administrative Law* 27 (1982)
14. Garner, *Administrative Law* 16; see also Wade, *Administrative Law* 28-9
15. Garner, *Administrative Law* 15

16. Schwartz and Wade, *Legal Control of Government* 7-8 (1972)
17. Schwartz and Wade, *Legal Control of Government* 11
18. Schwartz and Wade, *Legal Control of Government* 17
19. Barrington, *The Administrative System* 31-3 (1981)
20. See Devlin Report 430; Barrington, *The Irish Administrative System* 33-4; Ombudsmans Act 1980
21. *Administration Yearbook and Diary* 19-64; 113-45 (1984) for descriptive data on departments and state-sponsored bodies and composition of civil service.
22. *Administration Yearbook* 19-20 (1984)
23. Dooney, *The Irish Civil Service* 118-23 (1976)
24. See Barrington, *The Irish Administrative System* 37, 180 (1981); Dooney, *The Irish Civil Service* (1976) for a detailed analysis of the Irish civil service.
25. See Casey, *The Office of the Attorney General in Ireland [The Attorney General]* 40-41 (1980)
26. Casey, *The Attorney General* 145-7
27. Casey, *The Attorney General* 148-51
28. See Casey, *The Attorney General* 161
29. See Casey, *The Attorney General* 166-72 for an analysis of the Attorney General's fiat.
30. See Roche, *Local Government in Ireland* in general and 187-272 (1982); O'Donnell, *How Ireland is Governed* 53-70; *Administration Yearbook* 65-8 (1984)
31. O'Donnell, *How Ireland is Governed* 53-4
32. Barrington, *The Irish Administrative System* 44
33. Wade, *Administrative Law* 120 (1982)
34. Chubb, *Government and Politics* 270-71
35. Barrington, *The Irish Administrative System* 58-9
36. Devlin Report 29-41 (1969)
37. Golding, 'The Juristic Basis of the Irish State Enterprise', ['Irish State Enterprise'] *Irish Jurist* 302 (Vol. XIII, 1978)
38. Golding, 'Irish State Enterprise', 313-5
39. Golding, 'Irish State Enterprise' 310
40. Wade, *Administrative Law* 139
41. Kelly, *The Irish Constitution* 187-8 (1984)
42. Kelly, *The Irish Constitution* 189
43. Chubb, *Constitutional Change* 84: see analysis of EEC effect on Irish law 85-9.
44. See articles 5, 8-13, 15 and 16 respectively, 1958 Constitution, as discussed by David, *French Law, Its Structure, Sources and Methodology,* [*French Law*] 20-22 (1972): Macridis and Brown, *The DeGaulle Republic* 160-65 (1960). For analysis of restrictions on President's powers, see Pickles, *Problems of Contemporary French Politics* 124-30 (1982).
45. See David, *French Law* 22-6; Macridis and Brown, *The DeGaulle Republic* 168-172
46. See Brown and Garner (assisted by Galabert), *French Administrative Law* 6-9 (1983); David, *French Law* 29-30, Macridis and Brown, *The DeGaulle Republic* 169-171
47. Brown and Garner, *French Administrative Law* 9
48. See Brown and Garner, *French Administrative Law* 41-52; Schwartz, *French Administrative Law in the Common Law World* 1-14 (1954) and in general.
49. See Brown and Garner, *French Administrative Law* 21-35, and in general, together with Schwartz, 'French Administrative Law in the Common Law World' for detailed analyses of the organisation, procedures and jurisdiction of the Conseil d'État and of the principles of French administrative law,

including comparisons with the administrative law of Britain and common law countries.

50. Brown and Garner, *French Administrative Law* 132-43; Schwartz, *French Administrative Law in the Common Law World* 162-4

51. See Brown and Garner, *French Administrative Law* 172-5 and Schwartz, *French Administrative Law in the Common Law World* especially 154-67 on the political and social significance of the Conseil d'État, and 132-4, 140-67 generally.

3 Legislative, Executive and Judicial Powers

The significance to administrative law of those provisions in Bunreacht na hÉireann pertaining to legislative, executive and judicial powers becomes apparent only when one understands how the courts have interpreted the provisions in resolving certain fundamental issues. These issues include the constitutionality of delegation of legislative and judicial powers by the Oireachtas to the administration, whether a particular exercise of power by the legislature intrudes upon executive power, and whether certain applications of executive power invade the constitutional domain of the Oireachtas or the courts. Since the judicial resolution of such issues also involves the nature of the remedies which the courts can provide and the basis upon which courts will give or refuse them to the concerned parties, these aspects of judicial power must also be considered.

Legislative Power: Issue of Delegation

The grant of 'sole and exclusive power of making laws for the State' to the Oireachtas in article 15.2 of the 1937 Constitution has been the basis for raising the issue of delegation of legislative power in Ireland. This issue is not raised in England owing to parliamentary sovereignty or in France in view of the government's power to legislate by decree. While the separation of powers reflected in the allocation of law-making powers exclusively to the legislatures of Ireland and the United States has resulted in the constitutional issue of delegation being raised, it has not seriously deterred the extensive delegation of rule-making power to administrative agencies in either country. In the United States, the Supreme Court has held a delegation of legislative power to the administration to be unconstitutional in only two cases, *Panama Refining Company v. Ryan* 293 US 388 (1935) and *A.L.A. Schecter Poultry Corporation v. US* 295 US 495 (1935) and to private parties in one case, namely, *Carter v. Carter Coal Company* 298 US 636 (1936).

In Ireland, the initial and principal case in which a direct challenge to the constitutionality of a delegation of rule-making power was made is *Pigs Marketing Board v. Donnelly (Dublin) Ltd* 1939 IR 413. The Pigs and Bacon Acts of 1935 and 1937 had established a Pigs Marketing Board and prohibited bacon manufacturers who were licensees as defined under the Acts from purchasing pigs at prices other than those set by the Board. The Board was given power to fix production quotas, periods and prices. The defendants, in response to an action by the Pigs Marketing Board to recover some £14,000 payable under the Act in respect of the Board's price-controlling powers, claimed that the 1935 and 1937 Acts were unconstitutional on several grounds, including the allegation that Part IV of the 1935 Act conferred legislative authority on the Board contrary to article 15 of the 1937 Constitution pertaining to legislative power. In particular, the defendants attacked the power to regulate prices of pigs and carcasses through fixing a 'hypothetical price' as well as an 'appointed price'. Although the Oireachtas in Part IV, sections 116 to 154 indicated a number of specific matters the Board is to consider in fixing the 'appointed price', there was no statutory guidance as to the fixing of the 'hypothetical price' other than the provision stating the price was to be that 'which in the opinion of the Board, would, under normal conditions, be the proper price' (page 420).

Hanna J. in the High Court, after dismissing certain objections raised by defendants as being beyond determination by a court of law, turned to the main issue of delegation of legislative authority. He held that while the legislature cannot confer power to make laws on any other body or authority, it always has had authority to delegate to subordinate bodies or departments not only the making of administrative rules and regulations, but the exercise, within principles laid down by the legislature, of the powers delegated and the manner in which the statutory provisions shall be carried out. With respect to the broad phraseology in the statute granting discretion to the Board when it fixes the hypothetical price, Hanna J. stated:

> That is a statutory direction, it is a matter of such detail and upon which such expert knowledge is necessarily required, that the legislature, being unable to fix such a price itself, is entitled to say: 'We shall leave this to a body of experts in the trade who shall in the first place determine what the normal conditions in the trade would be apart from the abnormal conditions

prescribed by the statute, and then form an opinion as to what
the proper price in pounds, shillings and pence would be under
such normal conditions'. (page 422)

The Court thus concluded that the Board was not making a new
law but giving effect to the provisions of the Act on how the Board
should determine the price. It would be futile to ask the legislature
to fix the amount of the normal price.

The power of the legislature to 'entrust its mandates to subordinate agencies' was upheld by the High Court against a claim of
invalid delegation of legislative power to a trade union tribunal in
National Union of Railwaymen v. Sullivan 1947 IR 77, 81 ILTR 55.[1]
However, the Supreme Court held the statute unconstitutional on
the primary issue raised in that case pertaining to freedom of
association under article 40.6. The issue of delegation of legislative
power was addressed more directly in *The State (Devine) v. Larkin*
1977 IR 24, where McMahon J. held that it was not unconstitutional
for the legislature to give the Foyle Fisheries Commission power
under the Foyle Fisheries Act 1952 to make regulations with the
approval of· the Minister for Agriculture in Ireland and of an
authority not subject to Irish law, namely the Ministry for Commerce for Northern Ireland.

In the more recent case of *Cityview Press Ltd and Oliver Fogarty v.
An Chomhairle Oiliúna, Minister for Labour and the Attorney General* 1980
IR 381, the plaintiffs contended that the Oireachtas made an
unconstitutional delegation of legislative authority contrary to article 15.2.1 of the Constitution. The particular provision of the
statute under attack was section 21 of the Industrial Training Act
1967. Section 21 provided that An Chomhairle Oiliúna (AnCO)
could make a levy order imposing a levy on employers in any
particular industry which had been specified in an order made
under section 23 of the Act as a 'designated Industrial Activity' for
the purpose of better training of those employed or to be employed
in that industry.

The Supreme Court rejected this contention, O'Higgins C.J.
stating:

> The giving of powers to a designated Minister or subordinate
> body to make regulations or orders under a particular statute
> has been a feature of legislation for many years. The practice

has obvious attractions in view of the complex, intricate and ever-changing situations which confront both the Legislature and the Executive in a modern State. (page 398)

The judge noted that on occasion the legislature would provide that such regulations or orders are subject to annulment by either House as a safeguard, but that the ultimate responsibility is on the Courts to ensure that the exclusive law-making authority of the Oireachtas is not eroded by an unconstitutional delegation of its power. As to the criteria which the Court would apply:

The test, in the view of this Court, is whether that which is challenged as an unauthorised delegation of parliamentary power is more than a mere giving effect to principles and policies which are contained in the statute itself. If it be, then it is not authorised; for such would constitute a purported exercise of legislative power by an authority which is not permitted to do so under the Constitution. On the other hand, if it be within the permitted limits – if the law is laid down in the statute and details only are filled in or completed by the designated Minister or subordinate body – there is no unauthorised delegation of legislative power.

In this instance, in the opinion of the Court, there has not been an unconstitutional delegation of authority. The Act of 1967 contains clear declarations of policies and aims and it establishes machinery for the carrying out of these policies and the achievement of these aims. In particular, the fact that there will be a levy is provided for in s. 21 and the obligation to pay it is laid down. The only matter which is left for determination by AnCO is the manner of calculating this levy in relation to a particular industry. This is doing no more than adding the final detail which brings into operation the general law which is laid down by the section. (page 399)

The criteria which the courts applied in upholding the delegation of legislative power in the above cases parallel criteria applied in American courts, namely the statute should define the subject of regulation with sufficient specificity, and should provide statutory standards both as to the objectives to be achieved and the processes for attaining those objectives. (See *US v. Grimaud* 220 US 506 (1911); *J.W. Hampton v. US* 276 US 394 (1928); *A. L. A. Schecter Corporation v. US* 295 US 495 (1935); *US v. Rock Royal Cooperative Inc* 307 US 533 (1939); and *Arizona v. California* 373 US 546 (1963) as typical examples.)

Legislative Oversight: Administrative Rules and Orders

The increasing delegation of rule-making power to the administration has led to direct legislative control over rule-making in England and Ireland, and recently, the United States, through a process generally referred to as 'laying on the table'. In Ireland, as Asmal notes, statutes delegating rule-making power customarily require that the rules or 'statutory instruments' adopted be laid before either or both of the Houses of the Oireachtas in one of several ways. A common mechanism is that although the statutory instrument becomes effective upon being made by the administrative agency, it may be annulled by resolution of either House within the next subsequent 21 days on which the House has sat after the regulation is laid before it. An alternative is that a draft of a regulation be laid before the Houses and the regulation may not come into force until they have passed a resolution approving of the draft. An atypical form is for an Act to provide that an instrument acquires legal effect only if a confirming Act is passed.[2] Generally, similar processes are provided for in Britain.[3]

The objectives of the individual Acts requiring that statutory instruments be laid before the Houses of the Oireachtas are supplemented and reinforced by a statute having general application, namely the Houses of the Oireachtas (Laying of Documents) Act 1966. This Act defines a statutory instrument as:

> (i) any order, regulation, rule, scheme, bye-law, warrant, licence, permit, certificate, directive or other like document; or (ii) any statute for the government of a university or a constituent college thereof.

The Act sets forth details in section 2 as to interpretation of references in statutes in respect of the procedure for laying of statutory instruments. It also provides in section 3 for a minimum period in relation to laying of certain documents within which a statutory instrument or draft of a proposed instrument may be annulled, disallowed, or disapproved in whole or in part by means of resolution passed by either House.

In 1948, the Seanad established the Select Committee on Statutory Rules, Orders and Regulations, patterned after a comparable committee of the British House of Commons. Reconstituted in 1951 as the Select Committee on Statutory Instruments, the Committee was first established as a sessional committee (i.e. for the life of the House) and then constituted in the same way since 1948 at the beginning of every Seanad. The original terms of reference which repeated those of the comparable British committee have been modified. When constituted in 1978, the Seanad resolution, as reported by McGowan Smyth in his study of the Oireachtas, provided:

1. That a select committee be appointed to consider every statutory instrument laid or laid in draft before Seanad Éireann in pursuance of a statutory requirement with a view to determining whether the special attention of Seanad Éireann should be drawn to it on any of the following grounds:

(1) that it imposes a charge on the public revenues or contains provisions requiring payments to be made to the exchequer or any government department or to any local or public authority in consideration of any licence or consent, of any services to be rendered or prescribes the amount of any such charge or payments;
(2) that it appears to make some unusual or unexpected use of the powers conferred by the statute under which it is made;
(3) that it purports to have retrospective effect where the parent statute confers no express authority so to provide;
(4) that there appears to have been unjustifiable delay either in the laying of it before Seanad Éireann or in its publication;
(5) that its drafting appears to be defective; or
(6) that for any special reasons its form or purport calls for elucidation;
or on any other ground which does not impinge on its merits or on the policy behind it; and to report accordingly.[4]

The resolution also provided that the committee would consist of

nine members, with the power to require any government department or other instrument-making authority to submit a memorandum explaining any statutory instrument under consideration or
depute a representative to appear before it for the purpose of
explaining the statutory instrument. The committee may report to
the Seanad any such memorandum or evidence explaining the
instrument. However, the committee, before calling special attention of the Seanad to a statutory instrument, has the duty of giving
the government department or other instrument-making authority
the opportunity of providing explanations orally or in writing. The
committee shall lay any report it adopts before the Seanad together
with such memoranda or evidence given in explanation of any
statutory instruments.[5]

The Select Committee on Statutory Instruments has met regularly and has reported to the Seanad, calling the attention of the
House to various statutory instruments on the grounds set out in
its terms of reference as listed above, and has also provided minutes
of evidence given by witnesses appearing before the committee and
communications between the committee and departments or other
authorities making statutory instruments. The committee has also
made general recommendations. Cooperation with the committee
has been forthcoming from departments and instrument-making
authorities and the committee has had success in standardising the
form of statutory instruments and in having a brief note attached
to each instrument explaining its meaning and effect.[6] In Asmal's
view, 'the committee has performed a useful function and instruments are more intelligible, more carefully drafted by reference to
the parent act, and civil servants are more sharply aware of the
existence of a watchdog committee'.[7]

The Irish and British practice of laying regulations before the
legislature has not become a standard practice in the American
federal or state governments nor has a congressional committee
comparable to the Seanad Select Committee on Statutory Instruments been established, probably owing to the greater rigour of the
separation of powers provisions in the American Constitution and
the resulting Congress to President relationship.[8]

Nevertheless, as noted by Barry and Whitcomb, a Congressional
Research Service Study revealed that 159 laws enacted between
1932 and 1979 contained a provision for legislative veto, of which
24 were enacted in 1978.[9] A summary report by the National

Conference of State Legislatures stated that by 1977, 34 states had legislation providing for some form of legislative review of administrative regulations.[10] A growing controversy over the constitutionality of the legislative veto has included attacks by Presidents Truman, Eisenhower, Johnson and Carter,[11] and has been reflected in several lower court decisions. (See *Atkins v. US* 556 F 2d 1028 (1977); *Consumer Energy Council of America v. Federal Energy Regulatory Commission* (673 F 2d 425 (D. C. Cir. 1982)); *Consumers Union of the United States v. FTC* 691 F 2d 575 (D. C. Cir, 1982)). This controversy culminated in the US Supreme Court's decision in *Immigration and Naturalization Service v. Chadha* 103 S. Ct. 2764 77 L. Ed. 2d 317 (1983) that section 244(c)(2) of the Immigration and Nationality Act, 8 US C. Section 1254 (which authorised a veto by either House of the Congress of a decision by the Department of Justice to suspend the deportation of an alien) was unconstitutional. The judgment of the Court was that the veto by one House of the legislature violates article 1, section 7 of the Constitution, requiring that every bill passed by Congress be presented to the President who may veto a bill, subject to an override by two thirds of the Senate and the House. It also violates article I, sections 1 and 7, requiring every bill to be passed by both the House and the Senate (the interbranch check of bicameralism). The effect of the decision on over 200 Federal Acts now having legislative veto provisions, and potential spin-off effect on a variety of laws in 42 states providing for some form of legislative review of state regulations, is still in the process of being sorted out. For example, in *Equal Employment Opportunity Commission v. Hernando Bank* 724 F 2d 1188 (5th Cir. 1984) the Court of Appeals ruled that an unconstitutional legislative veto provision contained in the Act under challenge was severable even in the absence of a severability clause, so that the Act as a whole was not invalidated.

Legislative Investigation

The exercise of investigatory power by the Dáil and Seanad has not been the subject of controversy leading to judicial review in Ireland to the extent that it has in the United States (See, for example, *Kilbourn v. Thompson* 103 US 168 (1881); *McGrain v. Daugherty* 273 US 135 (1927); *Watkins v. United States* 354 US 178 (1957); *Barenblatt v. United States* 360 US 109 (1959)). This is largely owing to the

differences between the Irish parliamentary process patterned after
the British system in which the most immediate form of control
through inquiry is the parliamentary question.[12] The Oireachtas
does have committees exercising oversight and fact-finding
functions, such as the Dáil Committee of Public Accounts and
Committee on Public Expenditure, and the Oireachtas Joint Committees on Commercial State-Sponsored Bodies, on Legislation,
and on the Secondary Legislation of the European Communities
(in addition to the above-mentioned Seanad Select Committee
on Statutory Instruments). Based upon examination or review of
accounts, expenditures, reports, proposed domestic legislation and
EEC regulations and directives, these committees report back to
the Oireachtas with recommendations for appropriate action and
certain of them have the power to send for persons, papers and
records. In addition, a number of ad hoc committees on special
topics have been established, e.g. Joint Committees on Building
Land, Co-operation with Developing Countries, Small Businesses,
Marriage Breakdown, Women's Rights, and a Dáil Committee on
Crime, Lawlessness and Vandalism, for purposes of examining
the problems extant in these areas and making recommendations
thereon.[13] Despite this growth of committees in the Oireachtas,
there is not as comprehensive a system of standing and special
legislative committees and sub-committees with control over bills,
exercise of oversight functions, and investigatory powers comparable to that of the American Congress, which reflects the nature of
the American presidential system of government and separation of
powers. The investigatory power of congressional committees is
such that Gellhorn and Byse have referred to 'government by
investigation' as a major form of modern congressional activity, and
cite statistics showing that since the 80th Congress, each Congress
within its time period of two years made more investigations of the
national administration than all the previous Congresses of the
entire nineteenth century.[14]

However, on one occasion, a comparable effort was made by a
Dáil Committee to conduct an investigation which raised constitutional issues reviewed by the Supreme Court. In the case of *In Re
Haughey* 1971 IR 217,[15] an order was made by the Dáil to the
Committee of Public Accounts on 1 December 1970 to examine and
make a report on the expenditures of certain grant-in-aid money
for Northern Ireland relief, and on any money transferred by the

Irish Red Cross Society to a bank account into which moneys from the grant-in-aid were or might have been lodged. Subsequently, on 23 December, the Oireachtas passed the Committee of Public Accounts of Dáil Éireann (Privileges and Procedure) Act 1970. The Act provided that if a witness before the committee refused to answer a question to which the committee legally could require an answer, such committee, through its chairman, might certify this offence to the High Court. The High Court, after such inquiry as it thought proper, might punish the person in the same manner as if the person had been guilty of contempt of the High Court.

The Committee of Public Accounts received hearsay evidence containing serious accusations against Haughey, who appeared as a witness and made a statement but refused to answer questions. The committee certified to the High Court that Haughey's refusal to answer questions constituted an offence under the Act. In the High Court hearing, evidence was furnished on affidavit and Haughey did not ask for a jury trial. The High Court sentenced Haughey to six months imprisonment. The Act was upheld on the grounds that it merely authorised the legislative committee to complete a step preliminary to the criminal trial in the High Court and that no conviction would take place until after appropriate inquiry by the High Court. Moreover, even if the offence were not a minor one, there was nothing in the Act precluding a trial by jury under article 38.5.

On appeal, the Supreme Court reversed the decision of the High Court, holding that the Act did not create the offence of contempt of court. Rather, it created an ordinary criminal offence, which in view of the unlimited nature of the penalty authorised on conviction was not a minor offence under article 38.2 of the Constitution, so that the person charged should be entitled to jury trial under article 38.5 of the Constitution. From this perspective, the Act would violate article 38.5 since it authorises a summary trial in the High Court for an offence which was not a minor offence. If one took the converse view and assumed the offence was a minor one, to be tried by a court of summary jurisdiction, the High Court could not try a person accused of such an offence since it was not a court of summary jurisdiction. Moreover, the Act would allow a penalty appropriate to a non-minor offence to be imposed on conviction for a minor offence, in violation of article 38.

The Supreme Court also found such procedural deficiencies as the giving of evidence against Haughey by affidavit in the High Court rather than orally, as required in criminal trials, which denied him the right to cross-examine witnesses. In addition, when Haughey appeared before the Dáil committee as a person accused of serious offences, he was not afforded the right to cross-examine witnesses or present his case through a lawyer, thus violating article 40.3 of the Constitution.

Executive Controls over Policy-Making

Since a detailed analysis of the administrative law powers and processes of the executive branch will be made in later chapters, consideration of executive power at this point is limited to those situations where basic constitutional issues have been raised in the courts as to the nature of executive power versus legislative or judicial power. One of these basic issues is whether executive policy-making may be challenged through resort to judicial process.

In view of the central role of the Taoiseach and the government in formulating foreign policy, it is unusual to have a challenge to the exercise of this constitutional power of the executive take place in the courts, as it did in *Boland v. An Taoiseach and Others* 1974 IR 338.[16] The origin of this case was the Sunningdale conference in December 1973 between the Irish and British governments and parties involved in the Northern Ireland executive (designate). At the end of the first stage of the conference, the parties issued a communiqué which included in clause 5 parallel statements of the Irish and British governments that they accepted and declared there could be no change in the status of Northern Ireland until it was desired by a majority of the people in Northern Ireland. Clause 6 of the communiqué said that a formal agreement incorporating the statements in clause 5 would be signed at the formal stage of the conference and registered at the United Nations, and clause 20 said that such a formal conference would be held early in 1974.

The plaintiff (a former member of the Dáil and of the government) contended that if the Irish government signed any agreement in the terms of the communiqué, the provisions of clause 5 of the communiqué constituted an infringement of the territorial sovereignty of Ireland and the agreement would be repugnant to articles 1 to 6 and 34 of the Constitution. In particular, it would violate article 2 of the Constitution saying that the 'national territory consists of the whole island of Ireland, its islands and the territorial seas', and article 3 providing that 'pending the re-integration of the national territory, and without prejudice to the right of the parliament and government established by this Constitution, to exercise jurisdiction over the whole of that territory the laws enacted by the parliament shall have the like area and extent of application as the laws of Saorstát Éireann and the like extra-territorial effect'. Plaintiff requested certain declaratory orders, and asked for an injunction to restrain the government from acting upon or implementing clauses 4, 5, 6 and 20 of the communiqué, especially in respect to signing the agreement under clauses 6 and 20 and registering it at the United Nations. The injunction also would prohibit the government from entering into any agreement which would limit the exercise of sovereignty over any portion of the national territory or prejudice the parliament's and government's right to exercise jurisdiction over the whole of the national territory.

The Supreme Court (FitzGerald C. J., O'Keeffe P., Budd, Griffin and Pringle J. J.) held that the declaration and other acts of the government at the Sunningdale conference were an exercise of the executive power of government, and under the circumstances, the courts did not have the constitutional power to review the conduct or policy declarations of the government. The controversial clause 5 was a declaration of policy of the government since a further conference was to be held and a formal agreement reached, which was to be registered at the United Nations. None of these actions would confer additional validity on the agreement until a bill was introduced in the Dáil for approval of such agreement. Under the Constitution, the Executive is charged with formulating policy and is responsible to Dáil Éireann, and according to article 28 every international agreement must be laid before the Dáil and approved before the state is bound by such agreement. Although the Court has the duty to intervene on a complaint that the government is acting contrary to a constitutional provision, nevertheless, as Budd J. stated:

> The Judiciary has its own particular ambit of functions under the Constitution. Mainly, it deals with justiciable controversies between citizen and citizen or the citizen and the State and matters pertaining thereto. Such matters have nothing to do with matters of State policy . . . . I ask whether it could be said

that the Courts could be called upon to pronounce adversely or otherwise on what the Government proposed to do on any matter of policy which it was in the course of formulating. It would seem that would be an attempted interference with matters which are part of the functions of the Executive and not part of the functions of the judiciary. From a practical standpoint alone, what action would be open to the Courts? The Courts could clearly not state that any policy ought not to be pursued. (page 366)

The *Boland* case places the formulation and proposal of policy by the government beyond constitutional challenge in the courts until a proposed bill has been passed as an Act by the Oireachtas and signed by the President, subject to the one exception provided in Article 26 of the Constitution. Under that Article, the President, after consultation with the Council of State, may refer a bill to the Supreme Court for determination as to its constitutionality, not later than the seventh day after the date it has been presented to him for his signature by the Taoiseach, but before the President has signed it. Of the seven occasions on which the President of Ireland has applied this infrequently used power, the one bill dealing with executive power which was most directly related to administrative law was *In re Article 26 of the Constitution and the School Attendance Bill of 1942* 1943 IR 334.[17] Three of the bills so referred dealt with enforcement powers of the executive against criminal actions in the nature of offences against the state, namely, *In re Article 26 of the Constitution and the Offences Against the State (Amendment) Bill, 1940; In re Article 26 of the Constitution and the Criminal Law (Jurisdiction) Bill, 1975* 1977 IR 120; and *In re Article 26 of the Constitution and the Emergency Powers Bill 1976* 1977 IR 154. One reference, *In re Article 26 of the Constitution and the Housing (Private Rented Dwellings) Bill, 1981* 1983 ILRM 246 pertained to whether property rights of landlords in a phasing out of rent control would be considered to be unjustly attacked, contrary to article 43 of the Constitution. In two instances, bills referred to the Supreme Court have been related to Dáil constituencies, i.e. *In re Article 26 and the Electoral (Amendment) Bill, 1961,* 1961 IR 169 and most recently, *In re Reference under Article 26 of the Constitution and the Electoral (Amendment) Bill, 1983* unreported, Supreme Court, per O'Higgins C.J., 8 February 1984.[18]

The administrative law issue in the case of *In re Article 26 of the Constitution and the School Attendance Bill, 1942* 1943 IR 334, 77 ILTR 96, was the constitutionality of section 4(1) of that bill. That section provided that a child would not be considered to be receiving suitable education in any other manner than through attendance 'at a national school, a suitable school or a recognised school unless such education and the manner in which such child is receiving it, have been certified under this section by the Minister to be suitable'. The Bill also provided for the granting and withholding of the Minister's certificate. The Supreme Court held the 1942 Bill to be repugnant to the Constitution on the grounds that it would give excessively wide discretion to the Minister. In the court's view, even though the Minister were to construe the legislation in a reasonable manner, the proposed statute would permit him to require a higher standard of education than that which could be required as a minimum standard under article 32.3.2 of the Constitution. Moreover, that standard required by the Minister would not be a standard of general application as intended by the Constitution, since under the Bill the Minister's standard might vary from one child to another. A situation also could arise in which a parent could be in default and liable to penalties. For example, a child could reach the age of six and be educated at a private school or at home, but a time gap could ensue during the time that it took for the Minister to issue his certificate stating that such substitute education was acceptable.

Executive Control over Policy Implementation

A typical constitutional issue concerning the powers of the executive to enforce or implement a statute following its enactment by the legislature is that raised by a plaintiff who seeks to stop such enforcement or threatened implementation on the ground that discretionary powers delegated to the administration and their application to plaintiff are infringements upon his constitutional rights. For example, in the case of *In re Philip Clarke* 1950 IR 235, 85 ILTR 119,[19] plaintiff attacked section 165 of the Mental Treatment Act 1945, which authorised a member of the Garda Síochána to take a person who was believed 'to be of unsound mind' into custody when it was believed that it was essential for the public safety or the safety of the person to place that person under care and control. Plaintiff claimed that this was an infringement of a citizen's personal rights under article 40.3.1 of the Constitution. However, the Court upheld the constitutionality of the statute:

> The impugned legislation is of a paternal character, clearly intended for the care and custody of persons suspected to be suffering from mental infirmity and for the safety and well being of the public generally. The existence of mental infirmity is too widespread to be overlooked, and was, no doubt, present to the minds of the draftsmen when it was proclaimed in article 40.1 of the Constitution that, though all citizens as human beings are to be held equal before the law, the State may, nevertheless, in its enactments, have due regard to differences of capacity, physical and moral, and of social function. We do not see how the common good would be promoted or the dignity and freedom of the individual assured by allowing persons, alleged to be suffering from such infirmity to remain at large to the possible detriment of themselves and others . . . . The section cannot, in our opinion, be construed as an attack upon the personal rights of the citizen. On the contrary, it seems to us to be designed for the protection of the citizen and for the promotion of the common good. In our opinion the section in question is not repugnant to either the letter or the spirit of the Constitution. (ILTR, page 125)

In the more recent case of *The State (Craven) v. Frawley and the Minister for Justice,* 1980 IR 1, the power of the Minister for Justice to make an administrative transfer of an eighteen-year-old offender detained in St Patrick's Institution for a six-month period, to a prison for the residue of his detention term was upheld against a claim that this was a function constitutionally reserved to the courts.

The Minister's action was taken under section 17 of the Criminal Justice Administration Act 1914, provisions of the Criminal Justice Act 1960, and section 7, Prevention of Crimes Act 1908. Under section 7, when a person detained in a borstal institution is reported by the visiting committee to be incorrigible or exerting a bad influence on other inmates, the Secretary of State (now the Minister for Justice) may commute the unexpired residue of the term of detention to a term of imprisonment not exceeding the unexpired residue. The reason for his action was a report from the visiting committee of St Patrick's Institution, stating that Craven was exercising a bad influence on other inmates as manifested by his leadership in a riot and five other incidents of misconduct, and recommending his transfer to a prison.

In opposition to the transfer, counsel for Craven argued that a court must make the decision as to where a convicted person under 21 years of age should be detained based on judicial discretion, taking into account matters at the time of sentencing. Further, there is a distinction between a sentence of imprisonment and a sentence of detention in St Patrick's. The power to change a sentence of detention imposed by a court into a term of imprisonment is a function reserved under articles 34.1 and 38.1 of the Constitution to the courts, as part of the judicial process of trial of a criminal charge. In response, Gannon J. held:

> It seems to be implicit in *White's Case.* [*The State (White) v. His Honour, Judge Martin* (1976) 111 ILTR 21], and it is clearly shown in *The State (C.) v. The Minister for Justice* [1976 IR 106; 102 ILTR 177], that a change of place of detention may become necessary in the interests of the health of the prisoner or of the better administration of prisons and that the making of such change is an administrative, and not a judicial, function. The fact that the investigation of all relevant and pertinent facts before the decision to make such a change must be carried out in a manner consistent with natural justice and may be performed in a judicial fashion does not make the function one reserved solely for the Court under the Constitution.

I have no doubt that the matter now before me must be determined in accordance with the decision of the Supreme Court in *Sheerin's Case [The State (Sheerin) v. Kennedy* 1966 IR 379]. Furthermore, the decision in *White's Case [The State (White) v. His Honour Judge Martin]* makes it clear that the course taken by the Minister in this instance was appropriate in the circumstances, as is shown by the report of the visiting committee. (page 7)

The Executive and Privilege of State

In addition to policy-making and execution, another dimension of executive power in Ireland consists of certain legal prerogatives of the executive known as the Attorney General's fiat and as the 'privilege of state'. These prerogatives limit the legal rights of a citizen suing a minister or other governmental official exercising discretionary powers. They relate to basic legal doctrines concerning both the legal status of the sovereign state in litigation with its citizens, and to the tension between executive exercise of powers in the public interest versus judicial power to protect legal rights of adversely affected individual citizens. However, the Attorney General's fiat, which is the requirement that formal permission be obtained from the Attorney General to sue a minister, is more directly related to the concept that the sovereign immunity of the Crown from suit without its consent was transferred to the Irish state as an entity. Consequently it is discussed in the following chapter dealing with liability and immunity of the state to suits by its citizens. On the other hand the claim of executive privilege pertains primarily to the power of governmental officials to deny access to documents concerning internal administrative communication and processes to citizens suing those officials. The reason for denial is that it is in the public interest and a matter of public policy to ensure the candour essential to effective communication between officials and staff advice to executives making and implementing policy decisions. This conflicts with the power of the courts to protect citizens' legal rights which may depend on access to such documents in litigation. Thus it is more directly related to the present discussion concerning executive powers.

The claim of executive privilege had its origin as one of the prerogatives of the Crown, namely to be immune from being forced to produce documents or to give information in any criminal or civil proceedings of the Crown, on the grounds that producing such data would be against public policy interest or service.[20] The Irish courts have taken the position that the claim to executive privilege could be based upon state interest and public policy regardless of whether the proposition that the privilege of the Crown was transferred to Irish officials was accepted or not. In the early case of *Leen v. the President of the Executive Council and Others* (No. 1) 1926 IR 456, involving a claim for payment of compensation for malicious damage, the Court upheld the refusal of defendant to respond to interrogatories on the grounds that if the defendant had the privilege of the Crown, the judge could not go behind his objection that disclosures would be detrimental to the public interest and service and contrary to public policy. Even if the contention is correct that this privilege can only be claimed by the Crown, the Court could:

> find nothing, however, in the authorities on this privilege in respect of discovery to suggest that the rule of law which has always been in force, and which has to be administered as heretofore under the Constitution of the Irish Free State, is dependent upon the magic of any particular nomenclature . .
> . . The principle has its roots in the general conception of State interests and the functions of Courts of Justice, which make it independent of the particular type of constitution under which the body of law which recognises that principle is administered. (page 468)

Similar concepts of this privilege were asserted and upheld in *Kenny v. Minister for Defence* 1942 Ir. Jur. Rep. 81, involving a contract with the army in which the Minister made a claim of privilege concerning confidential documents. They also were upheld in respect of confidentiality of communication between superior and subordinate police officers in *People (Attorney General) v. Simpson* 1959 IR 105, 93 ILTR 33 and *The State (Quinn) v. Ryan and Others* 1965 IR 70, 100 ILTR 105.

Shortly after the *Quinn* decision, a case directly involving administrative law asserted the Court's powers of inquiry against the executive power to control access to documents on a claim of executive privilege. The case of *O'Leary and Others v. Minister for Industry and Commerce and Others* 1966 IR 676 arose when the Electricity Supply Board (ESB) submerged a bridge near plaintiff's lands while developing a hydro-electric scheme under the Electricity Supply (Amendment) Act 1945. The Act required the ESB to build a new bridge unless relieved of this requirement by an order of the Minister for Industry and Commerce, based on his satisfaction from relevant data that the bridge was not required. The Minister issued two orders which: (1) amended the scheme by eliminating the requirement that the public road over the bridge be diverted to another point and (2) relieved the ESB from constructing a new bridge. Plaintiffs claimed that the Minister's orders were null and void and that the ESB must construct a new road and bridge. Dissatisfied with the affidavits of discovery of documents filed by defendants, plaintiffs applied to the High Court for an order to make further and better discovery and to produce the documents disclosed. The High Court upheld the claim of the Minister for Transport and Power, who had succeeded to the duties of the Minister for Industry and Commerce, that the application should be dismissed, since further discovery by him was contrary to public policy and against the public interest and service.

On appeal to the Supreme Court by plaintiffs, the Minister filed a supplemental affidavit of discovery identifying individual documents. However, he claimed entitlement to refuse disclosure of their content as being against the public interest, since the documents were communications between his Department and the ESB, requiring 'utmost freedom and candour of communication' in advice and data from the ESB, plus communications with other departments on policy matters and with the Attorney General on the duties and powers of the Minister under the Acts. The Supreme Court held that the Minister's functions under the 1945 Act, rather than putting him in a relationship which would entitle such communications to privilege from disclosure, actually placed a duty on him to 'keep the parties at arm's length' (page 696). The Minister was balancing the conflicting interest of the ESB in being relieved of the obligation to provide a new bridge versus the interest of the public in general and local residents in particular in possible loss if the bridge is not built. Ó Dálaigh C.J. stated:

> He (the Minister) is an arbiter. The Act uses the verb satisfied. This implies a judicial consideration of all the facts and circumstances . . .the Minister is required to make an objective finding in effect as between parties. The communications of the Board to the Minister in this instance are not the communications of an adviser in relation to the discharge of a statutory duty but the representations of a party with an interest. (pages 696-7)

The Chief Justice refused the Minister's claim of privilege as a misinterpretation of the obligations placed on him, and did not consider the constitutional issue involved in the claim.

However, in the subsequent case of *Murphy v. Corporation of Dublin* 1972 IR 215, 107 ILTR 65, the Supreme Court not only determined the need for executive privilege based on the merits of the specific situation, rather than accepting the Minister's routine statement asserting that privilege, but also applied constitutional concepts pertaining to the role of the courts in deciding whether documents will be disclosed. In *Murphy*, plaintiff sought a declaration from the High Court that a compulsory purchase order for his land made by the Corporation of Dublin under section 76 of the Housing Act 1966 was invalid, and an injunction to restrain the corporation from acting on foot of the order. The central issue in the interlocutory proceedings was whether a report of a public hearing held under article 5 (2) of the third schedule to the Housing Act 1966 made by the inspector holding the hearing, which provided the basis for the Minister's confirmation of the purchase order, should be made available under an order of discovery to be issued by the High Court. An Assistant Secretary of the Department stated by sworn affidavit that producing the report would be 'contrary to public policy and detrimental to the public interest and service'; that proper performance of ministerial functions under the 1966 Act required the 'utmost freedom of communication between a presiding inspector at a public inquiry and the Minister'; and that the report was 'within a class of document which on grounds of public interest ought to be withheld from production or disclosure' (pages 230-31). Kenny J., for the High Court, held that although the High Court must decide the availability of a document in every case, there were certain categories of documents which under no circumstances should be produced for High Court inspection. These include minutes of government meetings, military and diplomatic documents or memoranda on policy formation or proposed legislation. Though an inspector's report on an inquiry is not in these categories, a Minister may claim the right not to produce the report as it would be against the public interest or as a matter of policy, and the courts should accept the Minister's view unless demonstrably not formed in good faith, unreasonable, or involving a misunderstanding of the issues. Kenny J. refused production of the report to plaintiff or High Court for inspection as there was no evidence that any of these three exceptions applied.

In the Supreme Court reversal of this decision, Walsh J. noted that the Constitution gives the administration of justice solely to the judiciary and that the power to compel attendance of witnesses and production of evidence is an inherent judicial power constituting the ultimate safeguard of justice. It follows that although an executive's or head of government's opinion in a situation involving safety of the state may be sufficient evidence to justify a claim of non-disclosure or production of a document:

> It is, however, impossible for the judicial power in the proper exercise of its functions to permit any other body or power to decide for it whether or not a document will be disclosed or produced. In the last resort the decision lies with the Courts so long as they have seisin of the case. (page 234)

Walsh J. granted that even routine administration not dealing with security may involve documents which should not be produced in the public interest. The courts can sometimes determine this without examining the documents, while at other times judicial inspection is essential. No document may be withheld simply because it belongs to a particular category; once the court is satisfied the document is relevant, the claim of privilege must be based on the nature of the document and the reasons for claiming privilege. The High Court should not have accepted the Minister's opinion without examination since the High Court did not express a view on the claims made in the Assistant Secretary's affidavit, and the subsequent confirmation by the Minister was merely a statement of a conclusion. The documents should have been produced at least for inspection by the Court, followed by a decision.

Given the *Murphy* decision, it is not surprising that in the subsequent case of *Geraghty v. Minister for Local Government* 1975 IR 300, discussed in detail in chapter 5, the High Court and Supreme Court judges examined all the documents concerning a planning decision sought by the plaintiff, despite the Minister's certification that their disclosure would be contrary to public policy and detrimental to the public interest and service. All but four of the documents were ordered to be produced; the four not disclosed involved legal advice and confidentiality of communication between civil servants. (See discussion at pages 207-211, see also *Folens v. Minister for Education* 1981 ILRM 21; *Hunt v. Roscommon VEC* unreported, High Court, McWilliam J., 1 May 1981.)

Judicial Independence and Power

One indicator of judicial power is the extent to which the previously described constitutional provisions granting independence to the courts and judicial process from intrusions by the legislature or executive had been upheld in practice. The Sinn Féin Funds case (*Buckley and Others v. Attorney General* 1950 IR 67)[21] led to the decision that the Oireachtas may not remove a case from the jurisdiction and judgment of the courts, while action is pending thereon, by passing an Act providing that all further proceedings in the case be stayed, the case be dismissed on application *ex parte* of the Attorney General and funds held by the Court be surrendered for distribution by an administrative board. In another instance, the Supreme Court in *The State (Coughlan) v. Minister for Justice*, 1967 IR 106[22] held that section 13, Lunatic Asylums (Ireland) Act 1875, constituted a legislative interference with an exercise of judicial power to administer justice. A District Justice had charged prosecutor with indictable offences and remanded him to an institution for psychiatric examination and he was certified insane. The Minister for Justice, under provisions of section 13 of the 1875 Act, then ordered the transfer of Coughlan to another institution for confinement until certified as sane. The Supreme Court held that this would prevent the accused person from appearing before the District Court on the return date of his remand, which was an interference with judicial power. More recently, in *Maher v. Attorney General* 1973 IR 140, the Supreme Court held that the combined effects of the Road Traffic Acts of 1961 and 1968 were to make an administrative certification concerning the results of tests for alcohol in the blood or urine final and incontestable, provided that compliance with the procedural steps for obtaining and testing the blood or urine sample prescribed by regulations can be demonstrated. Since section 44 (2) provided that the certificate shall be 'conclusive evidence', the Supreme Court per FitzGerald C.J. held that 'insofar as the statutory provision in question purports to remove such determination from the judges or the courts appointed and established under the Constitution, it is an invalid infringement of the judicial power' (page 146). At the same time the Court also refused to sever from the portion of the Act which was under attack, the critical offending word 'conclusive' which made it unconstitutional, on the ground that this would constitute a judicial intrusion on legislative power.

The courts invalidated executive intrusion upon judicial power in the case of *Irish Agricultural Wholesale Society v. St. Enda's Co-operative Society* 1924 (2) IR 41, 58 ILTR 14[23] in which the Court held that a statement or letter of the Minister for Home Affairs, indicating

D

that conditions during the civil war did not merit military escorts for summons servers, was not in any way binding on the courts, and must not affect a judge's determination. As indicated in the preceding discussion of executive power, the courts have asserted the power to arrive at their own discretionary decisions as to the validity of a claim of executive privilege from producing documents for examination, rather than automatically excluding certain documents falling within a particular class, or accepting a Minister's sworn affidavit as conclusive. (See *O'Leary v. Minister for Industry and Commerce* 1966 IR 676; *Murphy v. Corporation of Dublin* 1972 IR 215, 107 ILTR 65 and *Geraghty v. Minister for Local Government* 1976 IR 153). *In Macauley v. Minister for Posts and Telegraphs and the Attorney General* 1966 IR 435,[24] the requirement of obtaining the Attorney General's fiat to sue a Minister of State in the High Court was held unconstitutional and the right of access to the Court was upheld. In yet another aspect of access to the courts it will be seen in chapter 10 dealing with the availability and scope of judicial review that a statutory provision making certain Land Commission determinations final and conclusive was held not to be in violation of constitutional provisions protecting property rights in *Fisher v. Irish Land Commission and Attorney General* 1948 IR 3, 82 ILTR 50. However, it will be seen that the courts have also held in a number of cases that such grants of finality of determination to administrators will not preclude judicial review and invalidation of such determination when they are *ultra vires* the statute, as in *Waterford Corporation v. Murphy* 1920 (2) IR 165, 54 ILTR 32; *Murren v. Brennan* 1942 IR 466, 76 ILTR 120; *The State (Horgan) v. Exported Live Stock Insurance Board* 1943 IR 581; and *The State (McCarthy) v. O'Donnell and Minister for Defence* 1945 IR 126.

A strong statement for safeguarding access to the courts, against a potential form of legislative and executive evasion of the judicial power to review a claim of violation of constitutional rights, is made in *Condon v. Minister for Labour and Attorney General* 1981 IR 62. Plaintiffs were members of the Irish Bank Officials' Association who refused to be bound by the terms of the annual national wage agreements and entered into an agreement providing for pay rates and employment conditions for the year starting 1 June 1975 with the Bank Staff Relations Committee representing employing banks. Since the rates of remuneration were higher than the national norm, the government viewed this as potentially dangerous to the economy, and the Oireachtas enacted the Regulation of Banks (Remuneration and Conditions of Employment (Temporary Provisions)) Act 1975. The Act authorised the Minister for Labour to determine by order the days on which the Act would come into effect and expire. The Minister made an order bringing the 1975 Act into operation on 15 December 1985 and on the same date made another order prohibiting payment by the associated banks of more than the amounts of the national wage agreements.

In response to these actions, the bank officials (plaintiffs) initiated proceedings on 23 December 1975 and later delivered a statement of claim seeking a declaration that the 1975 Act and Minister's prohibition order were repugnant to the Constitution. On 1 April 1976 defendants filed a defence denying such claim and asserting the constitutionality of the Act. Following notice of trial on 12 April, the Minister on 29 June made an order that the 1975 Act expired as of that date. He then gave notice of intent to apply to amend his defence by submitting that the plaintiffs' statement of claim disclosed no cause of action, since the Act had expired on 29 June 1976, and moreover, the order prohibiting increases in pay had expired 15 June 1976. Consequently there was no subject matter in respect of which the relief claimed could operate.

The preliminary issue therefore was raised as to whether the action should be dismissed, and the High Court, per McWilliams J., found against the defendant. On appeal to the Supreme Court, O'Higgins C. J. rejected defendant's argument that since the impugned Act had expired, consideration of the validity of the Act would be an academic exercise outside the function of the courts under article 34 of the Constitution. He stated:

> In large measure, preservation of constitutional rights depends on the manner in which the Courts exercise the power of judicial review over legislation. A strong, healthy and concerned public opinion may, in the words of Edmund Burke, 'sniff the approach of tyranny in every tainted breeze', but effective resistance to unwarranted encroachment on constitutional guarantees and rights depends, in the ultimate analysis, on the Courts. If access to the Courts in denied or prevented or obstructed, then such encroachment, being unchallenged, may become habitual and therefore, acceptable. (page 69)

O'Higgins C. J. noted events leading to the appeal to the Supreme Court, the Minister's contention that the Act was not contrary to the Constitution which implied that similar legislation might be introduced in the future, and that identical legislation and process for termination had taken place in the past. Given these factors, there could be serious consequences if the Court held that this type of temporary legislation was immune from judicial review simply because it had expired before its validity could be examined. All legislation passed by the Oireachtas is presumed valid, and if the Oireachtas could enact temporary legislation which created offences and provided for serious penalties (as this Act did) but which could escape judicial review on expiry, 'a form of legislative intimidation could be exercised'. The Court would not be exercising the 'vigilance and care upon which constitutional rights and guarantees depend for their protection' (page 70).

In a similar vein, Kenny J. felt that given the minimum of six months between the signing of an Act by the President and the day a case challenging its validity is heard (during which time the Act is presumed valid) a refusal by the Court to decide the case, since the impugned Act has been made non-operative by ministerial order:

> would give the Oireachtas a most convenient way of avoiding judicial review by the Court of the constitutional validity of the Act. If a Bill is introduced which contains a provision that the Act shall cease to be in operation when a Minister makes an order having that effect, the Oireachtas by insertion of such a section in any bill could remove short term legislation from effective judicial review. But judicial review was intended by those who enacted the constitution to extend to all legislation whether it be long or short-term. (page 71)

Kenny J. concluded that the principle to be followed has been enunciated in analagous United States Supreme Court judgments pertinent to this issue (citing relevant judgments). The principle is that when the issue arises as to whether the Court should refuse to entertain a case because the legislation in question is no longer in force, the determining factor is whether or not similar legislation is likely to be introduced in the future. If similar legislation is likely to be introduced, the Court should decide the case. Since it is highly probable that legislation similar to the Act of 1975 will be introduced in the future, the Minister and officials should be aware of the constitutional validity of similar legislation in the future. 'Therefore on principle and on the authority of the cases decided in the United States of America, the action is not moot even though the Act of 1975 was not in force when the case came for trial' (page 75).

Judicial Power: Nature and Limits on Delegation

More directly related to administrative law is the question of whether there has been an unconstitutional delegation of judicial power by the legislature to the executive, which also raises the fundamental issue of what constitutes the nature of judicial power and functions under articles 34.1 and 37 of the Constitution. Kelly's analysis of judicial decisions under the 1922 Constitution, with *Lynham v. Butler* (No. 2) 1933 IR 74, 67 ILTR 75 as a focal point, and the interpretation of article 37 of the 1937 Constitution reflected in *Fisher v. Irish Land Commission* 1948 IR 3, 82 ILTR 50; *The State (Crowley) v. Irish Land Commission* 1951 IR 250, 85 ILTR 26, and *Foley v. Irish Land Commission* 1952 IR 118, 86 ILTR 44 leads to his statement:

> The result of article 37 and of the cases decided before and after its enactment could be summarised as follows. Firstly, there is an 'administration of justice' in 'justiciable controversies' such as must be reserved to judges in courts: Art. 34 (Art. 64 of the 1922 Constitution). Secondly, there is (in the Supreme Court's words in *Foley's* case) a power – such as was recognised in *Lynham's* case – of an administrative body 'by its determination within jurisdiction to impose liabilities and affect rights'. But thirdly, there appeared to exist a further type of power, one which the Courts hesitated to ascribe to either of the two former categories, namely, a 'limited power or function of a judicial nature within the meaning of Art. 37'.[25]

Given this situation, the courts under the 1922 Constitution did not define clearly administration of justice as being solely capable of performance by judges or what constituted an administrative determination of liabilities or rights, with a consequent lack of

demarcation between judicial power and administrative determination. Moreover, article 37 of the 1937 Constitution, rather than
resolving matters, led to a third category of power which also was
undefined. This 'uncertainty created by article 37 and reflected in
the *Fisher, Crowley* and *Foley* judgments, continued as did the somewhat hand-to-mouth approach to establishing what was an
"administration of justice" in the sense of article 34.1'.[26]

Judicial decisions following *Fisher, Crowley* and *Foley*, which
involve administative law issues most relevant to the nature of
and limits on delegation of judicial power by the legislature to
administrative bodies, would seem to affirm what Kelly characterises as a 'hand-to-mouth approach' or as it is referred to in the
United States 'a gradual and empiric process of inclusion and
exclusion' (Justice Frankfurter in *Wolf v. Colorado* 338 US 25
(1949)).

An important case in this regard is *In re Solicitors Act 1954 and In
re O'Farrell and Gorman* 1960 IR 239, 95 ILTR 167[27] involving a
challenge against the constitutionality of provisions in the Solicitors
Act which established a disciplinary committee appointed by the
Incorporated Law Society and prescribed a disciplinary process.
(See sections 14, 16, 13 (1), 23, Solicitors Act 1954.) A client of
the appellants, O'Farrell and Gorman, solicitors in partnership,
complained to the Incorporated Law Society that despite her repeated requests, they failed to deliver money belonging to her
which was in their possession. Appellants were found guilty by
the Disciplinary Committee following its inquiry, which neither
appellants or their counsel attended, nor did they file an affidavit
in response to the inquiry. The Committee ordered their names to
be struck off the solicitors' roll, that they pay costs to the Society,
and that the findings and order be published in three daily papers,
the Incorporated Law Society's *Gazette* and *Iris Oifigiúil*. This action
was appealed to the Chief Justice under section 23 of the 1954 Act,
alleging that sections 4, 5, 7 and 13 to 23 were *ultra vires* the
Constitution by delegating judicial authority to a group of persons
or body not created or sanctioned by the Constitution and not
appointed by the Chief Justice, as well as unconstitutionally limiting
and usurping the powers, rights and duties of the judiciary. Maguire
C.J. dismissed the appeal and the appellants appealed to the
Supreme Court.

Kingsmill Moore J., for the Supreme Court, quoting from the

judgment of Kennedy C.J. in the *Lynham* case, noted that this issue could be raised only where there is a written constitution embodying the theory of separation of powers. In *Lynham*, Australian and American judicial precedents were cited and Kennedy C.J. defined judicial power as the power to determine guilt or innocence of persons charged with offences against the state, punishment of those found guilty, and rights and obligations in a dispute between parties with finality, all enforceable by state authority. Judicial power includes authority to compel attendance of witnesses and order execution of judgments against persons and property. Kingsmill Moore J. also analysed what does not constitute an exercise of judicial power. For example, the Land Commission must *act* judicially in the exercise of its administrative power, but this does not mean that it is exercising judicial power, as established in *Fisher v. Irish Land Commission* 1948 IR 3, 82 ILTR 50; *State (Crowley) v. Irish Land Commission* 1951 IR 250; and *Foley v. Irish Land Commission* 1952 IR 118, 86 ILTR 44. As to a related claim that the Disciplinary Committee combined the roles of complainant, tribunal and hearing of the complaint, thus having a built-in bias, Kingsmill Moore J. held that the Constitution imposes restrictions on the composition of a body only if it is administering justice.

Applying these criteria to a detailed analysis of the powers of the Committee to compel attendance of witnesses through a summons, to make orders as enforceable as if they were a judgment or order of the High Court, to strike solicitors' names off the roll and award costs and restitution to an aggrieved party, the judge concluded that the Committee's powers constituted an exercise of judicial power of the state, entrusted to persons other than judges, in contravention of article 34 of the Constitution. Such powers were not merely limited powers and functions of a judicial nature permitted under article 37.

Further insight into the perspective of Irish courts as to what constitutes judicial power which cannot be delegated to bodies other than courts is afforded in *Cowan v. Attorney General and Others* 1961 IR 411.[28] In this case, plaintiff's election to the Dublin City Council was challenged through an election petition on grounds of his disqualification as an undischarged bankrupt. The trial of the petition was to be held by a practising barrister of not less than seven years' standing from a panel of five appointed for trial of municipal election petitions by three judges of the High Court on the rota for trial of parliamentary election petitions, in accordance with the Municipal Corporation Act 1882 and the Municipal Elections (Corrupt and Illegal Practices) Act 1884.

Plaintiff argued that by providing for election courts and giving them judicial functions, the two Acts were contrary to article 34 of the Constitution. Haugh J. for the High Court concluded that in contrast with powers exercised by the Adoption Board, or deciding officers in the Department of Social Welfare or the Land Commission, the election court 'is administering justice at the suit of those who request its aid'. It performs the same work the High Court had performed when trying municipal election petitions before the Acts established the election courts. The election courts may order attendance of witnesses, require testimony under threat of contempt, and summarily try any person prosecuted for corrupt or illegal practice with a maximum penalty of six months in jail or fine up to £200, subject to the option of being tried by jury rather than summarily. It may award costs against individuals under certain conditions. As Haugh J. stated:

> An election court when commencing the hearing of an election petition may know what it is about to try, but if and when, in any petition, the court should, of its own volition, order the attendance of a new witness or witnesses, entirely new issues may arise that may involve findings by the court that could well affect, in the most profound and far-reaching way, the lives, liberties, fortunes or reputations of those against whom they are exercised; and I am of opinion that the (election) court, availing of all the powers and duties conferred upon it in its ordinary day-to-day exercise of its powers and functions, is in fact not exercising the limited functions and powers allowable by Article 37, and is therefore unconstitutional. (page 423)

A more subtle delegation of judicial power was invalidated in *Deaton v. Attorney General and Revenue Commissioners*, 1963 IR 170, 98 ILTR 99.[29] The plaintiff alleged that section 186 of the Customs Consolidation Act 1876 was unconstitutional, since it empowered the Revenue Commissioners to elect which of the penalties therein prescribed would be imposed by the District Court if the District Court decided to convict the accused, and such determination of penalty is a judicial function which cannot be given to the executive. In the High Court, Kenny J. held that the election of the penalty by the Revenue Commissioners only determines what a person must pay if the courts find him liable; it does not affect the District Justice or Circuit Court Judge's decision on appeal as to *whether* the defendant should pay that penalty. However, on appeal the Supreme Court per Ó Dálaigh C.J. reversed, holding that the power of the Revenue Commissioners to elect the penalty was repugnant to the Constitution, because the legislature had not prescribed the penalty to be imposed on individuals but merely stated a general rule providing a range of penalties. Since the degree of punishment affects the liberty of citizens, it was inconceivable under a constitution based on separation of powers that the power to elect a punishment could be placed in the hands of the executive. However, in this instance, the Court did not declare the whole section unconstitutional. The Court felt it could sever the offending words 'at the election of the Revenue Commissioners' from the body of the Act, with the result that the Courts would have power to determine which of the alternative penalties would be imposed together with the issue of guilt or innocence of the accused.

Given the above reversals of the delegation of adjudicatory power, upon what grounds may such delegation meet the approval of the courts? In a later case, *In re Solicitor's Act 1954 and D., a Solicitor* 95 ILTR 60, the appeal was to the Chief Justice from a direction of the Incorporated Law Society to the Registrar of Solicitors to refuse the customary annual practising certificate under section 49 (1) and (2) of the Act. The Court distinguished this action from that of striking a solicitor from the roll of practising solicitors as in the previously discussed case of *In re Solicitors Act 1954 and O'Farrell and Gorman* 1960 IR 239, since this decision of the Disciplinary Committee was not final in the same sense as a decision to order the removal of a solicitor's name from the roll. The solicitor's name had not been struck off: he had been refused a practising certificate for the current year in a procedure which was not final as there was an appeal to the Chief Justice. Consequently, section 49 of the Act was not an unconstitutional delegation of power to administer justice.

It also was determined by the Supreme Court that judicial power had not been delegated in violation of articles 34 and 37 reversing a judgment of the High Court in *McDonald v. Bord na gCon and*

Attorney General 1965 IR 217, 100 ILTR 89 (Supreme Court).[30] In this case, plaintiff appealed from an exclusion order issued by Bord na gCon under section 47, Greyhound Industry Act 1958 with the consent of the Irish Coursing Club. The order prohibited McDonald from being on any greyhound racing track, being at any authorised coursing meeting or being at any public sales of greyhounds. His claim was that section 47 of the Act and the exclusion order were unconstitutional delegations of judicial power, in violation of articles 34, 37 and 38 of the Constitution.

Kenny J. stated in the High Court that with respect to the issue of whether the Board was administering justice:

> It seems to me that the administration of justice has these characteristic features: 1, a dispute or controversy as to the existence of legal right or a violation of the law; 2, the determination or ascertainment of the rights of parties or the imposition of liabilities or the infliction of a penalty; 3, the final determination (subject to appeal) of legal rights or liabilities or the imposition of penalties; 4, the enforcement of those rights or liabilities or the imposition of a penalty by the Court or by the executive power of the State which is called in by the Court to enforce its judgement; 5, the making of an order by the Court which as a matter of history is an order characteristic of Courts in this country. (IR, page 231)

Kenny J. felt that the exclusion order possessed all of the above characteristics of the administration of justice: the Board makes an exclusion order only when satisfied there is a violation of the code of conduct governing greyhound racing which necessarily involves a controversy; it is an imposition of a liability since the Board is given power to impose fines; and it involves a determination of guilt of some disreputable behaviour or conduct. Although an exclusion order can be enforced only by the licensee of a greyhound racing track rather than by executive authority of the state, any body or tribunal which may lawfully execute its orders by physical force does not differ from a court. An exclusion order would seem similar in form and effect to an injunction against trespass, which is an order characteristic of courts. Although not able to summon witnesses, administer oaths, or penalise for contempt, the test of whether a power is limited by article 37 of the Constitution when exercised lies in the effect of the assigned power when exercised, as indicated in *In re Solicitors Act 1954* 1960 IR 239. In the judge's opinion, 'the power to make such an order (by Bord na gCon) is calculated ordinarily to affect in the most profound and far-reaching way the fortunes and reputation of owners and trainees.'

The Supreme Court after detailed analysis of the Board's powers to investigate and make findings leading to an exclusion order held that those powers are such as to:

> require that the procedure which can lead to that result must conform to the principles of natural justice. In the context of the Constitution, natural justice might be more appropriately termed constitutional justice and must be understood to import more than the two well established principles that no man shall be a judge in his own cause and *audi alteram partem*. (page 242)

At the same time, the Court held that the bodies or persons conducting the investigations under sections 43 and 44:

> while bound to act judicially, are not constituted judicial persons or bodies nor do they exercise powers of a judicial nature within the meaning of Article 37 of the Constitution. . . . Accepting the characteristic features of a judicial body set out by Mr. Justice Kenny, these investigating authorities do not satisfy any of those requirements . . . . the Board . . . . or the Club in the exercise of its powers under the section [47]. . . are not constituted judicial bodies or do not exercise powers of a judicial nature as they would only satisfy one of the tests referred to. In the opinion of the Court the submission that the Act in s.47 violates the provisions of Articles 34, 37 and 38 of the Constitution fails. (page 244)

Four years after the *McDonald* case, Kenny J., in *Central Dublin Development Association Ltd & Others v. Attorney General* 109 ILTR 69, ruled on a constitutional issue involving article 37, in respect of the power of the Minister for Local Government to determine what was 'development' as against 'exempted development' under the Local Government (Planning and Development) Act 1963. Kenny J. held that despite being an administration of justice, this was a limited power, subject to appeal to the High Court. The Minister's decision as to what is 'development' as against 'exempted development' does not affect 'the fortune of citizens in a profound way'. The Minister's decision merely determines whether the obtaining of permission from the local planning authority to develop is or is not required. His decision does not entail the determination to grant or not grant such permission. That decision is made by the local planning authority, which thereby makes the determination as to whether a particular development may be carried out. Kenny J. also noted that it is not possible to establish a test to differentiate between limited and unlimited powers and functions of a judicial nature, since the scope and impact of such functions and powers must be determined in each individual case.

Two more recent cases show that the issue of constitutionality of delegation of judicial power continues to be raised. In *The State (Murray) v. Governor of Limerick Prison* 1979 IR 133, the issues were whether the Governor of Limerick Prison was administering justice in exercising disciplinary powers under rules 68 and 69 of the Rules for the Government of Prisons 1947, and if so, was he exercising a limited function of a judicial nature in a matter other than a criminal matter. The High Court, per Finlay P., dealt with the second issue at the outset, and held that the Governor was performing a limited function in making a determination as to whether the prosecutrix had committed a breach of prison discipline as set forth in the rules, and if there were such a violation of discipline, in determining which if any of the permissible penalties provided in rule 69 would be applied. At no time does the Governor determine whether the prisoner has committed a crime against the state or the public, but only a breach of prison discipline, and the appropriate penalty. The fact that the conduct also may be an offence against the state does not make his investigation one concerning a criminal matter. He therefore was exercising a power of a limited nature, and so by definition was not in violation of article 34.

A reaffirmation of previous determinations concerning articles 34 and 37, and an explicit, unequivocal ruling that a particular function of the Land Commission falls within the category of a limited judicial power under article 37 was made in *Madden v. Ireland, Attorney General, Land Commission and Others* High Court, unreported, per McMahon J., 22 May 1980. Plaintiff appealed from compulsory acquisition of his newly purchased farm of 230 acres by the Land

Commission to relieve congestion under section 25 of the Land Act 1936. That section prescribes procedures for publishing a certificate as to the need for the land and a provisional list, the hearing of objections to the list by the Lay Commissioners, and an appeal on a question of law or the price of the land to the Appeal Tribunal. It also provides for the procedure to be followed in fixing the price of such land under section 25 (2) of the Land Act 1923 as amended by section 5 of the Land Act 1950. The plaintiff's arguments were that the Lay Commissioners are deciding justiciable controversies about questions of fact when they hear an objection to a provisional list. Moreover, in fixing the price of the lands the Lay Commissioners and the Appeal Tribunal are deciding questions of legal right. In both instances, they are exercising judicial power in violation of article 34.1, since these functions do not fall within the category of limited functions and powers of judicial nature under article 37. Moreover, the guarantees of property rights under articles 40.3 and 43 demand that the law provide the best protection of such rights, namely a judicial, not an administrative, process.

McMahon J. held that the objections made by the plaintiff on constitutional grounds in respect of the functions of the Lay Commissioners when they hear objections to a provisional list, under section 25, Land Act 1936, could not be sustained, based on principles established in *Fisher v. Irish Land Commission* 1948 IR 3, 82 ILTR 50; *The State (Crowley) v. Irish Land Commission* 1951 IR 250, 85 ILTR 26; and *Clarke v. Irish Land Commission* 1976 IR 375. In those cases, it was determined that the Lay Commissioners and Appeal Tribunal must act judicially, but it does not follow from this that they are administering justice and exercising judicial power. Further, it was held in *Attorney General v. Southern Industrial Trust Ltd and Another* (1960) 94 ILTR 161, that property rights under article 40 are subject to the claims of social justice under article 43.2(1), which include the procedures by which jurisdiction to interfere with property rights may be prescribed by the legislature.

However, with respect to the fixing of the price of land acquired by compulsory process, McMahon J. stated:

> I find it difficult in regard to the function of the Lay Commissioners and on appeal the Appeal Tribunal in fixing the price of land compulsorily acquired as merely the exercise of an administrative power . . . . In this process there is no scope

for policy concepts and what is being decided is solely a
question of legal right. In my view the jurisdiction so exercised
by the Lay Commissioners and on appeal the Appeal Tribunal
constitutes the administration of justice and the exercise of
judicial power.

I am satisfied that it is an exercise of judicial power which is
sanctioned by article 37 of the Constitution. It is not the power
to dispossess the owner which is the question here but the power
to ascertain the fair market value of the land expropriated and
on that basis to fix the price to be paid to the owner. In my
view that is a power which is of limited nature . . . . Experience
has shown that modern government cannot be carried on
without many regulatory bodies and those bodies cannot function effectively under a rigid separation of powers. Article 37
had no counterpart in the Constitution of Saorstát Éireann and
in my view introduction of it to the Constitution is to be
attributed to a realisation of the needs of modern Government.
The ascertainment of the market value of a holding of lands
by an administrative body with special experience appears to
me to be the kind of judicial power contemplated by article 37.
(pages 8-9)

In this statement, McMahon J. identifies an administrative power
as clearly falling under article 37, and emphasises how it meets
the intent of article 37 to recognise the need for administrative
adjudicatory power in the modern state, in contrast with the somewhat equivocal rulings in certain preceding cases.

Forms of Judicial Remedies

Since the exercise of judicial power depends upon a controversy
being submitted to the courts for adjudication, two integral aspects
of judicial power are first, the forms of remedies through which
review and some type of judicial relief may be granted, and second,
the grounds for giving such review and relief. The forms of remedies
include specific statutory provision for review by named courts,
the 'prerogative' public law remedies of certiorari, prohibition,

mandamus and habeas corpus, and the 'ordinary' private law remedies of injunction, declaratory action, and action for damages.

Specific Statutory Review

Statutes conferring administrative powers may provide explicitly for appeal from determinations of the administrative authority on a point of law, or for full review and judicial substitution of judgment by a named court, or for a choice as to appeal to a court or a higher administrative tribunal (but not both). (See Land Act 1933, section 7 (6); Medical Practitioners Act 1978, section 47 (1)-(5) and section 49 (1)-(5); and Unfair Dismissals Act 1977, section 15 (11-31).) Such provisions normally resolve the question as to the authority for and form of appeal to the courts.

Certiorari

An order of certiorari is an order from a higher court to a lower court or administrative tribunal or authority requiring it to transmit the record of its proceedings leading to a determination or order to the higher court. By this means, the higher court may review the proceedings and determine whether, as may be claimed by appellant, (a) the order of the lower court or administrative tribunal is made in excess of its jurisdiction; (b) the elements of natural or constitutional justice were ignored in the procedure followed by the tribunal or authority; (c) there was an error of law on the face of the record which is reflected in the decision.[31] If any of these claims are proved, the proceedings and order of the inferior tribunal may be quashed.[32] With the growth of administrative law and administrative bodies making decisions affecting legal rights, the courts have broadened the application of the order of certiorari to include determinations of administrative authorities. However, the determining factor in certiorari depends upon the administrative decision having characteristics which require the authority to 'act judicially'.[33]

As indicated above and discussed in chapter 5, the type of decision- making requiring administrative agencies to act judicially is a matter of judicial opinion, so that certain processes which administrators may have viewed as primarily fact-finding or investigative, on occasion have been held by courts in recent years to have characteristics which the courts consider to be 'judicial'. See *The State (Costello) v. Irish Land Commission* 1959 IR 353 for example of using certiorari to quash a decision being refused, distinguishing *In re Estate of Roscrea Meat Products Ltd* 1958 IR 47, 92 ILTR 100; *The State (Doyle) v. Carr* 1970 IR 87 commenting on the High Court's discretion in matters of certiorari; *The State (McGuinness) v. Maguire* (Judge) 1967 IR 348; *State (Dowling) v. Leonard* 1960 IR 381, 95 ILTR 148; and *The State (Shannon Atlantic Fisheries Ltd) v. McPolin* 1976 IR 93 where certiorari was granted to quash decisions.[34]

Prohibition

Closely related to certiorari is the order of prohibition, which is an order issued by a higher court to an inferior court or administrative body to prevent or restrain that inferior body from initiating or continuing an action which would usurp a jurisdiction or function in excess of its statutory power. As with certiorari it is applicable only where the administrative body has the duty to act judicially. It is also not applicable where there is an error in law on the face of the record.[35] The requirement that the administrative agency must be acting judicially narrows the application of prohibition, as illustrated by the High Court judgment of Walsh J. in *State (Stephen's Green Club and Another) v. Labour Court* 1961 IR 85. The court first held that an order of prohibition would not lie against the Labour Court since the Labour Court did have jurisdiction under section 67 of the Industrial Relations Act 1946 inasmuch as the statutory definition of the term workers did encompass persons working for the Stephen's Green Club. Moreover, even if the Labour Court did not have jurisdiction, a prohibition order would not be granted, because the Labour Court could only make recommendations rather than decisions affecting or imposing liabilities. In such circumstances a proper remedy was an injunction.

Mandamus

A mandamus is an order by the court to an administrative body, officer, or inferior court requiring the performance of a function or legal duty assigned by law to that body, officer or court. In contrast to certiorari and prohibition, mandamus will be given in respect of non-judicial acts. Mandamus to overcome failure to perform a statutory function is illustrated by *The State (Modern Homes (Ireland) Ltd) v. Dublin Corporation* 1953 IR 202, 88 ILTR 79. In 1934, Dublin City Council passed a resolution to make a planning scheme, under section 29 of the Town and Regional Planning Act 1934, which provided that once a planning authority decided to make a planning scheme, it should do so with all convenient speed. Despite this resolution, no action to actually adopt a planning scheme had been taken as late as 1953 when plaintiff requested a mandamus to require such adoption. Plaintiff alleged their construction business was suffering in the absence of certainty as to what would be required under the planning scheme once it was adopted. The High and Supreme Courts held that the failure of the Council to have prepared either a planning scheme or even a draft of such scheme by the time of plaintiff's action was cause for a mandamus order to carry out the planning duty as prescribed by statute.

Consistent with the principle that mandamus may be applied to overcome failure to perform a statutory function as in the above *State (Modern Homes Ireland Ltd)* case is the concept that a public authority cannot be forced by mandamus to take an action unless there is a statutory provision creating a public duty to do so. In *The State (Finglas Industrial Estates Ltd) v. Dublin County Council* Supreme Court, unreported, per Henchy J., 19 February 1983, plaintiffs (the developers) submitted an application for development of a light industrial estate, although at that time they had no interest in the land in question and were not incorporated as a limited company. The Council refused the application in June 1975 on five grounds, the most critical being that since the only sewerage system in the vicinity was in the functional area of Dublin Corporation, and that was being used to full capacity, facilities for disposal of sewage and surface water were not available and could not be provided.

An appeal by the developers to the Minister for Local Government from this refusal resulted in a grant of the permission sought, subject to the condition that the developers pay a sum of money to the Dublin County Council and/or the Dublin Corporation:

> as may be appropriate as a contribution towards the provision of a public water supply and piped sewerage facilities in the area. The amount to be paid and the time and method shall be agreed between the developers and the said Council and/or the said Corporation before the development is commenced or, failing agreement, shall be as determined by the Minister for Local Government.

Subsequent offers by the developers failed because in the Council's opinion, the piped sewerage facilities could not possibly be made available within the legal lifetime of the permission. The resolution of this impasse necessary for implementation of the Minister's condition did not go back to the Minister, however, since in the interim the Local Government (Planning and Development) Act 1976 had been enacted, transferring most of the Minister's powers under the 1963 Act to An Bord Pleanála (the Board). Developers' advisors wrote to the Board requesting them to make the assessment or adjudication reserved to the Minister before the transfer of powers to the Board and after giving the parties involved opportunity to make representations, the Board issued an order in December 1980 determining the contribution of the developers payable to the Council, and in January 1981 the developers sent the Council a letter and a cheque for £180,000. The Council flatly refused to accept cheque or letter, and the developers took recourse to the courts, obtaining an order of mandamus directed to the Council ordering them to accept the cheque.

On appeal to the Supreme Court, Henchy J., for the Court, first noted that the Council had no sewerage system available, that the Dublin Corporation's sewerage system was overloaded, that the Corporation had not been a party to the planning application or appeal, and that the applicant developers had had no legal existence, not being incorporated until April 1981. If this last point were the only one at issue, it would be grounds for invalidating the Minister's permission as being granted to a non-existent legal person. However, the main point was that as he understood the law of mandamus, 'a public authority, be it a planning or sanitary authority, cannot be compelled by mandamus to accept money tendered to it unless there is a public duty to accept it'. His review of the Public Health (Ireland) Act 1878, sections 23 and 24, led him to conclude that where sewers do exist adjoining the premises in question, the granting of planning permission to build such premises may bring into force a legal obligation on the sanitary authority to make a connection. This in turn might raise the question of whether forcing the payment of a contribution towards provision of sewerage facilities can lawfully be made if its effect is to impose an obligation on the sanitary authority to overload their sewers.

In this situation, though, there is no sewerage system to which a connection may be made from the premises in question. To make such a connection possible, the existing sewerage system would have to be extended. Henchy J. could find nothing in the planning Acts which created any legal obligation on a sanitary authority to provide a sewerage system where none existed, or to permit a connection to an existing sewerage system. However, the Court was not called upon to make a comprehensive ruling on this question, since it is sufficient to say that the condition of a financial contribution imposed by the Minister must be construed as referring to a contribution towards the cost of providing a public water supply or piped sewerage facilities in the area *only* if the Council were either willing or legally bound to make such provision. He would discharge the order of mandamus.

Unlike the United States, where mandamus has been limited severely by the judicial doctrine in that its applicability is limited primarily to ministerial acts, mandamus in Ireland also will lie to review the exercise of discretion by administrative bodies. Thus an authority which allows its decision to be affected by consideration of factors not relevant to its decision, may be held to have declined jurisdiction as defined by the statute setting forth the purposes of the authority's decision making, and may be ordered to hear the case again and make its determinations properly according to law. In *The State (O'Mahony) v. South Cork Board of Health* 1941 Ir. Jur. Rep. 79, tension-ridden relations between tenant O'Mahony and the Board entered into (or dominated) the Board's decision to undertake an ejectment proceeding against Mrs O'Mahony rather than limiting its decision-making process to a consideration of the factors which the Labourers Act 1935 prescribed as relevant to a determination of her application to purchase the cottage. The High Court therefore issued a mandamus directing the Board to consider her application and decide it in accordance with law, and to exclude those extraneous factors involved in the conflict between Mrs O'Mahony and the Board which had influenced their first decision. A further illustration of this point is found in *The State (Keller) v. Galway County Council and Another* 1958 IR 142, in which the High Court ordered a reconsideration of a decision which had been made by certain health officers and the Council to reject an application for support by a disabled person based on factors which were extraneous to that decision. (See further discussion of the *O'Mahony* and *Keller* cases in chapter 5.) Finally mandamus will not be issued in respect of a review of errors in law within the agency's jurisdiction, if the administrative determination is one which may be categorised as judicial.[36]

Habeas Corpus

The order under article 40.4 of the Constitution, commonly known as habeas corpus, is a remedy in which a higher court in response to a complaint that someone is being unlawfully detained, may order the official in whose custody the person is held to produce the person before the court on a named day and certify the grounds of detention for review by the court. If the court is not satisfied that the detention is in accordance with law, the court may order the release of the person. Although primarily applied in criminal law, habeas corpus also is a remedy in administrative law when it is alleged that a person is being held in custody unlawfully as a result of an administrative action or determination. For example, in the case of *In re Doyle, an Infant* (1956) IR 217, the father applied for an order of habeas corpus against the Minister for Education who had refused to give up custody of a child being cared for in an industrial school. This led to a decision that section 10 of the Children Act 1941, insofar as it allowed a parent to deprive himself of the control of his child, was repugnant to the Constitution. On the other hand, in the case of *In re Philip Clark* 1950 IR 235, 85 ILTR 19[37] the Supreme Court upheld the processes of the Mental Treatment Act 1945. Section 165 (1) of that Act empowered a member of the Garda Síochána to take a person into custody when of the opinion it was necessary that a person, believed to be of unsound mind, should for his own safety and that of the public be placed forthwith under care and control; sub-section 2 required the Garda who took him into custody to apply forthwith for an order authorising his detention in a mental hospital. Plaintiff applied for an order of habeas corpus on the ground, inter alia, that his detention was unlawful since section 165 was repugnant to provisions of article 40 of the Constitution pertaining to the personal rights of the citizen. In response, the Court held that this section seemed to be designed for the protection of the citizen's safety and the promotion of the common good, and could not be interpreted as an attack upon the rights of citizens.

Injunction

In addition to the above prerogative remedies, there is the equitable remedy of injunction, which is a coercive order from the court to stop the recipient of the order from embarking upon an action if the applicant can show virtual certainty of its taking place and that it will cause irreparable injury. More commonly it is applied to stop an ongoing action which is causing or could cause substantial injury. Although resorted to infrequently, since mandamus normally is used to compel performance of duty, a court may grant a mandatory injunction to require performance of an act required by statute which an administrative agency is neglecting or refusing to perform. Injunctions also may be interlocutory, requiring interim cessation of an action so as to maintain the status quo pending final determination of a case. The applicant must show a threat of irreparable injury and that there are prima facie grounds for the eventual grant of a permanent injunction.[38]

The Law Reform Commission study of judicial review of administrative action cites a wide variety of cases in which courts have been requested to grant injunctions against administrative bodies from 1885 to the present. It notes the injunction's advantages of flexibility in form and scope, such as being applicable when an authority is not 'acting judicially' as well as when it is so acting. However, the injunction still is not sought as frequently as in the United States, where, as Davis states:

> Much the most important non-statutory forms of proceedings for review of federal administrative action are injunction and declaratory judgment, which probably account for more than nine-tenths of all cases involving non-statutory review. The two remedies are almost always combined . . . . the injunction has moved away from its historical foundations in equity and has become a general utility remedy for use whenever no other form of review proceedings is clearly indicated.[39]

From the perspective of the Law Reform Commission, the injunction has potential for expanded use in the future. Ireland does not have the equivalent of the British Crown Proceedings Act to constitute an impediment to granting of injunctions against ministers as in England. In *Boland v. An Taoiseach and Others* 1974 IR 338, discussed above, counsel for the government did not argue, nor did the Supreme Court hold that the injunction requested against the

Taoiseach and the government ministers was not an appropriate form of remedy; rather, the issue was resolved on the constitutional concept of separation of powers. Another indicator is that the legislature has provided in section 27 of the Local Government (Planning and Development) Act 1976 that any person may seek an injunction to restrain unauthorised development whether or not that person has an interest in the land. A similar provision has been enacted in the Local Government (Water Pollution) Act 1977.

The public policy implications and their relation to the role of the courts in respect of the availability and use of the injunction as reflected in section 27, Local Government (Planning and Development) Act 1976, are discussed in a comprehensive and illuminating decision by Barrington J. in *Stafford and Bates v. Roadstone Ltd* unreported, High Court, 17 January 1980. Plaintiffs asked for an interlocutory injunction to abate an alleged nuisance emanating from a recently increased quarry operation near their residences, and for an injunction under section 27 of the 1976 Act to prohibit continuance of increased blasting operations and reinstatement of conditions existing prior to the increase. Applying first the criteria appropriate to an interlocutory injunction where, as in this case, there was conflicting evidence, Barrington J. concluded that an interlocutory injunction totally disrupting defendants' business should not be granted if the defendants are in fact entitled to make such use of their lands. If defendants are not so entitled, the interlocutory injunction would be a proper remedy. He therefore examined the evidence from the perspective of the section 27 application and held that the greatly expanded quarry operation in fact constituted an unauthorised development and use which would justify the plaintiffs' case for an injunction under section 27. However, based on his analysis of section 27, he concluded that the High Court was given wide jurisdiction to balance competing interests. In this case, on the one hand, there is the statutory right of a citizen, as a watchdog for the public interest and regardless of his or her interest in the land, to ask for an injunction to stop a land development or industry because of a technical breach of planning law (and an inactive planning authority). On the other hand, there is the importance of that development or industry to its owners, its workers and the economic benefit to the community. Moreover, plaintiffs had not asked that the quarry be closed but be allowed to operate subject to conditions. Barrington J. therefore adjourned the case for a short time to give both parties an opportunity to consider his findings. He also withheld ordering the injunctions so as to allow the defendants to give certain undertakings to the court, namely to seek planning permission promptly and to ensure their activities in the interim did not cause a nuisance to local residents. These conditions had to be met if the Court were to refrain from issuing an interlocutory injunction.

Among recent examples of judicial determinations on applications for injunction and mandatory injunction which were not based on statutory authorisation is *Crowley v. Ireland, Minister for Education, Attorney General and Irish National Teachers Organisation* 1980 IR 102. Plaintiff as the mother of one child and on behalf of several other children claimed a declaration that the Minister was in breach of duty under article 42.4 of the Constitution by permitting a strike of members of the Irish National Teachers Organisation (INTO) in a dispute with the local board of management which resulted in 180 children having no schooling for a number of months. She also asked for a mandatory injunction against the Minister to provide free primary education in accordance with article 42.4, and an injunction against the INTO to compel it to withdraw a direction to its members not to enrol at other schools children from the strike-bound schools. The High Court granted the mandatory injunction against the Minister, which was affirmed by the Supreme Court, ordering the Minister to provide transportation for pupils to schools in other districts. The INTO withdrew its direction before the trial, obviating the need for that injunction. However, the High Court ruling that the Minister had been in breach of duty prior to the injunction was reversed by the Supreme Court primarily on the ground that the Minister's duty was to provide for education, rather than directly *supplying* education. Further, control of education by the state was limited by the interposition of local managers and boards of management between the state and child.

In the case of *Nolan v. Irish Land Commission* 1981 IR 23, plaintiff sued for a declaration that he was entitled to inspect documents and data considered by the Lay Commissioners prior to their certification on 21 May 1978 that plaintiff's lands were required by the Land Commission for purposes of a resale. Plaintiff also requested an injunction restraining or prohibiting the Lay Commissioners from determining plaintiff's objections to the proposed acquisition of his land until the documents and data had been made available for inspection. In the High Court, Costello J. granted interlocutory relief in the terms of the injunction sought and in an early trial decided plaintiff was entitled to the relief claimed. On appeal, the Supreme Court affirmed that decision, O'Higgins C.J., after detailed examination of the function of the certificate in the process of land acquisition, stated that 'in the absence of discovery and inspection of appropriate documents, considered by the Commissioners prior to certification, the requirements of natural justice would not be observed.' For examples of a declaration granted but mandatory injunction denied, see *Phelan v. Laois Vocational Education Committee and Parsons* High Court, unreported, 28 February 1977; *Hogan v. Minister for Justice, Superintendent Garvey and the Attorney General* High Court, unreported, 8 September 1976.

Declaratory Order

A plaintiff may seek an order declaratory of the rights and duties of the parties from the courts. This judgment is binding, despite the absence of the coercive or directive aspects of the prerogative orders or injunction, which are backed by the penalty of contempt of court for disobedience. It is assumed that an administrative body would comply with a judicial determination of the law. Moreover, there ultimately are sanctions, such as a subsequent action and order for an injunction, or an action for damages caused by non-compliance with the declaratory order. The declaratory order has the advantage that it is not limited to situations where the administrator must act judicially, but also can be used to challenge the constitutionality of statutes, the validity of administrative rule-making or the withholding of discretionary grants of benefits.[40] Moreover, such challenges do not necessarily exhaust the potential scope of the declaration as a remedy, and as Asmal states:

> With the development of the declaratory order, many of the procedural and technical weaknesses of the prerogative orders are obviated, and even in situations where the State has substantive immunities from being sued, the declaratory order can provide a suitable remedy.[41]

It should be noted, however, that the declaratory order is not designed to deal with error in law on the face of the record or to be a challenge to an inferior court's conviction in excess of jurisdiction. Moreover, as indicated by Gavan Duffy J. in *O'Doherty v̇. Attorney General and O'Donnell* 1941 IR 569, 75 ILTR 171 a declaration may not be made where there is an appropriate remedy which plaintiff should have used unless the plaintiff can show doubt as to the alternative remedy being open to him, or that it cannot give the relief due him, or that under special circumstances the usual remedy is useless or not adequate, or that excessive expense would result from additional litigation if a declaration were refused.

As in England and the United States, the declaratory judgment in Ireland may be combined with the coercive remedy of the injunction, or an award of damages. Examples of combining a declaratory order with an injunction in Ireland include *Boland v. An Taoiseach and Others* 1974 IR 338 and *Cowan v. Attorney General and Others* 1961 IR 411, previously referred to in connection with constitutional issues of executive policy-making and limits of delegation respectively. Further cases demonstrating the flexibility of the combined remedies to adapt to situations are those of *Crowley v. Ireland, Minister for Education, Attorney General and Irish National Teachers Organisation* 1980 IR 102 and *Nolan v. Irish Land Commission* 1981 IR 23 discussed above in the consideration of the injunction as a remedy. In *Crowley*, the injunction was granted but the declaration that the Minister had acted in breach of duty was refused; in *Nolan*, both the injunction and declaration were granted on the ground of protecting rights under natural justice.

Action for Damages

A person who is aggrieved by an administrative decision may under certain circumstances secure judicial review by instituting a suit for damages. The issues surrounding the liability and immunity of the government for suit for damages as defendants where negligence, non-feasance, or misfeasance are claimed by private parties are complex, as are other aspects of the position of the state as plaintiff or defendant in litigation with private persons, and thus are analysed in detail in chapter 4.

Disobedience

An alternative to the above forms of remedies for those wishing to contest the legality of an administrative action or decision is to refuse compliance, and in the subsequent judicial proceeding against him plead that the action or determination is unconstitutional, *ultra vires* the statute, or contrary to natural justice or constitutional justice. This approach is illustrated in *Pigs Marketing Board v. Donnelly* 1939 IR 413, discussed earlier in this chapter. This form of remedy is of little value, however, in those circumstances where compliance is not a significant factor, such as where the person has been refused a gratuity or payment from the government or has suffered damages as a result of negligence or misfeasance on the part of the government. It also may not be attractive in the light of possible penalties for non-compliance if the argument of the individual in defence of his disobedience to the administrative determination is not upheld by the courts.

Attorney General and Remedies
It will be recalled from the discussion of the relation of the Attorney General's functions to administrative law in chapter 2 that his roles of asserting the public interest, acting as relator and being defendant in suits against the state make him a necessary or advisable participant in certain types of cases to ensure or facilitate the grant and operation of a number of the above remedies.

Grounds for Granting Judicial Remedies

The above discussion of the forms of remedies does not explain the grounds upon which they are granted when private parties seek redress from administrative action or determinations or when administrative agencies wish to force compliance from private parties refusing to obey administrative regulations and decisions. The circumstances or grounds upon which the remedies will be granted, and judicial doctrines conditioning the availability of judicial review such as locus standi, exhaustion of administrative remedies and ripeness, are part of the detailed analysis in subsequent chapters. Consequently, the following discussion is limited to a summary of the basic aspects of grounds for granting remedies.

Unconstitutionality of Statute or Executive Action
A fundamental ground for requesting a judicial remedy is that the executive or administration is planning to take or has taken an action, or has made a determination under a statute which is

unconstitutional. A less frequent challenge is that the authority has acted unconstitutionally in the way it has exercised its powers. Examples of the first type of challenge such as *Pigs Marketing Board v. Donnelly (Dublin) Ltd* 1939 IR 413, *In re Haughey* 1971 IR 217, or *City View Press Ltd v. An Chomhairle Oiliúna* 1980 IR 381 and also of the second type of challenge such as *Boland v. An Taoiseach and Others* 1974 IR 338 have been discussed in the preceding sections above pertaining to legislative, executive and judicial powers.

Excess of Jurisdiction: Ultra Vires Actions

There is a want of jurisdiction if the administrative agency has acted without statutory authority over either the subject matter or the parties who are before it. This includes situations where although the agency may have had jurisdiction at the beginning of an action, it has gone beyond the limits of its authority by taking into account matters beyond its jurisdiction or by taking an extended or altered action not within the scope of its authority. Decisions under such circumstances are quashed as being *ultra vires* the statute. In the case of *Waterford Corporation v. Murphy* 1920 2 IR 165, 54 ILTR 32, it was held that the imposition of tolls for using a bridge was beyond the powers or in excess of the jurisdiction of the Corporation, which under the statute was empowered only to enact byelaws with respect to the time and mode of boats proceeding through the bridge. Again, in *Cross v. Minister for Agriculture* 1941 IR 55, Gavan Duffy J. held that since the Minister, in defining the boundary between tidal and fresh-water portions of a river, used the limits of saline vegetable growth under the water as his criteria rather than the statutory criteria of taking the limits of the tide, he had misconstrued his statutory jurisdiction and had arrived incorrectly at his order. And in *Minister for Industry and Commerce v. Hales* 1967 IR 50, 102 ILTR 109, Henchy J. in the High Court held that as they construed the statute:

> It is not conceivable that the legislature, having indicated that the scope of the Act was to be limited to persons employed under a contract of service or a contract of apprenticeship, should by the use of general words in sub-section 3 of section 3 of the Act have given the Minister power to broaden the scope of the Act to such an extent that he could, by the

making of regulations, import into work-contracts made with independent contractors a series of statutory terms such as holiday allowances, the breach of which would result in criminal liability. (page 76. See also pages 244-5 of this book.)

It should be noted that the courts have developed various categories of *ultra vires*, such as non-adherence to statutory purpose, bad faith exercise of discretion and unreasonable action, as discussed below.

Adherence to Purpose or Objective of the Statute

A concept which expands the grounds for the scope of judicial review is that in the absence of specific guidelines in the grant of discretionary power, the court may determine whether the administrative agency has complied with the general purpose or objectives of an Act as revealed in the general context of the Act as a whole. In *East Donegal Co-operative Livestock Mart Ltd v. Attorney General* 1970 IR 317, 104 ILTR 81, O'Keeffe P., in the High Court, considered allegations of plaintiffs that the Livestock Marts Act 1967 was repugnant to articles 40 and 43 of the Constitution by giving unfettered discretion to the Minister to grant or refuse a licence, to exempt, 'if he so thinks fit', any particular business or businesses of any particular class, and to attach to a licence such conditions as he thinks proper. The High Court rejected the arguments with respect to grant or refusal of the licence, but agreed that the Act did not subject the Minister's power to attach conditions in granting a licence to any of the procedural safeguards for which the Act had provided in regard to his determinations on the refusal or revocation of a licence. Since the provisions for attaching conditions were integral to the whole licensing system, there was no alternative but to hold that the licensing provisions of the Act as a whole were unconstitutional. On review, the Supreme Court, per Walsh J., stated that no particular part of the Act could be held unambiguous until each part was examined in relation to the whole. Upon examination of specific sections of the Act and its long title he concluded that the power given to the Minister to attach conditions was to enable him to add conditions peculiar to an individual application but not capable of being applied in general. Moreover:

All the powers granted to the Minister by section 3 which are prefaced by the words 'at the discretion' or 'as he shall think proper' or 'as he so thinks fit' are powers which may be exercised only within the boundaries of the stated objects of the Act and are ones which cast upon the Minister the duty of acting fairly and judicially in accordance with the principles of constitutional justice and do not give him an absolute or an unqualified or arbitrary power to grant or refuse at his will. (page 93)

Therefore, any condition not conforming with the objectives of the Act would be *ultra vires* and there were sufficient ways in a court proceeding to review the Minister's decision in this regard despite absence of procedural requirements in the statute. The Court upheld the Act, with the exception of the phrase empowering the Minister to exempt any particular business if he so thinks fit. The power to exempt individual cases, as against a particular *class* of businesses as defined by the legislature, may not be delegated by the Oireachtas to an administration unless such exemption is necessary to avoid an infringement of a constitutional right by virtue of the application of the statute. This did not seem to be the reason for the statutory provision under consideration.

In general, the Supreme Court decision in *East Donegal* would indicate that its review of administrative determinations goes beyond 'on the face of the record' indicators of an *ultra vires* action.

Failure to Perform Agency's Duty

Where an administrative body has failed to perform a duty which the courts consider to be required by statute, the courts will not only give judicial review, but under appropriate circumstances will issue a mandamus or a mandatory injunction to require performance of that duty. Illustrative cases of situations in which a mandamus or mandatory injunction will or will not issue are provided above in the discussion of mandamus and mandatory injunction as judicial remedies.

Procedural Defects

A court will quash administrative acts where an agency has failed to follow procedures prescribed by statute, provided the requirements are mandatory and not merely directory. However, statutory provisions are not a *sine qua non* for review of procedural defects, since to an increasing degree, Irish courts also will negate administrative action for procedural defects which are deemed contrary to what the courts refer to traditionally as 'natural justice'. These requirements of natural justice have been expanded in recent years to encompass the requirements of 'constitutional justice', the scope of which goes beyond the expectations of natural justice as indicated by Henchy J. in *The State (Gleeson) v. Minister for Defence and the Attorney General* 1976 IR 280,[42] as follows:

> while the common-law concept of natural justice is usually taken to comprehend no more than what is encompassed by the maxims *nemo judex in sua causa* and *audi alteram partem*, the requirements of what was . . . . called 'constitutional justice' and is sometimes called 'constitutional due process' cover a wider field . . . . The necessary implementation of express or necessarily implied constitutional guarantees means that decisive acts and procedures may be impugned for a wide variety of reasons depending on the circumstances of the case; for instance, because justice was not administered in public; or the decision was given by an unconstitutional tribunal; or the decision applied an unconstitutional law; or the accused was deprived of a fair, competent and impartial jury; or the person affected received unjustifiably unequal treatment; or the evidence was obtained in a manner not constitutionally permissible. (pages 294-5)

However, Henchy J. then made the qualifying statement:

> Because of the wide scope of such constitutional guarantees, whatever value 'constitutional justice' may have as a term of generic connotation, a plea of a denial of constitutional justice lacks the concreteness and particularity necessary to identify and bring into focus the precise constitutional issue that is being raised.

> When, as in this case, a person brings proceedings in which he seeks to have condemned as invalid a decision or a decisive process on the ground that it is incompatible with the Constitution, it is necessary for him to plead and prove, first, the application in the circumstances of the case of a specified constitutional right, either express or implied; secondly, that

the decision or decisive process in question has infringed that right; and, thirdly that he stands aggrieved by that infringement. (page 295)

In this case, the Court held that the plaintiff was denied natural justice by being discharged from the Army for a reason discreditable to him, without due notice and reasonable opportunity to respond to that notice, rather than on grounds of constitutional justice, since he could not identify a particular right of constitutional origin in support of his claim.

The range of specific issues illustrated by cases involving alleged procedural defects are analysed in detail in chapter 5, and also appear in subsequent chapters dealing with licensing and directing powers. As will be seen, they include the right to notice and hearing and certain procedural requisites of a fair hearing, plus institutional decision-making issues such as absence of bias, official notice of matters not in the record, and aspects of the interrelated roles of the hearing officer, departmental staff and minister or board ultimately making the decisions.

Bad Faith, Improper or Unauthorised Purpose
The courts will reverse or quash an administrative act if it can be shown that an administrative authority has abused its statutory discretion by acting in bad faith, or to effectuate an unauthorised purpose, or on considerations not relevant to the statutory purpose, or ignoring matters relevant to the purpose. Although these grounds for judicial reversal of administrative action are separable, they frequently overlap. For example, in *Listowel Urban District Council v. McDonagh* 1968 IR 312, Listowel UDC made a byelaw (order) under section 31 (1) of the Local Government (Sanitary Services) Act 1948, prohibiting erection or retention of temporary dwellings on certain streets as prejudicial to public health. The defendant, who owned and occupied a caravan, was prosecuted, convicted and fined a small sum in the District Court. On appeal to the Circuit Court, he claimed that the order was *ultra vires* because it was unreasonable; that the Council had not made proper inquiry into the matter before reaching their decision, and that their opinion or decision was not arrived at *bona fide*. The Circuit Court stated certain questions for determination by the Supreme Court, namely whether the Court may inquire into what transpired at the meeting of

Listowel UDC and the evidence it had available when making the order; the views expressed by UDC members concerning the order and whether the opinion was arrived at *bona fide*. The Supreme Court, per Ó Dálaigh C.J., referred to the distinction between an *ultra vires* act done *bona fide* and an act which on the face of it is regular but which will be held null and void if *mala fides* is discovered and brought to the Court's attention. Given this distinction, 'a discretionary statutory power, if exercised in bad faith, can be condemned as invalid and *mala fides* is a well-recognised ground of challenge' (page 318). In response to the question put in the case stated, the Supreme Court held that the Circuit Court in deciding the appeal was entitled to enquire into whether or not the opinion of the UDC was arrived at *bona fide*.

Insufficient Evidence
An absence of evidence, or of sufficient relevant evidence, may be the basis for reversal of an administrative decision. In the case of *In re Estate of Ole Anderson: O'Brien v. Irish Land Commission* unreported, Supreme Court, per Henchy J., 3 June 1975, the Lay Commissioners of the Land Commission certified that an entire holding of 51 acres, 1 rood and 10 perches was required for relieving congestion. On appeal from this certification, the Commissioners tended to the view that the Commission needed to acquire only 10 acres, 1 rood, leaving the objector with 40 acres, 2 roods. The objector then appealed to the Appeal Tribunal on the ground that his holding was so reduced as to be uneconomic. The Appeal Tribunal, per Butler J., held that there was nothing in the evidence, i.e. an absence of evidence, to show that such a holding was anything other than uneconomic. It was held by the Supreme Court that the owner might retain his original holding of 51 acres. In those cases where the issue is one of sufficiency rather than absence of evidence, the resolution of whether the evidence is sufficient to sustain a determination in an administrative hearing may depend upon the nature of the class of evidence involved and its consequent weight or probative value in reaching that decision. This is well illustrated in *The State (Kiely) v. Minister for Social Welfare* 1971 IR 21, 1977 IR 267, in which Kenny J. in the High Court in 1971, and Henchy J. in the Supreme Court in 1977, analysed categories of evidence for their probative value in relation to the procedures followed in an administrative hearing and the requirements of natural justice, with

particular reference to the weight of documentary as against oral evidence subject to cross-examination. In that case, the social welfare appeals officer allowed *prima facie* oral evidence of the appellant's claim to be rebutted by a written statement of an absent witness. The Supreme Court held that to do so made the hearing unfair and was contrary to natural justice. (See discussion of the *Kiely* case, pages 183-6.)

Unreasonableness
The plea of unreasonableness has not been resorted to with as much frequency as its American counterpart plea that a rule or exercise of power by an administrative agency was 'arbitrary and capricious' or against substantive due process. Until recently, the leading Irish case applying the test of unreasonableness was *Limerick Corporation v. Sheridan* 90 ILTR 59. At issue was a byelaw of Limerick City Council, enacted under the Local Government (Sanitary Services) Act 1948, prohibiting the erection or retention of any temporary dwelling on any street or land within 300 yards from the centre of such street or from any occupied dwelling thereon without previous written consent of Limerick Corporation. Defendant Mary Sheridan, living in a wheeled caravan on waste ground within 300 yards of the centre line of a street, was charged in the District Court with contravening the order. On appeal to the High Court, Davitt P. held that:

> if the order were a good one, then it made it illegal for anyone to erect or retain a temporary dwelling anywhere or, particularly, anywhere in the County Borough. Without such consent, nobody could camp out in a tent or a sleeping porch in his own garden. Harvesters could not camp out on agricultural land on which they were working. If the complaintents were correct, the common law rights sought to be safeguarded to a limited extent by that sub-section [34 (12) of the Local Government (Sanitary Services) Act 1948], might also go by the board. (page 64)

The Court held the order unreasonable since it was manifestly unjust, and involved an oppressive, gratuitous interference with common law rights which could find no justification in the minds of reasonable men, and therefore was *ultra vires* the 1948 Act.

In the previously discussed case of *Central Dublin Development*

E

Association and Others v. Attorney General 109 ILTR 69, the complex
and lengthy judgment dealt with various allegations questioning
the constitutionality of the Local Government (Planning and Development) Act 1963. During the process of rejecting all of these claims
in the High Court, Kenny J. also enunciated his concept of the role
of the Court in reviewing an allegation of unreasonableness. In this
case, if there were no reasonable grounds for a planning authority
to form an opinion that land contiguous to or adjacent to such lands
is necessary for satisfactory development and use of that land, and
includes such adjacent land in an obsolete area shown in a plan,
the High Court has jurisdiction to review their decision and set it
aside. In general then:

> When the exercise of statutory power depends on the formation
> of an opinion by any person or authority (except possibly, a
> Minister of State), the High Court has jurisdiction in a declara-
> tory action to inquire whether such an opinion was held and
> whether there were reasonable grounds for it. (page 88)

However, based upon dicta of Kenny J. in the case of *Kiely v. Minister
for Social Welfare* 1971 IR 21, Kelly concludes that Kenny J. does not
mean the criterion of unreasonableness to be that an administrative
decision is invalid because it is not the decision which the judge
would have made had he been the administrator. Rather, the test
of reasonableness is similar to the test an appeals court would make
when asked to reverse a jury decision, namely, it will reverse if it
feels that on the basis of the evidence, no reasonable jury should
have reached such a verdict.[43]

Further application of the concept of unreasonableness is illustrated by *Dunn Ltd v. Dublin County Council* 1974 IR 45. Pringle J.
held that the imposition of conditions on developers related to
notification of purchasers or tenants with respect to aircraft noise,
and the provision of insulation against such noise, were not related
to the planning and development of the area. Such conditions,
therefore, constituted an unreasonable restriction beyond the power
of the defendants to impose.

Error of Law in the Record
If on the face of the record the determinations of an administrative
body are based on an error in law, the courts will grant review. An

example of an administrative misinterpretation of the meaning of a statute and the applicability of a judicial precedent to a factual situation may be found in *Phillips v. the Minister for Social Welfare,* High Court, unreported, per Kenny, J. 28 February 1974. In this case, the issue was whether the statutory term 'agricultural worker' applied to one of five record keepers maintaining data on agricultural production and one of four lorry drivers who were employed on a large farm having 45 workers and selling its products directly to retail outlets. If they were classified as agricultural workers, a considerably lower 'special rate employment contribution' could be paid by the employer, rather than the higher ordinary rate employment contributions normally required under the Social Welfare Act 1952. The Court reversed the decisions made by the Department of Social Welfare deciding officer and appeals officer that these employees were not agricultural workers. The Court held that the interpretation of these officers would have been correct under the previous Unemployment Insurance Act 1920 and the case of *Warner v. Minister of Industry and Commerce* (1928) 62 ILTR 121. However, this would be a misinterpretation of the Social Welfare Act 1952 currently in effect, since the 1952 Act changed the basis for classifying workers from being determined by the type of work done by the individual worker, to the type of enterprise in which the worker was employed, regardless of what the individual worker was doing in that enterprise.

Notes to Chapter 3

1. O'Reilly and Redmond, *Cases and Materials on the Irish Constitution* [*Cases and Materials*], extract, *NUR v. Sullivan* 582-3 (1980). Note: for the convenience of the reader interested in details of court judgments summarised in this chapter, an alternative to reporting systems in libraries is provided by footnotes to extracts of cases in O'Reilly and Redmond's book which are relevant to the particular aspect of the case being summarised.
2. See Asmal, 'Administrative Law in Ireland ['Administrative Law']. *Survey of Public Administration and Administrative Law in Ireland* 73-4, extract from *International Review of Administrative Sciences* (Vol. 34, 1968)
3. See Wade, *Administrative Law* 769-77 (1982)
4. McGowan Smyth, *The Houses of the Oireachtas* [*The Oireachtas*] 47-8 (1979); Chubb, *Source Book of Irish Government* 119 (1983)
5. McGowan Smyth, *The Oireachtas* 48-9

6. McGowan Smyth, *The Oireachtas* 49; see also McGowan Smyth, *The Theory and Practice of the Irish Senate* 90 (1972); Jackson, 'Delegated Legislation in Ireland' *Public Law* 417-435 (1972) and reports of Select Committee on Statutory Instruments, 1949-present.

7. Asmal, 'Administrative Law', 73

8. Schwartz and Wade, *Legal Control of Government* 90, 100-101 (1972)

9. See Barry and Whitcomb, *The Legal Foundations of Public Administation* 175 (1981) citing *The New York Times* 16 April 1979 D2

10. See National Conference of State Legislatures, 'Legislative Review of Administrative Regulations' 9 November 1977 (unpublished)

11. Warren, *Administrative Law in the American Political System* 156-9 (1982)

12. See McGowan Smyth, *The Oireachtas* 25-7

13. *Administration Yearbook* 11-12 (1984)

14. Gellhorn and Byse, *Administrative Law* 880-90 (1970)

15. O'Reilly and Redmond, *Cases and Materials* extract: *In Re Haughey* 359-365

16. O'Reilly and Redmond, *Cases and Materials* extract: *Boland v. An Taoiseach and Others* 277-9

17. O'Reilly and Redmond, *Cases and Materials* extract, *In re Article 26 of the Constitution and the School Attendance Bill 1942* 616-22

18. For a detailed analysis of these cases, see Kelly, *The Irish Constitution* 145-61 (1984)

19. O'Reilly and Redmond, *Cases and Materials*, extract, *In Re Philip Clark* 494-6

20. See Kelly, *Fundamental Rights in the Irish Law and Constitution* 328-9 (1968), and *The Irish Constitution* 242-7 (1984), Donaldson, *Some Comparative Aspects of Irish Law* 221-2 (1957)

21. O'Reilly and Redmond, *Cases and Materials*, extract, *Buckley and Others v. Attorney General* 324-5; 657-9; 696-7

22. O'Reilly and Redmond, *Cases and Materials*, extract, *The State (C.) v. Minister for Justice* 255-6, 357-9

23. O'Reilly and Redmond, *Cases and Materials*, extract, *Irish Agricultural Society v. St. Enda's Co-operative Society* 323-4

24. O'Reilly and Redmond, *Cases and Materials*, extracts, *Macauley v. Minister for Posts and Telegraphs*, 501-503

25. Kelly, *The Irish Constitution* 216-17 (1984)

26. Kelly, *The Irish Constitution* 217; see also his detailed and authoritative analysis of this topic at 216-30, 363-8

27. O'Reilly and Redmond, *Cases and Materials*, extract, *In Re Solicitors Act 1954 and O'Farrell and Gorman* 410-16

28. O'Reilly and Redmond, *Cases and Materials*, extract, *Cowan v. Attorney General and Others* 416-19

29. O'Reilly and Redmond, *Cases and Materials*, extract, *Deaton v. Attorney General and Revenue Commissioners* 337-40

30. O'Reilly and Redmond, *Cases and Materials*, extract, *McDonald v. Bord na gCon and Attorney General* 382-6

31. See Law Reform Commission, *Judicial Review of Administrative Action: The Problem of Remedies* 9 (1979)

32. See Law Reform Commission, *Judicial Review* 9-12; Delaney, *The Administration of Justice in Ireland* 50 (4th Ed. Lysaght 1975)

33. See Law Reform Commission *Judicial Review* 12

34. See generally Law Reform Commission, *Judicial Review* 8-24 for detailed analysis of certiorari.

35. See Delaney, *Administration of Justice* 50-51; Grogan, *Administrative Tribunals in the Public Service* 47 (1961); Law Reform Commission, *Judicial Review* 37-45
36. See Law Reform Commission, *Judicial Review*, 59-68 for analysis of mandamus.
37. O'Reilly and Redmond, *Cases and Materials*, extract, *In re Philip Clark*, 494-6
38. See Law Reform Commission, *Judicial Review* 45-58; 68-69 for analysis of injunction.
39. Davis, *Administrative Law, Cases Tests Problems* 175-6 (1977)
40. See Law Reform Commission, *Judicial Review*, 26-29; Grogan, *Administrative Tribunals* 42
41. Asmal, 'Administrative Law', 76
42. O'Reilly and Redmond, *Cases and Materials*, extract, *The State (Gleeson) v. Minister for Defence*, 393-5
43. Kelly, 'Judicial Review of Administrative Action: New Irish Trends', *The Irish Jurist* 41 (Vol 6, 1941)

4 Citizen and Sovereign State in Litigation

After the establishment of the Irish Free State, the courts continued to apply judicial doctrines of sovereignty and the prerogatives of the British Crown. However, these were converted into concepts of the state as sovereign where the issue concerned the position of the state and its immunity or liability in litigation with its citizens. The doctrines have been made largely by judicial decisions, supplemented by Acts of the Oireachtas or previous statutes of the United Kingdom Parliament. Until recently, the main import of judicial decisions and legislative Acts has been to give the state (and its agencies) a special legal position conferring certain advantages and placing limits or conditions on the legal rights of private parties seeking a remedy against governmental action in civil litigation.

The situations in which the issues of the state's special position in litigation most commonly arise involve the following: (1) the general applicability of statutes and certain judicial processes to the state in litigation; (2) specific circumstances in which the state is (a) a plaintiff in debt and tort cases, and (b) a defendant in suits involving contract, debts or tort. Further situations are those where local authorities are defendants in tort actions or in suits under the 'Malicious Injuries Code'. The treatment of the origins and earlier development of judicial doctrines in critical court decisions summarise the analyses made by Kelly, Donaldson and Wade,[1] and discusses more recent judgments on the position of the state in litigation.

Applicability of Statute and Judicial Process to the State

One remaining judicial doctrine on the royal prerogative is that in the absence of an explicit provision or clear inference in a statute making it applicable to the Crown (later the Irish government), the Crown or government is exempt from being bound by the statute. Since the King of England constituted an element in the Irish Free State Constitution (articles 51, 73, 80) it was to be expected that the courts would assert the prerogative right of the Irish Free State not to be bound by its statutes. Such a ruling was made in the case of *In Re Moloney, a Bankrupt* 1926 IR 202 concerning a government claim of priority for money owed by a bankrupt to the Land Commission: the Court said the Commission could rely on the prerogative of the Crown and was not bound by the statute. Again, in *Galway County Council v. Minister for Finance* 1931 IR 215, the Court rejected the Council's argument that the statute blocked the Minister's claim to set off certain payments against the Council's claims, based on the prerogative right not to be bound by the statute in the absence of any indication of specific intent of the legislature to do so.

Following the adoption of the 1937 Constitution, judicial doctrine continued to uphold the concept of the state's not being bound by its own statutes. Although the Constitution omitted any reference to the King, articles 49 and 50 provided for continuation of the powers, functions, rights, prerogatives and laws existing before December 1936. In *Cork County Council and Burke v. Commissioners of Public Works and Others* 1945 IR 561, a claim was made by the local authority based on rating statutes for payment of rates on two houses which formerly were Crown property and exempt, and were now rented to two departments of the government. The government argued that the two departments were in the same position as that of the Crown, and therefore exempt in the absence of explicit statutory provision or implied requirement necessary to bind the government. The local authority claimed the statutes involved were of general application, eliminating the prerogative rights continued by article 73 of the Free State Constitution and articles 49 and 50 of the 1937 Constitution. Reference was also made to the legal doctrine in *United States v. Hoar* 6 Mason 311 (1821) quoting Justice Story's statements to the effect that legislative acts generally are meant to regulate the acts and rights of citizens so that the reasoning applicable to citizens is applied with different and often contrary force to the government. Thus it was, according to Justice Story:

a safe rule, founded in the principles of the Common Law, that the general words of a statute ought not to include the Government, or affect its rights, unless that construction be clear and indisputable upon the text of the Act. (IR, page 577)

The Irish Supreme Court in this manner emphasised that the

prerogative rights of the Crown were now the rights of the state and did not constitute an integral part of the institution of kingship.

Two other aspects of the legal position of the state in litigation are the claim of 'executive privilege' made by the executive and the statutory requirement of the Attorney General's fiat as a prerequisite to a suit against a minister by a citizen. The claim of executive privilege in which ministers may claim immunity from having to produce administrative documents for examination by the court or the defendant, on the grounds that disclosure would be against public policy or the public interest and service, was discussed in the preceding chapter.

With respect to the fiat of the Attorney General as a prerequisite for suing a minister of the government under section 2 of the Ministers and Secretaries Act 1924 the definitive case is *Macauley v. Minister for Posts and Telegraphs* 1966 IR 345.[2] The plaintiff, dissatisfied with the telephone service he had been receiving, claimed a judicial declaration that the Minister was obliged to provide a proper, reasonably efficient and effective telephone service in accordance with agreements for telephone service which he had signed. The Minister's response was that the plaintiff had not obtained a grant of the Attorney General's fiat which was necessary before any action could be brought against a minister in the courts, as provided in section 2 of the Minister and Secretaries Act 1924. The plaintiff challenged the constitutionality of this provision of the Act as representing a denial or impediment to the citizen's right of access to the courts.

Kenny J. in the High Court rejected the argument by the plaintiff that the Attorney General's fiat had its origin in the immunity of the British Crown and thus was inconsistent with the Irish state. In his view, the fiat was created by an Act of the Oireachtas of the Irish Free State and 'was not a legacy from the functions of the law officers of the Crown' (page 353). Nor was the fiat inconsistent with article 40 of the Constitution providing for equality before the law, as argued by plaintiff, since the fiat is required only when the minister is sued as a minister, and not as a human person. He also rejected plaintiff's claim that the fiat was an unconstitutional grant of power to the Attorney General to administer justice, since none of the usual characteristics of the judicial function were present in this regard. The Attorney General had complete discretion to grant or withhold the fiat which is the prerequisite for suing a Minister in the courts. He is not bound to hear the parties nor is he required to give reasons for his decision.

However, in view of the unfettered discretion of the Attorney General, Kenny J. upheld the plaintiff's primary argument that the fiat was contrary to plaintiff's right under the Constitution to have free access to the courts. Kenny J. stated:

> That there is a right to have recourse to the High Court to defend and vindicate a legal right and that it is one of the personal rights of the citizen included in the general guarantee in Article 40, sect. 3, seems to me to be a necessary inference from Article 34, sect. 3, sub-sect. 1°, of the Constitution which provides:— "The Courts of First Instance shall include a High Court invested with full original jurisdiction in and power to determine all matters and questions whether of law or fact, civil or criminal" . . . If the High Court has this original jurisdiction to determine all matters and questions and this includes the validity of any law having regard to the provisions of the Constitution, it must follow that the citizens have a right to have recourse to that Court to question the validity of any law having regard to the provisions of the Constitution or for the purpose of asserting or defending a right given by the Constitution for if it did not exist, the guarantees and rights in the Constitution would be worthless. (page 358)

This decision, in which section 2(1) of the Ministers and Secretaries Act 1924 was held invalid in respect of the fiat requirement, was not appealed to the Supreme Court. Consequently this aspect of the fiat has become inoperative.[3]

However, the Attorney General's fiat is definitely operative in a particular type of case which arises in connection with his important role as representative of the public interest in various situations.[4] In citizen suits against governmental authorities, a special aspect of the application of the Attorney General's fiat, namely the 'relator' action, comes into play. In such an action, the Attorney General is made a party, on the information of, or at the instance of, a person or organisation lacking standing *(locus standi)* to sue. An interesting illustration is provided by the recent case of *Attorney General (Martin) v. Dublin Corporation* 1983 ILRM 254, in which the relator, Fr F.X. Martin, sought an injunction to prevent Dublin Corporation from building municipal offices on the site of the Early Viking settlement at Wood Quay (which had been declared a national monument) without a valid consent under the National Monuments Act 1930. He also sought a declaration that the consents on which the Corporation claimed to act were of no legal effect. To bring this claim in the High Court, Fr Martin had to secure the fiat of the Attorney General, which was given subject to the understanding that Fr Martin would defray the costs and expenses of the Attorney General and that the Attorney General expressed no opinion on the legal issues involved. The action then proceeded as a relator action, i.e. the Attorney General was named as plaintiff 'at the relation of Francis X. Martin'. An interim order was obtained from the High Court on 10 January 1979 restraining the Corporation from carrying on further work on the Wood Quay site, on the basis of an undertaking given on Fr Martin's behalf that he would 'abide by any order this Court may hereinafter make as to damages in the event of this Court being of the opinion that the defendants or any of them shall have suffered any damages by reason of this order which the plaintiff ought to pay'. After further interim orders Fr Martin obtained an interlocutory injunction on 12 February 1979 prohibiting any interference with the national monument on the site until the determination of the action.

The making of the interlocutory injunction was appealed to the Supreme Court, which held that the consents upon which the Corporation were acting were valid and subsisting consents, discharged the injunction and dismissed the action as being unsustainable. At no stage in the proceedings did the Attorney General or his representative appear and the transcript showed that both counsel for Fr Martin and for the Corporation made it clear by explicit statements in court that the Attorney General's fiat did not extend to or include the undertaking as to damages, which were for the relator, Fr Martin. In fact, the Corporation counsel urged that the accepted inability of Fr Martin, if so ordered, to meet the alleged losses to Dublin ratepayers of £30,000 a week caused by the delay in work on the municipal building as a result of the court action should be ground for refusing the interlocutory relief which Fr Martin sought.

Despite these facts, the wording of the interim order given by the High Court recited that the undertaking had been given for the plaintiff (the Attorney General) by his counsel, and further errors appeared in the order of the Supreme Court when the interlocutory order was discharged and the matter was remitted to the High Court 'for an assessment of the damages in pursuance of the undertaking given by the plaintiff F.X. Martin'. Counsel for the Corporation then submitted a claim that: (1) the orders should be accepted as they stood and that the Attorney General should be held liable to pay damages; (2) alternatively, the Attorney General had implicitly accepted a joint and several liability to pay damages. In response, O'Higgins C.J. for the Supreme Court stated: 'In putting forward its claim, the Corporation seek to take advantage of what was clearly a slip or error in the description applied to Fr Martin in the first order made in the proceedings, which error was repeated in later orders' (page 255).

In dismissing the appeal, O'Higgins C.J. held that although the Attorney General clearly was the plaintiff in relator proceedings, he had not given the undertaking in this case. Rather, the undertaking was given by Fr Martin. The granting of the consent of the Attorney General does not necessarily indicate that he approves of the proceedings and the absence of his approval had been expressed on his behalf when the proceedings had started. He concluded that:

> The acceptance or otherwise of Fr Martin's undertaking was a matter for the court. It was stated on his behalf that his ability to meet the losses was limited ... The learned trial judge expressly declined to seek an undertaking as to damages from or a lodgment of such by the Attorney General. In these circumstances, I cannot see how any liability on the Attorney General's part could be implied. (pages 257-8)

The State as Plaintiff: Debts and Torts

The prerogative right of the Crown to priority in recovering debts due to the Crown as against other debts was part of Irish common law. This right was reinforced by a provision in section 38(2) of the Finance Act 1924, providing that money due currently or owing in the future to the Central Fund would have all the rights and privileges which had existed as to debts due to the Crown.[5] In early cases such as *In re K, an Arranging Debtor* 1927 IR 260 and *In re Hennessy, a Bankrupt* 1932 IR 11, the Supreme Court ruling indicated that not only had part of the Crown's prerogative been given effect by statute, but that those debts not covered by the Finance Act 1924 were also subject to the prerogative of preferential payment as previously asserted by the Crown. However, in subsequent cases, notably *In re Irish Aero Club* 1939 IR 204, the courts turned against the concept that the royal prerogative had survived in this regard and asserted that the extent to which a prior claim of the state existed with respect to a debt owed to it was dependent only on the scope or coverage of the statutory provisions of section 38(2) of the Finance Act 1924. In brief, the Crown prerogative based on the personal pre-eminence of the King over his subjects under common law in such matters had not been passed on to the government of the Irish Free State in 1922, and the common law of Ireland no longer supported the doctrine of the prerogative priority over debts owed to the state.[6]

With regard to the position of the state as plaintiff in tort actions, the Attorney General in his role as protector of the public interest may sue on behalf of the people on the same basis as a private plaintiff, using the same remedies and judicial forms, as determined in *Attorney General v. Northern Petroleum Tank Co Ltd* 1936 IR 450. However, on the substantive issue of whether the state may recover wages paid to a public servant incapacitated as a result of the negligence of a defendant, the Supreme Court in *Attorney General and Minister for Defence v. Ryan's Car Hire Ltd* 1965 IR 642 held that public servants do not fall within the category of ordinary master-to-servant relationships. Consequently, action *per quod servitum* does not apply to such public service members as the armed forces, police or civil service. The Court therefore overruled the *Attorney General v. Dublin United Tramways Co* 1934 IR 590, 741 ILTR 46 case, and also *Minister for Finance and Attorney General v. O'Brien* 1949 IR 91 and *Attorney General and Minister for Posts and Telegraphs v. Coras Iompair Éireann* 90 ILTR 139, which had held that members of the public service were servants of the public employed by the government and that their back wages for services lost during incapacity for work could be recovered.

The State as Defendant: Contract, Statute, Tort

Another dimension of the special position of the state as litigant is when it appears as defendant. In this role, it has enjoyed a privileged position in suits involving claims for compensation under contract or statute and in tort. However, a trend towards reduction of these special privileges has been evolving.

Suits Involving Contract or Statute

The background of Irish and English jurisprudence on the position of the state as defendant in suits involving claims by citizens against the state under contract, statute or in tort has been well delineated and analysed in the literature on public law.[7] Under English law, and in Ireland until the establishment of the Irish Free State, the Crown could not be sued in contract or tort on the same basis as a private person, since the courts were the King's courts. However, a person aggrieved by the Crown or its agents for not meeting an obligation of contract might ask for a Petition of Right (provided that the royal fiat was first obtained) with a reasonable expectation of satisfaction even though the court could not actually compel a payment. A plaintiff could also bring an action for a declaration of his or her rights under contract or statute and again it was understood that there would be compliance with the court's declaration.

Nevertheless, these remedies in British law were restricted. Servants of the Crown could not be held personally liable for contracts entered into in their official capacity, since the real debtor was the Crown under a ruling in *Macbeath v. Haldimand* 1786 ITR 172 (99 ER 1036). A public servant who exceeded his powers and offered himself as having authority to contract when he in fact lacked that authority could not be made personally liable on breach of warranty of authority, according to *Dunn v. MacDonald* (1897) 1 QB 401. Further, in *Rederiaktiebolaget 'Amphitrite' v. the King* (1921) 3 KB 500, it was held that the Crown could not bind future executive action through a contract. As a result, a suit for damages for breach of contract through Petition of Right failed, despite the fact that the British government clearly had broken its promise not to detain the ship Amphitrite if it were sent to England. With the enactment of the Crown Proceedings Act 1947, the Crown became liable for torts committed by its servants or agents acting in the course of their functions, provided such servants or agents were and would have been liable themselves. The Act makes the Crown liable for breach of duties an employer owes to his servants or agents at common law and for breach of duties which under common law attached to ownership, occupation or control of property. However, a contract made by a servant of the Crown under which money was to be payable by the Crown, was held to be subject to Parliament's appropriating money for the purpose of that contract, and thus a Petition of Right would not prevail where Parliament had not appropriated money, as determined in *Churchward v. the Queen* (1965) LR 1, QB 173.

Following the establishment of the Irish Free State, the Ministers and Secretaries Act 1924, section 2 abolished the Petition of Right. Instead, the Act provided that each of the ministers would be a corporation sole with power to sue and be sued subject to the grant in each case of the fiat of the Attorney General. To the citizen, this change merely substituted the fiat of the Attorney General for the Petition of Right. The basic legal rights of the citizen remained the same with respect to suits against the state for contract or tort, together with the existing judicial doctrines as to the restriction in such suits. This lack of change in the transition from English rule to the Irish Free State was demonstrated in *Kenny v. Cosgrave* 1926 IR 517. Mr Kenny, a builder, claimed that when he was confronted with the demands of striking workers, Mr Cosgrave, President of the Executive Council of the Irish Free State, told Mr Kenny that it was critical to the government that Mr Kenny not compromise with the strikers, and that the Executive Council would reimburse him against any financial losses suffered from an extension of the strike. Kenny did in fact suffer as a result of resisting the strikers' demands, and sued defendant for damages on grounds of a breach of the indemnity agreement. However, the Supreme Court dismissed plaintiff's claim since Mr Cosgrave could not be held personally liable on a contract into which he had entered as a Minister of State (per *Macbeath*) or on an implied warranty given by him in his public capacity (as under *Dunn*). Further, the contract was not enforceable against the Executive Council since the Council could not promise to pay plaintiff an indemnity out of public funds, unless the Oireachtas approved it by an appropriation, according to the *Churchward* doctrine.

Despite *Kenny*, a suit against the state over contractual rights was not always futile, as demonstrated in *Leyden v. Attorney General and Others* 1926 IR 334. Plaintiff claimed a declaration of his salary rights under his contract of service as a school teacher. The Supreme Court held that although an action for damages might not be successful in view of the doctrine in *Churchward*, i.e. it would take an appropriation by the Oireachtas to fulfil the contract, the *Churchward* doctrine would not stop the Court from entertaining a claim for and making a declaration of the rights of the plaintiff. It was presumed that given such a declaration, the government would respond accordingly.

In a more recent case, *Ryle v. Minister for Agriculture* 97 ILTR 127, the plaintiff had signed an application form for participation in the Bovine Tuberculosis Eradication Scheme in early 1960, in accordance with the terms prescribed in an explanatory memorandum. The Minister for Agriculture then granted free tests of the plaintiff's cattle and made a headage grant, as provided for in the memorandum, on four reactor cows owned by plaintiff. Six months later the Minister introduced amending measures to the scheme. Given these facts, the Court held that a binding contract between plaintiff and defendant had been created and that this contract could not be altered by the Minister's introducing amending measures.

The judicial perspective in respect of claims based on the liability of the state to make payments provided for in statutes parallels judicial views as to suits based on contract. In *Leen v. President of the Executive Council and Others* 1928 IR 408, the Supreme Court dismissed plaintiff's claim for a declaration that he was entitled to be paid a sum of money by the Compensation (Ireland) Commission for property maliciously destroyed during the Civil War, from a fund appropriated by the Oireachtas to compensate for malicious injuries to property. The basis for the decision was that payment of an award by the Compensation Commission could not be enforced by the Court by way of contract, estoppel or mandamus since it was subject to the discretion of the Minister for Finance, and there was no evidence to show that the sum of £4,000 claimed by plaintiff was specifically included in the appropriation made by the Oireachtas.

In the later case of *Galway County Council v. Minister for Finance and Attorney General* 1931 IR 215, the Council sought a declaration that they were entitled to payments from the Minister for Finance out of money granted by Appropriation Acts to enable local authorities to recoup compensation they had paid for malicious injury to property during the Civil War. The Court reiterated the doctrine of *Leen* as to what is the effect of lack of evidence concerning specific inclusion of payments sought, for which only a general appropriation of money had been made. However, it also held that in this case the Galway County Council was entitled to payment in view of a letter from the Minister for Finance which made reference to the amount claimed by the Council, based upon decrees for damage to property during 1919-21. In the Court's view, the content of the letter constituted the type of evidence which the Court in the *Leen* case had said was absent to support such a claim.

It is apparent from these decisions that judicial doctrine favours a strict construction of contractual claims against the state and requires specific legislative intent and proof that the claimant explictly meets that intent. Moreover, in the absence of such proof, administrators may not commit the state to payment of such claims.

Suits in Tort

The citizen has also occupied a less favourable position in suits against the state for torts committed by its agents. Griffith and Street state that this unfavourable position had its origins in the concepts of the immunity of the King from suit in his own courts save by Petition of Right, which was not available for suits in tort except in the instance of a real action. These concepts were founded in the underlying concept that 'the King can do no wrong'.[8] As Wade points out, when the theory that the Crown cannot exercise its powers wrongly was combined with existing judicial doctrines that the liability of employers for the torts of their agents depended upon implied authority given by the master to the servant, or negligent choice of incompetent agents, the net result was that the Crown could not be liable in tort.[9]

These doctrines were made explicit in the English cases of *Viscount Canterbury v. Attorney General* 1843 1 Ph. 306 and *Bainbridge v. Postmaster-General and Another* 1906 1 KB 178. The *Bainbridge* case was cited as precedent in an early leading case in Ireland, namely *Carolan v. Minister for Defence* 1927 IR 62. In *Carolan*, plaintiff sued for injuries suffered as a cyclist, alleging they were caused by the negligence of a soldier driving an army lorry. Plaintiff argued that section 2 of the Ministers and Secretaries Act 1924 made Ministers of State liable for torts committed by subordinates and that the Minister for Defence was the only person who could be considered to be the soldier's employer. The High Court, per Sullivan P., referred to the *Bainbridge* case in which it was held that a superior servant of the Crown could not be liable for a subordinate servant's tort and stated that in Ireland a master-servant relationship does not exist between superior and subordinate officers of the government, since both are fellow servants of the public. Soldiers are employees of the government and fellow servants of the Minister for Defence. Consequently the Minister is not liable for their torts. Moreover, section 2 of the Ministers and Secretaries Act 1924 authorises suit against a minister only in his corporate capacity for a wrongful act which as minister he committed, ordered or directed. The intent of the Act therefore is not to make a minister liable for all defaults or wrongful acts of every person working in a minister's department.

In commenting upon this case, Kelly in 1968 made what later proved to be a prophetic statement. After noting that *Carolan* was limited to declaring that a minister cannot be made liable for torts of his fellow-servant subordinates, Kelly stated:

> The case is in no way an authority for the proposition that the Irish State has inherited the immunity of the Crown from actions in tort, and it may be thought that in the present state of the law, the State in fact has no such immunity.[10]

Given the subsequent decisions of *Attorney General v. Dublin United Tramways Co.* 1934 IR 590, 74 ILTR 46, *In re Irish Employers' Mutual Insurance Association Ltd* 1955 IR 176, *Attorney-General v. CIE* 90 ILTR 139, and the *obiter dicta* of Kenny J. on the non-applicability of the sovereign immunity doctrine to the Irish state in *Macauley v. Minister for Posts and Telegraphs* 1966 IR 345, it was to be expected that eventually a decision would be made rejecting the concept of sovereign immunity from suits in tort. The case of *Byrne v. Ireland and Attorney General* 1972 IR 241 dealt directly with the liability of the state for the torts of its agents in a situation where there was no statutory waiver of immunity. The plaintiff was injured in a fall allegedly caused by a subsidence in a public footpath where a trench had been dug and then refilled by employees of the Department of Posts and Telegraphs. She brought an action in the High Court naming the 'People of Ireland' and the Attorney General as defendants, claiming damages from those defendants for the negligence of their agents. On the motion of the Attorney General, it was ordered by the High Court, per Murnaghan J., that 'Ireland' be substituted as a defendant for the named 'People of Ireland' as defendant, and that the following issues should be tried by a judge without a jury:

1. Whether the Court can exercise jurisdiction over 'Ireland' in this action as the judicial power granted by the Constitution does not of common right extend to actions against the sovereign authority.

2. Whether the action based on alleged tortious acts and omissions and breach of duty is maintainable in law by reason of the immunity of 'Ireland' as the sovereign authority against such actions.

3. Whether the action can be maintained against the Attorney General as representing 'Ireland' and the representative order sought can be made.

4. Whether the persons or any of them alleged to have committed any of the tortious acts alleged in this action were either servants, employees or agents of 'Ireland'. (page 244)

The decision of the High Court in each of these issues was negative. On appeal, the Supreme Court, per Walsh J. (Fitzgerald J. dissenting), reversed. Walsh J., in response to the issues posed in the High Court, noted that article 4 of the Constitution says the name of the state is 'Ireland' so if the state can be sued, it can be sued by its official name. Further, articles 6, 46 and 47 make it clear that the state was created by the people, to be governed under the constitutional provisions enacted by and amendable by the people, so that sovereign authority is in the people in the final analysis. Since article 6 of the Constitution provides that the legislative, executive and judicial powers can be exercised only by the organs of the state established by the Constitution, the issue therefore is whether the judicial power exercised by the courts may be applied to bind the state itself, one of whose organs is the judiciary. In this regard, *Comyn v. Attorney General* 1950 IR 142 and *Commissioners of Public Works v. Kavanagh* 1962 IR 216 established the state as a juristic person capable of holding property and it was implicit in these judgments that the state could have been sued as the state.

A review of the concepts underlying the privileges and prerogatives of the Crown by Walsh J. revealed that the immunity of the King from suits in tort was a judge-made rule, based on the presumption that the officer committing the wrong did so of his own accord since the King, who was incapable of committing a wrong, could not have authorised it. In contrast, under the Irish Constitution, it is the Oireachtas which makes the laws and the judiciary which administers them. Consequently, there is no reason why the activities of either of these organs of state should compel the state itself to be above the law.

Further indicators of widespread support for the view that immunity from suit is not a necessary ingredient of state sovereignty in the view of Walsh J. are statutes in the United States and England waiving such immunity and French jurisprudence making the state liable for torts of its agents (*faute de service*). Furthermore, there are constitutional or statutory provisions in Germany, Australia, Canada, New Zealand and South Africa waiving immunity.

Therefore, in response to the constitutional question, Walsh J. stated:

> Where the People by the Constitution create rights against the State or impose duties upon the State, a remedy to enforce these must be deemed to be also available. It is as much the duty of the State to render justice against itself in favour of individuals as it is to administer the same between . . . individuals. The investigation and adjudication of such claims by their nature belong to the judicial power of government in the State, designated in Article 6 of the Constitution of Ireland . . . .
>
> In my view, the whole tenor of our Constitution is to the effect that there is no power, institution or person in the land free of the law, save when such immunity is expressed or provided for in the Constitution itself. Article 13, s. 8, subs. 1 (relating to the President) and Article 15, ss. 12 and 13 (relating to the Oireachtas) are examples of express immunities . . . . There is nothing in the Constitution envisaging the writing into it of a theory of immunity from suit of the State . . . stemming from or based upon the immunity of a personal sovereign who was the keystone of a feudal edifice. English common law practices, doctrines or immunities cannot qualify or dilute the provisions of the Constitution. (page 281)

In respect of the responsibility of the state for tortious acts of employees of the Department of Posts and Telegraphs, as against the Minister's being responsible as head of the Department and suable under the Ministers and Secretaries Act 1924, the Court held that the employees of the Department are not the Minister's employees. Rather, both the Minister and the employees are persons employed by the state, so it is the state and not the Minister which is liable for a damage done by such employees.

As to maintaining the suit against the Attorney General, the determining factor is that the Attorney General under article 30 of the Constitution is an independent constitutional officer of state who has quasi-judicial and executive powers and duties. He is not answerable for acts of the government or its members or those in the service of the state. He is also responsible under section 6 of the Ministers and Secretaries Act 1924 for representing the government and the public in all legal proceedings. When the state is sued, it is entitled to defend itself, and the right to defend itself can be exercised only through the government under article 49 of the Constitution. In such cases, the correct procedure is to sue the state and join the Attorney General and to effect service on the Attorney General for both parties. If the claim succeeds, it is against the state, not the Attorney General. Walsh J. also held that although it was not necessary at that point to consider how such a decree would be executed, it could be said that an order for mandamus to compel compliance with the judgment would be appropriate and not without precedent.

Fitzgerald J., in a brief dissent, noted that no previous case has gone to the length of holding that the state is a juristic person liable in tort for the act or neglect of a public servant. Rather, since 1922, the liability of the state for tort did not exist unless created by statute. To extend the liability of the state as a juristic person to the law of tort is a radical change which should not be undertaken by the Court. If such a change is made, it should be done by the legislature, as in the Workman's Compensation Act 1934, and not by the courts, so he would affirm the High Court decision and dismiss the appeal.

Byrne v. Ireland is a significant decision which completed the trend towards reversing the concept that the prerogatives of a sovereign king applied to a republican state. From the private citizen's perspective, making the state liable to suit when constitutional and legal obligations of the state are involved transforms the previous legal irresponsibility of the state to legal responsibility for the acts of its agents. Moreover, the Supreme Court in *Byrne* took the initiative to develop a comprehensive rationale for eliminating the immunity of the government from suits, while the federal courts in America left this issue to Congress, which waived the immunity for the American national government from suits in tort by enacting the Federal Tort Claims Act 1946. Within this comprehensive rationale, however, the majority judgment at one point emphasises the Irish judicial doctrine of sovereignty resting solely in the people of Ireland under the 1937 Constitution as being in contrast to a position supposedly established by Chief Justice John Marshall, i.e. 'the United States was created by the States and the People of the States, and not by the people separated from the States' (page 262). However, in such early landmark cases as *Martin v. Hunter's Lessee* 1 Wheat 304, 4 L. Ed. 97 (1816) and especially *McCulloch v. Maryland* 4 Wheat 316, 4 L.Ed. 579 (1819) (judgment by Chief Justice Marshall) it was asserted that although the people could not be separated from the states, the United States Constitution was approved and brought into existence by the people, through conventions elected by the people for that purpose, and not by the States. The people, by so adopting the Constitution, allocated powers to, and limited the powers of, both the national and state governments. These and subsequent major American cases would seem to reveal that the views of the Irish and American courts on sovereignty resting in the people are quite similar.

The initiative of the Irish Supreme Court on this issue has been paralleled by that of the courts in a number of American states which have rejected the doctrine of the immunity of their governments from suits in tort, while in other states, the courts cling to the concept that this may be done only by legislative enactment (which often is of a qualified or piecemeal nature).[11] In this regard, it ultimately rests with the courts to reduce or reject the overall concept of sovereign immunity from suits in tort, despite legislative waivers of immunity setting the terms and conditions of such waivers. This is illustrated in Irish cases interpreting statutes such as the Road Traffic Act 1933, and in American cases interpreting statutes such as the Federal Tort Claims Act 1946. Under such Acts, the award or denial of compensation for injuries caused by the negligent actions of agents of the state depends on how narrowly or broadly the courts construe the legislative terms and conditions despite clear connection between action and injury in individual cases. (See as two examples, *Neill v. Minister for Finance* 1948 IR 881, interpreting the Road Traffic Act 1933, and *Dalehite v. the United States* 346 US 15 (1953) interpreting the Federal Tort Claims Act.)

Local Authorities as Defendants: Tort

Suits in Tort: Misfeasance

Local authorities in Ireland are subject to the common law remedy of suits in tort, in which the question of liability for damages hinges upon traditional doctrines surrounding actions in tort. This contrasts with legal doctrines in the United States which until recently extended the immunity of the states from suits in tort to their local governments in the performance of certain types of functions. As stated in *American Jurisprudence:*

> No liability attaches to it [the municipal corporation] at com-
> mon law, either for non-use or misuse of such power or for the
> acts or omissions on the part of its officers or agents through
> whom such functions are performed, or of the servants
> employed by agencies carrying out governmental functions of
> the corporation. This rule is not affected by a statutory or
> charter provision that the municipality may sue and be sued.
> Insofar, however, as a municipal corporation acts in its private
> or proprietary capacity, the general rule is that it is liable in
> tort in the same manner as a private corporation, although this
> rule is not adhered to in all jurisdictions.[12]

For example, with regard to different functions connected with public highways, it was held in earlier cases such as *Strickfadden v. Greencreek Highway District* 42 Idaho 738, 49 ALR 1057 (1926) that negligence in not providing adequate warning barriers incident to highway repair which led to damage to a motor vehicle made the Local Highway District liable for damages in a suit in tort, because the function of highway repair was 'proprietary'. On the other hand, the Court in *Harris v. District of Columbia* 256 US 650 (1921) ruled that flushing streets with a water tank truck was a public health or 'governmental function' and consequently the District of Columbia could not be sued in tort for the negligence of its truck driver who had dropped the water tank plug cover on a child's head.

Fortunately for the Irish citizen, no such distinction between functions (which in American cases has become rather esoteric at times) limits the legal right of the citizen to sue local authorities for damages arising out of negligence of their agents. In Ireland, rather than distinguishing between the types of functions in relation to possible liability, the issues turn on common law doctrines in respect of negligence, with the assumption that if negligence is demonstrated, and it is reasonable that the local authority might have anticipated the hazard, the local authority will be liable for damages. In *Kane v. Howth Urban District Council* 1939 Ir. Jur. Rep. 34, a suit for damages against a local authority was successful when the plaintiff's motorcycle was damaged owing to alleged misfeasance, i.e. negligence of the local authority in doing road repairs.

A further example of this focus of the Irish courts is the case of *Swift v. Westport Urban District Council* 1944 IR 259, where the critical test was whether the local authority in building and maintaining gully traps had failed to anticipate the presence of children and the likelihood of their injury, and thus had not taken reasonable precautions to guard against such injury. The Supreme Court held it was reasonably open to a court to decide the matter either way under this criterion. On referral back to the High Court, Gavan Duffy J. held that the defendants had failed to anticipate the presence of children and the likelihood of injury to them, and to take reasonable precautions against this; consequently damages should be awarded. In the same year as *Swift v. Westport*, the High Court in *McGovern v. Clones Urban District Council* 1944 IR 282, 79 ILTR 86 applied the precedent and criteria of *Swift* and held that, given the facts, the defendants could not fairly be expected to have anticipated that the type of gully trap which injured the plaintiff would be likely to be meddled with by young children and cause them injury. It was proved that no information had been made known to the Council of a record of three similar accidents in nine years involving children seeking to recover marbles. Consequently, the plaintiff's claim was dismissed. Again, the critical factor was the application of judicial criteria of negligence to the facts of the cases, and not the type of function being performed.

The scope and nature of the liability of Irish local authorities for torts are further illustrated by *Phelan v. Kilkenny County Council* 1943 Ir. Jur. Rep. 1 and *Lynch v. Cavan County Council* 76 ILTR 12: both reflect the basic doctrines applied in *Kane* and *Swift*. In the *Phelan* case it was held that if a highway authority does repair work on a roadway, it must leave the roadway in reasonably safe condition. Failure to do so constitutes misfeasance, for which the highway authority will be liable in damages to one who is injured while lawfully using the highway. Carrying this concept a step farther, in *Lynch* it was held that if a local authority enters a quarry to obtain road materials under contract with the Land Commission as owner of the quarry, and on its own volition erects a fence, although not required to do so under the contract, the local authority is bound to maintain that fence. Consequently, when plaintiff's horse fell into the quarry owing to the defective condition of the fence, the local authority was liable for damages for negligence.

Yet another dimension of local authority liability in tort is illustrated by the judgment in *Weir v. Corporation of Dun Laoghaire* 1983 IR 242, 1984 ILRM 113, 1983. *The Incorporated Law Society of Ireland Gazette* 23 (1983). In upholding a jury award of damages to the plaintiff, the Court first held that the evidence established negligence, since plaintiff's fall and resulting injury was caused by a two-inch difference in road levels along a line where a new lay-by for buses was being constructed, for which no warning of the difference in levels was given and the entire roadway of tarmacadam appeared to be uniform. The Court then ruled against the argument of defendants that as road authority under the Local Government Act 1925, they were not to be fixed with knowledge or made liable in respect of any licence or approval they may have given as the planning authority under the Local Government (Planning and Development) Act 1963. The Court noted that the defendants as planning authority when approving of the development of a shopping centre had imposed a condition that a bus lay-by be constructed. The developer hired a firm of contractors to construct such a lay-by and evidence from defendants' Assistant Borough Engineer showed that the layout of the bus lay-by was agreed upon with the defendants and that it appeared that the carrying out of the work was known to defendants.

Given this evidence, O'Higgins C.J. held that the defendants must be held to have known and approved of the work undertaken by the firm of contractors. Since the work was done with their knowledge, they had a responsibility to look to the safety of those using the roadway who might be endangered if the work being done caused a risk of injury. In his dissent to the majority judgment, Griffin J. stated that 'so to extend the liability of a road authority to include responsibility for the acts of a contractor engaged by a developer in doing work for which the latter had obtained planning permission, and equating this liability with that of the authority for acts of a contractor engaged by them, is in my view warranted neither by principle nor authority'.

It should be noted at this point that despite the contrast between Irish and American judicial doctrines on local government tort liability, American state courts and legislatures in recent years are moving in the direction of the position taken by Irish courts. In certain states, the courts are displaying impatience with the unwillingness to abandon the judicial sophistry involved in the 'governmental-proprietary' functional dichotomy. Instead, they are holding local authorities responsible for torts regardless of the nature of the function, with the exception of liability for adverse effects of such basic governmental policy-making functions as the enactment of local ordinances, adoption of administrative rules or local judicial determinations. (See especially *Muskopf v. Corning Hospital District* 55 Cal 2d 211, 35 359 P. 2d 457 (1961).)

Suits in Tort: Nonfeasance

Although local authorities are liable for torts resulting from misfeasance, the same is not true for nonfeasance, as demonstrated in *Kelly v. Mayo County Council* 1964 IR 315. Plaintiff in this case was injured when thrown from his bicycle owing to a rut in a public road which, according to a County Council road employee's testimony, was one of several ruts greatly enlarged to a six-inch depth and foot-and-a-half length by extensive driving on the road by County Council lorries. Plaintiff's suit was not for inadequate road maintenance but on the grounds that the County Council's lorries, by excessive user, had damaged the road so as to create a nuisance. The Supreme Court first stated that exceptional user of a highway to so affect a road as to constitute a public nuisance can be restrained by injunction, and might be a cause of action by a person showing himself to be damaged by such nuisance, citing *Guardians of Armagh Union v. Bell* 1900 2 IR 371. However, the facts concerning user by the County Council lorries did not show either excessive or unsuitable user. Secondly, the County Council was possibly dilatory in not filling the potholes. Nevertheless, it is well established law that while a road authority may be liable for damages for injuries caused by negligence in performing road repairs or in interfering with the road, they are not liable for injuries suffered or caused by want of repair of a road. This is founded on the well established distinction between misfeasance and nonfeasance, under which there is liability for the former but not the latter.

The *Kelly* case as compared with the *Kane, Swift,* or *Lynch* cases might cause the non-legal mind to speculate upon the potentially odd public policy impact of the doctrine concerning nonfeasance. A local authority which makes a positive effort to repair its roads or to build a fence around a quarry but fails to exercise sufficient care in doing so may have to pay damages, while the local officials who do nothing to repair potholes in roads will suffer at most verbal protests or abuse by those having to put up with such inadequate road surfaces. In the abstract, this seems to be an encouragement for inaction.

Local Authorities as Defendants: Malicious Injuries

In addition to the liability of local authorities to suits in tort under common law doctrines, a particular form of liability of local authorities for damages exists in Ireland under the 'Malicious Injuries Code', which as Kelly in his 1969 article, 'The Malicious Injuries Code and the Constitution', stated, is a series of enactments of the UK parliament during the nineteenth century applied in Ireland on the basis of being 'carried over' under continuance provisions of the 1922 and the 1937 constitutions.[12] The essential elements in the operation of the malicious injuries code have been that if an owner suffers malicious damage to his property, he may claim compensation through an application in the Circuit Court from the local authority for the district where the damage took place. If compensation is awarded, the local authority then increases the rate levied on ratepayers of the district by the amount necessary to meet the Circuit Court award. The system is impersonal in that while the claimant must prove malice on the part of some person or persons in connection with the damage to the satisfaction of the court, it is not necessary to identify positively who such person or persons are or might be. Neither is it necessary to show that the ratepayers, who in effect pay the claim, had any connection with the incident or, for that matter, that the instigator of the damage came from or had any connection with the district where it occurred.

Given the purpose of the malicious injuries legislation in the context of the periods in which it was enacted, judicial interpretations, and the current operation and effect of the code relating to pertinent constitutional provisions, Kelly concluded that the origins and operations of the code reflected the concept of community liability for prevention of crime. The system was inherently part of the criminal, not civil law, as indicated by the nature of its penal features. In his opinion it did not constitute an analogue of mutual community insurance or social adjustment through spreading the social cost of a common problem. In addition, the system was inconsistent with article 38.1 of the Constitution since it applied penal measures to individuals without charge or trial and made an assumption of guilt. It also conflicted with article 40.1 since the system may operate so that ratepayers in the area in which the person doing the damage lives do not have to contribute to a payment for the damage done, if that damage takes place in another district where the ratepayers have to pay through increased rates. On these grounds, pending a ruling of unconstitutionality by the courts, Kelly favoured legislation to make the compensation a charge on the central government.[13]

Despite the persuasiveness of Kelly's analysis, the malicious injuries code continued to be applied without basic policy changes. Kelly's criticism had been preceded by concern expressed by some county councils, leading to the appointment by the Minister for Justice in 1960 of an interdepartmental committee to consider the amendment or repeal of the existing statutes on compensation for malicious injuries. The committee in its 1963 report recommended keeping some system of compensation for malicious injuries, but felt that the existing law was unnecessarily comprehensive, that payments from insurance policies be taken into account and compensation be given for consequential loss. For a long period, the only action taken subsequent to the report was in 1974 when the increasing cost of compensation was recognised through a non-statutory arrangement in which if the cost of compensation to a local authority in any financial year was greater than the amount yielded by a rate of 20p in the pound, the excess could be recovered by the local authority from the central exchequer.[14]

The malicious injuries code therefore continued to be applied without basic policy changes (other than the arrangement for recovery of some compensation by local authorities from the national exchequer, reflecting something of Kelly's views). It was not until 1981 that the Malicious Injuries Bill 1980, which rewrote the code, was enacted. Typical of the judicial determinations up to 1981 interpreting the applicable statutes as to when, and on what basis, compensation might be awarded was *Borough Builders Ltd v. Dublin Corporation* 1966 IR 285 in which the maliciously damaged buildings involved were temporary and had been erected illegally in violation of section 27 of the Public Health Acts Amendment Act 1907.

Dublin Corporation conceded that there had been malicious damage but argued that since the buildings had been erected illegally, they could not be made the subject matter of a claim for compensation for malicious damage. The High Court, per Henchy J., cited section 135 of the Grand Jury (Ireland) Act 1836 and section 5 of the Local Government (Ireland) Act 1898, extending section 135 of the 1836 Act to make the compensation payable 'in all cases' to cover malicious damage to property of any description, provided that it is shown the act was a crime punishable on indictment under the Malicious Damage Act 1861. Based on these Acts, the Court held that the applicants must prove they own the property, that it was maliciously damaged and that the act of damage was a crime punishable on indictment under the 1861 Act.

The 1836 and 1898 Acts do not require that a building be legally erected or constructed. Section 135 of the 1836 Act simply says compensation may be awarded 'in all cases' of malicious damage and so Henchy J. could find no principle of statutory interpretation which would compel him to read the added requirement proposed by Dublin Corporation into the malicious injuries code. Nor could he apply to this case the legal maxim *ex turpi causa non oritur actio* which would defeat a statutory remedy if the claimant is seeking to profit from his illegality. In this situation it is not profit but merely compensation from ratepayers for malicious damage that is being sought. An award of compensation should thus be made.

Another issue is that of the causal relation between the alleged malicious action and the damage to be compensated. The Supreme Court, per Ó Dálaigh C.J., in *Rexi Irish Mink Ltd v. Dublin County Council* 1972 IR 123 held that the act of releasing 340 live mink from applicant's mink farm under circumstances demonstrating deliberate and malicious interference with the cages on the part of persons unknown constituted grounds for compensation. A large majority of the minks came back but then were fit only for pelting and not breeding since there was a loss of recorded identity of the mink; a smaller number were found dead and a few missing for a total loss estimated at some £9,000. The court affirmed applicant's claim that the damage arose not from the consequence of the release; rather, a direct loss occurred immediately upon the release as a result of that action, which constituted malicious damage under the statute. The value of the escaped mink as breeding mink minus pelting revenue was the basis for damages. This principle was applied in the more recent case of *Duffy v. Cavan County Council* unreported, High Court, per McMahon J., 6 November 1979 in which the court held that although the physical aspect of the malicious damage to plaintiff's car was completely repaired so as to restore it to its prior condition, the award of compensation could include the amount of depreciation in the value of the car since it was now a repaired car. Under the Malicious Injuries Code, the right to compensation is not confined to physical injury and extends to non-physical damage, as in the *Rexi Irish Mink* case. Since the depreciation of the value of the applicant's car was the direct consequence of the malicious damage done to it, which was incapable of being restored by repair, plaintiff was entitled to compensation for the reduced value of the car.

The issue most frequently raised is that of proof of malicious damage as against other cause, which is illustrated by *Fleming v. Cavan County Council* 1972 IR 159. A detailed analysis of the evidence by the Supreme Court, per Budd J., showed that before leaving his home on holiday, applicant had turned off the heating system fuel oil supply, disconnected electric fuses and locked all doors and windows. It was established that shortly before the fire which damaged the house, someone had broken into the house as indicated by windows forced open, the chain taken off the door and fuses replaced, but no property was stolen as indicated by melted silver from the house being found in the debris. Applicant's position in the local school system had involved him in controversial decisions which had resulted in letters of complaint. Qualified electricians testified that there was no electrical fault in the house. Given this evidence, the court held it reasonable to draw the inference that the intruder had started the fire deliberately and therefore maliciously within the meaning of the Criminal Injuries Acts.

A more complex ground of proof of malicious damage was involved in *McRandall v. Louth County Council* unreported, High Court, per O'Higgins J., 2 April 1974. Applicant's motor vehicle was stolen in Belfast. It was driven by two persons to Dundalk where they met a third man who was waiting for them, and the car was loaded with gelignite. Authorities, having later discovered that the car was loaded with gelignite, took it to a rifle range and blew it up, whereby McRandall suffered a loss of £1,375.

Under section 1 of the Malicious Injuries (Ireland) Act 1853, if any persons unlawfully assembled maliciously or unlawfully destroy or demolish any goods, all damages sustained by any person shall be recovered. O'Higgins J. concluded that the coming together of the two men in the car with the third man in Dundalk constituted an unlawful purpose, occurring when all available security forces were deployed on the border with strict lookout for the carrying of guns or explosives to the North. Consequently, the men stealing the car knew that one of two things would happen: if the car was stopped and the load detected, it would be destroyed; if not, the car would be used as a bomb. This unlawful act, combined with the other factors leading to destruction of the vehicle, provided the element of unlawful and malicious destruction under the statute and the applicant was entitled to succeed in his action.

Finally, a determination as to which of two competing judicial doctrines regarding the nature of proof of malice was made in *Cavendish v. Corporation of Dublin* 1974 IR 171. In considering applicant's claim for over £300,000 compensation for a fire alleged to be maliciously set in a commercial building, Pringle J. in the High Court stated that the onus is upon the applicant to prove the fire causing the damage was set maliciously. However, the question was whether that onus of proof is of the type required in civil proceedings, namely the 'balance of probabilities' as argued by applicant, or the type required in criminal proceedings, namely 'proof beyond a reasonable doubt' as advanced by the respondent.

Pringle J. considered analagous prior cases in relation to the position of an applicant under the Local Government (Ireland) Act 1898, referring to *Artificial Coal Co. v. Minister of Finance* 1928 IR 238 which indicated that the nature of proof is that of a criminal trial to convince the mind and conscience of the judge but did not expressly state how it must be proved that a crime has been committed. This is a central issue in malicious damage by fire where frequently there is no direct evidence of the origin of the damage. In the absence of such direct evidence it is possible that the facts adduced can be as consistent with the inference that the fire was caused by accident or negligence as with the inference that a crime was committed, as indicated in *Crowe v. Tipperary County Council* 1928 IR 255.

Given these factors, the test to be applied in the view of Pringle J. is that which operates in civil actions, namely the balance of probabilities applied in the maliciously-set-fires cases of *Morrison v. Dublin Corporation* 1948 IR 424 and *Prendergast v. Kerry County Council* (1950) 84 ILTR 185. The evidence in the present case of testimony by persons checking and leaving the premises of the building before the fire's occurrence and the discovery (albeit seven months after the fire) of charred remains of a commonly employed device to start fires (allowing for conflict of testimony on the device) and other indicators of incendiarism led to the conclusion that the fire was set through an incendiary device under the balance of probabilities rule. On this basis, the request for compensation should be approved.

Subsequent to the above judgments, the Malicious Injuries Act 1981 was enacted to rewrite the Malicious Injuries Code. It repealed the Malicious Injuries (Ireland) Acts, 1948 and 1953 entirely, as well as certain sections or schedules of the Grand Jury (Ireland) Act 1836, the Merchant Shipping Act 1894, the Local Government (Ireland) Act 1898, and the Courts (Supplemental Provisions) Act 1961 (see Schedule: Enactments Repealed at page 37). Partially new changes in existing provisions in previous Acts were made, particularly regarding provisions on the operation of the Act, e.g. joinder of other local authorities in proceedings, and stating of cases for the Supreme Court (sections 10, 18). The new provisions pertain to such matters as: the right to compensation for malicious damage during a riot (section 6); non-defence for damage by a person of unsound mind or a child (section 7); and reduction or exclusion of compensation based on a court's evaluation of (1) whether the damage was related to any precautions which the person suffering such damage reasonably might have taken to avoid the damage; (2) that a person connived at or assisted in causing the damage; or (3) that the damage was to a structure which was unauthorised under the Local Government (Planning and Development) Acts,

1963 and 1976 or under notice of existing non-compliance under those Acts (section 12). If compensation has been paid for property taken, and the property is then recovered, the local authority becomes the owner of the property to dispose of it as the authority sees fit, under section 22.

By providing for denial of claims for damage to or loss of property resulting from malicious damage to a structure if that structure was unauthorised under the Local Government (Planning and Development) Acts 1963 and 1976, the 1981 Malicious Injuries Act would seem to have responded to the issue in *Borough Builders Ltd v. Dublin Corporation* 1966 IR 285, (discussed above) in which the Court had held that as the statutes then stood, compensation would have to be granted for maliciously damaged buildings, even though they were temporary and had been erected illegally. On the other hand, Greer and Mitchell note that the 1981 Act, despite recommendations in the interdepartmental committee's 1963 report, and discussion in the debate on the Malicious Injuries Bill 1980 of the criticisms made by Kelly, retained and, in certain respects, expanded the ambit of entitlement to compensation. It did not repeal the existing provisions on non-deduction of payments under insurance policies, and retained provision for non-payment of compensation for consequential loss. The concept of liability of the local authorities was continued with the modification of putting into statutory form (in section 20) the non-statutory arrangements made in 1974 for compensation to local authorities from the central government referred to previously in which if the cost of compensation by a local authority in any financial year was greater than the amount yielded by a rate of 20p in the pound, the excess could be recovered from the central exchequer.[15]

It would appear that the 1981 Act did not make a significant change in policy as regards the potential for liability of local authorities for loss of or damage caused by malicious acts of unknown persons, as indicated by the recent decision in *Fitzgerald v. Limerick Corporation* Supreme Court, unreported per Henchy J., 7 June 1984. As Henchy J. stated, this was the first case stated under section 18 of the Malicious Injuries Act 1981 to come before the Court which raised the question of whether a person whose motor vehicle had been taken without authorisation and crashed while being driven, could recover compensation under the 1981 Act for malicious damage to the vehicle. In the malicious injury claim brought in the

Circuit Court, the applicant had to show under section 5 (2) (d) of the Act that the damage to the car was caused 'in the course of the committing of a crime against the property damaged', and the Circuit Court judge held the damage was so caused, and made an award to applicant of £600 compensation against Limerick Corporation. The case stated sought a ruling as to whether this decision was correct.

After noting that this issue is of 'considerable practical importance' considering 'how prevalent this kind of "joyriding" offence' is, Henchy J. held that there was clear evidence of an offence under section 112(1) of the Road Traffic Act 1961, as amended by section 65, Road Traffic Act 1968 which makes it an offence to 'use or take possession of a mechanically propelled vehicle without the consent of the owner . . . ' Once the offender took control of the vehicle and drove off, and until the crash, he was committing an offence contrary to section 112 (1) (a) by using the car without the owner's consent. To determine whether the offence was a 'crime against the property damaged' as provided in section 5 (2) (d) of the 1981 Act, he analysed section 5 (1) providing for a right to compensation when damage over £100 is 'maliciously caused to property' and section 5 (2) which has the purpose of giving an extended meaning to 'maliciously' as used in section 5 (1). He concluded that when (as in this case) damage was caused in the course of using the car contrary to section 112 (1) (a) of the Road Traffic Act 1961, the damage was caused 'in the course of . . . the committing of a crime against the property damaged'. Therefore the applicant was correctly held to be entitled to the compensation award.

The implications for local authorities of this decision applying the 1981 Act are yet to be determined, but as Henchy J. indicated, they may well be of 'considerable practical importance', presumably of a fiscal nature.

The authorisation of claims for compensation provided for under the Malicious Injuries Code in Ireland, and similar legislation in England, has no true counterpart in the United States. The closest approximation is typified by statutes in some fifteen states which permit citizens whose property was damaged as a result of civil disturbances which local authorities fail to control to sue their municipalities for damages. However with the growth of civil disturbances, earlier statutes of this nature adopted in the nineteenth century have been repealed recently in some states.[16]

F

Notes to Chapter 4

1. See Kelly, *Fundamental Rights in the Irish Constitution* 324-49 (1968); Donaldson, *Some Comparative Aspects of Irish Law* (*Comparative Aspects*) 218-28 (1957); Wade, *Administrative Law* 690-718 (1982) for details of these aspects. This summary treatment is followed by more detailed discussion of recent judicial determination on the position of the state in litigation.
2. O'Reilly and Redmond, *Cases and Materials on the Irish Constitution* [*Cases and Materials*] 501-503 (1983)
3. See Casey, *The Office of the Attorney General in Ireland* 166-72 (1980) for detailed analysis of the Attorney General's fiat, and judicial decisions leading to the *Macauley* decision.
4. Kelly, *The Irish Constitution* 202-204 (1984)
5. Donaldson, *Comparative Aspects* 219, and Kelly, *Fundamental Rights* 329
6. Donaldson, *Comparative Aspects* 219, 224 and Kelly *Fundamental Rights* 329-34
7. See Kelly, *Fundamental Rights* 334-40, Donaldson *Comparative Aspects* 210-12, 218-24, Wade *Administrative Law* 697-718 and 648-81 and 'The Public Service, the Citizen and the Law', *Léargas* 1-4 (Vol. 5, 1966)
8. Griffith and Street, *Principles of Administrative Law* 251 (1967)
9. Wade, *Administrative Law* 700
10. See Kelly, *Fundamental Rights* 347
11. See Barry and Whitcomb, *Legal Foundations of Public Administration* 288 (1981)
12. 38 American Jurisprudence, *Municipal Corporations* section 572. However, see *Monell v. Department of Social Services of City of New York* 436 US 658 (1978) holding that under section 1983, Civil Rights Act 1871, municipalities may be held liable for damages by actions of their officials 'pursuant to official municipal policy of some nature' which causes a constitutional tort (violation of a constitutional right).
13. Kelly, 'The Malicious Injuries Code and the Constitution' *The Irish Jurist* 221-33 (1969)
14. See Greer and Mitchell, *Compensation for Criminal Damage to Property* 22-3, (1982) and generally for analysis of Malicious Injuries Code.
15. Greer and Mitchell, *Compensation* 22-3
16. Barry and Whitcomb, *Legal Foundations* 317

5 Natural and Constitutional Justice in the Administrative Process

The operating aspects of administrative law within the Irish governmental framework discussed earlier involve the scope and nature of the administrative powers employed to achieve statutory purposes and the limits placed upon the application of these powers so as to protect the due process rights of individuals. The characteristics of such rights are established by constitutional provisions, statutes and judicial decisions based on concepts of natural and constitutional justice. At the same time, the extent of due process rights may be affected by the nature of the administrative power being applied. For example, perspectives of an individual's rights may be influenced by whether the courts consider a licence to be a state-granted privilege or a legal interest and whether a fact-finding process leading to a decision is thought to be investigatory or adjudicatory.

The dilemma of which to consider first – the nature of the powers or what constitutes the elements of procedural due process rights – would seem resolved best by dealing initially with the concepts of procedural due process *per se*, keeping in mind that they may be modified in view of the courts' perspective as to the nature of the administrative power being used. The scope and characteristics of rule-making, investigating licensing and ordering power will be explored in subsequent chapters with attention to how agencies must meet due process requirements in applying these powers.

Concepts of Natural and Constitutional Justice

Due process in administrative law includes the elements of natural justice, namely, *audi alteram partem* (hear the other side) and absence of bias in the decision-maker. These and additional rights are subsumed in the term 'constitutional justice'. This latter term has not been defined comprehensively in any one case, but it has been used increasingly in judicial decisions such as *McDonald v. Bord na gCon* (No. 2) 1965 IR 217, in which Walsh J. stated:

In the context of the Constitution, natural justice might be more appropriately termed constitutional justice and must be understood to import more than the two well established principles that no man shall be judge of his own cause and *audi alteram partem*. (page 242)

Later, in *East Donegal Co-Operative Livestock Mart Ltd and Others v. Attorney General* 1970 IR 317, 104 ILTR 81 the same judge noted as a general principle of judicial review that the presumption of constitutionality of a statute carries with it the assumption that the Oireachtas intended the administrative processes prescribed by the statute to be carried out in accordance with principles of constitutional justice. The term also requires the provision of legal assistance in criminal trials if the person faces a serious criminal charge and is not able to bear the cost himself, according to O'Higgins C. J. in *The State (Healy) v. Donoghue* 1976 IR 325.

The term constitutional justice was explicated further in *The State (Gleeson) v. Minister for Defence and the Attorney General* 1976 IR 280. This case involved the discharge of plaintiff who had served almost two years of a three-year enlistment, on the grounds of 'his services being no longer required'. This constituted a discreditable discharge. The High Court quashed the discharge on certiorari based on the submission that the discharge constituted 'an infringement of his [plaintiff's] constitutional rights and a denial of constitutional justice.' On the Minister for Defence's appeal to the Supreme Court, Henchy J. referring to dicta in *McDonald v. Bord na gCon (No 2)* 1965 IR 217, stated:

> while the common-law concept of natural justice is usually taken to comprehend no more than what is encompassed by the maxims *nemo judex in sua causa* and *audi alteram partem*, the requirements of what was there called 'constitutional justice' and is sometimes called 'constitutional due process' cover a wider field . . . . The necessary implementation of express or necessarily implied constitutional guarantees means that decisive acts and procedures may be impugned for a wide variety of reasons . . . for instance, because justice was not administered in public; or the decision was given by an unconstitutional tribunal; or the decision applied an unconstitutional law; or the accused was deprived of a fair, competent and impartial jury; or the person affected received unjustifiably

unequal treatment; or the evidence was obtained in a manner not constitutionally permissible. Because of the wide scope of such constitutional guarantees, whatever value 'constitutional justice' may have as a term of generic connotation, a plea of a denial of constitutional justice lacks the concreteness and particularity necessary to identify and bring into focus the precise constitutional issue that is being raised. (pages 294-5)

Therefore, in the view of Henchy J., a person seeking invalidation of an administrative determination on the ground that it is incompatible with the Constitution must specify the particular constitutional right applicable to the facts of the case, and show that he is aggrieved by its infringement in the administrative procedure or decision. Since counsel for the prosecutor could not specify a particular constitutional right to support his claim, he and counsel for the defence agreed the issue must be determined under the common law in the light of the Constitution. On this basis, the Supreme Court held the discharge invalid because there was a breach of natural justice, since Gleeson was never informed of the reason for his discharge until after it had taken place, or of any facts or findings relied on to support that reason until affidavits were filed in the court proceedings. Finally, no opportunity was provided to him to meet the case for discharging him. Since a discreditable discharge was involved, natural justice requires that the army authorities give him due notice of intent to discharge, the statutory reason for discharge and the essential facts and findings alleged to constitute that reason and a reasonable opportunity to present his response to that notice.

Adjudicative Versus Legislative Hearings

Details of procedural due process elements in the right to be heard according to natural and constitutional justice will be analysed later through judicial decisions providing insight into the characteristics and significance of those elements in practice. At this point, the basic issue is whether the individual has the right to be heard before a decision is made affecting his legal rights or vested interests. It also should be recognised that there are different types of hearings, namely adjudicatory or 'trial-type' hearings, and legislative or 'argument-type' hearings. An adjudicatory or trial-type hearing is held to resolve issues of disputed facts, leading to a decision on the legal rights of an individual affected by an existing or proposed action or determination. It should include a notice to the person or persons concerned, followed by an evidentiary oral hearing conducted by an independent, impartial hearing officer. In that hearing, the parties are entitled to be represented by a lawyer and to call witnesses on their behalf, to cross-examine opposing witnesses, and (subject to certain limitations) to have access to documents relevant to their case. It should result in basic findings of fact based on substantial evidence, and ultimate findings in law, plus recommendations by the hearing officer to higher deciding authority, or a decision if the hearing officer is also the deciding officer. As it will be seen, adjudicatory hearings may be required by the courts in certain situations on the grounds of natural and constitutional justice despite the absence of statutory requirement for such a hearing.

In contrast, the purpose of a legislative or argument-type hearing is to resolve issues of policy, discretion and law (which may also encompass factual questions) leading to the adoption of a statutory instrument such as a regulation or a development plan. It typically involves general notice to the public of the proposed regulation's or plan's content, and the opportunity to submit written statements by interested parties. Under certain circumstances, it may provide the right to make oral statements or arguments in a hearing, to express objections to, arguments for, or suggested modifications of, the proposed regulation or scheme. Although such statements may have factual components, it is not an evidentiary hearing. A legislative-type hearing is required by the courts only to the extent that it is specified in the statute authorising an authority to make rules or adopt plans or schemes. It is ordinarily not viewed as being required under natural or constitutional justice except in such situations as a direct nexus between an individual's property rights and a particular provision of a development scheme.

Right to Adjudicative Hearing

The circumstances under which Irish courts hold that natural justice requires notice and hearing even when not required by statute are illustrated by *Foley v. Irish Land Commission and Attorney General* 1952 IR 118, 86 ILTR 441. Under section 2 of the Land Act 1946, the Land Commission made a certificate for recovery of the land and house occupied by plaintiff on the grounds that he had not complied with their directive to reside continuously in the house built by the Commission on the allotted lands. The certificate is declared to be conclusive evidence for all purposes of the facts certified by section 2(2)(b)(v) of the 1946 Act. The Supreme Court held that when making such a certificate the Commission must act judicially. Since plaintiff had never been given notice of the intent of the Commission to make a determination concerning his non-compliance with their directive for continuous residence, and he had not been given an opportunity to plead his case in any sort of hearing, the certificate was held void and Foley's appeal was allowed insofar as it concerned the validity of the certificate.

The major objective of the right to a hearing under natural justice, as perceived by the Irish courts, is achieved if due process is provided in an operative sense, even though there may not have been exact adherence to specified details of statutory provisions on notice and hearing. This was illustrated by *The State (Curtin) v. Minister for Health* 1953 IR 93, involving a local hearing conducted by a Dr Kearney on a nurse's complaint as to a physician's conduct in a hospital. Plaintiff Curtin, a hospital employee and branch secretary of a trade union, attended the hearing to instruct a solicitor on behalf of certain hospital staff appearing as witnesses who were union members. During the hearing, Dr Kearney charged plaintiff with attempting to interfere with some of the witnesses. Though not summoned or obliged to do so, Mr Curtin volunteered to give evidence and under examination and cross-examination denied all allegations of his attempts to interfere with witnesses. However, Dr Kearney concluded on the evidence before him that Mr Curtin had tried to prevent the truth of the matter under investigation from being brought out at the inquiry. Based on this conclusion, Mr Curtin subsequently was removed from his position by the Minister for Health, under section 25(2) of the Local Government Act 1941, which contained specific provisions on notice and hearing before removal from office. On review of plaintiff's appeal against his removal from office, Davitt P. held that given the facts surrounding the local inquiry and the affidavits of plaintiff and of Dr Kearney, it seemed that plaintiff knew the charges against him. He also had been given an opportunity to confront witnesses whose evidence substantiated the charges, of seeing and hearing them examined by the union solicitor, and of presenting his own case orally with the assistance of the union solicitor. Thus the claim that the Minister had not observed the essentials of justice failed.

The *audi alteram partem* rule has been extended to determinations made by private associations such as trade unions. In *Kilkenny and Others v. Irish Engineer and Foundry Union* 1939 IR 1952, the executive committee of the union, without notice to certain of its members with whom the committee had differences, passed a resolution in their absence taking away their membership rights and expelling them from the union. The expelled members sought a declaration that the resolution was *ultra vires* and against public policy and natural justice, and an injunction to restrain the union from enforcing the resolution. In the High Court, Gavan Duffy J. held that the resolution was contrary to natural justice since it was passed without giving defendants an opportunity to be heard in their defence, and granted the declaration, but held that an injunction would be inappropriate since plaintiffs had since become members of another union.

As shown in the previous discussion of *The State (Gleeson) v. Minister for Defence* 1976 IR 280, the right to an adjudicatory hearing based on a general claim of 'infringement of constitutional rights and denial of constitutional justice' (upheld by the High Court) was rejected by the Supreme Court. It was held that a claim of infringement of constitutional justice must be supported by identification of the express or implicit constitutional right applicable to Gleeson's case, which plaintiff did not provide. Nevertheless the Supreme Court held for plaintiff's right to a hearing on the basis that the requirements of natural justice demanded that Gleeson be given due notice of the intention to discharge him, and the facts and findings alleged to constitute the statutory reason for the army's deciding to give him a discreditable discharge, together with the opportunity to present his response to that notice.

The linkage between the right to a hearing in accordance with natural justice and rights specified in the Constitution which was absent in *Gleeson* was established in the subsequent case of *Garvey v. Government of Ireland* 1981 IR 75, (1980) 113 ILTR 61. Plaintiff, Commissioner of the Garda Síochána from 1975 on, received a letter on 19 January 1978 delivered by hand to his private residence, which informed him that he was being removed from office as from that date and gave him the opportunity to resign from office within two hours of its receipt. Garvey instituted proceedings against the government claiming it was not entitled to remove him from office without first according him natural justice rights of notice which would give him information of the reason for removal and an opportunity to reply to matters relied upon as grounds for removal. Government counsel argued that Garvey was not entitled to these procedural protections since section 6(2) of the Police Forces (Amalgamation) Act 1925 states that 'every Commissioner . . . may at any time be removed, by the Executive Council . . .' thus indicating that the Commissioner holds office during the pleasure of the government. Cited in support of this position was *Ridge v. Baldwin* 1964 AC 40 containing statements based on earlier English decisions that an officer holding office at the pleasure of the government has no right to be heard before dismissal nor is the person making the dismissal bound to give reasons. Furthermore, the Commissioner is of such importance to state security that he must have the full confidence of the government or be removed, and disclosure of reasons for removal would be contrary to public policy.

O'Higgins C. J. held that the phrase 'may be at any time removed by' was not equivalent to 'at the pleasure of the government' since other Acts were passed by the Oireachtas in 1925 in which the phrase 'at the pleasure of the appointing officer' was used, signifying legislative cognition of the difference in the phrases. He and Henchy and Griffin J.J. rejected English case precedent because it was based on the royal prerogative not applicable in Ireland, and the cases were not analogous. On a more fundamental basis, all three judges held that the operation and application of the Police Forces (Amalgamation) Act 1925, and the common law in force when the 1937 Constitution became effective, must be in accordance with that Constitution. According to O'Higgins C.J.:

> The Constitution incorporates into our laws and their administration the requirements of natural justice, and by Article 40, s.3, there is guaranteed to every citizen whose rights may be affected by decisions taken by others the right to fair and just procedures. This means that under the Constitution powers cannot be exercised unjustly or unfairly. This applies as well to the Government as to any other authority within the State to which is given the power to take action which may infringe on the rights of others.

Therefore, in my view, it follows that, even if the office of the
Commissioner of the Garda Síochána (or, indeed, any other
office upon which the holder depended for his livelihood) were
stated to be an office from which the holder could be removed
at pleasure, this would not relieve those who sought to exercise
that power from the obligation and requirement to act in
accordance with natural justice. (page 97)

Henchy J., commenting in the same vein on the effect of article 40.3
modified his statements made in the preceding *Gleeson* case limiting
natural justice to two major principles of procedural rights, so as
to broaden the potential scope of natural justice as follows:

the statements in certain decisions of this Court to the effect
that the Constitution impliedly assures to the citizen basic
fairness of procedure mean that . . . he will be held entitled to
natural justice a concept which is not confined to the two main
principles of *nemo judex in sua causa* and *audi alteram partem*. It
should be noted that those guarantees are protective against
an unjust attack as well as vindicative in the event of an unjust
attack. (page 100)

From the above cases, and particularly *Garvey*, it would appear that
the courts in Ireland first expanded procedural rights beyond those
originally encompassed within the principles of natural justice by
developing the term constitutional justice, and then in *Garvey* have
asserted that the Constitution has incorporated natural justice into
the laws of Ireland. Incident to this assertion, the courts seem to
have implied a broadening of the concept of natural justice.
    In this regard, the extent to (and ways in) which the courts
currently emphasise the right to be heard, i.e. to tell one's side of
the situation to the deciding agency before a determination is made,
as being essential to natural justice, are illustrated by *O'Brien v.
Bord na Móna* 1983 ILRM 314 and *The State (Genport Limited) v. An
Bord Pleanála* 1983 ILRM 12. The judgment of the Supreme Court
on the constitutional issues raised by the plaintiff in *O'Brien v. Bord
na Móna* was delivered by O'Higgins C. J. who held that sections
29 and 30 of the Turf Development Act 1946 which authorised Bord
na Móna (the Board) to compulsorily acquire bogland were not
repugnant to articles 40.3 and 43 of the Constitution. In his opinion,

the statute constituted a decision that the common good requires that bogland should be available for compulsory acquisition. Moreover, the making or refusal to make an order for compulsory acquisition is essentially an administrative, not a judicial, act in which the Board is balancing the desirability of the production of turf on the one hand, and the agricultural interest of the individual on the other. Consequently the prohibition against an agency exercising judicial power from being a judge in its own cause did not apply, although the Board has an obligation to act judicially in making its decisions. (See *Fisher v. Irish Land Commission* 1948 IR 3, *McDonald v. Bord na gCon* 1965 IR 217, *Loftus v. the Attorney General* 1979 IR 221.)

However, as to the remaining procedural issues distinct from constitutional issues in the case, Finlay P., delivering the judgment of the Court (O'Higgins C.J., Walsh, Henchy and Griffin J.J. concurring), held that there had been a failure by the Board to hear properly the objections and representations of the owner of the land before deciding to acquire it. Plaintiff, following a notice published by the Board of intent to make an order to acquire permanently and compulsorily certain boglands, formed a Fardrum IFA Bog Committee which submitted written general objections to the acqui-ˈ sition. Subsequently, plaintiff and another member of the Committee met with officials representing the Board, and plaintiff made it clear that while he objected to his lands being acquired, he also, if such lands perforce had to be acquired, objected to their acquisition in fee simple. He gave reasons why it was his desire not to lose ownership of the lands, in order that after the period needed for defendants to remove the peat, the land in a cut-away condition would revert to him. The Board's representatives explained the reasons for the Board's policy of acquisition in fee simple but agreed to refer the matter to their principals, and later the Board's managing director told the Board representative that it was the Board's unchanging policy to acquire boglands in fee simple. When the Board met, they received recommendations from the managing director for permanent acquisition in fee simple of the land, and also the objections contained in the Fardrum IFA Bog Committee letter, but no reference was made to the particular objection made by plaintiff O'Brien to the acquisition in fee simple of his lands.

Finlay P. stated that the Board had given sufficient notice of intent to make a compulsory acquisition and opportunity to plaintiff to make his objections known to the Board's representatives. However, the precise objection of plaintiff that his land be acquired for only the time necessary to extract peat and thereafter revert to him was never brought to the Board's notice. It is not the function of the Court to determine the wisdom of policy of acquiring bogland in fee simple, but there was a failure to hear properly the representations of the landowner before deciding to acquire it. Such a deficiency could not be repaired by subsequent proof that even if such representations and objections had been heard and considered, it was improbable that a different decision would have been reached. Moreover:

> Whilst therefore it may be true as was contended on behalf of these defendants that if the present acquisition order is set aside and a further acquisition process instigated that the result will be the same as far as the plaintiff is concerned, I am satisfied that the plaintiff is nonetheless entitled to a declaration that the procedures were not in accordance with natural justice, and that accordingly the purported resolution to acquire the lands is null and void. (pages 322-3)

The same protection of the right to have a hearing (in which the concerned parties may make their representations before an administrative determination) was given in *The State (Genport Limited) v. An Bord Pleanála* 1983 ILRM 12.[1] Prosecutor lodged an appeal through its architects with An Bord Pleanála (the Board) against the planning authority's decision to refuse permission for retention of various extensions to an hotel. No grounds for the appeal were indicated but it was stated they would be provided in due course. The Board wrote to the architects requiring a statement of the grounds of appeal without delay, and on receiving no reply, wrote again on 14 July 1981 stating that if plaintiff wished 'any such submissions to be taken into account by the Board in its consideration of the appeal, please forward it to the Board within 14 days from the date of this letter otherwise the Board will be obliged to determine the appeal on the basis of the information available to it.' No reply was made within this time limit but on 6 August the architects wrote to the Board that the grounds of appeal were to be withheld since third-party objections were still being received. The receipt of this letter was acknowledged and thereafter the Board continued to forward objections from third parties to prosecutor as they were received, together with a statement that it was not necessary that plaintiff provide comments but if they wished to do so they should be 'forwarded at an early date if you wish to have them taken into consideration when the appeal is being determined'. No response in the form of comments or statement of grounds for the appeal was made, and on 4 November 1981 the Board decided to refuse permission. Prosecutor then brought certiorari proceedings and the order was granted by the Court on the grounds that the Board may not determine an appeal in the absence of representations from the appellant if the Board has unequivocally called upon the appellant to make such representations and it has failed to do so.

On appeal to the Supreme Court, Finlay P. held firstly that the notice of appeal was valid, that the Board's 14 July letter was in compliance with section 18 of the Local Government (Planning and Development) Act 1976, and that if they had proceeded within the 14-day period to determine the appeal, their decision could not have validly been challenged in any court. The Board's letters accompanying the objections received sent to the prosecutor's architects were in compliance with section 17 of the 1976 Act. He also stated that the burden of proof was on the prosecutor, and their position that they would make no submissions or even state their grounds of appeal until they had heard all objections from other parties was unusual and unjustifiable. However, the Board's reply to the 6 August letter from prosecutor raising no objections to prosecutor's proposal, coupled with sending objections and inviting observations by prosecutor, could be construed as a waiver by the Board of the right they originally had to determine the appeal within 14 days of 14 July without further reference to prosecutor.

In general, determination of an appeal against refusal for planning permission should not be concluded in the absence of representations on behalf of an appellant unless he has unequivocally been called on to make such representations and has not done so, therefore:

The possibility of an injustice having occurred in this case due to what I would consider to be the unusual and unreasonable attitude of the appellant but to some slight extent contributed to by the further communications sent by the Board to the

architects is sufficiently real to drive me to the conclusion that
I should quash the order and decision made in this case. It
seems to me that the Board should, bearing in mind the . . .
correspondence . . . between the parties before finally deciding
the appeal on the 4th of November, have written a letter in
similar terms to that which they sent on the 14th of July 1981.

The order was quashed, and the Board directed to proceed anew
to determine the appeal.

The stress in the *O'Brien* and the *Genport* cases upon protection
of the basic procedural right to be heard, that is, to make representations, would seem to indicate that administrative agencies must
develop awareness of how the actions they take in their processes
leading to an administrative determination must meet judicial
criteria of procedures required under the concepts of natural justice.
In both cases, the court indicated its approval of certain steps in
the processes of the agency, and also provided guidelines as to what
procedures should be followed to meet the requirements of natural
justice so as to avoid reversal and secure judicial approval.

Right to Legislative-Type Hearing
In the absence of a general Administrative Procedures Act such as
that of the United States which requires a notice-and-comment
hearing procedure for all legislative-type rule making, a hearing for
administrative rule-making in Ireland is required only if it is specified in the particular Act delegating rule-making power. The issue
confronting Irish courts in respect of rule-making hearings therefore
becomes whether the authority has complied with the statute. It is
at this point of statutory interpretation that the concepts of natural
justice may come into play, as illustrated in *Finn v. Bray Urban
District Council* 1969 IR 169.

In this case, the Urban District Council (UDC) as local planning
authority gave public notice in May 1967 of a draft of a proposed
development plan as required by section 21(1)(b) of the Local
Government (Planning and Development) Act 1963. Plaintiff, an
owner and rated occupier of property which would be affected
directly by a proposal in the draft, objected in writing and made
oral representations through a lawyer on 18 September 1967. The
UDC, confronted by a statutory 30 September deadline to make its
development plan, adopted a plan for the urban district on 26

September. This plan substituted a new and different provision for that objected to by plaintiff, together with other amendments. No publication of intention to make amendments was made nor was plaintiff informed of any result of her written and oral objections. The UDC planned to sign and seal the development plan on 30 September but plaintiff obtained an interim injunction on 28 September followed by an interlocutory injunction on the grounds that the UDC had acted *ultra vires* the Act.

Plaintiff's claim was that if a draft development plan is amended, the planning authority cannot adopt the final plan as so amended without further publication and opportunity for former objectors to inspect and object to the amendment. UDC counsel argued that section 21 of the Act dealt with both the draft of a plan and the final development plan, and since a draft plan was not required by the statute to be prepared, the statutory procedures pertaining to formulating a draft could be avoided by not making a draft. Even if a draft is made, the final plan may be adopted in an entirely different form which is not bound by the draft or objections made to it, provided those objections and representations alone were considered. The statutory protection for the property owner is the requirement to publish notice of a plan after its completion, to make it available for inspection, and to review objections and requests for alterations. However, the primary purpose of article 21 is not to protect individuals but to enable a planning authority to stimulate public interest and discussion and to obtain public opinion before adopting a plan, without necessarily being bound by that opinion.

Butler J. held that since a plan may affect private property adversely, the Act should be given that interpretation which gives the property owner the right to notice and opportunity to make objections and state his case before such adverse effect happens. Under the statute, once the final plan is made the only obligation of the planning authority is to make it available for inspection, to review it, and if on review the authority thinks it is needed, to make variations. Only if they make variations must they consider objections to such variations from objectors. Given this situation, Butler J. ruled that the correct interpretation of the Act is that it requires the planning authority to: (1) prepare a draft of their proposals; (2) give notice of the draft; (3) make the draft available for inspection; (4) receive and consider objections and representations and provide opportunity to state one's case. If any amendment is made in the draft materially altering its proposals, similar notice and like opportunities to make objections and representations, and to state one's case must be given. The UDC was not empowered to adopt its plan for Bray containing a major variation of its draft plan, since it had not followed this procedure.

This interpretation of the 1963 Act seemed to view its provisions on notice and hearing from the perspective of procedures bordering on adjudication to protect the property rights of individuals affected by a proposed development plan, rather than of procedures for general policy-making designed to secure citizen participation and public opinion inputs into the plan. Although a somewhat different issue is involved, this approach is comparable to certain instances in which some United States courts have applied what they call a 'substantial impact' analysis of the effect which an administrative rule has on private property or interests to determine whether the notice-and-comment procedure prescribed in the American Administrative Procedures Act for 'legislative-type' rule making must be followed, against claims of an agency that the rules are 'interpretative-type' rules which are exempt from such procedural requirements. (See *National Motor Freight Traffic Assn v. US* 268 F. Supp 90 (DDC 1967) affd. 393 US 18 (1968); *Pharmaceutical Mfgs Assn v. Finch* 307 F. Supp 858 (D. Del 1970); *Energy Reserves Group Inc v. Department of Energy* 589 F 2d 1082.) It is also noteworthy that among the amendments of the Local Government (Planning and Development) Act 1976, the Oireachtas limited the right of an objecting ratepayer to be heard in respect of amendments in drafts of development plans to a written representation.

Due Process Components of Adjudicative Hearings

The concepts of natural and constitutional justice expressed in the above judicial decisions require fair notice and hearing for persons whose rights are adversely affected by administrative determinations. Thus issues on the nature and scope of the components of an administrative adjudicatory hearing arise: (1) what constitutes a fair notice; (2) who has a right to be a party to a hearing; (3) is the hearing officer legally authorised to hold the hearing; (4) is the hearing officer independent in judgment and non-biased; (5) do the parties have a right to discovery of official documents; (6) may the parties call and examine witnesses (usually through a lawyer); (7)

what types of evidence may be considered sufficient to substantiate a determination; (8) to what extent should official notice of facts not introduced in the hearing be made known to the parties; (9) what are the requirements for findings and reasons in the decision together with the related roles of hearing officer, staff and minister in the making of decisions. These elements of a fair hearing are primarily procedural, raising issues comparable to those in judicial processes. However, the issues at times have a different character from that encountered in judicial processes owing to the fact that the hearing and decision-making processes are conducted by hierarchically organised administrative authorities charged with programmatic responsibilities, resulting in what has been termed institutional decision-making. Thus the issues as to whether the hearing officer is independent and unbiased may involve subordinate hearing officer to minister relationships, or commitment to achieving statutory goals. The issue of official notice of facts not in the record may involve inclusion in the report of the hearing officer to the minister of results of physical inspections as well as his findings of fact on what transpired at the hearing. The minister's determination may be influenced not only by this report but also by observations from experts on the departmental staff following the close of a hearing. These aspects of institutional decision-making raise questions as to the roles of the hearing officer, departmental staff and the minister in the making of decisions which are not typical of the traditional judicial process.

Fair Notice

The function of fair notice is to ensure that the parties have knowledge of the time, place and subject matter of the hearing within sufficient time to enable them to prepare their case. Operational aspects of giving notice can raise legal issues requiring judicial resolution based on the requirements of statutes and of natural justice. These include first, whether the substantive content of the notice provides the information necessary for the parties to prepare their case adequately and secondly, whether the notice gives them adequate time to prepare their case.

Whether the substantive content of notice was sufficiently explicit was the issue in *Dunraven Estates v. Commissioners of Public Works* 1970 IR 113. According to section 6(1) of the Arterial Drainage Act 1945, notice must be served on each person whose lands or rights may be interfered with, giving details of the drainage scheme and how each person's land, rights or property is affected by it. This is to enable the landowner to send to the Commissioners observations on the proposed acquisition, restriction, termination, interference, diversion or removal in respect of his lands, rights or property. The Commissioners must consider these observations before forwarding the scheme to the Minister for Finance for his confirmation.

In the Supreme Court Ó Dálaigh C.J. held that the notice, consisting of an excerpt from the proposed drainage scheme, was drawn in very general terms giving individual owners no indication of the rights with which it proposed to interfere. He rejected the Commissioners' rationale that it was in the landowners' interests to leave the scheme flexible to facilitate the Commissioners' consulting the landowners' wishes. Rather, this was a failure to appreciate the statutory purpose and the process necessary to effect it, namely giving the owners a specific proposal so that their observations are based on knowledge of the nature of interference with their rights. Flexibility is provided since the Commissioners, after considering the landowners' observations, may make alterations. Budd J., concurring, stated that given the statutory provisions for compensation, he did not see how an arbitrator could assess the value of any benefit to the property when compensation is being claimed unless the arbitrator knew in advance precisely what works were to be done and how any benefit would arise. He therefore agreed with the Chief Justice's judgment that the notices of the scheme as served were *ultra vires* the Act and invalid.

A further illustration of the requirement that a notice provide sufficient information to enable the recipient to prepare a response to charges against him is the case of *Hogan v. Minister for Justice, Edmund P. Garvey et al* High Court, unreported, per Hamilton J., 8 September 1976. Commissioner Garvey of the Garda Síochána issued a notice to plaintiff stating that under Disciplinary Regulation 34 he considered plaintiff 'unfit for retention in the Force', that he proposed 'subject to the consent of the Minister for Justice' to dismiss plaintiff from the gardaí; that he had 'set up a special inquiry board to inquire into the alleged breach of discipline' and that plaintiff was 'now being given an opportunity of advancing to me . . . reasons against the proposed dismissal on or before 1st day of April 1976'. Subsequently, on 29 March, plaintiff was served with a notice signed by a Chief Superintendent of the gardaí that a special inquiry would be held on 22 April 1976, at the Roscommon garda station under regulation 34, to inquire on oath into:

> among other things, an alleged breach of discipline committed by you by your attendance at and participation in a demonstration organised by Kevin Street Sinn Féin at Ballina on the 22nd day of February 1976.

Written requests by plaintiff's counsel for details of the charges evoked the response that the question of giving reasons against his dismissal was a matter for the accused, and under regulation 34 the Commissioner was not obliged to provide the information sought. However, the names of the garda officers appointed to hold the inquiry at which plaintiff could be legally represented would be supplied.

On appeal to the High Court, Hamilton J. rejected the argument that regulation 34 was repugnant to the Constitution for failing to provide constitutional and natural justice rights, for giving the Commissioner unrestricted power of dismissal subject only to the Minister for Justice's consent, and failure to protect the personal and property right to hold office as a member of the gardaí in accordance with article 40 of the Constitution. The precedents of *The State (Gleeson) v. Minister for Defence and Attorney General* 1976 IR 280; and *East Donegal Cooperative Livestock Mart v. Attorney General* 1970 IR 317, 104 ILTR 81 were cited in support of the necessity to have power to dismiss security force members and the presumption that discretionary powers impose a duty on the Minister to act fairly and judicially in accordance with principles of constitutional justice. However, Hamilton J. held that although the 9 March notice informed the plaintiff of the intention to discharge him and of the statutory reason:

> It did not give to him the essentials or any facts or findings alleged to constitute that reason, and consequently cannot be said to have given him a reasonable opportunity of presenting his response to that notice . . . .

> It is obvious from this notice that the inquiry was not to be limited to the alleged breach of discipline specified in the notice

but was to deal with 'other things' of which the plaintiff was
given no notice.

In addition the Commissioner specifically refused to give the
information in regard thereto sought by plaintiff's solicitors in
their letter dated the 13th day of April 1976.

Hamilton J. held that the plaintiff did not have adequate notice
and knowledge of the nature of the charge against him. Before the
inquiry proceeds, the plaintiff is entitled to full notice of the grounds
on which he is considered unfit to continue as a garda, the essential
facts and findings alleged to constitute the reason for considering
him unfit and particulars of the alleged breach of discipline.

An illustration of how the courts take a pragmatic approach
based on the factual situation to decide whether a notice is given
in sufficient time to make an appeal from an administrative decision
and proposed action is found in *The State (Fitzgerald) v. Ennis Urban
District Council* unreported, High Court, per Teevan J., 7 February
1968. The prosecutor, Fitzgerald, sought a conditional order of
certiorari on 7 July 1967 to quash the Ennis UDC compulsory
purchase (housing) order which included his property. Section 17(3)
of the Housing (Miscellaneous Provisions) Act 1931, as amended by
section 28 of No. 19 of 1932, together with sub-section 4 of section
17, in effect provide that a person aggrieved by an order alleged to
be *ultra vires* that Act may request that the order be quashed on
appeal to the High Court within three weeks after publication of
notice of confirmation of the order. However, if no appeal is made
within three weeks, the order becomes operative and may not be
questioned in any proceedings. Prosecutor and others had made
objections to the order and a public inquiry was held on 24 and 25
May 1965 attended by prosecutor and his solicitor. Notice of the
Minister for Local Government's confirmation of the order was
served on prosecutor on 15 January 1966, therefore the statutory
three weeks for appeal ended in Feburary 1966. Prosecutor also had
written to the County Manager after the public inquiry but before
the confirmation of the order, offering a compromise settlement
combined with a threat that if his offer were rejected and the
Minister confirmed the order, prosecutor would object through
legal proceedings. Prosecutor also refused to accept and returned a
mailed notice requiring acknowledgment of its receipt and tore up

and returned the pieces of a follow-up notice delivered personally to the prosecutor.

Teevan J. held that though the strict three-week time limit for appeal imposed by the statute could be considered drastic, it did not involve the slightest injustice, given the facts in this case. Prosecutor was an experienced builder and the evidence demonstrated that he was aware of his rights should the Minister confirm the compulsory purchase order.

In a more recent case, *Fanning and Fanning v. Incorporated Law Society of Ireland* unreported, 27 March 1980, Butler J. also resolved the issue of adequate notice on the basis of the factual situation. Plaintiff claimed damages for breach of his natural and constitutional rights caused by the Incorporated Law Society's making a stop order freezing his bank accounts. Butler J. stated that on 30 March 1977, the Compensation Fund Committee of the Incorporated Law Society concluded from reports on the solicitor that they should apply to the High Court for a freezing order on plaintiff's bank accounts as of 1 April. He further stated that the plaintiff had been given prior notification on two occasions of the Society's intention to do this and had once explicitly and once implicitly been given opportunity to furnish his accounts and to make an explanation to the Society and call any evidence he wished. Given this and subsequent inaction and delaying tactics by the plaintiff, Butler J. concluded:

> I have no hesitation whatsoever in finding on the facts of the case, without having to decide one question of law, that . . . the Law Society were more than fair. On the facts of this case the Plaintiff knew well everything that was going on . . . from the 28th of February on, if not sooner, the Plaintiff, Mr John Fanning, and his son, knew that unless they co-operated with the Society that the Society was going to apply for a stop order. So I have no hesitation in dismissing the plaintiff's claim.

The issue of statutory meaning and intent as to required time for giving and receipt of notice was raised in *The State (Murphy) v. Dublin County Council* 1970 IR 253. Mr Murphy sought to make absolute a conditional order of mandamus in the High Court to compel the County Council as planning authority to give him permission to build a five-floor hotel. He claimed that the County Council had

not given him notice of their decision to refuse his application within
the statutory time limit of two months beginning on the day of
receipt of the application, as provided in section 26(4) of the Local
Government (Planning and Development) Act 1963. This inaction
should be regarded as a decision by the planning authority to grant
permission as of the last day of that period, since the Act also
provided that failure to give notice of decision within the two-month
limit was to be construed as granting a permission.

   In fact, the County Council as planning authority had sent its
refusal of the application to Murphy by registered post on a Friday.
The Sunday following was the last day of the statutory time limit,
but the office address Murphy gave for purpose of serving notice
was not open on the intervening Saturday when the notice normally
would have been delivered according to customary postal schedules.
Consequently, the notice was not delivered until the Monday following the Friday posting of the letter. O'Keeffe J., in the High Court,
on review of the Interpretation Act 1937, section 18 on service of
notice by post and relevant English cases, concluded that resolution
of issues as to notice hinged upon legislative intent. As he interpreted
the Local Government (Planning and Development) Act 1963, the
legislature intended that the planning authorities decide without
undue delay and that notice of the decision to an applicant was to
be given by posting such notice within the statutory period. The
time the notice was received by the applicant was not the determining factor of statutory compliance. Consequently, notice in this case
had been given as of 10 January when it was sent by registered post
and was in accordance with the provisions of the Act as to service
of notice, thus bringing it within the ambit of the Interpretation
Act 1937.

   It should be noted, however, that in the more recent case of *Feeney
v. Bray UDC* 1982 ILRM 29, O'Hanlon J. enunciated a different
interpretation of the Local Government (Planning and Development) Act 1963 and the related Interpretation Act 1937, from that
expressed in the *Murphy* case. Plaintiff sought a declaration that he
had a planning permission by default because defendants had failed
to give notice of their decision to refuse permission in the time
period permitted by section 26 of the 1963 Act, in a situation which
O'Hanlon J. characterised as not unlike that in the Murphy case.
He noted that section 7 of the 1963 Act provides for four ways of
service of notice. Three of the methods involve either personal

delivery of notice to an applicant or delivery of notice at the applicant's residence or the address he or she has given for service purposes, or delivering it at the land to which the application relates—or affixing it conspicuously at or near the land. In all three methods time runs against the planning authority until notice is physically delivered to or brought to applicant's notice or left at his premises. The fourth method is to send it in a prepaid registered letter by post addressed to the applicant at the residence where he ordinarily lives or the address he furnished for service. Under the *Murphy* judgment the applicant would be bound by the notice from the moment it was posted to him by registered letter, even though the letter might never arrive or come after a long time. In his opinion, the applicant in such circumstances is an innocent party, and the consequences of the mishap should fall on the planning authority, who chose to use this means of communication.

O'Hanlon J. felt that section 7 in conjunction with section 26(4) of the 1963 Act indicates an intention by the legislature that planning applications were to be dealt with as matters of some urgency, that planning authorities were obliged to communicate their decisions within a strict time limit, and that notice of decisions reach applicants personally or at their premises within the 'appropriate period' of the Act. The related Interpretation Act 1937 creates a presumption in favour of the sender of statutory notice that it has reached an applicant at the time it would have been delivered in due course of post. However, if service was by registered post and applicant can show it did not in fact reach him within the appropriate period, then the planning authority must suffer the consequences of resorting to this method of service rather than the more conclusive methods of personal service or service at premises where applicant resides or to which he relates. He doubted that the alternative interpretation of the statute suggested by the *Murphy* judgment was likely to have been intended by the legislature, in view of the uncertainty of the legal position of the parties as illustrated by the present case, e.g. was the registered letter 'posted' when it was given to the post office during the 'hours of business', but after the time given as 'latest time for posting' for registered letters? In his view, the letter should be regarded as having been 'posted' when it was handed in to the post office, even though it was later than the latest time for posting, since the post office then had charge of it, although the letter could go no further on its journey to the addressee until the next day. However, notice was not given in this case for the purposes of the Act until 25 September 1979, a date clearly outside the five-week period prescribed by the statutory provisions, and in view of the importance of receipt of notice by applicants for planning permission, the Oireachtas must have meant planning authorities to be strictly bound by the time limits. O'Hanlon J. held that plaintiff in effect had received approval of his application, since with the expiry of the period for giving notice of decision, a decision to grant an approval is regarded as having come into existence by operation of the law.

Parties: Right to Participate in Hearing
An important element in the right to notice and hearing is that of who may be a party to an administrative hearing. The concepts involved are essentially those reflected in judicial doctrines of *locus standi*, or standing to sue in the courts, as modified by statutory provisions in a specific case. The right to be a party in an administrative hearing rests on the proposition that a person whose interests may be affected by a governmental determination resulting from a hearing should have the right to participate in the hearing. This raises the issues of the legal nature and directness of the interests and the effect upon them as claimed by those seeking to be parties to the hearing. In addition to private persons seeking to be parties, administrators have a direct concern with statutory and judicial requirements concerning who may be a party to a hearing. Administrators wish to limit the number of participants in a hearing only to those who have evidence to offer which the administrators consider to be directly pertinent to resolution of the issues of the hearing, but if they mistakenly refuse to allow participation to a person whom the courts feel has a legitimate interest the courts may remand or reverse the administrative determination.

The nature of the issues and concerns of both private parties and the administrative agency in regard to who may be a party in an administrative proceeding is portrayed in the well-known case of *The State (Nicolaou) v. Bord Úchtála and Attorney General* 1966 IR 567, 102 ILTR 1. Prosecutor, a Cypriot and Greek Orthodox Church member with British citizenship, was the father of an illegitimate child born in England of Miss Donnelly, a Catholic Church member and Irish citizen. Despite Nicolaou's offer of marriage, Miss Donnelly returned to Ireland with the child, requested the Catholic

Protection and Rescue Society to arrange for the adoption of the child, and gave her consent to an adoption order by An Bord Úchtála (hereafter the Board). Since Nicolaou felt he had an understanding with Miss Donnelly that he would be informed of any proposed adoption of the child (which he opposed) and had had his solicitors notify both the Society and the Board that they would institute High Court proceedings to prevent any proposed adoption he instituted action to quash the adoption order made by the Board. The first ground for this action was that the order was made without jurisdiction because of non-compliance with provisions of the Adoption Act 1952 specifying who may be parties to the proceedings of the Board. The second set of claims made by Nicolaou raised constitutional issues for which the case is primarily known and cited, namely that certain provisions of the Adoption Act violated his personal rights under articles 40, 41 and 42 of the Constitution.

In respect of his claims of right to be a party to the adoption proceedings, Nicolaou argued that the Board had violated section 14, sub-sections 1 and 2 of the Adoption Act requiring that an adoption order not be made without the consent of 'every person being the child's mother', or guardian or having charge of or control over the child, unless the person cannot give consent because the person is mentally infirm or cannot be found. Also violated was section 16, sub-section 1(d) and (i) providing that a person having charge of or control over the child and any other person whom the Board in its discretion decides to hear shall be entitled to be heard on application for adoption. These violations, Nicolaou asserted, had taken place when the Board had not made him a party to the determination leading to the adoption order for his child. He thus had not given his consent to that order, although at the time he was a person having charge or control over the child, and his consent to adoption was as necessary as that of the mother.

The Supreme Court, per Walsh J., held that the widest range of time during which a valid consent could have been given was a three-month period before the adoption order was made, and the evidence was clear that Nicolaou did not have actual charge or control over the child during that period since Miss Donnelly and the child were in Ireland and Nicolaou was in England. The evidence also showed that Nicolaou's claim to an understanding with Miss Donnelly that any adoption proposal would be referred immediately to him did not constitute a binding agreement that he would be so notified. Miss Donnelly took the child from England to Ireland, under her natural right, not as an agent of Nicolaou. The Court considered and rejected Nicolaou's argument that the Board had deprived itself of jurisdiction to make a valid adoption order by not hearing him on the application for the order despite Nicolaou's notification to the Board through his solicitor that he acknowledged the child as his, that he opposed adoption and intended to sue to prevent an adoption order being made, and that natural justice required he be heard on the application for adoption. In rejecting these arguments, the Court indicated its view on the discretion of the Board in determining to whom the right to be a party to an adoption order proceeding might be extended:

the persons specified [in the Adoption Act 1952] . . . have a right to be heard on an application for an adoption order in the sense that, if one of them applies to the Board to be heard, he cannot properly be refused. It does not, however, follow that before it can make a valid adoption order the Board must seek out all such persons and inquire of each whether he wishes to be heard. There could also be several persons not coming within any of the categories covered by sub-paras. (a) to (h) whose views as to the adoption of a particular child might be of assistance to the Board; and sub-para (i) enables the Board to hear them. However, no such person can be said to have a right to be heard unless and until the Board has decided to hear him. In this respect the drafting of the sub-section and sub-paragraph may be somewhat peculiar, but the purpose is plain enough. It would be a strange result if by failing to hear some person who could have been of assistance, and who did not ask to be heard, the Board could deprive itself of all jurisdiction to make a valid order. It might well be thought that in the particular circumstances of this case it was impolitic of the Board not to have afforded the appellant the opportunity to be heard but it had a discretion after proper consideration not to do so. The proper exercise of that discretion not to allow the appellant such opportunity left him without any right to be heard. The position would of course be different if the refusal was based on a general policy not to hear the fathers of illegitimate children in such cases and in such an event certiorari would go. There is, however, no evidence that such was the position in this case. (pages 638-9)

On this basis, and on the rejection of the constitutional issues raised by Nicolaou, the Court refused to grant an order of certiorari to quash the adoption order.

The circumstances of the *Nicolaou* case and ruling in support of administrative discretion to determine who may be a party to an administrative proceeding contrast with a later High Court decision upholding a plaintiff's right to be a party in an administrative hearing, *Andrew Law v. Minister for Local Government and Traditional Homes Ltd* unreported, High Court, per Deale J., 29 May 1974. Traditional Homes Ltd had applied to Dublin County Council under the Local Government (Planning and Development) Act 1963 for outline planning permission to erect 34 houses. On objection by Law and other local residents, the council refused permission, and Traditional Homes appealed to the Minister for Local Government. An inspector appointed by the Minister conducted the hearing on appeal, which was attended by representatives of the Council, Traditional Homes and 23 local residents including Law as objectors. Despite strong objections by Law and others to proposed septic tanks, the inspector's report to the Minister following the hearing included a recommendation that trial holes for soil tests for soakage be conducted before any decision on drainage arrangements was made and, if satisfactory, permission be granted for not more than thirteen houses.

The report was not made available to Law and other objectors, nor were they told of test results on which a decision was made that septic tanks could be used without risk of public injury. When outline planning permission for 27 houses was granted, Law sued on the grounds that since planning permission was given on evidence not contained in the report, his rights were denied as objector to be present at the tests or to be given test results so he could have his own tests carried out or otherwise try to controvert the tests as evidence. Therefore, planning permission was granted *ultra vires* the 1963 Act and in contravention of principles of constitutional and natural justice.

Defendants claimed that Law was not a party to the hearing by the inspector and lacking this right had no grounds for the appeal, according to article 2(2) of the Local Government (Planning and Development) Act 1963 (Appeals and References) Regulations 1964 (SI no 216 of 1964). This statutory instrument defines the word party as including an appellant, the planning authority whose decision is appealed, an applicant for permission where another is the appellant and any person served by the planning authority with notice or order in relation to which an appeal is brought by another person.

The High Court held that these definitions of who may be a party are highly artificial and confined to the statutory instrument. To determine whether plaintiff was a party, one must go beyond the statutory instrument and consider the realities of the plaintiff's position in relation to the planning application, administrative hearing appeal, and to the High Court. The Court felt that the facts led to the conclusion that:

> the Plaintiff took an active part in the whole affair from the very start; he entered into contention with the second-named Defendants at the appeal hearing; he succeeded by his contentions in preventing the granting of the permission; and he had an interest as a nearby occupier in conducting these activities. His position at the hearing . . . was almost indistinguishable from that of a Defendant in a civil proceeding who enters into contention with the Plaintiff and succeeds either in preventing the Plaintiff from recovering in the action or succeeds in having the Plaintiff's remedy postponed. The only difference between a Defendant's position and Mr Law's is that in the civil action the Plaintiff's remedy would be against Mr Law, whereas in the hearing by the Inspector the second named Defendant's remedy would be against the Dublin County Council.

The Court resolved the closely related second claim made by defendants that Mr Law lacked *locus standi* to sue in court on the issues he had raised in virtually the same manner. The Court noted that this second claim also rested on the argument that Mr Law could not be a party to the administrative proceedings under the statutory instrument, and thus lacked standing to sue in court. In this regard the Court held that Mr Law's standing to sue in court over the matters he complained of could not be taken away by a

statutory instrument which applies only to quasi-judicial proceedings. Law's participation in the events described, and his interest
as a resident in preventing septic tanks being used near his house,
gave him the legal right to protect that interest in a Court of
Chancery and he therefore could maintain this suit.

Legal Authority of Hearing Officer

In addition to a fair notice and being a party to administrative
hearings, citizens are protected from having their rights determined
by administrators who are not legally authorised to take part
in adjudicatory processes or who disregard their responsibilities
specified by statute. This is exemplified by *The State (McCarthy) v.
O'Donnell* 1945 IR 126, in which McCarthy had applied for a service
certificate under the Military Services Pension Act 1934. That Act
empowers the Minister for Defence to give a person to whom the
Act applies a service certificate and grant a pension with approval
of the Minister for Finance. The Act requires that the Executive
Council (now the government) appoint a Referee (a judge or barrister of ten or more years' standing) who is authorised to compel
attendance of witnesses; examine them under oath; compel submission of documents; and in the event of non-compliance, certify
on non-compliance to the High Court – an offence which, if the
Referee were a court of justice with contempt power, would be
contempt of court. The Act requires the Minister to refer every
application for a certificate to the Referee, who after investigation
makes a report to the Minister containing findings on whether the
person comes within the scope of the Act. The Referee's findings
are final, conclusive and binding on all persons and tribunals.
Section 6 of the Act requires that there be an advisory committee
appointed by the Executive Council to sit with the Referee and
assist him in exercising his functions. The Act places the burden of
proof on the applicant, and authorises the government to revoke a
pension under certain circumstances.

Despite these explicit statutory provisions, on McCarthy's
appearance before the Referee in accordance with the Referee's
notice and the Referee's administration of an oath to McCarthy, he
was examined orally in relation to his application in another room
not by the Referee, but by a civil servant attached to the Referee's
office. A transcript of this examination was forwarded to the Referee

and advisory committee. Subsequently some members of the committee heard evidence of verifying officers of the Brigade Area in which applicant claimed to have served in the Forces, and these Committee members advised the Referee that applicant had not served continuously during certain periods. Following this the Referee found the applicant did not qualify under the Act. On notice of this finding and of the right to submit additional evidence, McCarthy submitted evidence reviewed by some members of the advisory committee who reiterated their advice to the Referee that service still was not considered continuous. At no time did the advisory committee sit as a group with the Referee to consider the claim or matters related to the claim.

On notification he had not qualified for a service certificate, and on refusal by the Minister of the names of witnesses examined by the Referee and the nature of the evidence on which the decision was based, McCarthy appealed to the High Court and subsequently to the Supreme Court asking that a conditional order for certiorari and mandamus discharged by the High Court be made absolute by the Supreme Court. The Supreme Court, per Sullivan C. J., held that the Referee's determination was a judicial act, thus meeting the first condition for certiorari. The Court also held that the Referee had exceeded the jurisdiction conferred upon him by the Act and had not acted judicially in two respects. In view of the extensive compulsory fact-finding powers delegated to the Referee, the Act intended that the Referee be present when any person attends for examination as a witness, especially since non-compliance by a witness may lead to certification to the High Court for contempt. Therefore, the civil servant officer attached to the Referee's office was not legally authorised to examine McCarthy in the absence of the Referee. Further, section 6 of the Act states the functions of the advisory committee in clear and unambiguous terms, namely that it was intended to ensure that the Referee will sit with the committee to consider applications in light of the information acquired in the investigation before making his report to the Minister, so that the views of each member of the committee would be made known to the Referee. This provision was imperative not directory, and since it was disregarded, the findings of the Referee and his report to the Minister must be treated as invalid.

The legal authority of five members of the planning staff of the Dublin Corporation appointed by the Assistant City Manager to

hear objections by ratepayers to proposed plans was challenged in
O'Hora v. Dublin Corporation The Incorporated Law Society of
Ireland Gazette, 87 (Vol. 67, 1973). Plaintiff alleged that Dublin
Corporation had acted *ultra vires* the statute concerning proposed
plans in this regard, since the function of hearing objections to a
proposed plan from ratepayers was reserved by statute to the City
Council. The Dublin Corporation argued that there was a difference
between the preparation of a draft and the actual making of a plan
since there may be preliminary steps in preparing a draft and the
statute did not provide that such preliminary steps were a function
reserved to the Council. Teevan J. held that the appointment of
persons to hear statements objecting to a proposed plan was not a
reserved function, since the legislature was always specific about
what constituted a reserved function. In the absence of a specific
provision, the hearing of those objections was an executive function.

Another issue as to who is authorised to hold a hearing may arise
out of an unavoidable institutional decision- making situation such
as the change or substitution of hearing officers over the course of an
adjudicatory process. In *Hession v. Irish Land Commission* unreported,
Supreme Court, per Henchy J., June 1975, an objection was heard
by Lay Commissioners Kelly and Mac Piarais in June 1970, to the
acquisition of lands under section 31 of the Land Act 1923, as
extended by section 30 of the Land Act 1950. Grounds for the
objection were that the lands were not needed for the purpose
certified and that Hession qualified for the benefit as one of the
persons entitled to the land under section 32 of the Land Act 1933,
as amended by section 35, Land Act 1950. After listening to evidence
from both sides, the Lay Commissioners announced that the lands
were nonproductive and that objector had no answer to the proceedings, but for purposes of 'giving Thomas Hession a chance' they
adjourned the proceedings to the summer of 1972. However, when
the adjourned hearing took place in June 1972, Commissioner
O'Sullivan replaced Commissioner Mac Piarais. After listening to
further evidence these Commissioners held that 'deserving congestion' had been proved, that the lands were not in full production
during the qualifying period, and there had not been a change in
entitlement to or use of lands by Hession, therefore the objection
was disallowed.

On the appeal which eventually reached the Supreme Court,
Henchy J. for the Court held that when the Lay Commissioners

held the second hearing after a two-year adjournment of the first hearing, and they determined that the lands were required for the relief of congestion and that the objection was not sustained, the Commissioners were obliged to make the determination based on proper evidence. Neither of these findings could have been made without making use of the evidence given at the first hearing. Since one of the two Commissioners at the second hearing, Mr. O'Sullivan, was not one of the two Commissioners who sat for the first hearing, the final determination and order made at the second hearing could not be supported as a valid order, based on evidence before the tribunal making the order.

In making this rigorous requirement that 'he who decides must hear' the Court did not comment on the existence or non-existence of a record of the first hearing to which Commissioner Sullivan might have had recourse, or of the importance of a hearing officer's observation of the demeanour and thus the credibility of witnesses. Consequently, it cannot be discerned whether these factors were influential in the Court's decision.

Independent Hearing Officer and Forms of Bias
Another problem of institutional decision making which is the product of the hierarchical structure of administrative agencies is that of maintaining the decision-making independence of administrative hearing officers from the influence of high executive authority such as that of a minister, especially if the hearing involves a matter pertinent to a public policy concern of the minister. The well-known case of *McLoughlin v. Minister for Social Welfare* 1958 IR 1 dealt directly with this issue, resulting in a judicial decision that the independence of a hearing officer must be maintained. Appellant McLoughlin had been informed by letter from a social welfare deciding officer that his employment was insurable employment under the Social Welfare Act 1952, part 1, para 3 (3) which applies to those employed 'in the civil service of the Government'. He had appealed from this decision to an appeals officer of the Department under section 44 (1) of the Social Welfare Act 1952. At the conclusion of McLoughlin's personal appearance before the appeals officer, in which he made certain submissions, McLoughlin was told by the appeals officer that the officer had a minute from the Minister for Finance which in effect directed that McLoughlin was in the employment of the civil service of the government. The appeals

officer also stated that he was bound to adhere to the direction of the Minister. Despite McLoughlin's request, the appeals officer refused him permission to see the minute.

McLoughlin appealed, claiming that the appeals officer was in error in law in holding that appellant's employment was in the civil service of the government and that the decision was contrary to natural justice and made in disregard of his rights. Following a High Court decision dismissing McLoughlin's claims, the Supreme Court held that McLoughlin was a public servant of the state, and not 'in the civil service of the government.' In regard to the role of the appeals officer, the Court held that since that officer said he was bound to adhere to a direction from the Minister for Finance, it was evident this did not show concern for the probative value of the direction. Rather, it showed that the appeals officer believed that a public servant in his position had no choice except to act on the direction of the Minister for Finance. Such a belief was an abdication of his duty as an appeals officer. Therefore appellant was correct in his claim that there was a failure on the part of the appeals officer to hear his appeal, and McLoughlin could have moved the High Court for an order quashing the 'pretended decision' of the appeals officer. Instead, appellant chose to appeal to the High Court and there re-argue the point of law as to whether he was in the civil service, on which there was not a proper hearing. The Court held there was no purpose in sending this matter back to the appeals officer, but the appeal, as Ó Dálaigh J. pointed out, would serve to 'make it known that appeals officers under the Social Welfare Act 1952, and equally deciding officers, are, and are required to be, free and unrestricted in discharging their functions under the Act'.

Although the issue of bias is not confined to administrative decision-making since it may appear in judicial determinations, the characteristics of institutional decision-making by agencies with a statutory charge to carry out certain public policies, and their more direct interpersonal dealings with private parties, do call for administrators to be alert in guarding against various forms of bias. The most recognisable forms of bias to the person not trained in law are those of the decision-maker with personal animosity towards a party or having a personal gain in the outcome of a decision. Less obvious but still possible grounds for reversal by the courts are when administrative determinations are biased by prejudgment of

G

adjudicative facts, or the influence of excessive commitment to a policy, or the giving of the appearance of bias even when none exists in fact. There is also that form of bias within the natural justice concept that no person should be a judge in his own cause which in the United States is referred to as 'combination of functions', namely combining adjudicatory with other functions which may be considered incompatible with the adjudicatory function. The special characteristics of this form of bias are peculiar to structural aspects of administrative agencies and decision-making and merit the separate identification given to them below.

The case of *The State (O'Mahony) v. South Cork Board of Public Health* 1941 Ir. Jur. Rep. 79 provides an example of bias owing to personal animosity. The prosecutrix, Mrs Rose O'Mahony, applied to the court to make absolute a conditional order of mandamus that the Board of Health be directed to consider her application for purchase of a cottage and determine according to law whether she was qualified and entitled to buy it under the Labourers Act 1936, as amended by the Housing and Labourers Act 1937. Mrs O'Mahony had been a tenant for some years of the cottage under the jurisdiction of respondents, during which difficulties arose between Mrs O'Mahony and the Board when she made repairs to the cottage and then obtained a decree against the Board for the expenses of the repairs, claiming she had done them owing to the Board's default. Following this the Board served notice to quit on Mrs O'Mahony, the notice then expired, and summons for possession of the cottage was served. Shortly thereafter, Mrs O'Mahony served her application for purchase of the cottage, as a tenant of the cottage, an agricultural labourer, and a child of the deceased previous tenant of the cottage.

The evidence of minutes of a subsequent Board of Health meeting showed that the Board considered and decided to refuse Mrs O'Mahony's application for purchase with regard to the circumstances, including past decisions and actions of the Board to make her vacate the cottage, and her responses thereto. The Court's evaluation of the evidence was that nothing in the minutes showed that the Board directed their minds to the one issue properly before them, namely was Mrs O'Mahony a qualified person within section 16 of the 1936 Act, although as far as the Court could judge, she was within the purchase scheme. If the Board wished to be rid of her, they could have allowed her to buy the cottage under the Act where their relation with her would be the minimal one of receiving an annuity which she would be obliged to pay. Based on the affidavits, the Court concluded that there was a close connection between her legal action against the Board to recover cost of repairs to the cottage and the Board's refusal of her application to purchase the cottage. As the Court stated:

> Mere pique at an unfavourable judgment in the High Court seems to me to be no justification for attempting to deprive the applicant of her legal rights . . . . The Board of Health have failed to consider her application. This court must direct the Board to consider it. I have indicated clearly what . . . . are the matters to which they should have regard in deciding whether the applicant can establish that she is a qualified person within Section 16 of the Act . . . the conditional order will be made absolute. . . . (page 83)

Bias in the form of prejudgment of adjudicative facts concerning the individual as a result of previously formed opinions concerning that person appeared in *The State (Horgan) v. Exported Live Stock Insurance Board and Committee of Assessors* 1943 IR 581. In this case, a claim by prosecutor for loss of cattle under the Exported Live Stock (Insurance) Act 1940 was at issue. The Act establishes a Board with power to create a fund to meet such claims and provides that claims will be referred for investigation to a committee of assessors composed of three of the Board's members who will determine whether a claimant is entitled to compensation and fix the amount to be granted. The committee's determination is final and conclusive as to the right to and amount of compensation. Prosecutor's claim was based on his having telephoned the agent of the Board, concerning two incidents of cattle injured in shipment from Ireland to England and complying with his instructions to have a veterinary surgeon examine the cattle, with the result that the veterinarian issued certificates that the cattle should be slaughtered. The cattle were sent to Horgan's lands and disposed of, cheques for the amounts realised on the cattle were sent to the Board, and Horgan then filed claims with the Board. Affidavits filed by the Board to the High Court revealed that earlier dealings between Mr Horgan and the Board led the Board and committee of assessors to view his claims with suspicion. Since the committee assessors, on review of the claims, felt they were not *bona fide,* the committee deferred decision until they had made a verbal report to the Board with general discussion of the claims during which dissatisfaction was expressed over moving injured cattle until they were inspected by an officer of the Board, and with the way Horgan carried out his duties. Following this meeting, the committee met again and, after further consideration of the claim, reported in writing that they had decided claimant was not entitled to compensation. Subsequently, the assessors discussed the matter further with other members of the Board, and the Board then adopted the reports, which had no legal effect but demonstrated Board agreement.

Maguire P. held that the actions of the committee of assessors contained several fatal flaws. Mere study of documents before the committee is not an investigation unless the documents contain evidence to support the finding of non-entitlement to compensation. The finding was not so supported since the only evidence the committee had was the shipper's statements, reports and cheques from the Board's agent, the veterinarian's certificates enumerating cattle found injured on arrival at destinations, and prosecutor's claim forms. The committee did not use its statutory powers to require Horgan to verify his claim by statutory declaration or to appear with witnesses. Moreover, deferring consideration of the claim until discussion with Board members put the committee in the position of inviting the Board who, as payers of compensation if a claim is granted, had the status of an interested party, to discuss the claim in the absence of Mr Horgan. The Board members could be called as parties to give evidence, but not in a general conference behind the claimant's back, and this was sufficient to void the whole proceeding.

The Court's opinion was that the claim was rejected not on evidence, but suspicion by the committee members, augmented by feelings of Board members, that Horgan's claim was an effort to perpetrate a fraud abetted by the Board's agent and the veterinary surgeon. This perspective led to prejudicing of facts in disregard of the evidence before the committee and Board. Certiorari was issued to the Board to send all reports made on claims of prosecutor to the Court to be quashed.

The less obvious bias caused by excessive commitment to a policy which prejudices fair evaluation for a claimant's supporting evidence is illustrated by *The State (Elizabeth McGeough) v. Louth County Council* 107 ILTR 13. The elderly prosecutrix holding a labourer's cottage in fee simple wished to sell her interest to support herself when she went to live with her niece. She applied to the Louth County Council for permission to sell in compliance with the legal prohibition against sale without consent of the local authority. The County Manager refused permission to sell and to give any reason therefore, on the ground that he was empowered to deny consent and decline to give reasons. Following extensive correspondence between prosecutrix's solicitor, the County Manager and the accountant to the County Council, a conditional order of mandamus was granted on appeal by the High Court directing the County Council to consider and determine on its merits prosecutrix's application for permission to sell. On further appeal to the Supreme Court, it was held that the manager's sworn affidavit and his cross-examination in the High Court showed that a County Council resolution entitled 'prohibition on the sale of vested cottages' influenced him strongly since he said he paid great attention to the resolution on each application for sale; moreover, he personally did not favour sale of cottages except in special situations. The Court also noted there had been twelve applications for consent since the Council's resolution and all were refused.

The Supreme Court held that the intent of applicable provisions of the Labourers Act 1936 is for the County Manager to consider fairly each application. However, the effect of the County Council's resolution on policy was such that the Manager was implementing those provisions of the Act in a very limited way, thus thwarting the purpose of the Act. Consequently, the resolution was both *ultra vires* and improper as an effort to amend the statutory conditions on which purchasers hold their cottages. The resolution should never have been passed or should have been ignored, since it influenced the manager improperly in his approach to a decision in the prosecutrix's case depriving her of a fair and unbiased consideration of her application for consent to sell her vested cottage as she was entitled to do under the law.

In contrast to the *McGeough* case, it was held that a commitment to a public policy by a district council did not constitute bias in the recent case of *The State (Divito) v. Arklow Urban District Council and Byrne* Supreme Court, unreported, per Henchy J., 7 June 1984. Mr Divito (the applicant) wished to convert his premises in Arklow into an amusement hall for gaming. This requires a certificate (licence) from the District Court under section 15 of the Gaming and Lotteries Act 1956, to be issued only if there is in force for the area containing the premises a resolution by the local authority under section 13 adopting Part III of the Act. Such a resolution by the Arklow Urban District Council (the Council) was in force when the applicant first sought and was granted a certificate by the District Court in April 1982 notwithstanding the objection of the Council. On appeal the Circuit Court considered that the four existing licences in the urban area were sufficient and was not satisfied as to the suitability of the premises or the type of customer the enterprise probably would attract. Applicant then carried out some modifications to the premises with the intent of making a new application to the District Court, and in January 1983 published statutory notice of such intent. The Council then passed a resolution on 9 February 1983 rescinding their adoption of Part III of the 1956 Act, thus negating any application to the District Court for a certificate for issue of licence for any premises. Applicant did re-apply for a certificate to the District Court on 7 March. The application was not moved and was adjourned, and continued to be adjourned. On 13 March 1983 the Council passed a resolution which re-adopted Part III of the 1956 Act, limited so as to enable the four existing amusement halls to be licensed, but preventing a licence from being issued for the central area of the town where applicant's premises were located. Applicant then instituted certior-ari proceedings in the High Court to quash both the 9 February and 13 April resolutions, so that he could then proceed with his adjourned application. The High Court discharged a conditional order of certiorari obtained by applicant who appealed to the Supreme Court.

Henchy J., for the Supreme Court, rejected applicant's first argument that the Council's conduct was an unconstitutional inter-ference with the administration of justice and the independence of the judiciary. There was no *lis* before the District Court when the Council intervened, i.e. no pending proceeding of which the District Court was seised, since applicant had only published notice of intent to make an application on a specified date. The District Court had not acquired jurisdiction to make any order in the matter, pending applicant moving his application before which time the Council's resolution removed the application of the Act to the premises.

As to the claim that the resolutions were made in bad faith in that they were *ad hominem* and discriminatory, Henchy J. held that administrative decisions which do not disclose invalidity on their face have a presumption of being made within jurisdiction. The burden of proof rests on the applicant to show otherwise, i.e. that the Council acted out of personal animus rather than in the exercise of their powers under the Act. He found ample evidence on affidavit that the Council were motivated by such considerations as the undesirability of having an amusement hall in the vicinity of five schools, the sufficiency of four existing halls, and the declared wishes of the community. The applicant's further claim that the Council's resolution was invalid for personal interest or bias since one of the existing amusement halls is located in a civic centre in which the Council has an interest was rejected. Henchy J. found that the nomination by the Council of one of the members of the Arklow Development Company Ltd which runs the civic centre, and the Council's yearly contribution towards running the swimming pool, did not constitute financial connections deflecting the Council from fairness in dealing with the applicant. Finally, the decisions of the Council did not disregard the essentials of justice. The Council justified the steps they took in consistently opposing applicant's efforts to establish an amusement hall by claiming it would be socially undesirable to have an amusement hall in that part of the town, and that the gaming needs of the Arklow population of 8,000 with a very high rate of unemployment were amply met by the four existing amusement halls. He therefore dismissed the appeal.

The judicial stress upon absence of bias is shown in *The State (Hegarty) v. Winters* 1956 IR 320, in which the Court held that there should not be even the appearance of bias, regardless of the reality of the situation. An official arbitrator, under the Acquisition of Land (Assessment of Compensation) Act 1919, sat to determine the compensation, if any, to be paid to Hegarty by Clare County Council for damage to his lands alleged to be caused by widening and cleaning of a stream under the Local Authorities (Works) Act 1949. The affidavits filed revealed acrimonious exchanges between the arbitrator and Hegarty during the proceedings, but the High Court did not find it necessary to resolve Hegarty's claim as to the Arbitrator's hostility towards him in view of another manifestation of potential bias. Following the administrative proceedings, the arbitrator had asked a county staff engineer to show him the lands.

They went in the arbitrator's car to the land where the county engineer accompanied the arbitrator on his inspection, and then drove back with him to the court house. Subsequently, the arbitrator made a nil award and ordered Hegarty to pay towards the costs of arbitration.

The arbitrator stated he had not discussed Hegarty's claim with the engineer during the land inspection, and the President of the High Court accepted this statement. However, the Supreme Court held that even if the making of an inspection is not a taking of evidence, technically, the basic rule applies that 'in proceedings before any tribunal called upon to decide an issue between parties, not alone must justice be done, but it must be seen to be done' (page 334). The inspection was so closely allied to the taking of evidence that the same rules regarding equal treatment and fair play between parties must apply. The action of the arbitrator might 'reasonably give rise in the mind of an unprejudiced onlooker to the suspicion that justice was not being done' (page 336). Therefore the basic rule was broken and the nil award could not be allowed to stand.

Closely related to avoiding the appearance of bias is the problem in which the structure of the agency may lead to the same administrators combining investigating and reporting, or accusatory functions and adjudicatory functions. This can result in claims that the natural justice rule against any person acting as a judge in his own cause has been violated, which in effect parallels the American doctrine that certain combinations of functions violate the concept of separation of powers and therefore due process. Three fairly recent cases in Ireland pertaining to this issue reveal the difficulties of adjusting these legal concepts to the realities of institutional decision-making.

In *O'Donoghue v. Veterinary Council* 1975 IR 398 the Minister for Agriculture and Fisheries provided information to the Veterinary Council indicating that plaintiff had duplicated blood samples in a brucellosis testing programme and issued false certificates so as to deceive the Department. Since the Attorney General advised the Minister that he should not act as complainant in the case, the Council asked a member of the Council, Mr O'Nualláin to allow his name to be used as complainant. Mr O'Nualláin did not participate in the Council's special investigating committee in obtaining evidence against petitioner, and did not instruct solicitors acting for him; they were instructed by the Council's registrar. However, plaintiff appealed to the High Court to cancel the Council's decision on the claim that there had been a breach of constitutional justice. The grounds were that Mr O'Nualláin was the complainant, and also was a member of the Council who participated in the Council hearing and determination that the report of its special investigating committee should be adopted, and that the acts constituted disgraceful professional conduct meriting punishment. In response to this argument, Kenny J. held:

> It is a fundamental principle of our law that no one should act as a judge in his own cause. Although Mr. O'Nualláin took no part in the preparation of the case for hearing and although he was a nominal complainant (the real complainant being the Minister), he must be regarded as being the complainant and, as he took part in the determination and as he voted on the resolution that the petitioner committed the acts charged and was guilty of conduct disgraceful in a professional respect, the decision of the Council must be cancelled. (page 403)

In an *obiter dicta* response to the Council's request for guidance as to how they could constitute themselves as an impartial tribunal, Kenny J. stated that since many complaints to the Council come from the Minister, the only way to avoid suspicion of bias is that no one working in the Department of Agriculture and Fisheries should be on the Council.

The *O'Donoghue* case figured prominently in two subsequent cases which involved the roles of Lay Commissioners of the Land Commission. In *Corrigan v. Irish Land Commission* 1977 IR 317, counsel for Dr Corrigan appealed to Butler J., sitting as the Appeal Tribunal, from a Land Commission hearing in which it was decided that his land was needed for acquisition for relief of congestion. On the morning of the hearing before Butler J., Dr Corrigan's counsel sought an amendment of notice of appeal so as to strike out all previously stated substantive grounds for appeal. He proposed to substitute one new ground, namely that the Land Commission hearing was invalidated by the fact that the two Lay Commissioners who earlier had certified that the lands were required for the relief of congestion under section 25 of the Land Act 1936 were also the

Lay Commissioners who held the Land Commission hearing on the objection to that certification.

In the Supreme Court review of the refusal by Butler J. of this claim, Henchy J. stated that there are four Lay Commissioners whose functions may be exercised by a quorum of two. When two of them sign a certificate that lands are required for relief of congestion, they are recording an administrative decision reached *ex parte* on consideration of internal Land Commission material that a *prima facie* case has been made out for acquisition. If an objection is lodged, a plenary hearing by at least two of the four Commissioners must be held to confirm (or reject) the certification decision for acquisition. Henchy J. also noted that counsel for Dr Corrigan disavowed any claim that the two Lay Commissioners who held the hearing acted unfairly or improperly or that they were influenced by bias or evidence outside the hearing. Rather, the argument was that they were open to suspicion of bias in the possibility that they may have brought to the hearing opinions or preconceptions unfavourable to the landowner resulting from dealing with the material on which they formed the provisional *ex parte* decision to acquire the lands.

Henchy J. stated that this issue had not been ruled on specifically in any recorded judgment and that the two experienced counsel appearing for Dr Corrigan throughout the process had full knowledge of the fact that the two Lay Commissioners who conducted the hearing were the same Lay Commissioners who had signed the certificate. However, they had raised no objection prior to or at the time of the hearing, or between that hearing and the seven months leading up to the appeal to the Appeal Tribunal. It was only on the morning of the hearing before the Appeal Tribunal that the allegation of bias was first made by a newly added counsel. He ruled that if an individual:

> with full knowledge of the facts alleged to constitute disqualification of a member of the tribunal . . . expressly or by implication acquiesces at the time in that member's taking part in the hearing and in the decision, he will be held to have waived the objection on the ground of disqualification which he might otherwise have had. (page 324)

Kenny J. dissented from this majority opinion based on the doctrine of estoppel. Citing his decision in the *O'Donoghue* case and related English cases, he stated that:

> it is altogether wrong that either of the commissioners who signed the original certificate should hear and determine the objection because there is a risk that justice will not be done, and a certainty that justice will not be seen to be done. (page 323)

The *Corrigan* case provided the basis for the issue raised in the subsequent case of *The State (Curran) v. Irish Land Commission* High Court, unreported, per Doyle J., 12 June 1978. A provisional list for acquisition of lands for resale accompanied by a certificate signed by two of the four Lay Commissioners of the Land Commission led to a hearing on the objection to the certificate. The hearing was held by the two other Lay Commissioners not involved in issuing the certificate, but they could not agree as to the effectiveness of the provisional list and certificate. They adjourned the hearing to a later date with the intent that the hearing would be held by three Commissioners, one of whom would have to be a Commissioner who had signed the certificate to which objection was being made.

A request for an order of prohibition against constituting the tribunal to hold the hearing in this manner was made by Curran on the grounds that the third commissioner, Mr O'Sullivan, who would be one of the reconstituted three-person hearing panel, was disqualified because he had signed the certificate to which objection was being taken. He thus already had formed a view on relevant information supplied to him by administrators of the Land Commission, which information was not available to Curran.

Doyle J. pointed out that this case differed from the *Corrigan* case, particularly in that the objection to the composition of the hearing panel or tribunal was raised in advance of, rather than after, the hearing, and also in the reason for the land acquisition. After extensive references to the opinion of judges Henchy, Griffin and Kenny in the *Corrigan* case, Doyle J. stated that the issue still had not been the subject of a reported judgment which could provide clear guidance to him. However, he accepted what had been presented as evidence to him in this case, namely that Teevan J. and Butler J., acting as Appeals Tribunals on former occasions, had ruled on this issue. They had held that the signing of a certificate by a Land Commissioner did not disqualify that Commissioner from later hearing an objection to making the certificate and affirming the action to acquire the land. He concluded:

> I feel myself unable to depart from rulings by the two learned Judicial Commissioners (Teevan and Butler) whose collective experience of Land Commission procedure extends over such a lengthy period. One should be wary of too facile application of legal maxims . . . but in the present case I feel justified in applying the presumption; *omnia rite esse acta.*

On this basis, Doyle J. discharged the conditional order of prohibition.

A further aspect of the combination of functions issue as well as the constitutional issues of an alleged exercise of judicial power and absolute discretion by an administrative agency is illustrated by *McCann v. the Attorney General and the Racing Board* 1983 ILRM 67. This case arose under section 24 of the Racing Board and Race Courses Act 1946 which provides that the Racing Board may in its 'absolute discretion' as 'it so thinks fit' grant, refuse, suspend or revoke a betting permit, subject to informing a licensed bookmaker of a refusal, suspension or revocation in writing and giving the bookmaker the right to make written or oral representations to the Board if he requests within seven days to do so. Plaintiff had been operating as a licensed bookmaker for over five years when the Racing Board (the Board) officials complained that plaintiff's clerk had entered two bets on his race card instead of on the standard racing sheet during races at Navan, and that plaintiff refused to hand over the race card on the ground it was his clerk's property and he could not compel the clerk to hand it over to him. Plaintiff was warned that this would, at the least, result in his suspension (since permitting bets to be recorded on the race card instead of the racing sheet indicated evasion of the betting levy) but plaintiff, thinking at worst he would face a short suspension, told the Board officials 'I will take my suspension if I have done anything wrong'. Subsequently the Board wrote to plaintiff that they would consider the revocation of his permit as recommended by the Board's officer at the Navan race, and invited him to make written or oral representations. Plaintiff's solicitors made a written submission that the clerk had carried out the transactions in question as his own personal business, and since plaintiff could not do anything to help the Board in this regard, he should not be penalised under these circumstances. The Board and plaintiff treated this as a written representation, and on 18 December revoked the permit. Plaintiff appealed this decision, the Board heard his oral appeal, and confirmed the revocation on 21 December 1973.

Plaintiff brought proceedings to the High Court, where Barron J. first rejected plaintiff's argument that the Supreme Court judgments in *In re Solicitors Act 1954* 1960 IR 239 and *McDonald v. Bord na gCon* 1965 IR 217 supported his position that the Racing Board was administering justice. In the view of Barron J., the similarity of the Greyhound Industry Act 1958 and the Racing Board and Race Courses Act 1945, the judgment of Walsh J. in the *McDonald* case, and the propositions of Kingsmill Moore J. in the *Solicitors* case as to what constituted exercise of judicial power, all led to the conclusion that the powers given the Racing Board were administrative, not judicial.

Plaintiff also submitted that section 24 of the Act is repugnant to article 40(3) of the Constitution by giving absolute discretion to the Board which denies the right to fair procedures; that even if fair procedures are required by section 24, no proper hearing was given before the revocation order; and the hearing by way of appeal against the original order was contrary to natural justice since the Board by hearing an appeal from itself acted as a judge in its own cause. These submissions were treated as interrelated by Barron J. and in response to the claim of repugnance to article 40(3) he cited the judgment in *East Donegal Co-Operative Society Limited v. Attorney General* 1970 IR 317 holding that whenever a statutory discretionary power is granted, there is a presumption that the Oireachtas intended that fair procedures be exercised. Although an inference can be drawn from section 24 that the legislature intended the Board to decide whether allegations against an individual justified either suspension or revocation without hearing representations, the Board in this case notified plaintiff of the allegation against him by letter, gave him the opportunity to make representations which plaintiff did make by letter, and after its decision, gave plaintiff the opportunity to appeal the decision in person before the Board. Consequently, the Board's exercise of its powers were in accordance with fair procedures. Though plaintiff's rights could have been adversely affected by the statute, they were not so affected in actual practice, and he thus lacked *locus standi* to challenge section 24. Finally, regarding the combination of functions implied in the Board's hearing an appeal from itself, and thus acting as a judge in its own cause, together with the composition of the Board in the context of the matter with which it had to deal, Barron J. noted again that under section 24, plaintiff was entitled to and in fact was given a first hearing (in which he chose to make a written representation) and also a second hearing (this time in person). If the first hearing was valid, he could see no grounds upon which further consideration of the matter should become an appeal which should have been heard by another body, citing the statement of Kingsmill Moore J. in *In re Solicitors Act 1954* 1960 IR 239 that:

> It is true that in a hearing before the Committee a solicitor will not have the protections he would receive in a Court of Justice. Complainant, tribunal and the person who conducts the complaint are inextricably interconnected . . . . In many cases the person against whom a complaint is made will be a solicitor with whom members of the tribunal have had professional dealings which may have predisposed them in his favour or against him . . . . In the opinion of the Court these considerations . . . are not in point. If the Committee are not administering justice the Constitution imposes no restrictions on the composition of the body. (page 272)

Since the Racing Board was exercising an administrative function (although its power had to be exercised judicially), and its composition could not be faulted, Barron J. held that he could see no reason why a fair hearing of a complaint of misconduct should be held to be invalidated because that decision is reviewed by a further fair hearing held by the same body.

Right to Discovery of Documents

The right of access to governmental documents raises issues important to the individual seeking to protect interests threatened by an administrative determination, as against the administrator wishing to protect the confidentiality of his written communications. The private citizen justifies right of access to documents on the ground that they are evidence critical to proving his claim. The administrator argues that denial of access to the documents is essential if he is to have the freedom and candour of interdepartmental and intradepartmental staff communication necessary to formulate and carry out public policy effectively in the public interest. The issues raised by a claim of right of discovery of documents versus the assertion of executive privilege were discussed in the previous analysis of *Margaret O'Leary v. Minister for Industry and Commerce* 1966 IR 676 and the first case of *Murphy v. the Corporation of Dublin* 1972 IR 215, in chapter 3. (See pages 63-6.)

The judicial doctrines of the *O'Leary* and *Murphy* cases prevailed in the later case of *Geraghty v. Minister for Local Government* 1976 IR 153. Plaintiff Geraghty sought a declaration against the Minister for Local Government's refusal to grant outline planning permission for a housing development. This involved a factual situation and issues of official notice and relationships between inspecting officer, departmental staff and Minister (see pages 207-211). Plaintiff raised the additional issue of discovery of certain documents in the possession of the Minister. In response, the Assistant Secretary of the Department of Local Government claimed that certain documents, including those covering normal departmental procedure for handling an appeal, should not be produced on the grounds that disclosure would be contrary to the public interest. This claim was reinforced by a Minister's certificate to the same effect.

Kenny J., in the High Court, allowed production of all but three of the twenty-two documents. The exceptions were: (1) a draft order with written comment by the legal adviser to the Department of Local Government, held to be the same as advice by a solicitor or barrister to client and thus privileged; (2) another draft of that order formulated as a result of the advice given by the legal adviser, held to be a confidential document; and (3) a document written by an officer who had heard appeals analogous to the Geraghty appeal, held to be a confidential communication from one civil servant to another civil servant. On appeal by the Minister that all the documents were privileged, the Supreme Court affirmed Kenny J.'s decision, with one exception in which the Supreme Court ruled that a fourth document was privileged since it was an internal communication giving an outline of the steps in the appeal sent to the legal adviser, which had been written to determine whether the draft order was legally correct. These exceptions parallel the *O'Leary* rulings that communications on statutory duties from the Attorney General to the Minister for Industry and Commerce were privileged.

In view of certain aspects of bias and combination of functions
in the *Corrigan* and *Curran* cases as discussed above, the establishment of the right to the discovery of documents for the Land
Commission issue of certificates of acquisition, as established in a
recent Supreme Court decision, is of particular interest. In *Nolan v.
Irish Land Commission* 1981 IR 23 plaintiff sued for a declaration that
he was entitled to inspect the documents and data considered by
the Lay Commissioners of the Land Commission prior to their
certification that his lands were required for purposes of resale, and
an injunction to restrain the Lay Commissioners from hearing and
deciding on plaintiff's objections to their certification and proposed
acquisition of his land until the documents had been made available
for his inspection. Plaintiff contended that he could not adequately
present his objection without knowing through discovery the kind
of case he had to meet, consequently the absence of discovery
violated concepts of *audi alteram partem.* The Land Commission
argued that natural justice rules do not extend to evidential or
procedural matters, but only to the actual hearing before the tribunal (except for informing a person of a charge against him in
advance of a hearing). O'Higgins C. J. noted that the certificate is
not conclusive of the facts certified when the cause for acquisition
is resale of the land, inasmuch as the relevant Act states that
the objector can resist acquisition by establishing that during the
qualifying period, the lands had not been offered for sale, that he
had complied with the residence test, and that the lands had
provided adequate agricultural products and employment. Since at
the hearing by the Lay Commissioners of an objection to acquisition
three separate issues of fact may arise, any one of which if decided
in favour of the objector will entitle him to succeed, the landowner
should be given a fair opportunity to make that challenge.

As Griffin J. noted in his concurring opinion, Henchy J. in the
Corrigan decision had stated that all the essential legal requirements
of *a lis inter partes* have to be observed in a hearing before the Land
Commissioners; furthermore an essential legal requirement of *a lis
inter partes* is that discovery of documents may be obtained so as to
put both parties on an equal footing at the hearing.

The Court (O'Higgins C.J., Griffin, Parke J. J.) concluded that
an absence of discovery and inspection by the plaintiff of appropriate
documents considered by the Lay Commissioners prior to their
issue of certificates of acquisition would mean that the requirements

of natural justice would not be observed. However, that right to discovery of documents was limited by the Court to those reports made officially by Land Commission inspectors to the Commissioners describing and dealing with the lands as to their suitability for resale, while other kinds of communications or 'data' which might contain opinions and views could be properly subject to the claim of executive privilege.

Further affirmation of the right of access to evidence posed by a deciding administrative authority was given by the Supreme Court more recently in *The State (Williams) v. The Army Pensions Board and The Minister for Defence* 1983 ILRM 331. Sergeant Williams had served in the Army from 1939 until his death in 1978, including two tours of duty with United Nations forces in the Congo and in Cyprus. The latter tour of duty ended with his being flown home for medical attention, and for the following eleven years he received regular medical treatment, recorded in a voluminous medical dossier of three medical books, test and X-ray results and a central medical file of clinical notes. Following his death Mrs Williams applied to the Army Pensions Board (the Board) for those allowances and gratuities which the Army Pensions Act 1962 provides may be granted by the Minister for Defence if a husband's death was attributable to a wound or disease incurred in service with a United Nations force.

The vague provisions of the 1962 Act on how the Board is to exercise their functions are supplemented by article 8 of Regulations (S.I. No. 6 of 1928) providing that they 'shall make such inquiries, summon such witnesses and take such evidence as they may deem necessary to report on such applications'. In this instance, as was their customary practice, the Board decided against an oral hearing. The Board report rejected Mrs Williams's claim, and she then applied for reconsideration, under article 10 of the Regulations permitting an applicant to request reconsideration in the light of 'any additional evidence' the applicant might submit. The extensive medical record on Sergeant Williams had been made available to the Board, but when Mrs Williams and her son sought access to that record as evidence, the Board refused on the basis it was not their practice to make such evidence available, leaving her with only her husband's death certificate as medical evidence. The Board's second report on reconsideration was again adverse, on the grounds that no additional evidence had been received on Mrs Williams's behalf.

On appeal from a High Court decision against plaintiff's application for a conditional order of certiorari to quash the two reports of the Board, Henchy J. held that the Board's functions were adjudicative, not administrative, and that if they find an applicant entitled to allowances and gratuities, the Minister must grant them. He identified the applicant's primary and only valid complaint, namely that she was in no position to offer any evidence concerning factors causing or contributing to her husband's death, and yet she was denied the opportunity of knowing and thus being able to rebut the evidence in Sergeant Williams's medical dossier available to the Board. In his view:

> The result was that the Army's side of the case was fully presented to the Board. As against that, Mrs Williams, who was left in the dark, had nothing to offer except her completed claim form and the death certificate.

> I consider that this one-sidedness amounted to a breach of natural justice. Mrs Williams was unfairly and unjustifiably prevented from rebutting, if that was possible, the conclusion reached by the Board. (page 334)

Henchy J. concluded that though there may be cases where for reasons of state security or public policy the Board may be privileged from disclosing evidence, this was not one of those cases. In his judgment the Board unintentionally and in good faith breached natural justice and relevant regulations and thus divested themselves of jurisdiction. Their reports and the Minister's consequent rulings therefore fall to be quashed and an order of certiorari should issue in absolute form.

Right to Call and Examine Witnesses

The right of an individual to call and examine witnesses on his or her behalf and cross-examine opposing witnesses can be critical to their defence in an administrative hearing. It is also vital to the official of the agency conducting a hearing, if the agency is to develop all the evidence needed for an informed determination. Statutory recognition of the agency's need to call and examine witnesses under oath is frequent. Typical examples include the

Social Welfare (Consolidation) Act 1981, Part VIII, section 298 (7-10) giving such powers to appeals officers and the Restrictive Practices Act 1972, First Schedule, section 7 (1) (a)-(c), (2), (3) and (4) providing for powers of the Restrictive Practices Commission to require attendance of witnesses and submission of testimony under oath, or documents, under threat of contempt. The Solicitors (Amendment) Act 1960, section 15 (1), (2) and (3) gives the disciplinary committee the powers, rights and privileges vested in the High Court to enforce attendance of witnesses, to examine them under oath, and compel production of documents, subject to contempt proceedings which on certificate to the High Court will be tried as though the offence were a contempt of the court.

This right may also raise questions as to the powers of an officer conducting the hearing to maintain a certain modicum of control over the course of proceedings. In *Fitzpatrick v. Wymes and Others* unreported, Supreme Court per Walsh J., (Budd and Henchy J. J. concurring),13 February 1974, the issue was the extent to which the individual's right to call witnesses on his behalf may be restricted by the hearing officer in the interest of calling only witnesses whose testimony is relevant to the matter at hand. Plaintiff, a member of the Garda Síochána, was charged with disobeying a lawful written order and an inquiry was held on this charge. Plaintiff had been furnished with names of the persons to hold the inquiry, witnesses to be called and a summary of the evidence. Counsel for plaintiff had furnished a list of witnesses whose attendance was desired under regulation 10 of the Garda Síochána (Discipline) Regulations 1926, which provides that a defendant may submit names of witnesses of material fact whom defendant wishes to be present, and that such witnesses must be ordered to attend under penalty of a fine and possible brief imprisonment. The list included the Minister for Justice and the Minister for Industry and Commerce, but Fitzpatrick's counsel refused to give any indication as to the materiality of witnesses. When asked to do so during the hearing he and Fitzpatrick left the inquiry in protest. The inquiry proceeded in their absence without hearing witnesses for Fitzpatrick. It was decided that Fitzpatrick was guilty and he was dismissed from the Garda Síochána.

Fitzpatrick's challenge of his dismissal, on the grounds that this application of regulation 10 of the Garda Síochána (Discipline) Regulations 1926 amounted to a denial of the *audi alteram partem* rule, eventually reached the Supreme Court. Walsh J., for the Court, held that if witnesses whom plaintiff asked to be called were those who *prima facie* could give material evidence, the administrative tribunal should not require plaintiff's counsel to state what the evidence was that witnesses called would give, nor should the tribunal rule as to whether or not they be called. However, if the names on the list of witnesses to be called included those whose materiality of testimony to the issues was *not* clear on the face of it, then it would seem that the regulations would require the administrative tribunal to be satisfied on this matter by an indication from plaintiff as to why their testimony would be material before issuing summons. This is particularly true since a person so summoned may be punished for not complying, and it is not unreasonable that a prospective witness should not be compelled to attend a hearing unless his evidence is relevant to the proceedings. Refusal to issue a summons until an administrative tribunal is thus satisfied does not constitute a breach of a fundamental right. Fitzpatrick's appeal from dismissal on these grounds was refused.

The right to cross-examine witnesses would appear to be implicit in the power provided in statute and regulations to call witnesses and examine them under oath. This right to cross-examination in administrative hearings is supported also in judicial decisions. Moreover, it will be seen in the discussion which follows of evidence in administrative hearings, illustrated particularly in *Kiely v. Minister for Social Welfare* 1971 IR 21, 1977 IR 267, that the right to cross-examination may be a critical factor in judicial determination of the nature and sufficiency of evidence necessary to substantiate an administrative determination.

Evidence

The types and amount of evidence which the courts will accept as sustaining an administrative decision is a central issue in administrative adjudication. In general, the courts in Ireland, England and the United States do not impose the requirements of evidence traditionally associated with criminal trial processes. The American Administrative Procedures Act codified existing judicial doctrine when it provided that a decision must be supported 'by and in accordance with reliable, probative and substantial evidence'. (See Administrative Procedures Act 5 US Code, section 556 (d).) Substantial evidence is defined by the US Supreme Court as that evidence, which, upon consideration of the record as a whole, 'is more than a mere scintilla. It means such relevant evidence as a reasonable mind might accept as adequate to support a conclusion'. (See *Universal Camera Corporation v. NLRB* 340 US 474 (1951), quoting *Consolidated Edison Company v. NLRB* 305 US 197, at 229 (1938).) Under the substantial evidence rule, hearsay evidence may be admitted and used for the probative value it may have. (See *Richardson v. Perales* 402 US 339 (1971).) In England, the 'legal rules of evidence do not apply, which eliminates a certain source of technicality', and a medical appeal tribunal has been held not to be bound by legal rules of evidence and may take:

> into account medical reports in comparable cases even though their authors are not available and the evidence is thus techni-cally hearsay. This makes an interesting parallel with the American Law as laid down in *Richardson v. Perales*. It is probably true to say that the law is the same for British Tribunals generally.[2]

In Ireland, the weight of oral as against written evidence, the use of written evidence not subject to examination and cross-examination and official notice of written evidence were analysed in the case of *Kiely v. Minister for Social Welfare* 1971 IR 21, 1977 IR 267. Plaintiff claimed death benefit under the Social Welfare (Occupational Injuries) Act 1966 on the grounds that her husband had sustained an accident in 1968 in the course of his insurable employment which caused his incapacitation for work, first by physical injuries and later by depression, culminating in a coronary thrombosis. Upon rejection of her claim by a deciding officer and an appeals officer of the Department of Social Welfare, the High Court on further appeal held that plaintiff had not been given adequate opportunity to controvert evidence adverse to her case contained in a written report made to the Department by Dr Mulcahy, a cardiac specialist. The case was referred back to be heard by a different appeals officer and medical assessor. The result of the hearing in 1972 again was adverse to plaintiff's claim. From a negative ruling by the High Court on appeal, a further appeal was made to the Supreme Court, claiming that the departmental appeals officer violated natural justice in requiring plaintiff's wit-nesses to give evidence on oath and submit to cross-examination, while receiving Dr Mulcahy's evidence in the form of his original letter of January 1969, and denying plaintiff's counsel an opportunity to cross-examine him. It was also contended that the medical assessor's role in the hearing negated the decision of the appeals officer.

Henchy J., for the Supreme Court, noted that the intent of the Social Welfare (Occupational Injuries) Act 1966 and Social Welfare (Insurance Appeals) Regulations (S.I. No. 376, 1952) was that the appeals officer has jurisdiction to conduct a full oral hearing where only one side gives evidence. He also stated that the Regulations allow admission of a written statement as *prima facie* evidence of any fact in any case in which the appeals officer thinks it just and proper to do so. However, case law and treatises make clear that once a fact provided by a written statement is controverted by probative evidence to the contrary, it ceases to be *prima facie* evidence of the fact.

Henchy J. referred to the fact that two doctors appeared for the plaintiff. One of the doctors had attended her husband after the accident and the other was an expert in cardiac medicine. Both maintained under oath and cross-examination by the appeals officer and medical assessor that the coronary thrombosis resulted from the accident. He also noted that the appeals officer stated he would take into account a letter from Dr Mulcahy, which had been written in response to a summarised case history which a medical adviser to the Minister had sent to Dr Mulcahy, in which Dr Mulcahy had stated:

> On careful perusal of the evidence presented to me, I could find no evidence of any sort to suggest the accident led directly or indirectly to the subsequent coronary attack and to the patient's death. (page 280)

The appeals officer had also ruled that he would not require Dr Mulcahy to attend the hearing, and did not deny using Dr Mulcahy's written opinion in rejecting plaintiff's claim.

Henchy J. held that natural justice and *audi alteram partem* means that both sides must be fairly heard, and that:

> Where essential facts are in controversy a hearing which is required to be oral and confrontational for one side but which

is allowed to be based on written and therefore effectively unquestionable evidence on the other side, has neither the semblance nor the substance of a fair hearing . . . Dr Mulcahy's written opinion was three years old. It was a hypothetical opinion given on the basis of an incomplete version of the case history. Dr Mulcahy was given no opportunity of reconsidering his opinion in the light of a fuller version of the clinical facts . . . nor an opportunity of reviewing his opinion in the light of the opposing medical opinions which his letter was used to controvert. In short, its use as a determining piece of evidence was so unfair as to invalidate the hearing. (pages 281-2)

Moreover, the social welfare regulations do not allow a written statement to be received in evidence in rebuttal of a *prima facie* case (established by the testimony of plaintiff's two medical witnesses) which was the purpose for which Dr Mulcahy's letter was used; there was no jurisdiction to receive and use a written statement.

Finally, it was held that under the social welfare regulations, the medical assessor is not to participate in the proceedings, but only to make his medical expertise available, if requested, to enable medical evidence to be properly understood and assessed. However, a letter was written by the medical assessor to the appeals officer during the interval between the hearing and notification of the decision which asserted that the deceased had been a great risk for coronary heart disease owing to his physical condition and personal habits previous to the accident, and that the medical examiner's personal experience and the relevant literature showed that anxiety and tension brought on by deceased's accident had no causal effect in regard to his death. Since this constituted new evidence in writing, given without notice to the plaintiff, and received and acted on without giving plaintiff or her witnesses an opportunity to comment on or controvert that evidence, it was not admissible. It was contrary to natural justice and to the relevant statute and regulations, in that it nullified the oral hearing processes and constituted evidence addressed behind plaintiff's back, when she thought the only evidence contrary to her claim was Dr Mulcahy's letter. Although the appeals officer and medical assessor were not shown to have acted otherwise than in good faith, the decision was flawed and could not be allowed to stand. A fresh oral hearing before a different appeals officer and medical assessor was ordered by the Court.

Another evidential issue is the effect on interpreting statutory intent as to burden of proof in relation to inferences drawn from conflicting evidence, illustrated by *In the Matter of the Redundancy Payments Act 1967: The Minister for Labour and O'Connor and Irish Dunlop Company Ltd* unreported, High Court, per Kenny J., 6 March 1973. There was conflicting testimony over what had been agreed to in a conference between the plaintiff, O'Connor and Locke, personnel manager for Dunlop. Mr Locke's recollection of the agreement was that £500 would be paid upon Mr O'Connor's dismissal for redundancy, which included the lump sum payable under the Redundancy Payments Act 1967, while Mr O'Connor's understanding was that he would receive £500 plus the statutory payment. Mr O'Connor was not given and did not sign a redundancy certificate when he was dismissed, as required by the Redundancy Certificate Regulations, SI No. 3 of 1968.

On appeal by plaintiff from an adverse decision by the Redundancy Appeals Tribunal, Kenny J. held that the deciding factor was the company's failure to issue a redundancy certificate at the time of dismissal or reasonably thereafter in view of the statutory obligation to do so. This is especially true since the purpose of the certificate is to ensure that the employee knows the amount of the statutory redundancy payment which the employer thinks is payable to the employee. The certificate also establishes that the lump sum has been paid so that the employer can claim payment of the rebate from the redundancy fund, and the burden of responsibility is on the employer to make certain the employee signs the redundancy certificate when the lump sum is paid.

Kenny J. found that the evidence showed neither plaintiff nor defendant company knew the exact amount of the statutory lump sum during the negotiations or when the £500 was paid; and that a redundancy certificate was never issued to the employee. When this occurs, the payment made to an employee can be treated as payment of the statutory lump sum only if the employer proves to the satisfaction of the Appeals Tribunal that (1) the employee at the time of payment knew the amount of the statutory lump sum to which he was entitled at the time of dismissal and (2) the employee had agreed to accept the amount paid by employer in discharge of the statutory lump sum. Mr O'Connor therefore was entitled to the statutory lump sum of £132 in addition to the £500 already paid to him.

In addition to burden of proof, the sufficiency of evidence necessary to sustain an administrative determination was an issue in *Clark and Clark v. Irish Land Commission* 1976 IR 375. Plaintiffs had completed a contract to purchase a 188-acre farm shortly before the Land Commission instructed its inspector to make an offer for the land. It then issued a certificate that the lands were required for relief of congestion. In a hearing before two Lay Commissioners on an objection lodged by the plaintiffs against the Land Commission purchase, the inspector of the Land Commission testified that there were fifteen people in the immediate locality with uneconomic holdings, there were no other lands on hand in the area and the farm was a 'kingpin holding', since if nine other holdings close to it were acquired, land congestion in the locality would be totally relieved.

The inspector on cross-examination by plaintiff's solicitor admitted there were farms in the locality owned by elderly people or not being properly worked which constituted a potential source of land for relief of congestion. However, further cross-examination as to individual owners of other farms led one of the Lay Commissioners holding the hearing to state he would not like the hearing to be used to bring other farms to the Land Commission's notice (although he made no formal ruling in this regard). The solicitor thereafter did not seek to adduce any evidence as to other holdings and ceased this line of cross-examination.

On disallowance of the objection by the Lay Commissioners and by the Appeal Tribunal, plaintiffs on appeal to the Supreme Court argued that an objection against compulsory acquisition to relieve congestion cannot be disallowed unless the evidence shows there is local congestion and the particular lands in question and not other lands are required to relieve that congestion. Furthermore, the order of the Lay Commissioners was void because they wrongfully had excluded evidence which would have shown that other lands were available for relief of congestion.

Henchy J. for the Court held that the Lay Commissioners are bound to act judicially in hearing an objection to the compulsory acquisition of lands for relief of congestion, citing *The State (Crowley) v. Irish Land Commission* 1951 IR 250, 85 ILTR 26 and *In re Estate of Roscrea Meat Products* 1958 IR 47, 92 ILTR 100. He knew of no rule of evidence or statute which cast the onus on the objector to rebut the correctness of a certificate that lands are required for relief of congestion. The certificate's correctness depends on the assessment made by the Land Commission of its scheme for re-deploying the land and the objector normally will not know enough of Land Commission data and proposals to evaluate the basis of the certificate. Since this question is one of mixed fact and law, involving assessment of facts against the statutory meaning of relief of congestion and Land Act objectives, the Lay Commissioners must not only feel there is a need for relief of congestion but that the particular land in question is *required* for that purpose. The degree of proof is more than merely showing the lands could be used for that purpose, since the Commission could then arbitrarily ignore more suitable lands and select those less suitable.

Henchy J. accepted counsel for plaintiff's submission that he was entitled to give evidence to the Lay Commissioners by cross-examination or otherwise as to other specified holdings to show their suitability for relieving congestion. However, he would not accept the second claim that the Lay Commissioners' decision was invalidated because they had refused to allow such evidence to be given. There was no refusal to hear such evidence, no application was made to receive such evidence, and in fact, such evidence was given as shown by the Land Commission's inspector conceding in cross-examination that there were other holdings which might be acquired for relief of congestion. However, in the final analysis, the cross-examination did not change the evidence that the holding in question, owing to its size and location, was crucial to the Land Commission's scheme for relief of congestion and this was sufficient evidence to support their and the Appeal Tribunal's conclusions.

Another type of challenge against evidence used in an administra-tive determination is that the administrative agency has exceeded its jurisdiction by considering factual matters which are not within the scope of authority or duty of the agency to take into consideration as defined by the statute. In *The State (Keller) v. Galway County Council and Another* 1958 IR 142, plaintiff claimed a disablement allowance under section 50 (5) of the Health Act 1953, providing that a health authority shall provide for payment of maintenance allowances in accordance with regulations made by the Minister to disabled persons over sixteen who are unable to provide for themselves and whose relatives also cannot provide maintenance. The Disabled

Persons (Maintenance Allowance) Regulations 1954 (SI No 207 of 1954) provide that the allowance will be payable by a health authority to an applicant who:

(a) by reason of injury, disease, congenital deformity or physical or mental illness or defect, which has continued or may reasonably be expected to continue for at least one year from its onset, is in the opinion of the Chief Medical Officer of the health authority substantially handicapped in undertaking work, of a kind which, if he were not suffering from that injury, disease, or congenital deformity . . . would be suited to his age, experience and qualifications.
(b) is not maintained in an institution by or at the expense of a local authority.

The High Court's statement of Keller's condition, based on an orthopaedic specialist's analysis, was that owing to an early injury his left hip joint was destroyed, pelvis distorted, left leg shortened some six inches, bent inwards and underdeveloped with gross limitation of movement. A lump on the left buttock made sitting for any length of time uncomfortable, and his back was under strain. At age 26, he obtained a surgical boot and could walk without crutches and cycle, but his effort to become a barber had to be abandoned since long periods of standing caused severe pain. He had never worked, had earned nothing, and lived with his old-age pensioner father and a brother who earned £5 to £6 a week.

Keller's application for disablement allowance at age 36 was accompanied by a certificate attesting to his condition from Dr Dyer, his Loughrea District dispensary doctor. On the direction of Dr McConn, Chief Medical Officer of Galway County Council, Dr Ida Gallagher, Assistant Medical Officer, came to the Loughrea dispensary, interviewed Keller and read his application form and Dr Dyer's certificate. Her affidavit to the Court was that Keller was in good health, but the left hip condition was obvious and in accordance with Dr Dyer's certificate, so she did not expose or examine the hip. Dr Gallagher's report to Dr McConn included her opinion that given Keller's intelligence and his surgical boot correction he should have learned a trade not requiring standing; that he was fit for work other than heavy labour and could contribute to his maintenance. Dr McConn concurred in this and wrote a note on Keller's application form that 'This boy should have learned some suitable trade which would not require standing - as however, his deformity is adequately corrected by a surgical boot, he is not in my opinion eligible' (page 146).

On the County Council's refusal of Keller's application based on Dr McConn's refusal of a certificate, Dr Dyer requested reconsideration, sending photographs of the deformity, and calling attention to the fact that the lump on his left buttock made sitting work unsuitable and to Keller's lack of experience or qualifications. Dr McConn, after further review and discussion with Dr Gallagher, and certain inquiries as to Keller's father's and brother's incomes, adhered to his initial refusal of a certificate.

In response to Keller's request for an order of mandamus requiring Dr McConn and the Galway County Council to hear and determine his application in accordance with law, Davitt P. held that Dr McConn's function in forming his opinion was a quasi-judicial function. Further, when an inferior tribunal which is hearing and determining questions according to law considers matters which it has no right to take into account, and allows its decision to be affected by such matters, it can be held to have declined jurisdiction and may be required on mandamus to hear and determine the issue properly in accordance with law.

On review of the evidence, Davitt P. held that if Dr McConn accepted Dr Dyer's view of Keller's incapacity for a sitting job and confined himself to the evidence he was supposed to consider under the specific provisions of the Minister's regulations, then Keller's complete lack of experience, qualifications, or knowledge of a trade meant that the only work he could perform was unskilled labour for which he was clearly unfit. It was clear that Dr McConn must have considered and been influenced by matters he was not entitled to consider, namely Dr Gallagher's opinion that Keller should have learned a trade not requiring standing and that he was fit to contribute substantially to his own maintenance. Moreover, while the County Council may consider Keller's father's and brother's earnings in determining whether and how much of an allowance to give, this is not of concern to Dr McConn, although he seemed to have given this factor consideration.

Davitt P. concluded that since Dr McConn took into account matters extraneous to his function and outside the scope of his duty according to law which affected his decision, he must be considered as having declined to carry out his duty according to law. The County Council, having accepted Dr McConn's position, based their refusal on it and were party to Dr McConn's refusal to carry out this duty and so failed to carry out their duty. An absolute mandamus was issued to Dr McConn and the Council to consider and deal with the application in accordance with law.

Official Notice
Another procedural issue in natural and constitutional justice which in part results from the institutional decision-making processes of administrative agencies is that of official notice. This issue also arises in the courts when judges take notice of facts external to evidence presented in court which presumably are commonly known, but it is more likely to occur in administrative adjudication owing to the factors which also contribute to the previously discussed problems of hearing officer independence and forms of bias. Administrative determinations are often a composite of inputs from departmental field officers making inspections or studies which become part of the findings in a report on a hearing, plus staff officer analyses and the minister's or appeal board's assessment and reaction to this data. This increases the potential for use of facts or opinions not introduced as evidence in a hearing or made known to the parties at any time in the process leading up to the decision.

To administrators who see what they are doing as an administrative function in carrying out public policy, the determination by the courts that such functions require them to 'act judicially' in the procedures they follow may come as a rude surprise, even though the precedent for such judicial rulings existed in prior cases. In the earlier case of *In re Estate of Roscrea Meat Products Ltd* 1958 IR 47, 92 ILTR 100, plaintiffs had lodged an objection in accordance with Land Purchase Act Rules against the Land Commission's certification of their 545 acres of untenanted lands being sought for compulsory acquisition and subsequent resale under the Land Acts. Their claim was that these were very high quality grazing lands and unsuitable for the purposes of the Land Commission.

Plaintiff's appeal to the Supreme Court made from a hearing before the Lay Commissioners of the Land Commission and from the Appeal Tribunal stressed the question of law as to whether the Commissioners might properly consider reports from an official of the Land Commission on the lands in question when such reports were not disclosed to the objector. The Supreme Court, per Maguire C. J., held that the Lay Commissioners must act on reports of its officers, since they must have prior knowledge of the nature and use of the lands they intend to acquire. However, the statutory provisions on the right to object and right to a hearing show an intent that there be a hearing analogous to that taking place in a court of law. All those safeguards which in the interest of parties concerned have been held necessary in proceedings in court must be provided, most important of which 'is the requirement that the objector must have an effective opportunity of meeting the case against him' (page 58). Kingsmill Moore J., in his concurring opinion, stated:

> Any matters which have or may have any bearing on the questions at issue or which might influence the decisions of the Commissioners must be brought before them in open court so that the objector may know of them, be able to test them on cross-examination, and may meet them if he thinks fit, by evidence given in support of his objection. (IR, page 59)

Consequently, reports made to the Lay Commissioners by a fact-finding or investigating officer must be made known to the objector so that the objector may have opportunity to refute such reports by submission of contrary evidence or cross-examination.

However, the applicability of official notice as a basis for challenge to an administrative determination is dependent upon there being a legal ground in the first place for making an objection to the determination. In *The State (Costello) v. Irish Land Commission* 1959 IR 353, prosecutor had inherited 110 acres of land in 1937 which were poor in quality, without buildings and non-viable; in 1952 the Land Commission initiated the process to acquire the land for resale under section 25 of the Land Act 1936. For five years the Commission notified prosecutor of the steps it was taking. The only response from prosecutor occurred in 1953 when his solicitors notified the Land Commission that Costello objected to the acquisition since the lands were the means of livelihood for himself and family and that he was working in County Dublin to earn money so as to return and work the lands and build a house. Despite the *ad misericordiam* or personal hardship nature of this objection, which was not a legal objection under the statute, the Lay Commissioners heard the appeal and disallowed the objection. Costello did not appeal this decision and the land acquisition, but did appeal the price to be paid for the land to the Appeal Tribunal, which raised the price and the sum was deposited to his credit. Costello made no effort to have the land bonds paid to him, and when the Land Commission started work on the land in 1957, Costello entered on the land and stopped the workmen from working. On the Commission's obtaining an interlocutory injunction against Costello, he claimed certiorari to quash that order on the ground that the order of acquisition of the land had been made without jurisdiction since the Lay Commissioners who heard and decided against his objection had received and considered a report from Land Commission officials which was not disclosed to Costello before the hearing was conducted.

In the High Court, Teevan J. refused certiorari (as did the Supreme Court on appeal) first noting that the *Roscrea* case was undoubtedly the inspiration for prosecutor's claim. However, *Roscrea* did not apply, since in that earlier case a legal issue had been raised immediately to the Appeal Tribunal as to the right of the Land Commission to acquire lands by using information obtained from an inspector behind the objector's back. In this case, he saw no valid objection to the completion of the Lay Commissioners' acquisition in the manner they had followed, particularly in view of prosecutor's long failure to respond to multiple legal opportunities to object to the land acquisition except for his one objection based on hardship, and his appeal on the price fixed, which could be implied as accepting the acquisition. On the appeal to the Supreme Court, Maguire C. J. stressed that the Lay Commissioners' hearing of objections was solely on grounds of personal hardship, not on legal grounds as in *Roscrea*, and the appeal now before the Supreme Court was in the nature of an *ad misericordiam* appeal. This type of ground is not open under the Land Acts, nor must Land Commissioners consider such grounds. However desirable it might be that reports available to Lay Commissioners should be made available to objectors, there is no obligation to do so; the discretion of the Lay Commissioners is unfettered and the rule of *Roscrea* does not apply.

The concept of official notice appearing in the earlier cases of *Roscrea* and *Costello* was further confirmed in the later case of *Killiney and Ballybrack Development Association Ltd v. Minister for Local*

Government and Templefinn Estates Ltd unreported, High Court, per
Finlay, J., 1 March 1974. Under the Local Government (Planning
and Development) Act 1963, defendants Templefinn Estates Ltd
had applied to Dun Laoghaire Corporation as planning authority
for permission for a housing development. Their application was
opposed by plaintiff, but permission was granted in the first
instance, subject to conditions. The plaintiff appealed to the Minister, an oral hearing was held before a departmental inspector
appointed by the Minister to which plaintiff and defendants called
witnesses. A written report by the inspector was submitted to the
Minister, who decided the appeal in favour of Templefinn Estates.

On appeal to the High Court, the inspector's report and Minister's decision were presented together with plaintiff's argument
that the Minister was performing a function of a judicial nature
and under natural justice may act only on evidence made known
to the other party and may make findings or inferences only from
facts supported by evidence. If the inspector's report contained
evidence not made known to the plaintiff, the Court must presume
the Minister acted upon that evidence unless proved otherwise,
since the Minister does not have to give reasons for his decision
under the Planning and Development Act. Plaintiff also alleged
that there was no evidence in the published report of the hearing
to support the claim by defendants that the proposed development
would not cause pollution on the seashore at Killiney, in view of
the demands made upon, and the inadequacy of, the existing
sewerage facilities.

Finlay J. in the High Court noted that there was conflict between
the evidence given at the hearing by defendant's architect that he
had visited the site about twenty times, had often walked the
seashore and on no occasion had seen any evidence of pollution nor
was he conscious of any undue smell, and the evidence of an expert
witness for the plaintiff who stated there were signs of raw sewage
and rubbish along the beach. In addition to this testimony, the
inspector's report stated that he had discussed the overloading of
the sewage works with the Department's sanitary inspectors and
had made inquiries of local authorities and there was no doubt that
the works were coping with a vastly greater load than originally
planned. His report also stated that he had walked along the river
bank and foreshore, and had seen no evidence of raw excreta, but

that both the stream and river did indicate substantial discolouration. In regard to this report defendants had argued that section 83 (5) of the Act gives the person holding the hearing power to visit the site, thus endorsing the right to report the result of that visit to the Minister. Moreover, the right of inspection under the Act may be assumed since it enables the inspector to understand evidence given before him and thus accurately report on those matters to the Minister.

In the opinion of Finlay J., the discussion of the inspector with sanitary inspectors and local authorities was not a fact upon which the Minister might act or which might influence his opinion. However, the inspector's statement of visual observation with regard to pollution and sewage unquestionably was a statement of fact resulting from observation, and there is no indication that this visit or the observations were disclosed at the public hearing. The Minister in considering the report of the visual inspection would thus be acting on what is in fact evidence not disclosed at the oral hearing which the other party has had no opportunity to refute or challenge. Since the inspector's report was not strongly worded, and there was a direct conflict of evidence between witnesses in the hearing as to what was found or seen, a factual account by the inspector was capable of influencing the Minister. The inclusion of the account by the inspector in his report on the result of his visual inspection of the area was fatal to the validity of the decision of the Minister who was carrying out a function of a judicial nature, and the application to quash the Minister's order was granted.

Findings, Reasons for Decisions: Roles of Hearing Officers and Agency Heads
Certain components of adjudicative hearings discussed above, notably the independence of hearing officers, absence of bias, right of parties to discovery of documents, weight accorded to forms of evidence, and official notice of data not in the record, also reflect problems arising from the nature of institutional decision-making. Judicial decisions concerning these components infer the need for findings and reasons and to some extent express judicial views as to what should be the roles of inspecting or hearing officers, agency staff and agency heads in making adjudicatory determinations. However, it is in the judicial resolution of issues concerning the making of findings of fact and law, and providing reasons for

H

administrative determinations that legal questions about the roles of hearing officers, internal agency staff and agency heads or tribunals become a major focal point in judicial decisions.

With regard to the requirement of findings and reasons, the courts expect documents relating to an administrative determination, such as transcripts or notes or oral testimony and documentary evidence submitted at a hearing, to be accompanied by a report of basic findings of fact. In essence, such findings should be a distillation (not a mere summary) of the oral and documentary evidence reflecting what the inspecting or hearing officer considers to constitute the key facts of the case. Thus, conflicting lengthy testimony by several witnesses pertaining to an incident or situation may be subsumed in a few sentences stating what the hearing officer considers to be the established fact as to what happened or existed. In addition, an ultimate finding in law is expected, in which the hearing officer or tribunal states a conclusion that, given the findings of fact, the pertinent statutory provision or administrative regulation has been violated. Finally, as with a judicial opinion, the reasons or rationale for the decision should be provided. Giving reasons becomes increasingly important in relation to the degree of complexity of issues, possible inferences or differing interpretations of the statute's application to the situation.

The practical grounds for requiring administrative findings and reasons have been delineated effectively by the well known American administrative law authority, Kenneth Culp Davis. They may be summarised and supplemented for application in Ireland as follows:

1. Without administrative findings and reasons, the judiciary would be overburdened by having to review detailed transcripts or notes and accompanying documentary evidence of hearings in appeals from large numbers of administrative determinations, in order to evaluate the evidence and decide whether the agency decision correctly applies the law.

2. Findings and reasons help prevent the judiciary from usurping the functions of administrative agencies in determining facts. If findings are not made or are unsatisfactory, the court usually will remit the case to the agency to make findings which meet judicial expectations rather than substituting judgment

for that of the agency through review of the detailed evidence appearing in the hearing record.

Ultimate findings in law and reasons for the decision given by the administrative agency further inform the court so as to reduce judicial remission of cases or substitution of judgment for that of the agency.

3. Findings and reasons help guard against arbitrary or careless determinations by forcing administrators into the mental discipline of reducing a hearing record of testimony, documentary evidence, and inspection results to succinct written form in which the ultimate finding in law must flow from basic findings of fact based on the hearing record. Initial impressions or conclusions reached during the oral hearing may be modified through this more disciplined review.

4. Findings and reasons help to keep agencies within their statutory jurisdiction and guard against abuses of official notice, by reducing potential for using facts beyond the scope of the agency's statutory authority or evidential material not part of the hearing record.

5. Findings and reasons forwarded with the record of the hearing to the minister or administrative tribunal making the final decision are valuable to both the minister and the parties. If parties involved are provided with the administrative findings and reasons prior to their submission to the minister, parties may forward observations replying to those findings to the minister or tribunal who thus will have the advantage of knowing the views of both the hearing officer and of the parties to the case. If findings are not made available to parties at this stage the minister at least will have findings of an experienced administrator to help overcome his lack of time (and expertise) for detailed review of a lengthy hearing record and documents, and his not being able to observe the demeanour of witnesses who testified or see the potential housing site or development area.

6. Findings also assist parties in making appeals to the courts. Alternatively they may persuade parties not to appeal if the findings convey fairness and rationality in the decision, rather

than the suspicion which may be generated by an absence of findings and a rationale.[3]

The judicial insistence that administrative determinations should be accompanied by findings of fact based on a record of the proceedings is illustrated by *In re Dunleavy's Estate* 1952 IR 86. Plaintiff Dunleavy owned lands certified by the Lay Commissioners of the Land Commission to be required for resale to persons under the Land Act 1923, section 31 as amended by section 33, Land Act 1933. Following publication of the provisional list of lands and the hearing of appellant's objection to that list, the Lay Commissioners gave their decision, stating:

We have given further consideration to the evidence and submission but feel . . . we would not be justified in allowing his [the owner's] objection in view of the considerable congestion existing in the vicinity for the relief of which they are required. . . . We are . . . satisfied that the objector was cognisant of the congestion . . . and of the need for its relief before he purchased these lands. (page 86)

During plaintiff's appeal to the Appeal Tribunal, which included several adjournments at the request of plaintiff's counsel, an application was made for an order directing the Lay Commissioners to produce to the Appeal Tribunal and plaintiff's solicitors their original notes of the evidence taken during the hearing on his objection. The Appeal Tribunal, per Maguire J., noted that plaintiff's counsel at the earlier stages of the hearing had expounded grounds for objection at length, and elected to go into evidence. He thus found it difficult to understand why at a later stage application was being made to limit the hearing to what might appear upon notes taken by the Lay Commissioners. Such a request had never been made before to the Appeal Tribunal and there was no rule, practice or precedent requiring Lay Commissioners to take proper notes. Inquiry to the Lay Commissioners revealed that no official notes were taken; whatever notes made are only for the Commissioners' assistance. Consequently, the question of furnishing notes or a transcript of them could not arise. Moreover, if the Appeal Tribunal's hands were tied to such notes as may appear to exist, it would be hard to see how justice could be done in a case of importance, therefore the application was refused.

However, on appeal to the Supreme Court, a judgment was given which supported plaintiff's argument. Maguire C. J. for the Court held that the issue was whether an appeal on a question of law from the Lay Commissioners should be determined through a rehearing, or should be determined on a report from the Lay Commissioners of the proceedings which took place before them. In response to this issue, the Court stated:

> This Court is of opinion that the appeal should be decided on a report from the Lay Commissioners of the proceedings before them. This should include a note of the evidence and of their findings of fact.
>
> It is the duty of the Lay Commissioners, as it is of any tribunal from which an appeal lies and has been taken, to supply, so far as they can, a note of the proceedings before them and of their findings of fact. If in a particular case no note can be supplied it will be for the Appeal Tribunal to decide how it will inform itself as to what took place. (page 90)

Though succinct, this decision indicates that judicial doctrine expects administrative tribunals from which appeals may be taken to make findings of fact based on some form of record of the hearing, and that the appeal should be decided on the record and findings. From the dicta, it might be inferred that a higher appellate body in the absence of such record and findings might opt to remit the case to the tribunal with instructions to make findings or engage in a *de novo* proceeding and decision which would supersede the original decision of the administrative tribunal.

The judicial expectation that an administrative determination should be accompanied by reasons or a rationale for the decision is demonstrated by the case of *The State (McGeough) v. Louth County Council* 107 ILTR 13, discussed above in conjunction with the issue of bias. It will be recalled that the strong policy predilection of the County Manager precluded his consideration of the merits of Miss McGeough's application in accordance with standards prescribed by statute. It also developed that the County Manager adamantly declined to give any reasons or state any policy as grounds for his refusal to give Miss McGeough permission to sell her cottage. In response to written requests from plaintiff's solicitor for reasons for withholding consent, the Manager stated 'I do not give reasons for withholding consent in cases of this nature', and the Secretary, on behalf of the Manager, wrote that 'I am to state that the County Manager is not prepared to give reasons for withholding consent in the case of any application for transfer of a vested cottage'. Further requests for reasons were refused and a satisfactory response ultimately was achieved only through a court mandamus. Kingsmill Moore J. for the Supreme Court, in a cogent statement on the importance of providing reasons for a decision, noted that a local authority might adopt a policy for the better implementation of a statute, and that the County Manager may have had in mind the merits of that policy but that:

> If so, he has refused to divulge the policy or principle which he has in mind to the applicant, and so has deprived her of the opportunity to which I think she is entitled, of conforming with or contesting such a principle or policy. Nor has he thought it right to enlighten the Court except in so far as he admitted under cross-examination that he personally did not favour sales ... and that over a period of some six years he had never consented to a sale ... in the absence of any further elucidation or explanation on his part, he had unfortunately left himself open to the suggestion that his attitude towards applications for consent to sell has been arbitrary, capricious and obstructive. Such a suggestion may be unfair and entirely erroneous. The Manager may have acted on grounds ... which may have been reasonable. ... It is ... regrettable that he has made no effort to meet this suggestion. He could clearly have done so by stating his reasons for the information of the Court, which could then have given him guidance as to their legality. Instead ... he contends that the Act gives to him the unfettered right to refuse or give consent ... according to his personal views which are to remain unexplained and unrevealed. (page 25)

The requirement that findings be made and reasons given, and the judicial concepts of what the respective roles of hearing officers, departmental staff and ministers should be in meeting that requirement have been developed further in certain key cases subsequent to the *Dunleavy* and *McGeough* decisions. The major cases include *Murphy v. Dublin Corporation and Minister for Local Government* 1972 IR 215 and *Murphy v. Dublin Corporation* (No. 2) 1976 IR 143; *Geraghty v. Dublin Corporation* 1976 IR 153; and *Russell v. Minister for Local Government* 1976 IR 195.

As indicated in the previous discussion of the first *Murphy* case, the Court dealt only with the issue of right to discovery of documents against the claim of executive privilege as being the sole questions at that point, and did not rule on Murphy's claim that the Dublin Corporation's compulsory purchase order for acquisition of his land was *ultra vires* the 1965 Housing Act. (See pages 64-6.) Incidental to the Court's decision that the Minister for Local Government could not deny access to the report of the Department of Local Government inspector conducting the public hearing on Murphy's objection, Walsh J. analysed the function of the inspector as related to that of the Minister, with relevance to findings and what use may be made of them. His statement, though possibly obiter dicta, has been quoted or referred to in subsequent cases:

In this context, it is necessary to examine the precise function of the inspector in this role. By statute the Minister is the one who has to decide the matter–not the inspector. In doing so, the Minister must act judicially and within the bounds of constitutional justice. . . . It is clear . . . that in so far as the conduct of the inquiry is concerned, he (the inspector) is acting as recorder for the Minister. He may regulate the procedure within permissible limits of the inquiry over which he presides . . . the inspector's function is to convey to the Minister, if not a verbatim account . . . at least a fair and accurate account of what transpired and one which gives the Minister the evidence and the submissions of each party because it is upon this material that the Minister must make his decision and on no other. The inspector has no advisory function nor has he any function to arrive at a preliminary judgement which may or may not be confirmed or varied by the Minister . . . If the Minister is influenced in his decision by the opinions of the inspector or the conclusions of the inspector, the Minister's decision will be open to review. It may be quashed and set aside if shown to be based on materials other than those disclosed at the public hearing. (pages 238-9)

The significance of the availability of the inspector's reports to the plaintiff, in terms of providing one of the bases upon which he made his appeal to the courts in *Murphy* (No. 2) is best demonstrated by an analysis of the content of the reports submitted by the inspector to the Minister for Local Government. The reports are particularly revealing since they show that the inspector viewed his role as making findings of fact amounting to a distillation and evaluation of the relative worth of the testimony and documentary evidence offered and of his own direct inspection and observation. They also included his recommendations which amount to findings in law. In this regard they go beyond merely 'acting as recorder for the Minister'. The first 'interim' report of the planning officer of the Department of Local Government acting as inspecting officer dealt with the suitability of the area for housing development in view of its proximity to Dublin airport, and was resolved in favour of the land's suitability based on appraisal by departmental staff and observations from the Department of Transport and Power. It was the content of the second and third reports of the inspecting officer dealing with critical evidential conflicts arising out of the enquiry and their submission to and consideration by the Minister, which led to further discussion in the second *Murphy* case of findings and the roles of inspector and minister.

In the second report, the inspecting officer focussed on objections of holders of small areas of land required for development by Dublin Corporation rather than those of Murphy and one other large land holder, so as to deal comprehensively with the broader issues raised by the proposal for extended Corporation housing development in the area. In addition to attaching a 200-plus page transcript of evidence to his report, the inspecting officer also gave his evaluation of the land as first-class farm land suitable for virtually any use based on his personal inspection of lands related to the objections made against the purchase order. In his detailed evaluation of the need for acquisition grounded on evidence submitted and his inspection, the officer commented on balancing that need versus the hardship of persons involved. He expressed his hope that a generous settlement would be made or that persons be allowed to rebuild on what was left of their property. Statements from his report provide insight into the inspector's evaluation of evidence and interpretation of his role:

These occupied dwellings all front on the northern portion of Jamestown Road. The reason put forward for their acquisition is that this road needs to be widened. The sworn evidence given by two of the Housing Authority's officers . . . failed entirely to substantiate this need. These two gentlemen are both able and honourable. Through no fault of theirs they had not been required to make a study of this particular portion of the . . . project.

A public Enquiry of this type has two purposes. One is to enable the Local Authority to prove to the Minister that the acquisitions are essential. The other is to provide the objectors with an opportunity to indicate why they object. To my mind, I must advise the Minister on the weight of the sworn evidence given. It would not accord with natural justice were I to canvass road experts for their views which had not been available to the objectors to examine and if possible rebut. I must advise that, subject to three partial exceptions, these properties . . . should be excluded from the Order. (Report No. 2 of Inspecting Officer, 5/7/68 at 2-3)

The third and final report of the inspector made conclusions and recommendations based upon findings from the evidence on the following major aspects which may be summarised as follows:

1. The inspector would ignore the defendant Corporation's layout plans since they were produced in a hurried one week's effort under a previous limitation on noise restrictions since removed, for a project which would cost over seven million pounds. He also was ignoring layout plans produced by plaintiff Murphy, since they were a Radburn type less than ideal for Irish conditions. Since neither layout had the plaintiff's or the authority's approval, the final design undoubtedly would differ considerably from those submitted.

2. The inspector found that of the two principal objectors, Murphy had much more standing. In addition, there was possible ambivalence in the situation where the City Manager, City Planning Officer, and City Engineer were also the County Manager, Planning Officer and Engineer, since as county

officials they potentially could refuse permission for development, while as city officials they could argue strongly for it.

3. The inspector found that the Corporation wanted the land to build houses to fulfil their responsibilities as housing authority, and sought to prove that Murphy and the other objectors would cater for a restricted class of persons, while the Corporation would cater for a wider spectrum including citizens unable to secure houses from their own resources. Objectors are equally anxious to build, and claim that their plans provide for types of houses suitable for meeting existing housing needs and, as owners of the land and reputable builders with ample resources, they could erect houses more speedily and at lower cost than the Corporation.

4. The inspector also found that (a) the Corporation's claim of catering for the greater variety of citizens was unsupported by evidence (citing specific pages of testimony in the transcript); (b) objectors would be more effective than the Corporation in speed and efficiency (again citing testimony in the transcript); (c) consequently the compulsory acquisition of objectors' lands by the Corporation would be of no help in speeding up provision of new houses and might even hinder it. The two firms are competent builders impartial as to whom they build for, and in a position to make a contribution towards attaining the target figures set by the Corporation.

Based upon the above findings, the inspector concluded:

It is my recommendation therefore that the Minister be not advised to confirm this Order in respect of these lands for the reason that the Corporation failed to prove that their acquisition was essential to, or even the most expedient way of securing, the speedy erection of new houses.

It may be that greater benefit would accrue if the Corporation and these objectors, instead of wrangling, cooperated in devising the most suitable type of residential development for these lands and for speeding provision of the much needed houses. (Report of Inspecting Officer, Lands of Messrs Wates and Murphy, 30 August 1968 at 8-9)

Despite these findings and recommendations of the inspector, the compulsory purchase order was confirmed by the Minister for Local Government. In *Murphy* (No. 2), the High Court, while dismissing Murphy's appeal challenging the Minister's order, made a significant comment concerning the dicta of Walsh J. in the first *Murphy* case, which had inveighed against an inspecting officer making conclusions and recommendations and had warned that if they influenced a minister certiorari would lie against a minister's decision. In respect of these dicta, the President of the High Court stated:

> . . . 'in spite of what is said in the judgment of Mr Justice Walsh in the Supreme Court, I do not think for one moment that he intended to indicate that the Minister should not receive in the report of an inspector holding an inquiry of this kind views of the inspector derived from the consideration of the evidence–views which the Minister might or might not accept. I rather think that what was intended was that an inspector, in making a report to the Minister, should not include in his report matters extraneous to the public inquiry, information obtained from some other source, or views of his own not the subject of any discussion at the inquiry. . .' (1976 IR 162)

Following the High Court decision in *Murphy* (No. 2), Murphy appealed to the Supreme Court, on the grounds that the compulsory purchase order was *ultra vires* the 1966 Housing Act since Dublin Corporation as housing authority had not entered into an agreement with Dublin County Council for building on the Council's land before making the order, although the County Council were themselves housing authority for the area. Moreover, the Minister was not only wrong in ignoring the requirements for such arrangements, but he was also wrong in that he disregarded the recommendations of the inspector holding the inquiry as well as the evidence at the inquiry.

The Supreme Court, per Henchy J., rejected the issues concerning the respective jurisdictions of the County and City of Dublin based upon its interpretation of the Housing Act 1966 and the Local Government (Planning and Development) Act 1963. Henchy J. then turned to the procedural questions regarding the respective roles of the Minister and the inspecting officer and the claim that the Minister had acted *ultra vires* by confirming the purchase order in the face of evidence at the public inquiry that plaintiff could better put into operation the purposes of the Housing Act.

Henchy J. characterised the inspector's role as that of being responsible for making a fair and accurate report of what took place at the inquiry. The Minister's function was to reach his own decision, unfettered by any conclusions of the inspector, but on the same evidence as that before the inspector. The claim that the Minister had rejected the inspector's findings without and contrary to evidence given at the inquiry was based on the false assumption that the Minister had rejected the finding, whereas the fact that the Minister had confirmed the compulsory purchase order did not mean he rejected the finding. Even if he were in full agreement with the finding, the Minister was still entitled to confirm the order, since it was sufficient that he be satisfied that the land was being acquired compulsorily for the purpose of the Act, and that there had been compliance with the provisions of the third schedule of the Act. Neither of these statutory requirements demanded that he be satisfied that the land was needed for, or would result in, the speedy erection of new houses. Although in certain cases these requirements were intended to eliminate overcrowding, the Act also enabled housing authorities to take a longer view so that housing authorities could acquire land compulsorily if the Minister was of the opinion that there is a reasonable expectation the land will be required in the future to achieve objectives under the Act in preparing a building programme. It was also erroneous to consider the public inquiry as a contest between plaintiff and the Corporation as to which would be permitted to build on plaintiff's land, with the winner the one who could do it more rapidly. Once there was evidence that the land was required by the Corporation immediately for the purposes of the Act, or alternatively, there was a reasonable expectation that the Corporation would require the land in the future to attain objectives of the Act, the Minister was entitled to confirm the compulsory purchase order. The evidence did not demonstrate an immediate need for acquisition of the land for housing, but there was unquestionable evidence that the Corporation would use it in the future to provide housing to meet needs arising from obsolescence of dwellings or prospective increase in the population.

The importance of findings of fact and law, and the reasons for the conclusions reached by the administrator making the final decision, to the parties involved in the situation and the courts becomes obvious from the *Murphy* cases and the inspecting officer's report. It is also obvious that there are various views as to the roles of the inspector as hearing officer and the Minister as ultimate decision-maker. These appear in the contrast between the obiter dicta of Walsh J. in *Murphy* (No. 1), the statements of the inspecting officer in his report and claims made by Murphy's counsel. However, the President of the High Court in *Murphy* (No. 2) reduced the potential conflict of these views in his interpretation of the dicta of Walsh J. The Supreme Court in *Murphy* (No. 2) clarified and further diminished the contrast of views by emphasising the discretion of the Minister to make a decision contrary to the inspector's recommendations as long as there was evidence to support the conclusion that one of the multiple objectives of the pertinent statute would be met.

The judicial concepts expressed in the two *Murphy* cases provided the foundation for the case of *Geraghty v. Minister for Local Government* 1976 IR 153 for an expanded judicial analysis and exposition of the interrelated roles of the departmental inspector, technical planning staff and minister in making findings and a reasoned conclusion. As it was mentioned in the previous discussion of the concept of the right to discovery of documents, the *Geraghty* case also involved a discovery of documents issue, as did *Murphy* (No. 1). Moreover the *Geraghty* case contained an official notice issue, demonstrating again the close connection or overlap of issues which arises in the context of institutional decision-making. In this case, the application of the plaintiff, Mrs Geraghty, for outline planning permission for a housing development on her lands from the Dublin County Council as planning authority was refused. The stated reasons for refusal were: (1) development of the property for housing purposes would generate extensive additional traffic hazard; (2) no water or sewerage facilities were available to serve the project; (3) the development was premature since it was not clear when the additional water and sewerage facilities that would be required might become available; (4) the project would interfere with the proper development and operation of the airport, according to the Department of Transport and Power and (5) occupants of the houses would suffer loss of amenity due to aircraft noise.

On appeal from this refusal to the Minister for Local Government, an oral hearing was held by a departmental inspector at which the plaintiff, the planning authority and the Department of Transport and Power were represented and called witnesses. The inspector's report was forwarded to the Department where various additional materials were appended by the staff of the department, and then to the parliamentary secretary to the Minister for Local Government to whom the duty of determining such appeals was delegated by SI 216 of 1964, made under the Ministers and Secretaries (Amendment) Act 1939. The parliamentary secretary after review affirmed the local planning authority refusal of the outline planning permission for essentially the same reasons.

Plaintiff appealed from this decision to the High Court on the grounds that it was based on and influenced by materials, objections and advice which could not properly be considered by the parliamentary secretary acting in a judicial capacity, and that for these and other reasons the decision was improperly made. The defendant agreed to produce as evidence all documents in his possession relating to plaintiff's appeal.

O'Higgins J. took official notice of the fact that four months before the oral hearing of plaintiff's appeal, the planning and development committee of Dublin County Council had passed a resolution for consideration and ultimate determination by the full Council that Mrs Geraghty's lands be zoned for residential purposes. However, at the time of the oral hearing on plaintiff's appeal the planning officer of the County Council had drawn up a draft plan also for consideration by the elected members of the Council for adoption, and in that plan it was proposed that Mrs Geraghty's land be zoned for agricultural purposes. One month after the oral hearing, the members of the County Council exercised their statutory powers to zone Mrs Geraghty's land for residential purposes. From the facts in the documents before him, O'Higgins J. felt that the decision by the elected members of the County Council was made against the advice of the planning officer of the County Council, which aroused opposition and indignation among certain planning advisers of the Minister. This meant that the determination of Mrs Geraghty's appeal was regarded virtually as a test case for the application of what the planning section of the Department of Local Government regarded as proper planning principles.

The internal departmental processing of the inspector's report following the oral hearing was traced in detail in the High Court and later in the Supreme Court decisions. The report of the inspector dealt with the submissions and evidence of the oral hearing, his inspection of the lands, his opinions and comments on the evidence and his recommendations for refusal of permission and grounds for such refusal. The report had on its margin notes by a senior officer of the planning section which had resisted efforts to erase them. The report did not go directly to the parliamentary secretary but was treated in the manner of a departmental file. It accumulated en route to the parliamentary secretary recommendations from the officer in charge of the planning section and a long memorandum of an interpretative nature from a senior planning section officer, which had been sent to the inspector with a suggestion that the report be submitted to yet another planning section officer who had conducted an oral hearing in another appeal concerning lands owned by Mrs Geraghty's husband. This latter planning officer's comments included a recommendation that Mrs Geraghty's application be dealt with by the Minister through use of his powers under section 22 (2) and (3) of the 1963 Act and the officer also attached a copy of a report he had made on an appeal in an oral hearing he had held concerning lands of Mrs Geraghty's husband. That report contained a criticism of the action of the elected county council representatives for passing the resolution zoning Mrs Geraghty's lands as residential. An inquiry from the parliamentary secretary to the inspector concerning access to the site, which also indicated an intention to grant the permission, received the response that there was no way of disposing of domestic drainage from the site and at the nearest point there was only a six-inch drain (a fact not found in the original report), and that another planning section member also advised that even if the developer could get access to the Forrest Hill Road, the sewerage and airport problems would still remain.

O'Higgins J. stated that as a judge his duty was to see that the decision made by the parliamentary secretary was based exclusively on the report of the person he appointed to conduct the oral hearing and on the evidence and submission there given and made, in accordance with constitutional justice, article 9 of the Planning Appeal Regulations and the precedents of the *Murphy* cases, the *Killiney* and the *Templefinn* cases. If it appeared that the decision may have emanated from advice and materials not proper to be considered and which could not have been countered by the appealing party, the decision could not stand no matter how well based the reasons might be upon the evidence at the oral hearing. In his view the case illustrated the impracticality of processing through a Department of State the exercise of a judicial function conferred by statute on the head of that department, in that such function must be carried out by the holder of the office personally, and not with assistance or advice of persons not contemplated by the statute. Accordingly, he would grant the plaintiff the declaration she sought.

On appeal to the Supreme Court, it was held that the High Court judgment should be affirmed and that the oral hearing be treated as a nullity and a new oral hearing granted to Mrs Geraghty. Of particular interest are the similarities, with some variations, in the perspectives of Justices Gannon, Henchy and Walsh. Their opinions dealing with the nature of the roles of the inspecting officer, departmental staff and the parliamentary secretary as the deciding officer indicated what the judges thought those roles should be, thus providing judicial guidelines for the manner in which they should be carried out. The areas of agreement among the three judges, with indication of the more important variations or differences, can be summarised in general terms, although appreciation of the nuances requires reference to the original opinions.

As to the role of the inspector, all three agreed that the inspector must not simply record for the Minister what happened at the hearing. He must submit a report which fairly and accurately informs the Minister of the substance of the evidence and arguments for and against the issues raised by the parties through findings of fact and conclusions. Gannon and Henchy J.J. further indicated in some detail that in addition to findings of fact, the inspector should also present inferences which he would draw from the evidence and the reasons for those inferences, together with the attitudes of parties and the issues of law. Henchy J. also referred to inferences in the report drawn from any inspection or visit the inspector made of the site involved. Both Gannon and Henchy J.J. further held that the resolution of disputed questions of fact in the hearing should be made by the inspector who heard and observed the witnesses. Conflicts of fact of this nature should not be resolved by a person who learns of the evidence from a report, and whose conclusions might be contrary to those of the person seeing and hearing the witnesses. In this regard, Henchy J. would even make the findings of fact binding on the Minister, and generally would assign the most positive role to the inspector.

All three judges agreed that upon receipt of the inspector's report, the Minister's role is to consider the report and decide upon the appeal as though it had been made to him in the first instance. Walsh J. stated that the Minister is not bound by the findings of fact of the inspector, while as noted above, Gannon and Henchy J.J. in this regard would make an exception, particularly where a conflict of evidence is best resolved by the person who could observe the demeanour of witnesses. All three judges held that the inspector's inferences, conclusions or recommendations are in no way binding on the Minister. The Minister's own findings of fact, conclusions in law, reasons and decisions must be founded on the evidence before him, and as Walsh J. put it, he not only makes the decision but determines the constituent elements which go to make up the decision. Finally, the Minister must make his decision within the scope of statutory policy, notwithstanding other policy considerations.

The role and functions of the internal departmental staff, as related to the role of the Minister, were treated inferentially by Walsh J. in his discussion of what the Minister may properly consider, and specifically by Henchy and Gannon J.J. The latter two judges indicated that it may be necessary for the Minister to inform himself as a layman through seeking advice of experts within (and without) his Department. These experts may include a legal adviser, a planning adviser or other technical assistants. He may also seek assistance from the High Court on a point of law. All three judges agreed that expert advice and technical assistance should be obtained only with respect to matters within the scope of the report and of the oral hearing and must not involve factual matters extraneous to their subject matter which have the effect of adding to, reducing or affirming the factual proof of the oral hearing or report. In accordance with the concept of official notice, the judges stated that if the Minister finds it necessary to utilise new facts or probative material related to the appeal which was not made known at the time of the oral hearing, he must not consider such facts unless the oral hearing is reopened and such data are introduced into evidence with an opportunity to all parties to rebut or refute such evidence.

Given the comprehensive opinions of the Supreme Court in

Murphy (No. 2) and *Geraghty* concerning the functions and roles of
the inspector and Minister in making findings of fact and law, and
giving reasons for an administrative determination, the treatment
of these aspects by the High Court in the subsequent case of *Russell
and Others v. Minister for Local Government* 1976 IR 185 is somewhat
puzzling in certain aspects. Plaintiff Russell objected to an order of
Cobh Urban District Council to acquire a portion of her lands
compulsorily for purposes of the Housing Act 1966. An inspector
held a public inquiry and transmitted a full transcript of the
evidence together with his report to the Minister, who made an order
confirming the compulsory purchase order.

Plaintiff Russell then sought an order in the High Court to quash
the compulsory purchase order. A major part of the ground for the
order was criticism of the inspector's report and his conduct of the
inquiry, and a second part was the claim that the Council had not
prepared a building programme as required by the Housing Act.
In response to the plaintiff's criticism of the inspector's report,
Parke J. at the outset of his judgment stated that it was clear from
the inspector's report that he had 'grossly exceeded his functions'
and it was 'lamentable' that despite a number of judgments (citing
the *Murphy* cases, *Killiney* and *Geraghty*), 'the Inspector had done
just what the courts had directed Inspectors not to do'.

Following these statements, Parke J. analysed what the inspector
had done. However, in each instance he indicated that although
the inspector's actions were not correct, or could be criticised, he
did not consider the actions sufficient ground to merit reversal of
the Minister's decision, which raises a question as to why the
inspector was so severely criticised at the outset for having 'grossly
exceeded his functions'. As the opinion of Parke J. indicates, and
the inspector's report accompanying the transcript of the hearing
reveals, a summary was provided in the report of the points made
and evidence given. The inspector did comment briefly on certain
aspects of the evidence, and in one instance made a finding constituting a conclusion by saying that the evidence of the town clerk
showed that the existence of the housing need had been fully
demonstrated. He summarised the evidence of another plaintiff and
made a finding that the plaintiff's objection had no substance. The
inspector also visited the lands and based on that visit found that
they were suitable for building purposes. The report ended with a
brief conclusion or finding in law that the inspector felt the land

was suitable for the purpose of the Act, and one sentence recommending that the order be confirmed.

In commenting upon these aspects, Parke J. held that in accordance with the previous cases he had cited, the inspector's duty is to record and report and not to advise or recommend. He exceeded his functions by giving his own views and a recommendation and by commenting on the lack of substance of the third plaintiff's objection. However, since those same previous cases had also held that the decision to annul or confirm an order is for the Minister alone, he may, and in fact, must disregard any opinions which the inspector may express. Therefore, given the nature of the inspector's comments in this situation, these discrepancies were not fatal to the validity of the hearing. Parke J. also distinguished the inspector's visit to the lands from that involved in the *Killiney* case, since in that case the inspection was on a matter directly in issue between the parties, while in this case both parties had made it clear they regarded the lands as suitable for building purposes, so the inspection merely confirmed for the inspector what both parties were contending. Parke J. did not accept the criticism of the plaintiff as to the inspector's conduct of the hearing, but did uphold the claim on the substantive ground that the Council had not prepared a building programme as required by the Housing Act, and thus could not proceed to acquire land compulsorily for housing purposes.

On appeal to the Supreme Court, the treatment by Walsh J. of the procedural issue was limited to noting that counsel for the Minister had expressed concern over the High Court's criticism of the inspector's failure to observe and follow judicial opinions in the *Murphy*, *Killiney* and *Geraghty* cases. Walsh J. stated he accepted counsel's explanation that at the time of making the inquiry and report the inspector was not fully aware of the effect of those prior individual decisions, and that he was satisfied that the learned trial judge would not have expressed those criticisms had he known of this lack of knowledge. He also concurred with the ruling of the High Court that the criticisms of the inspector's actions did not afford a ground in law for quashing the order of the Minister since the Minister had a complete transcript of the evidence given at the inquiry and submissions made by parties. Furthermore:

The amount of material written by the inspector himself in the report is only three and a half pages, virtually all of which is a summary of the evidence. In so far as his report consists of comments by himself they are but brief comments. His recommendation consists of one line only. It is quite clear that the Minister had more than ample evidence on which to base the decision he made and there is nothing whatsoever to indicate he arrived at the decision because the inspector so recommended. (page 190)

In addition to this statement which implicitly moderated the High Court's criticism of the inspector's role in making findings with evaluative comments and a recommendation to the Minister, Walsh J. reversed the High Court decision on the substantive issue of the case. He devoted most of his opinion to his interpretation of the Housing Act, and why the failure of Cobh County Council to prepare a building programme did not preclude their acquisition of land for housing purposes.

A possible explanation of the High Court's criticism of the inspector's actions and report in this case is an adherence to the *obiter dicta* of Walsh J. in *Murphy* (No. 1), which posited a more limited role for inspectors in making findings, and inveighed against a Minister's being influenced by an Inspector's opinions or conclusions. It does not reflect the more expanded role of inspectors as envisaged by Gannon, Henchy and Walsh J.J., in the later *Geraghty* case, especially in regard to the inspector's drawing inferences from oral evidence and inspection of the site, commenting on the attitudes of parties, and making recommendations. It is in accord, of course, as to the ultimate independence of the Minister in making his own findings and conclusions.

From the earlier *Dunleavy* and *McGeough*, and more recent *Murphy* Nos. 1 and 2, *Geraghty* and *Russell* decisions, it is clear that the courts in Ireland insist upon adherence to statutory provisions for findings and reasons, or in the absence of statutory provisions, will require findings and reasons as a necessary part of fair procedure or due process in adjudicatory determinations. These decisions reveal an increasing appreciation of the realities and complexities of administrative institutional decision-making by the inspector or hearing officer, departmental staff and minister in relation to meeting procedural rights under natural and constitutional justice. They also show an understanding of the practical reasons (summarised above) for requiring findings and reasons.

The issues raised in these cases as to the respective roles of inspector, departmental staff and minister have been of concern to the legislature and the government as well as to the courts. Beginning in 1967 initiatives were taken by members of the Dáil and the Minister for Local Government (now Environment) to introduce bills to establish a planning appeals board to decide appeals against planning authority decisions. Finally, the Local Government (Planning and Development) Act 1976 became law, amending the Local Government (Planning and Development) Act 1963, so as to transfer appeals which had been taken to the Minister for the Environment to an independent corporate body, An Bord Pleanála (the Planning Board). Further amendments to the 1963 Act have been made in the Local Government (Planning and Development) Acts 1982 and 1983.[4]

The Planning Board now consists of a chairman and five other members (section 3, Local Government (Planning and Development) Act 1983). The chairman is appointed by the government from among nominees proposed by a special committee (specified in section 5) and five Board members, four of whom are appointed by the Minister for Environment from nominations made by organisations designated by the Minister and one from established civil servants in the Minister's department (section 7).

The Planning Board hears appeals brought by applicants for planning permission or by third parties under the 1963 Act as amended by sections 5 and 6 of the 1982 Act (relating to applications for permission which have been abandoned). In the performance of its functions, the Planning Board, under section 5, 1976 Act, is to keep itself informed of the policies and objectives of the Minister, planning authorities and any other public authorities with functions related to planning and development. The Board is provided with the services of clerical, executive, administrative and professional staff by the Minister for the Environment.[5] In view of the judgments made in the *Murphy* and *Geraghty* cases, it is of particular interest that inspectors of the Board, when making an inspection or conducting an oral hearing on behalf of the Board, are required by section 23 of the 1976 Act to make a written report on the inspection or hearing, and include in the report a recommendation relating to the matter with which the inspection or hearing was required, and

the Planning Board must consider the report and any recommendation contained therein. Inspectors have the power to administer
and take evidence on oath from witnesses; may require planning
authority officers to give evidence; may visit and inspect any land
to which the reference or appeal relates; and may require any person
to attend, to give evidence or produce documents (sections 82 and
83 of the 1963 Act). Witnesses are given the same immunities and
privileges as if they were testifying in the High Court.

The Planning Board has absolute discretion with regard to holding an oral hearing of any reference or appeal, under section 15,
1983 Act, which also provides that regulations may be made under
which the Board must hold oral hearings on references of a class
specified in the regulations. Each planning appeal is considered *de
novo* under section 26(5)(b) of the 1963 Act, and additional information may be requested by the Board from the planning authority
and appellant. The Board may take into account aspects other than
those placed before it by the interested parties (section 17 of the
1976 Act). Since the appeal is treated as if it were an original
application to the Board, the Board may refuse the appeal, or
uphold the appeal, with or without conditions and, under section
14(8) of the 1976 Act, may grant a permission or approval even if
the proposed development contravenes the development plan or
any special amenity area order pertaining to the area of the planning
authority to whose decision the appeal relates. The Board makes
public its reasons for its decisions, whether negative or positive.
Insulation of the Board from certain forms of external influence is
provided for by section 14 of the 1983 Act:

> It shall not be lawful to communicate with the chairman or an
> ordinary member for the purpose of influencing improperly his
> consideration of an appeal, reference, or other matter with
> which the Board is concerned or a decision of the Board as
> regards any such matter.
>
> In addition, if either chairman or ordinary member believes a
> communication is in violation of this provision, it is his duty
> not to entertain the communication further.

It will be seen in the following chapters analysing the scope and
nature of regulatory powers delegated to agencies and issues raised
in their application that the right to a fair hearing and its procedural

components under natural and constitutional justice are critical factors in the resolution of those issues.

Notes to Chapter 5

1. See O'Sullivan and Shepherd, *A Sourcebook on Planning Law in Ireland*, 288-91, (1983) statement of facts, excerpt of judgment, *The State (Genport Limited) v. An Bord Pleanála* (1983) IRLM 12, upon which this case summary is based.
2. Schwartz and Wade, *Legal Control of Government* at 146 and 154-155 (1972)
3. See Davis, *Administrative Law, Cases, Text, Problems* 424-9 (1977) upon which summary with modifications is based.
4. See descriptive analysis pertaining to origins, powers, and operations of An Bord Pleanála in Zimmermann, 'An Bord Pleanála', *Administration* 329-344 (Vol. 28, No. 3, 1980); O'Sullivan, *Irish Planning and Acquisition Law* Chs. 2 and 4 (1978); and comprehensive analysis with extensive documentation of Acts, regulations and excerpts of judicial decision on planning law in O'Sullivan and Shepherd, *A Sourcebook on Planning Law in Ireland* (1984).
5. *Administration Yearbook* 119 (1984)

6 Rule-Making Power

The regulatory powers of rule-making, investigating, licensing and directing constitute the control processes through which the administration implements statutory objectives, subject to the requirements of natural and constitutional justice and the context of legislative, executive and judicial constitutional powers discussed in previous chapters. Each of the administrative regulatory powers has its distinguishing characteristics of function and process, together with legal concepts ascribed by the courts (e.g., concepts of privilege versus right in licensing and directing powers). These characteristics may modify the application of due process requirements under natural and constitutional justice when conflict between private parties and governmental agencies arises out of the exercise of regulatory powers, with their attendant problems of maintaining a balance between administrative effectiveness and individual rights. Such factors are of importance in determining which of the regulatory powers are most appropriate for securing compliance with statutory purposes from individuals or organisations.

Although the characteristics of, and the statutory and judicial restraints on, regulatory powers must be considered individually and in a logical sequence for purposes of conceptual and operational understanding, this does not mean that they are mutually exclusive or that this is the order in which they occur in the administrative process. There may be occasionally an intermingling of such powers or a blurring of distinctions between them in statutes, in their application by administrative agencies and in judicial decisions.

Since it is not feasible (or meaningful) to delineate the instances in all of the Acts of the Oireachtas in which there is delegation of regulatory powers, certain statutes will be referred to as a representative sample. They illustrate the range and extent of regulatory powers delegated, diversity of policy issues and interests affected, degrees of statutory sophistication in specifying procedures, and variations in time of enactment. The court decisions which will be discussed will also bring into play still other statutes.

The Acts referred to in this and ensuing chapters include the Censorship of Publications Acts of 1929, 1946 and 1967 which may

218

affect freedom of expression and consumer choice as to what may be read. The Restrictive Practices Act 1972, the Unfair Dismissals Act 1977 and the Safety in Industry Act 1980 provide for governmental intervention to protect consumers and workers in a broad range of economic enterprise. The Social Welfare (Consolidation) Act 1981 pertains to various social services and forms of financial aid to those within specific categories of need. Also of interest are the Solicitors Act 1954, Solicitors (Amendment) Act 1960 and the Medical Practitioners Act 1978 which delegate governmental and regulatory powers over leading professions to a quasi-private Incorporated Law Society and a quasi-public Medical Council. In addition the Land Act 1923 and subsequent Land Acts such as those of 1933, 1950, and the Local Government (Planning and Development) Acts 1963 to 1983 involve planning, redistribution of land and controls over land use, development, environment and amenities. These have extensive socio-economic and legal implications for large numbers of individuals and corporations as to their property and other rights.

Statutory Delegation

The importance of administrative rule-making as a major component of administrative law has been recognised in publications of authorities on Irish, English and French administrative law.[1] American authorities give similar weight to the significance of administrative rule-making in their studies, typified by the following statement made by Davis:

> Rule-making procedure is one of the greatest inventions of modern government . . . The main tool all over the world for getting governmental jobs done may soon be rule-making, authorised by legislative bodies and checked by the courts. If neither the legislative bodies nor the courts are able to produce the elaborate law that is needed by a modern society, the natural resort is to specialised administrators who have the needed capacity, and their main tool may be the notice and comment procedure laid down by the Administrative Procedure Act.[2]

The pervasiveness of administrative rule-making, and the breadth of discretion granted in the various delegations of rule-making power by the Oireachtas to the Administration in Ireland, is exemplified in key provisions of the Acts outlined above. The Censorship of Publications Act 1946, section 20(1)(a) and (b) provides that the Minister may make regulations in relation to 'any matter or thing referred to in this Act', and 'any other matter about which the Minister considers it necessary or desirable to make regulations for the purpose of carrying into effect the objects of this Act', following consultation with the Censorship of Publications Board or the Censorship of Publications Appeal Board. In this Act, as in the rule-making provisions of the other Acts discussed later, the standard requirement is made that rules must be laid before the Houses of the Oireachtas, either house of which may annul the regulation by resolution within 21 days.

Section 4 of the Restrictive Practices Act 1972 authorises the Restrictive Practices Commission to make rules on fair practice conditions on recommendation of the Examiner of Restrictive Practices or on request of an association of persons engaged in supply and distribution of goods or provision of services. The same Act in section 8 provides that the Minister for Industry, Trade, Commerce and Tourism, after consideration of a report of the Commission, may issue an order (i.e. rule) prohibiting restrictive practices and unfair methods of competition. To ensure equitable treatment of persons regarding supply or distribution of goods or provision of services, he may make such other provisions in this regard 'as he thinks fit'. The Minister for Labour under section 16 of the Unfair Dismissals Act 1977 is given power to: amend specific subsections of the Act to extend its application to certain classes of employees; vary the amount of compensation granted for unfair dismissal; vary its effect in relation to dismissal where employment is for a fixed term or purpose, and vary it to comply with international obligations. In general under section 17, he may make regulations for the purpose 'of enabling any other provisions of the Act to have full effect.' The Minister for Labour is also authorised by section 4 of the Safety in Industry Act 1980 to amend any provision of the Act to comply with international obligations which the state has decided to assume, to extend the meaning of factory, and under section 5 may make special regulations after consultation with the Minister for Health pertaining to any noise pollutant or vibration in a factory to protect health of workers. He may also make under Part II, section 9 of the

Act regulations to prescribe specifications or other requirements with which the design and construction of any plant of a prescribed class or description will comply.

One of the broadest delegations of rule-making power is given by the Social Welfare (Consolidation) Act 1981 in section 3(1) : (a) providing that the Minister may make regulations 'for any purpose in relation to which regulations are provided for by any of the provisions of this Act, and (b) 'for prescribing any matter or thing referred to in this Act as prescribed or to be prescribed.' Section 3(3) states that any regulations 'may contain such incidental or supplementary provisions as appear to the Minister to be expedient for the purposes of the regulations'. However, section 3(4) requires the sanction of the Minister for Finance for regulations pertaining to 25 of the sections, and drafts of regulations in respect of 14 of the sections, out of the 313 sections in the Act. Section 3(5) contains the typical provision for laying regulations before each House of the Oireachtas and their annulment by resolution of either House within 21 days. In addition the Minister under section 310 may determine by his order the day the Act comes into operation, a power not delegated by US legislation to heads of departments.

It is particularly interesting that the Oireachtas in section 5(1) of the Solicitors Act 1954 made a broad delegation of rule-making power to the Incorporated Law Society of Ireland, a non-governmental organisation, to 'make regulations in relation to any matter or thing referred to in this Act as prescribed or to be prescribed or as being the subject of regulations'. Sub-section 2 of the same section authorises the Society to 'make regulations for the purpose of the execution of the provisions of this Act'. The Society's disciplinary committee with the concurrence of the President of the High Court may make rules regulating proceedings of the committee under section 16, Solicitors (Amendment) Act 1960. In respect of the medical profession, on the other hand, authority to make rules under the Medical Practitioners Act 1978 is given to the Minister for Health, not to a private professional society. Section 37 of that Act provides that the 'Minister may, if he thinks fit, on the recommendation of the Council by regulations made under this section, amend the provisions of the Fourth Schedule of this Act' (which specify the primary qualifications for a person to be placed on the register of medical practitioners). The Minister is also authorised under section 66 to make by regulation any adaptation

or modification necessary in respect of any statute, order or regulation in force at the time of the passage of the Medical Practitioners
Act 1978 to ensure conformity with that Act. Under section 36(1),
the Medical Council must ensure that education and training
requirements for qualification as medical practitioner meet minimum standards of any directive adopted by the Council of the
European Communities, and with the consent of the Minister also
determines under section 38 the specialities it will recognise under
the Act, and the titles and designations of those specialities.

The Incorporated Law Society also has an advisory function
according to section 3(1), Land Act 1933 which empowers the
Minister for Lands and Fisheries (now Minister for Agriculture) to
make rules to carry out the Land Acts after consultation with the
President of the Incorporated Law Society and with the concurrence
of a committee composed of the Judicial Commissioner, the Secretary of the Land Commission, and a Lay Commissioner appointed
by the Minister. Rule-making power is also shared with the Minister
for Finance who is empowered to make regulations to give effect to
the provisions of the Act in relation to land purchase, a power
continued under section 3 of the Land Act 1950.

The Local Government (Planning and Development) Acts, 1963
to 1983 also merit notice in regard to delegation of rule-making
power, particularly if the concept of rule-making is broadened to
encompass the power given to planning authorities to establish
policy on which administrative determinations affecting property
rights are made. Sections 19-23 of the 1963 Act require that a
development plan be made within three years of the appointed
day by the planning authority showing its objectives for future
development. The development plan is not explicitly referred to as
constituting regulations with the force of law. However, section 21
of the 1963 Act is explicit as to the procedure involved in making
a plan or variations in the plan, including notice and a hearing
on objections and representations of ratepayers. The previously
discussed case of *Finn v. Bray Urban District Council* 1969 IR 169
viewed the provisions for notice and hearing on a draft of a proposed
plan as having adjudicatory as well as legislative purposes since the
plan affected property rights. This implies that the development
plan has a legal effect on individuals comparable to that of a rule
or regulation (although section 37(3) of the 1976 Act has reduced
the right of an objecting ratepayer to be heard on amendments

of a draft development plan to making written rather than oral representation). Further indicators of the legal effect of a development plan are the extensive provisions of sections 24-33 for control of land development through a licensing system which pertains to the enforcement of the objectives of the development plan. More direct delegations of rule-making power in the Local Government (Planning and Development) Acts, 1963 and 1976 include the provision in section 10 in the 1963 Act that the Minister for the Environment may make regulations for any matter referred to in the Act as prescribed or as the subject of regulations. Section 25 of the 1963 Act virtually compels the making of regulations governing grants of development permission and section 86 authorises the making of building regulations. With the creation of An Bord Pleanála by the 1976 Act, the Minister was authorised by section 20 to make rules 'providing for any matter of procedure in relation to references or appeals to the Board' and by section 35 to make regulations providing for payment of application fees to planning authorities for waiver notices, publication by planning authorities of notices for permission to develop land or for waiver notice, enabling applicants to appeal to the Board against refusal of an approval, and making 'such incidental consequential, transitional etc. provision as may appear to him to be necessary . . . for any purpose of this Act'. Section 42 gives the Minister power to make procedural regulations on appeals to him on building regulations.

Equally broad powers of rule making are delegated to the Minister for the Environment in the recent Act of 1982. Section 11 authorises the Minister to make regulations on procedures for applications under section 4 of the Act, and to make such supplementary provisions as appear to him to be necessary 'to give full effect to any of the provisions of sections 2, 3 or 4 of this Act'. Section 7 states that the Minister shall 'issue such general directives as to policy in relation to planning and development as he considers necessary' which may apply to planning authorities as well as An Bord Pleanála. Section 10 authorises the Minister to make regulations, with the consent of the Minister for Finance, providing for prescribed fees related to various types of applications under the Acts of 1963 to 1982. Again, the 1983 Act after specifying the organisation and composition of An Bord Pleanála then gives rule-making power to the Minister to amend or implement statutory provisions concerning officials or organisations involved in the nomination of candidates for appointment to the Board. (See sections 5(6) and 7.)

The breadth of discretionary rule-making power delegated in these statutes equals and in certain instances, such as the expressly delegated power to modify statutory provisions, would seem to exceed that given to American administrative agencies. However, this must be viewed in the context of the delegation of rule-making power in a parliamentary system where, as in the case of each of the above statutes, it is customary to require the submission of rules to the Oireachtas, either House of which has the power to annul such rules by resolution within a certain time limit. In the United States, as discussed in chapter 3, the requirement that rules be submitted to the legislature for review and possible annulment started relatively late (1920) and in a limited way; it then accelerated significantly in more recent years with resultant executive branch opposition, culminating in the Supreme Court's holding the legislative veto to be unconstitutional on 23 June 1983, in *Immigration and Naturalization Service v. Chadha* (No. 80-1832), 77 L.Ed 2d. (See pages 52-3). In this respect, the 'laying on the table' provisions in the delegation of rule-making power in Ireland are typical of such delegation in England while in French administrative law the issue of delegation of rule-making power and legislative review of rules does not arise because of the nature of the constitutional allocation of legislative powers between the executive and legislative branches.

Rule-Making Contrasted with Adjudication

Before defining rule-making power as distinguished from adjudication, a possible semantic problem may be avoided by noting that when an Irish Act states that the Minister has the power to 'make orders' it often means the power to make regulations of general application. However, to 'make orders' in certain instances may also mean the authority to issue a directive to a particular party, as in the Censorship of Publications Act 1929, the Unfair Dismissals Act 1977 and the Safety in Industry Act 1980. This dual use of the term 'order' (also characteristic of the term 'statutory instrument') contrasts with the more restricted use of the term 'order' in American law to mean primarily the exercise of directing powers to tell a particular party to stop an unlicensed operation, or an unfair trade or labour practice and/or to perform a remedial act such as reinstatement of a dismissed employee with back pay. Consequently, in using the term order, when discussing regulatory powers, a distinction will be made between the order as an exercise of rule-making power and the order as an exercise of directing power.

In the absence of an administrative procedures Act of general application in Ireland, the definition of rule-making and of different types of rule-making must be based on a combination of the Statutory Instruments Act 1947 and individual Acts delegating rule-making power and judicial decisions. The Statutory Instruments Act provides in section 1 that: 'The expression "statutory instrument" means an order, regulation, rule, scheme or byelaw made in exercise of power conferred by statute.' Section 21(a)-(d) amplifies this definition by stating that the provisions of the Act 'primarily' apply to every statutory instrument made by the President, the government, any member of the government, parliamentary secretary (now Minister of State), person or body, corporate or unincorporated, exercising any function of government or public duties in relation to public administration which either is required by statute to be laid before the Houses of the Oireachtas or is of such character as to affect the public generally or any particular class or classes of the public.

Section 3 of the 1947 Act, as amended by the Statutory Instruments (Amendment) Act 1955, requires that every statutory instrument to which the Act applies must within seven days of making be sent to ten specifically named repositories, and notice of the making of the statutory instrument and location where copies may be obtained must be published in *Iris Oifigiúil*.

The Act does not supersede any Act delegating rule-making power which contains specific provisions of its own for publication of rules in *Iris Oifigiúil*. If any question arises as to whether a person, body or statutory instrument falls within the statutory prescription of categories covered by the Act, it is referred to the Attorney General who may issue a certificate affirming or exempting the agency or instrument from application of the Act. He has broad discretion to determine that the instrument is exempt as of merely local or personal application or 'for any other reason' (section 2). This last ground would seem to make it difficult to challenge the Attorney General's decision to exempt as being *ultra vires* the statute.

In addition, all statutory instruments of a particular class qualifying for exemption may be exempted from the Act by the Attorney General. Finally, failure to comply with the requirements of publication and sending copies to repositories will not, under section 3(2) and (3), affect the validity or coming into operation of any statutory instrument except when a person is charged with violating that instrument, and the prosecutor cannot prove publication of the instrument in *Iris Oifigiúil*. In such an instance, charges will be dismissed unless the prosecutor can prove that steps had been taken to bring the purport of the instrument to the public, persons to be affected by it or to the defendant.

Certain criteria as to what constitute rule-making in Ireland may be inferred from the Statutory Instruments Acts. There must be a statutory delegation of rule-making power, exercised by bodies carrying out governmental functions or public duties related to public administration, and their rules either are required to be laid before the Oireachtas or must have a general effect on the public or particular class of the public. Unless exempted by the Attorney General, their adoption requires adherence to certain procedures for notice to the public, deposit in specified repositories, and notice of where copies may be obtained. In this respect the Statutory Instruments Acts in combination with the Houses of the Oireachtas (Laying of Documents) Act 1966 (see chapter 2) represent a partial move towards a general administrative procedures Act in Ireland: they establish criteria and prescribe certain procedures generally applicable to all authorities exercising rule-making powers in Ireland. However, these Acts do not, to use the *Devlin Report* phraseology, place Ireland in the category of one of the 'administrative procedures act countries' when they are compared with the American Administrative Procedures Act 1946 (APA). The APA defines and differentiates between rules and rule-making, order, licence and licensing, and adjudication. It prescribes details of procedures to be followed in the exercise of rule-making as opposed to adjudication. It also provides for access to public documents and for the scope and nature of judicial review of administrative determinations, as well as for the appointment and roles of hearing examiners.

In the absence of provisions in Irish legislation comparable to those of the APA, the Irish courts are not confronted with issues of interpreting statutory definitions and differentiations between types of regulatory powers and procedure in their application. Typical of such issues faced by American courts is the case of *Willapoint Oysters v. Ewing* 174 F. 2d 676 (CCA 9th Cir. 1949) (cert. denied 339 US 945; 70 Supreme Court 793) arising three years after the APA was enacted, in which the plaintiff claimed the agency did not provide the procedures of a trial-type or adjudicatory hearing in reaching an administrative determination as required under the APA. The agency claimed that the nature of the administrative action or determination was rule-making, and therefore the much less rigorous 'notice-and-comment' rule-making procedure specified by the APA was applicable. In resolving this issue the court defined rule-making as against adjudication generically (thus it could apply as well in Ireland or England) by stating:

> Rule-making is legislation on the administrative level, i.e. legislation within the confines (standard) of the granting statute as required by the Constitution and its doctrines of non-delegability and separability of powers . . . . rule-making is normally directed primarily at 'situations' rather than particular persons. Individual protestations of injury are normally and necessarily lost in the quantum of the greater good.

> Adjudication . . . comports with the judicial function. Its primary concern is with individual rights, liabilities for past conduct, or present status under existing law, and tends to be accusative and disciplinary in nature.

> Each definition is couched necessarily in terms of 'tendency' . . . The concepts are not wholly mutually exclusive but each to a degree contains elements of the other . . . . In the twilight region . . . intermediating the poles of clarity, the doctrine of primary purpose controls. So tested, we are without serious doubt that this was a rule-making proceeding. This is true even though the result . . . is of immediate and grave economic import to practitioner. (pages 693-4)

On this basis, the Court held that permitting the chief government witness and governmental counsel to aid in preparing portions of the findings and conclusions reached did not violate the APA or constitutional right to a fair hearing since it was a rule-making proceeding.

Despite the absence of an Irish administrative procedures Act to provide a statutory basis for suits of the nature of the *Willapoint Oysters* case, Irish courts are confronted with issues requiring differentiation between rule-making and adjudication. A basic issue which arises frequently in a variety of circumstances is what constitutes action and decision of an administrative or executive nature as against an adjudicative or judicial nature. Regardless of how administrators may perceive the type of power being exercised or categorise it, if the Irish courts consider the process involved and determination reached to be adjudication or as requiring that the administrative body 'act judicially', then constitutional justice requires the procedural due process protections discussed in chapter 5. On the other hand, if the administrative actions are considered by the courts to be rule-making, the only procedural requirements which the courts insist be adhered to are those required by the statute delegating the rule-making powers. There are, of course, borderline situations in both Ireland and the United States since rule-making can involve conflict over purely factual matters as well as those of policy and opinion, and have an impact on legal rights both of which may lead the courts to require a trial-type hearing.

A distinction was drawn by Gavan Duffy J. in *Cross v. Minister for Agriculture* 1941 IR 55, between rule-making and adjudication, based on the nature of the process and determination made under the governing statute. In this case plaintiff appealed from restriction of his fishing rights resulting from definition by an order or rule made by the Minister for Agriculture establishing the boundary between the tidal and fresh water portions of the River Corrib, under the Salmon Fishery Act 1863. Gavan Duffy J. stated that under that Act, the Minister had inherited powers of the special commissioners of Irish fisheries, who were given important judicial powers over weirs and fixed nets, and also under section 17 were empowered to define certain boundaries. In setting boundaries section 7 treated the commissioners not as a judicial but as an administrative body with wide discretion from which there was no appeal.

Under these powers the Minister for Agriculture drew the boundary to mark off the fresh from the saline portion of the river on the basis of tests which showed fresh-water vegetation to grow on one side of the line and sea-water vegetation to grow on the other side. Appellant argued that since the river was confined by vertical banks, the boundary between tidal and fresh water must be drawn at the highest points across the river at which spring tides cause a vertical motion of the water (although the sea water there displaced the fresh water). These competing modes for determining the boundary line would produce widely differing results.

As Gavan Duffy J. read section 17 of the Act, the words 'by reference to maps or otherwise' do not impose a statutory duty to take evidence before the boundary is determined, leaving the Minister in control of the situation as long as he acts *intra vires* the statute. He must make some examination of the river and based on this data and such other information he sees fit to gather, he must decide a boundary line and show it on a map and publish it. Beyond this, the sole question is whether the Minister has exercised a particular jurisdiction conferred on him, since he is not administering justice, and the court therefore has no concern with the practical merits or demerits of the line he sees fit to mark out. On this basis Gavan Duffy J. concluded that the Minister had not exercised the jurisidiction conferred upon him, since in his opinion section 19 of the Act requires the Minister to make his boundary lines by ascertaining tidal limits, not saline limits. However, within that tidal limit approach, the Minister is unfettered by any particular time, and may make out his line at any place where visible tidal action normally ends, whether at neap, spring, high or low tide.

Gavan Duffy J. also warned that his admission of evidence in this instance to support appellant's case (to which the Minister had made no objection) should not be understood as establishing a normal course where evidence is forthcoming on appeal in support of the Minister's definition, nor as prejudging any objection that might be made in a future case. His reason for this warning was that this case was not the re-trial of a *lis* in which appellant is entitled to show error in the order of an inferior court by adducing further evidence. The proffering of such evidence might seem to imply that if it were believed, it would give appellant a right to annulment of the Minister's boundary marking which would be a dangerous unfounded postulate in that neither appellant nor the court hearing the appeal can insist that the Minister's discretion, if exercised *intra vires*, should take a particular course of action.

Although the judgment in this case does not employ the terms, administrative rule-making versus administrative adjudication, Gavan Duffy J. clearly denotes the differences between these two types of power. This is achieved by his emphasis upon the Minister's discretion to adopt a standard or rule for the boundary line between fresh and salt water subject to judicial review only as to whether the Minister has stayed within the statutory guidelines in making that policy. His policy-making discretion is not subject to judicial review of the weight of evidence as to the validity of the boundary line, since the Minister is not making an adjudicatory determination.

Types of Rule-Making

In the development of administrative law, certain types of rule-making have emerged which have been categorised as 'legislative' and 'interpretative'. 'Legislative'-type rule-making involves an explicit statutory grant of rule-making power by the legislature to an administrative agency to make rules having the force and effect of law, violation of which is subject to a statutory penalty. 'Interpretative' rules are not made under an explicit statutory delegation of rule-making power. Rather they are statements of specific policy constituting the agency's interpretation of general or broadly phrased statutory provisions which are issued in various forms to provide guidance to administrators, private parties and the courts as to how the agency will construe and apply the statutory provisions. They are intended to reduce uncertainty as to statutory meaning (or even the meaning of general legislative-type rules) and provide consistency of application, so as to make for more effective implementation of the statute.

The Statutory Instruments (Amendment) Acts of 1947 and 1955 do not differentiate between the types of rules and related rule-making procedures. This is also true in England where earlier legislative efforts to define rules according to their nature have been abandoned.[3] This is in contrast to the United States where the APA defines legislative and interpretative-type rules and specifies certain procedures for legislative-type rule-making while exempting interpretative-type rule-making from such procedural requirements. The result of this contrast is that there is an absence of issues raised before Irish courts on the basis of statutory provisions requiring distinctions to be drawn between legislative as against interpretative-type rules in regard to administrative adherence to rule-making procedures, while in the United States this is a frequent issue. (See for example *National Motor Freight Association* US, 168 F.

Supp 90 (D.D.C 1967) affd. 393 US 18 (1968) *US v. Florida East Coast Railway Co* 410 US 224 (1973).) Moreover, American courts differentiate between the two types of rule-making in respect of their legal and binding effects, and the extent to which the courts are more inclined to substitute their judgment for that of the administrator. (See *Kelly v. Zamerello* 486 P. 2d 906 (Alaska, 1971) citing the leading case of *American Telephone and Telegraph Co. v. US* 299 US 232; (1936) (legislative-type rule making) and *Skidmore v. Swift & Co* 323 US 134 (1944); *Chrysler Corporation v. Brown* 441 US 281 (interpretative -type rule-making).)

Legislative Rules
Irish courts are not directly confronted with the question of whether rules are legislative or interpretative as defined by statute, but they seem to recognise such a distinction implicitly in the process of resolving appeals on the issues that rules are *ultra vires* the statute or contrary to constitutional rights. This is revealed in dicta in judgments on the statutory authority for rule-making, the mode of adoption and promulgation of rules, their legal effect and the role of the courts in reviewing rules.

An example of how the court views its role in reviewing what was essentially legislative-type rule-making is the *Cross v. Minister for Agriculture* case discussed earlier. Gavan Duffy J. stressed the explicit statutory delegation of power to the Minister to make policy on the dividing line between salt and fresh water, and the statutory treatment of this power as an administrative, rather than an adjudicatory, function. He emphasised that it was not the function of the court to judge the merits or demerits of the line drawn, provided that the Minister's rule was made within statutory guidelines. The sole basis for a court judgment on the rule was whether it was *intra vires* or *ultra vires* the statute.

A later case dealing with what was clearly a legislative-type rule is *Minister for Industry and Commerce v. Hales* 1967 IR 50, in which the Minister brought a test case against the trustees of the Royal Liver Friendly Society for alleged failure to grant holidays to one of the Society's insurance agents or in the alternative to pay an amount equal to two week's salary. The rule provided that 'wholetime insurance agents whose ordinary remuneration is by way of commission for premiums collected by them and who are engaged under a contract *for* services shall be deemed workers for purposes of the

Act' (emphasis added). It was adopted under section 3(3)(a) of the Act which gave the Minister power to make rules in respect of who may be a 'worker' under the Act, as follows:

> that any person or any class or description (defined in such manner and by reference to such things as the Minister thinks proper) of persons shall be deemed to be a worker or workers for the purposes of this Act . . .

> Any regulations made by the Minister under this subsection may contain such supplemental and consequential provisions or modifications of the provisions of this Act as he considers necessary for giving full effect to the regulations.

The defendant Society claimed that the Minister's rule was *ultra vires* the Act, which defined a worker as any employed person over fourteen (with exclusions) and defined the term 'employee' as one who is 'employed under a contract *of* service . . . or a contract *of* apprenticeship, and cognate words shall be construed accordingly' (emphasis added). As a consequence, many of the provisions of the Act were unsuitable for workers under contract *for* service now covered under the Minister's regulations. For example, a worker could now receive 54 weeks' pay for 50 weeks' work, while the Act would require only 52 weeks' pay. In opposition to this, the Minister claimed that section 3(3)(a) of the Act was meant to enable him to bring workers, such as the Society's insurance agents paid by commission under contract for service, within the purview of the Act.

Henchy J. for the High Court held that the regulations were *ultra vires* the Act, stating:

> it is not conceivable that the legislature, having indicated that the scope of the Act was to be limited to persons employed under a contract of service or a contract of apprenticeship, should by the use of general words in sub-s. 3 of s. 3 of the Act have given the Minister power to broaden the scope of the Act to such an extent that he could, by the making of regulations, import into work-contracts made with independent contractors a series of statutory terms as to holiday allowances, the breach of which would result in criminal liability. (page 76)

Moreover, according to Henchy J., the Act could not be operated effectively for persons under contract for services since many amendments to the Act would be needed to make its provisions applicable, and the Minister does not have power to amend the Act.

Butler J., in dissenting, felt that the Act did not have words limiting the Minister's rule-making power to persons employed under a contract of service, and the Act intended that the Minister be able to 'extend its operation to any persons engaged in earning their livelihood by engagement to another whether under contract of service or for services' (page 86). In addition, the fact that application of a power may cause difficulty or incongruous results is not adequate ground for holding the power has not been conferred.

Both the *Cross* and *Hales* cases illustrate legislative-type rule-making in that the courts emphasised the nature of the explicit delegation by the legislature to the administrator of the power to make rules which have the effect of law, including a penalty for violation. The courts focused their review on whether the rule was *ultra vires* the statute, and not on its wisdom or desirability, although Henchy J. also added a subordinate note as to the feasibility of the application of the rule, which was rejected by Butler J.

Interpretative Rules

Cases in which departmental policies or rules with the characteristics of interpretative rule-making have been reviewed by the courts are not common in Ireland, as indicated by the limited number of such decisions. The determination in *Mulloy v. Minister for Education and Attorney General* 1975 IR 88 illustrates certain characteristics of interpretative rule-making and the judicial perspectives concerning its legal effect or status. The plaintiff, Father Mulloy, appealed a decision which would have excluded teaching service accrued while assigned to a seminary in Nigeria from being considered in calculating his incremental salary under the terms of a scheme set out in supplemental rules in the Department of Education Circular M 30/3. The scheme had been adopted to encourage secondary teachers to teach in certain underdeveloped countries by allowing such teaching service to be computed in calculating incremental salary. The evidence proved that Father Mulloy was an Irish citizen, a priest and member of a missionary and teaching religious order, a highly qualified teacher who had taught in Blackrock College. He had registered as a secondary teacher under Department of

Education regulations, which qualified him to be paid incremental salary by the Department. However, since the supplemental rules pertaining to teaching in underdeveloped countries applied only to lay secondary teachers, the Department refused Father Mulloy's claim for consideration.

Father Mulloy's appeal for a declaration was based on his claim that the exclusion of himself and other religious from the benefits of the scheme was repugnant to article 44.2(3) of the Constitution which provides that the state will not impose disabilities or make any discrimination on the ground of religious profession, belief or status.

In his review of the rules setting forth the scheme, Butler J. did not use the term 'interpretative rules'. However, the way he expressed his doubt as to their legal force and effect, in view of the absence of adherence to normal rule-making procedures in the making, is a typical characterisation of interpretative-type rule making:

> It is difficult to know by whom these rules are made or under what authority. Some are stated to have been made by the Minister; many are not signed by him. The rules with which we are here principally concerned are not attributed to or signed by anybody. None of the rules appear to me to have any statutory force or effect; they have never been considered by the Oireachtas. The amount of the incremental salary is calculated on the number of years of approved teaching service of the teacher. . . . (pages 89-90)

Beyond this ruling on the lack of the legal force and effect of the rules, the Court held that under article 44 of the Constitution, the distinction between a lay and a religious person is a matter of religious status within the meaning of that article and thus plaintiff's submission was logical and unanswerable. The exclusion of religious from the scheme under the rules cannot be justified on the grounds that the scheme was designed to help developing countries by providing incentives to lay teachers to teach in those countries, while such incentive is not needed for missionaries in view of their vocation. Nor is it relevant that under the rules, the granting of incremental payments is at the discretion of the Minister. What is decisive is that plaintiff was excluded under the rules of the scheme because he was a priest, a discrimination repugnant to the Constitution.

Another form of policy-making with certain characteristics of interpretative rule-making is illustrated by an earlier case, *Devanney v. Dublin Board of Assistance* 113 ILTR 83 (1949). Plaintiff, Mrs Mildred Devanney, a registered nurse holding office under the Dublin Board of Assistance, sought a declaration that she was a permanent pensionable officer whose termination of service by the Board in 1946 was *ultra vires*. She also sought an account of the loss and damage for thirteen months of non-employment suffered before reinstatement by the Board after a review of her case by the Minister for Local Government and Public Health who advised that she had been improperly removed.

After concluding that plaintiff was a permanent officer, and her removal *ultra vires* and void, Gavan Duffy J. dealt with her claim to damages. He noted that the pertinent regulations were issued by the Minister together with a letter from his office in regard to salaries and emoluments. The regulations, Local Government (Minor Officers) Order S.R. & O. No. 46 of 1943 stabilised remuneration of holders of a scheduled office at the existing rate until otherwise directed by the Minister. The letter, dated 24 November 1944 from the parliamentary secretary's office, implied that the new salary scale for nurses at St Kevin's Hospital emanated from the local Board of Assistance and differentiated between categories of nurses for purposes of the scale and variations within it. Plaintiff was considered to belong to one of the categories.

Based on the letter, the Board had paid plaintiff from 1945 on an improved scale as 'sanctioned' without any salary increments. Gavan Duffy J. commented on the legal effect of the Minister's letter:

> The delegation to the parliamentary secretary, presumably authorised by one of the Ministerial Delegation Orders, is not challenged, but the letter has given me some difficulty. The Minister may by his order (under section 14 of the Act of 1941, read with section 15(3) of the Interpretation Act, No. 38 of 1937) amend former orders directing the kind and number of officers to be appointed by a local authority for any purpose; but the letter does not purport to amend a former order, and the grotesque classification of nurses, presumably now made

here for the first time, has the authority of no statutory order of which I am aware. The letter is not an order under section 11 of the Act. . . . Again, while the Minister may under section 19(1) of the Act, make regulations determining remuneration for the officers of a specified class, description or grade, I find no power in him to lay down a special scale for the Dublin nurses; their class or description or grade, once determined, must, I think, carry its appropriate remuneration under official regulations and we have seen that the two sets of 1943 regulations left remuneration where it was, determining no new scale. . . .

The letter of sanction seems to me a very informal method of altering so important a matter as a scale of salaries, and I have had to ask myself whether the plaintiff could sustain her right to the increased emoluments which she has received as a result of this letter, though the Board has not raised this point against her. (pages 121-2)

Given this situation, Gavan Duffy J. held that he preferred to say that the Board under section 10(1)(b) of the Local Government Act 1941 had to pay every officer such remuneration as it might assign, and that it did so assign and pay plaintiff the improved salary contemplated in the letter. The letter may be treated as an approval by the Minister under article 4 of the Local Government (Minor Officers) Order S.R. and O. No. 46 of 1943 to vary plaintiff's remuneration as authorised by section 19(3) of the 1941 Act and as a departure with consent of the plaintiff and the manager within 11(2) of the said Act. On this basis, the plaintiff's remuneration was lawful.

It can be seen that Gavan Duffy J. gave very limited legal effect to the parliamentary secretary's letter, treating it as an approval under the Act by the Minister of a departure from established regulations. This in effect was a rule interpreting a legislative-type rule, typical of interpretative rule-making.

The most definite example of the difference between the legal effect of legislative and interpretative-type rules is the case of *Cahill v. Irish Motor Traders' Association* 1966 IR 430. Plaintiff, a retailer of petrol and motor accessories, sought an injunction claiming that defendants had made representations to his tyres supplier to induce

him to discontinue supplying tyres in breach of an order made by
the Minister for Industry and Commerce, entitled the Restrictive
Trade Practices (Motor Cars) Order 1956 made under section 9 of
the Restrictive Trade Practices Act 1953. The Order was based on
a fact-finding report and confirmed later by statute, giving it the
force of law. The Order prohibited a trade association from coercing
a supplier to withhold goods because of prices charged or because
a person is not approved by a trade association. It also prohibits
agreements limiting or restricting entry to trade in goods and the
publishing of lists of approved traders.

However, the Fair Trade Commission in 1959 also had made
certain fair trading rules on 'Entry into and Trade in the Sale
and/or Repair of Motor Vehicles', which were adopted under the
powers granted by section 4 of the 1953 Act to make rules representing the Commission's opinion of fair trading conditions with regard
to supply and demand and distribution of any kind of goods. The
rules defined a 'motor trader' in terms of employing a specified floor
space, equipment and skilled assistants, and made it an unfair trade
practice for a 'supplier to supply goods for resale to a person other
than a motor trader.' Defendants claimed that any representations
they made were legally justified as being designed to implement
these fair trading rules.

In the High Court, Budd J. held that plaintiff did not in fact
meet the requirements of a 'motor trader' under the Fair Trade
Commission's rules. These rules, if they had a prohibitory effect in
law, would debar plaintiff from receiving supplies of tyres from the
supply company. But the Minister's Order makes no exceptions to
the fair trading rules of the Fair Trade Commission and therefore
the trade association was not empowered to take any action. However the Association had tried with authority 'backed by a fear of
sanctions' to make the supply company stop supplying tyres to the
plaintiff.

To resolve this dilemma, Budd J. noted that section 4 of the 1953
Act did not give power to the Commission to command or prohibit
any act by a citizen. Rather, the rules reflect only the Commission's
concern with what in its opinion represent fair trading conditions
and thus they 'form a guide to those concerned in the trade' (page
448). On the other hand, section 9 of the Act gives the Minister
power to prohibit certain acts by order and by implication to
command acts to be abstained from or done. Moreover, section 6

of the Act requires the Commission to report any non-observance of its rules to the Minister who under section 9 may then make an appropriate order of a remedial nature. Since the fair trading rules have no directory or prohibitory effect in law, and in no way affected the operation of article 15 of the 1956 Order made by the Minister, the defendant Association was prohibited from any attempt to coerce the supply company to withhold a supply of tyres from the plaintiff. Even if the Association's actions were an effort to compel compliance with the fair trading rules, this cannot affect plaintiff's right to obtain an injunction.

From the *Mulloy, Devanney* and *Cahill* decisions, it would appear that interpretative rule-making takes place in Ireland. It is characterised in the first two cases by the absence of explicit authorisation by statute and by formal adoption and promulgation procedures. In all three cases the most important common denominator is judicial relegation of interpretative-type rules to a status of less legal effect than legislative-type rules. Nevertheless, interpretative rules have sufficient effect to lead to judicial review and determination of their constitutionality as in *Mulloy*, and their application and validity in relation to statute and existing legislative-type rules, as in *Devanney* and *Cahill*.

Given the characteristics of legislative as against interpretative rule-making as elaborated in the above judicial decisions, it becomes apparent that the Acts discussed above also delegate legislative-type rule-making power. The provisions of those Acts show that there is an explicit delegation of power to adopt rules, following procedures specified in the Acts, including a virtually universal requirement of laying the proposed rules or orders before the Houses of the Oireachtas, which have the power of nullification. The rules are given the force and effect of law through statutory provisions with penalty for their violation. (See, for example Restrictive Practices Act 1972, section 23; Social Welfare (Consolidation) Act 1981, sections 114-19; Local Government (Planning and Development) Act 1963 sections 31-5, as amended by section 38, 1976 Act and sections 8 and 9, 1982 Act.)

Challenges to Rules and Rule-Making

The types of challenge to administrative rules vary with the nature of their substantive content, their impact on the parties affected,

the procedure through which the rules were made and the circumstances of a particular case. Rules may be challenged on constitutional grounds, namely that the provisions of an Act which delegate
the power to an administrative agency to make rules are repugnant
to the Constitution, thus invalidating any rules made thereunder
or, even if the statutory provisions delegating rule-making power are
constitutional, the rules made thereunder are in and of themselves
repugnant to the Constitution. An issue or challenge raised more
frequently than constitutionality is the claim that the rules or
regulations are *ultra vires* the statute. Other issues are that the rules
are unreasonable or made in bad faith, the question of the binding
effect of rules on the rule-maker, and whether the procedure in the
adoption and application of rules has been complied with. The
following illustrations of challenges in the courts against rule-
making involve 'legislative-type' rules; the relatively few instances
of cases in which the courts were reviewing 'interpretative' rule-
making have already been discussed above.

Unconstitutionality
The case of *Cooke v. Patrick Walsh* 1983 ILRM 429, involved both
types of constitutional challenge referred to above, and the related
claim that the regulations at issue were *ultra vires* the statute. Plaintiff
was nine years old when he was struck by an automobile driven by
defendant Walsh, and suffered injuries which required that he be
given constant medical care and attention for the remainder of his
life, at a cost estimated at £325 per week. Plaintiff ordinarily would
have had full eligibility for all the services to which an eligible
person is entitled free of charge under the Health Act 1970, but was
made ineligible by section 72(1) and (2) of the 1970 Act and
the implementing article 6(3) of the Health Services (Limited
Eligibility) Regulations 1971 (SI 105 of 1971). Section 72 of the
1970 Act gives power to the Minister for Health to make regulations
providing that any service under the Act is available only to a
particular class of persons who have eligibility for that service. The
implementing 1971 regulations in effect render persons requiring
treatment for injuries received in a road traffic accident to be
ineligible to receive services under the 1970 Act if they cannot
establish to the satisfaction of the Chief Officer of the related Health
Board that they have not received damages or are not entitled to

receive compensation in the nature of damages from another person in respect of the injuries.

After ruling that the defendant had standing to raise constitutional issues since he was materially affected by the provisions of the 1970 Act and related regulations, and was liable to compensate plaintiff for the losses he had sustained, Hamilton J. rendered the High Court judgment with respect to the following issues: (1) was section 72(1) and (2) of the Health Act 1970 (a) contrary to article 15.2 by going beyond what the legislature may delegate and thus an abrogation of its power, and (b) contrary to article 40.1 of the Constitution by enabling the Minister of Health to differentiate between citizens without due regard to differences of capacity, physical and moral, and of social function; (2) if section 72(2) of the 1970 Act is not unconstitutional, was article 6(3) of the Health Services (Limited Eligibility) Regulations 1971 invalid as being contrary to provisions of the Constitution; and (3) if neither statute nor regulations were unconstitutional, was the Minister for Health acting *ultra vires* the statute in making the regulations?

As to the claimed violation of article 15.1 of the Constitution, Hamilton J. followed the Supreme Court decision in *City View Press v. An Chomhairle Oiliúna* 1980 IR 381, quoting the statement of O'Higgins C.J. on the growth of delegation of rule-making power to meet complex problems of the modern state, the judicial responsibility to guard against unconstitutional delegation, and reasons for upholding a delegation of rule-making power in that case. (See pages 48-9). He held that the provisions of section 72(1) and (2) of the 1970 Act were not repugnant to article 15.1 of the Constitution, based on the *City View Press* decision and the presumption of constitutionality of an Act of the legislature as enunciated in *McDonald v. Bord na gCon* 1965 IR 217, namely that the powers conferred on an administrative agency are only for the purpose of giving effect to policies contained in the relevant Act. As to the alleged violation of article 40.1 of the Constitution, Hamilton J. determined that given the Supreme Court decision in *East Donegal Co-operative v. Attorney General* 1970 IR 317, it was within the competence of the Oireachtas to vest the power of deciding what class of persons had eligibility for the services were entitled to avail themselves of such services. This was especially true since the power given to the Minister for Health is the power to differentiate between classes of persons and not between individuals, and such powers give the

Minister the duty of acting fairly and judicially in accordance with the principles of constitutional justice.

Concerning the claimed unconstitutionality of article 6(3) of the 1971 Regulations, and its invalidity as being *ultra vires*, Hamilton J. determined that its effect is to exclude from the benefit of the Act only persons requiring treatment for injuries incurred in a traffic accident who have received damages or are entitled to receive damages from another person. Such exclusionary factors must be established to the satisfaction of the Chief Executive Officer of the Health Board who must act judicially in the exercise of this administrative function, subject to review by the court should he fail to so act. In making the regulation the Minister for Health acted in accordance with constitutional justice principles since persons excluded from health services either had, or were entitled to receive as part of their damages from another person, the cost of such services, and that other person by law was so obliged to be insured in respect of such damages. The regulation therefore was not repugnant to the Constitution and the Minister for Health acted *intra vires* in making the regulation.

A claim that an administrative regulation was contrary to the Constitution was made in *Quinn's Supermarket and Fergal Quinn v. Attorney General and the Minister for Industry and Commerce* 1972 IR 1. The rule-making powers given by section 25 of the Shop (Hours of Trading) Act 1938 to the Minister for Industry and Commerce empowered him to make orders designating certain areas as trading areas and regulating the hours in which any shop situated in a trading area could keep open on any weekend. Under these powers the then Minister made an order in 1948 applying to certain victuallers' shops in the County Borough of Dublin, the Borough of Dún Laoghaire and Bray Urban District which in effect exempted shops selling only meat killed according to the Jewish ritual (kosher meat) from closing hours so that they could sell such meat after 6.00 pm on weekdays (and 6.30 pm on Saturdays), while stores selling non-kosher meat were required to stop sales after 6.00 pm. Both types of stores could be open on Sundays if they so wished. In actual practice, owing to blackout requirements during World War II, it developed that the kosher meat shops shifted from being open Saturday night to being open Sunday, while the non-kosher meat stores did not open on Sundays.

Plaintiff Fergal Quinn, managing director of Quinn's Super-market, was prosecuted by the Superintendent of the Garda Síoch-ána for keeping his supermarket's meat department open in the evening on a weekday in violation of the 1948 Order. Plaintiff sought a declaration that the entire order was invalid as contrary to article 40.1 of the Constitution stating that all citizens shall as human persons be held equal before the law, and article 44.2(3) providing that the state shall not impose any disabilities or make any discri-mination on the ground of religious profession, belief or status. The High Court, per McLaughlin J., held that the 1948 Order was invalid because it (1) effected a discrimination contravening the provisions of article 44.2(3) of the Constitution and (2) it was *ultra vires* the 1938 Act.

On appeal by defendants to the Supreme Court, Walsh J. for the Court held that the provisions of article 40.1 of the Constitution were a guarantee of equality as human persons and against treatment of any human beings as inferior or superior to other individuals in their community. Since under no possible construction of the constitutional guarantees could a body corporate or other entity save a human being be considered a person under this provision, it had no bearing on the point to be considered in the case.

With respect to the claimed contravention of article 44.2(3) of the Constitution, there was no evidence that the plaintiff's deprivation of ability to sell meat after the hours established by the rules has anything to do with the religious profession, belief, or status of Mr Quinn or of the shareholders of his supermarket. Granted that the exception made in the rules in relation to the sale of kosher meat would seem to be *prima facie* a discrimination on the ground of religious profession, it is still a fact that a person practising the Jewish religion would be faced with the choice of going without meat or acting in breach of his religion's commands. The rules or Order would thus interfere with the free profession and practice of that religion.

A conflict therefore is created between the constitutional guar-antee of free profession and practice of religion and the constitutional guarantee against discrimination on ground of religious profession, belief or status. Of five decisions of the United States Supreme Court on conflict of constitutional guarantees, Walsh J. felt that only *Abington School District v. Schemp* 374 US 203 (1963) dealt directly with this type of conflict. In his view, the concurring opinion of

Brennan J. in that case was the correct approach, namely that certain practices which might violate the prohibition against the establishment of religion clause in the US Constitution would, if invalidated on that basis, constitute a serious interference with religious liberties protected by the First Amendment (such as the provision of churches and chaplains in military establishments for those in the armed services). Similarly, under the Irish Constitution, if the implementation of the guarantee of free profession and practice of religion requires a distinction to be made to assure the guaranteed right of persons to profess a particular religion, such distinction is not contrary to the Constitution. Consequently the exemption of kosher meat shops for the evening hours is not invalid (even if not utilised) and any proposal to make it unlawful to sell kosher meats on Sundays as a means of maintaining a balance of trading hours would be contrary to the intent of the constitutional provisions. Therefore, the appeal by plaintiff was dismissed.

Excess of Jurisdiction: Ultra Vires
More prevalent than the claim of unconstitutionality of rules is the claim that the rules are made in excess of jurisdiction and thus are *ultra vires* the statute. An early example is that of *Waterford Corporation v. Murphy* 1920 2 IR 165 in which a delegation of rule-making power in section 10 of the Waterford Corporation Bridge Act 1906 (6 Edw 7, c. 76) provided that as soon as reasonable after purchase by the Corporation of the bridge undertaking, and thereafter, the Corporation:

> may alter bye-laws, rules, and regulations with regard to the time and mode of vessels passing through the existing bridge, or any new bridge which may hereafter be substituted . . . subject always to this provision, that all such by-laws . . . shall in the first place have been approved of by the Waterford Harbour Commissioners . . . and . . . submitted for confirmation to the Board of Trade . . . . A printed copy of such by-laws, rules and regulations . . . signed by an Assistant Secretary of the Board of Trade, shall be conclusive evidence of the validity of such by-laws, rules . . . in any proceedings or prosecution under the same for any purpose. (pages 166-7)

Bye-law No. 1 was adopted under this rule-making power. Together with setting the times when there would be free passage of vessels, it also provided that at all other times the bridge would be opened for passage of steam vessels on giving notice to the bridge overseer as to the time for such opening and on payment of a charge of £1.

The bye-law was challenged on the grounds that the imposition of a charge was *ultra vires* the 1906 Act. The Court held that the object of the Act was to enable the Corporation of Waterford to purchase the undertakings of the owners of the old bridge. The Act provided that either the old bridge or any new bridge should be toll free, and in the delegation of rule-making power as to time and mode of vessels passing through, no reference was made to any toll or charge. This indicated legislative intent that the public right of passage should be preserved by regulating passage of vessels in a manner not to interfere unduly with road traffic or river navigation.

The Court also rejected the Corporation argument that section 10 of the Act put its bye-law in the same position as an Act of Parliament, since once the Board of Trade confirmed a bye-law the power to make it cannot be questioned. Although it might be reasonable to enable the Corporation to impose a charge for extra work in opening the bridge at certain times, the Act as it now stands would make such a charge *ultra vires,* and section 10 of the Act does not preclude the Court from inquiring into the validity of the bye-law, in contrast with such an Act as the Patent Designs and Trade Marks Act 1907. That latter Act explicitly provides that rules made thereunder would be of the same effect as if contained in the Act and should be judicially noticed; moreover, such rules must be laid before the Houses of Parliament, either House of which may annul such rules.

The more recent case of *Minister for Industry and Commerce v. Hales* 1967 IR 50, discussed previously as an example of legislative-type rule-making, also provides a cogent illustration of divergent judicial viewpoints as to the bases upon which the courts make a determination that a rule is or is not *ultra vires* the statute. (See pages 231-3.) In that case Henchy J. decided that the Minister for Industry and Commerce's rule extending coverage of the Act to insurance agents engaged under a contract *for* services was in excess of jurisdiction and *ultra vires*. This was based on his analysis of the regulations in relation to the purpose of the Act as reflected in the long title, combined with many expressions in the Act referring to a contract *of* service and not one *for* service. Further, the Act could not be effectively operated in respect of persons engaged under a contract for service since the Minister lacked power to amend portions of the Act which would be necessary to accommodate the new rule.

The dissent of Butler J. stressed that the doctrine of *ultra vires* involved determining whether the rules not only give wider application than necessary but also whether the rules exceed or interfere with, or negate, the provisions and intention of the Act as a whole. Although there is a long line of authority supporting use of the title of a statute to aid in its interpretation, there is also a line of authority that the title cannot be used to control express provisions of an Act. As he interpreted the Act, its express provisions permitted extension of coverage of the Act, so that the use of the term 'contracts of service' did not exclude extension to 'contracts for service'. Moreover, difficulty in application of the Minister's rules is not sufficient ground for holding that the power to make such rules has not been conferred, unless it interferes with other provisions and applications of the Act, and providing holidays with pay for whole-time insurance agents does not interfere with the same benefits for the remaining workers under the Act.

Despite this division of opinion, all three judges of the Court agreed that in determining the intent of a statute related to the question of whether a rule is *ultra vires*, the function of the Court is to make its determination based on construction of the wording of the Act. The Court should not be influenced by argument or evidence submitted as to the 'parliamentary history' of the Act, and thus debates in parliament, reports of commissions, or other contemporaneous circumstances should not be taken into account – a view of judicial methods of interpretation of intent which contrasts with that of American courts.

Both the *Waterford* and the *Hales* cases involved administrative rule-making which, though in excess of jurisdiction and *ultra vires*, was an administrative effort to implement the parent statute delegating the rule-making power. In *McCrumlish v. Pigs and Bacon Commission and Minister for Agriculture and Fisheries* unreported, High Court, per Gannon J., 28 May 1975, the issue concerned the making of administrative rules by the Pigs and Bacon Commission under the Pigs and Bacon Acts to protect domestic agriculture from foreign competition, a purpose which seemed to be more related to implementing the Customs Acts than the Pigs and Bacon Acts.

Plaintiff, a dealer who bought and sold a large number of pigs for slaughter to factories, claimed that under statutory instruments Nos. 109 and 293 of 1972, made by the Pigs and Bacon Commission, he had sustained substantial losses in his sale of pigs to factories by reason of deductions made from statutory minimum prices to which he claimed he was entitled. The specific issues which Gannon J. was asked to resolve were first, whether or not these statutory instruments were invalid and unenforceable because they were made *ultra vires* the statutory powers of the Commission. Alternatively, were they made partially invalid and unenforceable with respect to that portion of the schedules in the statutory instruments containing the words 'other than pigs in respect of which the Minister for Agriculture and Fisheries is not satisfied that the pigs were produced in the State' (such quoted words referred to as 'the formula' in the judgment of Gannon J.).

The Court considered evidence relating to the making of the rules by the Pigs and Bacon Commission under section 3 of the Pigs and Bacon (Amendment) Act 1956, with the consent of the Minister for Agriculture and Fisheries, as required by section 21 of the Pigs and Bacon Act 1951. The evidence included a series of administrative documents showing that the two statutory instruments were made following consideration by the Commission and Department of Agriculture of ways to ensure that the benefit of subsidies payable out of state funds under the Pigs and Bacon Acts would not reach persons dealing in pigs illegally imported into the state.

Gannon J. stated that the regulation of the recovery, control and distribution of money collected by the Commission in fees and levies, including payment of subsidies on exported bacon, is entirely within the powers of the Commission, and the Acts also provide penal sanctions for violations of law and regulations. However, none of these statutory provisions have any association with powers, functions or duties related to matters within the scope of the Customs Acts. Therefore, in regard to the application of section 67 of the Customs Consolidation Act 1876 to the export of bacon, it cannot be assumed that the Commission has any implied authority to withhold payments as a sanction for breach of provisions of the Customs Acts in relation to the import of pigs.

A detailed review of the Pigs and Bacon Acts led Gannon J. to conclude that the legislature did not intend that grading of carcasses be affected by the pigs' country of origin, nor were the Commission or Minister empowered to authorise a licensed factory to make deductions from the minimum price fixed by the Commission, which would make a licensee liable to prosecution. By the 'formula' (the clause pertaining to the Minister's being satisfied as to the country of origin) the Commission, as makers of the two statutory instruments, purport to confer on the Minister the function of determining the place of origin of pigs without guidance by regulation as to how the question for determination is to be submitted. To the extent that the Minister participated in making these statutory instruments, he seemed to arrogate to himself a quasi-judicial function of imposing penal consequences on his own licensees. Neither he nor the Commission has the authority to grant such power.

Gannon J. therefore ruled that both the statutory instruments were invalid and unenforceable with respect to the 'formula', i.e. that part of the schedule in each of the statutory instrumemts containing the words 'other than pigs in respect of which the Minister of Agriculture and Fisheries is not satisfied that the pigs were produced in the State.' Otherwise the instruments are valid and enforceable as if the words had been omitted therefrom.

In addition to this pragmatic resolution of the issues by separating out the *ultra vires* portion of the rules on the grounds that rules made under objectives of one statute cannot be used to enforce different objectives of another statute, it is of interest that Gannon J. accepted administrative documents, newspaper advertisements, conditions of sale and evidence on the process of making rules as evidence of the intention of the Pigs and Bacon Commission and the Minister and of the purpose of the 'formula' part of the regulations. Such evidence would seem to be of the nature referred to in the *Hales* case as 'parliamentary history', albeit in this case it would be 'rule-making history'.

Unreasonableness or Bad Faith

Another ground for claiming that an administrative regulation is *ultra vires* is that it is unreasonable and/or made in bad faith. A case illustrating an unreasonable rule is *Corporation of Limerick v. Sheridan* 90 ILTR 59, which involved an order (i.e. rule) made by the Mayor, Aldermen and Burgesses of the County Borough of Limerick acting as sanitary authority pursuant to section 31 of the Local Government (Sanitary Services) Act 1948. The 1948 Act conferred upon sanitary authorities powers to regulate the erection and use of temporary dwellings (tents, vans, sheds). Under section 30, sanitary authorities were authorised to make bye-laws regulating use of temporary dwellings within the district; section 31 enabled a sanitary authority to prohibit erection or retention of temporary dwellings in its district if they were of opinion it would be prejudicial to public health or amenities or interfere unreasonably with traffic; section 32 brought to bear provisions of the Public Health Act 1978 to a temporary dwelling which had become a nuisance; section 33 extended court powers in proceedings related to temporary dwellings; and section 34 provided comprehensively for licensing of land for use as a camping grounds, to come into effect in a district when the Minister for Local Government made an order to that effect. However, sub-section 12 of section 34 provided that nothing should prohibit or restrict use of land for camping if (1) the land is agricultural land and the camping is done annually by persons in farming operations or (2) the land is occupied in connection with a permanent dwelling situated on the land and the camping is only by persons occupying the permanent dwelling and household members. Under section 31 of the 1948 Act, the County Borough of Limerick, acting as sanitary authority, made an order which prohibited:

> the erection or retention, without the previous written consent of the said Sanitary Authority, of any temporary dwelling on any street or roadway within the area of the County Borough of Limerick, being of opinion that any such erection or retention thereof would interfere to an unreasonable extent with traffic on such street or roadway, or on any land in said County Borough situate within the distance of 300 yards from the centre of any such street or road or from any occupied dwellinghouse therein, being of opinion that any such erection or retention thereof would be prejudicial to the amenities of the locality. (page 60)

The defendant, Mary Sheridan, was living in a caravan on some waste ground at the rear of 9 Parnell Street, Limerick within 300 yards of the centre line of the street. She was charged by the Corporation with contravening the order in question (an offence under section 31(4) of the Local Government (Sanitary Services)

Act 1948) before a district justice who ruled that the order was *ultra vires* section 31 of the Act and dismissed the complaint on the merits. The only question submitted to the High Court was whether the District Justice was correct in point of law in his ruling that the order was *ultra vires* the statute.

The High Court noted that the District Justice had found as a fact that excepting some areas of private land not within 300 yards from any occupied dwelling or the centre lines of any road, the order affected all land within the County Borough. If this order were held valid, any sanitary authority by adopting a sufficiently great distance could bring all land in its district within the ambit of its order. In the opinion of Davitt P., section 31 required that before making such an order the sanitary authority should form the opinion that the erection of temporary dwellings on a particular piece of land or on a particular category of land would be prejudicial to public health or the amenities of the locality involved or interfere unreasonably with traffic on some roads. The sub-sections of the Act could not be read as enabling the sanitary authority to say that in their opinion, all temporary dwellings are prejudicial to public health or to amenities or interfere unreasonably with traffic on roads. Since the terms of the order in question did not indicate that before it was made the Corporation had formed any of the requisite opinions with regard to any particular dwelling or group of dwellings, or particular area of land or specified class of land or locality, the order was *ultra vires* the powers conferred in the Act.

Moreover, in the opinion of Davitt P., the order was unreasonable since it would make it illegal for anyone to erect or retain a temporary dwelling anywhere in the County Borough without written consent of the Corporation. No one could camp in their own garden, nor could harvesters camp on agricultural land where they were working without such consent, yet if section 34 of the 1948 Act were brought into operation such bye-laws could not affect such common law rights guaranteed by sub-section 12 of section 34, and the same would be true of certain other exceptions created by sub-section 10 of section 34. In short, if the bye-laws were enforced, the common law rights contained in these sub-sections would 'go by the board'. In the view of Davitt P.:

> Their [the Corporation's] order was manifestly unjust, and involved such oppressive gratuitous interference with the

common law rights of those affected as could find no justification in the minds of reasonable men. It might well be said that
the legislature never intended to give authority to make such
an order. *It was unreasonable, and therefore ultra vires.* (page 64,
emphasis added)

A more recent case turning on the issue of whether the rule-making
power was exercised *bona fide* as well as a claim of unreasonableness
of a regulation is *Cassidy v. Minister for Industry and Commerce* 1978
IR 298. The Minister had developed a voluntary system whereby
suppliers of goods and services would not increase prices without
advance notice to the Minister, who on review would approve an
increase if acceptable, or refuse it if it were found unjustifiable. The
licensed vintners' associations in Ireland were co-operating with
this system, but the Minister learned that this voluntary agreement
was being broken by publicans in Dundalk selling drink at increased
prices without advance notice to him, and subsequent correspondence and conference failed to dissuade them from continuing this
practice. The Minister then used his powers under the Prices Acts
of 1958 to 1972 to issue statutory instruments establishing maximum
prices for liquor in the urban district of Dundalk, which exempted
hotels but applied equally to public bars and lounge bars. In
response, Dundalk publicans as plaintiffs sought to have the price
orders declared invalid on the grounds that (1) the orders were not
made for the statutory purpose of maintaining price stability but to
force compliance with the non-statutory system of prior notification
of proposed price increases to the Minister; (2) the orders were
unreasonable since the single scale of maximum prices forces publicans operating lounge bars to charge the same prices as publicans
operating public bars.

On the first issue, Henchy J. stated that the evidence led him to
conclude that the Minister's primary purpose in making the orders
was to eliminate unwarranted price increases, while a subsidiary
objective was to return the publicans to the voluntary system. He
held that where a power is delegated to make rules for a purpose
and that power is exercised *bona fide* and primarily for that purpose,
the exercise of the power is not vitiated if it also seeks achievement
of a subsidiary purpose not inconsistent with the permitted purpose.
In regard to the second issue, Henchy J. noted that when parliament
delegates the power of subordinate legislation, it must be exercised

within the limits expressed or implied in the statute, otherwise it
will be held *ultra vires*, since 'it is a necessary implication in such
statutory delegation that the power to issue subordinate legislation
should be exercised reasonably'. *Mixnam's Properties Ltd v. Chertsey
UDC* 1964 1 QB 214 at 237 was quoted as to what constitutes
unreasonableness, namely:

> that kind of unreasonableness which invalidates a bye-law
> . . . is not the antonym of 'reasonableness' . . . but such mani-
> fest arbitrariness, injustice or partiality that a court would say:
> 'Parliament never intended to give authority to make such
> rules; they are unreasonable and *ultra vires*'.(IR, page 311)

Henchy J. held that the Oireachtas could not have intended that
licensees of lounge bars be treated unfairly by maximum price
orders. The Minister understandably exempted hotels from the
maximum price orders, in that if hotel owners had been forced to
sell liquor at the same price as public bars, despite the necessary
capital outlay and overhead expenses of hotels, there would be
general agreement that such a requirement would be ruinously
unfair. By like token, orders which do not distinguish lounge bar
prices from public bar prices unreasonably ignore the fact that
lounge bar owners, like hoteliers, have extra capital outlay and
overhead expenses. Moreover, while the maximum prices fixed for
Dundalk bring prices in public bars in Dundalk down to the level
charged by public bars outside Dundalk, the same prices also apply
to lounge bars in Dundalk, while such maximum prices do not
apply to lounge bars outside Dundalk. Henchy J. therefore ruled
that the orders were not *ultra vires* so far as they apply to public
bars, but they must be construed as not having any application to
lounge bars. If the Minister wishes to fix lounge bar maximum
prices, he may do so, but they should not be marred by unjustifiable
discrimination.

Since reasonableness of a rule may be the determining factor in
a judicial decision that the rule is *ultra* or *intra vires*, the question is
raised as to what is the role of the court and on what basis does it
make such a determination? This was dealt with in *Maloney and
Lenihan v. Minister for Fisheries and Forestry* High Court, unreported,
per McWilliam J., 30 March 1979. The Fisheries (Consolidation)

Act 1959 and Fisheries (Amendment) Act 1962 delegate comprehensive rule-making powers to make such bye-laws which in the Minister's opinion are 'expedient for the more effectual government, management, protection and improvement of the fisheries of the State' dealing with fisheries, times, seasons, places, nets, engines used, types of practice or 'any other matter . . . relating to government and protection' of fisheries. The Minister made a Salmon and Trout Conservation bye-law, No. 606 of 1978, which increased the annual close season for salmon fishing in several ways under section 11 (1) (d) of the 1959 Act. Appellants brought action to have this bye-law annulled. They claimed that the High Court should conduct an inquiry into the propriety of the restrictions so imposed, based on the precedent of *Dodd v. Minister for Fisheries* 1934 IR 291, in which the Court on the basis of evidence tendered had concluded that there was no reasonable ground for supposing that the alteration in the close season made by the bye-law then in question would make any improvement in the fisheries sufficient to outweigh the injury inflicted on appellants.

   In responding to arguments made by plaintiff and defendant on his role in determining the issue, McWilliam J. stated:

> It seems to me that I should approach the matter on the basis of examining the evidence given before me to ascertain whether that evidence, if it had been given before the Minister, is such that he could, for the purposes set out in Section 9 of the Act, and notwithstanding the detriment to the Appellants, reasonably have made the bye-law which he did make, whether I would have made the same bye-law or not.

On review of the statistics and reports produced by the Department, and evidence from witnesses on both sides, McWilliam J. held that the restrictions imposed seriously affected the appellants and that they were persons aggrieved within the meaning of the Act, although they would be able to make a living despite a reduction in income: the evidence demonstrated that salmon stocks were declining and a major cause was the fishing practice which the bye-laws sought to restrict. He concluded that:

> On the main issue I am satisfied on the evidence put before me, that the Minister could reasonably have formed the opinion

that the two bye-laws were expedient for the more effectual government, management, protection and improvement of the fisheries of the State and that this expediency was such as to outweigh the serious detriment to the Appellants. The fact that additional steps, particularly with regard to illegal fishing, could also have been taken appears to me to be irrelevant.

As to the claim that one effect of the bye-laws may be to discriminate against drift-net fishermen in favour of draught-net fishermen, McWilliam J. held that this was a subsidiary effect and not, as it was in *Dodd's* case, the sole effect of the bye-law.

The *Maloney* case provides a classic statement of the role of the courts in reviewing an administrative regulation. The judge is to determine whether the Minister could reasonably have made the regulation given the facts at hand, *not* whether the judge would have made the same regulation had he been the rule-maker. In deciding that a rule is or is not *ultra vires* the statute, it is not for the judge to determine the wisdom of the rule or whether in his opinion a more effective rule could have been made.

A claim that an order (regulation) is unreasonable may be accompanied by a related claim that it was made *mala fides*, and the accompanying question as to the extent to which the court may probe into the rule-making processes. In *Listowel Urban District Council v. McDonough* 1968 IR 312, the Supreme Court heard a case stated from the Circuit Court to which defendant had appealed from a prohibition order issued by the complainants as sanitary authority for the Listowel UDC. The order prohibited the erection or retention of temporary dwellings on a number of named streets, stating that the order was made since the Council were 'of the opinion that any such erection or retention thereof would be prejudicial to public health'. Defendant was convicted and fined ten shillings in the Listowel District Court for contravention of the order as an owner of a wheeled caravan on one of the named streets. On appeal to the Circuit Court, defendant argued that the order was *ultra vires* section 31, Local Government (Sanitary Services) Act 1948, in that it was (1) unreasonable; (2) complainants had not taken reasonable steps to inquire into the matter before arriving at their opinion; (3) the opinion of the complainants was not arrived at *bona fide;* and (4) the order referring to his particular street was bad since his street did not appear on any official map. Counsel for the defence further argued that to resolve these issues, the Court was entitled to enquire into various aspects of the rule-making process. This argument was disputed by counsel for the complainants. In order to resolve this argument, the President of the Circuit Court referred to the Supreme Court the questions as to whether (1) the Court is entitled to enquire into what transpired at the Council meeting and the evidence available to the Council concerning the making of the bye-law; (2) the views expressed by Council members and officials of the Council on the bye-laws and the veracity of the opinion they expressed; and (3) whether or not the said opinion was arrived at *bona fide*. A technical question on the identification of the streets in the order was also referred to the Supreme Court.

After disposing of the technical question on street identification, Ó Dálaigh C. J. referred to the opinion of Lord Russell of Killowen C. J. in *Kruse v. Johnson* (1890) 2 QB 91, stating that there may be cases in which it is the Court's duty to condemn bye-laws as invalid since they were unreasonable by virtue of being partial or unequal in their operation on different classes, or manifestly unjust or if they disclosed bad faith. In addition the views of Lord Somervell in *Smith v. East Elloe District Council* 1956 A.C. 736 were cited first, to the effect that *mala fides* has not ever been precisely defined but it covers fraud or corruption and second, that a distinction exists between an *ultra vires* act done *bona fide* and an act which, although on the face of it regular, nevertheless will be held null and void if *mala fides* is discovered and brought before the court.

Given this precedent, Ó Dálaigh C.J. stated that a discretionary statutory power, if exercised in bad faith, can be condemned as invalid and that *mala fides* is a well-recognised ground of challenge. Although the defendant's challenge could be by way of certiorari and litigation of the matter by action in the High Court, he saw no reason for limiting the defendant to that mode of redress. There was nothing to preclude the defendant from raising *mala fides* as part of his defence in the criminal action against him. In respect of unreasonableness and *mala fides* being used as part of defendant's defence, Ó Dálaigh C. J. stated that his answers to the questions in the case stated by the Circuit Court would be in the affirmative, i.e. the lower court was entitled to make all three types of enquiries into the process of making the bye-laws as delineated in the questions the lower court had asked.

The issue of reasonableness of a rule based on the weight of evidence also raised the related questions of the procedures through which such evidence was submitted for review on appeal, and the role of the court in exercising judgment on the validity of a rule, in the case *In the Matter of the Fisheries (Consolidation) Act 1959; Dunne and Others v. Minister for Fisheries and Forestry* High Court, unreported, per Costello J., 10 February 1984. The Minister under section 8 of the 1959 Act gave notice that he was considering the justification for three bye-laws made in 1913 prohibiting drift net fishing for salmon in a specified area of the tidal waters off the Kerry coast. A subsequent three-day enquiry in October 1980 was presided over by Dr Gibson, a senior inspector and scientific advisor in the Department of Fisheries and Forestry, who heard oral evidence and submissions by legal advisers of interested parties. A new South Western Fisheries Region Bye-Law No. 620, 1981 was then made which revoked all three of the 1913 bye-laws, opened up large tracts of water off the Kerry coast for drift net fishing of salmon, and abolished what had been referred to as a 'sanctuary area' for some 70 years.

Appellants as persons aggrieved under section 11 of the 1959 Act appealed to the High Court against the 1981 bye-law, submitting affidavits which included a transcript of the evidence taken at the public enquiry. Appellants through an order of discovery of documents and reply from the Minister also brought before the Court copies of a report and memoranda by Dr Gibson, after the Minister's demand for formal proof of these documents was met. The report and oral evidence of Dr Gibson, considered by the court to be 'a highly experienced scientific expert', strongly advised the Minister against revoking the bye-laws. The only evidence adduced for the respondent Minister, other than copies of the former and new bye-laws, was that of a departmental inspector junior to Dr Gibson who had attended the enquiry. She admitted she was in agreement with Dr Gibson's opinion as to what was likely to happen if drift net fishing in the sanctuary area was permitted, but nevertheless supported the main arguments of the Minister for revoking the 1913 bye-laws. The affidavits for the Minister averred that he was satisfied that salmon conservation policy did not require the continuing prohibition of drift netting in the Kerry region, and that in arriving at this decision the Minister had available a volume of expert technical advice together with the report of the public

enquiry. However, Costello J. noted that although it was a reasonable inference that the report of the public enquiry and the volume
of technical evidence referred to in the affidavits supported the
Minister's decision to make the 1981 bye-law, the actual facts did
not warrant that inference. It was clear from the evidence that there
was no 'volume of expert technical advice' available to the Minister;
the only expert technical advice was that of Dr Gibson that revocation of the 1913 bye-laws would be contrary to proper salmon
conservation policy. Although the Minister undoubtedly had available a great deal of technical scientific data on the subject of
conserving salmon stocks in general, no reference was made in his
affidavits of scientific studies of a general nature in support of the
new bye-law, nor did the studies quoted by witnesses at the enquiry
provide such support.

Prior to drawing conclusions on the evidence, Costello J. dealt
with submissions of the Minister that, based on treatise references
and British precedents, the Court had no jurisdiction to substitute
its judgment for that of the Minister, and could annul a bye-law
only in such exceptional situations as the Minister acting entirely
unreasonably. Costello J. distinguished between the exercise of
common law power of judicial review and appellate jurisdiction
given by statute. In view of the judgment in *Dodd v Minister for
Fisheries* 1934 IR 291, the similarity of the appellate jurisdiction
conferred by the Fisheries Act 1925 and the current 1959 Fisheries
Act, he concluded that the court's statutory jurisdiction on an
appeal should be wider than its powers when exercising its inherent
jurisdiction at common law. Moreover, the right of an appeal in
the 1959 Act is not limited to a point of law only as in section 45,
Social Welfare Act 1952. Furthermore, a court's power to confirm
or annul instruments under the 1959 Act can arise in a variety of
circumstances in which a party may or may not have had opportunity to present his case to the Minister, so a court might have to
allow a witness to give evidence and decide the matter on material
not available to the Minister. This indicates that in cases where
new evidence is given and also where the appeal is decided on the
same data before the Minister, the court may annul a bye-law or
other instrument if in the court's opinion the bye-law is not expedient for the statutory objective of 'the more effectual government,
management, protection and improvement of the fisheries of the
State'.

As to procedure in the development and review of evidence, Costello J. noted that where an appeal from a bye-law is preceded by a public enquiry, it is desirable that the appeal be heard on the evidence given in that enquiry and on all other materials the Minister had before him. However, the Court also has power to hear additional evidence by way of affidavit or oral testimony, and 'it should exercise this power if the Minister declines [as happened in this case] to make available to the Court the report of the Inspector who held the enquiry and the other material on which the opinion of the Minister was based.' Secondly, if an enquiry relating to the justification for retaining existing bye-laws is made, the Minister and the court on appeal must consider not only the effect of a new bye-law on the fisheries in the immediate area but also how new bye-laws may affect fisheries elsewhere, and all probable consequences which flow from the new bye-law.

His evaluation of the conflicting evidence in the enquiry between witnesses for and against repeal of the 1913 bye-laws led Costello J. to decide that the issue was essentially one for expert scientific assessment. He thus had to be guided by Dr Gibson's uncontradicted evidence concerning the rapid decline of salmon stocks in Cork and Waterford rivers, in the Kerry coastal district and in other areas. He felt Dr Gibson was correct in concluding that the principal cause had been excessive legal and illegal drift netting although poaching, pollution and disease were contributing causes, and that the facts established at the enquiry supported Dr Gibson's opinion. To abolish the Kerry sanctuary and license extra drift netting would exacerbate the excessive exploitation of salmon in the area, and would not be conducive to the statutory objective of proper management, protection and improvement of salmon fisheries either locally or nationally. Given this, he rejected the argument that Kerry fishermen should be granted drift net licences equal to such grants in other areas (which ignores the statutory objectives) and the argument that since the former bye-laws were considered arbitrary thus contributing to illegal drift net fishing, the new bye-law would contribute to compliance with conservation and regulatory measures. The evidence did not suggest that the previous bye-laws were unenforceable, nor did it show that repeal of a major conservation bye-law would result in remaining conservation measures being obeyed. He concluded that the evidence is that the new bye-law did not achieve the statutory objectives and that it must be annulled.

The *Limerick, Cassidy, Maloney, Listowel* and *Fisheries (Consolidation) Act 1959* cases demonstrate that the courts do not see their role as that of substituting their judgment for that of the administrators on the content of regulations which are *intra vires*. However, the courts will nullify an order or rule as *ultra vires* the statute when the evidence shows it was arrived at through exercising rule-making power *mala fides* or that the regulation is *prima facie* so unreasonable that it could not have been intended by the statute, *e.g.* an all-encompassing and gratuitous control over temporary dwellings as in *Limerick*. Again an unjustifiably discriminatory treatment of a class of parties falling within the regulations will be held to be *ultra vires* as in *Cassidy*. Moreover, the cases, notably *Listowel* and *Fisheries (Consolidation) Act 1959* demonstrate that administrators should exercise their discretionary rule-making power to provide not only a rationale but also sufficient evidence for their rules. *Listowel* and *Fisheries (Consolidation) Act 1959* open the door to judicial review and evaluation of evidence concerning the veracity of the opinions or inputs and processes of administrators participating in the making of rules, the adequacy of the information relied on for making rules and attention to the range of consequences resulting from the adoption of rules.

Binding Effect of Rules

Another issue concerning the validity of administrative rules involves the extent to which the rule-making authority is limited or bound by its own rules. In *O'Callaghan and Ó Cinneide v. Minister for Education* unreported, Supreme Court, per Kingsmill Moore J., 1955, plaintiffs claimed a number of declarations constituting two overall contentions. The first was that those rules and regulations governing the position, duties, rights and emoluments of national teachers in force and effect when any national teacher was employed in a national school, formed a continuing contract of employment which persists as long as the teacher remains so employed. Thus any representations contained in such rules and regulations are binding on the Minister for Education. Secondly, the provisions in the rules introduced in 1946 granting greater remuneration to married than to unmarried teachers were unauthorised and void, in so far as they affected those teachers who entered the service before 31 October 1946, as in the case of the two plaintiffs.

Kingsmill Moore J., for the Supreme Court, made an analysis of the Department of Education's system of rules on curriculum, the qualifications, payment and promotion of teachers, functions of school managers, the rules extant when plaintiffs were appointed and the effect of the 1946 rule changes on them. Based on this analysis and judicial precedents, he first concluded that the making and publication of these rules constitute representations to managers and teachers as to the way funds granted by parliament would be applied. To the extent that parliament granted discretion in this respect, the Minister for Education is legally bound by the representations he has made: the representations made to a teacher are those contained in the rules in force when he or she was appointed. Thus when agreements with teachers are renewed owing to a change in managers, this would not import a change in the rules in force to the detriment of a teacher and at variance with representations made in rules existing at the time of appointment. Since teachers enter service with intent to make it a lifelong professional career, and the rules extant when they enter the service represent the conditions of the service, the teachers should be able to rely on the continuance of such conditions, subject to whatever provisions for change are contained in those rules. At the same time, the Minister for Education must be able to make general alteration of pay rates for all teachers to enable the Department to operate within the funds allocated by the Oireachtas to education. However, a change in the rules on salaries to impose new qualifications for teachers to receive the same salary rates they were entitled to receive under their previous or existing conditions should not be made.

In this regard, plaintiffs argued that the revised salary scale introduced by the 1946 changes in the rules by the Minister granting more remuneration to married than unmarried teachers constituted an alteration of the rules prevailing when they entered the service to the detriment of their position and status, since a junior married teacher might earn more than a senior unmarried teacher, and an unmarried teacher cannot reach the top of the salary scale unless he or she marries. Kingsmill Moore J. ruled against this argument, since plaintiffs' emoluments were not reduced, but rather increased by the 1946 and subsequent rules. Although emoluments of married teachers were increased to a greater degree, this cannot be regarded as a financial detriment to plaintiffs.

This decision appears to have established that an administrative

K

authority is bound by its own rules and should not change or apply rules to adversely alter or to deny legal rights of individuals provided for in those rules, in circumstances where the persons affected were entitled to expect the continuation of those rights. Subject to this limitation, changes in rules which affect all those covered by the rules (although some may benefit more than others, or may reflect fiscal constraints) are not prohibited.

Improper Procedures
The provisions which are of general application pertaining to procedures for rule-making in the Statutory Instruments Act 1947 (as amended by the Statutory Instruments Act 1955) and in the Houses of the Oireachtas (Laying of Documents) Act 1966, have been outlined above, together with the functions of the Select Committee on Statutory Instruments. (See pages 225-6 and 50-52 respectively.) However, these Irish statutes of general application to rule-making do not require participatory procedures in rule-making to the extent found in the American Administrative Procedures Act 1946, as provided for in the following excerpts from section 553 of that Act:

(b) General notice of proposed rule-making shall be published in the Federal Register, unless persons subject thereto are named and either personally served or otherwise have actual notice thereof . . . . The notice shall include–
(1) a statement of the time, place, and nature of public rule-making proceedings;
(2) reference to the legal authority under which the rule is proposed; and
(3) either the terms or substance of the proposed rule or a description of the subjects and issues involved. . . .

(c) After notice required by this section, the agency shall give interested persons an opportunity to participate in the rule-making through submission of written views or arguments, with or without opportunity for oral presentation. After consideration of the relevant matters presented, the agency shall incorporate in the rules adopted a concise general statement of their basis and purpose. *When rules are required by statute to be made on the record after opportunity for an agency hearing, sections 555 and 557 of this title apply instead of this sub-section.* (emphasis added)

Exceptions to these procedural requirements are made in section 553(a) with regard to military or foreign affairs, and matters of agency management, personnel, property, loans, grants, benefits or contracts. Similarly, modifying clauses (A) and (B) in section 553(b) exempt interpretative rules, policy statements, rules or agency organisation, procedure or practice or when the agency gives findings and measures in rules that notice-and-comment procedure is impracticable or contrary to public interest (unless required by statute). Finally, substantive rules must be published not less than 30 days before their effective date under section 553(d) (except for interpretive rules, policy statements or as otherwise provided by the agency for good cause) and section 553(e) gives interested persons the right to petition for issue, amendment or repeal of a rule. These provisions, and sections 554-7 on adjudication, have been the basis for much litigation in the United States on whether an administrative action is rule-making or adjudication (thus calling for different procedural requirements) and, if it is rule-making, whether rule-making is interpretative-type and exempt from, or legislative-type and subject to, section 553 notice-and-comment requirements.

A more recent issue raised with varying success has been the claim that even if the rule is interpretative, the impact of the rule on parties is such that basic fairness requires adherence to section 553 procedures. And although there is an absence of explicit statutory language in a statute requiring that rules 'be made on the record' after an opportunity for hearing, it may be claimed that the statutory *intent* as implied in its language was to require rule-making to be 'on the record', and thus the more rigorous procedures of a trial type or adjudicatory hearing is required, per sections 556-7 of the APA.[4]

A relatively early case in which the procedures for making of rules was at issue is that of *Pigs Marketing Board v. Donnelly (Dublin) Ltd* 1939 IR 413, in which the Board sued for payment of over £14,000 levied on defendant amounting to the difference between the 'appointed price' and the 'hypothetical price' in certain sale periods, under the Board's 'Appointed Price Orders'. The major issue in this case as discussed in chapter 3 was that the Act involved was unconstitutional as an invalid delegation of legislative power by the Oireachtas, and as being contrary to social justice and the guarantee of private property in the Constitution. Hanna J. upheld the constitutionality of the Act against all these challenges in the High Court. In addition, defendant claimed that there were procedural defects in the Board's making of appointed price orders for pig carcasses. The first was that all the Price Orders, Classification Orders, and Hypothetical Price Orders made under the Acts were invalid, since the Board did not comply with the requirements of section 134(2)(b) of the 1935 Act. The Board had not passed a resolution specifying the terms of the order. Moreover, the making of the order was not in the first place referred to the ordinary members for their vote thereon, nor was it decided by the unanimous vote of the ordinary members or by the chairman in default of a decision by a unanimous vote of the ordinary members. In regard to these assertions, Hanna J. held that although certain minutes which were submitted and impeached were brief, they were sufficient in terms of stating that a resolution was passed to a certain effect by the Board without going into the details of the voting and other matters relied upon. This, together with the evidence submitted by the chairman of the Board, satisfied Hanna J. that all the requirements of the 1935 Act for rule-making procedure had been met. Moreover, the orders or rules were protected by section 77 of the 1937 Act which states that the making of an order by the Board shall be *prima facie* evidence that such order was validly made in all respects.

On the other hand, a procedural defect in the Board's application of its orders resulted in a ruling partially in favour of the defendants. The claim made by the Board for some £5,500 out of the total £14,000 claimed was based on the 1935 Act, and was distinct from the remaining claim of over £9,000 alleged to be due under the 1937 Act. The 1935 Act in section 147 provided for a very simple procedure whereby the Board must serve a 'notice' stating the money required to be paid and upon service of that 'notice' the money became a debt due to the Board recoverable as a simple contract debt. These provisions had been complied with by the Board making the same £5,500 claim recoverable. However, under the 1937 Act, section 70 calls the sum payable a 'levy' and prescribes a procedure for recovery as follows: (1) ascertain the amount; (2) make a certificate which certifies the amount payable by a particular person in respect of the appropriate periods, and (3) serve a copy of the certificate on that person. These procedures must be executed by the Board, as a corporation sole with a seal, and not by a subordinate official. Despite these different provisions, the old procedure of the 1935 Act had been followed for recovering the £9,000 under the 1937 statute. As a consequence, Hanna J. ruled that the Board had not put itself into a position to recover the total balance of over £14,000, although he also held that this discrepancy could be remedied in future proceedings.

Judicial perspectives on precise adherence to procedures in rule-making as against quasi-adjudicative enforcement action against an individual are implied in this decision. The Court rejected a probe into the minutes supporting the resolution establishing the general price orders and was satisfied that there had been general adherence to the rule-making provisions in the statute. On the other hand, where there was non-adherence to procedure as specified in the statute for enforcement of the rule with a direct monetary impact on the individual, the Court expected strict adherence to the terms of the statute.

The decision in the *Pigs Marketing Board* case focussed on the sufficiency of adherence to statutory provisions on procedure in making a general rule or order. In the later case of *Finn v. Bray Urban District Council* 1969 IR 169, the broader issue of the purpose of rule-making procedure was raised. As the discussion of that case in chapter 5 indicates, the Court rejected defendant's argument that the main purpose and statutory intent was to provide machinery for a public authority to stimulate public interest and discussion of a draft local development plan and to sound out public opinion when the planning authority considered it desirable to do so. Instead, the Court held that given the potential adverse effect of a development plan on private property, the primary statutory intent of the rule-making procedures was to protect individual rights. Consequently the Court held that a draft development plan should be prepared, and notice given, with opportunity to inspect the draft and make written and oral objections. Moreover, this process should be repeated if amendments were made in the draft to be incorporated in the final plan.

The emphasis upon providing procedural rights in the rule-making process in the *Finn* case was extended in the more recent case of *Burke v. Minister for Labour* 1979 IR 354, in which the Court stressed 'constitutional propriety', natural justice and fairness in procedures to be followed in rule-making if the agency is to remain *intra vires* the statute. Plaintiffs were employer representatives on the Hotels Joint Labour Committee (hereafter the Committee) together with worker and independent representatives and an independent chairman, which was established by the Labour Court under the Industrial Relations Act 1946 to make regulations fixing minimum rates of pay for hotel workers. Under the Act, the Committee initiates proposals for employment regulation orders for submission to the Labour Court which may: (1) approve the proposed order or (2) send it back with observations to the Committee for reconsideration and resubmission to the Labour Court with or without amendments in response to the observations. Following either step (1) or (2), the Labour Court publishes a notice of the proposals to allow representations which must be considered by the Committee and the Committee then may re-submit proposals with or without amendment to the Labour Court, which may approve or disapprove of the proposed order. A remuneration order has the force of law, with criminal and civil penalties for non-compliance by employers. Remuneration rate orders are not subject to ministerial control or parliamentary control through laying on the table, and are not subject to change or revocation for six months.

Plaintiff's claim was that a new remuneration order, S.I. No. 156 of 1978, Employment Regulation Order (Hotels Joint Labour Committee) 1978, to which they took exception and made objections when the order was being made, had been formulated without including in the wage increase calculations the increases in the true values of board and lodging supplied to workers which should be deducted from gross earnings.

Henchy J. for the Supreme Court noted that the initiative for the formulation of the Order came from the workers' representatives on the Committee. Moreover in the formulation and adoption of the Order, there had been consistent refusal during the Committee's meetings by a majority of the Committee who were workers and independent representatives to consider the data the employers' representatives wished the Committee to consider. The process followed was one of rejecting the motions put forward by the employers' representatives in one informal vote, and then reaching agreement informally without a vote. He held that it was within the statutory power of the Committee over its own internal procedures to decide, after discussion in its meetings, that the motions of the employers' representatives did not require a formal vote of rejection during the Committee meetings. However, whether the Committee had the power to reject the employers' representatives' motions and make the order without regard to the real cost to employers of board and lodging supplied was another matter, particularly in view of the extensive nature of the rule-making power delegated to the Committee. The Labour Court could only veto or accept orders proposed by the Committee, making the Committee the order-making body, not subject to ministerial or parliamentary controls. When such powers are delegated by parliament:

> it is to be necessarily inferred as part of the legislative intention that the body which makes the orders will exercise its functions, not only with constitutional propriety and due regard to natural justice, but also within the framework and terms and objects of the relevant Act and with basic fairness, reasonableness and good faith. The absoluteness of the delegation is susceptible of unjust and tyrannous abuse unless its operation is thus confined. . . . (page 361)

Given this legislative intent, Henchy J. felt that the wish of employer representatives on the Committee that the Committee give consideration to the actual cost to employers of board and lodging supplied to workers was a reasonable proposal, pertinent to assessing a fair figure for computing remuneration, and therefore:

> By the self denying restraint by which the Committee debarred themselves from looking at the data necessary to determine the true cost to the employer of board and lodging, the Committee left themselves open to the charge that the consequent minimum-remuneration order may be unjust and unfair . . . . Nor is it a good answer to say that, if the Committee had taken into account the true, rather than the estimated, cost of board and lodging the figures fixed as minimum rates of remuneration would not have been materially affected. . . even if such evidence would have made no difference, the Committee, by rejecting it unheard and unconsidered, left themselves open to the imputation of bias, unfairness and prejudice . . . Elementary fairness required that the employers as well as the

employees . . . should have been allowed to present and see
consideration given to material . . . crucially relevant to the
question of minimum rates of remuneration . . . .

By failing to receive and consider that evidence, the Committee
failed to keep within the confines of their statutory terms of
reference as those must necessarily be inferred. In other words,
the order of 1978 was made in excess of jurisdiction to that
extent. (pages 362-3)

The *Finn* and the *Burke* cases demonstrate that the courts in interpreting statutory provisions concerning rule-making procedures
tend to require adherence to concepts of natural justice by administrative bodies carrying out such procedures, despite the fact that
what is involved is a quasi-legislative, rather than adjudicative,
function.

The remaining issue which has been raised in respect of administrative rule-making procedures is whether the rule-making authority
has complied with statutory requirements concerning submission
of rules to the Oireachtas for scrutiny and possibly nullification by
a resolution of one or both of the Houses. In *Premier Meat Packers
(Ireland) Ltd v. Minister for Agriculture and Fisheries* unreported, High
Court, per O'Keeffe P., 30 July 1971, plaintiffs claimed two declarations. The first was that the defendant had collected certain money
levies for a purpose which had failed. The second was that the
statutory instruments under which the levies were made were null
and void for not having been laid before each House of the Oireachtas as soon as possible after being made. For these reasons, plaintiffs
claimed a return of the levies paid by them.

These issues and the manner of their resolution by the courts
stemmed from a complex sequence of events and negotiations
between officials of the Department of Agriculture, the Director of
An Foras Talúntais (the state-sponsored Agricultural Institute) and
representative bacon curers, fresh meat exporters and canners, in
regard to the establishment of a research unit under the rubric of
the 1958 *Programme of Economic Expansion*. The stated purpose in
the programme was to make state aid available for research into
economic problems of the meat industry and specifically to provide
state assistance to establish a full-scale research unit to keep abreast

of technical developments, to do research on expansion of the bacon-curing industry, and to investigate problems common to the pig and cattle processing industries.

The prolonged negotiations between the Minister and representatives of the meat industry started with an assumption by the parties involved that the research unit would be separate from An Foras Talúntais. As time went on, this assumption changed in favour of tying the research unit in certain ways to An Foras Talúntais to facilitate several forms of subsidisation from the government so as to meet anticipated costs of the proposed research unit. There was also a request from the meat associations that the Minister increase rates of slaughtering fees, the increase to be used for a state support grant to the research unit. However, with the selection of a director for the proposed research unit by the newly formed Irish Meat Association, and on his advice, the Meat Association reverted to the original position of the meat industry that they should have a research unit of their own, separate from and not tied to An Foras Talúntais. This would require additional fiscal assistance.

Unfortunately this return to the concept of an independent research unit was not conveyed to the Minister for seven months, during which time he had laid before the Dáil and the Seanad drafts of regulations to provide for the special additional levy requested by the representatives of the meat industry. The drafts of regulations were accompanied by explanatory notes and copies of the Minister's speeches covering the origin and purpose of the research unit, the proposed allocation of the increased levies solely to the Research Unit, and the organisation of the research unit and its relationship to An Foras Talúntais. The drafts of regulations were approved by the Dáil and the Seanad by mid-December. The final official rules or orders were made by the Minister on 24 February 1964, despite the fact that almost immediately after the Dáil and Seanad approvals in mid-December, he had received a letter from the Meat Association stating their change in view and abandonment of the scheme as outlined by them to the Minister prior to the development of the drafts of the regulations.

Following this, correspondence between representatives of the meat trade and the Department continued at length over a number of years, but no agreement was reached on establishing a Meat Research Institute. During these years money was collected in levies under the orders issued in 1964 by the Minister, and was placed in a suspense account during the early years (since it supposedly was for a research institute), but later the Comptroller and Auditor General gave advice leading to the levies being spent as an ordinary revenue of the state.

The High Court refused to accept the contention of the plaintiffs that since they had been unable to agree with the Minister as to the manner of organising the research institute and the extent of state fiscal support, the fees that had been levied had been collected for a purpose which had failed and therefore plaintiffs were entitled to repayment of the fees. Inasmuch as agreement theoretically might be reached at any time, and the fees collected then applied to the purpose for which they were collected, plaintiffs were not entitled to a return of their fees. Moreover, the Minister's argument that the fees collected are to be applied for the benefit of the Exchequer in such manner as the Minister for Finance might direct was strictly in accordance with section 52, Agricultural Produce Act 1954. Although the Court felt this was a breach of faith by the Minister for Agriculture towards the trade interests at whose instance the regulations were made, and the Oireachtas which approved of the draft regulations on the basis of the Minister's statements, the fact remained that the fees had been put into the general revenue of the state and had been diverted from the purpose for which they were collected. Consequently it was not open to the Court to order any direction for their restoration to a suspense or other account.

As to plaintiffs' second claim that the regulations were void since only the drafts, and not the final regulations had been laid before the Oireachtas, the Court held that it apparently was assumed by the Minister that once approval for the draft regulations was obtained by resolution of each House, it was unnecessary to lay the final regulations before the Houses. Since the final regulations were not laid before each House as soon as they might have been after they were made:

> having regard to the change of mind on the part of the Plaintiffs it is not possible to say that if they were so laid they would not have been annulled within the period prescribed by the statutes.

At the same time, the Court noted, counsel for the Minister argued that the statute did not specify that if the regulations were not so laid they became invalid, and in this respect counsel was correct. However much the Court might like to think that when a Minister ignores a statutory direction of this kind the regulations as a result would be regarded as null and void *ab initio*, the authorities, such as they are, did not justify such a ruling. In view of this situation, the Court held that the Minister had an obligation even at this late date to comply with the law by laying the regulation before each House of the Oireachtas: each House may consider whether they should be allowed to stand or be annulled by resolution. If plaintiffs wished, the Court would make a direction to that effect; otherwise, plaintiffs were entitled to no relief in their action.

Legislative Policy and Judicial Doctrines

It is apparent from the statutory provisions and judicial decisions on rule-making discussed above that there is absence of explicit statutory definition distinguishing rule-making from adjudication or legislative as against interpretative-type rule-making in either an administrative procedures Act or individual statutes in Ireland (thus relieving Irish, like English, courts from litigation based on statutory distinctions which may seem artificial when applied to specific situations). However, the courts in their decisions have made distinctions by delineating the courts' role in reviewing rule-making versus adjudication and the legal effect of legislative as against interpretative rules.

The legislative delegation and exercise of rule-making by administrative agencies in Ireland has been largely legislative-type rule-making. In this regard, the grounds for challenge and issues raised concerning legislative rule-making generally parallel those found in the United States, namely claims that the rules are made under an unconstitutional delegation of legislative power; are themselves unconstitutional, are *ultra vires* the statute for reasons of excess of jurisdiction or unreasonableness; contravene the binding effect of rules on the rule-maker; or were not made in compliance with statutory requirements of procedure in making rules. One area of contrast is that since Ireland does not provide for generally applicable procedures in rule-making in an administrative procedures Act comparable to the American APA, the Irish courts are free to apply their judicially developed standards as to the application of natural and constitutional justice concepts when interpreting the rule-making procedure provisions in individual statutes. In this respect, the *Finn* and the *Burke* cases discussed above indicate that the Irish courts may tend to require procedures more akin to those of an adjudicative rather than a quasi-legislative process when direct impact upon individual legal interests or rights is involved. The conflicting arguments in the *Finn v. Bray* case as to the purpose of rule-making procedures, i.e. public participation to inform the rule-maker versus protection of individual rights, is symptomatic of a basic conceptual problem running through issues of rule-making. Although the legislature delegates, and the courts uphold that delegation of legislative power, both bodies seek to impose controls on administrative exercise of rule-making power (occasionally with frustration, as indicated when the Court in the *Premier Meat Packers* case was unable to reverse a *fait accompli* despite non-compliance with statutory requirements for laying of the final rules on the table).

This tension in Ireland, as in England and the United States, is between the legislature's need to delegate rule-making power to administrators for the reasons discussed in chapter 3, and its concern that administrators, immune from electoral controls, may be insensitive to electoral reaction and to the legal rights of individuals or groups affected by the rules. A feeling also can develop in the legislative and judicial branches that the administration has supplanted the legislature and judiciary in certain areas of their traditional powers and roles. These factors, as will be seen, also arise in the legislative delegation and judicial review of investigating, licensing and directing powers.

Notes to Chapter 6

1. See Gavan Duffy, 'Administrative Law: The Urgent Need of Systematisation and Publicity', *The Irish Jurist* 34-6, Vol I. No. 5 (August 1935); Asmal, 'Administrative Law in Ireland' in *Survey of Public Administration and Administrative Law in Ireland*, 72-74; extract from *International Review of Administrative Sciences* Vol.34, 1968; Wade, *Administrative Law* 733-75 (1982); Schwartz and Wade, *Legal Control of Government* 84-106 (1972); David, *French Law*, 22-23 (1972); Brown and Garner, *French Administrative Law* 8, 9, 11-12 (1983)
2. Davis, *Administrative Law, Cases-Text-Problems* [*Administrative Law*] 241 (1977)
3. Schwartz and Wade *Legal Control of Government* 98-100 (1972)
4. Davis, *Administrative Law* 241-269; see also Jaffe and Nathanson, *Administrative Law, Cases and Materials* 497-524 (1976)

7 Investigating Powers

Information is essential to the administrative implementation of statutory goals and with the increased complexity of functions performed by the modern state, there is a corresponding increase in the need for a wide variety of information. Administrative fact-finding may even include research on scientific and socio-economic factors in planning and budgeting for 'service'-oriented functions such as subsistence payments. For example, section 66 of the Social Welfare (Consolidation) Act 1981 provides that the Minister may promote research into preventing occupational accidents or diseases through employing research personnel, contributing to research expenses or otherwise assisting researchers. However, the investigatory power is more commonly associated with regulatory functions, such as requiring safety measures in factories, issuing orders which prohibit unfair methods of competition, the sale of obscene literature, the licensing of professions and private enterprises and control over land use. Legal controversy over the application of investigatory power arises most frequently in programmes of a regulatory nature, although administrative fact-finding may be resisted by those adversely affected by research in public health or social service programmes on the grounds of invasion of privacy.

Purposes of Investigating Power

Investigating power has three purposes. The first is to provide a means for continuing supervision to ensure compliance with standards set by a statute or regulation. Its most typical form is the on-site inspection, which induces the operator of an enterprise to maintain required standards to pass the inspection. If the inspector finds non-compliance, the usual process is educational and correctional in that the inspector states what must be done to rectify matters within a given time limit before reinspection, unless the non-compliance is so dangerous as to require suspension of the operation until correction is made. This process may vary in the use of oral and/or written warnings and the length of time allowed for the enterprise to come up to the prescribed standards.

Such continuing supervision through inspection usually secures adherence to administrative standards without further coercive measures. If non-compliance should continue, the second purpose of investigating power is to provide facts to sustain an action for administrative enforcement such as revocation of a licence or an administrative order when reviewed by the courts.

A third purpose of the investigating or fact-finding power is to provide information as a basis for policy-making, either in the formulation of rules or orders or the drafting of proposed legislation.

The three major types of investigating power consist of the physical inspection or audit by agency administrators; the requirement that oral testimony be given and documents submitted to the administrative agency; and the requirement that records be maintained and reports submitted in the form and content specified in advance by the agency.

Inspections

The on-site inspection or audit by an administrative inspector of an enterprise results in the gathering of facts which typically are recorded on a form or checklist to show compliance or non-compliance with standards contained in Acts and statutory instruments. An inspection or audit may range from checking the safety of physical equipment in a plant to evaluating the potential and actual use of land to asking employees and employers questions in relation to alleged restrictive business practices. For example, sections 35 and 36 of the Safety in Industry Act 1980 provide that employees may chose either a 'safety representative' or a 'safety committee' which then appoints a 'safety delegate'. Section 37 of that Act specifies that if neither a safety representative nor a committee have been so appointed within six months, the relevant occupier (of the place of work) must appoint from among the employees a safety representative or a safety committee, depending on whether the work force is 20 or less or has over 20 employees. The safety representatives or delegates represent the employees in consultations with the employer and assist the employer in matters of safety measures under the Act and related regulations. They also make representations to inspectors of the Department of Labour on safety, health, and welfare of the employees. The safety delegate is entitled to accompany the inspector on his tour of inspection. Under section 38 the Minister for Labour may cause an inspection in response to a request from a safety committee or officer and convey the outcome to the requesting party. The Minister may also designate an industrial medical adviser under section 50 who may invite employees to be medically examined for purposes of the Act. An inspector, in accordance with section 53, on entering a factory may take samples of air and samples of any substance in the factory, take any measurement or photograph or make any tape or electrical recording he considers necessary under the Act. Section 11 provides that the results of inspections may lead to a prohibition notice or directive to cease activities being undertaken or about to be undertaken in a factory.

Broad inspection powers are granted under section 83 (1) and (2) of the Local Government (Planning and Development) Act 1963 as amended by section 42(c) (i), (ii) and (iii) of the 1976 Act, to authorised persons to enter land during normal business hours and to do all things necessary to carry out the purposes of the Act, such as surveying, making plans, taking levels, making excavations and examining depth and nature of the subsoil. Similarly, inspectors according to section 264 of the Social Welfare (Consolidation) Act 1981 may enter premises covered by the Act to make such inquiry as necessary, and require any person on the premises whom the inspector has reason to think is an insured person to sign a declaration of the truth of the matters in respect of which he has been examined. The Act requires employers and their employees to produce documents on wages, registrations and other documents as the inspector may reasonably require, subject to penalty for delay, obstruction or refusing to respond to requisitions. Under section 61, regulations may provide for disqualifying a person for receiving an injury or a disability benefit if the person does not submit to periodic medical examination and prescribed treatment.

The power to evaluate certain aspects of the contents of books or to enter on land and make enquiries to determine adherence to standards of a broad subjective nature are given, respectively, to the Censorship Board in respect of alleged obscenity or indecency in books, and to the Land Commission in regard to ascertaining the 'extent and character' of land. (See the Censorship of Publications Act 1946, sections 6 and 7 and the Land Act 1923, section 40(6).

Requiring Testimony and Documents

With regard to requiring testimony and submission of documents concerning past actions or existing situations, the Restrictive Practices Act 1972 provides that based on an investigation by the Examiner of Restrictive Practices of business practices alleged to be in restraint of trade or unfair competition and his recommendation thereon, the Restrictive Practices Commission may hold a formal enquiry. The Commission may summon witnesses, examine them on oath and require them to submit any documents in their control. Refusal to comply, or any other act which, if the Commission were a court, would constitute contempt of court, is an offence. The Commission may make such enquiry also on the request of the Minister for Industry, Trade, Commerce and Tourism conveyed by the Examiner or on application by a person whose request for an enquiry has been refused by the Examiner. The Commission must submit its report to the Minister for his final decision and action, such as an order or rules to prevent restrictive practices in an industry. (See sections 5, 6, 7, 14 and 16, First Schedule, Restrictive Practices Act 1972.)

Section 40(1) of the Land Act 1923 provides that every owner, tenant, or rent collector of any land to which the Act applies must give the Land Commission, on its request, such particulars concerning the land in the form and verified in the manner and time as specified by the Land Commission. Non-compliance or giving false information is subject to a fine and/or imprisonment under section 40(5) of the 1923 Act. Failure to furnish information or to prosecute proceedings by any person (or their agent) can result in appointment of a solicitor or agent or engineer to act in the matter (replacing the person's solicitor or agent if necessary) by the Judicial Commissioner, with costs for his services to be paid by the owner, according to section 41(1)-(3), Land Act 1923.

Similarly, the Local Government (Planning and Development) Act 1963, section 9 empowers the local planning authority to require an occupier or receiver of rents to give information as specified in the statute, subject to punishment for non-compliance. More extensive powers are granted under section 82, as amended by section 42 of the Local Government (Planning and Development) Act 1976, which provides that a person conducting an oral hearing on a reference or appeal may require any officer of a planning authority to give him any information in relation to the hearing which he reasonably requires for the hearing. The inspector or hearing officer appointed by An Bord Pleanála may inspect land to which the hearing relates and may take evidence on oath, give notice in writing requiring a person to attend at the time and place specified to give oral evidence or produce any documents available to him relating to the matter of the hearing. Failure to appear or suppressing, altering, or refusing to give evidence is an offence punishable on summary conviction by a fine. Following this fact-finding enquiry, section 23 of the 1976 Act requires that the inspector must make a report with a recommendation on the matter at issue, which must be considered by the Board or the Minister as appropriate before making a determination.

Prescribing Records and Reports

The power to require maintenance of records and submission of reports as prescribed differs from requiring submission of testimony and the existing documents of a regulated enterprise in that the administrative agency anticipates the data it needs for control purposes. It is the difference between requiring regulated enterprises to keep records or accounts and to make reports in specified ways which are designed to facilitate administrative agency inspections, review of reports, or hearings to carry out statutory goals, as against inspecting or demanding submission of existing records and accounts which private enterprises maintain for their own purposes and testimony based on such records.

A statutory provision which prescribes in advance the nature of a report is section 10 of the Safety in Industry Act 1980 under which the Minister for Labour may require that an owner who has an accident in his factory must have it investigated by a competent person, who must make a report in the form and with the factual matter required by the statute and the Minister. The report is submitted to the owner and the Minister, and if the Minister is dissatisfied with the report, he may appoint another investigator at the expense of the owner.

Under the Social Welfare (Consolidation) Act 1981, sections 58 and 59, the Minister for Social Welfare may make regulations prescribing the notice to be given of any accident in respect of which occupational injuries benefits may be payable and the time within which the notice is to be given; regulations may also require employers to make reports and to furnish information required for the determination of claims for an occupational injuries benefit. Again, section 31(1) and (2), Solicitors (Amendment) Act 1960 requires that every solicitor to whom the provisions of the Solicitors' Accounts Regulations apply must submit annually a certificate stating that in compliance with section 31 and regulations made thereunder, an accountant has examined the books, accounts and documents of the solicitor or his firm for the accounting period specified in the certificate. The accountant either must state that the solicitor has complied with the Solicitors' Accounts Regulations or specify the matters on which he is not satisfied. The accountant must meet the qualifications specified by the Society in the Accountants Certificate Regulations and conduct his audit according to those regulations.

Challenges to Investigating Power

The application of investigating power to obtain information for decisions which affect a wide range of rights and privileges of individuals or organisations, illustrated by the Acts discussed above, leads to resistance and appeals to or prosecution in the courts. The challenges to investigating power in Ireland have been made on the following grounds: (1) the investigating power as delegated is unconstitutional; (2) the application of the investigating power is in excess of jurisdiction, hence *ultra vires*; (3) the application of the investigating power is not relevant to the statutory purpose, and thus *ultra vires*; and (4) the investigating power as applied requires that the administrator 'act judicially' and the procedures which were employed did not conform to natural justice concepts.

Constitutionality
The delegation of investigating power was challenged on the grounds that it actually constituted a delegation of judicial power contrary to articles 34, 37 and 38 of the Constitution in *McDonald v. Bord na gCon and Attorney General* 1965 IR 217. As discussed in chapter 3, Kenny J. for the High Court held the contested section 47 of the Greyhound Industry Act 1958 (No. 12 of 1958) to be an unconstitutional delegation of judicial power, since the investigation culminating in the exclusion order against McDonald by Bord na

gCon had the characteristics of the administration of justice. The order was made for a violation of the greyhound racing code of conduct, it imposed a liability, a determination of guilt was made, and it authorised the licensees of any greyhound racing track to remove the excluded person from the track by force. Since making an exclusion order would affect seriously the fortune and reputation of the person excluded, it came under the doctrine of *In re Solicitor's Act 1954* 1960 IR 239 (see pages 72-3), as the powers and functions conferred are not limited in the sense of that word as interpreted in the decision in the *Solicitor's* case. However, the Supreme Court reversed the High Court decision. It was held that the exclusion order may affect the rights of a prohibited person so that the investigatory process leading to the order must conform to the principles of natural justice and that in the context of the Constitution, natural justice might be more appropriately termed constitutional justice. At the same time, section 47 must be read in conjunction with sections 43 to 46, and based on those sections and the nature of 'occurrences' to be investigated as defined in the Act, Walsh J. concluded:

In the Court's view the bodies or persons conducting the investigations under ss. 43 or 44, while bound to act judicially, are not constituted judicial persons or bodies nor do they exercise powers of a judicial nature within the meaning of Article 37 of the Constitution. This is an essential difference between the judgment of this court and the judgment of Mr. Justice Kenny. Accepting the characteristic features of a judicial body set out by Mr. Justice Kenny these investigating authorities do not satisfy any of those requirements. In particular, it is to be noted that the investigating authorities do not themselves by virtue of anything in ss. 43 or 44 affect any right or impose any penalty or liability on anybody. So far as the Board is concerned in the exercise of its powers under s. 47, or the Club in its exercise of the powers under the section, they are not constituted judicial bodies or do not exercise powers of a judicial nature, as they would only satisfy one of the tests referred to. (page 244)

A constitutional provision more directly related to the delegation and exercise of investigatory power than the articles on judicial power, is article 40.5 of the Constitution which states that the 'dwelling of every citizen is inviolable and shall not be forcibly entered save in accordance with law'. However, this article has not been developed as a ground for contesting the delegation or application of investigatory power in criminal law, let alone in administrative law in Ireland, to an extent comparable to the application in the United States of the Fourth Amendment of the American Constitution forbidding unlawful searches and seizures. For example, in addition to an extensive number of decisions involving Fourth Amendment issues in criminal law, the American Supreme Court has invalidated local ordinances which provided penalties for refusal to submit to an administrative inspection without a warrant or its equivalent, and negated federal factory inspections without a warrant. (See *Camera v. Municipal Court* 387 US 523 (1967); *See v. Seattle*, 387 US 541 (1967); *Marshall v. Barlow's Inc* 436 US 307 (1979).

In contrast, article 40.5 of the Irish Constitution, as Kelly states, 'has received very little judicial attention'. He notes that the one case in which article 40.5 was directly at issue, namely *The People (Attorney General) v. O'Brien* 1965 IR 142, 'provided the occasion for dicta which have had an important effect in the law of criminal evidence'.[1] In that case, the Supreme Court upheld the admission of evidence from a search not conducted in accordance with law on the ground that there had been an innocent clerical error in the warrant. The dicta of the court included statements by Walsh J. as to the meaning of article 40.5:

> In my view, the reference to forcible entry is an intimation that forcible entry may be permitted by law but that in any event *the dwelling of every citizen is inviolable save where entry is permitted by law and that, if necessary, such law may permit forcible entry.* (page 169, emphasis added)

Walsh J. also referred to 'the competing interests of the trial and conviction of criminals and the frustration of police illegalities'. In his view:

> When the illegality amounts to infringement of a constitutional right the matter assumes a far greater importance than is the case where the illegality does not amount to such infringement

.... The Courts ... must uphold the objection of an accused person to the admissibility at his trial of evidence obtained or procured by the State as a result of a deliberate and conscious violation of the constitutional rights of the accused person where no extraordinary excusing circumstances exist, such as the imminent destruction of vital evidence or the need to rescue a victim in peril. (page 170)[2]

Although the *O'Brien* case pertained to criminal law evidence, there are times when the dividing line between searches made in criminal law and entrances made into private domiciles or business locations to carry out an inspection under administrative law, becomes somewhat thin or tenuous (as in the *Camera, See* and *Marshall* cases in the US, see pages 277-8). Consequently, judicial concepts and dicta expressed in criminal law cases such as *O'Brien* can have implications for administrative law investigating power.

An additional challenge to investigatory power made in the United States, namely, that its exercise invades Fifth Amendment rights of protection against self-incrimination, has no constitutional basis in Ireland, in the absence of an explicit provision in the Irish Constitution comparable to the American Constitution's Fifth Amendment.

However the Oireachtas has explicitly provided for protection against unlawful searches or self-incrimination in various statutes delegating investigating power in Ireland. For example, the Censorship of Publications Act 1929 requires the oath of a high-ranking garda officer that there are reasonable grounds for suspicion that a building is housing indecent pictures or prohibited books for sale, before a judge will issue a warrant to enter and search the building and seize such pictures, books or periodicals. (See section 19(1) and (2) and section 12(1) and (2).) The Restrictive Practices Act 1972 requires the agent of the Examiner of Restrictive Practices to provide advance warning of inspection and gives the owner a right to refuse access and then apply to the High Court for a declaration as to whether the 'exigencies of the common good' justify the inspection. (See section 15 (2) and (3).) Similarly the Local Government (Planning and Development) Act 1963 requires either consent of the owner or a 14-day notice to the owner or occupier of intent to enter on the land, during which time an order may be sought from the District Court prohibiting or specifying the conditions of the entry. (See section 83 (3) and (4).) If the entry is for the purposes of Part IV of the Act (control of development), entry may be made without previous notice unless entry is refused in which case the administration must obtain an order from the District Court for entry. (See section 83(6) (a) and (b).)

Witnesses testifying under oath to the disciplinary committee of the Incorporated Law Society or to an inspector holding a hearing for the Minister for the Environment or the Planning Board are given the same immunities and privileges as if they were witnesses before the High Court, under the statutes pertaining to those administrative agencies. (See Solicitors (Amendment) Act 1960, section 15 (3); Local Government (Planning and Development) Act 1963, section 82 (6).) Moreover, under the Solicitor's (Amendment) Act 1960, section 19(1) and (2), when the issue of dishonesty in management of a trust by a solicitor is involved, the refusal of a person to produce or deliver documents pertinent to that issue, although punishable on summary conviction by a fine, can be overcome only by the Incorporated Law Society applying to the High Court for an order requiring their delivery. The protection against self-incrimination is directly stated in the Social Welfare (Consolidation) Act 1981: section 264(6) states that 'no one shall be required under this section to answer any question or give any evidence tending to incriminate himself' to an inspector appointed by the Minister for Social Welfare.

The statutory protections against unlawful searches through inspection, or forcing self-incrimination through requiring testimony contained in these Acts provide the grounds for appeal to the courts based on a claim of an *ultra vires* act if the administrator denies such statutory protections. However, a question remains as to what extent rights guaranteed in certain articles of the Constitution could form the basis for a claim that the delegation or exercise of investigatory power is unconstitutional where the statute involved does not contain such protection. The decision in the *People (Attorney General) v. O'Brien* case discussed above provides only obiter dicta on this issue, and the more recent *Abbey Films* case (discussed below) involves a direct attack upon the constitutionality of the delegation of administrative investigatory power, under a statute which contained a provision giving protection against an unwarranted inspection and from self-incrimination.

Although not answering the question just raised, *Abbey Films Ltd*

v. Attorney General and Kennan 1981 IR 158 is significant in upholding
the delegation and exercise of administrative investigatory power
in general. An attack on the constitutionality of the investigatory
power as delegated was made based on several constitutional
articles as well as on a claim of action *ultra vires* the statute. The
focus of the claims made by *Abbey Films* was section 15 of the
Restrictive Practices Act 1972, which authorises an Examiner of
Restrictive Practices to investigate unfair trading practices by entering and inspecting premises at reasonable times and requiring
persons therein to produce any documents or records under their
control and give him information related to entries in such documents and records. The Examiner or his agents must inform the
owner or other persons providing information of both the investigatory powers of the Examiner, and of the owner's right to refuse
entrance or to give information, provided that the owner applies
within seven days to the High Court for a declaration that the
'exigencies of the common good' do not warrant the Examiner's
investigation. The Examiner's report to the Restrictive Practices
Commission may result in a formal Commission inquiry, and a
report to the Minister for Industry and Commerce who may issue
an order to control or prohibit the unfair trading practices in the
industry as determined by the investigation.

Based upon an initial investigation in May 1976 in response
to complaints from independent cinema owners, the Examiner
concluded that three organised groups of cinema owners and two
major distributors of films were financially interconnected. Through
interlocking control over the distribution and showing of films they
had a monopoly, resulting in a diminishing number of independent
cinemas in Ireland.

The Examiner attempted to get one of the major distributors,
Kinematograph Renters Society, to modify its policy through persuasion and through threats to make a report recommending a
formal inquiry by the Restrictive Practices Commission, which
he publicised in statements to the press and in radio interviews.
Subsequently, in October 1976 the Examiner sought additional
evidence from ten firms to support his initial conclusion that a
monopoly existed. One of the firms, Abbey Films Ltd, refused to
allow an inspection. Advance notice of the inspection had been
given, and three directors of Abbey Films were present when the
Examiner's agents produced their authorisations, informed the

directors of their statutory powers and of the directors' right to
refuse inspection and apply for a declaration from the High Court.
The directors admitted the relevance of the information sought, but
were not satisfied with the way the Act was being administered in
regard to the Examiner's use of the press and radio incident to his
investigation.

Three allegations of unconstitutionality of the statute were made
by Abbey Films in its appeal to the High Court. The one claim
which was not repeated in its appeal to the Supreme Court was
that section 15(1) of the 1972 Act gave a power of entry and
search without an order of a court, contrary to article 40.5 of the
Constitution that 'the dwelling of every citizen is inviolable' and
'shall not be forcibly entered save in accordance with law.' McWilliam J., in ruling against all three claims, held in regard to the
article 40.5 issue that office premises were not a 'dwelling', that a
company was not a 'citizen' and that in view of the expression
'human persons' in article 40.1 human rights cannot be attributed
to a company.

On appeal to the Supreme Court, Abbey Films reiterated its
claim that section 15 of the Act was contrary to the Constitution:

1. It makes acts infringements of the law which were not so at
   the date of their commission (Article 15).

2. . . . it imposes . . . an onus on the defendant to prove that
   the exigencies of the common good do not warrant the
   exercise of certain powers and, as these proceedings are
   connected with a criminal offence, the provisions imposing
   this onus are repugnant to the Constitution.

3. It offends against Article 6 because it entrusts a decision as
   to the exigencies of the common good to the Courts while,
   as the plaintiffs contend, this is a function of the legislature
   alone.

4. It usurps the function of the legislature by empowering the
   High Court to create a new offence.

5. A company is required to retain a solicitor to act for it in
   proceedings under the section; while a citizen may appear
   in person. It is thus a breach of the principle of equality
   before the law (Article 40, s. 1).

6. It is an unjust attack on the right of private property and

so offends against Articles 40, s. 3 and Article 43. (pages 168-9)

Kenny J. for the Supreme Court held that the offence is committed when an authorised officer is impeded or not given the information required. If the owner's request for a declaration is decided in his favour, it is a complete defence to any subsequent prosecution. As to the second claim, the legislature may require an accused in a criminal prosecution to establish a limited and specified matter, and thus such an onus may be imposed in a civil action though it is connected to criminal proceedings. The onus is not to prove innocence, rather it is a means of resisting prosecution by showing that the common good did not require the investigation. Regarding the third claim, article 6 divides powers between the three branches of government but the constitutional framers did not adopt a rigid separation between legislative, executive and judicial powers. Promotion of the common good may be primarily a legislative function but nothing prevents the legislature from investing courts with jurisdiction to determine whether a particular act is required by the exigencies of the common good. In respect of the fourth claim, the function of the Court is not to create offences but to determine whether the exercise of the Examiner's power in a particular instance was or was not warranted by the exigencies of the common good. The legislature creates that offence, the courts decide whether it is committed. Kenny J. rejected the fifth claim in view of the difference in the capacity of a company from that of a natural person. Finally, in regard to the alleged attack on private property, he held that none of the powers affected the right of private ownership or the right to transfer, bequeath and inherit property under article 43.1.

In addition to upholding the constitutionality of the investigating power delegated by the legislature, the Supreme Court overruled the High Court's decision on the statutory issue that the investigation was not 'warranted by the exigencies of the common good', on grounds to be explicated in the discussion of the requirement that the administrator 'act judicially' in certain investigations. (See pages 292-4.)

Despite the importance of the High and Supreme Courts' rejection of these multiple constitutional grounds for attacking the validity of the statutory delegation of investigatory power, it is conditioned by being made in the context of a statutory provision for the right to resist investigation by asking for a declaration by the High Court to determine the legitimacy of the investigation, and the fact that the plaintiff was a corporation, not a natural person or citizen.

Excess of Jurisdiction

A typical challenge to the exercise of investigatory power is the allegation that the administrative agency is acting in excess of jurisdiction and therefore *ultra vires* the Act from which it derives its authority. In *The State (Stephen's Green Club and Another) v. Labour Court* 1961 IR 85, the issue was whether a conditional order of prohibition obtained on behalf of the Stephen's Green Club and directed to the Labour Court to stop it from starting an enquiry concerning wages and employment conditions of certain employees of the club should be continued or discharged on the grounds that the enquiry was in excess of jurisdiction and therefore *ultra vires* the Industrial Relations Act 1946.

The Stephen's Green Club argued that it is an unincorporated members' club of a social and domestic nature, not carrying on a trade or industry whose employees were domestic servants, i.e. they were not engaged in trade or industry. Therefore there could not be a trade dispute between the Club and its employees under section 67 of the Industrial Relations Act 1946. The Labour Court position was that the terms 'trade dispute' and 'worker' were intended to encompass all employers, employment and workers, whatever the scope and nature of employment, and worker would mean any person working under contract with an employer. Walsh J. in the Supreme Court held that the omission of the words 'employed in trade or industry' from the definition of workers contained in the Industrial Relations Act 1946 signified awareness of an intention to avoid the strict construction placed on those words in the previous Trade Disputes Act 1906, and to give a much wider definition of the term 'worker'. The Stephen's Green Club employees, as persons under contracts of employment with the Club, and not being persons expressly excluded by section 4 of the 1946 Act, are workers within the meaning of that section. Any dispute between them and the Club connected with their employment, its terms or conditions is a trade dispute under the Act, which the Labour Court has power to investigate. Such an enquiry is not *ultra vires* the Act. Moreover, the writ of prohibition cannot lie against the Labour Court on the basis of its having judicial powers under the Act. The Labour Court is empowered to summon witnesses, examine them under oath, and require them to produce documents, and a penalty is provided for non-compliance with these demands. However, all the Labour Court ultimately can do is to make recommendations. No means is provided for enforcing the recommendations or making the findings binding on the parties, or for action by a superior authority affecting rights of the parties.

The *Stephen's Green Club* case not only illustrates the basis upon which the Court holds an action *intra* rather than *ultra vires*, but also highlights the basic difference between investigatory and adjudicatory powers as perceived by the Supreme Court. However, the resolution of whether an investigation is in excess of jurisdiction is not always as clear as in the *Stephen's Green Club* case. This is revealed in the divided opinions of the Supreme Court in *The State (Pharmaceutical Society and Another) v. Fair Trade Commission* 99 ILTR 24 (1965). The Fair Trade Commission had issued notice of intention to hold an enquiry under the Restrictive Trade Practices Act 1953 into the conditions of the 'supply and distribution, by wholesale and retail, of proprietary and patent medicines, and infant foods, and medical and toilet preparations'. The Chairman of the Commission stated that he would require the attendance at the forthcoming enquiry of a licensed pharmaceutical chemist to give evidence on compounding prescriptions issued by doctors and methods used for computing charges. The Pharmaceutical Society then sought to test this aspect of the proposed investigation by applying for a writ of prohibition. The Society's claim was that this aspect of the enquiry would be in excess of the Fair Trade Commission's jurisdiction under the Act, and outside the stated terms of the enquiry, although the Society had no objection to the enquiry concerning patent or proprietary medicines, infant food, or drugs, medicines or toilet preparations in the ordinary sense. The High Court decided in favour of the Commission holding that the compounding and dispensing of medical prescriptions was a trade and not a profession, or at least was not exclusively a professional activity and thus not exempt from the application of the Act.

The Supreme Court, in a judgment by Maguire C.J. (Davitt and Lavery J.J. concurring), noted that in *Pharmaceutical Society v. Revenue Commissioners* 1938 IR 202, it had been held that although the

Pharmaceutical Society is a professional body and that a member to be qualified as a licentiate must undergo careful training ensuring a very high degree of knowledge in pharmacy, the Society only examines and registers chemists and has no disciplinary control over chemists once they are registered. Moreover, the interests of the registered chemists as traders are looked after by an independent trade society. Given these factors, the Chief Justice held that the fact that a medical prescription is made expressly for one customer does not support the claim that this transaction is not the supply of goods or a trading transaction, since this also applies to many articles, such as boots or clothes made to measure for an individual customer. The price lists issued by the Irish Drug Association to its members establish the price of items compounded and dispensed based on the price of materials involved and a charge for services. A chemist who sued for non-payment for a prescription would claim a price based on goods sold and delivered. It would seem that the prices so established constitute a sale in the process of the trade. Although he felt the Commission would have due regard to the nature of the trade and professional qualifications of chemists, he would uphold the High Court order and dismiss the appeal.

Kingsmill Moore J. dissented since he found that an article compounded and dispensed under prescription is adapted for one specific ailment of one person, specifying the time and amount to be used according to directions from the doctor to the patient. It is not to be used by others, and cannot be sold by recipients since it might be injurious to another. No such article could be described as an article of trade goods. The price of a prescription includes remuneration for the professional skill of the pharmaceutical chemist, and the responsibility for providing a correct dosage is that of the chemist, since if there is a failure in this respect, the liability rests with the chemist, not the doctor. Moreover, the terms of the notice and the definition of the enquiry by the Commission could encompass prescriptions only under the phrase 'medical preparations'. This term reflects the existence of remedies sold without prescription, not articles compounded and dispensed by individual prescription.

Ó Dálaigh J. concurred with Kingsmill Moore J. that the appeal should be allowed. In his opinion, given the acknowledged characterisation of compounding and dispensing of a prescription as a professional activity, he was:

unable to follow the process by which the dispensing and compounding, *ex concessis* a professional activity, is divorced from the payment which the chemist receives in exchange for the preparation. The Commission's argument is in substance that there are two activities involved, a professional activity and a trading activity. It seems to me that this division is unreal, and in effect, it operates to deny the professional status of the pharmaceutical chemist. In my opinion there is but a single indivisible activity of a professional character and I cannot agree the activity loses that character because it terminates in a money payment . . . . (page 44)

Failure to follow statutory processes essential to establish the basis for exercising investigatory power may also constitute an *ultra vires* action, as in the case of *Bord na Móna v. James Heavey and Robbie Heavey* unreported, High Court, per Kenny J., 26 July 1974. Bord na Móna (the Board) sought an interlocutory injunction to restrain defendants from preventing the Board's bringing a large machine across certain lands which the Board claimed it had acquired, so as to work on part of those lands. Defendants claimed plaintiffs had not actually acquired the lands and had no power to enter on them or bring the machine across them. In the opinion of Kenny J., the right to enter and work on the lands depended upon the content of a resolution passed by Bord na Móna under certain sections of the Turf Development Act 1946. The resolution stated that 'the Board considered it advisable to acquire permanently the lands' and ordered that documents identifying the land, in accordance with the Act and related regulations, be deposited at certain offices, that public notice in newspapers be published, and individual notice be given to the occupier of the land of intent to acquire the land and of the Board's entitlement to enter on and take possession of the land one month from service of notice.

Kenny J. agreed with defendants' contention that plaintiffs had not made an order or passed a resolution for compulsory acquisition of the land. Under the relevant sections 29 and 30 of the 1946 Act, the Board's power to acquire land depends on the Board's making a definite order to acquire such land. A statement in a resolution that the Board 'considered it advisable' to acquire land does not give them the right to enter and take possession of it. Moreover the related section 24 of the Act authorising the Board to enter any lands to do anything the Board is authorised to do by the Act or make any enquiry prior to the doing of any such thing, merely authorises the Board and its servants to enter on land, but not to take possession or bring a large machine across it. The application for an interlocutory injunction therefore was dismissed.

Relevance to Statutory Purposes
A challenge to a demand for information may also be made as to whether the inquiry is relevant to the statutory purpose, as in the case of *The State (Attorney General) v. Matthew Bruton* 76 ILTR 56 (1942). Defendant was prosecuted under the Emergency Powers Act 1939, section 6(2) and (3), and the Emergency Powers Order (S.R. & O. No. 224 of 1939) article 78 which requires a person on request on behalf of the Minister to furnish any information or article specified which the Minister's representative considers necessary or expedient to obtain or examine in the interest of the public safety or preservation of the state. The Minister's representative (administrator) in this case requested defendant to furnish further information after defendant had made a statement to the administrator. He showed the defendant an authorisation from the Minister for Supplies, in the form prescribed by regulation, to request any information concerning the source from which defendant obtained petrol coupons which defendant had sold. This additional information was considered by the administrator to be necessary in the interest of the public safety, but the defendant refused to give the additional information and was prosecuted.

However, the Court held that a conviction under article 78 of the 1939 Order could not be supported since the administrator did not give any direct evidence to substantiate his opinion that the information which he had requested was necessary or expedient for the safety of the state nor could this be inferred from the fact that the administrator had produced an Order of a Minister stating the information must be furnished to the administrator. The Special Criminal Court decision was reversed and the conviction quashed.

Natural Justice: Investigation and Adjudication
An important issue in the exercise of investigatory power is whether the fact-finding process has certain characteristics which the courts feel require the administrator to 'act judicially' in accordance with procedural protections of natural justice. A second and closely related issue is whether the divulgence of certain information in-

fringes substantive individual rights under natural justice. The reaction of the courts to these issues when raised would seem to depend upon the extent to which an adverse effect upon the interests or rights of those being investigated can be demonstrated and, in regard to the first issue, whether the investigatory process has certain aspects of an adjudicatory nature, although not constituting adjudication *per se*. The nature of the procedural issue and its treatment by the courts was discussed as a part of the analysis in chapter 5 of various aspects of institutional decision-making in the two *Murphy* cases and the *Killiney* and *Geraghty* cases in regard to the fact-finding, evaluating evidence and reporting functions of the inspector as related to the deciding function of the Minister. (See pages 193-5 and 201-212.) However, the border line is not always clear in statutes or judicial precedents between what is an administrative investigation not requiring natural justice protections, and what is an investigation or fact-finding process having characteristics requiring the administrator to 'act judicially'.

In *McDonald v. Bord na gCon and Attorney General* 1965 IR 217, Walsh J. made the distinction that administrative bodies conducting an investigation under the Greyhound Industry Act 1958 'while bound to act judicially, are not constituted judicial persons or bodies, nor do they exercise powers of a judicial nature.'

This differentiation between having to act judicially in conducting an investigation, and exercising powers of a judicial nature may seem like an exercise in semantics but it has consequences for administrative agencies in the expectations which the courts place on agency administrators. It may be difficult for an administrator to anticipate that he should 'act judicially' to provide procedural due process when he is finding facts and reporting them to a Minister who makes the final decision, particularly if he perceives his role as merely making findings from the evidence and not drawing conclusions or making recommendations to his superior.

This problem is illustrated by *The State (Shannon Atlantic Fisheries Ltd) v. Minister for Transport and Power and McPolin* 1976 IR 93.) Plaintiff applied to make absolute a conditional order of certiorari which required Captain McPolin to send the report of his inquiry and its related records and entries concerning the wrecking of the fishing vessel *Colm Padhraig* owned by plaintiff to the Court for the purpose of being quashed. The Minister for Transport and Power had appointed Captain McPolin to hold a preliminary inquiry, and under section 465 of the Merchant Shipping Act 1894, he had obtained from the Shannon Atlantic Fisheries Company (Shannon Company) the names and addresses of the vessel's crew and information on logs and records connected with the vessel. He interviewed and took sworn depositions from three members of the crew (the fourth could not be traced). Officers or members of the Shannon Company were not interviewed nor was any company representative given the opportunity to learn the facts set forth in the depositions or to cross examine or ask questions of the members of the crew. Captain McPolin's report provided a factual account of the circumstances surrounding the wrecking of the vessel: (1) the time it had sailed from Galway; (2) the number of persons constituting the crew; (3) the length of time it had fished before the accident; (4) the course it was taking at the time of the accident; (5) the position and duties of crew members when the accident occurred, and (6) a very short description of the accident.

Following this report, a Minister for Transport and Power letter was sent to the Shannon Company stating that the preliminary inquiry showed that contrary to sections 413 and 457 of the Merchant Shipping Act 1894 the *Colm Padhraig* went to sea having neither a duly certificated skipper or certificated second hand. The vessel was in an unsafe condition owing to undermanning, i.e. three men and an apprentice with no previous experience as against the normal crew of five to six. The duration of the fishing trip was far in excess of the normal efficient working capacity of such a small crew. The letter requested early observations from the Shannon Company as to the circumstances under which these legal requirements were not observed.

The Shannon Company refuted the letter, protested against Captain McPolin's not having heard representatives of the Company before concluding his preliminary inquiry, and claimed that the inquiry was not conducted in accordance with the principles of natural justice. Defendants contended that there was no want of natural justice, since Captain McPolin's only function was to ascertain the immediate facts of the wrecking of the vessel through interviewing available witnesses who were on the vessel and could give evidence. This was not a decision-making function such as is capable of being quashed on an order for certiorari, if not carried out in accordance with natural justice, since the report made no finding or charges against the company. Moreover, the breaches of law alleged in the letter from the Minister for Transport and Power were summary offences no longer prosecutable at the time the letter was written, so the company did not have sufficient interest in quashing the report to justify making absolute an order of certiorari.

Finlay P. noted that the person appointed under section 465 of the Merchant Shipping Act 1894 has extensive powers to enter on and inspect boats and premises, summon persons and examine them, administer oaths and require production of documents. No reference is made in the Act to a report or to what it should contain. Given these statutory powers, and the fact that the report, finding and depositions indicated that Captain McPolin had decided between the conflicting evidence of the witnesses relating to times of sailing and length of fishing, the Court held that:

> the investigating officer was necessarily reaching a decision and, in a sense, was entering a verdict in precisely the same way as a jury is asked to reach a decision and to enter a verdict on facts. (page 98)

Although the Minister must decide whether any further action relating to prosecution should be taken, this did not affect 'the true decision-making role of the person carrying out the preliminary inquiry'. This is further supported by the fact that section 446 of the Act authorises the person making the preliminary inquiry to initiate an application to a court of summary jurisdiction to hold a formal investigation, binding the court to hold such investigation, and the fact that the Minister's letter showed that he had relied on the report and depositions.

Consequently, the preliminary inquiry by Captain McPolin was a quasi-judicial investigation affecting the interest of the Shannon Company, which as a matter of natural justice was entitled to be heard and to know of matters arising from evidence given by other persons which might affect their interests. The inquiry was not carried out in accordance with the principles of natural justice. Although the time had expired for prosecution of Shannon Company, enough reason existed for the company to challenge the reports and documents in the records of the Department, since the owner of any registered vessel has a considerable interest in his record or shipping character as it exists in the files of the Department of Transport and Power. The conditional order of certiorari was made absolute.

The conclusion reached in this case would seem to be an extension of the rulings in *Murphy, Killiney* and *Geraghty*. (See pages 193-5 and 201-212.) However, there is a modification of the emphasis of those preceding cases. The primary rationale in *Shannon Atlantic Fisheries* for requiring natural justice rights was that the person making the preliminary investigation was engaged in decision-making by exercising judgment on conflicting evidence gained from his interrogations and depositions when making his report to the Minister. In *Murphy, Killiney* and *Geraghty*, the stress was on the extent to which inspectors holding oral hearings and inspecting development sites should evaluate evidence and make recommendations in their reports in view of the possible influences on the adjudicatory decision of the Minister who received the reports. In those cases the courts held that natural justice required the inspecting officers to 'act judicially' but not because of decision-making powers being ascribed to the inspecting officers. The rationale in *Shannon Fisheries*, if taken to an extreme or too literally, may obscure the important distinction between the fact-finding role of the investigating officer and the decision-making role of the Minister. It deals in an oblique way with the basic problem. That problem is that the Minister's decision was based on incomplete information or evidence obtained in an investigation process in which the investigating officer did not obtain evidence from or allow controverting evidence to be given by *Shannon Fisheries*, one of the directly affected parties, contrary to natural justice.

However, the later case of *Abbey Films Ltd v. Attorney General and Kennan* 1981 IR 158 (see page 280) indicates that the distinction between administrative fact-finding and reporting processes and formal enquiry or fact-finding hearings is maintained in regard to the application of natural justice requirements. In addition to the constitutional issues raised concerning section 15 of the Restrictive Practices Act 1972, the Supreme Court dealt with Abbey Films' claim that the exercise by the Examiner of Restrictive Practices of his investigatory powers was not warranted 'by the exigencies of the common good' as required by section 15. Based on the facts of the investigatory process carried out by the Examiner (which are detailed in the discussion above of the constitutional issues of the

Abbey case), McWilliam J. in the High Court held that although it might:

> be for the common good that the supply and distribution of films should be more fairly and equitably carried out . . . some of the methods of doing it may not, themselves, be conducive to the common good . . . . One of the things which are conducive to the common good is that it should be seen that an enquiry by a State body is fair, impartial and unprejudiced. If it is not or appears not to be so, this is against the common good. The distinct impression that I got from evidence, (including that of the examiner) was that he did not enter upon this investigation in an impartial manner. I consider it to have been unsatisfactory that radio and newspaper interviews were given during the course of such an investigation. Evidence was given before me about the interviews and the plaintiffs' directors and servants took a strong objection to them. Although the examiner was preparing a report for a Commission which would then hold an enquiry if he recommended it, the information for the report ought to have been obtained and the report prepared in a reasonably judicial manner and without exacerbating feelings during its assimilation. (page 167)

On appeal to the Supreme Court, Kenny J. noted that prior to enactment of the Restrictive Practices Act 1972, the Fair Trade Commission (now the Restrictive Practices Commission) combined the functions of investigating a complaint of an unfair trade practice and holding a formal public enquiry on the matter at which all parties would be represented. The 1972 Act divided these functions. An examiner of Restrictive Trade Practices is charged with investigating the supply or distribution of goods or services and with making a report to the Restrictive Practices Commission on his findings if he feels an enquiry should be made. The Commission is responsible for holding an enquiry into matters in the Examiner's report and making recommendations to the Minister as to whether he should make an order. If the Minister issues an order prohibiting a restrictive practice, the order becomes effective only after it is confirmed by an Act of the Oireachtas. Given these statutory provisions, Kenny J. held that it was 'essential to keep in mind the differences between the investigative function of the Examiner and

the semi-judicial powers of the Commission and of the Minister'
and noted that this division was almost completely ignored in the
High Court.

Kenny J. therefore disagreed with the High Court determination.
On review of the actions of the Examiner, he held that the Examiner's function was to investigate, not adjudicate, and thus he had
to have the information essential for preparation of a report if he
were compelled to do so. Such a report would have to be made
unless his negotiations with the plaintiffs to persuade them to
change their patterns of supply and distribution were successful.
The evidence showed that after starting his investigation in May
1976, he had formed strong views by November 1976 on the existence of a monopoly and abuse of a dominant position. In the view
of Kenny J., he began the investigation in an impartial manner and
the press and radio interviews he gave were part of his plan to
employ the threat of an enquiry as a means of obtaining agreement.
Since this failed, he felt that the information he sought from plaintiffs
was essential in order to prepare an adequate report for submission
to the Commission. Since unfair or restrictive trade practices by
their nature are contrary to the common good, the preparation of
a fair and balanced report by the Examiner required that he should
have access to the information sought.

In their concurrences, O'Higgins C.J. and Griffin J. agreed that
plaintiffs had failed to establish that the exigencies of the common
good did not warrant the exercise of the Examiner's powers,
although Griffin J. indicated that he gave his concurrence 'notwithstanding the criticism to which the Examiner left himself open in
giving interviews to the press, to *Business and Finance*, and on radio.'

In addition to procedural protections, natural justice concepts
have been applied to assert a natural right of a substantive nature
against the exercise of investigatory power in *Murphy v. PMPA
Insurance Company* High Court, per Doyle J., unreported, 21 February
1978. The Road Traffic Act 1961, and Road Traffic (Compulsory
Insurance) Regulations 1962 S.I. No. 14 of 1962 require insurers to
issue to insured persons a certificate with the person's name and
address, period of coverage, limits on use, persons whose liability
is covered, vehicles covered and drivers or classes of drivers covered.
They also require the insurer to keep records at his place of business
of the particulars and other matters required to be stated on the
certificate, its issue and the loss, destruction or defacement of any

such certificate. An insurer on request must admit a member of the Garda Síochána to inspect these records and make copies, and must furnish any information related to an approved policy which the officer requires.

PMPA Insurance Company (hereafter PMPA) had issued an insurance policy to Michael Mellon, a member of the Garda Síochána. When Inspector Murphy of the Garda appeared at PMPA to seek information on Mellon's insurance policy, an employee refused to provide the data until he received authorisation from his superior. PMPA wrote to Inspector Murphy the next day asking what he required to know and Inspector Murphy wrote that he wished to have a copy of the certificate and copies of all applications, proposals, statements and other documents submitted by Mellon to obtain insurance. Not receiving a reply, Inspector Murphy went to PMPA, whose manager said legal advice was being sought to determine whether the information requested was that required by law.

The case stated by the District Court was that Inspector Murphy charged PMPA with failing to comply with the Road Traffic Act and Regulations by not furnishing information to him. PMPA had argued before the District Justice that it owed a duty to its insured clients to treat certain information which might be supplied to PMPA for purposes of obtaining insurance coverage as confidential. Although information contained in, or related to, the records which insurers had to keep according to regulations would have to be given to the Garda Síochána, this did not include information which the insurers were not obliged to keep by statute or regulation, and which was kept in the insurer's private records. Consequently, PMPA did not have to divulge all the information concerning their insured client which might be in their possession as demanded by Inspector Murphy's letter. On the other hand, Inspector Murphy argued that insurers were obliged to disclose any information they had in their possession when requested to do so by a member of the Garda Síochána or other authorised person.

The High Court held that the contract between insurer and insured appeared to be a contract *uberrimae fidei*, i.e. based on the exercise of utmost good faith by each party. The insured is obliged to disclose every material circumstance which might influence the insurer's judgment in fixing the premium or even taking the risk of giving insurance. Such disclosures might involve very personal and private matters, e.g. the insured's health, which if concealed might cause insurers to void the contract. It follows that insurance companies contract an obligation of confidentiality as to such personal information, especially since disclosure might in certain circumstances lead to the detriment of the insured.

Consequently, Inspector Murphy's claim that the statute gives him the exceptional privilege of obtaining information sought despite this cloak of confidentiality, in the view of Doyle J:

> appears to constitute an encroachment . . . on natural liberty or natural rights. It seems to me therefore that any such encroachment . . . . must be manifested with reasonable clearness (and) . . . that the encroachment to be justified must be demonstrated to fall within the general spirit and scope of the enactment.

Doyle J. stressed that the encroachment on natural rights claimed in this case does not stem from constitutional articles. Certain natural and personal rights may coexist with constitutional rights, as held in *The State (Gleeson) v. Minister for Defence* 1976 IR 280 (see pages 134-5) and personal rights are not exhausted by guarantees in the Constitution as indicated in Kelly's book on *Fundamental Rights in Irish Law and Constitution.*

Doyle J. concluded that in as much as:

> the contract between the insurers and their insured was one of *uberrimae fidei;* it carried a corresponding obligation of confidentiality on the part of the insurers because of the special relationship which the contract set up between themselves and their insured. It must also be taken into account that in the special circumstances of this contract the disclosure sought by the complainant may operate to the detriment of the insured Mr. Mellon because of his particular status as a member of the Garda Síochána, in which force the complainant occupies a position of authority. To give effect to the regulation in the present case would entail an encroachment on the natural rights of . . . Mr. Mellon and also in my view conflict with the obligation springing from a natural right which lies upon the insurers.

He considered that the Road Traffic (Compulsory Insurance) Regulations 1962 did not manifest with reasonable clearness an intention to invade the natural rights in question in this case. Therefore, Doyle J. answered the query of the District Justice by finding that defendant insurers should have been acquitted.

Notes to Chapter 7

1. Kelly, *The Irish Constitution* 559 (1984)
2. See Kelly, *The Irish Constitution* 559-61

8 Licensing Power

Administrative agencies can impose specific standards and determine whether there is compliance through rule-making and investtigating powers (discussed earlier). If there is a refusal to comply, they must resort directly to prosecution in trial courts if they do not also have licensing or directing powers. Under a statutory grant of licensing or directing powers, administrative agencies exert systematic control processes which include administrative sanctions for non-compliance, such as the refusal, suspension or revocation of a licence or issuing a negative or positive order to a particular party. Resort to the courts by the agency to overcome defiance of such sanctions, or appeals to the courts from the sanctions by the affected parties, involve what is essentially an appellate review of the administrative record and arguments submitted by opposing lawyers, rather than a trial *de novo*, especially if there has been an intervening appeal from the initial administrative decision to a minister or administrative tribunal.

Concepts and Nature of Licensing Power

A licence may be referred to in Acts and regulations as a 'permit', 'practising certificate', 'approval', 'permission' or 'registration' and the word 'licence' has been used by legislatures to denote activity which is primarily taxation. The components of a complete licensing system which distinguish it from other regulatory powers may be summarised as follows:

1. The statute requires that a licence be issued before the operation of an enterprise, or undertaking an activity, or practice of an occupation or profession, and imposes a penalty for unlicensed operation or practice.

2. The statute prescribes minimum standards to be met to qualify for the licence, or at least general standards or objectives to guide the administrator's adoption of specific standards to be met to qualify for a licence.

3. A prospective licensee must initiate an application for a licence. Administrative receipt of the application is followed by inspection or some process for examination of data concerning the applicant or the enterprise as to compliance with standards, upon which the agency may issue or refuse to issue a licence.

4. Following grant of the licence, there is normally a means or process for determining whether there is continuing compliance with the standards (also referred to as requirements or terms and conditions of the licence).

5. In the event of discovery of non-compliance by the licensee with the required standards, the agency has the power to suspend a licence to prevent immediate danger to the public, pending a decision on whether to revoke the licence based upon proof of non-compliance with the terms and conditions of the licence.

Licensing, therefore, is a system of prior and continuing consent given by the state, under which operation of an enterprise or practice of an occupation or profession without a licence is illegal and subject ultimately to judicially imposed penalties. The publicised rationale is to protect persons affected by the activity or enterprise or using the product or services of the enterprise, the entrepreneur, or professional person, by specifying a certain level of competence and prohibiting practices which would endanger public health, safety, morals or convenience.

The agency may also be granted rule-making and investigatory powers to establish detailed requirements for licensees beyond those of the authorising Act, and to investigate for compliance with such requirements. A licensing system combined with rule-making power enables an agency to raise the standards of an occupation or profession over time, especially if a short-term licensing system is involved in which annual or biennial expiry of the licence requires re-application for and renewal or refusal of the licence by the agency. The agency can gradually raise the qualifications for renewal of the licence, exercising care to avoid too extreme an impact on existing short-term licensees, or, if more permanent licences are involved, using 'grandfather clauses' to continue existing licensees under older standards while requiring new standards to be met by new licensees.

An unpublicised concomitant objective of a licensing system may be to limit entrance into a trade or profession, especially if representatives of the occupational or professional group being regulated have influence over the development and raising of standards or control over the application of the requirements for a licence. Restricting competition increases occupational security and helps to maintain a certain level of charges or fees. The growth of the licensing of occupations and professions is often attributable to the demands by an occupational group to be licensed, rather than to the demand of the consuming public or the government.

Licensing is closely related to but not synonymous with compulsory registration and the grant of a franchise. Compulsory registration requires the regulated person or enterprise to divulge prescribed information to the administrative agency sufficiently in advance of operation to enable the agency to refuse registration pending corrective action or to prohibit the proposed activity. The grant of a franchise gives a state-approved monopoly to an enterprise and in return the entrepreneurs must expect administrative control over prices, quality, quantity, convenience and safety of services and even managerial aspects such as accounting systems or mergers with comparable enterprises. Licensing thus falls between registration and franchise in the degree of controls exercised, but these systems are not mutually exclusive, since some systems called registration may involve more control than some licensing systems, and some licensing systems may have elements of a franchise.

Statutory Grants of Licensing Power

The prevalence of licensing power as a system of administrative control in Ireland is indicated by a review of statutes listed in the *Indexes to the Statutes:* licensing power is provided with respect to over forty occupations, enterprises, business relationships or subjects of regulation and control. These include the licensing of animal slaughtering, bull breeding, betting and bookmakers, shift work, imports, dairy produce, dogs, films, firearms, multiple aspects of land development and use, fishing, the importation and sale of flour and exporting of fresh meat. Also licensed are game dealers, gaming and lotteries, sale of intoxicating liquor, livestock marts, load line certificates in merchant shipping, prospecting for minerals, money lenders, motor vehicle drivers, pawnbrokers, aspects of the pigs and bacon industry, potato exporters, merchandise transport, tobacco manufacture, trade union negotiating, wheat milling, wireless telegraphy and wool marketing. Certain statutes which provide for control through registration are virtually licensing systems, such as those pertaining to doctors, nurses, pharmaceutical chemists, solicitors, trade marks, the egg industry, millers and milling of oatmeal, since they provide for application, registration, continuing supervision and power to cancel registrations.

Of the statutes selected for illustration of regulatory powers in chapter 6, the Solicitors Act 1954, sections 24-63 and Solicitors (Amendment) Act 1960, sections 6-17 and the Censorship of Publications Act 1946, sections 18-19 establish licensing systems. The Local Government (Planning and Development) Act 1963, sections 24-41, supplemented by sections 26 and 27 of the Local Government (Planning and Development) Act 1976 and also by sections 1-4, Local Government (Planning and Development) Act 1982 establish licensing in relation to land development. The Medical Practitioners Act 1978, sections 26-34, and 45-55 delegates licensing power in regard to medical practitioners. However, it should be noted that the above statutes may use such terms as 'registration', 'permit', 'practising certificate' and 'permission' rather than the term 'licence', although in fact licensing systems are established by the statutes.

The Medical Practitioners Act 1978 exemplifies a statutory delegation of power for a complete licensing system masquerading under a statutory label of 'registration'. The Medical Council (hereafter the Council), charged with establishing a register of medical practitioners under section 26 of the 1978 Act, is composed of general practitioners, medical specialists and lay persons as provided in section 9 of that Act. Medical practitioners not already on the register under the previous statute must apply to be registered, meet statutory standards, and satisfy the Council that they have been trained and passed examinations specified by the rules of the Council to qualify for registration. It is an offence punishable by fine and/or imprisonment to falsely represent oneself as a registered medical practitioner under section 61(1)(b) and a nonregistered person may not sue for recovery of medical fees or sign various required medical certificates. The Council may refuse to register a person otherwise entitled to be registered on grounds of unfitness to practise medicine (the reasons must be given in writing) or may grant a provisional registration or a temporary registration as specified by the statute. The Council may register or refuse to register doctors in medical specialties. A doctor may apply to have his name removed from the register, and later apply to have it re-registered, subject to approval or disapproval by the Council on the grounds of unfitness. (See sections 27-34 of the 1978 Act.)

Under sections 45-55, the Council may initiate an inquiry to be conducted by its Fitness to Practise Committee into alleged professional misconduct or unfitness to engage in medicine. The Committee has the power vested in the High Court to force attendance, testimony under oath, and production of documents by witnesses who have the same immunities and privileges as if appearing before the High Court, and also are subject on summary conviction to fines for non-compliance. Based on findings of the Committee in its report to the Council, the Council may erase a practitioner's name from the register or suspend his registration. The Council at any time may restore a practitioner's name to the register and may attach conditions for such restoration. Upon a practitioner's conviction of an indictable offence, the Council may erase his name from the register. All the Council's disciplinary determinations, except Council admonitions or censures of a practitioner, are subject to appeal by the practitioner within 21 days to the High Court, which may affirm or cancel the Council's decision, and in the case of conditions, may add conditions other than those made by the Council. If no such appeal is made, the Council may apply *ex parte* to the High Court for a declaration confirming the Council decision. Appeal to the Supreme Court may be made only on issues of law.

Another statute of particular interest is the Solicitors Act 1954 as amended by the Solicitors (Amendment) Act 1960 since licensing power in effect is delegated to a private association, the Incorporated Law Society. Basic requirements for becoming a solicitor are contained in the 1954 Act, sections 24-45 and the Society may prescribe supplementary requirements. Upon meeting these qualifications and admission as a solicitor of the Courts of Justice, a solicitor, in order to practise his or her profession, must submit an application with specified data for a practising certificate from the Society. Data from the application must be entered on the register of practising solicitors by the Society's Registrar and the applicant is issued a one-year practising certificate which must be renewed annually. (See sections 46-8, 1954 Act and section 31, 1960 Act.)

The Society may refuse a certificate on grounds specified in the Acts or may direct the Registrar to issue a certificate with attached terms and conditions with written reasons for the conditions, from which an appeal may be taken to the President of the High Court under section 49, 1954 Act and section 25, 1960 Act. Requirements must continue to be met, such as submitting an annual certificate with data signed by an accountant that the solicitor has complied with the Solicitors Accounts Regulations under section 31, 1960 Act, and a certificate may be suspended in cases of bankruptcy according to sections 50-52 of the 1954 Act. Sections 6-7 of the 1960 Act provide that solicitors may be subjected to an inquiry by the Society's disciplinary committee appointed by the President of the High Court, which has all the powers of the Court to require attendance of witnesses, their testimony and production of documents. The committee may decide that there is not a *prima facie* case, must make a finding based on the inquiry and give their opinion on the fitness of the solicitor to be a member of the profession. If misconduct is found, sections 8-14 of the 1960 Act provide that the Society shall bring the committee's report before the President of the High Court or a judge of that Court assigned in that behalf by the President who may strike the solicitor's name from the register, suspend him for a fixed period or remit the case to the committee to take further evidence and submit a supplemental report. He may also censure the solicitor, require a money penalty, direct restitution to an aggrieved party, or freeze a solicitor's bank account, under section 8, 1960 Act. A solicitor may apply to the High Court to have his name restored to the register, with prior notice to the Society which is entitled to be heard on such application, and the President may allow or disallow the application. (See section 10, 1960 Act.)

In effect, the Incorporated Law Society administers a short-term licensing system for solicitors with the participation of the President of the High Court who not only appoints the disciplinary committee but also makes the final decisions on such matters as the equivalent of revocation of a licence to practise law and related penalties. The President's role would seem to combine the administrative adjudicatory role of a minister making a decision based on a report from a subordinate enquiry officer together with the appellate role of the High Court.

The Local Government (Planning and Development) Acts 1963, 1976 and 1982 illustrate the statutory provisions for licensing an entrepreneurial activity, such as proposed development of land involving construction of new or added structures, or change in use of land, adding appurtenances to the land, or retention of existing structures, as related to the local development plan. Once the planning authority has adopted a development plan, permission must be obtained from the local authority for any new development of land not exempted or commenced before the appointed day (1 October 1964) and for the retention of existing structures which became unauthorised on that day, in accordance with sections 19, 24, and 25, 1963 Act. Carrying out any development for which permission is required except in accordance with the permission as granted, is prohibited, and there are penalties for non-compliance (section 24(3) of the 1963 Act).

Application for permission to develop land must be made in accordance with the Minister for the Environment's regulations made under section 25 of the 1963 Act, section 35 of the 1976 Act and section 11 of the 1982 Act and his power to issue 'such general directives as to policy related to planning and development as he considers necessary' which apply to both planning authorities and An Bord Pleanála under section 7 of the 1982 Act. The planning authority may grant permission to develop land, with or without conditions, or may refuse permission, based on the relation of the proposed development to the development plan. Permission may not be granted which would contravene materially the development plan or a special amenity area order unless the consent of An Bord Pleanála (the Board) is obtained. (See section 26, 1963 Act, section 14, 1976 Act.) In this process public awareness and participation is provided for by requiring the applicant to give public notice of the project with details as specified in regulations adopted under section 25(2)(b) of the 1963 Act, and any person may appeal within two months to the Board against the planning authority's decision. The Board will determine the application as if it had been made to the Board in the first instance, either refusing or granting permission with or without conditions. The decision and its notification must comprise a statement specifying the reasons for the Board's decision, according to section 26(5) and (8) of the 1963 Act and section 14 of the 1976 Act. Essentially the same process is involved in application for permission to retain an unauthorised structure, under sections 27 and 28 of the 1963 Act and sections 14 and 24 of the 1976 Act. It should be noted that according to section 22(1) of the Local Government (Planning and Development) Act 1983, section 26(5)(b) of the 1963 Act as amended by section 14(9) of the 1976 Act is to be construed subject to sections 16, 18 and 19 of the 1983 Act, (i.e. powers of the Board over frivolous appeals, to direct production of evidence and direct planning authorities regarding conditions of a permission); furthermore, that other provisions concerning appeals to the Board in the 1963 to 1982 Acts will be construed subject to section 17 of the 1983 Act (power of Board to require that grounds for appeal be submitted in writing).

Planning authorities may modify or revoke permission to develop land based upon consideration of the proper planning and development of the area and preservation of its amenities as related to the development plan or any amenity area order, with appeal to the Board which may confirm the notice to modify or revoke a permission, with or without modification or may annul the notice. (See section 30 of the 1963 Act as amended by section 39 of the 1976 Act.) Sections 2-4 of the 1982 Act supplement the 1963 and 1976 Acts with provisions concerning what amounts to cancellation of planning permission when nothing is done on a development, or nothing on what remains to be done after the expiry of the appropriate period for the development (except for certain categories of permission specifically listed as being exempt from this provision). Power is also given to the planning authority to specify the period for development in its permission and to extend the appropriate period, subject to regulations of the Minister under the 1963 to 1982 Acts.

Enforcement of the licensing system against unauthorised development of land, or non-compliance with conditions for permission to develop or continuation of an unauthorised structure, through notice to correct deviant activity and subsequent prosecution in court, is provided for in sections 31 and 35 of the 1963 Act and section 26 of the 1976 Act, with provision for penalties as revised in section 8 of the 1982 Act. Section 27 of the 1976 Act also enables the planning authority or any other person (whether or not the person has an interest in the land) to apply to the High Court for a negative order to cease certain actions or a positive order to force compliance with the development permission. Orders requiring corrective action, with the alternative of such action being taken by the planning authority with recovery of costs against the owner, may be issued by the authority under sections 32 and 35 of the 1963 Act. Related licensing powers are given to planning authorities under section 89 of the 1963 Act in respect of the erection, construction or maintenance in, on or under a public road, of appliances for servicing motor vehicles, vending machines, advertising structures and pipelines which the Minister's regulations designate as appropriate for licensing.[1]

Constitutional and Conceptual Issues

The delegation to and exercise of licensing power by administrative agencies raise constitutional issues of due process and equal protection under the law with related legal-conceptual issues as to whether a licence is a privilege or right, preventive or punitive in purpose, whether there is a presumption of illegality of unlicensed operation and where the burden of proof lies. Additional legal-conceptual issues are the legal effect of a licence and the difference between licensing and taxation.

Right Versus Privilege and Due Course of Law
In *Conroy v. Attorney General and Another* 1965 IR 411, plaintiff was charged with violation of section 49 of the Road Traffic Act 1961 and claimed a declaration that section 49 was repugnant to article 38 of the Constitution. His argument was that the offence created by section 49 was not a minor offence which could be tried by a District Justice but must be tried by a judge sitting with a jury, in accordance with article 38 which provides that no person shall be tried on any criminal charge without a jury, except for minor offences which may be tried by a court of summary jurisdiction. Under section 49, a person charged with a first offence of driving while drunk may be tried by a court of summary jurisdiction with a maximum of six months imprisonment and/or £100 fine, and disqualified from having a driver's licence for a year; for a second or repeated offence causing death or serious bodily harm, the District Justice must impose a minimum of three years' disqualification from holding a driver's licence, with no maximum limit on such disqualification.

Kenny J. in the High Court cited *Melling v. O Mathghamhna* 1962 IR 1, 97 ILTR 60 applying principles established by the United States Supreme Court as to what is a 'petty offence', namely (1) how the law stood when the statute in question was passed; (2) the severity of the penalty; (3) the moral quality of the act; (4) its relation to common law crimes. His analysis of the 1922 and 1937 constitutional provisions and legislation enacted in the years between them led him to conclude that the 1961 Act was far more severe than the earlier law on drunken driving since that legislation was not a reliable guide as to what was a minor offence, and assessment of comparative severity of punishment thus should be based on the maximum penalty existing in 1922. As to severity of penalty, disqualification from driving can be very serious punishment for those whose occupation requires driving automobiles as indicated in *State of Minnesota v. Hoben*, 98 N.W. 2d 813, as follows:

Much has been said as to whether a licence to operate a motor vehicle is a right or a privilege. It has been variously denominated as a privilege in the nature of a right and is an important privilege or right under our present mode of living . . . . Clearly one's inalienable right to liberty and the pursuit of happiness is curtailed if he may be unreasonably kept off the highways maintained by him as a citizen and taxpayer.

Kenny J. referred to evidence from Canon John McCarthy, Doctor of Theology and Canon Law that it is a dereliction of moral duty to drive a car with lack of control owing to alcohol or drugs, since it risked life and bodily integrity of others and of the driver, with the gravity of the act inherent in the act itself regardless of the outcome. From a common law standpoint, a person driving when intoxicated could be prosecuted for committing a public nuisance, namely unreasonable and excessive use of the highway which is an indictable offence not triable summarily. Based on these factors, he held that a section 49 offence was not a minor offence, and plaintiff was entitled to a declaration that section 49 was repugnant to article 38 of the Constitution.

On appeal to the Supreme Court, Walsh J. disagreed as to how the law stood when the Road Traffic Act was passed, holding that the procedures for prosecuting drunken driving prescribed in the

Road Traffic Act 1933 were widely known in 1937 when the present Constitution was adopted, and the procedures prescribed by section 49 of the 1961 Road Traffic Act correspond to the pattern existing in 1937. He agreed that driving while intoxicated and thus risking the life or bodily integrity of others is a dereliction of moral duty, but stated that there is a large area between serious and minimal moral guilt which must be left to the legislature's discretion in deciding whether an offence is minor. In the Court's opinion, punishment of six months imprisonment and £100 fine is in the category of a minor offence.

Regarding the severity of punishment in disqualifying a person for a licence (perhaps indefinitely), the Criminal Justice Act 1951, section 23, distinguishes between punishment and forfeiture or disqualification, even though both are imposed by a court exercising criminal jurisdiction. However, classification of every punishment requires analysis of its basic nature rather than its statutory description. Section 38 of the Road Traffic Act 1961 makes driving an automobile without a driving licence a criminal offence, and in the prosecution of that offence, the presumption is that the defendant did not have a driving licence until he shows the contrary. Regarding the possession of a driving licence, the effect of Part III, 1961 Act is that every person has a statutory right to a driver's licence if he has reached the prescribed age and proves he has the prescribed skill and is not disqualified by a court order or for health reasons. As to the right/privilege dichotomy in this respect, Walsh J. stated that:

> The Court uses the term 'right' in this context in contrast to 'privilege' in the sense that a driving licence is not something which is granted at the discretion of the licensing authority. The grant of a driving licence is not made a judicial act. The Act however does make declarations of disqualification of persons from holding a driving licence judicial acts . . . . consequential and ancillary disqualification orders can only be made by the Court when a person has been convicted of the appropriate offence or offences . . . . before any such order is made the Court concerned must act judicially in respect of the disqualification order in addition to hearing and determining the charge which leads to the conviction referred to in sects. 26 and 27. (page 440)

Given this, Walsh J. felt that the right to a driving licence granted
by the Act may be lost temporarily or even permanently while the
Act is in force. Despite the American precedent that to some persons
a driver's licence is as valuable as an occupational or professional
licence, it is the 'primary punishment' which must be examined to
determine the seriousness of an offence. Such punishment is that
where crime is concerned, it consists either of the loss of liberty or
the intentional penal deprivation of property by fine. The possibility
that any conviction may have other consequences, even though of
a punitive nature affecting his very livelihood, is too remote to be
taken into account in evaluating the seriousness of an offence. The
disqualification order is essentially a finding of the lack of fitness to
hold a driving licence and recognition of the public interest that an
improperly driven vehicle is a hazard to all others and the driver.
This view is supported by provisions in section 29 for removing
consequential and ancillary disqualification orders, through judicial
consideration of the applicant's character, the nature of the offence
and other matters the court considers relevant, to determine if the
applicant has ceased to be unfit to hold a driving licence.

The High Court and Supreme Court disagreement over the
meaning and severity of punishment in loss of a driving licence has
significant conceptual connotations as to the nature of a licensing
system which have operational consequences. Had the High Court
perception that losing a driving licence is a serious punishment
requiring trial by jury prevailed, the licence revocation or disqualification process would have been taken largely out of the realm of
administrative law and process, with implied emphasis on the
punitive over the preventive purpose and effect of this aspect of the
licensing process. The decision by the Supreme Court that loss of
a driving licence is not a primary punishment requiring jury trial
kept the disqualification within the category of administrative law.
Although the District Justice who decides on disqualification must
act judicially, he essentially is performing the role of an administrative tribunal since the disqualification is primarily for the preventive
purpose of safeguarding the public and the driver from his drunken
driving, rather than imposition of penalty. This is further indicated
by the Supreme Court's dicta concerning the illegality of the unlicensed person who must bear the burden of proving innocence, in
contrast with the presumption of innocence and burden of proof on

the state in criminal law cases.

Equality Before the Law and Private Property Rights
Equal protection of the law and rights of private property under
articles 40.1, 40.3 and 43 of the Constitution were the grounds
for challenging the licensing powers granted to the Minister for
Agriculture and Fisheries under the Livestock Marts Act 1967, in
East Donegal Co-operative Livestock Mart Ltd and Others v Attorney General.
1970 IR 317. Sections 1 and 2 of the 1967 Act make it an offence
to operate a livestock mart without a licence and sections 3(1)-(8)
provide for detailed licensing procedures. An application must be
made providing data required by the Minister who at his discretion
may grant or refuse a licence to operate a livestock mart and may
'attach to the licence such conditions as he shall think proper and
shall specify in the licence'. The Minister must give notice, and
reasons, of his intention to refuse a licence. When a licensee is guilty
of an offence under the Act, which includes violating regulations of
the Minister or conditions attached to the licence the Minister may
'if he so thinks fit' revoke the licence. The Minister must give notice
of intent to revoke an existing licence, and reasons for the proposed
revocation, and if the licensee requests an inquiry within seven
days, the Minister must appoint a barrister of ten or more years
standing to hold an inquiry and give notice to the licensee of the
right to appear and adduce evidence. The barrister may take
evidence on oath, and must make a report of findings to the Minister
who must consider them before revocation of the licence, give
reasons for the revocation, and lay them before both Houses of the
Oireachtas.
    In contrast with the substantive and procedural provisions sur-
rounding the issue of revocation of permits, section 4 of the 1967
Act provides:

    (1) The Minister may, if he so thinks fit, grant exemption from
    the provisions of this Act in respect of the carrying on of any
    particular business or business of any particular class or kind.

Moreover, the Minister may withdraw an exemption at any time.
He must, however, lay the details of an exemption or its withdrawal
before each House of the Oireachtas.

Plaintiffs, constituting three co-operative societies and four stock-holders of a society engaged in livestock mart operation, argued that the Act was contrary to equal protection of the law under article 40.1 of the Constitution, since where there is regard in an Act to differences of capacity or social function, the Act must prescribe the way in which those differences are to be given effect. However, the 1967 Act delegated unfettered discretion to the Minis-ter to grant or refuse a licence, to attach conditions more onerous for one licensee than another, to amend or revoke such conditions at will, and finally, to exempt any particular business or business of any particular class. Moreover, holding livestock marts is a property right under article 43 of the Constitution and though such rights may be regulated in the public interest, the Act does not provide criteria by which the rights in question may be regulated.

An appeal to the Supreme Court was taken from the High Court decision rejecting the claim of repugnance to article 40, but holding that the absence of procedural safeguards in regard to attachment of conditions was fatal to the Act as a whole since it meant that the legislation could be applied to differentiate between citizens in a manner not reflecting differences of capacity. Walsh J. for the Supreme Court held that the extensive procedural protections afforded to an applicant for a licence, or a licensee threatened with revocation by the Minister, demonstrated that it was not the intent of the Oireachtas to empower the Minister to act in a manner contravening the provisions of the Constitution or to place his actions beyond review by the courts. He also concluded upon analysis of the Livestock Marts Act that every reference to an offence by a licensee meant a criminal offence to be adjudicated by a court. Consequently the Minister could revoke a licence only after the licence holder had been convicted by a court of an offence, although the Minister still had discretion to decide whether to revoke a licence after such court conviction. This interpretation of the Act was contrary to the Attorney General's submission on behalf of the Minister for Agriculture, arguing that the word 'offence' in section 3(4) could also refer simply to a breach of a condition of a licence, or to the Minister's opinion that there had been a breach, based upon which the Minister might revoke the licence without a prior court conviction.

Regarding the claim of unfettered discretion in imposing con-ditions, Walsh J. referred to the presumption of parliamentary

intent that proceedings, discretion and adjudication under any Act
are to be conducted in accordance with the principles of natural
justice as held in *McDonald v. Bord na gCon* 1965 IR 217. He held
that a departure from natural justice would be corrected by the
courts, stating:

> That conditions must be of the character already indicated in
> this judgment and must be related to the objects of the Act . . .
> Any condition which did not conform with these tests would
> be *ultra vires* the Act . . . it is not a valid inference that because
> a specified procedure is prescribed for . . . revocation or refusal
> of a licence that the Minister is not bound to act in accordance
> with the principles of natural justice in respect of the imposi-
> tion, amendment or revocation of conditions attached to a
> licence. (pages 95-6)

Moreover, Walsh J. held that the provision in section 4 of the Act
granting power to the Minister to exempt 'any particular business'
was invalid. The constitutional power of the Oireachtas to recognise
social function differences in physical and moral capacity does
not extend to delegating such power to the executive to decide
independently of the Oireachtas which individuals from among
those covered by the legislation shall be exempted from its
application, unless such exemptions are necessary to avoid infringement of a constitutional right because of unique circumstances.
This prohibition does not apply however, to delegation of power by
the Oireachtas to exempt all business of a particular class or kind,
since such exemption would not distinguish between individuals.
The Act as a whole was determined to be constitutional, with the
exception of the words 'any particular business' in section 4(1) and
'a particular business' in section 4(2).

   Thus the Minister's power to impose conditions under the Act
was upheld on the presumption it would be exercised in accordance
with concepts of natural justice which would be imposed in any
court review, and his power to issue or revoke licences was approved
in part because of the statutory procedural protections surrounding
the issue and revocation of licences. However, the approval of power
to revoke licences was also based on the rationale that all offences
under the Act were criminal offences so that the Minister could
revoke a licence only after conviction of an offence in a court of law,

which makes the administrative revocation of a licence subordinate to criminal court processes. An interpretation more in accord with concepts of administrative law would have been that the Minister was also empowered to initiate proceedings for and revoke a licence following statutory procedural provisions, based on substantial evidence in an administrative hearing of violation of licence requirements, subject to subsequent appeal to the courts as to sufficiency of evidence and adherence to statutory procedures and natural justice.

Fair Procedures, Free Expression, Social Policy
In *Nova Media Services Ltd and Brady v. Minister for Posts and Telegraphs, Ireland, and the Attorney General* 1984 ILRM 161, Murphy J. held that it was not possible or appropriate for him to resolve the constitutional issues of fair procedures, free expression and social policy raised by Nova at that stage of the proceedings where he was determining the more immediate issue of Nova's application for interlocutory relief (an injunction) against the Minister's enforcement actions. However, his comment in his judgment that 'a stateable case has been made out' indicated that serious consideration should be given to the constitutional issues raised in this case concerning the Wireless Telegraphy Act 1926, although they were unresolved at that point by the High Court. The 1926 Act prohibits the use of apparatus for wireless telegraphy without a licence from the Minister and penalises unlicensed operation by a minimal fine on summary conviction and also by forfeiture of all apparatus for broadcasting. Under section 8(1) of the 1926 Act, a District Justice may issue a search warrant to enter, by force if need be, search for and seize all broadcasting equipment used contrary to the Act or related regulations.

Radio Nova, a 'pirate' radio station with some 50 employees and £350,000 investment in equipment, had operated since 1981 but had never applied for a licence. In May 1983 officials of the Minister, under a warrant issued by a District Justice, entered Radio Nova premises and removed broadcasting equipment. A plenary summons was issued the same day as the entry and seizure in which Radio Nova claimed that certain provisions of the 1926 Act were repugnant to the Constitution and violated the EEC Treaty of Rome. Radio Nova then resumed broadcasting with alternative but

less powerful equipment, and applied to the court for interlocutory
relief to restrain the defendants from interfering with their broadcasting and to require them to return the seized equipment pending
trial of the full action. Subsequently a District Court summons was
issued on complaint of the Minister, that Radio Nova unlawfully
kept apparatus for wireless telegraphy.

Radio Nova argued that the seizure procedure provided for by
section 8 of the 1926 Act authorised imposition of a penalty without
a charge being made or a hearing, contrary to fair procedures
guaranteed by the Constitution, and the seizure itself represented
an administrative decision to impose a penalty contrary to article
38 of the Constitution, which required criminal charges to be tried
by court of law. In addition, the licensing provisions of the 1926
Act violated the article 40 guarantee to citizens of the right to
express their opinions through the media, including radio and press.
Finally, article 45.3 of the Constitution recognises an ideological
preference for private enterprise over state monopoly, but a monopoly in effect had been created in favour of the national broadcasting
system through the Minister's use of his powers under the Act. In
this regard, the reason an application had never been made by
Radio Nova for a licence, as claimed by Nova's managing director
in his affidavit, was that he was informed and believed it was the
policy of theMinister for Posts and Telegraphs not to issue licences
for the type of broadcasting Radio Nova proposed to engage in, as
demonstrated by the fact that despite applications, no such licences
had ever been issued.

Regarding these claims of unconstitutionality of the Act, Murphy
J. held first that it would not be possible to resolve such far-reaching
submissions at this stage of the judicial process, and it would not
be proper for him to express his tentative views. However, he did
state:

It is sufficient to say – as indeed the defendants virtually
concede – that 'a stateable case' has been made out. (page 167)

On the immediate issue of interlocutory relief in his judgment, the
balance of convenience had to be made out in the light of the
circumstances. On the one hand, the plaintiffs, by being prevented
from broadcasting for more than twelve months before these proceedings would come on for hearing would suffer a very substantial

financial loss which would be difficult to foresee or to calculate. On the other hand, the Minister for Posts and Telegraphs would be unable to perform the duties placed on him by the 1926 Act, since the effect (of an injunction to restrain the Minister from interfering with their broadcasting, removing their equipment and an order to return the seized equipment) would be to suspend control and regulation of radio broadcasting until the issues were resolved by the courts.

In this respect, it was difficult not to sympathise with plaintiffs, since they had been broadcasting for almost two years without interference from the Minister, had co-operated with revenue authorities, planning authorities and the Garda Síochána, and two bills entitled Independent Radio Authority Bill had been introduced but not yet passed, all of which might lead to the assumption that the 1926 law would not be enforced against Nova without reasonable warning. However, except in special circumstances, it would be most unusual for the courts to intervene to prevent the Minister from exercising a function with which he is charged under express terms of a statute made for the public good. The fact is that the plaintiffs started and continued their enterprise knowing that they were in conflict with the 1926 Act and they did not seek to obtain a licence or challenge the constitutionality of the licensing provisions or any other portion of the Act at any time before these proceedings. It would thus be improper for the court to make an order restraining the defendants from exercising the powers conferred on the Minister by the 1926 Act.

Preventive, Not Punitive, Purpose

A fundamental concept of licensing power indicated in the *Conroy* case (page 306) is that it is designed to prevent or minimise in advance the potential injury which might be caused by the incompetence of individuals providing services or the unsafe, negligent or deceptive operation of an enterprise. This contrasts with traditional criminal and civil punitive deterrence through imprisonment and monetary penalties after the injury or damage has taken place, or even equitable remedies such as the injunction to avert an imminent threat or continuance of injury in a particular instance when it would result in irreparable or incalculable damage.

A cogent statement emphasising the preventive nature of licensing appears in the case of *In the Matter of the Moneylenders Act 1933 and of*

Lynne and Others, Applicants v. Attorney General 74 ILTR 96 which involved four appeals from the refusal of the Dublin District Court to grant a renewal of moneylenders' certificates to four appellants, on the ground that they were not fit and proper persons to hold such certificates. The evidence demonstrated non-fulfilment of requirements under the Act as to memorandum of contract, charging of excessive interest, employment of agents, making loans to married women without knowledge or consent of their husbands and failure to disclose rates of interest. On appeal to the Circuit Court, Davitt J. noted that all four applicants felt that they were entitled to engage in all the transactions and forms of actions demonstrated by the evidence, provided they did not specifically violate any of the penal provisions of the Moneylenders Act 1933. Moreover, they did so knowing that as moneylenders they were taking the risk that they would be unable under the Act to secure their enforcement to recover the money lent.

Davitt J. refuted this line of reasoning stating that:

> I regard section 11 of the Moneylenders Act, 1933, as the Magna Carta of that class of people who have recourse to moneylenders and I consider that if that section is allowed to be infringed with impunity then the protection given by the statute to borrowers is removed, and the way is left open to abuse. It is not an answer that the borrower can refuse to repay the loan if there is a breach of section 11 of the Act, or can come to the courts for protection against the moneylender who charges excessive interest.

The reason for this, in the judge's view, is that in many instances those who borrow are not in a position to refuse to pay or come to the Court for protection since they are unaware of their rights or the high rates of interest being charged. He wanted it to be clearly understood by future applicants for moneylenders' licences that evidence of continued or frequent failure to comply with the provisions of the Moneylenders Act is a definite ground for refusal to grant a certificate. He adjourned the request for renewal of the four certificates to a later day and allowed the applicants to continue their temporary licences on probation with the warning that he would refuse their applications for permanent licences at the time of the resumed hearing if any infringement by them should be brought to his attention.

Further insight into the preventive as against punitive nature of licensing is provided by *In re Crowley* 1964 IR 106, 99 ILTR 118. The plaintiff, Crowley, was refused a practising certificate for the year 1961-2 because the Incorporated Law Society were not satisfied with the explanation he had given to its registrar's committee in response to allegations of professional misconduct, namely 'touting' for business (he had 'stolen' a client by offering to provide a legal service without or for less than the fixed fee normally charged). Crowley appealed to the President of the High Court and in accordance with section 49 of the Solictors Act 1954, the registrar was required to issue a certificate pending the outcome of the appeal. The President of the High Court refused the appeal and suspended the certificate, but granted a stay of suspension if Crowley lodged a notice of appeal to the Supreme Court within 21 days. That appeal was made but was not listed until February 1962. By that time the period for which the practising certificate was effective had ended, so the Supreme Court adjourned the matter. In effect, Crowley through the timing of statutorily provided-for appeals continued to hold a certificate to practise during the year for which the Society sought to refuse the certificate.

Subsequently, when the plaintiff Crowley applied for a practising certificate for 1962-3, he was invited in writing by the Secretary of the Society to make further representations at a meeting of the registrar's committee to consider again the original complaint of touting. Crowley did not attend the meeting on the ground that the charges and evidence were identical with those given at the previous registrar's committee meeting on the matter, and he could not conjecture what he could say beyond his previous explanation and representation unless he were to say they were false. Assuming his first explanation was true, he could not alter it despite its inadequacy to explain his action to the committee's satisfaction.

The registrar's committee again directed the registrar to refuse to issue a practising certificate for 1962-3, Crowley again appealed to the President of the High Court, who confirmed the refusal. Crowley then appealed to the Supreme Court, arguing that: (1) the complaint against him could be dealt with only by the disciplinary committee established by the Solicitors (Amendment) Act 1960 as the one body empowered to make an order striking a solicitor off

the registrar's roll; (2) the conduct complained of was for one
transaction, not continuing conduct so it could not be the subject
of a second investigation and refusal of a certificate for a succeeding
year; (3) refusal of the certificate for two years was too severe a
penalty.

The Supreme Court (Ó Dálaigh C. J., Kingsmill Moore and
Walsh J. J., Lavery and Haugh J. J. dissenting) held the Society
was not justified in refusing to issue the practising certificate for
1961-2 or 1962-3. Kingsmill Moore J., for the Court, stated that
logically the High Court decision could mean that the Society might
refuse a certificate 'forever after'. This was because the refusal
would not be for continued misconduct or seriousness of the offence
but for continued failure of the accused to give any explanation of
his previous conduct other than his original explanation, which
rightfully was considered inadequate by the registrar's committee.
Kingsmill Moore J. was reluctant to impute that such an action
was intended by the legislature. Moreover, though section 4 of the
1954 Act provided that the Council was to perform the Society's
functions and under section 73 could delegate Council functions to
its own committees, a disciplinary committee was also established
in Part III of that Act, with prescribed powers and procedures. It
thus appeared that the legislature intended that only the disciplinary
committee could suspend a solicitor from practice. Moreover, the
later Act of 1960 gave power to withhold a certificate to the High
Court acting on a report from a new disciplinary committee
appointed by the President of that Court.

Kingsmill Moore J. stated that situations can arise where the
interests of the public, the profession and the individual solicitor
may warrant the severe penalty of withholding a certificate, but
that in such circumstances:

> Such restraint is not a matter of discipline for past offence but
> of precaution lest future practice by the solicitor should prove
> dangerous to the public or the profession . . . . The fact that a
> solicitor has misbehaved himself in the past may indeed be an
> element in arriving at the conclusion that he is likely to mis-
> behave himself in the future . . . but in such a case the certificate
> is not to be withheld, or conditions imposed, as a discipline for
> past misdoing. Such action is only justified as a necessary

precaution against the likelihood of future misdoing reasonably to be inferred from past misconduct. (page 129)

Therefore the Society can take appropriate disciplinary action through its disciplinary committee and the High Court, but it can not bypass the proper disciplinary procedure and use the registrar's committee as an indirect method of inflicting discipline as such, which is precisely what the Society had done by refusing the certificate based on one past instance of misconduct.

Lavery and Haugh J. J. in dissent held that the Solicitor's Acts permit the Society to deal with refusal of a certificate through its registrar's committee as well as its disciplinary committee, with review by the President of the High Court and Supreme Court available. It was doubted that the Society would abuse its power by refusing a certificate *ad infinitum*; such abuse is subject to judicial review. Plaintiff's claim that it was futile to appear at the second registrar's committee meeting overlooked the approaches of either admitting to the complaints and apologising, or providing evidence that this was the only instance of misconduct with no subsequent improprieties together with assurances of proper future conduct and offering compensation for losses his misconduct may have caused. Previous cases showed that such an approach meant it was possible the Society might have imposed a less severe penalty.

The divergence of judicial opinion in this case reflects differences in interpretation of legislative intent in statutory provisions. However, underlying the majority and dissenting opinions is a conceptual difference in perception, namely the refusal to issue a practising certificate as a preventive measure to protect the public or as a punishment for a past offence.

Burden of Proof and Presumption of Illegality
Licensing as a preventive control system is supported by the legal concept that the burden of proof rests on the applicant for a licence as illustrated by *Irish Cinemas Ltd (Applicants) In Re the Intoxicating Liquor Act 1960*, unreported, High Court, per McLoughlin J., 8 November 1968. Section 14 (1) (e) of the Intoxicating Liquor Act 1960 provides that if a licence holder for an existing premises applies for a licence for a new premises which will not be located on the same site, the new premises must be located either partly on that

site or in the immediate vicinity. Moreover, the site of the new premises must not be likely to have a materially adverse effect on the business carried on in any other licensed premises in the neighbourhood.

The Gresham Hotel and the owners of other licensed premises in the surrounding area opposed the grant of a licence which Irish Cinemas Ltd had sought for the new premises which would adjoin the Gresham. Their grounds were that the new premises would have a materially adverse effect on their businesses, and that the new premises would not be located in the immediate vicinity of the original premises, known as the Cosmo Bar, located some 733 yards away and on the other side of the river Liffey from the proposed new premises.

McLoughlin J. held that the objectors had not made a case that the new premises would materially affect their business, but this factor did not subsume the other requirements that the new premises must be located in the immediate vicinity of the original premises, and he stated that 'the burden of proof is on the applicant to satisfy me that such is the case'. Some meaning must be given to the outer limit of the statutory term 'immediate vicinity' and in this regard:

> If a visitor standing outside 19 O'Connell Street which is beside the Gresham Hotel were to enquire of an average well-informed Dublin person as to the whereabouts of the (original premises of the) Cosmo Bar, he would, I think be told — 'you are in the wrong part of the City . . . it is in a different neighbourhood altogether . . . go south, cross the bridge, and continue to the end of D'Olier Street'.

Since no evidence was given which satisfied him that the new premises was in the immediate vicinity of the original premises, he felt that he must refuse the application, despite an inclination to accede to an application of this kind.

Placing the burden of proof upon an applicant as in *Irish Cinemas Ltd* does not conflict with the traditional assumption that the individual is innocent and the burden is on the state to prove guilt since refusal of a licence is not a penalty or loss of property. However, since a penalty is usually imposed for unlicensed operation there is a potential conflict between the traditional criminal law concept and the licensing power presumption of illegality of an unlicensed operation and concomitant burden of proof on the individual to show that he is licensed so as to make an operation or activity legal. In *Attorney General v. Duff* 1941 IR 406, 76 ILTR 8, defendant was accused of operating without a licence in violation of an Emergency Order (regulation) made under the Emergency Powers Act 1939 which prohibited the export of specified goods unless (1) they were exported under and in accordance with a licence issued by the Minister, and (2) such licence was, prior to exportation, delivered to the appropriate officer. The Act also provided penalties for violation of Emergency Orders. The Court held it was not incumbent upon the prosecution to prove that the defendant's licence did not exist or that it had not been delivered to the defendant, if the defendant could not produce evidence of the existence and delivery of that licence.

The presumption of illegality of unlicensed operation and burden of proof on the defendant also informed the determination of the Court in *Attorney General (Lew) v. Marmion* unreported, High Court, per Davitt P., 8 August 1956. Defendant was charged with violating the Road Transport Act 1933, as amended by the 1934 Act, which made it unlawful for a person in the merchandise road transport business to carry any merchandise anywhere in the state without the necessary licence or unless the area in which he carries it is an exempted area and his carrying of merchandise is only in such an exempted area. Davitt P. noted that section 8, County Officers and Courts (Ireland) Act 1877 placed the burden on the defendant of proving that he comes within either exception. In addition he held that apart from the Act, the general principle that the burden of proof rests on a defendant when a matter to be proved is peculiarly within his knowledge would apply in this case. The defendant did not have a licence so Davitt P. felt that to prevail in his defence, he had to bring himself completely within the Transport Act by proving he was carrying the goods only in an exempted area and that his journey must never have taken him outside an exempted area. Since his journey did take him from an exempted area into a non-exempted area, an offence was committed when he carried the merchandise in any area and at all stages of the journey.

However, in *McGowan v. Carville* 1960 IR 330, the Supreme Court qualified the presumption and burden of proof concept expressed in *Marmion* by introducing the element of statutory intent related to the importance to the public interest of compliance with licensing requirements. Defendant Carville could not produce his driving licence when stopped by garda McGowan but stated he would produce it later at a specified police station. Carville was notified of but did not attend a subsequent hearing on the charge of driving without a licence in violation of section 22(1) of the Road Traffic Act 1933, where the garda gave evidence of the above facts, but no evidence as to whether he had produced his licence at the specified police station. The District Justice dismissed the summons on the grounds that the burden lay upon the garda as complainant to prove that defendant had no licence, which the garda had failed to do. The decision of the District Justice was affirmed by the High Court.

On appeal to the Supreme Court, Lavery J. for the majority of the Court also affirmed the lower courts' decisions. He held that proof of offence was dependent upon the intent of the legislature as shown in provisions of the particular statute involved. For example, violation of a motor vehicle owner's obligation to have third party insurance may have important consequences, so the Road Traffic Act 1933 positively places the burden on the vehicle owner to prove he holds insurance coverage. In contrast, the statutory 'obligation to have a driving licence is relatively insignificant. Such a licence can be obtained without any formality other than the payment of the fee. It is purely a revenue tax' (page 355). Moreover, road traffic regulations require the licensing authority to keep a register of driving licences so the garda can readily determine whether or not a licence has been issued.

Maguire C.J. dissented, stating there are two exceptions to the burden of proof lying on the prosecutor, as a matter of law and pleading in criminal cases based on a presumption of innocence. The first is where a disputable presumption of law exists or a *prima facie* case has been proved. The second is where the subject matter of a party's allegation is peculiarly within the knowledge of the opposing party. The Road Traffic Act 1933 required a driver to produce a licence if it is with him or within five days at a police station for perusal if it is not. This seems to put the burden on the driver to satisfy the Garda Síochána he has a licence. Moreover, once a person drives a vehicle, the burden of proof of possession of a licence is on him since it is peculiarly within his knowledge whether he has a licence or not.

The concepts of the *Marmion* and *McGowan* cases were considered and applied in the later case of *Bridgett v. Dowd* 1961 IR 313, 94 ILTR 101. Defendants were charged under section 9, Road Transport Act 1933 with carrying cattle outside an exempted area in a jointly owned motor lorry without a merchandise licence. Davitt P. noted the evidence from the identical cases stated on appeal from decisions of the District Court dismissing the complaints. The complainant, garda Bridgett, saw the lorry being driven into Dublin along the Navan road and while it was under his observation it was within 15 miles of Dublin's centre and thus in an exempted area. However, when the lorry was first seen, it could have been coming from Bective, County Meath, outside the exempted area. Although there was no apparent connection between Bective, cattle and defendants, there was an underlying suggestion that the cattle were being driven from Bective to Aughrim Street (Dublin).

Davitt P. held that the *McGowan* case was distinguishable from this case since the obligation to have a driver's licence is 'relatively insignificant', obtainable primarily through paying a fee or revenue tax, under the Road Traffic Act 1933. In contrast, as the *Marmion* case shows, a merchandise licence under the Road Transport Acts has an important regulatory purpose making it a valuable piece of property difficult to acquire. However, given *McGowan,* he would modify the view expressed in his opinion in applying *Marmion* to this case, and hold that it is clear from *McGowan* that in a prosecution for carrying goods without a merchandise licence, the burden of proof that defendant has no such licence rests initially upon the prosecution with a ready means of doing so provided under the statute. Once the absence of a licence is established, together with the fact that the defendant has carried merchandise in a lorry, the burden of proof shifts to the defendant to bring himself within one of the exceptions under the Road Transport Acts if he is to escape liability, as in *Marmion.* Defendants in this case did not have a licence, and had carried cattle in a lorry, and did not prove that on the occasion in question the cattle were carried only within an exempted area. In this regard, the District Justice was wrong in his decision, and the question he submitted was answered accordingly.

Licensing as Regulation, Not Taxation
Although the legal effect and implications of a licence for regulatory purposes, as against a licence with the purpose of revenue through

M

fees, had not been raised as the central issue in cases, the *dicta* of the courts in *McGowan, Bridgett* and *Marmion* indicate that the courts do make a differentiation. The distinction can be significant, since as these three cases indicate, it affects judicial perspective as to which party has the burden of proof. In *McGowan*, Lavery J. emphasised the seriousness of the motor vehicle owner's obligation to have third party insurance in view of the important consequences of non-compliance, and the resulting burden of proof on the owner to show possession of insurance coverage under the Road Traffic Act 1933, while in contrast:

> The obligation to have a driving licence is relatively insignificant. Such a licence can be obtained without any formality other than the payment of the fee. It is purely a revenue tax. (page 355)

Given this difference and the relative administrative ease of determining whether a person has a licence, the initial burden of proof was placed on the Garda Síochána to show non-possession of a licence.

Again, as indicated immediately above, Davitt P. emphasised the limited application of *McGowan* as against the direct and determining application of *Marmion* to the *Bridgett v. Dowd* case. In large part, this was based upon the contrasting purposes of the Road Traffic Act 1933 requirement of licences for drivers, and the Road Transport Acts' requirement of licences for merchandising. As he noted, the former was primarily for revenue purpose, the latter for serious regulatory purposes. As a consequence, the burden of proof in the latter instance fell upon the defendant to demonstrate that he came within one of the statutory exceptions to the requirement of having a merchandise licence.

Effect of Licence on Legal Relationships

Being without a licence may have an adverse effect upon the legal relationships of the unlicensed person with other parties, in that the legal rights of the unlicensed may be nullified or restricted in transactions with other persons. In *Dolan v. The Corporation of the Corn Exchange Buildings Company and Vico Estates Ltd* 1975 IR 315, plaintiff sought a new tenancy in his licensed premises in Dublin and was held to be entitled to a new lease by the Circuit Court. Defendants appealed to the High Court on the grounds that the Corn Exchange Corporation had agreed to sell the building to Vico Estates with vacant possession, free from existing tenancies including that of plaintiffs; that the Minister for Local Government had granted outline planning permission for the construction of an office block requiring demolition of the Corn Exchange Building; and that subsequently Vico Estates had purchased the building and submitted an application to Dublin Corporation for planning approval to construct a new office and commercial block on the site of the Corn Exchange building. The application still involved discussion and correspondence between Vico Estates, its architect and Dublin Corporation.

The High Court held that Vico Estates had a *bona fide* intention to develop the property which would necessitate demolition of the building and that it was probable the necessary planning approval would be granted, which would require possession of plaintiff's premises. However, on appeal to the Supreme Court, Henchy J. stated that the demolition required for the development could not begin until planning permission was actually obtained. At best the vacant premises might be required some time in the future and at worst they might never be required, since planning permission might be refused. Until the planning permission (licence) was actually granted, the owners could not satisfy the Court that they required, and had the legal right to, vacant possession for demolition.

A similar adverse effect upon legal rights of an unlicensed person is demonstrated by *Somers v. Nicholls* 1955 IR 83. Plaintiff claimed that a commission from defendants G. and K. Nichols was due to him under an agreement that defendants would pay a sum for his introducing to them or obtaining a purchaser for a hotel they owned. Plaintiff's evidence was that he had not been authorised by defendants to make a binding contract for sale of the hotel, but had been promised £250 by defendants for an introduction to the purchaser with whom they subsequently negotiated the sale of the hotel. Plaintiff admitted he had never held a house agent's licence as required by the Auctioneers and House Agents Act 1947 which defines an agent in section 2 as:

a person who, as agent for another person and for and in expectation of reward, purchases, sells, lets or offers for sale or letting, or invites offers to purchase or take a letting of, or negotiates for the purchase, sale or letting of a house, otherwise than by auction, or attempts to effect such purchase, sale or letting.

Defendants argued that in acting in this transaction for reward, plaintiff was acting as an unlicensed agent in violation of the statute which negated his claim against them for a commission since enforcement of his claim depended upon his being licensed. Plaintiff countered that he was not claiming to be an agent since he could not bind defendants contractually but rather was only claiming to be an independent contractor. Ó Dálaigh J. held for the defendants, since what plaintiff did in promoting the sale was done on the authority of defendants on their behalf and the ordinary meaning of the term 'agent' cannot mean anything other than one who acts on behalf of another. Plaintiff was not any the less an agent because he was unrestricted as to the means of persuasion he might use, or did not have authority to complete a sale of property. Plaintiff's failure to have a licence barred enforcement of any claim he might make against defendants.

Legal Issues in Operation of Licensing Process

The statutory provisions and judicial determinations resolving basic constitutional and legal-conceptual issues in licensing provide the frame of reference within which administrators and courts resolve issues raised in the operation of licensing systems. These issues arise in connection with processes for application for licences, the administrative imposition of terms and conditions and procedures followed in the grant and revocation of licences.

Issues in Application for Licence
The initial step of application for a licence requires that care be exercised by both applicant and agency to meet statutory standards and administrative regulations as interpreted by the courts, pertaining to the grant of licences. The basic question of who may be considered an applicant for a licence arose in *Frescati Estates v. Walker* 1975 IR 177. The Supreme Court held that a person who had no

interest in the land but applied for planning permission under section 26 of the Local Government (Planning and Development) Act 1963 in order to impede another party from carrying out a development was not an applicant within the meaning of the Act. Though the Act intends that persons with no direct legal interest, such as would-be purchasers, may apply for permission to develop, the Court felt the term applicant must be restricted to avoid:

> unnecessary or vexatious applications, with consequent intrusion into property rights and demands on the statutory functions of planning authorities beyond what could reasonably be said to be required, in the interests of the common good, for proper planning and development . . . . an application for development permission, to be valid, must be made either by or with the approval of a person who is able to assert sufficient legal estate or interest to enable him to carry out the proposed development, or so much of the proposed development as relates to the property in question. (page 190)

Whether an application for permission to develop land was duly made in compliance with planning permission regulations and the date on which the application was received by the planning authority were issues in *Frank Dunne Ltd v. Dublin County Council* 1974 IR 45. The application was delivered personally to the Council's offices shortly before 5 pm on Friday, 8 August 1969. Subsequently, the applicant received a postcard acknowledging receipt of the application on Monday, 11 August. On 10 October, the Council wrote to the plaintiff requiring further information and gave notice of approval of the plans subject to meeting specific conditions.

Plaintiffs claimed that the defendants had not given a decision on their application or requested further information within two months from 8 August and therefore permission by default must be regarded as having been given, and the approval subject to conditions nullified, in accordance with section 26(4) of the Local Government (Planning and Development) Act 1963. The defendants contended that permission should not be regarded as given by default since plaintiff had not complied with section 26 of the 1963 Act because the application was not made in accordance with the permission regulations. The non-compliance alleged was that: (1) the application did not contain particulars of the applicant's interest in the land; (2) the notice of the application published in a newspaper did not contain as a heading the name of the area in which the land was situated and (3) the scale on which the plans were drawn and the north point were not indicated on the plans.

It was held by Pringle J. that the day on which the application was made to the Council was 8 and not 11 August and therefore permission would be regarded as having been given (by default) on 8 October. After consideration of the regulations, and the documentary details of the information submitted by plaintiff with his application, Pringle J. further held that plaintiff had met the basic purposes of the permission regulations regarding notice in the newspapers. Moreover, in his view, the requirements of all these regulations relied on by the defendants were directory and not imperative. Consequently, although plaintiff's application did not comply with the precise requirements of those regulations, the application was not thereby invalidated.

The issue of compliance with planning regulations regarding the information to accompany a planning application arose again in the later case of *McCabe v. Harding Investments Ltd* Supreme Court, unreported, per O'Higgins C.J., 27 October 1982. Plaintiff challenged the validity of a planning permission granted to defendants on the ground that the application was not made in compliance with article 17(a) of the 1977 regulations, which requires an application to be accompanied by particulars of the interest held in the land by the applicant. It was claimed that defendant had stated on a form issued by Dublin Corporation as planning authority that its interest was a freehold interest when such was not the case.

In the judgment of O'Higgins C.J., the information given by the defendants on the form was not so inaccurate, wrong and misleading as to constitute a failure to give particulars of the defendants' interest in the site and therefore a breach of the statutory requirements. The facts were that Harding Investments Ltd, at the time of making the application, were only entitled to a conveyance of the land under a contract yet to be completed. Under that contract they were purchasing the fee simple interest for £300,000, of which they had already paid £200,000, and were withholding the balance for the completion of the conveyancing steps already agreed to by the vendors. Given those circumstances, defendants obviously had a beneficial interest in the site, in view of the amount of purchase money already paid, which, as the purchasers of the fee simple, 'could fairly be described as a freehold interest'. In addition, even if the description of the defendants' interest lacked accuracy (which O'Higgins C.J. did not accept), the divergence from accuracy was 'so insignificant and trivial as proper to be ignored', citing Henchy J. in *Monaghan UDC v. Alf-A-Bet Promotions Ltd.* Supreme Court, unreported, 24 March 1980 (see pages 332-4) on the application of the *de minimus* rule to permission regulations. In discussing that rule, Henchy J. had stated that to excuse deviation from a requirement of the legislature, it must be so trivial, technical or peripheral, that given the principle that it is the spirit rather than the letter of the law that matters, the requirement had been substantially and therefore adequately complied with. In conclusion, O'Higgins C.J. held that plaintiff's claim lacked reality and was without foundation, admittedly being made only to deprive defendants of the planning permission and that this could not excuse the mounting of an action which could not succeed and is vexatious. The plaintiff's claim was therefore dismissed.

A combination of interrelated issues in the licence application process which also raises questions as to respective responsibilities of applicant and administrative agency arose in *The State (Alf-A-Bet Promotions Ltd) v. Bundoran UDC* 112 ILTR 9. In this case, the issues involved the timing of notice of agency decision, whether there was a qualified applicant and whether honest administrative error excused delay in notification of agency decision in response to the application (further complicated by belated monitoring of applicant's actions). The complex sequence of events leading to this case, characterised by McWilliams J. as a 'somewhat casual approach to the formalities of an application for planning permission evinced by both parties', began when James Gorman, one of the organisers of Alf-A-Bet, contracted to purchase certain premises from Irvine Hamilton and instructions were given to incorporate Alf-A-Bet on 9 January 1974. That incorporation actually did not take place until October 1976 but architects hired by Alf-A-Bet wrote to the District Council's clerk on 26 February 1974 detailing alterations proposed for the property and indicating future development in the rear of the premises. On 22 April 1974 the clerk to the Council mistakenly wrote to Hamilton requesting information on his application for permission for development; the mistake was corrected, after the architects telephoned on 3 March to inquire about progress of their planning application, by sending a similar letter to Gorman, the architects and Alf-A-Bet on 3 May 1974. By that date alterations had been made to the premises according to the originally submitted plans and the premises were thereafter operated as an amusement arcade despite a further letter of 11 June sent to Alf-A-Bet by the Council requesting that a proper planning permission application be made. No further action was taken by either Council or Alf-A-Bet until late 1976 when Alf-A-Bet started extensive structural development not detailed in the original 24 February application, followed by an application for permission for such development on 7 January 1977. The Council then moved to obtain an injunction to restrain such development, in response to which the architects first wrote to require a grant of the original application for permission contained in the February 1974 letter on grounds of the Council's default under section 26 of the Local Government (Planning and Development) Act 1963. When the Council refused, Alf-A-Bet then applied for a mandamus to direct the Council to grant development permission based on the failure of the Council to give notice of its decision within the requisite two-month period under section 26 of the 1963 Act.

In the High Court, the Council argued that the original application was made for a non-existent person with no interest in the property, citing *Frescati Estates v. Walker* 1975 IR 177; moreover, although the letter of 19 April 1974 was sent by mistake to the wrong person, the letter was sufficient to stop the running of the statutory time limit under the precedent of *Norfolk County Council v. the Secretary of the Environment* 1973 All ER 673. Moreover, section 26 of the 1963 Act is not mandatory and the subsequent application for planning permission made in January 1977 included part of the premises which were the subject of the original February 1974 application.

McWilliams J. held that apart from the unusual circumstances of the *Frescati* case where the application was not genuine:

> the mere fact that a company was named which had not been formed or was inaccurately . . . named would not of itself be sufficient to render the application invalid . . . . The application by the architects on behalf of their clients was perfectly genuine and I am satisfied that the clients had sufficient interest to support the application (pages 15-16)

As to the requirement of notice of decision within two months, the letter sent to Irvine Hamilton was within the statutory period but the subsequent 3 May letter to the architects and Gorman was not. The letter of application from the architects had given James Gorman's name and address and named him as secretary of Alf-A-Bet, and also gave the address of the architects, and the reference in the letter to purchase of premises from Hamilton did not explain the sending of notice to Hamilton rather than to Gorman and the architects.

McWilliams J. distinguished the *Norfolk* case, because in the present case no decision had been taken by the Council within the requisite time whereas in the *Norfolk* case a permission had, in fact, been refused and a council employee inadvertently notified the applicant that he had been granted a permission. Although principles regarding mistake and absence of detriment are applicable, he held that in the light of the facts:

> I am of opinion that the Council having made a mistake and having been made aware of it, should have taken some steps to ascertain what was going on and not relied merely on the letters of 3rd May and 11th June, 1974. Accordingly . . . the Council is not entitled to rely on this ground . . . .
>
> On the question of the Company's right to an Order of Mandamus, I do not see how the original application can be affected by the fact that there is an application for a further development of part of the premises the subject-matter of the original application . . . . the Company is entitled either to a declaration that a decision by the Council to grant the permission is to be regarded as having been given on 27th April, 1974, or to an Order of Mandamus. In my view, if a decision to grant permission is regarded as having been given, the Council is bound to grant the permission and I will make the Order sought. (page 16)

A further issue in the licence application process is whether the applicant has given adequate notice of the proposed development to the public as required by regulations. In *Keleghan and Others v. Corby and Another* unreported, High Court, per McMahon J., 12 November 1976, it was held that there was a failure to comply with section 26 of the Local Government (Planning and Development)

ADMINISTRATIVE LAW

Act 1963 which authorises the planning authority to grant permission for a development, provided the application is made in accordance with implementing regulations. The regulations required publication in a newspaper of a notice containing a statement of the extent and nature of the development for which permission was requested. McMahon J. held that the published notice of application for permission to erect a temporary pre-fabricated classroom on six acres of school grounds did not convey to the people living in a cul-de-sac that the development might include a roadway giving access to the school through their cul-de-sac. Such access is not a normal part of constructing prefabricated buildings and there was evidence that the access was for an entirely separate reason than serving the classrooms. Although a planning authority may give permission subject to conditions that require certain work to be done, the conditions must be specified in the permission so that a person who considers himself aggrieved by the decision to grant permission can appeal against it. In this instance, the authority gave permission for the access road subject to details which would be submitted later for agreement by the developer. Since the public could have no knowledge of what those details might be and no way of appealing against them, the planning permission as granted was invalid.

The importance of adequate notice of the public concerning a proposed development plan was repeated and the *Dunne* case judgment (see page 327-8) concerning directory rather than mandatory regulations was distinguished in the later case of *Monaghan UDC v. Alf-A-Bet Promotions Ltd* Supreme Court, unreported, per O'Higgins C.J., (Henchy and Griffin J.J. concurring), 24 March 1980.[2] The Monaghan UDC received from Alf-A-Bet on 26 April 1977 an application under the Local Government (Planning and Development) Act 1963 for change of user of premises at the Diamond in Monaghan town, accompanied by an extract from a local newspaper as proof of compliance with article 14 of the Local Government (Planning and Development) Regulations 1977. The extract was a notice stating that Alf-A-Bet was applying for planning permission in respect of alterations and improvements at their premises at the Diamond. The Town Clerk on behalf of the UDC wrote to Alf-A-Bet on the same date, 26 April 1977, that they should publish a notice of intention to the UDC for planning permission, since the UDC, not the County Council, was the body to apply to for permission. On 28 April 1977, Alf-A-Bet published the notice and on 11 May sent an extract to the UDC. On 24 June 1977, the UDC refused permission and sent notice of refusal to Alf-A-Bet on 28 June.

Alf-A-Bet claimed that if the application received by the UDC on 26 April was in order, then notice of decision on the application under section 26(4)(b) of the 1963 Act should have been served on 26 June. Since notice of refusal was not given until 28 June after the two-month period for notice prescribed by the statute had expired, a decision to grant permission (by default) must be deemed to have been given under section 26 (4) of the 1963 Act.

Alf-A-Bet's claim thus hinged upon whether the application received by the UDC was in order. It was noted by O'Higgins C.J. that it was conceded that the notice as published was not headed, nor did it contain the particulars on the nature and extent of the development as required by article 15 of the regulations (Part IV of SI 65 of 1977). However, Alf-A-Bet had argued that given the *Dunne* decision, these requirements were directory and not imperative. In this respect, O'Higgins C.J. held that the Dunne decision related to former regulations and provisions differing materially from the requirements in the present article 15, and in his view the wording of article 15 is mandatory and the requirements imperative. The application therefore was not in accordance with permission regulations since the newspaper notice did not meet the requirements of those regulations, and the contention of Alf-A-Bet failed.

Regarding this issue, Henchy J. stressed the fact that one objective, if not the primary objective, of requiring the published notice is to enable interested members of the public to determine whether there is a reason to object to the proposed development. The notice as published by Alf-A-Bet omitted any indication of the actual nature or scope of the proposed development, namely that the terms 'alterations and improvements' as advertised really meant conversion of a drapery shop into a betting office and amusement arcade. As he interpreted the 1963 Act, the requirements the legislature prescribed in that Act or mediately through administrative regulations as being obligatory, may not be reduced to being merely directive except on application of the *de minimis* rule, namely:

what the legislature has prescribed, or allowed to be prescribed, in such circumstances as necessary should be treated by the courts as nothing short of necessary, and any deviation from the requirements must, before it can be overlooked, be shown, by the person seeking to have it excused, to be so trivial, or so technical, or so peripheral, or otherwise so insubstantial that, on the principle that it is the spirit rather than the letter of the law that matters, the prescribed obligation has been substantially and therefore adequately, complied with.[3]

As he viewed the combination of section 26 of the 1963 Act and articles 14 and 15 of the Regulations, the legislative intent clearly was that permission for development should not issue by default unless the newspaper notice specified the nature and extent of the proposed development since every member of the public has an interest in seeing that undesirable development will not be allowed. The newspaper notice that the nature of the development was 'alterations and improvements' lacked compliance with the spirit and purpose of the Act and regulations and therefore the application was nullified, the UDC was entitled to treat it as a nullity, and there was no obligation on them to point out to the applicant that the notice was defective.

In the view of Griffin J. in his concurring judgment, what he had said in *Ready Mix (Eire) Ltd v. Dublin County Council*, i.e. that the planning authority 'were meant only to be watch dogs and not blood-hounds', was also appropriate in relation to members of the public regarding notices published under articles 14 and 15. Notices which are calculated to give as little information as possible are repugnant to the spirit of the Acts and to be discouraged.

In addition to the issues raised in the above cases regarding application for a licence, a further issue is illustrated by *Athlone Woollen Mills Co. Ltd v. Athlone Urban District Council* 1950 IR 1, namely the extent to which an applicant is bound by the stated purposes of an application once permission has been granted and affirmed on appeal with conditions. Plaintiffs applied for planning permission to the Urban District Council. Permission was granted subject to conditions which, plaintiffs claimed, gave rise to compensation under the Town and Regional Planning Acts, 1934 and 1939. However, during an exchange of communications in which the date of the Minister's order responding to plaintiff's appeal from the conditions was not specified, and plaintiff also submitted a claim for compensation, plaintiff failed to meet the time limit for making the claim, and it was denied. Plaintiffs then sought to revive their claim for compensation by submitting a new application for repair and renewal, rather than reconstruction, but the plans were identical with those of the first application. This was rejected as invalid by the Council and by the Minister on appeal. On an application to the High Court for a declaration that the application for permission was valid, Gavan Duffy J. stated that the Acts contained no provision which would enable a disappointed applicant who was granted special permission by the local authority with an attached condition affirmed by the Minister on appeal to go back to the local authority and there have the Minister's decision reversed. These decisions are an exercise of limited powers of a judicial nature and thus judicial decisions in relation to which the doctrine of *res judicata* applies with consequent estoppel. In the view of Gavan Duffy J., the plaintiffs might as well have come into court and claimed a right to a re-hearing and reconsideration of their original application for a special permission.

Grant or Refusal of Licence: Imposition of Conditions
A major factor in the decision of an administrative agency (or lower court) to grant or refuse a licence is whether an applicant meets the requirements prescribed by statute, agency regulations, or conditions attached by an agency to an individual licence. The most common issues involved are whether the substance of the conditions or the way in which they are imposed are *ultra vires* the statute or contrary to natural or constitutional justice. An example of the imposition of condition attached to a particular licence considered by the Court to be *ultra vires* the statute, both as to its substance and the manner or process of imposing it, is afforded by *Irish Trust Bank Ltd v. Central Bank of Ireland* unreported, High Court, per O'Keeffe P., November 1973.[4] This case arose under section 10, Central Bank Act 1971, which provides that a grant of a licence to a bank is subject to such conditions as the Central Bank may impose to promote an orderly and proper regulation of banking. The licence may be amended, added to, or revoked after it has been granted. Section 10 further provides in sub-section 3 that the Central Bank must give notice to the licensee when it intends to add conditions. Similarly, it must notify a person (or organisation) who is in the process of being granted a licence that the Central Bank intends to attach conditions to the new licence. In both instances, reasons for those conditions must be given. The person notified has 21 days to

make representations in writing to the Central Bank, which must consider them before a final decision to impose the proposed conditions.

When the Central Bank Act 1971 became operative, Irish Trust Bank, which had a licence obtained prior to the 1971 Act, applied for a new licence to the Central Bank. A licence was granted with effect from December 1971 subject to a notice that the Central Bank intended to attach conditions at a later time. In January 1972, the Secretary of the Central Bank learned that the curriculum vitae which Mr Kenneth Bates, one of Irish Trusts' directors, had supplied to meet one of the requirements for Irish Trust to obtain a licence, had omitted mention of his association with the English firm of Howarth of Burnley. That firm has been in difficulties to the order of a million pounds, although this occurred after Mr Bates had ceased to be a director or shareholder.

The Central Bank's Board informed Irish Trust that under section 10 of the 1971 Act it proposed to make it a condition of the Irish Trust licence that Mr Bates cease to be a director, that company shareholders should not include Mr Bates or his nominees and shareholders should not include those having an interest exceeding ten per cent of any company in which Mr Bates had an interest of ten per cent or more. After a delay owing to administrative error, reasons were officially given that the condition was imposed in the interest of orderly and proper regulation of banking arising from inquiries of a confidential nature in England concerning Mr Bates's association with Howarth of Burnley, which provided substantial grounds for doubts as to Mr Bates's suitability to engage in the banking business. Any submission by Irish Trust objecting to these conditions would have to be supported by an unqualified testimonial as to Mr Bates's suitability to be a bank director from the chairman or chief executive of one of the London clearing banks. The Central Bank then wrote to Irish Trust notifying them of its final decision to impose these conditions with effect from 6 April 1972.

On appeal by Irish Trust to the High Court, O'Keeffe P. held that the conditions were not validly imposed and that Irish Trust could hold its licence without such conditions. He indicated that it was natural for the Central Bank to be concerned over the omission in Mr Bates's curriculum vitae; that drawing an inference from this was within the authority of the Central Bank's directors; and his decision was not a reflection of whether Mr Bates was a suitable person to be a director or whether the ownership of Irish Trust should be unrestricted in its composition. However, when the Central Bank required that any representation must be supported by an unqualified testimonial as to Mr Bates's suitability to be a bank director from the chairman or chief executive of a London clearing bank, the Central Bank was imposing a condition which limited the statutory right to make representations. O'Keeffe P. further noted that the delivery date of the letter giving notice of the final decision to impose the conditions was Holy Thursday, when most business concerns would be closed until the following Tuesday. Even the Central Bank's own legal adviser had indicated that it would be unreasonable to expect compliance with the conditions imposed by the date as required. O'Keeffe P. concluded that no person empowered to impose conditions may do so if it is unreasonable to expect compliance with the conditions so imposed, and for this reason the conditions required by the Central Bank were unwarranted. Moreover, even if they had been warranted, it is only the Governor of the Bank who can impose the conditions.

The *Irish Trust Bank* case turned on the imposition of an *ultra vires* condition limiting procedural rights under the statute and an unreasonable time limit for compliance. The substantive aspects of conditions may also be grounds for holding conditions *ultra vires*, as in the *Dunne* case (page 327-8). In addition to the issues of whether the application complied with regulations and agency notification of its decision within two months, a further issue in this case was whether the conditions imposed by the agency as prerequisites to a grant of permission to develop under section 26(2) of the Local Government (Planning and Development) Act 1963 were legally valid. The conditions were that: (1) the developers had to 'notify all purchasers or tenants that the Department of Transport and Power have stated that aircraft noise will be significant in the area of the proposed development'; and (2) the houses as proposed had to be modified in accordance with specifications of some six types of modification of walls, roof spaces, window glazing and other matters.

In the High Court, plaintiffs not only claimed that defendant had not met the statutory requirements for giving notice of proposed changes in the original plans but also made an alternative claim that the substance of the conditions sought to be imposed were *ultra vires* the statute. With respect to the substance of the first condition on warning of aircraft noise, Pringle J. held:

> In my opinion, this condition can have no relation to the planning and development of the area and is an unreasonable restriction which the defendants had no power to impose. . . . (page 53)

In regard to the second condition, he also ruled:

> With some doubt, I consider that this condition is also invalid, as it is not sufficiently connected with the planning and development of the area, or the preservation of or improvement of the amenities thereof. The requirements of this condition would seem to me to be more appropriately dealt with by building regulations which can be made by the Minister under s. 86 of the Act of 1963. (page 54)

In view of the decision in *Dunne*, it is of interest to note that the Local Government (Planning and Development) Act 1976, section 39(c) authorised planning authorities to include conditions pertaining to noise or vibration. This illustrates the cycle of legislative policy-making in an Act, administrative application, judicial interpretation, and consequent legislative modification of policy through an amending Act. It is also of interest that occasionally the imposition of conditions may raise substantive issues which though of a relatively minor nature can consume the valuable time of the Supreme Court, as in *Flannery v. Superintendent Colleran* Supreme Court, unreported, per O'Higgins C.J., 21 March 1980. A case was stated by the Circuit Court judge concerning provisions of section 16 of the Courts of Justice Act 1947, in which the grant or refusal of a special exemption to enable sale of liquor at a particular dance hinged solely upon the profound question of whether provision by the applicant of music for disco dancing by gramophone records and tapes rather than by live musicians constituted a 'dance' within the meaning of the Intoxicating Liquor Act 1927 as amended by section 12, Intoxicating Liquor Act 1962. The District Justice had refused the licence since a band or orchestra of musicians would not provide the music in person, although all other requirements had been met.

O'Higgins C.J. responded by stating:

A dance within the Section is simply the occasion on which dancing takes place. Dancing itself is to move with measured steps, especially to music. It does not seem to me to matter from what source the music comes or indeed whether in fact any music is provided. In this case I have no doubt that the provision of music by tapes or gramophone records on an occasion when people dance constitutes a dance within the meaning of the appropriate statutory provisions.

The Court held that the applicant was entitled to the special exemption licence (incidentally furthering technological unemployment of musicians).

The issue of whether a condition is *ultra vires* the statute becomes more complex when it involves subjective questions of social policy which give the governmental agency broader discretion than in the *Irish Trust* and *Dunne* cases. In the case of *In the Matter of the Licensing Acts and in the Matter of an Application of Connellan* unreported, High Court, per Finlay J., 19 October 1973, an appeal was brought by applicant Connellan against the refusal of the Circuit Court judge for a declaration under section 15, Intoxicating Liquor Act 1960, that premises he proposed to construct at Bayside, Dublin, would, if in accordance with plans submitted, be fit to be licensed. The application was opposed by the local church authorites and over 900 residents of Bayside, on the statutory grounds of unfitness of the applicant, unsuitability and inconvenience of the premises and the number of licensed premises in the area.

Based on the evidence, Finlay J. held there were no grounds against the applicant on the basis of his being a fit and proper person, or the number of existing licensed premises. The key objection was as to the suitability and convenience of the premises in respect of siting related to parking facilities and traffic hazards, the parking of cars around the church and possible damage to church property, noise at night and finally, the intention of the area residents' association through a joint committee to build a community centre close to the proposed licensed premises. The community centre financing would be economically viable only if they had the sole right to sell liquor, and it was considered socially desirable to limit premises where young persons might buy drink to a club operated by the community, rather than a public house.

Finlay J. concluded that the objectors' claims concerning traffic hazards, parking, noise and similar matters were not supported by the evidence. As to the final reason for objection, he noted that previous cases indicated that the suitability and convenience of the premises were not confined to design and layout but included everything arising from the location, thus allowing for a wide range of objection. However, he felt that the heart of the complaint, namely that a grant of the application would interfere with objectors' proposed monopoly to provide profits for the worthy cause of establishing a community centre, was:

> outside the scope of the discretion conferred upon the courts by the licensing code. No matter how much I might, as a matter of social policy, favour the provision of a community centre and favour a situation in which it could from a monopoly sale of intoxicating liquor in its own area fund itself in an economic and profitable way, I do not consider that the licensing code gives me a discretion to implement that view. The licensing code was intended to restrict the proliferation of public houses; to prevent inconvenience, disturbance and noise to residents . . . nearby; to prevent a poor standard in the sale and provision of facilities for the consumption of . . . liquor and was designed to prevent . . . illegal carrying on of the trade of a publican. It is in all these matters essentially a negative or restrictive code and can not fairly and properly be construed as a positive weapon of social policy.

Therefore, the applicant was entitled to his licence, by meeting the prescribed statutory requirements to the satisfaction of Finlay J.

An even broader grant of discretion to consider the impact on the community is given in the Public Dance Halls Act 1935, as revealed by *Application of Quinn* 1974 IR 19. Section 2 (2) of the 1935 Act provides that a District Justice considering an application for a public dance hall shall:

> in addition to any other matter which may appear to him to be relevant, have regard to the following matters . . .

(a) the character and the financial and other circumstances of the applicant . . .
(b) the suitability of the place. . .
(c) the facilities for public dancing existing in the neighbourhood of such place . . .
(d) the accommodation for the parking of vehicles . . .
(e) the probable age of the persons . . . likely to make use of such place . . .
(f) whether the situation of such place is or is not such as to render difficult the supervision by the Garda Síochána of the management of and proceedings in such place;
(g) the hours during which the applicant proposes that public dancing should be permitted . . .

The applicant had run public dances in his hall since 1968, and applied for renewal of licence in 1970. No fault was found with the hall, supervision of dances, noise from the hall, prevention of disorderly conduct or suitability of the applicant or his employees, but the District Court refused renewal of the annual licence. On appeal to the Circuit Court, the evidence established that on weekend nights and public holiday periods many persons from Dublin and surrounding areas came to the dances. Some came by bus and their behaviour intimidated the bus crews and other passengers so that garda assistance was requested. In addition the lives of Clondalkin residents were disrupted by disorderly behaviour, assault and malicious damage to property incident to the incursion of dance hall patrons. Consequently, expanded garda control was necessary at the dance times. Although the misconduct did not occur in the dance hall or its immediate vicinity and admittedly was out of the applicant's control, the Garda Síochána, CIE and its employees' trade union submitted evidence of this disorderly behaviour in opposition to the application, on the ground that the dances seemed to be the occasion for the misconduct.

The Circuit Court judge asked in a case stated (i.e. referred the matter to a higher court as to) whether he should treat the misconduct as a relevant matter under section 2 (2) of the Public Halls Dance Act 1935, although it could not be controlled by, nor was it the fault of, the applicant for the licence. The applicant argued that the general words 'any other matter which may appear to be relevant' in section 2(2) of the Act should be confined to the matters specifically listed in that section, so that the District Justice should not consider the difficulties the Garda Síochána might encounter beyond their supervision of the management and proceedings in the dance hall. Counsel for the Garda Síochána submitted that the provisions are framed in wide terms and should be read in the context of section 4 of the Act which authorises a District Justice to insert into a public dancing licence such conditions and restrictions as he shall think proper.

Henchy J. for the Supreme Court held that the generality of the expression 'any other matter which may appear to him to be relevant' is not narrowed by the requirement that such regard be given 'in addition' to the requirements or matters specifically listed following this general clause. As long as the discretion is exercised in good faith, the only grounds for challenging the relevancy of considerations are first, that a matter may not be considered which would make the decision *ultra vires* the Act, and secondly, the discretion may not be exercised so as to infringe a constitutional right. He further noted that the wide and imprecise discretion given by section 2 contrasts with the narrow and clear discretion given by other statutes in respect of the grant of other kinds of licence. The breadth of section 2 (2) not only authorises but requires the District Justice to consider evidence concerning the impact of the grant of a licence on the lives of local residents, since it is the ground for evaluation of probable social and environmental consequences of renewal of a licence, and enables him to balance the merits of the applicant's claim against the adverse impact which the grant of a licence would have. However, the Justice should also consider whether the evidence indicated that the adverse behaviour could be eliminated or reduced by increased garda activity. If the Justice gives due appraisal in good faith to all the relevant evidence and then decides to grant or refuse, it is difficult to see how the decision could be challenged as *ultra vires* the Act.

This judicial perspective concerning broad discretion to consider the impact of the grant of a licence on the surrounding community was reiterated in *Dublin Corporation v. Raso* High Court, unreported, per Finlay P., 1 June 1976. Defendant had obtained permission from Dublin Corporation for a change of user of his shop from a food shop to a fish and chip take-away shop. Local residents appealed to the Minister. The Minister confirmed the permission but a condition was added that the premises should not be used for the permitted use between the hours of 11 p.m. and 8 a.m. The District Justice convicted defendant of a violation on the evidence of a person who had purchased fish and chips after 11 p.m. Defendant argued that under rule 4, Local Government Planning and Development Act 1963 (Exempted Development) Regulations 1967, his was an exempted development within the classes of use in Part IV of the Schedule to those Regulations, which exempts use as a shop for any purpose except as a 'fried fish shop' (not a fish and chip shop). In this regard the evidence before the District Justice proved only that fish and chips had been sold, which could describe fish which was not fried.

In response to this argument while upholding the District Court decisions, Finlay J. held:

> It is in my view within the power of the Planning Authority or of the Minister on appeal to impose a condition upon the granting of a permission governing the hours of opening of a shop for the purpose as undoubtedly occurred in this case of cutting down nuisance, noise and the frequenting or gathering of people which would disturb the residential aspect of a neigbourhood. Such an object . . . is clearly within the planning code. It would therefore in my view have been open to the Planning Authority even if the proper application had been made for permission, (that is to say, permission only for use as a fried fish shop without any reference to chips) to have imposed a condition that the shop would not open for the purpose of selling either fried fish or chips after 11 p.m. – although on the strict interpretation of the regulations change of user from a foodstore to a store selling chips only would be an exempted development. The words 'permitted use' contained in the condition imposed . . . by the Minister . . . must be interpreted . . . as referring back to the use referred to in the decision itself which . . . was use as a fried fish and chip shop. The defendant who applied for permission in that form can not . . . be heard now to assert that because the inclusion of the words 'and chip' may have been strictly unnecessary that the condition must be construed as prohibiting only the sale of fried fish but not prohibiting the sale of fried chips after 11 p.m.

A complicating factor concerning the imposition of conditions inci-

dent to issue of a licence is that in Ireland certain enterprises are
regulated by and must meet requirements of both the national and
local governments. The issue raised is whether and to what extent
the primary licensing authority is responsible for determining compliance with all requirements imposed by both levels of government.
In the case of *Application by Thomas Kitterick* 105 ILTR 105, a case
stated by the High Court to the Supreme Court asked:

> whether the Court in the exercise of the jurisdiction granted to
> it by section 15 of the Intoxicating Liquor Act 1960:–
>
> (a) Must require proof of the compliance with the requirements
> of the Local Government (Planning and Development) Act,
> 1963 and the Building and Fire regulations in relation to the
> premises or may grant the declaration as sought by the appli-
> cant without requiring proof of such compliance and
>
> (b) May grant the declaration sought subject to the terms that
> the applicant shall obtain proof of the compliance with the
> requirements of the said Act and regulations in relation to the
> premises as shown on the plan accompanying the application
> or proof of the compliance with the said requirements in
> relation to the premises as shown on the said plan with alter-
> ations which are not substantial in character. (page 106)

Walsh J., for the Supreme Court, held that the grant of a certificate
entitling the applicants to obtain a licence for premises yet to be
constructed, altered or acquired was subject to the Circuit Court
granting the application on such terms as the Court might think
fit. The Act requires that the Court be satisfied and the Court
cannot delegate its functions to a local planning authority. Concomi-
tantly, it would be contrary to the Court's policy in the administration of the law that any court order should establish grounds for
the commission of an illegal act, such as violation of the Local
Government (Planning and Development) Act 1963. Upon analysis
of alternate actions open to the courts in various situations in
which an applicant might meet the courts' standards under the
Intoxicating Liquor Act but not local standards under the Local
Government (Planning and Development) Act or vice versa, Walsh
J. answered the case stated, by noting that the two questions

constituted four questions in all and answered them accordingly. First, the Circuit Court or High Court on appeal does not have to require proof of compliance with requirements of the Local Government (Planning and Development) Act 1963, or with the Building and Fire Regulations. Second, and relatedly, the courts may grant the declaration sought by the applicant without requiring proof of such compliance. Third, the Court may grant the declaration sought subject to the terms that the applicant obtain permission of the appropriate planning and other authorities in relation to the plan of the premises which the Court declared to be fit and convenient to be licensed without any alterations. Fourth, the Court may grant the declaration subject to the terms that the applicant obtain the permission of appropriate planning and other authorities to the plan of the premises declared by the Court to be fit and convenient to be so licensed with alterations which are not substantial in character.

In effect, the Supreme Court designated the Circuit Court and the High Court as the licensing agencies with authority and discretion to impose conditions they considered best adapted to reduce conflict between governmental jurisdictions without condoning the violation of either national or local laws or regulations.

Similar concepts are applied in *The State (Foxrock Construction Co Ltd) v. Dublin County Council* High Court, unreported, per Finlay P., 5 February 1980, involving terms and conditions imposed by the local authority and An Bord Pleanála on a proposed development. The prosecutors had agreed to purchase land for building houses under a contract (subject to planning and bye-laws approval) from a previous owner who had been given planning permission by the respondent council subject to nineteen conditions.

Certain objectors had appealed this permission to An Bord Pleanála which eventually granted permission to the previous owner subject to eight conditions. When Foxrock Construction applied to the Council for building bye-law approval of the development it was given notice by the Council of disapproval of the plans for surface water drainage of the site. To overcome the reasons for disapproval would require a complete re-routing of the proposed system.

Foxrock Construction argued that the reasons given for the disapproval by the Council were *ultra vires* the bye-laws. In this regard, certain bye-laws, they argued, should be construed narrowly, since to construe them broadly would permit the local authority to require a major design amendment to the plans which had already received planning permission on the appeal to An Bord Pleanála. Although Finlay J. disapproved of certain reasons advanced by the Council for their requirements as being *ultra vires* their bye-laws, he accepted as *intra vires* the reasons for requirements which would prevent the buildings from being adversely affected by moisture from adjoining earth. As to the local authority requiring amendment to a plan which already had planning permission, he held:

> In law no building development may take place even though it is the subject of a planning permission unless it also has obtained building bye-law approval where that is necessary
> . . .

> There appears to me therefore to be no inconsistency in a planning authority or An Bord Pleanála confining its consideration to the proper planning and development of an area leaving such matters as the protection of a building against weather as specifically dealt with in building bye-laws to the Bye-law Authority.

He further held that An Bord Pleanála must have been aware that the planning authority had from the beginning consistently disapproved of the drainage route as it had been proposed, and:

> Had the Board decided, as the prosecutors contend, to overrule that disapproval, they would it seems to me have done so either by imposing no condition, giving to the Planning Authority any remaining discretion concerning the drainage system or by imposing a condition markedly different from that which the planning authority had decided to impose.

Finlay J. concluded that the Board's condition meant that the planning authority could set out detailed requirements for the drainage system and that the plaintiff developer must comply with them.

Effect of Compliance or Non-Compliance with Conditions
Since an applicant must meet conditions to acquire a licence an important issue is that of the rights of an applicant who demonstrates compliance with conditions despite opposition by other parties to the granting of the licence. In the case of *In re Murray's Application* 91 ILTR 4 1957, the question involved was Murray's right to a seven-day licence under section 3 of the Licensing (Ireland) Act 1902. Section 3 provides that when a licence (that is included in a lease) for the sale of intoxicating liquors on a premises is extinguished or surrendered because the lease has expired, 'the licensing authority may . . . grant a licence for suitable premises in the immediate vicinity of the premises to which the licence so extinguished or surrendered was attached.' In this instance, O'Reilly, the former yearly tenant of the premises to which a seven-day licence was attached, fell into arrears with his rent. A consent was entered into whereby he agreed to surrender possession of the premises, the seven-day licence was allowed to lapse, and no renewal was applied for at the annual licensing sessions. Murray, under section 3 of the 1902 Act, then requested that he be granted the lapsed seven-day licence in place of a six-day early-closing licence which he held for his own premises. However, O'Reilly appeared as an objector testifying that although he had surrendered his interest in the formerly licensed premises owing to his advancing years, he wished that his son, who was in the licensed trade in England but too young at that time to take over the business, would get the seven-day licence at a future date.

In this regard, Judge Binchy stated that if he held other than that O'Reilly's licence was extinguished because of expiry of the lease under which the premises were held, he would be making a forced construction of the facts which would not meet approval of any reviewing court. Given the situation:

> Once the applicant is, under the law, entitled to the licence sought, the only discretion which the Court can exercise to refuse the application is by sustaining an objection on one of the usual grounds, according to the circumstances of the particular case. No such objection arises for consideration in the present case. (page 7)

The fact that applicant Murray had a six-day licence attached to the premises for which the seven-day licence was sought was not a ground for refusal under the statute and all other statutory requirements having been met, the application would be granted.

The rights of a person who has complied with conditions for a licence may be grounded in common as well as statutory law, as in the case *In re McLoughlin's Application* 1963 IR 465. Appellant purchased a premises, notified the necessary parties on 3 March 1960 of intent to apply to the Circuit Court on 7 April for a new hotel licence for the premises, under the Licensing (Ireland) Act 1902, and invested over £8,000 in reconstruction ending in May. When the application came on for hearing on 31 May, objections were entered by the Garda Síochána and certain parishioners, but the Circuit Court judge was inclined to grant the application subject to completion of furnishing the ten bedrooms of the hotel. He therefore adjourned the hearing to give appellant an opportunity to complete such furnishing. On completion of the furnishing, appellant's solicitor inquired at the Circuit Court office as to when the application would be relisted for hearing. This was urgent since the approaching passage of an Intoxicating Liquor Bill would amend the existing 1902 law on hotel licensing so as to include a provision raising the minimum number of bedrooms to twenty. However, the relisting for hearing was not mentioned to the judge sitting for criminal business in the Circuit Court and he did not sit again for civil business until four days after the Intoxicating Liquor Act 1960 came into effect. Given the 1960 Act's requirement of twenty bedrooms for a hotel licence, the Circuit Court judge refused the application when the relisted hearing took place.

On appeal to the High Court, Davitt P. held that section 21 (1) of the Interpretation Act 1937 was of no assistance to appellant since it protects only her rights acquired under the previous 1902 Act which was amended by the 1960 Act. Furthermore, the only previous adjudications made by the Circuit Court were first to adjourn the hearing on the application, and then on the later adjourned hearing to dismiss the application. Consequently, the appellant's right to have her application determined in accordance with section 2 of the 1902 Act before it was amended had to derive from the common law principles. Under those principles, the issue was whether it was a right taken away by the 1960 Act, which depended on whether that Act showed legislative intent that it should apply to proceedings pending before it came into operation.

Since the Intoxicating Liquor Act 1960 merely repealed one provision of section 2, 1902 Act and substituted another, there was nothing to indicate that the substitution was intended to affect any pending proceedings at the date of its enactment. Davitt J. thus was satisfied under common law principles that appellant's application must be decided according to section 2, 1902 Act as unamended and held that during the course of the hearing before him:

> I gave expression that, if the application had to be dealt with on that basis, it should be granted. There was never any objection concerned with the appellant's suitability. I am satisfied on the evidence . . . that the premises are now suitable. No objection on the grounds of the number of licensed premises in the neighbourhood was sustained; and the application being otherwise in order, I am prepared to grant it. (pages 471-2)

Although the rights of appellant in *McLoughlin* were readily resolved, a more complex issue as to compliance with terms and conditions was present in *Readymix (Eire) Limited v. Dublin County Council and Minister for Local Government* unreported, Supreme Court, per Budd J., 30 July 1974, as indicated by a three-to-two division in the Court on the matter. Readymix acquired an option on 4 June 1969 through a written agreement with James McGurk to purchase his site in Blackrock, County Dublin, with its conventional plant to make concrete blocks or bricks where all processes of manufacture were completed, including a limited amount of readymix concrete; a small amount of traffic movement to and from the site took place. There was also an oral agreement that McGurk would apply for development permission to replace his plant so that once such permission was obtained, Readymix could exercise its option to purchase and thereby use the development permission granted to McGurk.

McGurk applied for planning permission on 27 June to erect a replacement concrete plant in substitution for the existing plant, enclosing copies of the existing site layout and the site layout of new structures and the new plant layout, which actually were drafted by an engineer employed by Readymix. An advertisement was published on 28 June giving notice that approval was being sought 'for replacement of concrete plant . . . at Newtown Park Avenue' (Blackrock) for J. McGurk. The application and supporting docu-

ments were examined by three engineers for the County Council
and permission was granted on 29 August subject to certain conditions. The permission terms stated it was for the 'replacement' of
the 'existing' concrete plant. Notice of permission to McGurk on 9
October was followed by conveyance of the site to Readymix on 12
December. Readymix proceeded with the construction and then
wrote to the planning authorities in January 1970 referring to the
use they proposed to make of the site. In contrast to the McGurk
operation, the Readymix operation was large. For ten hours a day
large 22-ton trucks were receiving materials for concrete from the
plant and continuing to mix them on route from the plant to
customers at a rate of a truck coming or going every ten minutes,
plus other trucks delivering raw materials to the plant. Local
residents complained about the contrast in traffic to and from the
plant with that of the previous McGurk operation. The planning
department of the County Council then notified Readymix that the
operation described in their letter constituted a change of use which
was a development according to the Local Government (Planning
and Development) Act 1963 and that they had requested the
Minister for Local Government to decide whether or not the proposed change of use was a development or an exempted development
under sections 4 and 5 of that Act.

Readymix then issued a plenary summons against the County
Council and the Minister claiming declarations which were granted
by the High Court, namely that the permission of 9 October 1969
was a valid and subsisting permission; that the County Council was
not entitled to derogate from this permission; and that no question
arising within the meaning of section 5 had risen for reference to
the Minister. On appeal to the Supreme Court by the County
Council, Budd J. for the Court majority stated that McGurk's
application for permission, the newspaper notice to the public and
the permission as granted all specified that the purpose was to erect
a modern concrete plant in substitution for the existing plant, with
no suggestion it was to be a different kind of structure. On all three
counts, the purpose and intention were not for a completely new
type of plant for readymix concrete. Although the County Council
engineers were mistaken or initially misled as to applicant's inten-
tions and did not raise the question as to whether 'development'
was involved, the Council now realised such was the case and
section 5(1) of the 1963 Act required that such a question must be

referred to and decided by the Minister for Local Government. He rejected plaintiff's argument that under section 28(6) of the Act, if there is an absence of specification of the purpose for which a structure may be used in a permission, that permission must be construed as approval to use the structure for the purpose for which it was designed (i.e. making readymix concrete). He held this was answered by the fact that the County Council permission did specify the purpose for which the structures were to be used.

Griffin J., concurring, emphasised the unlikelihood that anyone reading the public notice and reviewing the plans would realise the intent was to build a readymix concrete plant, since every significant external feature was omitted which might have indicated that it was to be a readymix plant. Contrary to plaintiff's contention that the council officials' duty was to determine plaintiff's intention and not the duty of applicants to show precisely their intention he felt that 'the function of the officials of the County Council is that of watchdogs, not blood hounds.'.

In dissenting, Henchy J. granted that the agreement between McGurk and plaintiffs showed the intent that McGurk obtain permission, to enable plaintiffs 'stepping into McGurk's shoes and . . . becoming free to use the development permission . . . not for the purpose of manufacturing concrete products on the site but for the distribution by lorry from the site of "readymix concrete".' However, when permission is granted under section 24(2) it then, under section 28(5), enures (i.e. continues to have effect) for the benefit of not only the person to whom it is issued but also anyone acquiring an interest in the property and under section 24(4) a planning permission is a good defence against prosecution for carrying out a development without permission. The permission must stand on its own as do all public documents, and in particular, a permission not specifying a purpose for which a structure may be used, shall be construed under section 28(6) as including permission to use the structure for the purpose for which it was designed. It cannot be said the permitted structure was not 'designed' to produce readymix concrete and although the County Council could have narrowed that purpose so as to exclude readymix concrete, it did not do so. He would hold the plaintiff's use of the plant for readymix concrete was within the permission granted.

In this regard, Henchy J. commented on desirable administrative processes, noting that though the application ranged from that of

a 'successfully uncommunicative ploy' to that of being 'devious . . .
almost to the point of sharp practice' the permission nevertheless
was granted by the planning authority with a breadth not intended,
which 'is unfortunate, but the experience may provide a cautionary
lesson for future cases'. He noted that existing regulations authorised thorough inquiry into applications, which would have unco-
vered the use of the proposed structures, and stated that a planning
permission should be clear, specific and to the extent possible, self-
contained.

Underlying these contrasting opinions are different perspectives
as to what constitutes meeting conditions for a licence, the legal
effect of complying or not complying with conditions and in particular the respective roles of applicant and agency in this regard. The
majority of the Court would place the burden on the applicant to
indicate clearly the purpose of a development, subject to careful
review but not investigation to uncover concealment of actual
purpose. If subsequent construction reveals a purpose beyond conditions of the permission, the legal effect may be to nullify the
permission. The dissent places the burden of determining actual
purpose of an application on the agency through investigation and
verification of information submitted so that a more precise decision
on the statement of conditions to be met can be made, since failure
to do so may bind an agency to an incorrect licensing decision.

Fair Procedures in Grant or Refusal of Licence
A basic question in licensing is whether procedural requirements
of statutes or natural justice have been met by the agency in reaching
a decision to grant or refuse a licence in response to an application.
The importance of this question is revealed in the previously discussed case of *East Donegal Co-operative Livestock Mart Ltd and Others
v. Attorney General* 1970 IR 317, 104 ILTR 81 where the courts in
resolving the constitutional issues raised emphasised the statutory
procedural protections surrounding the grant or revocation of a
livestock mart licence, and the presumption that discretionary
powers must be exercised in accordance with constitutional justice.
In response to one of the claims made by plaintiffs that the legislation
was unconstitutional since it gave the Minister 'an unfettered discretion to grant or refuse a licence', O'Keeffe P. held that section 3(6)
of the Livestock Marts Act 1967 controls that discretion by requiring
the Minister to give notice of his intention to refuse to grant or to

revoke a licence and of the reasons therefore to the applicant. The applicant may make representations to the Minister which the Minister must consider. As a result, his discretion 'must be exercised fairly and impartially and is . . . subject to review by the Courts in the event of his exercising the discretion in a manner not contemplated by the section' (IR, page 334). Walsh J. for the Supreme Court in its review of the appeal agreed that all the powers given to the Minister in section 3 which are preceded by the words, 'at the discretion' or 'as he so thinks fit' are powers which:

> may be exercised only within the boundaries of the stated objects of the Act; they are powers which cast upon the Minister the duty of acting fairly and judicially in accordance with the principles of constitutional justice and they do not give him an absolute or an unqualified or an arbitrary power to grant or refuse at his will. Therefore, he is required to consider every case upon its own merits, to hear what the applicant or the licensee (as the case may be) has to say, and to give the latter an opportunity to deal with whatever case may be thought to exist against the granting of a licence or for the refusal of a licence or for the attaching of conditions, or for the amendment or revocation of conditions which have already attached, as the case may be. (IR, page 344)

The elements of procedural fairness, i.e. due process in licensing, include the administrative agency's giving adequate notice within a statutory time limit of any changes in the application which the agency thinks are needed, and of the agency decision to grant or refuse the application. They also include the applicant's meeting statutory requirements for giving notice in a newspaper of the proposed development for which permission (licence) is sought, which sufficiently informs the public of the nature of what is to be done under that permission if it is granted. The procedural requirements which the administrative agency must meet were illustrated in the *Dunne* case (page 328) and the responsibility of the applicant for giving sufficiently descriptive notice to the public to enable the public to make informed objections were delineated in the *Keleghan* and *Monaghan UDC* cases (pages 331-2).

Two of these requirements, namely adequacy of published notice to the public by the applicant, and notice by the agency of its decision within the prescribed time limit were involved in *The State (Stanford and Others) v. Dun Laoghaire Corporation and Others* 1981, Supreme Court, unreported, per Henchy J., 20 February 1981.[5] This case reveals that an agency must keep both requirements in balance, particularly as regards the time factors involved in considering applications for planning permission. In this instance, the local authority was dissatisfied with the description of the proposed development in the newspaper notice submitted with the application, and required the developer to provide a more complete description of the development in a second advertisement. This was published and submitted to the planning authority. However, towards the end of the two-month period from the date of the submission of the second advertisement, the planning authority required a third advertisement in accordance with its opinion that a more exact address for the development should be published. This third advertisement was published in the newspaper very close to the expiry of the two-month period from the date of receipt of the second advertisement. Since the planning authority felt compelled to decide on the application within the two-month period starting from that date, it granted permission for the development on the first business day after receiving the third advertisement.

Henchy J. considered the tenor of the regulations (articles 14, 15, 17, 25 and 32 (2) implementing section 26 (1) of the Local Government (Planning and Development) Act 1963), which provided for publication and submission of notice of intention to apply for planning permission, the power of the planning authority to require re-publication of a corrected notice, and the right of the public to make written representations or objections to the proposed development. In his view, the intent of these regulations and the statute is not just to enable the public to learn of a planning application and then to appeal against a grant of permission, if the permission has been granted. Rather:

> The grant or refusal of a development permission involves three parties: the developer, the planning authority and the public. It is to be said that the exercise of this quasi-judicial function would be flawed if the public . . . whose interests do not necessarily coincide with those of the planning authority, were to be denied the opportunity of yielding forth interested persons who could make representations or objections. The

right of such persons to make representations or objections in writing would seem to be impliedly recognized by the regulations, for art. 32 (2) provides [here article 32 (2) is quoted] . . . . That sub-article recognizes the intervention, *at the pre-decision stage*, of members of the public by submitting representations or objections in writing. (emphasis added)[6]

The purpose of the advertisement of a proposed application is to give interested members of the public opportunity to make representations or objections. In his opinion, when, as in this case, the grant of permission was given on the day after the third advertisement was published, the interested members of the public (such as the prosecutors) were deprived of the opportunity to submit representations or objections in writing. Even if a resident chanced to note the advertisement the day it was published and wrote his objections and posted them that same night, it was unlikely that his letter would reach the planning authority before permission was granted the next day. The planning authority thus breached an essential pre-condition for the grant of a valid permission, *viz.* to give objectors a reasonable opportunity to submit written representations; it acted *ultra vires* and so the permission was invalid.

An additional procedural issue is that of meeting the requirements to be followed in obtaining evidence upon which the decision to grant or refuse a licence is based, as in the case of *The State (Doyle) v. Carr and Delap* 1970 IR 87. Section 1 of the Public House (Ireland) Act 1855 provides that upon the sale of premises licensed to sell liquour, a District Justice after examining under oath all necessary parties, may transfer the licence to the purchaser, who is thereby authorised to carry on the licensed business until the next annual licensing session of the District Court. Under this Act, Bernard Electrical Holdings Ltd, a company registered in Scotland which had purchased a licensed premises in Bray, County Wicklow, gave appropriate notices for application for the interim transfer. When the application was heard, the conveyance of the premises, together with a certified copy of a resolution appointing Fallon as the company's nominee to hold the licence, were handed in. The District Justice was told Fallon was in court and a Garda Síochána officer informed the District Justice that the gardaí had no objection to the application. The District Justice thereupon granted the application without examining the nominee, Fallon, or any other

N

person under oath. Later the existence of the interim transfer came to the notice of the prosecutor, Doyle, who was in business as a publican, and he applied to the High Court for an order of certiorari directed to the District Court to bring up the interim transfer order to be quashed, followed by a motion to make absolute the interim order. The grounds were that the District Court had made the order in excess of jurisdiction since there was no examination on oath of the company's nominee, Fallon, or any other person on behalf of the company, as required by section 1 of the Public House (Ireland) Act 1855 and the related rule 97 (1) of the District Court Rules, 1948 (as amended by rule 12 of the District Court Rules, 1955) providing in detail for the process of transfer of licences.

It was held by Henchy J. that the requirement of examination on oath of the necessary parties under the 1855 Act and related District Court rules before an interim transfer of a licence was made was mandatory rather than directory and that the one necessary party probably was Fallon. On being examined under oath, it might have developed that the company whose nominee he was were not qualified by their memorandum and articles of association to hold a public house licence, or it may have become apparent (as it seemed in this case) that the company had no intention of running a licensed business on the premises. Henchy J. felt that since an interim transfer application is an unadvertised proceeding of a summary nature, to treat the requirement of oral testimony on oath to support the application as directory would be to treat it 'as a peripheral . . . detail, which it is not, rather than as an essential prerequisite to the making of the order, which I believe it to be' (page 92). However, Henchy J. also considered the prosecutor not to be a person aggrieved by the order of the District Justice since the interim transferee never traded as a publican, the transfer was spent and replaced by another licence, and prosecutor has not been nor will he be damnified by the transfer order. In view of the discretion of the Court regarding certiorari where a prosecutor is not a person aggrieved, and his judgment that the quashing of the order would be pointless, he discharged the conditional order.

A further evidential issue in grant or refusal of a licence is that of the nature of the proof which the applicant must provide to qualify for the licence, as in *Savoy Cinema and the Licensing Acts* unreported, High Court, per Butler J., 1967. In this case, Butler J. held that the burden of proof is on the applicant to show that all the requirements of section 14 (1) (a)-(e) of the Intoxicating Liquor Act 1960 are met, with one exception, since they are capable of being demonstrated. The one exception, clause (ii) of sub-paragraph (c) is not demonstrable, since it requires an applicant to show that locating a proposed premises on a new site is unlikely to have a materially adverse business effect on other licensed premises in the neighbourhood. As a consequence:

> the applicant is required to establish a negative . . . with regard to conditions which do not exist at the time of the application and in relation to the business carried on in other premises of which, in the ordinary way, he can have no first hand knowledge. It follows, in my view, that all the applicant can be required to do is to establish *prima facie* by evidence of existing conditions or of what has happened and/or by competent opinion as to what is likely to happen, that the granting of the licence to him will not have the materially adverse effect mentioned in the section. If such a *prima facie* case is established the court can find the requirement satisfied and grant the licence. An objector . . . must either run the risk of the Court so acting or . . . adduce affirmative evidence, from experience of his own trade and figures . . to show that the new licence . . . would have this materially adverse effect.

Applying these concepts to the case before him, Butler J. felt that the applicant had given evidence of his experience in his present establishment and in other restaurants and cinemas owned by his company, the type of trade planned, and observations over time of the number of customers from the Savoy cinema who went into the premises. None of the objectors to his licence produced figures or a concrete estimate of how the new licence might adversely affect their business. The holding of conferences and other functions in the new Savoy premises will tend to increase business in the neighbourhood for other licensees, and the possible adverse effect on other hotels due to the Savoy's capacity, will be counterbalanced by increased need for hotel accommodation generally owing to the holding of conferences in the Savoy. He therefore felt the licence requirements had been met, and ruled in favour of the applicant, thus showing that the burden of proof varies with the objectivity or subjectivity of the statutory requirements to be met.

The evidence which may or may not be considered by an agency in deciding to grant or refuse planning permission was raised in *The State (Fitzgerald) v. An Bord Pleanála* Supreme Court, unreported, per Henchy J., 4 April 1984. Application was made by Figgis and Co (Ireland) Ltd (the developers) in July 1975 to Dublin Corporation as planning authority for permission to build six three-storey houses in the garden next to prosecutor's house on Clyde Road, Ballsbridge with access from Clyde Lane. Permission was refused by both the planning authority and An Bord Pleanála (the Board) on appeal, and a second application in August 1975 to build six two-storey houses was refused again by the planning authority and the Board. In July 1978, application was made for permission for four houses; this was granted on appeal by the Board, after refusal by the planning authority, as not being seriously injurious to residential amenity or contrary to proper planning and development of the area. However, as the development proceeded, the prosecutor noticed early in 1981 that the house being built on Site D. was not in accordance with the permission as granted. This deviation was such that in March 1981 Dublin Corporation brought proceedings against the developers for an order requiring the removal of the house. The developers thereupon undertook in the subsequent court proceedings, that no further development would be carried out on Site D. without planning permission.

The developers then made two further applications for permission, both of which were refused by Dublin Corporation and by the Board on appeal. Finally, in 1982 the developers applied for permission to retain the unlawfully erected house on Site D. which Dublin Corporation refused on the grounds that it was visually obtrusive on the prosecutor's house and was 'seriously injurious to existing residential amenities'. On appeal to the Board, permission was granted, as Henchy J. stated, 'to retain on Site D. the house they had built in flagrant violation of the permission they had got'. The grounds the Board gave for allowing the appeal were:

> Having regard to the development on adjacent sites and Clyde Lane, generally, it is considered that the retention of this house would be in accordance with proper planning and development of the area. The degree of injury and departure from original plan are not such as to warrant removal of the structure.

The prosecutor contended successfully for an absolute order of certiorari in the High Court to have the Board's order quashed on the grounds that the reason given in the order showed that the Board acted without jurisdiction. On appeal to the Supreme Court, Henchy J. noted that under section 26(1) of the Local Government (Planning and Development) Act 1963, as amended by the 1976 Act, a planning authority, and the Board on appeal, are:

> restricted to considering the proper planning and development of the area of the authority (including the preservation and improvement of the amenities thereof), regard being had to the provisions of the development plan, the provisions of any special amenity area order relating to the said area and the matters referred to in subsection (2) of this section.

In this respect, he further noted that the matters referred to in subsection 2 do not include consideration of the removal of a structure unlawfully erected. In his judgment, the reason given by the Board for allowing the appeal included their opinion that the degree of injury and departure from the original plan was not such as to warrant removal of the structure, and in taking that matter into consideration, the Board exceeded its jurisdiction. Such a matter falls to be considered by the High Court only when an application is made under section 27 of the 1976 Act for prohibition of development carried out without the required permission. The decision of the Board was invalid, since they considered a matter which the statute excluded from the scope of their jurisdiction.

Renewal of Licence: Basis for Grant or Refusal
The fact that a person or enterprise has been granted a licence in previous years when the licence requires annual renewal would seem to create a presumption for the applicant and shift the burden of proof for refusal to the administrative agency comparable to the burden of proof in the revocation of a licence. Although this view is reflected occasionally in the United States (see *Bankers Life and Casualty Co. v. Cravey* 68 SE 2d 87 (1952)) it is not an established doctrine, nor does it seem to be so established in Ireland. As the *Quinn* case in connection with discretion in imposing conditions shows, the burden of proof did not change despite the facts that the proprietors had received licences and operated their dance hall in accordance with licensing requirements from 1968 on, and that no

fault was found with the hall, supervision of dances, noise from the
hall, prevention of disorderly conduct or suitability of the applicant
or employees. At best, these factors appeared to be mitigating or
qualifying evidential factors as indicated in the Supreme Court's
dicta that the District Justice as the licensing authority, when
evaluating the consequences for the community of future disruptive
behaviour of dance hall clientele outside the dance hall, should also
consider whether the evidence showed that such adverse behaviour
could be eliminated or reduced by increased Garda Síochána
activity. Given due appraisal in good faith of all relevant evidence,
the decision to grant or refuse renewal could not be challenged as
ultra vires the Act or contrary to applicant's rights (see pages 340-
42).

A distinction was drawn between refusal to renew a short-term
licence, and revocation of a licence modified by circumstances in
the case of *In the Matter of the Solicitors Act 1954*, and in *The Matter of
D., a Solicitor and the Constitution* 95 ILTR 60. The Incorporated Law
Society directed its registrar to refuse to issue a practising certificate
(in effect, an annual licence) to D. for the year 1958 under section
49 of the Solicitors Act 1954. This refusal was based on three
separate instances of misuse of client's funds, which resulted from
his continuing to run an old country business inherited from his
father on lines in which separate banking accounts were not kept
for the clients' moneys and the firm's moneys, and advances were
made to clients on account of moneys to become due to them for
estates to be administered or sales to be completed. Inadequate
accounts led to clients owing money not immediately collectable,
and D. owing other clients money he could not immediately pay,
so that the Incorporated Law Society obtained a High Court order
under the Solicitors Act preventing any banking company from
making payment out of any account in D.'s or his firm's name.

Mr D. appealed the refusal of his certificate to the Chief Justice
(as provided for by the Act at that time), who refused the appeal,
noting that there is a distinction between an order to remove a
solicitor's name from the roll of solicitors (revocation of licence) as
against the refusal to issue (i.e. renew) a certificate. In the latter
case, the solicitor's name still remains upon the roll and he may
renew his application for a certificate at any time, subject only to
deprivation of the right to practise for the current year. In his view,
the facts of D.'s allowing his affairs to result in confusion of his

clients' moneys with his own and his living beyond his means at the expense of his clients made it impossible for the Society to accept as a reasonable explanation that this was because of bad business methods. Though he was much impressed by appellant's efforts to meet his debts to his clients and plans to continue to meet them through instalments, Maguire C.J. did not feel he could overturn the Society's decision on the grounds that it was too severe a punishment or that this would make D.'s efforts to bring his affairs in order impossible.

On appeal from this determination to the Supreme Court, Davitt P. for the Court held that the Society had good cause to consider that D. had failed to give them an explanation for his conduct which they could regard as satisfactory, and thus had jurisdiction to refuse to issue the practising certificate. Nevertheless, the Society should take into account all relevant circumstances with due regard to the interests of the public, the profession, the solicitor's clients and the solicitor himself. On reviewing the circumstances, the Court held:

> Having regard to all the circumstances . . . in particular to:–
> . . . the way in which the business of the D. firm was being carried on when Mr. D. took it over; the efforts which he has made in the past few years under exceptionally difficult circumstances to straighten matters out . . .; the success which . . . has attended these efforts . . . the fact that in the three cases which gave rise to the present proceedings he has met his obligations in full . . . the fact that if he is not allowed to practise his task of attempting to meet his obligations will be rendered much more difficult; we are of the opinion that neither the interests of the public, nor the interests of the profession, require that Mr. D. be prevented from practising . . . and that the interests of his clients and . . . of Mr. D. himself will be served by allowing him to practise. (page 65)

Another issue pertaining to licence renewal is whether the annual renewal of a licence over a period of years by the licensing authority, despite non-compliance of the applicant with the same specific requirement for the licence each year, signifies that the applicant is entitled to further renewal when an objector for the first time raises the previously ignored or unrecognised question of such non-compliance. In the case of *In the Matter of the Licensing Acts, 1833 to*

1981, and In the Matter of an Application by Declan Bannerton High Court, unreported, per Barron J., 23 February 1984, applicant sought renewal of his licence under the 1883 to 1968 Acts for the Mount Hotel, Ballinasloe. The hotel had first been licensed in 1960 under section 2(ii) of the Licensing (Ireland) Act 1902, and its licence was renewed annually until 1975, was then transferred *ad interim* in 1976, and following that, renewed annually from 1978 to 1981. However, at the annual licensing sessions for 1982, objection was made on behalf of the Garda Síochána that the hotel was not registered in the register of hotels kept by Bord Fáilte, as required of licences granted under the 1902 Licensing Act by section 20 of the Intoxicating Liquor Act 1960.

Applicants argued that since the hotel had been licensed under the 1902 Act well before the 1960 Act was passed, the licence granted in 1978 was not a licence to which the 1960 Act applied. Moreover, since the hotel had never been registered at any time in the Bord Fáilte register of hotels, it was now too late to go behind the orders made since 1978 and the Court must presume that the hotel was so registered, as in *Application of Doreen Riordan* 1981 ILRM 2. In short, the orders, though made in error, are nevertheless valid and subsisting orders and cannot now be contradicted.

Regarding the first argument Barron J. held that section 20, Intoxicating Liquor Act 1960 refers to a licence, not to any premises, so that it was immaterial whether or not the premises to which the licence relates was or was not so licensed prior to the passing of the Act. The licence under which the premises were now licensed was granted after the passing of that Act, which applies to such licence. As to creation of a presumption through error in orders renewing the licence over several years, Barron J. distinguished the *Riordan* case. In that case, the orders made over a four-year period ignored a record of convictions which normally would result in forfeiture of the licence. The orders could not be quashed on certiorari because such orders were made within jurisdiction and the error involved a vitiating element which arose once and for all. Once an order was made within jurisdiction, and not quashed on certiorari or reversed on appeal, the vitiating element, i.e. forfeiture of the licence, was deemed never to have existed, with the effect that the licence had never been forfeited.

In the case before him, however, Barron J. held that the vitiating element is one which continues from year to year. He granted that the past orders made in error were not quashed by certiorari nor reversed on appeal in effect were declarations that the hotel was on the Bord Fáilte register of hotels and certiorari would no longer lie to quash such past orders. However, this proof is one which arises each year. It is now open to the Garda Síochána to make the point that the licence may not be renewed in the absence of proof that the hotel is registered in the register of hotels, since the past orders renewing the licence do not in effect declare that the licence is now so registered.

Revocation of Licence: Due Process Requirements
A differentiation in both statutory provisions and judicial interpretation was made between the extent and rigour of procedural due process requirements associated with revocation as against refusal to issue a licence in the previously discussed case of *East Donegal Co-Operative Livestock Mart Ltd v. Attorney General* 1970 IR 317, 104 ILTR 81. The Livestock Marts Act 1967 requires that in both the refusal and revocation of a licence, the Minister must give notice of intent to refuse or revoke, that the individual may respond within seven days and that the Minister must consider any written representation before final action (see also pages 310, 352). However, in regard to revocation, the Minister must wait a month before final revocation of a licence, and if within seven days the licensee requests the Minister to hold an inquiry, the Minister must appoint a practising barrister of at least ten year's standing to hold the inquiry. Notice of the time and place of the inquiry must be given, and the licensee is entitled to appear personally or by counsel and adduce evidence. The barrister may take evidence on oath and must make a report of the findings to the Minister who must not revoke the licence until he considers the report of findings. Reasons for the decision to revoke must be laid before both Houses of the Oireachtas. See section 6 (a)-(f), and section 7, Livestock Marts Act 1967. Despite this full complement of administrative protections, and representations by the Attorney General as to their sufficiency in providing due process, Walsh J. for the Supreme Court insisted that a major reason for upholding the constitutionality of the Act was that the Minister could revoke a licence only after a court conviction of a licensee for the criminal offence of violating any of the licence requirements, following which the Minister then could choose to

apply or not to apply the administrative process leading to revocation. This decision, which placed a severe limitation upon the exercise of the discretionary powers of the Minister by requiring prior court conviction despite the procedural protections surrounding the administrative procedure for revocation, illustrates the judicial emphasis in Ireland for more exacting due process requirements in licence revocation, as against the issue of, or imposition of conditions on, a licence.

The judicial perspective in *East Donegal* has been shown to be significant in its application in later determinations. In *Ingle v. O'Brien* 109 ILTR 7, plaintiff, who was licensed to drive a taxi by the carriage office of the Garda Síochána, under the Road Traffic (Public Service Vehicles) Regulations 1963, was convicted in July 1972 of three offences of forgery of cash dockets given him by a passenger. The District Court sentenced him to three months' imprisonment for each offence, and the convictions were confirmed but sentence suspended on appeal to the Circuit Court. Ingle previously had been convicted of two similar offences and in 1971 had been convicted of nine minor offences connected with his taxi operation and fined a total of £23.

Although the question of revocation of Ingle's driving licence also was argued, the Circuit Court judge indicated that licence revocation should be dealt with by the carriage office of the Garda Síochána. Subsequently, a sergeant of that office handed plaintiff on 15 January 1973 a notice (dated 16 November 1972 and signed by Superintendent O'Brien) stating that as the officer designated by the Commissioner of the Garda Síochána, he considered that Ingle was 'no longer a fit and proper person to hold a licence to drive small Public Service Vehicles' and thereby revoked his licence.

On an application to the High Court, to make absolute a conditional order of certiorari against the revocation, the principal claim made was that the revocation disregarded the requirements of constitutional and natural justice since no opportunity was given to Ingle to make representations against the proposed revocation. The judgment of Walsh J. in the *East Donegal* case was cited, as to the Minister's considering every case on its own merits to hear what the licensee has to say and that the Act did not make it mandatory to revoke a licence after conviction of an offence. In opposition, counsel for the Garda Síochána argued that the revocation was purely administrative, and not a judicial or quasi-judicial act.

Consequently, certiorari did not lie, as in *Reg. v. Metropolitan Police Commissioner Ex Parte Parker* (1953) 1 WLR 1150, in which it was held that revocation of a licence by the Commissioner of Police was a disciplinary, not a judicial or semi-judicial, power. In this regard, article 36, Road Traffic (Public Service Vehicles) Regulations, 1963, as amended by 1970 regulations, provides that the Commissioner may revoke a licence to drive small public service vehicles at any time if he considers the licence holder:

> no longer a fit and proper person to hold such a licence, or if at any time during its currency the holder is convicted of an offence under section 53 of the Road Traffic Act, 1961, or of an offence which in the opinion of the Commissioner renders him unsuitable to hold such a licence.

On such revocation the Commissioner must send a notice to the licensee, although the failure to send such notice, or error in the notice, will not invalidate the revocation. Appeal to the District Court from the revocation is provided for by the article 37 of the regulations.

Pringle J. held that the cited English decision was not in accordance with Irish law, referring to *The State (Crowley) v. Irish Land Commission* 1951 IR 250 for the test of a judicial act. Revoking Ingle's licence clearly affected his right to earn a living by operating his taxi. Although there was force to the argument that the Commissioner should have power to revoke a taxi licence immediately (subject to appeal to the District Court) where the driver through a heart condition or alcoholism was a dangerous driver, it is significant that the legislature did not make provision for immediate revocation of ordinary driving licences. In those cases, there must be an application to, and hearing before, a District Court before revocation. In this case, urgency was not involved, since notice of revocation was not given until two months after being made. Finally, Pringle J. rejected the argument that the licence holder is sufficiently protected by right of appeal to the courts from the revocation. He referred to a classic statement on natural and constitutional justice in the administrative process involving the relationship of administrative agency as original decision-maker and the courts as appellate reviewing bodies:

I must say I am impressed by the judgment of Megarry, J., in the case of *Leary* v. *National Union of Vehicle Builders*, (1971) 1 Ch. 34, in which he held that, whilst a complete rehearing by an original tribunal, or by some other body competent to decide an issue, might satisfy the requirements of natural justice, a plaintiff, where there was a right of appeal from an original decision, was entitled to natural justice . . . before the original tribunal and the appellate tribunal. At page 49 the learned Judge said: 'If a man has never had a fair trial by the appropriate trial body, is it open to an appellate body to discard its appellate functions and itself give the man the fair trial that he has never had? I very much doubt the existence of any such doctrine', and again on the same page he said: 'As a general rule at all events, I hold that a failure of natural justice in the trial body cannot be cured by a sufficiency of natural justice in an appellate body'. (page 11)

Pringle J. held that he agreed with this statement, and was satisfied that Superintendent O'Brien's decision was null and void by reason of the applicant being given no opportunity to be heard as to why such a decision should not be made. Although plaintiff's licence had expired, plaintiff could not apply for renewal for twelve months if the revocation were upheld, and for this reason he was setting aside the revocation.

The *East Donegal* and *Ingle v. O'Brien* determinations were reiterated in the subsequent case of *Moran v. Attorney General, Kearney and O'Brien* 1976 IR 400. Plaintiff, a holder of small public service vehicle licences and of licences to drive such vehicles for hire, was served with notices of the revocation of each licence by Superintendent O'Brien under the same statutory provisions and regulations as applied in the *Ingle v. O'Brien* case. The notices stated that the authorised officer considered the plaintiff to no longer be a fit and proper person to hold such licences. Plaintiff's appeal to the District Court was dismissed and he appealed to the High Court on the ground of having been given no notice that revocation of his licences was being considered, and no opportunity to make representations, and claimed a declaration that the revocation was invalid and asked for damages for the loss caused by the revocation.

Doyle J. quoted from the dicta of Walsh J. in the *East Donegal* case and also cited the judgment of Pringle J. in *Ingle v. O'Brien* stating:

> In that case the learned judge was considering revocation of a licence .. in circumstances .. similar to those now under review. He [Pringle J.] quoted with approval the decision of the Supreme Court *[East Donegal]* to which I have referred. He appears to have concluded that disregard of the rule *audi alteram partem* by the failure of the Commissioner to afford an opportunity to the licensee to make representations against the proposed revocation of his licence was contrary to constitutional and natural justice. With this view I agree, and I consider that the purported exercise of the powers created by the Minister by the regulations exceeded the canons of fair and judicial procedure as laid down by the Supreme Court in the authority cited. (page 404)

In response to defendant's argument that the hearing by the District Justice was a proper judicial investigation which would cure any defects in the earlier revocation procedure, and that plaintiff by following the procedure prescribed in the regulations had conceded jurisdiction to the District Justice, Doyle J. quoted the dicta of Megarry J. in *Leary v. National Union of Vehicle Builders* (1971) 1 Ch. 34, namely[6] 'a failure of natural justice in the trial body cannot be cured by a sufficiency of natural justice in an appellate body'. Consequently, the licence revocations in this case were null and void.

The *Donegal, Ingle* and *Moran* cases establish the concept that once an individual has been granted a licence, the revocation of a licence is looked upon by the courts as taking away the 'right to make a living' and thus there is greater insistence that revocation procedures must be more rigorous and carefully followed in order to meet the requirements of natural and constitutional justice than in the case of grant of a licence. Implicit in this is the shifting of the burden of proof to the agency in revocation, as against the burden being on the applicant in the grant of a licence.

This stress upon natural justice and where the burden of proof lies is applied whether the courts hold that the administrator must follow due process requirements (even though administrative revocation may occur only after a judicial conviction of a statutory violation as in *Donegal*) or whether the administrative agency may revoke a licence without a court conviction, as in *Ingle* and *Moran*. In the latter two cases, there is emphasis upon the role of the administrative agency as a 'trial' body so that procedural rights of natural justice must be provided at that juncture, despite ultimate review by the courts. In a third situation, where the High Court in effect becomes the 'trial' body making the final decision as to a revocation, and the administrative agency constitutes a fact-finding and initial decision-making body, the same emphasis is still placed upon the agency's burden of proof and the procedural rights of the individual during the agency's process. This is illustrated by the court laying down explicit rules of procedure to supplement a statute in the recent case, *In the Matter of the Medical Practitioners' Act 1978, James Magill v. the Medical Council* High Court, unreported, per Finlay P., 8 March 1984. After due notice from the Medical Council the Fitness to Practise Committee of the Council held an enquiry attended by Dr Magill, his counsel and solicitor. Following Council consideration of the report made to it by the Committee, the registrar of the Council notified Dr Magill that they had decided his name should be erased from the register of general medical practitioners (which made any further practice of medicine by Dr Magill a violation of the 1978 Act). Reasons were given for the decision and information provided of his right to appeal within 21 days to the High Court for cancellation of the decision.

Dr Magill sought such an order under section 46 of the 1978 Act to cancel the Council's decision, claiming that although he was heard and represented by counsel at the enquiry by the Committee, he was not given an opportunity to be heard by the Council before it made its decision, and to make representations concerning a plea for leniency to the Council. This lacked natural justice, since a situation could develop where if such a plea were successful, a lesser penalty of retention on the register with conditions or even a smaller penalty of admonition or censure might have been imposed by the Council. To achieve the same result by appeal to the High Court, the medical practitioner would have to go through a public hearing of the complaint against him. There also is the practical difficulty of making a case against a finding of misconduct while simultaneously making a plea for leniency before the Fitness to Practise Committee, especially since the Committee does not announce a decision as to whether or not there was misconduct but conveys its decision only in its report to the Council. In opposition to this viewpoint, counsel for the Council argued that since any penalty under the statute other than admonition or censure had to be imposed by the High Court, the convicting and sentencing body is the Court, and the requirements of natural justice are to be met before that Court.

After holding that the reasons for the decision of the Council were given adequately, Finlay P. first noted that if the Committee finds a medical practitioner to be guilty of professional misconduct, the Council under section 46 of the 1978 Act may decide that the practitioner's name be erased from the register, or will not be in effect for a stated period (i.e. suspension of licence to practise), and under section 47 of that Act may attach conditions incident to retention of the medical practitioner's name in the register. The Council may also advise, admonish or censure a medical practitioner. The medical practitioner may within 21 days apply to the High Court for cancellation of these Council actions (except for Council advice, admonition or censure), and may cancel or confirm the erasure or the suspension of the name or the attachment of conditions as well as add conditions. If the medical practitioner does not apply for cancellation, the Council may apply *ex parte* for confirmation of its decision to the High Court which will so confirm unless it sees good reason to the contrary. In his opinion, it was clear that no penalties other than admonition or censure may be imposed unless and until they are so directed to be imposed by the High Court.

Given the submissions made and the 1978 Act provisions, Finlay P. held that in the absence of procedures in the 1978 Act relating to the application of a medical practitioner to the High Court, he was obliged to enunciate such procedures and make them consistent with natural justice, and he assumed that this was the intent of the legislature. In this respect he held that when a medical practitioner made application to the High Court under either sections 46 or 47 to cancel a Council decision, the burden of proof of the alleged misconduct of the practitioner and the appropriateness of the penalty rests upon the Council. Secondly, he felt that this procedure is not a mere appeal from the combined decisions of the Committee and Council, but rather an entire trial of the issues involved. Consequently, the absence of the right of the practitioner to be heard by the Council before they reach a decision is not an unfair procedure or want of natural justice. However, under this construction of the Act, the Council must deliver to the medical practitioner applying for High Court review a copy of the Committee's report on the case. Furthermore, the practitioner must by notice in writing indicate within fourteen days to the Council what findings of fact made by the Committee he disputes. On delivery of the practitioner's notice, the Council must present to the High Court such evidence as it sees fit to discharge the burden of proof of, first, establishing the facts relied on as misconduct, second, that such facts do constitute misconduct, and third, such evidence as is necessary to support its decision. The practitioner is entitled to present evidence on all these topics. The Court then reaches a conclusion as to whether professional misconduct has been proved. If not, the Council decision is cancelled. If misconduct has been proved, then the Court should give further opportunity to the practitioner who has appealed to the Court, and if necessary to the Council, to be heard and present evidence as to the appropriate penalty to be imposed.

Enforcement Against Unlicensed Operation
If there is continued operation without a licence after administrative refusal or revocation of a licence, a further sanction is to secure a court fine for such an operation. However, there are instances when the entrepreneur may regard the fines as an overhead cost of making a profit by operating illegally, and so the final sanction of a judicial order to stop illegal operation without a licence must be sought, as in *Galway County Council v. Connacht Proteins Ltd* unreported, High Court, per Barrington J., 28 March 1980. The County Council sought an order under section 27 of the Local Government (Planning and Development) Act 1976 prohibiting the unauthorised use of land by respondents.

Originally, the respondents' predecessors-in-title, Galros Meats Ltd, received permission in 1966 for alterations to a recently acquired unused corn and storage mill for extraction of oils and fats from slaughterhouse offal and manufacture of meat and bone meal, which the Council regarded as encompassing change of use. Subsequently a fire completely gutted the mill, which in the opinion of Barrington J. meant that the permission to use the premises for a specific purpose also perished nor could permission be implied to use the outbuildings of the mill for the main business. In 1973, the

Secretary of the Council was informed that the firm of Connacht Proteins Ltd had bought the premises (the principal being a Mr McGann, who was a director of both firms). An exchange of correspondence in 1973 between Connacht Proteins and the County Council took place, in which Connacht Proteins applied for a retention order for reinstated buildings and the County Council notified Connacht Proteins that their work on buildings was unauthorised. In sum, defendants built an entirely new factory and other works on the site without planning permission. In the view of Barrington J., defendants had not obtained planning permission for the use of any of the buildings for extraction of oils and fats from slaughterhouse offals or for the manufacture of meat or bone meal, and they were in fact engaged in unlawful use of land. He also noted that the defendants had been refused permission for retention of the new factory by the County Council, An Bord Pleanála had rejected Connacht's appeal from the Council's decision, and that respondents had been convicted three times in the District Court between 1975 and 1978 for carrying out a development without planning permission, with successive fines of £10, £1,000 and £3,035.

Barrington J. therefore concluded that he was satisfied the premises were being operated so as to be 'a health hazard and an appalling nuisance to local residents' (citing among other things that the forecourt of the premises had a three-foot depth of rotting organic matter). Finding that respondents had no merits upon which he could exercise any discretion to postpone making the order requested, he granted the County Council an order prohibiting respondents from using their lands and premises to cook or render animal offal or extract oils from same or for manufacture of meat or bone meal or storing animal waste or greaves.

As in *Galway v. Connacht,* enforcement action against unlicensed operation was upheld in the later case of *Nova Media Services Ltd and Brady v. Minister for Posts and Telegraphs, Ireland and the Attorney General* 1984 ILRM 161. As the previous discussion of that case in relation to constitutional issues in licensing revealed, the principal point established by the judgment of Murphy J. was that in determining whether to grant interlocutory relief against the Minister's enforcement of the statute through seizure of the radio station's equipment, the balance of convenience had to be determined in the light of the circumstances. On the one hand, the plaintiffs would suffer a very substantial financial loss, difficult to foresee or calculate, by being stopped from broadcasting while waiting a year for a final hearing if interlocutory relief were denied. On the other hand, the grant of such relief would in effect prevent the Minister for the same period from controlling and regulating radio broadcasting until the issues were resolved by the courts. Despite circumstances which might have led Radio Nova management to assume that the law would not be enforced against them without reasonable warning, the fact remained that they started and continued broadcasting without a licence knowing that they violated the law and did not seek a licence or attempt to challenge the constitutionality of the Wireless Telegraphy Act 1926 until the enforcement action against them. Moreover, it would be most unusual for the courts, except in special circumstances, to intervene to stop the Minister from carrying out a function with which he is specifically charged under a statute made for the public good. On balance, Murphy J. held that it would not be proper for the court to make an order restraining the Minister from exercising the powers conferred on him by the 1926 Act and refused to issue an injunction against his enforcement of the Act by seizure of Radio Nova's broadcasting equipment. On this basis, the concept of the illegality of unlicensed operation was affirmed.

Notes to Chapter 8

1. See O'Sullivan, *Irish Planning and Acquisition Law* (1978); O'Sullivan and Shepherd *A Sourcebook on Planning Law in Ireland [Planning Law]* (1984); and Zimmerman, An Bord Pleanála', *Administration* Vol 28 329-344 for detailed analyses of substantive and procedural provisions and judicial interpretations of the 1963, 1976, 1982 and 1983 Acts and their application in practice.
2. See O'Sullivan and Shepherd, *Planning Law* 188-193 for extracts of opinions of O'Higgins, C.J., Henchy and Griffin JJ. in *Monaghan UDC v. Alf-A-Bet Promotions Ltd* unreported, Supreme Court, 24 March 1980, upon which this case summary is based.
3. O'Sullivan and Shepherd, *Planning Law* 189 (1983)
4. As reported in *The Gazette* Incorporated Law Society of Ireland, 19-20, (Vol. 68, Jan-Feb 1974)
5. See O'Sullivan and Shepherd, *Planning Law*, 215-17 (1983) for the statement of facts and opinion of Henchy J., in *The State (Stanford and Others) v. Dún Laoghaire Corporation and Others* unreported, Supreme Court, 20 February 1981, upon which this case is based.
6. O'Sullivan and Shepherd, *Planning Law* 216-17 (1983)

9 Directing Power

Some areas of regulation in governmental programmes are not amenable to the promulgation of specific standards in statute or rule in advance of their application to persons or organisations, typical of licensing systems, for such reasons as inadequacy of information on the subject or lack of operating experience. Other factors include the complexity and rapidity of change in the subject matter to be regulated or in the circumstances surrounding application of standards which make it difficult to anticipate when currently permissible modes of activity may later be against the public interest. Today's legitimate trade or labour practices may become tomorrow's illegitimate practices owing to changed economic conditions or the circumstances surrounding a particular situation. In such programmatic areas, the legislature normally enacts a statute which states overall objectives, provides general standards, and delegates directing power to an administrative agency. Such power usually encompasses authority to investigate, to make a determination as to alleged violation of the statute, and to issue a direction to the violator to stop and to rectify those actions found to be contrary to the purposes of the statute.

The dividing line between a direction (also termed an 'order' or a 'notice') and an administrative rule, especially an interpretative rule, is not absolute; it may be further obscured at times by the use of the term 'order' in statutes to denote rule-making power and at other times, directing power.[1] However, a direction, unlike a rule, is not normally of application to all those falling within a category of persons or organisations. Rather it is usually addressed to a particular party, arising out of a specific situation, and directs or orders that a certain practice or operation be stopped (a cease-and-desist order or direction). It may also order a specified remedial action (positive direction), such as reinstating a person improperly dismissed. A third direction (called a 'blanket order' in the United States) may be issued to supplement a cease-and-desist order so as to prohibit future specific actions which, though nominally different, are of the same nature as the actions prohibited by the cease-and-desist direction. In certain instances, all three types of direction may be issued, e.g. 'stop dismissing persons for union activity, reinstate those already dismissed with back pay and do not engage in comparable anti-union activities in the future.'

Given the nature of directing power, the burden of proof does not rest on the individual as in the licensing power. There is a presumption that the individual has a right to engage in the regulated enterprise or occupation, such as publishing a book or making a particular use of land, and the burden is on the agency to demonstrate that this is contrary to the applicable statute. At first it would appear that directing power is an after-the-violation punitive approach, compared to the prior-permission, preventive approach of licensing. However, as in cases of defiance of a licence revocation, the refusal to comply with an administrative direction can be overcome by an agency only through resort to the courts. Judicial support through imposition of a statutory penalty is granted only after judicial review and approval of the administrative direction. In view of the broad discretion given to administrative agencies to fashion directions of particular effect on the individual or organisation, the courts place emphasis upon the provisions of procedural due process and whether the directions are *intra vires* and reasonable.

Statutory Grants of Directing Power

Among the examples of statutory grants of directing power are the Censorship of Publication Acts 1929, 1946 and 1967 (of which the 1946 Act is the effective Act for most purposes). Directing power is delegated to a Censorship of Publications Board, which under section 6 of the 1946 Act examines books referred to them by a customs officer or on a complaint made by any person as prescribed by the Act, or on its own motion. The Board's examination is guided by broad standards in section 6(2)(a)-(e), which provides that the Board shall have regard to the following matters:

(a) the literary artistic, scientific or historic merit or importance and the general tenor of the book;

(b) the language in which it is written;

(c) the nature and extent of the circulation which, in their opinion, it is likely to have;

(d) the class of reader which, in their opinion, may reasonably be expected to read it;

(e) any other matter relating to the book which appears to them to be relevant.

The Board may also communicate with the author, editor or publisher in conjunction with examining a book, under section 6(3).

If the Board decides that a book is 'indecent or obscene' or advocates the procurement of abortion or miscarriage or use of any means for such purposes, it may issue a 'prohibition order' under section 7 of the 1946 Act forbidding its sale and distribution. An appeal may be taken by the author, publisher or any five members of the Oireachtas acting jointly to the Censorship of Publications Appeal Board under section 8(1)-(4). That Board is composed of a chairman who must be a judge of the Supreme, High, or Circuit Courts or a practising barrister or solicitor of seven years' experience plus four ordinary members. The Appeal Board may affirm, revoke or vary a prohibition order, or vary an order to exclude any edition of the book published after the date of the order, in respect of which no appeal has been previously made. Essentially the same powers are given to the Censorship and Appeal Board under section 9(1)-(3), section 10(1)-(2) and section 14 in respect of periodicals as well as books.

The Board must maintain a register of prohibited publications to ensure notice to those selling, keeping or distributing books. To facilitate enforcement of prohibition orders, section 17 of the Act provides that a District Justice may issue a warrant for a named Garda Síochána officer to search a place suspected of containing prohibited books for sale or distribution and to remove them. Violation of prohibition orders constitutes an offence under section 14(1)-(2) punishable on conviction by a specified fine and/or imprisonment, and forfeiture of the prohibited publication.

Given the broad standards and grant of power to issue negative directions with provisions for administrative and judicial appeal, the Censorship of Publications Acts clearly embody the concepts of directing power, which is the primary means for effecting the purposes of those Acts.

The Land Act 1923 and Land Law (Commission) Act 1923, as amended in subsequent Land Acts, give directing powers to the Land Commission. These Acts reflect the evolution of public policy in Ireland from a voluntary to a compulsory system of transferring land from landlords via the Land Commission to tenant-purchasers. The Land Act 1923 provides that land held under a contract of tenancy with less than sixty years to run ('tenanted land') would vest in the Land Commission automatically. Through what is termed the 'appointed day' procedure, landlords were considered to have agreed to sell their land to the Commission, and tenants on 'tenanted' land were considered to have agreed with the Land Commission to buy their holdings. Also vested in the Commission was 'untenanted' land in districts deemed congested. In general, the system has enabled the formation of viable holdings by transferring ownership of land to suitable tenants.[2]

The Land Commission consists of four Lay Commissioners and a Judicial Commissioner who is a judge of the High Court assigned under section 7, Courts of Justice Act 1936. The Judicial Commissioner also constitutes the Appeals Tribunal of the Land Commission. The Commission has been given extensive discretionary powers under the numerous Land Acts, among them being the power to make orders or directions (or 'declarations') incident to the variety of determinations authorised under the Acts. The types of determination which the Land Commission may make are illustrated by the matters excepted from ministerial direction and control under section 12, Land Act 1950. These included the determination of the persons from whom land is acquired or resumed, the actual lands to be so acquired or resumed, the price to be paid for such land, the persons to whom the land is to be allotted and the amount to be paid for the land by the person to whom the land will be allotted. Also included in such determinations are whether or not a holding has been used by a tenant or proprietor as a farm in accordance with proper methods of husbandry, whether a holding of tenanted land or parcel of untenanted land will vest in the Land Commission, the sporting, fishing rights and fisheries to be vested in the Land Commission, persons to whom fishing rights or fisheries are to be resold and prices for them, and easements and rights to be conferred, defined, extended or extinguished. The Commission may determine the bogs for which turbary regulations are to be made and make the regulations.

Over the years, the Land Acts have also authorised the Commission to make directions, such as conferring and defining rights of way to and from land and fixing compensation to the landowners under the Land Act 1923, section 43. When part of a holding charged with an advance under the Land Purchase Acts is permanently submerged by coastal or other erosion not the fault of the tenant, the Land Commission may apportion the land purchase annuity or annual sum between submerged and non-submerged land, so that the tenant is liable only for the portion of the land purchase annuity on non-submerged land, according to the Land Act 1933, section 37. The Commission may by order consolidate two or more holdings when necessary or desirable in the Commission's opinion for the purpose of the Land Purchase Acts and when the tenant or proprietor consents to such consolidation. (See Land Act 1965, section 25(1)-(3).)

The Local Government (Planning and Development) Acts 1963 to 1983 illustrate how an administrative programme may require both licensing and directing powers. As noted in chapter 8, the primary mode of regulatory control is through licensing, in that any development or use of land, including continuation of existing structures without permission of the planning authority after the 'appointed day' (1 October 1964) is illegal, under sections 24, 26, 27 and 28 of the 1963 Act. However, that Act also anticipates that situations may arise in which an existing structure may be, or may be developed so as to become, contrary to the proper planning and development of the area. In such instances, section 36 of the 1963 Act authorises a planning authority to serve on the owner and occupier a 'notice' (in effect a direction) requiring removal or alteration of the structure together with any replacement which seems suitable to the planning authority if a removal is required. A notice may also be served on the owner or occupier under section 37 of the Act requiring discontinuance of, or imposing conditions on, a particular use of land before the expiry of five years from construction or commencement of a use. Directions may be issued under sections 44 and 45 in respect of removing or altering any hedge, preservation of any tree, group of trees or woodlands. This may include any replacement specified in the direction. A planning authority may direct the 'repair or tidying' of advertisement structures within a specified period under section 54.

Section 26 of the 1976 Act provides that a 'warning notice' (a direction or order) may be served on a landowner by a planning authority requiring that any proposed or ongoing development in contravention of section 24 of the 1963 Act shall not be started

or shall be discontinued. A warning notice to discontinue any
unauthorised use of land may also be served, as well as a notice
that any tree or other structural or natural feature which was
required to be preserved as a condition of the permission to develop,
shall not be removed or damaged. In addition, a warning notice
may require that any reasonable steps necessary for such preservation shall be taken by the owner of the land. The notice also warns
that failure to comply with the notice is an offence.

As is typical of delegation of such directing powers, the statutory
provisions to guide the administrators exercising those powers are
general and broad in nature. Sections 36 and 37 of the 1963 Act
require planning authorities to consider the 'proper planning and
development of the area' with emphasis on the relationship between
the provisions of the overall development plan and of any special
amenity area order. In all instances, appeals from directions of
the planning authorities originally made to the Minister for the
Environment under the 1963 Act are now made to An Bord Pleanála, under section 14 of the 1976 Act. Compliance with directions
of local planning authorities is encouraged by statutory provisions
for compensating persons for expenses incurred in carrying out
removal, alterations, or replacements. Non-compliance is discouraged by provisions in the sections of the 1963 Act referred to above
authorising the planning authorities to enter the area and perform
the work required by the directive and in certain instances charging
the non-complier the costs so incurred (see section 54, 1963 Act).
Non-compliance is also an offence under the 1963, 1976 and 1982
Acts: conviction may lead to a fine or imprisonment.

The Safety in Industry Act 1980, discussed in chapter 5 as an
illustration of the investigatory power, also provides for directing
power in section 11. If the Minister for Labour as a result of facts
based on an investigation is of the opinion that activities in a plant
being carried on, or about to be carried on, involve or are likely to
involve a risk of serious bodily injury to employees, he may issue a
'prohibition notice.' This negative order specifies the matters which
in his opinion create the risk, the provisions of the statute or
regulations contravened by such matters, and directs that the
activities will not be carried on by the person on whom the notice
is served unless the matters have been remedied. The direction may
take effect on receipt of the notice if the Minister states his opinion
that the risk of injury to employees is imminent. Otherwise, the

direction takes effect on the expiry of the seven-day period during which a person may appeal to the District Court. The Court may confirm the prohibition notice with or without modification, cancel or suspend the operation of the notice for such period as it thinks appropriate. Non-compliance with the direction may be overcome by an order of the High Court on application of the Minister, and a fine imposed for such contravention. (See section 11(2)-(5), (8), (9) of the 1980 Act.)

Directing power has been delegated to administrative agencies in labour legislation. Examples of directing power in new legislation or amendment of previous legislation and related regulations during the period 1973-7 may be found in such statutes as the Unfair Dismissals Act 1977, the Employment Equality Act 1977 and the Anti-Discrimination (Pay) Act 1974.[3] The Unfair Dismissals Act 1977, section 6 provides that a dismissal for reason of trade union membership or activities, religious or political opinions, acting as a witness in civil or criminal proceedings against employers or for reasons of race, colour or pregnancy constitutes an unfair dismissal. Certain categories of public employees, certain trainees and apprentices, and persons working for relatives in a private establishment or persons who have reached retirement age are exempted under section 2 from the application of the Act. An employee covered by the Act may, under sections 8 and 9, bring a claim against an employer for redress before one of several Rights Commissioners, or may bring his case directly to the Employment Appeals Tribunal. The claim is initiated by notice in writing containing particulars, as specified in regulations made under the Act, to the Rights Commissioner or the Tribunal within six months of the dismissal, with a copy to the employer. If the appeal is to a Rights Commissioner, the Commissioner will make a recommendation, and on further appeal, the Tribunal will hear the claim only by way of an appeal from that recommendation, unless one of the parties in the case has notified the Rights Commissioner in writing that he objects to the Commissioner's hearing the claim. If the appeal is taken directly to the Tribunal, the Tribunal will make a determination related to the claim, which precludes the claim being heard by the Rights Commissioner. The Rights Commissioner or the Tribunal may issue a direction requiring reinstatement of the employee in his previous position or in a different position reasonably suitable for that person. Furthermore, he may require payment of such compensation not exceeding 104 weeks' remuneration for any financial loss incurred by the employee attributable to the dismissal as is just and equitable having regard to all the circumstances. The Minister for Labour under section 10 of the Act may institute proceedings in the Circuit Court on behalf of the employee against an employer who fails to carry out a Tribunal decision on a claim for redress under the Act. Section 15 provides that nothing in the Act will prejudice the right of a person to recover damages through a common law action for wrongful dismissal as an alternative mode of redress, but such common law action eliminates access to the administrative process under sections 9 and 10.

In similar vein, the Employment Equality Agency of the Department of Labour may initiate action in cases involving an overall discriminatory practices policy, advertisements which discriminate or put pressure on persons to discriminate. Upon making formal investigation and arriving at a conclusion that there are practices contrary to the Employment Equality Act 1977 or the Anti-Discrimination (Pay) Act 1974, the Agency may issue a non-discrimination notice i.e., a direction requiring that such discriminatory practice cease and the Agency may bring injunction proceedings in the High Court against persistent discrimination.[4]

Constitutional Issues in Delegating Directing Power

In *Foley v. Irish Land Commission* 1952 IR 118, 86 ILTR 44, the issue was raised as to whether a delegation of directing power in section 2, Land Act 1946 was contrary to property rights under articles 40.3 and 43 of the Constitution. Section 2 provides that where a holding of land was allotted to but not vested in a purchaser before or after the 1946 Act, and the land includes a house built before or after the allotment of the holding, the Land Commission may give a direction to the purchaser to reside continuously to their satisfaction in the house until the holding is vested in him. If the purchaser does not comply, the Land Commission may recover possession of the holding, and a certificate of the Land Commission, that a direction was given to the purchaser and that he failed to comply, will be conclusive evidence for the facts so certified. Plaintiff had been allotted land by the Land Commission (the Commission) in 1937, and the Commission had built a house on the land in 1939. In 1949 the Commission instituted proceedings in the Circuit Court to recover possession of the parcel of land and put in evidence a certificate made in 1948 certifying that the Commission had served a direction in 1947 on plaintiff requiring him to reside continuously in the house until the land was vested in him, and that he had failed to comply with the direction. Plaintiff brought proceedings in the High Court to test the validity of section 2 of the 1946 Act and the related certificate. On dismissal by the High Court, he appealed to the Supreme Court, claiming that section 2 of the 1946 Act in effect attached a new condition or requirement to his proprietary interest in the land, failure to comply with which involved a forfeiture of the land. Therefore, section 2 contravened articles 40.3 and 43.1(2) as they pertained to property rights. On this issue, O'Byrne J. stated:

The argument before this Court on behalf of the appellant, when reduced to its logical conclusion, seems to involve the proposition that any limitation placed by the Oireachtas on private property, which may result in the loss of that property by the owner, is repugnant to the Constitution and, accordingly, void. If this argument be sound, the Constitution has certainly placed serious fetters upon the Legislature in dealing with property rights and the Court is not prepared to such a far-reaching proposition. (IR, page 153)

The Court concluded that the Land Purchase Acts were an important part of Ireland's social legislation and, given their purpose and mode of financing, the imposition by direction of conditions or requirements as to residence, with the statutory penalty of forfeiture for non-compliance with those conditions was not an abolition of the right to private ownership under article 43.1(2) of the Constitution.

In response to the further argument that the 1946 Act was also repugnant to the Constitution by conferring the power to hear and determine justiciable controversies *inter partes* upon the Commission, the Court stated its view that the function of the Commission constituted a limited power of a judicial nature under article 37 of the Constitution or, alternatively, that the Act gave the Commission as an administrative body the power to impose liability and affect rights. In either case however, when making a certificate which constituted conclusive evidence, the Land Commission had to act judicially.

A challenge to the constitutionality of delegation of directing power for want of statutory standards and procedural protections was made in *Central Dublin Development Association and Ors. v. Attorney General* 109 ILTR 69. Plaintiffs were property and business owners who were members of the Central Dublin Development Association. The Association promoted and protected interests of property owners in a particular area of Dublin, by various means including legal action related to administrative plans or orders affecting the interests of Association members. Dublin Corporation had made a draft plan, and in response to objections, a revised plan under the Local Government (Planning and Development) Act 1963. This plan included compulsory acquisition of an area and an arrangement with a private company to develop the area with fiscal returns of mutual advantage to Dublin Corporation and to the company. Within the compulsory acquisition area, there was a sector encompassing business properties of plaintiffs which would be declared an 'obsolete area' in the future.

Plaintiffs attacked the constitutionality of virtually every major part of the 1963 Act in the High Court, but their main argument was against the grant of directing power to declare an area to be an 'obsolete area' as defined in section 2 of the Act, in combination with rule-making powers in Part III of the Act requiring local authorities to make development plans, and related powers of acquisition and development of 'obsolete areas' under sections 74, 77 and 79. Section 2 of the Act defined 'obsolete area' as follows:

> an area consisting of land (in this definition referred to as the principal land) which, in the opinion of the planning authority, is badly laid out or the development of which has, in their opinion, become obsolete, together with such land contiguous or adjacent to the principal land as, in the opinion of the planning authority, is necessary for the satisfactory development or user of the principal land.

Section 2 was claimed by plaintiffs to be repugnant to articles 40.3 and 43 of the Constitution for failure to give property owners a right to a hearing or opportunity to answer the decision that the property was an 'obsolete area', or to provide for review by any other tribunal or court. Moreover, the statutory definition of 'obsolete area' did not prescribe a precise standard by which the planning authority should: (1) determine when the 'principal land' referred to may be held to be badly laid out or when its development had become obsolete; (2) determine what land was contiguous to the principal land; and (3) determine when or under what circumstances such land is necessary for satisfactory development or user of the 'principal land'. This vagueness violated rights of property owners, and the definition of 'obsolete area' could be construed by the Court so that almost any land or property could be designated an 'obsolete area' and then compulsorily acquired.

In regard to plaintiff's claims concerning lack of due process, Kenny J. stated that the draft development plan must show the boundaries of any area the planning authority considers obsolete and be made available for inspection. Further, under section 21 (2) of the Act, any objector must be given opportunity to state his objections to obsolete area boundaries in an oral hearing before a person appointed by the planning authority, which must be considered by the planning authority. An error in law or unreasonableness of the subsequent decision is reviewable by the courts. As to the standards defined in section 2 of the Act, Kenny J. held they were sufficiently explicit so that the High Court:

> could decide whether an area is badly laid out, and whether the development of it had become obsolete, and that it could decide whether contiguous or adjacent land was necessary for the satisfactory development of the principal land because the Court would have the advantage of expert evidence. It is probable that prosperous businesses will be situate in such an area and that the building in which they trade will be compulsorily acquired, but this is the necessary price of declaring an area to be obsolete. (page 89)

Furthermore, the absence of a property owner's right to be reinstated in the same or similar premises in an obsolete area was not an unjust attack on property rights. The property owner is entitled to compensation for not only the value of his property but for a disturbance, in which an arbitrator must consider costs of acquiring new premises if the owner wishes to continue in business.

Central Dublin illustrates not only the breadth of discretion delegated to local planning authorities, but also the interdependency of
administrative powers. The formulation and adoption of a plan is
a form of rule-making for an area as a whole, while the declaration
that a specific sector is an obsolete area within the general area is
essentially an exercise of directing power, because it affects certain
individual business and property owners only.

The Supreme Court more recently dealt with the issue of the
citizen's right to express convictions and opinions freely under
article 40.6(1) of the Constitution in *The State (Lynch) v. Minister
for Posts and Telegraphs and Attorney General* 1983 ILRM 89. The
prosecutor, Lynch, was one of seven Sinn Féin candidates in the
general election of February 1982. He was designated by Sinn Féin
to broadcast on its behalf after Radio Telefís Éireann (RTE) agreed
to give it time for a series of party political broadcasts, since Sinn
Féin had qualified for broadcasting time by having the requisite
number of seven candidates in the election. However, the Minister
for Posts and Telegraphs (the Minister) made the Broadcasting
Authority Act 1960 (section 31) (No. 2) Order 1982, (SI 21 of 1982)
which directed RTE not to broadcast any matter made by or on
behalf of Provisional Sinn Féin advocating or inviting support for
them. The amended sub-section of the 1960 Act upon which the
order was based provides that:

(i) Where the Minister *is of the opinion* that the broadcasting of
a particular matter or any matter of a particular class would
be likely to promote, or incite to, crime or would tend to
undermine the authority of the State, he may by order direct
the Authority to refrain from broadcasting the matter or any
matter of the particular class, and the Authority shall comply
with the order. (emphasis added)

Under the sub-section, such an order may remain in force for a
period not to exceed 12 months, and may be extended by a further
order of the Minister or resolution of the Houses of the Oireachtas
for another 12 months. Every order must be laid before each House
and either House may annul it within 21 days without prejudice to
the validity of the order prior to annullment.

In support of his claim that section 31(1) of the 1960 Act violated
article 40.6(1) of the Constitution, prosecutor argued that under this

sub-section, the Minister may make an order which discriminates against some citizens and is inconsistent with the democratic nature of the state. Moreover, the sub-section contains no standards for determining when, how, or to what extent a given use of public media is calculated to undermine public order or the state's authority. Finally, the Minister's exercise of power is not subject to any appeal except for possible annulment by either House of the Oireachtas, nor does the Act subject it to any procedural safeguards to ensure that the power is exercised in accordance with the requirements of constitutional justice, and not exercised arbitrarily.

In the High Court, O'Hanlon J. (as noted by O'Higgins C. J. in his judgment for the Supreme Court) held that in view of the use of the word 'opinion' in the sub-section and citing a statement made in *In re Article 26 of the Constitution and the Offences Against the State (Amendment) Bill* 1940 IR 470:

> I am not aware of any case where the use of the expression 'is of opinion' has admitted of judicial review into the reasonableness of the decision made, and the decision of the Supreme Court in the case already cited would appear to be conclusive against any such interpretation. (page 93)

In his view, the amended version of section 31 gave the Minister a far reaching power of veto over material for broadcasting which is *prima facie* not susceptible to control by the courts once the Minister has formed his opinion. He concluded that the section empowered the Minister to act in an unfettered and un-reviewable manner contrary to article 40.6(1) of the Constitution.

On appeal to the Supreme Court, O'Higgins C.J. first dealt with the constitutional issue raised. He noted that the case cited in the High Court judgment was also followed by the Supreme Court in the subsequent case of *In re O Laighleis* 1960 IR 93. However, while the opinion expressed in these two cases 'reflected what was then current judicial orthodoxy, judicial thinking has since undergone a change.' Recent decisions show that the power of the courts to subject the exercise of administrative power to judicial review has a 'wider reach' than that limited by those earlier decisions, as shown by the later cases of *McDonald v. Bord na gCon* 1964 IR 350 and *East Donegal Co-Operative v. Attorney General* 1970 IR 317. In those later decisions, it was established that the correct approach is that in construing a statute which may lend itself to more than one construction, and where one of the constructions would not be repugnant to the Constitution while others would be, there is a presumption that the Oireachtas intended only the construction which was constitutional. This approach was applied in *Loftus v. Attorney General* 1979 IR 221 which considered the effect of the word 'opinion' in relation to the exercise of powers by the registrar of political parties.

As he construed the legislation in question and article 40.6(1), O'Higgins C.J. held that the article enables the state in certain circumstances to control freedom of speech and expression based on the overriding considerations of public order and morality.

The article places the obligation on the state to ensure that organs of public opinion not be used to undermine public order or the authority of the state through broadcasts on radio or television intended to secure or advocate support for organisations which seek by violence to overthrow the state or its institutions. At the same time:

> These, however, are objective determinations and obviously the fundamental rights of citizens to express freely their convictions and opinions cannot be curtailed or prevented on any irrational or capricious ground. It must be presumed that when the Oireachtas conferred these powers on the Minister it intended that they be exercised only in conformity with the Constitution. (page 94)

Consequently, section 3(1) of the 1960 Act as amended does not, in the Court's opinion, confer on the Minister the wide, unfettered powers claimed by the prosecutor. The sub-section does not exclude review by the courts, and any opinion of the Minister reached under the Act must be one held *bona fide* and be factually sustainable and not unreasonable. The constitutional invalidity claimed by the prosecutor has not been established.

Legal Scope of Directions

Assuming that the delegation of directing power is constitutional, a major issue raised by adversely affected recipients of a direction is whether the scope of the direction is *ultra vires* the statute. This issue is raised concerning negative, positive and blanket directions, and is concerned essentially with the substantive aspects of directing power. Incident to this issue, a further preliminary question may also be raised as to 'coverage', i.e. does the party to whom the direction is issued fall within the jurisdiction of the statute and therefore of the agency.

Negative Direction and Coverage
An example of a negative direction which raised the issue of coverage is *Dun Laoghaire Corporation v. Alliance and Dublin Consumers' Gas Company* unreported, Dun Laoghaire District Court, January 1972 *Gazette,* Incorporated Law Society of Ireland, 90-91 (April, 1973). Dun Laoghaire Corporation as sanitary authority served a notice, i.e., a direction under section 7(2) (b) of the Fire Brigades Act 1940, on the defendant company stating that as proprietors of a potentially dangerous building with fire hazards, they must discontinue using that part of the first floor known as the Gas Company Theatre until certain requirements contained in the notice were met. This direction was based on two inspections by the Chief Fire Officer which showed non-compliance with fire regulations on two occasions when a play was staged. Although the notice or direction clearly stated that under the Act the proprietors could appeal within fourteen days to the District Court they did not do so, and then later applied for extension of time to appeal to the District Court which was refused.

Complainants then stated in a summons that their direction had not been complied with since a contravention had been permitted contrary to section 7(4) of the Fire Brigades Act 1940. The Gas Company's Secretary gave evidence of ownership and that the premises had been let to a theatre group. Defendants argued it was not established that they were the proprietors as defined in the Act, since there were different proprietors of different parts of the building, and the sense of section 7(1) of the Act is that in such circumstances, each different person will be considered to be the proprietor of a building.

The District Justice held that since the defendant company had not appealed to the District Court from the requirements of the notice and then later applied for extension of time to appeal, they were estopped from denying they were proprietors. In the absence of a definition of 'proprietor' in the Fire Brigades Act, the word
o

would be taken in its ordinary sense as defined in the Concise
Oxford Dictionary, namely 'owner'. The evidence proved that
defendants were the owners and proprietors within the meaning of
the Act, and the Court would convict for contravention of the
direction.

A negative direction and the related issue of coverage was also
illustrated by *The State (Lynch) v. Minister for Posts and Telegraphs and
the Attorney General* 1983 ILRM 89. In addition to the constitutional
issue of freedom of speech dealt with in the discussion of the *Lynch*
case, the plaintiff also challenged the validity of the order itself as
not coming within the ambit of the enabling section 31(1) of the
Broadcasting Authority Act 1960. Plaintiff argued that the power
to veto a broadcast under that section is limited to prohibiting the
broadcasting of a 'particular matter or any matter of a particular
class' which only authorises banning of broadcasts dealing with a
particular subject matter. This power can not be extended to the
banning of broadcasts by particular persons or classes of persons,
which is what the Minister's order is designed to do, and therefore
is outside the powers granted by the sub-section.

This claim was rejected by O'Higgins C. J. on the grounds that
the word 'matter' in the sub-section 'is wide enough to cover a
broadcast on behalf of a named political party irrespective of the
contents of any broadcast, however described, by any person or
group of persons representing a named political party.' It is the
matter which is prohibited by the order, and not a broadcast by a
particular person or group of individuals, since the order is against
a broadcast on behalf of Sinn Féin or anyone representing that
organisation. In his view, it appeared that such a prohibition is
fully contemplated by the sub-section.

Positive Direction
The issue of whether the specificity in the substance of a positive
direction was *ultra vires* the statute was raised in *Minister for Agriculture
v. Donnelly (Dublin) Ltd* 83 ILTR 24. Under article 13, Emergency
Powers (No. 3353) Order 1945 made under the Emergency Powers
Act 1939, as subsequently amended by the Emergency Powers
(Continuance and Amendment) Act 1942, rules were made which
provided that the Pigs and Bacon Commission could at any time
issue a direction requiring a person to sell to another person 'any
specified quantity of bacon in the possession or under the control

of the vendor and requiring the purchaser to buy from the vendor the specified quantity of bacon'. Such a direction might contain provisions 'requiring the vendor to deliver the bacon to which the direction for sale relates, to the purchaser at a specified place and specified time', and 'fixing the time at which, or before which, the sale and purchase . . . is to be completed'.

The Pigs and Bacon Commission issued an order to the defendants to sell a specified quantity of bacon in the form of Green Wiltshire sides which were in their possession. Defendants contended that under article 13, paragraph 1 of the rules the Commission were not empowered to specify the type of bacon required to be sold, but only to make a direction for sale of a specifically stated quantity of bacon, and thus the direction was *ultra vires* and void.

The High Court, per Maguire and Dixon J. J. (Haugh J. dissenting), held that this argument ignored the terms of article 13 which referred to bacon in the possession or under the control of the vendor, and thus referred to bacon which could be identified or described. In this instance, the words used in the direction were words of description or identification of the bacon, which was proved to have been in the defendant's possession. Each direction also specified the quantity which the defendants were required to sell. In the Court's view, article 13 did not limit the terms of the direction for sale to those items or matters specified in the article, nor could it be construed as implying such a limitation. The contention that the direction for sale was *ultra vires* must fail.

Haugh J., dissenting, felt that the Pigs and Bacon Commission were limited to the specific powers granted by the statute, namely authority to order delivery or collection at a specified time and place and the time when sale and purchase were to be completed. Given the way in which 'bacon' was defined by article 2 of the Agency's rules, it was clear that 'bacon' included more than 'Wiltshire sides'. On the dates in question, defendant had bacon other than 'Wiltshire sides' on their premises. The Commission 'was entitled to direct defendants to sell a specified quantity of bacon, without reference to quality or type, to name time and place for delivery, and fix the date for completion, and no more' (page 28). It was within defendant's discretion to select the type of bacon to be sold and, as long as they delivered at a specified time and place the designated quantity of any type of bacon, they had complied with the law. That part of the direction specifying 'Wiltshire sides' therefore was *ultra vires*.

Negative and Positive Directions Combined

A decision to augment the scope of a negative direction to demolish a dangerous structure by adding a positive order that lateral supports to adjoining buildings be provided was at issue in *The State (McGuinness) v. Maguire* 1967 IR 348. The Local Government (Sanitary Services) Act 1964, section 3(1) authorises a sanitary authority (here Dublin Corporation) to serve notice on the owner of a dangerous structure to perform such work, including demolition, 'as will' in the opinion of the authority, prevent the structure from being a dangerous structure.' Section 1 defines a dangerous structure as '(a) any building, wall or other structure, or (b) any part of, or anything attached to, a building, wall or other structure of any kind that, in the opinion of the sanitary authority . . . is or is likely to be dangerous to any person or property'.

The three-storey structures in question owned by prosecutrix, Nos 125 and 126, were adjoined by non-detached premises, Nos 124 and 127. There also were braces running between Nos 126 and 128 above the roof level of the one-storey No 127 to give lateral support to No 128. Although No 128 is not the property of prosecutrix, taking down prosecutrix's premises meant removal of the braces. Given this situation, the order to prosecutrix which required her to take down the entire structure owned by her, also required her to provide lateral support to adjoining structures. Prosecutrix accepted her obligation to take down the entire structure but challenged the Corporation's order to require provision of lateral support for adjoining premises as being *ultra vires* the Act; moreover, the order to provide lateral support for premises No 128 would involve prosecutrix in continuing trespass over premises No 127.

The Supreme Court, per Ó Dálaigh C.J., held that although requiring provision of temporary shoring of a building during demolition might be within the power granted by the statute, once the buildings are demolished, they cease to be dangerous structures, and nothing can be required to prevent the structures from being dangerous, since they have ceased to exist. In disposing by demolition of two dangerous structures (Nos 125-6) the administrative agency would shortly have two other dangerous structures (Nos 124 and 128) to deal with, and thus it may have seemed proper to place the burden of preventing these additional structures from also becoming dangerous on prosecutrix. However such a solution ignores the complexities of the law of easements governing rights of adjoining owners in respect of support. What the agency overlooked was that the provisions of the 1964 Act in relation to dangerous buildings:

> are drawn in narrow terms. . . . Where, as a result of the demolition of a dangerous structure, an adjoining building also becomes a dangerous structure, the sanitary authority's power is to act against the owner of such adjoining building; it is he, and only he, who can be required to carry out such works as will . . . prevent the building from continuing to be a dangerous structure. (page 362)

Consequently, respondents were held to have erred in requiring prosecutrix to provide permanent lateral support for adjoining structures.

Blanket Direction

Appeals from blanket directions or orders made by the Minister for Industry and Commerce in *Roche and Bula Ltd v. Minister for Industry and Commerce and Others* and *The State (Randles) v. Minister for Industry and Commerce* were heard together by the Supreme Court and are reported in 1978 IR 149. The situation leading to the Minister's blanket orders in *Roche* and *Randles* involved minerals under lands owned in fee simple by Patrick Wright at Nevinstown, Navan, which the Minister in February 1971 had concluded were not being worked. He wished to negotiate a lease for working the mines in the area and felt that the mining rights should be controlled. Such control could be achieved under section 14 of the Minerals Development Act 1940, which provided:

> (1) Whenever it appears to the Minister that there are minerals . . . under any land . . . not being worked or . . . not being worked efficiently, and the Minister is of the opinion that it is desirable in the public interest . . . that the working of such minerals should be controlled by the State, the Minister . . . may by order either . . . compulsorily acquire such minerals or

compulsorily acquire an exclusive mining right in respect of such minerals.

(2) The following provisions shall apply and have effect in relation to every minerals acquisition order . . . (a) such order shall specify the nature, situation, and extent of the minerals to which it relates; (b) such order may be in respect of all the minerals on or under any particular land or in respect of any particular such mineral or any particular class of such minerals.

On 15 March 1971 the Minister issued the following order:

The Minister for Industry and Commerce in exercise of the power conferred on him by section 14 of the Minerals Development Act 1940 . . . and with the consent of the Minister for Finance hereby orders as follows–

1. This order may be cited as the Minerals Acquisition (Nevinstown and other townlands, County Meath) Order, 1971.

2. All minerals . . . under the land described in the Schedule to this Order are hereby vested in the Minister for Industry and Commerce in fee simple. (page 152)

Notice of this order was not published until 23 March 1971, and on 1 April the Minister under section 13 of the 1940 Act initiated action to grant to Tara Exploration and Development Co. Ltd or its subsidiary, Tara Mines Ltd, a state mining lease under certain conditions.

During this period, defendant Wright on 18 March agreed to sell his lands to plaintiff Roche, who on the same day entered into a second agreement to form a company, Bula Ltd, with nominal capital of £1,000,000. On the following day, Wright executed a conveyance of the lands to the company. An application was then made by Bula Ltd to the Land Commission for consent to vesting the lands in Bula, under section 45, Land Act 1965, but such consent was not given. Roche and Bula subsequently obtained a conditional order of certiorari on 21 March 1972 to quash the 1971 order of the Minister for Industry and Commerce and later sought to have the conditional order made absolute.

In the High Court, plaintiffs Roche and Bula claimed that the order of the Minister was *ultra vires* for the reasons: (1) a Minerals Acquisition Order under the 1940 Act can pertain only to specific minerals, and not be a blanket reference to all minerals, and (2) the Minister could not know whether all the minerals under the Nevinstown area had been worked. Other claims by plaintiffs regarding the Minister's grant of a lease, and property rights under the Constitution, and violation of natural justice rights to notice and hearing, were rejected by O'Keeffe P. in the High Court, but he did invalidate the order in view of its 'blanket' nature. In his view, the ministerial order must specify the nature, situation and extent of the minerals; further, no machinery was created to compensate a person for the existence of unknown minerals which might be of great value and thus could be acquired by the Minister without adequate compensation.

On appeal to the Supreme Court, Budd J. noted that section 14(2)(a) of the Minerals Development Act 1940 explicitly states that the Minister's order must specify the nature, situation and extent of minerals to which it relates, all of which could have been determined by experimental boring, and the location could have been delineated by reference to the townland. Similarly, Henchy J. stated that section 14(1) of the 1940 Act posits three criteria for the making of an order. First, it must appear to the Minister that there are minerals on or under the land; second, that such minerals are not being worked effectively; and third, that the public interest demands that the state should control the working of such minerals. Thus, he held the Minister's orders to be bad for they:

> are blanket orders to cover 'all minerals' under the land (other than minerals which are already State minerals) and thereby show a want of the discrimination and appraisal necessary on the part of the Minister to comply with the three pre-requisites set out in the section. (page 156)

He also stated that the 'scheme of compensation seems . . . incompatible with the blanket acquisition of all minerals on or under the land' since determination by the Mining Board as to what should be the royalty rent must be based on information as to what a willing grantee and willing grantor would agree to in a given situation taking into account the nature and extent of the minerals. In this instance, these factors were unknown (page 157).

From the foregoing judicial determinations, it is apparent that administrative agencies must exercise care in formulating the substantive content and scope of negative, positive or blanket directions or orders. The courts will uphold administrative directions if their content and scope comply with and implement the statutory purposes and guiding standards as construed by the courts. Conversely, administrative orders will be nullified if the content of the order or jurisdiction asserted exceeds the authority granted by the statute. An agency may impose requirements which are not explicitly stated in a statute provided that such requirements are related to achieving the purpose of the statute, as in the *Minister of Agriculture v. Donnelly* case. However, administrative directions specifying a line of action when authority to do so does not exist explicitly or by implication in the statute, or a blanket order ignoring statutory requirements as to the content of an order, will be held *ultra vires* as in the *State v. Maguire* and the *Roche* cases.

Procedural Requirements in Directing Power

In addition to substantive questions concerning the scope of administrative directions, issues also arise in respect of requirements of procedural due process to which the administrator must adhere in exercising directing power. Since the due process requirements of natural and constitutional justice have been dealt with in detail in chapter 5, the illustrations below are limited to those sufficient to demonstrate the applicability of procedural due process requirements to directing power.

Right to Notice and Hearing
The basic right to notice and hearing was the determining factor in *Foley v. Irish Land Commission* 1952 IR 118, also discussed above as an example of a challenge to the constitutionality of delegation of directing power. In *Foley*, the Land Commission, under section 2 of the Land Act 1946, had issued a direction to plaintiff that he must dwell continuously on the land allotted to him by the Commission. Upon his non-compliance with this direction, the Land Commission, in accordance with section 2, issued a certificate stating that he had not complied with their order and sought to recover possession of the land. Although plaintiff's challenge to the constitutionality of section 2 failed, his claim as to denial of procedural due process succeeded. In view of the fact that section

2(v) provided that the certificate of the Land Commission shall be conclusive evidence for all purposes of the facts so certified by the Commission, the Supreme Court held that the Commission were bound to act judicially in making their determination and issuing the certificate. Since the Commission had failed to notify plaintiff that they proposed to consider and determine whether he had complied with their direction for continuous residence, and plaintiff had no opportunity to present his case before the Commission, the certificate was held to be void and of no effect.

Judicial support of the right to notice and hearing under natural and constitutional justice was reiterated in the more recent case of *Irish Family Planning Association v. Ryan* 1979 IR 295. The five defendant members of the Censorship of Publications Board (the Board) issued in November 1976 a prohibition order against a book entitled *Family Planning* published by the plaintiff company on the grounds that it was 'indecent or obscene', thus prohibiting the sale and distribution in the state of that book. Plaintiffs sought declarations that the proceedings of the Board relating to the prohibition order were irregular, *ultra vires* and unconstitutional, and that sections 6 and 7 of the Censorship of Publications Act 1946 were repugnant to the Constitution. The grounds for the declarations were that with regard to the contents of the prohibited book, the Board could not, acting reasonably, have concluded that it was indecent or obscene; that the prohibition order had a lack of precision fatal to its validity; that the order should not have been made without giving plaintiffs the opportunity to be heard; and that even if the procedure followed was permitted by sections 6 and 7 of the Censorship of Publications Act 1946, those sections were repugnant to the Constitution.

The High Court concluded that the claim could be decided solely on the basis that prior to making the order the Board had not communicated with or heard plaintiffs under section 6(3) of the Censorship of Publications Act 1946 which provided:

(3) When examining a book under this section, the Censorship Board may communicate with the author, editor or publisher of the book and may take into account any representation made by him in relation thereto.

In the High Court, Hamilton J. held that given this statutory provision:

I fail to see how they [the Board] could exercise their powers
fairly and judicially in accordance with the principles of natural
justice if they fail to notify the author, editor, or publisher of
the fact that the book is being examined or if they fail to afford
such persons an opportunity to make representations in relation
to the book prior to the Board making an order which would
affect their rights . . . [the Board] failed to have regard to the
canons of fair and judicial procedure as laid down by the
Supreme Court in *East Donegal Co-Operative v. The Attorney
General* [1970 IR 317]. (page 309)

The High Court's decision that the prohibition order was void was
appealed to the Supreme Court. O'Higgins C.J. for the Court held
that contrary to the High Court's determination, section 6(d) of
the Act was discretionary rather than mandatory on the Board.
However, the High Court was correct as regards the nature of the
Censorship of Publications Act 1946. Since the statute was enacted
after adoption of the Constitution, it is presumed to be constitutional, and in accordance with the decisions in the *East Donegal* and
in the *Loftus v. Attorney General* cases:

this presumption of constitutionality carries with it the consequent presumption that powers of a discretionary nature conferred by such a statute are not intended to be arbitrary powers,
and are only exercisable in a constitutional manner . . . This
requires, at the very least, an exercise of the power at a time
and in circumstances in which it is fair and proper to do so.
(page 313)

Despite this judicial reiteration of administrative responsibility
for exercising discretionary powers in a constitutional manner,
O'Higgins C.J. stated that the Court could not give the Censorship
Board clear and precise guidelines to follow, since a prohibition
order implies conduct deserving of public condemnation and probably guilt of criminal offence, while the main statutory goal of
such an order is to prevent sale and distribution of unwholesome
literature. At best, the Court can only say that the facts and
circumstances of each case should indicate whether fairness and
justice require communication with the author, editor or publisher
of a book. Where the publication is manifestly indecent or obscene,

or the editor, author or publisher cannot readily be contacted, the exercise of discretionary power to communicate with the author or publisher would be wrong. On the other hand, where the publication is not patently obscene, and fair questions of points of view arise, then the Board should consider the appropriateness of such communication and give consideration to what the author or publisher have to say.

Given the facts and circumstances in this case, O'Higgins C.J. held that the Board acted unjustly in prohibiting the publication of the book since it should have exercised the power to communicate with and consider representations by plaintiffs. There would have been no difficulty in communicating with the Irish Family Planning Association at 15 Mountjoy Square, Dublin as the responsible publisher of the book. Concerning the book itself:

> As the evidence given in the High Court shows, it was produced as a part of the information services of a family-planning clinic conducted by responsible and qualified people . . . . An edition of the plaintiff's book had been on sale freely in Irish bookshops for some three years without let or hindrance from the Board. Far from being pornographic or lewdly commercial or pandering to prurient curiosity, it simply aimed at giving basic factual information on a delicate topic as to which there is genuine concern. . . . In those circumstances it is not possible to hold that this book would have been banned for being 'indecent or obscene' if the publishers had been given the opportunity of giving the Censorship Board the information that was adduced by them in the High Court.

The basic right to notice and hearing under concepts of procedural due process were also at issue in *The State (Lynch) v. Minister for Posts and Telegraphs and Attorney General* 1983 ILRM 89. Among the issues raised in this case (others of which have been discussed above), was the claim by Lynch that the order of the Minister prohibiting him from broadcasting as the person nominated by Sinn Féin to present that party's viewpoint was made without regard to the requirements of justice. These requirements were not met since no sufficient notice of the making of the order was given, and no opportunity afforded to offer representations or reasons why the order should not be enforced. In the view of O'Higgins C.J., the Minister was bound to act as he did, by both section 31(1) of the Broadcasting Authority Act 1960 and by the Constitution, assuming that he *bona fide* held the opinion which his order declared that he held.

> The time was short and a decision was urgent. There was no opportunity for debate or parley, and, indeed, to permit or seek such might, in the circumstances, have defeated the very object and purpose of the section. There may be many cases in which justice requires that those to be affected by action of this kind should receive notice and be heard. I am quite satisfied that this was not one of such cases. (page 97)

A similar viewpoint was expressed by Walsh J., who held that with regard to the argument that the Minister's order should be quashed, because he did not follow the procedure of seeking the views of the party affected in advance:

> In view of the time factor, in my view he was justified in acting as a matter of urgency having regard to the cogency of the evidence already available to him. Nothing has been shown to indicate that his decision would have been or ought to have been any different if he had gone through that procedure [of notice and hearing] even if the time for doing so was available. In my view no grounds have been established upon which the court should quash the order of the Minister. (page 103)

The *Foley* case, the *Irish Family Planning Association* and the *Lynch v. Minister for Posts and Telegraphs* cases are examples of the extensive administrative discretion which the legislature grants when delegating directing powers in varied areas of governmental regulation. They also illustrate the importance of statutory provisions for and judicial emphasis upon administrative adherence to procedural due process in the exercise of that broad discretion, as in *Foley* and *Irish Family Planning Association*. This emphasis is tempered, however, by judicial concern for protecting the public interest defined in statute within a situation involving the exigencies of limited time and available evidence which in *Lynch v. Minister for Posts and Telegraphs* was considered to be justification for an order made without prior notice and hearing.

Adequate Notice

Assuming that the basic right to notice and hearing is provided for by statute or required by the courts, the related issue of what constitutes adequate notice arises in the exercise of directing power. Failure to fully comply with statutory requirements of notice may lead to judicial refusal to impose a penalty for non-compliance with an administrative order, as in *Cootehill Town Commissioners v. Brigadier O'Gowan* 1958 Ir. Jur. Rep. 19. Plaintiffs made a clearance order under section 5 of the Housing (Miscellaneous Provisions) Act 1931, in respect of certain houses in Cootehill, County Cavan, including defendant's property, and made a demolition order under section 6 of the Act. The making of the clearance order was advertised in *The Anglo-Celt* newspaper on 12 April 1955 and defendant was served on 14 April with notice of the order by registered post and of its submission to the Minister for Local Government for confirmation. After a public local hearing by the Minister's designated inspector in Cootehill, attended by two occupiers of the houses but not by defendant, the Minister by order confirmed the clearance order on 20 November, all of which was published in *The Anglo-Celt*. No one made application within the statutory three weeks to the High Court to question the validity of the order. However, no notice or copy of the order having become operative was served on defendant under section 17(5) of the 1931 Act, which provides:

> So soon as may be after an order has been operative, the local authority shall serve a copy thereof on every person on whom a notice was served by them of their intention to submit the order to the Minister for confirmation.

Defendant failed to demolish the houses (which were vacant after 13 May 1956) so plaintiffs advertised for and contracted with a local contractor to carry out the work and then issued a summons against defendant to recover the amount paid to the local contractor, and an order was made to that effect in the District Court. The defendant pleaded that section 17(5) of the Act was not complied with so that it was possible he would not know of the demolition date. Plaintiff argued that once the clearance order is confirmed by the Minister it becomes operative unless attacked in High Court. In response to the arguments, the Circuit Court held:

The respondent local authority in making and seeking to give
effect to the clearance order affecting the appellant's property
appears to have complied with all the relevant statutory provisions of the Act with the exception of those contained in
s.17(5). Now this is an Act which gives wide and far-reaching
compulsory powers to local authorities to interfere with the
rights of private property owners . . . . In the exercise of such
powers local authorities must, in my view, strictly adhere to
and comply to the letter with all the relevant provisions of the
Act . . . . It is admitted that the respondents failed to comply
with the provisions of s.17(5) in the present case . . . . compliance with s.17(5) was mandatory . . . and . . . while their
admitted failure to comply with that sub-section may not affect
the validity of the clearance order, it does . . . . disable the
respondents from penalising the appellant by the recovery from
him of the expenses claimed. (page 21)

The *Cootehill* decision indicates that a statutory requirement as to
notice will be applied strictly by the courts. However, judicial
emphasis is upon achieving the actual purpose of fair notice rather
than compliance in a purely legalistic sense which might thwart
that purpose, as in *F. & C. Ltd v. District Justice Wine* unreported,
High Court, per Finlay P., 23 July 1979. Prosecutors claimed that
an order made by District Justice Wine to enforce an administrative
order affecting their lands was bad because it was made in the
absence of prosecutors without their having an opportunity to be
heard, and for failure by the Dun Laoghaire Corporation to serve
notice on the actual owner of the premises that they were obtaining
that judicial order. The events leading to the contested order began
in this case with an application by T. & J. Nolan Builders Ltd
who had applied for planning permission to the Dun Laoghaire
Corporation. The Corporation responded by serving notice pursuant to section 3, Local Government Sanitary Services Act 1964,
that the floors and ceilings of the four premises involved were
dangerous and specified certain works to be carried out. Later, the
Corporation notified Nolan Builders of its application to the District
Court for an order requiring Nolan Builders to carry out those
works, and in the event of non-compliance, for a court order
authorising the Corporation to perform the works, which order
was issued by the District Court. These actions culminated in an

application under section 3(8)(a) of the 1964 Act by the Corporation
for a final order by the District Justice, with due notice to Nolan
Builders prohibiting repair, letting of premises, or carrying out any
works on the site, until payment was made to the Corporation of
£1,289. This order was granted.

Subsequent to these actions the prosecutor, F. & C. Ltd, which
had full planning permission for certain works on the lands in
question, commenced construction of foundations for those works.
F. & C. Ltd had the same registered office and identical directors
as Nolan Builders. The corporation engineer then gave F. & C. Ltd
a copy of the District Court prohibition order which had been issued
to Nolan Builders with a warning that if work continued, those
responsible would be liable to imprisonment.

Finlay J. in the High Court concluded that section 3(8)(a), under
which the final District Court order was made, applied to the site
not just to the owner of the site. Consequently:

> the mere fact that a person who at a particular time owns land
> was not represented at the hearing on which an application for
> an Order under section 3(8)(a) was made could not be a
> grounds for invalidating that Order . . . . a person purchasing
> lands in respect of which an Order under section 3(8)(a) had
> already been made takes them subject to and affected by that
> Order and he cannot be heard to challenge it on the grounds
> only that he did not have an oppportunity of being heard in
> the proceedings at the time of the making of that Order.

In the opinion of Finlay J., the fact that Nolan Builders had claimed
to be the owners and ignored proceedings charging them with being
owners indicated acceptance of ownership. Moreover, the directors
of F. & C. Ltd, the actual owners, were also the directors of Nolan
Builders, and they failed to assert the true situation, which meant
they were misleading the Corporation and the Court as to the real
ownership. Thus, despite the mandatory statutory requirement for
notice to be served on the actual owner of intent to enter lands and
repair a dangerous building as a requirement for exercise of such
powers, there are no grounds for setting aside the District Court
order, which is good on its face. There is no suggestion it was made
without evidence, and all that is proved is that the District Justice
incorrectly determined who was the owner of the lands, and an

incorrect conclusion of fact by an inferior court is not subject to review by way of certiorari.

Sufficient Evidence

An important issue in directing power is whether there is sufficient evidence to support the determination upon which an administrative direction is based as part of the broader requirement of acting judicially. An earlier case turning primarily on this issue was that of *Price v. Leitrim Board of Health and Public Assistance* 1941 IR 123. Plaintiff owned two small farms a short distance apart and lived on the smaller one, over half of which the Leitrim Board of Health and Public Assistance sought to acquire compulsorily for purposes of the Labourers Acts, 1893-1931 as amended by the Housing (Financial and Miscellaneous Provisions) Act 1932. The compulsory purchase order was confirmed by the then Minister for Local Government and Public Health. In effect the plaintiff would be left with a strip of the field 72 feet wide and 321 feet long and low-lying swamp land adjoining the yard and garden house of his dwelling house. The plaintiff claimed this would interfere seriously with the amenity of his residence and with the field which he customarily used together with the residence, and would make his lands uneconomic, inconvenient and useless, diminishing the value seriously.

Gavan Duffy J. for the High Court held that the evidence before him showed that the Board was taking:

> not merely a large part of this man's land, but the best part of it. They are taking the high land and leaving the remainder. On the remaining land there is the plaintiff's own little house . . . byres . . . out-offices, a cottage which is sublet, a haggard, on which no crop can be grown, and a very small strip of field . . . . He has been using the field . . . for ordinary farming purposes and in particular for raising young cattle. The evidence is that if the local authority are allowed to acquire the portion of the land as set out in the Order, what is left will be swampy in wet weather . . . . The uncontradicted evidence is that the plaintiff would be left with the worst part of the field and that it would be utterly uneconomic. (page 126)

Gavan Duffy J. stated that plaintiff brought himself within section 17 of the Housing (Miscellaneous Provisions) Act 1931 which provides that any person aggrieved by such an order can obtain redress if the order is not within the powers of the Act or the interests of the applicant have been substantially prejudiced by failure to comply with any requirement of the Act. Moreover, section 6 of the Labourers (Ireland) Act 1882 provides that the scheme must avoid interference with the demesne and amenity of residence of the land immediately adjoining and customarily occupied with such residence, and in all cases land must be selected with regard to the general situation and convenience of the property so as to diminish the value as little as possible. The local authority had no jurisdiction to act in contravention of this last requirement since if the best of the owner's land is taken, and he is left with a poor patch, this is not the 'due regard' required by the Act, even though he has a larger field not far away, but less suitable to his purpose than what was taken. The compulsory purchase order therefore was quashed.

The function of the administrative hearing as the means for developing a record of evidence sufficient to sustain an administrative direction or order, and deciding what constitutes sufficient evidence is further brought out in *Hughes v. Wicklow County Council* 90 ILTR 167. In this case, Judge Fawsett in the Circuit Court was asked to quash or at least vary a demolition order made under section 23(1) of the Housing (Miscellaneous Provisions) Act 1931 which provides:

> Where a local authority, upon consideration of an official representation, or a report from any of their officers, or other information in their possession, are satisfied that any dwelling-house . . . occupied, or . . . of a type suitable for occupation by persons of the working classes, is unfit for human habitation and is not capable at a reasonable expense of being rendered so fit, they shall serve upon the person having control of the house, upon any other person who is an owner . . . notice of the time (. . . not less than twenty-one days after service of the notice) and place at which the condition of the house and any offer with respect to carrying out of works, or the future use of the house, which he may wish to submit will be considered by them, and every person upon whom such a notice is served shall be entitled to be heard when the matter is so taken into consideration.

Wicklow County Council, acting on the determination of the County Manager, issued a notice on 26 November 1953 to plaintiff, Mrs Hughes, of their satisfaction that the house was unfit, and could not be rendered fit for human habitation, and of the opportunity to be heard on the matter on 23 December. Following the meeting, at which plaintiff's architect testified on her behalf, the Council made a demolition order on 28 December, under section 23(3) of the 1931 Act.

In review, Judge Fawsett concluded there was only one relevant item in the evidence which the County Manager identified in his testimony to the Court as being in his possession to provide the basis for his decision to issue a notice of intention to make a demolition order (on which the Council acted). That item was a letter of 4 December from the acting Chief Medical Officer to the Staff Officer in Rathdrum. The other evidence, i.e. a County Engineer's inspection form of 21 December 1953, and a County Architect's report of 26 July 1954, obviously were not available for consideration prior to the 26 November 1953 notice of intention to make a demolition order. The Acting Chief Medical Officer's report described the house as dry with a sound roof, but noted insufficient lighting, that the back wall was damp, being four feet under ground level, and the external plaster and gutters were defective. The final evaluation was that, though some repairs had been carried out, it was not fit for human habitation, with no opinion stated as to whether the house could be made fit at reasonable expense.

The testimony of the participants in the 23 December meeting as to the substance of that meeting was conflicting. Plaintiff's architect's impression was that the inquiry was a mere formality since his efforts to discuss the particular defects and proposals to limit use of the cottage until agreement was reached on repairs were negated by an overall statement from the manager that the house was too small. The County Manager testified he was not satisfied by plaintiff's architect that the proposal as submitted would make the house habitable at a reasonable cost. The testimony of plaintiff's architect and the County Architect were in direct conflict, despite their reinspection of the house during the hearing before the Circuit Court. It was evident that the Acting County Engineer's report of 21 December, which the County Manager had in hand before issuing the final demolition order was made without inspection of the house interior, since the Engineer could not gain entry, and

Judge Fawsett noted that the report had incorrect measurements upon which the opinion was expressed that the ceiling heights were below standard. Similarly, it was reported that the ground covered the rear wall to a height of six feet and could not be easily excavated, when it actually was four feet and had been excavated after his inspection. Again, no costs of repairs necessary to put the house in adequate condition were provided. In the opinion of Judge Fawsett no private property should be demolished based on evidence of this character.

In regard to the 23 December meeting or hearing which formed the basis for the demolition order, Judge Fawsett stated that for future reference:

the holding of a statutory meeting of the character envisaged by section 23 of the Act is by no means a mere formality. . . . The Council or County Manager . . in convening and in holding such a meeting is acting not as a mere executive or administrative body but as a quasi-judicial tribunal exercising what is essentially a judicial function and as such should feel itself bound by the accepted rules of public justice . . . . I repeat these observations here for the guidance in the future of the local authority of this county when exercising its functions under the Act of 1931. (page 176)

Given Judge Fawsett's views on the purpose of the statutory meeting and his analysis of the evidence on which the order had been based, his conclusion was that the demolition order should be quashed. He did not think the County Manager had evidence before him upon which he could be satisfied that the house was not capable of being made fit for human habitation at reasonable expense. Based on his own inspection of the house, Judge Fawsett stated that he had inspected houses elsewhere with far more sanitary defects and in his opinion this house was capable of being repaired and made fit for habitation.

In addition to the question of sufficiency of evidence to support an administrative direction, there is the issue of the adequacy of evidence as it is related to the statutory purpose of the order, under the provisions of the Act delegating directing power. In *Ulster Bank Ltd v. Irish Land Commission* Supreme Court, unreported, per Henchy J., 16 December 1977, the Land Commission initiated proceedings to acquire certain lands, issuing a certificate that it was required for the purpose of resale to persons or bodies mentioned in section 31, Land Act 1923 as extended by section 30, Land Act 1950. Objectors to the acquisition appeared before the Land Commission, which disallowed the objection, and then appealed to the Appeal Tribunal. The Tribunal held that once evidence was given before the Lay Commissioner that other lands in the locality had been available for acquisition, the Land Commission were obliged to prove that it was objectors' lands, rather than any other land, which were required to satisfy the purposes of the acquisition. Since such evidence had not been given, the objection should have been allowed and the appeal was held to succeed.

On appeal to the Supreme Court, Henchy J. for the Court noted that there were two distinct sets of circumstances under which the Land Commission may acquire lands compulsorily, namely: (1) the lands are required for relief of congestion in the immediate neighbourhood, under section 32(3) of Land Act 1933, amended by section 35(1) of Land Act 1965; or (2) the lands are required for the purpose of resale to persons or bodies mentioned in section 31 of the Land Act 1923, extended by section 30 of the Land Act 1950. If the acquisition is for relief of congestion, then *Clarke v. Irish Land Commission* 1976 IR 375 applies, in which it was held that on the hearing of an objection in such cases, the onus is on the Land Commission to prove that the lands are required for the 'relief of congestion' in the 'immediate neighbourhood' in the statutory sense of those phrases and it is open to the objector to establish by cross-examination or otherwise, that such is not the case. In this regard it was held in *Cassels v. Irish Land Commision* 1963 IR 193, that the disallowance of an objection was bad because the opportunity of presenting evidence to show that the lands were not required for the relief of local congestion was denied to the objector.

However, if acquisition is for resale, *Clark v. Irish Land Commission* does not apply, since there are a multiplicity of purposes in terms of persons or bodies to whom the lands so acquired may be resold, constituting a broad grant of discretion which does not lend itself to plaintiff's argument that the Land Commission must designate in advance of acquisition the persons or bodies to whom the land will be sold. When the Lay Commissioners sit to hear an objection to acquisition which is certified for resale, they must consider: (1) whether the lands actually are required for the certified purpose, which objector may challenge through cross-examination or otherwise; and (2) whether the objector during the qualifying period (a) has not offered lands for sale, (b) has complied with residence tests and (c) has complied with the test as to production of agricultural products and provision of employment. If he has met these requirements, the objection must be allowed.

The hearing before the Lay Commissioners provided no evidence which impugned the intention of the Land Commission to acquire and apply the land for the certified purposes of resale. In addition, the Lay Commissioners found that objectors failed two of the three statutory tests for exemption from acquisiton, namely the residence requirement, and the required production of agricultural products. These findings had not been questioned in the appeal to the Supreme Court, and so that case for the objectors failed, as having been properly disallowed by the Lay Commissioners. The Commissioners' decision was upheld.

The question of whether the evidence was sufficient to support the direction made by the Minister for Posts and Telegraphs to RTE to refrain from broadcasting any matter made by or on behalf of Sinn Féin was also one of the issues raised in *The State (Lynch) v. Minister for Posts and Telegraphs and the Attorney General* 1983 ILRM 89. In addition to the claims of unconstitutionality of section 31(1) of the Broadcasting Authority Act 1960, lack of jurisdiction, and denial of fair procedure discussed above, plaintiff Lynch also argued that while the Minister may have acted in a *bona fide* manner, the reasons why the Minister acted should not have led to the banning of broadcasts by Lynch, since the content of the broadcasts was in fact harmless.

In this respect, O'Higgins C. J. summarised the evidence disclosed to the court by the Minister as his reasons for his action, including an extract from a Sinn Féin newspaper under the headlines 'By Ballot and Bullet', a report in the *Irish Times* of a statement by the president of Sinn Féin that 'we want to disestablish both States, North and South', an extract from a Provisional IRA staff report and the conviction records of Sinn Féin candidates and members of the officer board of the party.

Although these matters were not controverted by the prosecutor, he contended that his broadcast itself contained no materials which merited condemnation and was available for examination before being transmitted. However, in the view of O'Higgins C.J., this was irrelevant, since the broadcast, whatever its content:

> was intended to seek and rally support for the Sinn Féin organisation. On the basis of the information which he had, the Minister had cogent grounds for believing that Sinn Féin aimed at undermining the authority of the State. Any broadcast, therefore, which sought support for such an organisation could properly be regarded by him as being likely to promote or incite to crime or tend to undermine the State's authority .... A democratic State has a clear and binding duty to protect its citizens and its institutions from those who seek to replace law and order by force and anarchy .... it is abundantly clear that the Minister was not only justified in forming the opinion that he did form, but also, that he could not have formed any other. (pages 98-9)

In their judgments in this case, both Walsh and Henchy J.J. also held that the evidence justified the Minister's direction. In the view of Walsh J., the Minister 'put into evidence a considerable body of material which could fairly lead to the conclusion that one of the aims of the Sinn Féin Party is not merely to weaken the authority of the State but to overthrow it as it at present exists', the evidence justifying the opinion that the objectives of Sinn Féin would not be confined to constitutional methods. Again, Henchy J. held that the Minister's opinion was formed in 'good faith and justified by the facts'. An opinion to the contrary would have been perverse, since the uncontroverted evidence showed that Sinn Féin was a part of the Provisional IRA, an 'illegal terrorist organisation which by both its avowed aims and its record of criminal violence, is shown to be committed to ... the dismantling by violent and unlawful means of the organs of State established by the Constitution'. The Minister therefore was justified in his opinion that the broadcast would, as provided in section 31 of the 1960 Act, 'be likely to promote or incite to crime or would tend to undermine the authority of the State'.

Absence of Bias: Standing
The exercise of directing power may lead to controversies in which

single issues such as fair notice or sufficiency of evidence to support a direction are linked with issues as to the legal authority of the deciding officer, his possible bias and the standing of plaintiff to sue. This mixture was present in *Cassells v. Dublin Corporation* 1963 IR 193. Plaintiff had been a tenant of, and had ceased paying rent on, 5 John Street in 1942, claiming that the premises were in disrepair. In February 1951, the Dublin Corporation, under section 23(3) of the Housing (Miscellaneous Provisions) Act 1931, made a demolition order requiring that 5 John Street be vacated 30 days from the date the order became operative, the house be demolished and the site cleared within six weeks of the order, or if the house was not then vacated, the demolition must take place within six weeks of its being vacated.

A notice signed by the Assistant City Manager was served on Mrs Cassells's son-in-law, Mr Byrne, then residing in 5 John Street in January 1953, with a deadline of 10 April, and a summons on 23 April requiring Byrne to appear in the District Court to show cause why he had not left the house. Mrs Cassells then had a plenary summons issued on 9 July against the Corporation claiming a declaration that the demolition order was made in excess of jurisdiction and thus was not operative, and an injunction restraining Dublin Corporation from recovery of vacant possession. Following her death, proceedings were continued in the name of her daughter, Mrs Byrne. The High Court held that plaintiff had no interest in the proceedings as a tenant without control of the house and not the owner, and thus lacked standing to bring the proceedings. Consequently, the other issues raised were not considered.

The Supreme Court on appeal considered: (1) standing of plaintiff to sue; (2) subdelegation of power over administrative proceedings to issue the administrative order from the City Manager to the Assistant City Manager; (3) whether the notice contained a fatal defect; (4) the extent to which the Assistant City Manager should act judicially as to evidence to support the making of the order and relatedly, whether there had been bias in the decision to issue the demolition order.

Kingsmill Moore J. for the Court held that section 27(4) in the 1931 Act did not preclude a tenant whose interests were damnified by a demolition order from applying to the High Court for a declaration that the order was *ultra vires* the Act, and asking for an injunction against the local authority to stop it from proceeding under the Act, inasmuch as:

> It is one thing to conclude that the Legislature intended to exclude tenants from questioning the . . . rightness of an order . . . properly made after complying with the antecedent requisites prescribed by the statute. It is another to conclude that it is intended to exclude them from showing that the Corporation had acted *ultra vires* and that the order was . . . a legal nullity. (page 210)

As to the claim that the order was invalid *ab initio* by reason of the City Manager's subdelegation to the Assistant City Manager, Kingsmill Moore J. held that section 13(5) of the County Management Act 1940 empowered the Dublin City Manager to subdelegate all the powers which a County Manager would have to the Assistant City Manager. These include action as a local authority under Part II of the Housing of the Working Classes Act 1890 and Part II of the 1931 Act to sign notices and take all steps required by the Acts to be done by a local authority. In regard to issuing notices the Court stated that although the notices in this instance had been sent to Miss Guinness as owner of the premises after she had died, and not to the Public Trustee as her representative, this otherwise fatal defect was counteracted by the fact that the Public Trustee must have obtained the notice, since he was represented by his solicitor who appeared for him at the meeting held after notice of intent to demolish had been given.

   Plaintiff also argued that the Assistant City Manager had to be satisfied irrevocably and with finality of the facts to justify demolition prior to issue of the notice of intent to require demolition, and thus had to act 'judicially'. Plaintiff claimed that this was not done since the facts before the Assistant City Manager were insufficient for any person considering the matter judicially to be so satisfied. Kingsmill Moore J. rejected this argument, noting that section 23(1) of the 1931 Act refers to consideration of the 'condition' of the house at the subsequent meeting within 21 days, although he would agree that the Assistant City Manager was bound to approach consideration of facts 'in a judicial spirit and to be judicially satisfied.' Before directing the issue of the notice he must have:

either an official representation, a report from one of his officers, or other information, upon which he may reasonably . . . be satisfied that the state of the house is such as to make it probable that a demolition order should be made; and at the subsequent meeting he must be judicially satisfied that a demolition order should be made . . . (page 216)

In this regard, Kingsmill Moore J. noted correspondence and interviews which showed that the Dublin Housing Association Ltd was pressing Dublin Corporation to demolish 5 John Street, which was blocking a scheme for development and rebuilding of the surrounding area, and that the Corporation was anxious to further a scheme to improve housing in the neighbourhood. However, although cases do come before a person acting in a judicial capacity in which that person may have a predisposition to decide in a certain way, he is expected to overcome that leaning and decide on the facts before him. The Assistant City Manager had before him data from an advisory board composed of officials from the Dangerous Buildings Department, Health Department, City Engineers Department and Housing Department that owing to the shoring undertaken by the Corporation, the premises were no longer dangerous. At the same time, that advisory board, based on inspection of the house during the period in question, had also certified over the signatures of all five department officials that the premises were unfit for human habitation and not capable of being rendered fit at a reasonable expense. The board had also recommended service of notice under section 23 of the Housing Act 1931 providing for such notice when insanitary conditions are found to be of such a nature as to justify service of the notice.

This certification in the view of Kingsmill Moore J. was all that was necessary to enable the Assistant City Manager to consider the matter in a judicial spirit and arrive at the conclusion that the statutory conditions existed for serving the notice. Moreover, at the meeting called by the notice, evidence was given as to the dilapidation of the house, and no objection was made to the demolition order by the solicitor appearing for the Public Trustee, or anyone on whom the notice was served, and no offer was made to put the house into repair. Further, a report was submitted from the Deputy City Medical Officer who declined to find the house to be fit for human habitation on sanitary grounds, and the occupying tenant had refused to pay rent on the ground that the house was out of repair. This evidence provided an ample basis for the Assistant City Manager's decision and the appeal was dismissed.

The standing of the prosecutor Lynch to raise the issue of the constitutionality of section 31, Broadcasting Authority Act 1960 was also one of the questions raised in *The State (Lynch) v. Minister for Posts and Telegraphs and the Attorney General* 1983 ILRM 89, discussed above in respect of other issues in the exercise of directing power. It was the argument of the Minister's counsel that the prosecutor lacked standing since no right of his was interfered with by the Minister's order, he was not a person aggrieved by the order and should not be heard to challenge its validity. While article 40 of the Constitution contains a guarantee of freedom of speech it does not guarantee access by any individual citizen to the press, radio or television, thus prohibition of prosecutor's broadcast did not breach any constitutional right. Only Radio Telefís Éireann is entitled to question section 31 of the 1960 Act.

In response to this claim, O'Higgins C.J. held that although the order was directed to RTE and not to Lynch or his party, and neither Lynch nor his party had any right of access to RTE to make election broadcasts, they nevertheless were given such access by RTE and would have been entitled to act on the invitation made to them were it not for the Minister's order. RTE did not withdraw the invitation, rather, it was rendered inoperable by the Minister's action, thus depriving Lynch and his party of a benefit lawfully accorded to them in the first instance, and they were entitled to complain if this deprivation were unlawful. Consequently Lynch had sufficient standing to complain that section 31 of the 1960 Act was invalid in regard to provisions of the Constitution. Following a review of judicial precedent, including *Regina (Bridgman) v. Drury* (1894) 2 IR 489, *Transport Salaried Staffs Association v. CIE* 1965 IR 180, and *Cahill v. Sutton* 1980 IR 269 to emphasise the point that the circumstances of a case are the determining factor in whether a person can show sufficient interest to have standing, Walsh J., held that whether the RTE invitation to Lynch was a privilege or a right was immaterial. The point was that the invitation was never revoked by RTE, and if the Minister had revoked his order, the broadcast would have taken place. Consequently Lynch and his party suffered a loss, i.e. access to television in an election campaign, and were affected in a material way, and thus had sufficient interest to pursue the proceedings.

Findings as Basis for Direction

A further procedural requirement for issuing an administrative direction is that following a hearing the administrative agency should make findings to enable the reviewing court and the parties involved to understand the basis for its decision and consequent direction. The requirement of a finding was at issue in *The State (Crowley) v Irish Land Commission and Others* 1951 IR 250. The Land Commission published a notice in *Iris Oifigiúil* stating that the Land Commission intended to resume the lands owned by Mr Crowley for the purpose of relieving congestion under section 73 (4), Land Act 1923, and for resale to any of the bodies specified in section 31(1) of that Act, as amended by section 33(1) of the Land Act 1933, unless a petition were submitted within one month asking that the holding not be resumed without further inquiry. Crowley presented such a petition on the grounds that he was producing an adequate amount of agricultural products and providing an adequate amount of employment on the said holding and that there was no congestion in the locality in which the holding was situated. Crowley and his valuer gave evidence before the Lay Commissioners who reserved judgment at the conclusion of the hearing of Crowley's petition. On the day they delivered their judgment in written form, they stated that 'The Commissioners being of opinion, for the reasons stated in their written judgment that the said petition has not been sustained, it is ordered that the petition be and the same is hereby refused' (page 201).

Crowley then obtained conditional orders of certiorari from the High Court to quash the Commission's orders and written decision, in response to which the Lay Commissioners filed affidavits to show cause against the conditional orders. The matter thereupon came before the High Court and Maguire J. by orders disallowed the cause shown and made absolute the conditional orders, and appeals were taken by the Land Commission against the orders of Maguire J. to the Supreme Court.

O'Byrne J., for the Supreme Court, held that on the basis of allegations made in Crowley's petition and objection, a determination by the Lay Commissioners was required by section 39(6), Land Act 1939, and section 32(3), Land Act 1933. However, in

regard to those allegations, the only relevant finding made by the
Lay Commissioners was that 'admittedly this large area, including
the lands the subject of these proceedings, which it is to be noted,
are some ten miles from the home farm at Wallistown, is well
worked by the owner and employment is being afforded.' In his
view, this finding of the Lay Commissioners fell short of actually
determining whether or not they were satisfied that the lands were
producing agricultural products and providing an adequate amount
of employment. The finding was not in favour of Crowley, but it
certainly was not a finding against him, as the Land Commission
had claimed. An effort by the Land Commission to supplement its
orders and written judgment with a reference to a sworn affidavit by
the Lay Commissioners must be rejected, since their determination
appears in, and must be gathered from, their formal order. The
affidavit cannot be used to add to, explain or contradict the written
order.

The Lay Commissioners thus did not actually determine whether
the lands were producing an adequate amount of agricultural
products and providing an adequate amount of employment, which
was the basis Crowley had for stopping the acquisition, assuming
he could satisfy the Commissioners such was the case. In respect of
the relief to which Crowley was entitled, O'Byrne J. held that
the Lay Commissioners were not exercising merely executive or
administrative functions. Rather, the petition and objection listed
for hearing before the Lay Commissioners required them to act
judicially, i.e. to hear, consider, and determine the factual aspects
of allegations made by plaintiff, because their decisions on the facts
were final and affected Crowley's rights. They thus were subject to
control by certiorari, and since the Lay Commissioners did not
make these determinations, but nevertheless refused the petition
and disallowed the objection, they had exceeded their jurisdiction.
This refusal and disallowance was 'dependent upon a finding
against the petitioner on the question of production and employment, and their orders should, in my opinion, be brought up for
the purpose of being quashed'.

Judicial Role in Review and Enforcement

If the party to whom the direction is issued resists compliance, the
final step in directing power is for the agency to request a judicial

order in support of the administrative direction. Alternatively, the party may appeal to the courts against the direction. An example of the role of the court when there is a refusal to comply is *Bray Urban District Council v. Bray Greyhound Racing Association Ltd* 84 ILTR 164. Bray UDC, acting as planning authority for the area, issued an order prohibiting any further construction of a greyhound racing track at Bray, followed by a further declaration that any violation of this prohibition would be unlawful. Upon continuation of construction of the track by the Bray Greyhound Racing Association, the Council resorted to court action which resulted in a case being stated for the opinion of the Supreme Court as to whether the UDC as planning authority, being a corporate body was authorised in law to bring a prosecution for violation of a special prohibition which it had made. The Supreme Court held that the planning authority indeed was authorised by law to prosecute for non-compliance with its special prohibition.

The necessity for an administrative agency to have resort to the courts for enforcement is obvious from the *Bray* case; otherwise, the issuing of an administrative direction by the agency could become pointless if the recipient of the order could refuse compliance with impunity. However, an agency's request for judicial enforcement, or a private party's request for judicial review as to the validity of the direction of the agency, raises the question of the role of the courts in reviewing administrative directions in response to such requests. Insight into that role has been provided in judicial decisions discussed above in which administrative orders either were affirmed or were held to be *ultra vires* the statute if the content of the order did not relate to the statutory purpose, or did not comply with concepts of natural or constitutional justice. However, more explicit discussion directed to the question of the role of the courts and the scope of their review of administrative directions was provided by the *State (McGuinness) v. Maguire* 1967 IR 348, also referred to above as an illustration of an *ultra vires* order. In the course of arriving at the final decision that the local authority could order demolition of a dangerous structure but not require the provision of supports to adjoining buildings, Ó Dálaigh C.J. also considered another contention of the respondents. Their claim was that prosecutrix's objection to providing lateral supports to adjoining buildings had been considered and adjudicated by the Circuit Court, and since this adjudication was within the Circuit

Court's jurisdiction, certiorari did not lie. On review of this claim, which the High Court had overruled, Ó Dálaigh C.J. held that the governing words were in section 3(5) of the Local Government (Sanitary Services) Act 1964, providing:

(5) Where a person upon whom a notice under subsection (1) of this section in relation to a dangerous structure has been served does not comply with the terms of the notice, the District Court may, on the application of the sanitary authority by whom the notice was given, by order–

(a) (i) direct the person to carry out, within such time as the Court may consider reasonable and may specify in the order and in accordance with the terms of the notice, the works specified in the notice and authorise the sanitary authority to carry out the works aforesaid if the person does not comply with the provisions of the order, or

(ii) authorise the sanitary authority to carry out the works specified in the notice, and

(b) prohibit the use of the structure or any part of it or prohibit the use of the structure or any part of it for such purpose or purposes as may be specified in the order.

(6) Where a person does not comply with an order of the District Court under subsection (5) of this section, he shall be guilty of an offence and shall be liable on summary conviction to a fine not exceeding one hundred pounds.

In the view of Ó Dálaigh C.J., the determining words of these provisions were that the District Court 'may be order direct . . . or authorise . . . and prohibit' which, as he interpreted them, did not indicate that the Court could refuse to make the order applied for by the administrative agency. Rather, the wording of section 3(5):

is uncompromising in its insistence that, except for the time modification which is necessary because the original time limit has expired, the court's order must be in respect of the works specified in the notice, and that they must be carried out in accordance with the terms of that notice. The use of the term 'may' is explicable by the choice afforded to the court under the powers conferred by para. (a) of sub-sect. 5. The court can in no way alter or modify the works directed . . . or the conditions under which they are to be carried out, or review the opinion of the sanitary authority as to the appropriateness of the works required . . . or enter on the question of whether the structure is, or is not a dangerous structure.

An owner brought before the court by the sanitary authority can therefore ask for nothing except that he should be allowed another chance to carry out the works specified . . . a person served with a notice could . . . object that he was not the owner; and an owner could submit that the requirements of the notice were in excess of the powers conferred by the Act. The District Justice would have to inquire into both these matters. In the latter instance, if he came to the conclusion that the point was well taken, the proper course for him would be to decline to make any order; he could not, however, amend the notice to bring it within the powers conferred by the Act.

The objection raised by the prosecutrix was in fact that the notice exceeded the powers conferred by the Act . . . . The ruling of the District Court thereon, and the affirmation by the Circuit Court on appeal are therefore clearly reviewable by certiorari. (pages 359-60)

The Supreme Court thus made the role of the Court quite clear, given the terms of the Local Government (Sanitary Services) Act 1964. The Court, on application by the administrative agency for a judicial order to enforce an administrative direction, is not to substitute judgment on facts as to degree of danger in the structure or the wisdom of the agency's remedy, or to exercise discretion in modifying the order. The Court's function does include, however, review of the substance of the order as to whether it is within the authority of the governing statute, and if it is not, to hold the entire order *ultra vires* and void. In this last respect, it should be noted that a previous case, *The State (Moloney) v. Minister for Industry and Commerce and New Ireland Assurance Co. Ltd* 1945 IR 253, indicated that there may be circumstances in which a particular portion of an administrative directive which is *ultra vires* might be held to be

separable so that the entire direction is not voided. Mrs Moloney
sought to have quashed an order made by the Minister for Industry
and Commerce under the Insurance Act 1936, following an inquiry
by the Minister on a claim by the insurance company that there
was a breach of warranty invalidating two life insurance policies on
which Mrs Moloney was seeking payment. The Minister made an
award that a return of premiums paid should be made under section
72 of the 1936 Act, 'subject to the deduction of the costs and
expenses of the Company' in assessing the amounts to be paid. Mrs
Moloney applied for an order quashing the Minister's direction on
the grounds that the Minister lacked jurisdiction to order payment
of costs or deduct costs from sums paid as premiums, and also was
ultra vires because the insurance company in fact was accusing her
of fraud or misrepresentation. On appeal from the High Court,
which had allowed the cause shown against a conditional order of
certiorari, the Supreme Court, per Murnaghan J., held that the
Court was not concerned with the second of the two grounds. The
sole question was whether the Minister had jurisdiction to order
deduction and payment of costs, since under the statute, such
payment can be ordered only where the person was represented or
appeared at the inquiry, and Mrs Moloney and her solicitor had
refused to attend the Minister's inquiry on the ground it was held
in excess of jurisdiction.

In resolving the question, Murnaghan J. considered whether the
award was really an award of costs. As he analysed the situation:

> Firstly, the award measures the costs, and then directs taxation
> at the request of either party: if there were a taxation, what
> would be taxed except the Company's costs of the Inquiry?
> Secondly, the award awards witnesses' expenses and repay-
> ment of a lodgment fee. In substance the Minister inflicted on
> the appellant the payment of a sum for costs and expenses
> which he had no authority to impose. (page 263)

However, this *ultra vires* action did not invalidate the Minister's
order as a whole. That part of the order pertaining to payment of
costs and expenses was severable, and only that part of the order
should be quashed.

Notes to Chapter 9

1. This practice was criticised in the *Report of the Committee on Ministers' Powers,* CMD. 4060 (1932) [Donoughmore Report]. The report stated that 'the expressions "regulation", "rule" and "order" should not be used indiscriminately in statutes' and urged that 'regulation' and 'rule' be used to denote the instruments for the power of a minister to make substantive law and procedural law respectively, while the term 'order' be used to denote both the instrument for the exercise of executive power and the power to take judicial and quasi-judicial decisions (page 64).
2. See Donaldson, 'Some Comparative Aspects of Irish Law' 258-69; see also 'Eighty Years of the Irish Land Commission', 96 *Irish Law Times and Solicitor's Journal* Part 1, 245-6, 15 September 1962 and Part 2, 251-2, 22 September 1962.
3. See Ercus Stewart, 'Current Trends in Employment Legislation', *Personnel and Industrial Relations Directory, 1978* 300-313 for a succinct analysis of the scope of legislation and the reasons for its enactment.
4. See 1984 *Administration Yearbook and Diary* 47-8 for summary of Employment Equality Agency functions related to Employment Equality Act 1977 and Anti-Discrimination (Pay) Act 1974.

10 Availability and Scope of Judicial Review

A major concern reflected in the statutes and judicial decisions pertaining to administrative discretionary power discussed in preceding chapters has been the means of legislative and judicial control to maintain a balance between individual rights and the public interest. In addition to judicial review of administrative determinations for their compliance with constitutional, statutory and natural justice standards, there are other previously noted means for holding administrative agencies accountable. These include legislative review of regulations and administrative appellate review by ministers and appeals boards. Further means of oversight yet to be considered include a central administrative court, an administrative procedures Act, a central administrative oversight authority such as a commissioner for administrative justice, and an ombudsman who was appointed in 1984 under the Ombudsman Act 1980 (see chapter 11).

However, the judiciary has been and will be the principal institution to exercise direct and final control to keep administrative agencies in compliance with the statutes granting them their authority and with concepts of natural and constitutional justice. Consequently, judicial concepts or doctrines concerning the availability of judicial review, and the scope of that review, are critical to individuals or organisations seeking to protect their legal rights, and to administrators desiring judicial approval and enforcement of their determinations. Such concepts are also important in determining the relative roles of the courts, the legislature and the administration in the operation of administrative law.

Doctrines of Availability of Review: Comparative Aspects

Statutes often specify the availability and scope of judicial review of administrative determinations but such matters are ultimately determined by the courts applying judicial doctrines or concepts which they have developed in defining their roles and functions in maintaining the rule of law. These doctrines have been developed extensively in the United States and categorised as 'finality of

420

administrative determinations', 'standing to secure review', 'primary jurisdiction', 'exhaustion of administrative remedies' and 'ripeness for review'. Finality of administrative determinations and standing to secure review (*locus standi* in England and Ireland) play an important part in English law, but not the doctrines of primary jurisdiction, exhaustion of administrative remedies or ripeness for review. All of these doctrines, save that of primary jurisdiction, are applied in Irish administrative law. A consideration of the meaning of these doctrines in the United States, with a comparative reference to English doctrines, facilitates an appreciation of their application in Ireland.

A contributing factor in the development of the doctrines of availability of judicial review in the United States is the constitutional separation of powers, resulting in self-imposed limitations on judicial review established by the American courts based on the underlying premise that courts should not grant review unless an actual 'case or controversy' is before them. The Supreme Court has enunciated criteria for an actual case or controversy meriting review in such key decisions as *Muskrat v. the United States* 219 US 346 (1911) and *Nashville, Chattanooga and St Louis Railroad v. Wallace* 288 US 249 (1933). These include the existence of adverse parties whose claims have been submitted to the courts in regard to legal interests requiring the protection or enforcement of rights, or the prevention, redress or punishment of wrongs. Such criteria are distinguished from a friendly or collusive suit to pose an agreed-upon or hypothetical set of facts and issues so as to secure the opinion of the court on the interpretation or validity of a statute, as discussed in *Lord v. Veazie* 8 How. 249 (1850) and *United States v. Johnson* 318 US 302 (1943).

The doctrine of finality of administrative determinations deals with the extent to which the legislature can preclude judicial review by declaring in a statute that certain administrative determinations are final and conclusive. For example, the US Supreme Court has held that the courts should not review an administrative inquiry and recommendations which had been made by the Civil Aeronautics Board leading to a presidential decision to award an international air route or certain discretionary determinations of the Secretary of the Interior or the Administrator of the Veterans Administration. (See *Chicago and Southern Airlines Inc. v. Waterman Steamship Corp.* 333 US 103 (1948), *Ferry v. Udall* 336 F. 2d 706 (9th Cir.) 1964, cert.

denied 381 US 904 (1965), and *Kletschka v. Driver* 411 F. 2d (2nd
Cir. 1969) respectively.) However, the tendency of American courts
is to presume reviewability in the absence of 'clear and convincing
evidence of a . . . legislative intent' to limit access to judicial review
(*Abbott*, page 141), in accordance with sections 701-702 of the
Administrative Procedures Act that agency action is subject to
judicial review except where there is a statutory prohibition or
agency action is committed to agency discretion by law. This is
illustrated by *Abbott Laboratories v. Gardner* 387 US 136 (1967) and
Associated Data Processing Service Organization v. Camp 397 US 150
(1970).

The doctrine of standing to secure review or *locus standi* pertains
to criteria upon which the courts determine whether an individual
or organisation has the kind and sufficiency of legal interest to
challenge governmental action in the courts. The earlier restrictive
views of the American courts were that adverse economic impact
of a governmental corporation's competition on private enterprise,
or the interest of a taxpayer in an allegedly unconstitutional use of
taxes, did not constitute standing to sue in *Tennessee Electric Power
Co. v. TVA* 306 US 118 (1939) and *Frothingham v. Mellon* 262 US 447
(1923) respectively. These views have been liberalised considerably
in more recent years. In *Associated Industries* v. *Ickes* 134 F. 2d 694
(2nd Cir.) dismissed as moot (i.e. already decided) 320 US 707
(1943), the Court held that an organisation of industry members
had standing to appeal a determination of minimum prices by the
Bituminous Coal Commission on the ground that the organisation
helped to represent the public interest in a role comparable to that
of a 'private attorney general'. Standing was also given to a private
firm engaged in data processing services, based on its claim of
adverse economic competitive effect resulting from a ruling of the
Comptroller of the Currency that national banks could give data
processing services to other banks and bank customers, in *Association
of Data Processing Service Organisations Inc. v. Camp* 397 US 150 (1970).
A taxpayer was granted standing to sue, in part since a first
amendment right was also involved, in *Flast v. Cohen* 392 US 83
(1968).

The concept of primary jurisdiction applies when a claim is made
over which the courts and the administrative agency both have
jurisdiction, but issues are involved which have been allocated to
the particular competence of the administrative body by the statute.

In such instances, the judicial consideration is normally suspended until the administrative body has made its determination, according to *United States v. Western Pacific Railroad Co.* 352 US 59 (1956), although there may be instances in which the individual may justify direct resort to the courts without reference to the administrative agency or tribunal, as in *Nader v. Allegheny Airlines Inc.* 426 US 290 (1976).

On the other hand, the concept of exhaustion of administrative remedies applies where a claim by a party is cognisable in the first instance only by the administrative agency, and usually requires the party to follow those remedies available under the agency's process prior to requesting the courts for review, as exemplified by the leading case of *Meyers v. Bethlehem Shipbuilding Corporation* 303 US 41 (1938). Exceptions have been made by the courts to requiring exhaustion of administrative remedies if it is demonstrated that the agency lacks jurisdiction, that the statute involved is unconstitutional, or the administrative remedies are inadequate, according to *Lone Star Cement Corporation v. FTC* 339 F. 2d 505 (9th Cir.) 1964; *PUC of California v. US* 355 US 534 (1958) and *McNeese v. Board of Education* 373 US 668 (1963) respectively.

Primary jurisdiction and exhaustion of administrative remedies are both concerned with whether the administrative agency or the courts first take jurisdiction of a case, particularly since the agency's determination may satisfy the party and obviate the need for appeal to the courts, or at least, its initial consideration of the claim will provide agency fact-finding and expertise to enrich the court's understanding on review. In contrast, ripeness for review is concerned with the broader issue of when a controversy is far enough advanced to have a present, or imminent, adverse effect on a legal interest which merits judicial consideration, and for which the available judicial remedy is appropriate and meaningful in resolving the conflict. The leading case expounding in depth the precedents and concepts of ripeness is *Abbot Laboratories Inc. v. Gardner* 387 US 136 (1967). The Supreme Court held that the situation was ripe in this case for judicial review of a challenge from the drug industry against certain rules which the Food and Drug Administration had adopted, but had not yet taken action to enforce, in regard to major changes required in the contents of labels on drug products. In essence, the majority of the Court held that the adoption of the rules in and of itself had sufficient impact on the plaintiff drug firms

to merit review and determination of the issue in law as to whether
the rules were *ultra vires* the Act. The Food and Drug Administration
position and the dissenting opinion argued that granting review of
the rules in the absence of any action to apply them would open
the door to future challenges of agency rule-making prior to the
raising of the kind of issues and knowledge to be gained from
controversies which involved enforcement of the rules.

In respect of the development and application of these doctrines of
availability of review in Britain, Wade's analysis of court judgments
involving administrative determinations made under statutes granting finality through 'no certiorari', 'as if enacted' or 'shall not be
questioned' clauses shows that the courts have not permitted such
legislation to impede judicial review and application of remedies to
maintain the rule of law. This is epitomised in the leading case of
Anisminic Ltd v. Foreign Compensation Commission (1969) 2 AC 147 in
which the House of Lords held that an absolute 'ouster clause'
(providing that a determination of the Commission shall not be
questioned in any legal proceeding) does not protect a determination
which was made outside jurisdiction, and that the determination of
the Commission in this case was *ultra vires*. *Anisminic*, and subsequent
cases, in Wade's view apply a presumption that 'is tantamount to
saying that judicial control is a constitutional fundamental which
even the sovereign Parliament cannot abolish, at least without some
special and exceptional form of words'.[1]

The doctrine of standing, or *locus standi* as perceived by Schwartz
and Wade, is inherent to all legal systems including that of Britain,
but unlike the United States, where it can be analysed as a single
topic, in Britain it has been made up of various rules applying to
different remedies and procedures. Despite their technicalities, the
effects of certain rules on standing such as those pertaining to relator
action, to obtain an injunction, and the prerogative remedies of
certiorari and prohibition, have been liberal.[2] However, as Wade
has noted recently, 'The law about standing is at present [1982] in
a transitional stage which makes it difficult to expound'. The reason
for this is that the different rules on standing for different remedies
have been affected by an amendment of order 53 of the Rules of the
Supreme Court (SI 1977, No. 155). As Wade states:

> The new Order first provided that an application for an order
> of mandamus, prohibition or certiorari . . . 'shall be made by

way of an application for judicial review'. It added that an application for a declaration or an injunction 'may be made' in the same way, and may be granted if the court considers that it would be just and convenient, having regard to the matters in respect of which mandamus, prohibition or certiorari may lie, to the persons and bodies against whom they may lie, and to all the circumstances of the case . . . . All of the remedies mentioned are then made interchangeable by being made available 'as an alternative or in addition' to any of them.[3]

Although it would be premature, in Wade's opinion, 'to consign to oblivion' the rules previously distinguishing between the various remedies, his analysis of the House of Lords decision in *R. v. Inland Revenue Commissioners ex. p. National Federation of Self-Employed and Small Businesses Ltd* (1982) A.C. 617 leads him to conclude that 'The House of Lords has made it clear that Order 53 signalises a rationalising and simplifying of the tangle of different rules which used to complicate the subject of remedies'.[4] Granted that not all of the law lords agreed that the technical rules could be forgotten and that there were differences among them as to the discretion of the Court, the 'House of Lords is clearly now determined to prevent technicalities from impeding judicial review so as to protect illegalities and derelictions committed by public authorities'.[5]

Although doctrines pertaining to finality of administrative determinations and standing to sue or *locus standi* are of importance in both British and American administrative law, the other American doctrines in respect of availability of review are not, according to Schwartz and Wade:

> The American doctrines of primary jurisdiction, ripeness for review, and exhaustion of administrative remedies play little or no part in British law, thereby saving it a good deal of complexity and confusion. The main reason for this is that the British law is squarely founded on the doctrine of *ultra vires*, i.e. jurisdiction, and on this basis the function of the courts is more clear-cut than is that of the American Courts, with their preoccupation over the constitutional meaning of 'case or controversy' and their doubts about their relationship with administrative agencies. An English judge approaches a challenged administrative act on the footing that it is either lawful

or unlawful, *intra vires* or *ultra vires*. In the former case he has no concern with it. In the latter he will quash it or declare it void.

. . . . It follows that there is no need to discuss whether judicial review is 'available' at common law. It is always available for that is what is meant by the rule of law. The only possible question is whether the inherent right to it has been taken away or limited by statute.[6]

Since contrasting constitutional factors contribute to the differences in doctrines of availability of judicial review which are applied in Britain and the United States, it is to be expected that constitutional factors in Ireland would also affect concepts of availability of review in Ireland. The contrast between the Irish and British constitutional factors influencing availability and scope of judicial review has been expressed cogently by Donal Barrington, then Senior Counsel and now judge of the High Court, in his illuminating article on 'Private Property under the Irish Constitution' in which he states:

If the Constitution protects each citizen's natural right to his property and if the High Court has full original jurisdiction to determine 'all matters or questions whether of law or fact', and if, moreover, it is pledged to defend and vindicate the citizen's property rights, this may have very far-reaching effects in the whole sphere of administrative law.[7]

He notes that Parliament may allocate certain disputes to the courts, and other disputes to administrative tribunals concerned with implementing parliamentary policy. In the latter case, the concern of British courts is with whether the tribunals comply with the law enacted by Parliament and whether they preserve basic standards of fairness but not with whether the policy itself is just or unjust. No legal wrong is done to the individual deprived of property by an administrative tribunal under the theory of legal positivism, since all rights are derived from Parliament and what Parliament has given Parliament can take away. However:

The question is whether this system and all the legal learning derived from it relating to justiciable and non-justiciable disputes can be reconciled with a Constitution [i.e. the Irish Constitution] which guarantees natural rights, subordinates social policy to social justice and appears to make the Supreme Court the final arbiter of how the demands of individual right can be reconciled with those of social justice?[8]

The Irish courts, Barrington J. states, have held in the past that as long as the Oireachtas respected the separation of powers in the Irish Constitution, the British pattern in regard to justiciable issues concerning administrative tribunals could be followed, as in *Fisher v. Irish Land Commission* 1948 IR 3 and *Foley v. Irish Land Commission* 1952 IR 118. However:

> if, in fact, the rights protected by the Irish Constitution are natural rights, the philosophies underlying the Irish and British systems are logically irreconcilable. It is not that the Irish system does not allow very considerable scope for the operation of social policy. Article 43 of the Constitution, with its reference to the exigencies of the common good, clearly does. The difficulty appears to arise from the duty placed on the courts to defend both individual right and social justice. It is, therefore, arguable that any dispute in which either of these issues is raised is a justiciable dispute and that courts pledged to defend property and other individual rights as far as possible may find it difficult to opt out and say that a particular dispute is not 'justiciable'.[9]

Availability of Judicial Review in Ireland

The analysis of Barrington J. of the implications of constitutional factors in Ireland would appear to be borne out by Irish judicial decisions in respect of the availability of judicial review. These decisions reflect English law, modified by Ireland's written constitutional provisions and the perspectives of the Irish judiciary in regard to certain aspects of the role of the courts which are more characteristic of the American legal system.

Finality of Administrative Determinations
In *Fisher v. Irish Land Commission and Attorney General* 1948 IR 3, the constitutionality of a statute delegating finality to an administrative agency's determinations was upheld on a basis reflecting the British view concerning justiciable issues. Plaintiff, a yearly tenant of an extensive holding of land vested in the Land Commission, appealed

from the Commission's action to resume ownership of the entire holding for the stated reason of relieving congestion and providing land for resale to authorised buyers. The procedures followed by the Land Commission were governed by section 39(2) of the Land Act 1939, which, as outlined in the judgment of the Court, are as follows:

> 1, notice of the Land Commission's intention to apply for leave to resume; 2, a petition to the Land Commission (if the occupier so elects) against resumption without further inquiry; 3, consideration of the petition and all questions arising under it by Lay Commissioners, whose decision is final, subject to appeal to the Appeal Tribunal on a question of law; 4, in the absence of a petition or on its refusal, a certificate by the Lay Commissioners that the Land Commission requires the holding for purposes mentioned in sub-s. 1; 5, an order of the Appeal Tribunal for resumption on receipt of the certificate, which is conclusive; and 6, ascertainment of the resumption price. . . .
> (page 9)

The Commission had given notice of its intention to apply for leave to resume land; the petition of plaintiff to the Land Commission for further inquiry before resumption was heard and rejected, and soon after the Commission notified plaintiff it intended to apply to the Appeal Tribunal for leave to resume the holding, at which point plaintiff brought action in court claiming declarations against the Commission and the injunction to restrain its application.

Plaintiff argued that this procedure was repugnant to the Constitution because it assigns to laypersons the final determination of a justiciable controversy, namely the judicial question as to title in property in land. Relatedly, the right to appeal to the Appeal Tribunal was illusory since the plaintiff had no access to the evidence on which the Lay Commissioners reached their conclusions after hearing a petition. He thus had no way to determine the points of law which might be open to argument if he knew of the evidence.

Gavan Duffy J. held that the legislature had decided that the public interest demanded more equitable distribution of certain estates, even to the point of total expropriation. Only public policy could justify such interference with property rights, which the courts of law were not suited to weigh and determine. By choosing the

Land Commission to appraise the claim of the public interest against the claim of existing proprietors or tenants, the Oireachtas clearly indicated that the measures involved were extra-judicial in scope. The power given the Land Commission is basically legislative or, if not, administrative; its primary function is to make policy decisions, not to dispense justice, and in resolving issues between individuals and the public 'it was not to adjudicate upon any *lis inter partes'*. The Commission was not determining a conflict of legal rights, consequently its decision, if kept within its statutory jurisdiction, would involve no legal wrong. Even though an honest decision is 'an injustice in fact, the proprietor, failing to get the decision reconsidered . . . suffers only a *"damnum sine injuria"*. A similar mishap may befall a man even in a court of law'. Since article 43 of the Constitution subjects private ownership to the claims of social justice, but does not allocate public policy especially to the judiciary, the power conferred in this instance may be vested by the legislature wherever it thinks proper, i.e. in the Land Commission. As to the related complaint concerning the statutory remedy of appeal to the Appeal Tribunal on questions of law, Gavan Duffy J. held that since the appeal does not originate in a quasi-judicial proceeding, there can be no appeal from the Land Commission as having made a decision wrong in law. There is no *lis* to warrant a claim to discovery from an opponent and thus no right of access to the agency file.

The Supreme Court, per Maguire C.J., confirmed the decision of Gavan Duffy J., stating that given the impracticality of the Oireachtas expropriating land by statutory specification, the power to expropriate was delegated to the Land Commission. In regard to the Land Commission procedures specified in the Act:

> we are of the opinion that all the steps contemplated by sub-s. 2 are . . . of a purely administrative character . . . the subsection does not . . . intend the determination of any question of legal right . . . . In operating the machinery set up by sub-s. 2, the Lay Commissioners and the Appeal Tribunal are . . . bound to act judicially . . . but it does not follow . . . that they are administering justice or exercising judicial power. (pages 25-6)

Since the determination of matters committed under section 39(2)

to the Lay Commissioners is an administrative process, the maintenance of the Appeal Tribunal to hear appeals on questions of law is
not inconsistent with the clear intent of section 39(1), and consequently the section is not repugnant to the Constitution.

It was this determination which Donal Barrington (now Barrington J.) criticised, since as he stated in his article:

> it seems difficult to see how the High Court could be fulfilling
> its constitutional duty if, once being put on notice of an
> 'injustice in fact', it refused to interfere to vindicate the rights
> of the party oppressed. Likewise, it is difficult to see how the
> Oireachtas may properly exclude from the jurisdiction of the
> High Court any dispute which may involve a consideration of
> the question of whether an injustice has or has not been
> committed.[10]

In view of the decision in *Fisher*, the primary basis for contesting
an adverse decision by an administrative agency when the Oireachtas has given finality to decisions of the agency, is that the
agency has acted *ultra vires* the statute, especially when the administrators have not complied with statutory procedures with consequent denial of natural justice. In *The State (Horgan) v. Exported Live
Stock Insurance Board* 1943 IR 581 (discussed in detail in chapter 5),
prosecutor made a claim for loss of cattle injured in transit from Irish
ports to Great Britain under the Exported Livestock (Insurance) Act
1940. That Act required a committee of assessors to investigate and
determine whether a claimant is entitled to compensation, and to
fix the amount to be granted by a Board administering a fund for
that purpose. Section 2(4) of the Act provides that the Committee's
determinations in this regard are 'final and conclusive'.

Given the statutory provision for finality of administrative determinations, Maguire P. stated that the Court 'must be very wary
therefore of interfering with its [the committee's] decisions on the
ground that the ordinary rules which regulate investigations in a
Court of law are not obeyed' (page 600). However, the failure of
the Committee to investigate the claims, their deferral of consideration of the claim until they could discuss it with the Board (whose
members, as Overend J. stated in his concurrence, were the persons
most interested in opposing compensation), and their failure to call
the prosecutor before them to produce evidence in support of his

claim, all constituted 'a most improper proceeding' (page 600). Maguire P. held that the committee must act judicially and have regard to the essential requirements of justice, and, 'there is, to my mind, more than reasonable suspicion that justice does not seem to have been done' (page 601). The committee had rejected the claim 'not from anything which appeared in the claim or the supporting documents, but by reason of a suspicion formed in the minds of the Committee and apparently strengthened by the views of members of the Board to which they listened that the claim was fraudulent' (page 602). The High Court therefore quashed the committee report and directed the administrative agency to reconsider prosecutor's claim in accordance with procedures under both the statute and natural justice.

The concepts present in *Horgan* were also applied in *The State (McCarthy) v. O'Donnell and Minister for Defence* 1945 IR 126 (chapter 5). The Military Services Pensions Act 1934, section 9, provides that the findings of the referee's report as to whether an applicant for a pension is entitled under the Act are 'final and conclusive and binding on all persons and tribunals', and confers extensive adjudicatory powers upon the referee. In this instance, the referee's failure to sit with an advisory committee when considering McCarthy's application, as required by the 1934 Act, and his delegation to a subordinate civil servant of the referee's statutory function of examining the applicant under oath, constituted actions *ultra vires* the procedural requirements specified in the Act, and thus were held invalid by the Court, despite the statutory provision for finality of determinations.

An *ultra vires* action may involve a substantive rather than procedural question, as in *Corporation of Waterford v. Murphy* 1920, 2 IR 165 (chapter 6). A provision of the Waterford Corporation Bridge Act 1906 (6 Eds 7, c. 76) which empowered the Corporation 'to alter bye-laws, rules and regulations with regard to the time and mode of vessels passing through the existing bridge', stated that 'printed copy of such bye-laws, rules and regulations . . . signed by an Assistant Secretary of the Board of Trade, shall be conclusive evidence of the validity of such bye-laws, rules . . . in any . . . prosecution under the same for any purpose'. This provision for finality did not deter the court from holding that a bye-law adopted by the Corporation which would have imposed a toll was *ultra vires* the Act, given the Court's interpretation that the intent of the Act was that the bridge should be toll free.

Another issue of finality is whether the legislature may give finality to administrative determinations on a question of law, which normally is decided by the courts accompanied by appropriate judicial procedure. In *Murren v. Brennan* 1942 IR 466, plaintiff, a homeless, elderly agricultural labourer, requested and was given employment by Brennan (despite absence of need for a labourer at that time of year) on the basis, according to Murren, that Brennan would provide board, keep and seven shillings a week. This arrangement between Murren and Brennan was later influenced by the local curate who intervened to secure Murren's attendance at church. As a result, Brennan agreed to give Murren meals as a member of the family, tobacco, clothing, and pay his doctor's bills and church contributions, in return for receiving a reasonable amount of work from Murren, though there was little to be done in the winter months. Murren left two years later, after signing an acknowledgment with the word 'settled' and the date, which Brennan claimed he obtained as a release from any claims by Murren. However, Murren soon returned, and claimed that he wanted his wages and that he repeatedly had asked for them, which Brennan denied. Although there was no resolution of this dispute, Murren stayed on until he had been at Brennan's farm over ten years without wages.

Murren's claim before the High Court was for a minimum wage under the Agricultural Wages Act 1936, for several years' labour as an 'agricultural worker' within the definition in section 2(1) of that Act, requiring such claim be made only by a person employed under a contract of service. In this regard, Gavan Duffy J., in the High Court, characterised the arrangement between Murren and Brennan as largely eleemosynary on Brennan's part, terminable at any time by either without notice and lasting as long as it suited both parties and no longer, thus:

> there was no obligation upon Murren to cut turf when he wanted to smoke a quiet pipe, and there was no obligation upon Brennan to keep a man who preferred a quiet pipe, when he was told to cut turf. (page 474)

Although this 'free and easy arrangement' suited both parties, 'it did not constitute a contract of service, and is outside the purview of the statute' (page 474).

However, Murren's claim also rested on the ground that the Minister for Agriculture had certified that Brennan's business was agriculture, and therefore his employment by Brennan made him an 'agricultural worker' under the Act, especially since the Minister's certificates in this regard are by statute final. Gavan Duffy J. conceded that allowing the Minister to decide who was a farmer and who was a farm labourer would facilitate administration of the statute and was not unreasonable, but then held:

> I should be much surprised to find the Oireachtas entrusting to the Minister so technical a question of law as the decision whether or not there existed an employment under a contract of service between A and B, the kind of question which an official is not well fitted to determine and the kind of question which a Judge is trained to determine upon evidence, subject to appeal to a higher Court of law. (page 475)

The sub-section of the statute could be read as empowering the Minister to determine whether a person was a farmer or farm labourer, but not as authorising him to determine the legal quality of the relationship established between parties, thus his decision could not imply that Murren was employed under contract of service. In this regard, Gavan Duffy J. further stated:

> The question of the finality of the Minister's decision is not directly before me; but I may point out that, while a Court of law would be slow to interfere with any decision clearly entrusted by statute to a Minister of State, the phrase 'whose decision shall be final' in the sub-section cannot exclude the constitutional jurisdiction of the High Court in a case deemed by the High Court to call for interference. (page 476)

Standing to Sue: Locus Standi

The issue of standing to sue based upon interest as a taxpayer arose in *The State (Kerry County Council) v. Minister for Local Government* 1933 IR 517, incident to a conflict between the Kerry County Council and the Minister for Local Government over who should be appointed as

a replacement for the Council's solicitor when he resigned. When
the Council rejected the Minister's suggestion that the Council's
Secretary also undertake its legal work so as to save money, the
Minister subsequently issued a sealed order under the Local
Government (Temporary Provisions) Act 1923, stating that since
the Secretary of the Council was a qualified solicitor willing and
able also to perform legal duties, the Council thereby was directed
that its Secretary would act as its solicitor. In response, and acting
on a Council resolution, the Vice-Chairman of the Council and five
ratepayers applied to the High Court for an order of certiorari to
set aside the Minister's order. However, when the motion came
before the High Court, the Council had been dissolved, and the
Commissioner exercising the Council's powers had recorded a
resolution that no further proceedings be taken on behalf of the
Council, consequently only the ratepayers were left as prosecutors.

On appeal from the High Court to the Supreme Court, Murnaghan J. held that it would be unsatisfactory to dispose of the
application for certiorari merely on the basis of the standing to sue
of the ratepayers. He therefore dealt first with the substantive issue
at hand, namely the Minister's claim that he had authority under
section 15 of the 1923 Act to assign to every officer of a local
authority his duties, which in effect would mean the Minister could
repeal all statutory enactments on appointment of officers of local
authorities, their tenure, remuneration and duties. The Supreme
Court held that the Minister's construction of his powers was 'far
fetched and impossible', that the Minister had no power to specify
the duties of the Council's Secretary, and agreed with Hanna J. of
the High Court, who had emphasised the improbability that the
legislature intended the entire scheme of local government created
by statute to be subject to ministerial orders as if the statute had
not existed.

However, as to whether prosecutors had standing and thus could
be granted a writ of certiorari, Murnaghan J. cited *Weir v. County
Council of Fermanagh* 1913 IR 193, holding that a ratepayer suffered
no individual private wrong beyond that of the public or a class of
the public and thus could not restrain an illegal county council act
by injunction without the Attorney General as plaintiff. On this
basis, the ratepayers in the present case are not persons aggrieved
within the rule of *Reg. v. Surry* JJ LR 5 QB 466 establishing that
where an application is made by a person aggrieved, the grant of

the writ, although discretionary by the court, is *ex debito justitiae*. Although under a different set of facts there may be cases in which a ratepayer may be a person aggrieved, such is not the situation in this case. If the Kerry County Council (by this time reconstituted) were now to move in this matter, they would be persons aggrieved and legitimate prosecutors, since their statutory rights were interfered with, and the solicitor they had nominated to be their solicitor might also be considered to have sufficient interest. If the Council did not move in this matter, there would be no reason to grant the writ to the ratepayers.

The *Kerry County Council* case demonstrates how a court may maintain established judicial doctrine vis-a-vis standing to sue, while in effect also rendering an opinion (albeit without remedial enforceable order) on who would have standing to sue, and how a court would resolve the basic conflict of authority at issue if those having standing did sue. Even without a subsequent suit, it would seem dubious that a minister would continue to insist upon the powers he had asserted over local officers.

Although paying taxes does not give would-be litigants standing to sue, the Irish courts are willing to grant standing based upon complainants' showing potential or actual adverse impact of administrative action upon their personal interests or rights, or property rights, rather than stressing abstract legal concepts or literal interpretation of statutory provisions. In the case of *Cassels v. Dublin Corporation* 1963 IR 193 (chapter 9), one of the issues raised was the standing of the plaintiff. After the death of the original tenant and plaintiff, Mrs Cassels, the action was continued in her daughter's name, and it was the son-in-law, Mr Byrne, who was served with notice to quit the house, followed by a court summons in the matter. The trial judge did not consider plaintiff's allegations of errors and deficiencies in the procedure prior to making a demolition order, since he decided that although section 23 of the Housing (Miscellaneous Provisions) Act 1931 provides that a person aggrieved by a demolition order may appeal to the Circuit Court, it also states that notice of demolition need only be served on the person having control of the house, any other person who is an owner, and on mortgagees. A yearly tenant of a house does not come within these provisions. Further, no appeal will lie against a demolition order from a person under a lease with an unexpired term of under three years, which would exclude a yearly tenant from the right to appeal.

The Corporation argued that these provisions meant that if the demolition order were not appealed by those authorised to do so, it was the equivalent of a judgment *in rem*, binding on everyone as to any matters which would have been raised on appeal.

In regard to the effect of the Corporation's argument if accepted, Kingsmill Moore J. for the Supreme Court held that the occupying tenants had a valuable interest based on various statutes and cannot be evicted except for special reasons. They are the persons most directly affected by a demolition order, but since by statute they are not among those served with the original notice of intent to demolish, they ordinarily will not have a chance to give evidence at the meeting held upon such notice. Even if they gain knowledge of the demolition order, they are excluded by statute from making an appeal. The statutory policy thus is to exclude them from contesting the merits of a demolition order if it is made correctly as to form and procedure, which assumes that the tenants' interests are the same as those of the owners or persons having control. Kingsmill Moore J. rejected the validity of this assumption, holding that although the legislative intention might seem to be to preclude occupying tenants from having any voice as to whether a demolition should be made, it is, in his opinion:

> one thing to conclude that the Legislature intended to exclude tenants from questioning the merits or rightness of an order which was properly made after complying with the antecedent requisities prescribed by the statute. It is another to conclude that it intended to exclude them from showing that the Corporation had acted *ultra vires* and that the order was, as a result, a mere paper order and a legal nullity. I find it impossible to impute such an intention to the Legislature. . . Accordingly, I cannot agree with the decision of the learned trial judge that the plaintiff has no *locus standi*. (pages 210-11)

Standing to sue related to the sufficiency of interest of the party involved was also a significant issue in *Central Dublin Development Association Ltd and Ors v. Attorney General* (1973) 109 ILTR 69, analysed in respect of the constitutionality of delegation of directing power in chapter 9. The plaintiff, Central Dublin Development Association Ltd, was a company registered under the Companies Act 1963 to promote and protect interests and property rights of persons residing, carrying on business, owning, occupying or using property in a particular part of Dublin, by originating and promoting improvements in the law, and instituting support of or opposition to legal proceedings or to administrative orders, plans or decisions in the interests of its members. All of the individual plaintiffs had residence or business property within the area concerned. Their legal action opposed Dublin Corporation's draft plan under the Local Government (Planning and Development) Act 1963, which included compulsory acquisition of a 35-acre area designated as an 'obsolete area' under the Act, to be developed by a company so as to provide a rent to the Corporation, interest to the development company, and profit sharing between the company and the Corporation.

One of the defences raised by the Attorney General against the broadside attack made by plaintiffs upon the constitutionality of the 1963 Act was that none of the plaintiffs had sufficient interest in the Corporation's proposed town plan to warrant success in this action. He argued that a declaratory action to have an Act adjudged invalid required plaintiffs to show that at the time of the administrative hearing on the draft plan, they had been deprived of a constitutional right or that 'matters had been put in train which would have the result that they would be deprived of a constitutional right unless the Court intervenes'. Counsel for plaintiff argued in opposition that any citizen may successfully challenge any provision in any Act of the Oireachtas on constitutional grounds.

Kenny J. in the High Court held that he did not need to determine the issue of standing based on constitutional rights or grounds. In his opinion the plaintiffs had sufficient interest for them to bring the action, based on several facts. These included the stated objectives of the Central Dublin Development Association in the specific area of concern; the ownership of business by individual plaintiffs in this area; the detailed analysis of the development scheme; and the draft plans and recommendations of the planning officer and maps accompanying the plans. All of these aspects led him to conclude:

> The Dublin Corporation intend to show the obsolete areas in the final plan and the argument is that as the Corporation have not as yet decided on the boundaries of any obsolete areas the plaintiffs cannot now challenge the Act. I think it is probable that the area surrounded by the green line on plan No. 2191

will be declared to be an obsolete area at some time in the future and that the third, fourth and fifth plaintiffs, who carry on business in that area and whose property will certainly be affected, if not compulsorily acquired, have a sufficient interest to enable them to maintain this action. The scope of the matters which may now be dealt with in a declaratory action have been greatly extended in recent years (see the judgment of Mr. Justice Walsh in *Transport Salaried Staffs Association* v. *C.I.E.* (1966) 100 I.L.T.R. 189; (1965) I.R. 180 which was not cited in the argument) and the plaintiffs' interest in the definition of obsolete areas and the powers of planning authorities within it is sufficient to enable them to bring this action. (page 87)

The decision by Kenny J. showed a readiness to resolve uncertainty by holding that the situation was sufficiently advanced (thus illustrating also the doctrine of ripeness for review) with enough potential direct effect upon the property interests of plaintiffs to give them standing to sue. A similarly pragmatic test of *locus standi* was illustrated in *Law* v. *Minister for Local Government and Traditional Homes Ltd* unreported, High Court, 29 May 1974. As indicated in the earlier discussion of this case in chapter 5 with respect to the right of a person to be a party to an administrative hearing, a closely related issue of standing to sue in the courts was also involved. In essence, the facts analysed by the High Court and the rationale it gave for holding that Law was a legally qualified party to participate in the administrative hearing also constituted the Court's rationale for Law's having standing to sue in the High Court. In the view of the High Court, a right to litigate cannot be taken away by a statutory instrument applying only to quasi-judicial proceedings, and plaintiff's participation in the administrative hearing conducted by the inspector representing the Minister for Local Government, and Law's interest as a resident in preventing septic tanks from being used near his house, gave him a right to have his interests protected in a Court of Chancery and he therefore was entitled to maintain this action. In response to the argument by defendants that Law had 'no right to act as a watchdog for the public seeking correction by the Courts of injustices or infringements of legal right coming from such errors of procedure', based on *Buckley* v. *Holland Clyde Ltd* per Kenny J., unreported, in which *Simpson* v. *Edinburgh*

Corporation and University of Edinburgh (1960) S.C. 313 was followed, the High Court held:

> Here there is no question of departure from planning permission, or an attempt to enforce planning policy, as in Simpson's case. Here the Plaintiff claims—and has shown—a right in law springing from the appeal hearing regulations and procedure, which he says has been infringed by a wrongful act of the first-named Defendant and this has damaged him—the Plaintiff—but not any outside member of the public. The Plaintiff appears to me to have the same right as any other citizen to come to this Court and seek a remedy for the infringement of his legal right.

Thus in *Law*, as in *Central Dublin Development Association* and *Cassels*, the courts cut through impediments to *locus standi* which could have resulted from a too literal application of statutory provisions or administrative regulations, and granted standing based on the factual realities of the impact of administrative action upon an individual's legal interests.

In the more recent case of *The State (Lynch) v. Minister for Posts and Telegraphs and Attorney General* 1983 ILRM 89 (chapter 9), the question of Lynch's standing to secure review of the constitutional issue he had raised was resolved by the court in a manner similar to that followed in the cases delineated directly above. In giving his judgment, O'Higgins C.J. granted that the Minister's order issued under section 31(1) of the Broadcasting Authority Act 1960 was directed to Radio Telefís Éireann (RTE) not to allow the prosecutor, Lynch, broadcasting time and that prima facie Lynch and Sinn Féin had no right of access to RTE to make election broadcasts. However, RTE's invitation to Sinn Féin did give such access and Sinn Féin had designated Lynch as its spokesperson, prior to the Minister's order. Since such invitation could have been acted on except for the Minister's order, Lynch and Sinn Féin were deprived of a benefit legally given them in the first instance. They thus had sufficient standing to complain that section 31(1), under which the order was made, was unconstitutional.

On this point, Walsh J. noted that it has been observed 'that restrictive rules about standing are in general inimical to a healthy system of administrative law'. Based on his review of judicial precedent regarding standing in the cases from *Regina (Bridgeman) v. Drury* (1894) 2 IR 489 through to *Cahill v. Sutton* 1980 IR 269, he felt that the general conclusion was that the person concerned must be able to show sufficient interest and that such 'real interest' depends upon the circumstances and the context of the particular case. Whether one regarded the permission given by RTE to Lynch as a privilege or a right, in either case the permission was not revoked by RTE, and if the Minister had revoked his order the broadcast would have gone ahead. Therefore Lynch and Sinn Féin suffered a loss and were affected in a material way, since access to the public via television and radio is of value in an election campaign. From a comparable perspective, Henchy J. held that although Lynch did not begin by having a right to make a political party broadcast, once RTE decided and notified Sinn Féin and the public that they would allow Sinn Féin to make broadcasts, Lynch and Sinn Féin had a vested right to make the broadcast, subject only to approval of its content by RTE. However, before the broadcast text could be submitted for approval, the Minister made the impugned order nullifying Lynch's right to make the broadcast. Given the power vested in the Minister by section 31(1) and the circumstances dictating that in the interest of public security, the power be exercised promptly without a hearing, it was not open to Lynch to invoke the rule of *audi alteram partem* as a ground for invalidating the Minister's order. In view of this, Henchy J. considered that Lynch had *locus standi* to question the constitutionality of the statutory section under question.

The discretion of the courts in Ireland to adopt a liberal perspective in respect of standing to sue may not only be granted, but encouraged by statute in Ireland as illustrated in *Morris v. Peter Garvey* 1983 IR 319, 1982 ILRM 177.[11] Section 27(2) of the Local Government (Planning and Development) Act 1976 provides that:

> Where any development authorised by a permission granted under Part IV of the Principal Act has been commenced but has not been, or is not being, carried out in conformity with the permission. . .the High Court may, on the application of a planning authority or any other person, whether or not that person has an interest in the land, by order require any person specified in the order to do or not to do, or to cease to do, as

the case may be, anything which the Court considers necessary to ensure that the development is carried out in conformity with the permission and specifies in the order.

The defendants in this case were building flats and were not complying with conditions attached to planning permission in respect of the positioning of a gable wall and front wall. Plaintiff obtained an order of the High Court to require the removal of the walls. On appeal, the Supreme Court upheld the order. Henchy J. noted that section 27(2) of the 1976 Act explicitly 'recognised for the first time that a member of the public (as well as the planning authority)' despite not meeting qualifications based on property or propinquity, upon discovery of non-compliance by a developer with conditions in the development permission, may apply to the High Court to issue either a negative or a positive order to do or not do anything the court considers necessary to ensure compliance with the planning permission. In his view, the jurisdiction vested in the High Court by section 27(2) is extremely wide, and recognises that in all planning matters (as stressed in other decisions of the Court) there are three parties, i.e. the developer, the planning authority (or Planning Board if there is an appeal) and members of the public. Section 27(2) also recognises that compliance with statutory conditions for development is a legitimate concern of any member of the public:

> We are all, as users or enjoyers of the environment in which we live, given a standing to go to court and to seek an order compelling those who have been given a development permission to carry out the development in accordance with the terms of that permission. And the court is given a discretion sufficiently wide to make whatever order is necessary to achieve that object. (page 179)[12]

If section 27(2) were interpreted as only giving the Court the power to stop the continuance of the unauthorised development, it would be self-defeating in the view of Henchy J. The Supreme Court has judicial notice from other cases that developers for a variety of motives of self-interest have knowingly proceeded rapidly with an unauthorised development so that they then can argue that the Court's discretion should not be exercised against them under section 27(2) to undo the work already done, since this would involve undue expense or trouble. This type of conduct is not a reason for claiming that the Court should not make an order requiring demolition of the unauthorised building, since under section 27(2) the Court is balancing the duty and benefit of the developer against the environmental rights and amenities of the public, particularly those closely affected by the violation of the permission. Only exceptional circumstances (genuine mistake, acquiescence over a long time, technicality of infraction, gross hardship) would be grounds for not issuing a demolition order. A restraining order merely worsens matters by leaving a partly completed structure. In this case, the demolition expenses will be substantial. However, they were foreseeable and avoidable, since the developer, after receiving due notice of his unpermitted building operations, continued them despite threat of legal proceedings. It was true that a planning department official of the Dublin Corporation did state (no doubt in good faith) that he did not look upon the unpermitted work as materially deviating from the terms of the permission. Nevertheless, the uncontroverted evidence on the extent of the deviation and its effect on the amenities of Dr Morris's home is such that the High Court, per Costello J. , correctly refused to act on that opinion. If the builder wished to retain the unpermitted walls, he should have applied for a new development permission, thereby enabling Dr Morris or any member of the public to raise objections. A planning official's opinion cannot be allowed to defeat the rights of the public, especially those of a next-door neighbour.

Exhaustion of Administrative Remedies

The doctrine of primary jurisdiction as developed by American courts does not seem to have been raised as an issue in administrative law in Ireland. However, the closely related concept of exhaustion of administrative remedies was applied in two previously discussed case, namely *In re Crowley* 1964 IR 106, and *Readymix (Eire) Ltd. v. Dublin County Council and Minister for Local Government* unreported, Supreme Court, per Budd J., 30 July 1974, although the dicta in those cases do not explicitly refer to or discuss the doctrine as such.

As the details of *Crowley* delineated in chapter 8 reveal, Crowley was refused a solicitor's practising certificate for 1961-2 by the Incorporated Law Society based on dissatisfaction of the Society's registrar's committee with Crowley's explanation of his conduct at a hearing before the committee which resulted in a charge of touting. However, through exercise of his statutory right of appeal to the High Court and Supreme Court which suspended the refusal of the certificate during appeals, combined with the time factor involved, Crowley in effect retained his practising certificate throughout 1961-2. A second determination by the Society to refuse a practising certificate for 1962-63 was made on the same set of facts, following a second hearing of the registrar's committee, which Crowley refused to attend on the ground that short of saying his original explanation was false and altering it accordingly, he could not add or change anything in that explanation, which the Committee had found unsatisfactory during the previous year's hearing.

Following appeal by Crowley to the High Court which again affirmed the Society's refusal of the certificate, Crowley again appealed to the Supreme Court. Kingsmill Moore J., for the Supreme Court, emphasised that given the circumstances of this case, and the High Court's affirmation of the Law Society's second refusal to issue a practising certificate, a logical projection of future events could be:

> if a solicitor has been asked by the Society to give an explanation of his conduct and has failed to give an explanation which the Society regard as sufficient and satisfactory – because in fact the only explanation available *is* insufficient and unsatisfactory – the Society may for ever after refuse him a practising certificate: and that the reason why they may refuse is not the continuance of the conduct, or the seriousness of the offence, but the *continued* failure to give an explanation other than the one originally given, which, however true *it may have been,* yet may rightly have been regarded as inadequate to excuse his conduct in the matter. I should be loth to impute such an intention to the Legislature if the section can be construed in a more reasonable and equitable way. Such a reasonable construction appears to me. . .to be clearly indicated when the other provisions of the Socitors Act 1954, and the Solicitors (Amendment) Act 1960 are examined. (page 127)

The construction by Kingsmill Moore J. of the provisions of the Solicitors Acts 1954 and 1960 led him to conclude that continued refusal to grant a certificate owing to past misconduct was justified only as a preventive measure to protect the public if that past conduct indicated the probability of its continuation in the future. Moreover, the disciplinary committee was the committee authorised to impose disciplinary measures, and it was the intent of the legislature that only the disciplinary committee had jurisdiction to impose such a severe penalty as refusal of a certificate of practice, and not the registrar's committee.

The Supreme Court decision reflected the doctrine of exhaustion of administrative remedies first, by holding that a plaintiff should not have to exhaust an administrative process as a prerequisite to judicial review and remedy if that process is manifestly futile, i.e. Crowley's claim that his attendance at the second registrar's committee hearing would be useless since he could not change his original explanation which had already been found unsatisfactory. Secondly, exhaustion of administrative process is not required if the administrative body involved lacks statutory jurisdiction, and in this instance, it was the disciplinary committee, not the registrar's committee which had jurisdiction. Also reflecting these concepts of exhaustion of administrative remedies in their dissenting opinions, Lavery and Haugh J.J. held that Crowley's participation in the second registrar's committee hearing would not have been futile, since he could have given proof of no subsequent misconduct, assurance of future correct behaviour, and offer to compensate for the loss he had created. This could have ameliorated or changed the decision to refuse the certificate. Further, there was nothing in the two statutes which prohibited both the registrar's committee and the disciplinary committee having jurisdiction.

Application of the doctrine of exhaustion of administrative remedies was also implicit in the judicial resolution of the issues raised in *Readymix*. The case, as previously described in detail in chapter 8, involved a conflict between Readymix and the Dublin County Council. The Council claimed that Readymix's use of a site and its newly constructed plant for production and transport of readymix concrete constituted a change of use amounting to a development made without permission since it did not conform to the original permission as granted. If it was a change of use, reference to the Minister for Local Government (now Environment) was required under sections 4 and 5 of the Local Government (Planning and Development) Act 1963, for his decision as to whether the change of use constituted a 'development' or an 'exempted development'.

Readymix as plaintiff issued a plenary summons against the County Council and the Minister claiming declarations in the High Court that the permission originally granted was valid and that no question arising within the meaning of section 5 of the Planning and Development Act had been raised which required reference to the Minister for Local Government. On grant of the declarations and injunctions sought by Readymix by the High Court, the County Council appealed to the Supreme Court reiterating its claim that plaintiff's production of readymix concrete was outside the scope of the original permission and that reference to the Minister for decision was lawful. Readymix argued that using the premises to produce readymix concrete was not a material change constituting a development and moreover, under section 28(6) of the Act, in the absence of specification in a permission of the purpose for which a structure may be used, that structure may be employed for the purpose for which it was designed, and in this instance the plans clearly showed the structures were for making readymix concrete.

Griffin J., for the majority of the Court, held that the plans submitted and advertisements made did not indicate sufficiently the true purpose of the new plant, and that the intent and purpose of the permission granted by the County Council was to approve a new plant to replace the old plant in order to manufacture bricks and concrete blocks. Given this decision on the factual issue, Griffin J. concluded that:

> In my view, there is a very strong case to be made for the proposition that the use to which the land has been put does in fact constitute a material change in the use of the land. As this is, however, a question which has been referred to the Minister for Local Government under section 5 of the Act, and which must be decided by him, I do not wish to deal further with that question at this stage.

> When the structures for which a grant of permission was made are used as a readymix plant they are not, in my view, 'concrete plant' within the meaning of the permission granted. In my judgment, a question does arise as to whether the plaintiffs have made any material change in the use of the structures or the land and this question was properly referred to the Minister

by the County Council for decision by him under and in
pursuance of the provisions of section 5 of the 1963 Act.

Budd J. also held that the grant of permission did specify the
purpose for which the structure was to be used, and that there was
a question for the Minister to decide as to whether the structures
constitute development, and so he too would refuse to make the
declarations and injunctions sought.

In this manner, both judges applied the concept of exhaustion of
administrative remedies, by holding that the process specified in
the governing Act for submitting the question of whether the new
structure and its use constituted a development or exempted development to the Minister must be followed before the Court would
give judgment on the matter.

The rationale for exhaustion of administrative remedies is
thoroughly illustrated in the Supreme Court judgment reviewing a
High Court grant of an absolute writ of certiorari in *The State
(Abenglen Properties Ltd) v. Dublin Corporation* 1982 ILRM 590.[13] In
certiorari proceedings in the High Court, Abenglen Properties Ltd
claimed that the outline planning permission granted by Dublin
Corporation (the planning authority) was so radically different from
the original plan Abenglen had submitted (i.e. reduction of, and 40
per cent limit on, the use of office space and increase of proposed
residential use) as to constitute a completely different development.
It therefore was a failure to adjudicate on Abenglen's application.
On this basis, the planning authority's determination was a non-
decision, and in this situation should be treated as an unconditional
grant of permission by default at the end of the required two-month
period for notification of the planning authority's decision. Another
claim made was that if the planning authority were disposed to
grant permission subject to modification the authority should have
invited Abenglen to submit revised plans showing a modified development, under Local Government (Planning and Development)
Regulations 1977, article 77.

In the High Court, D'Arcy J. held contrary to these claims. On
the other hand, a further claim made by Abenglen that the Dublin
Corporation failed to interpret certain provisions of its city development plans correctly when making its determination (and thus was
ultra vires) was successful and the High Court issued a writ of
absolute certiorari which quashed the planning determination.

Prior to making his judgment on these claims, D'Arcy J. also considered an argument of counsel for the planning authority since it pertained to all of Abenglen's arguments. The planning authority submitted that the remedy of certiorari did not lie in this case since Abenglen had the alternative remedy of an appeal to An Bord Pleanála which was not only more convenient but also more appropriate than proceeding on the state side, since if Abenglen succeeded in certiorari proceedings, it would be entitled to planning permission by default without restrictions or conditions two months after making the application for planning permission. In regard to this submission, which was essentially an argument for exhaustion of administrative remedies, D'Arcy J. held that were he free to do so, he would not issue an order absolute in view of the alternative and appropriate remedy. However, in contrast with the past, when certiorari was not granted if an alternative remedy existed, it would appear to be the accepted practice and usage for the past 25 years that certiorari proceedings are not restricted or prohibited because there is an alternative remedy, and thus he had to reject the argument made by counsel for the planning authority.

An appeal was made to the Supreme Court by the planning authority against the absolute order of certiorari on the same grounds, namely that certiorari should not lie since Abenglen could appeal to An Bord Pleanála, which could deal with all of the claims Abenglen had made and Abenglen's failure to make such an appeal and the reasons for that failure justified the refusal of certiorari even if sufficient grounds for certiorari existed. O'Higgins C.J. held that if Abenglen had appealed to An Bord Pleanála rather than the High Court, they would not have suffered in any respect. In fact, their original application would be considered *de novo*, the Board would hear all the arguments and submissions for allowing the full development sought, and moreover, the Board was not bound to restrict the development to the limits prescribed by the Dublin City Plan. Consequently, it could waive the 40 per cent restriction on office development if it considered it appropriate to do so, or alternatively, state a case to the High Court on the correct interpretation of paragraph 3.4.20 of the Dublin City Development Plan of '1980 relevant to that restriction. He would find it difficult to think of a more effective means of dealing with Abenglen's complaints. However, Abenglen did not so appeal, but waited until the two months had almost expired and then applied for certiorari. The purpose was not to correct a grievance Abenglen had suffered as a result of a process they claimed to be without legal authority. Rather it was to take advantage of an alleged irregularity to obtain a benefit not intended by the planning code, since if the planning authority's decision were nullified, Abenglen could ask for a declaration that they had obtained a default permission under section 26(4) of the Local Government (Planning and Development) Act 1963. This would silence all opposition to the original development, and thus bypass the scrutiny of planning proposals provided by the planning Acts. In his view the absolute order of certiorari should not have been issued.

Similarly, Henchy J., as one of the several reasons he gave in regard to why he would refuse to quash the Dublin Corporation's decision by certiorari, even if that decision was made in excess of jurisdiction, stated:

> the correct procedure for the correction of the legal errors complained of lay in an appeal to the Board. The statutory scheme for making applications for development permission to the relevant planning authority – giving prior notice, as prescribed, to the public and complying with the requirements of the regulations; allowing interested parties to make representations by way of objection or otherwise; requiring the planning authority to deal with the application within a given time and according to prescribed standards; requiring that the decision shall contain prescribed essentials; allowing an appeal from the planning authority's decision to the Board, who may hold oral hearings, who are not bound to comply with the development plan (s. 14(8) of the 1976 Act), and who may refer a question of law to the High Court (s. 82(3) of the 1963 Act); and the fact that the Board's decision is put beyond the reach of certiorari or other legal proceedings questioning its validity unless such proceedings are brought within two months of the giving of the Board's decision (s. 82(3A) of the 1963 Act) – these and other features of the Acts envisage the operation of a self-contained administrative code, with resort to the courts only in exceptional circumstances. The present case does not seem to me to exhibit the exceptional circumstances for which the intervention of the courts was intended. On the contrary, certiorari proceedings would appear to be singularly inapt for

the resolution of the questions raised by Abenglen. Certiorari proceedings, based as they are on affidavit evidence, can result only in a stark and comparatively unilluminating decision to quash or not to quash; whereas an appeal to the Board would have allowed all relevant matters to be exploited (if necessary, in an oral hearing, with the aid of experts in the field of planning), thus allowing an authoritative exposition to be given of the appropriate practice and procedure, aided, if necessary, by a reference to the High Court of a question of law. (pages 606-607)[14]

Ripeness for Review

Whether a delay of action of a governmental agency affected legal interests of the plaintiff sufficiently to constitute a controversy for which the court had an effective remedy was at issue in *The State (Modern Homes Ireland Ltd) v. Dublin Corporation* 1953 IR 202. The plaintiff sought an order of mandamus directing defendants to prepare and adopt a draft planning scheme with all convenient speed in accordance with article 12, Town and Regional Planning Regulations 1934, to make with all convenient speed a planning scheme pursuant to section 29 of the Town and Regional Planning Act 1934, and to submit that scheme to the Minister for Local Government for his approval.

This suit originated in a resolution passed by the City Council in 1936 to make a planning scheme for the County Borough of Dublin under the Town and Regional Planning Act 1934. The City Manager had fully apprised the Council in a report of the reasons for and against this action, and had warned that once the Council voluntarily resolved to make a planning scheme, the making of that scheme was irrevocable and would have to be with all convenient speed. He recommended a more detailed study be made before passing the resolution, but the Council chose instead to adopt the resolution. Subsequent implementing actions were limited to appointment of planning consultants, a planning officer and assistant in 1937, establishment of a town planning department in 1938, and preparation of a sketch development plan in 1939 adopted by the Council in 1940 at which time it also was ordered that a draft scheme be prepared. However, a planning scheme had not been prepared by the time the Supreme Court reviewed the case.

Maguire C.J. for the Supreme Court identified four questions for consideration; (1) had a demand been made to Dublin Corporation to perform their duty; (2) had there been a refusal to perform that duty; (3) were the complainants competent prosecutors; and (4) should the remedy requested be denied on the grounds it would be useless or futile to grant it. As to the first question, the legislature recognised that delay was inevitable between passing of a resolution to make a planning scheme and its being carried out, when it gave planning authorities powers to use during the interim period between a resolution and adoption of a final plan, in order to prevent private development which might cause problems in implementing the final plan. However, the legislature intended there should not be an unreasonable delay to ending the interim period with its burden of uncertainty on private builders and developers. Whether the Corporation had refused to perform its duty by delaying unreasonably is a factual issue which a jury must decide if either party requires such a decision. In the Court's view, complainants had made a sufficient case to entitle them to have that issue decided, as a company in the building business claiming to have made applications to the Corporation for special permission to erect buildings, a number of which were refused, or when granted, conditions were attached to which the company objected. The Company thus was affected by Corporation exercise of its powers of interim control and suffered from the failure of the City Council to make and submit a planning scheme.

Regarding the right to maintain an action as related to its meaningfulness, the Court held it was not a prerequisite that the prosecutor must have a right to recover damages through an action. Prosecutors had sufficient interest to entitle them to apply for an order of mandamus, and it was not shown that there was any alternative specific remedy at law which was more convenient or effective. The Court does not have to pass judgment on the adequacy of the planning scheme, but only to decide whether in fact a planning scheme had been submitted to the Minister. Finally, as Maguire C.J. stated:

> An objection more strongly pressed is that the order should not be made because it would be futile. It is argued that there can be no certainty that the scheme will be made even if the order of *mandamus* is issued. It is, of course, correct that an order will not be made if it is clear that it would be impossible

of performance by reason of the circumstances that the doing of the act would involve a contravention of law or if the defendants have not the means of complying with the order . . . . The position here is far different. The appellants are asked to carry out their legal obligation and they have the means to carry out the order. It is to be assumed that they will obey an order of the Court to do that which it is their statutory duty to do . . . . If those who are held to have failed in a public duty prove recalcitrant, the Court has ample powers to compel compliance with its order, and does not necessarily seek other means of having the duty performed. (pages 229-30)

Subsequent to this decision, the issue on the order of mandamus was tried before McLoughlin J. sitting with a jury, which found that the Dublin Corporation had not proceeded with all convenient speed to prepare and adopt a draft scheme and make a planning scheme and submit it to the Minister. A peremptory order of mandamus was issued. The case thus illustrates the criteria for ripeness for review, i.e. an actual controversy existed, plaintiff's legal interests were sufficiently affected, the time was appropriate for the court to provide a remedy which was meaningful, and the court felt it had the means to enforce the remedy.

Ripeness for review was also the basis for resolving the issues raised in *Lynch v. McMahon and Others* unreported, High Court, per Teevan J., 25 July 1967. Plaintiff and defendants were members of the County Clare Law Association, an organisation of solicitors governed by rules regulating relationships and professional practice of its members. One of those rules (rule 19) which set forth what closing days would be observed by members was amended by a large majority vote at a general meeting of the Association in 1966 held after due notice that the meeting was for the express purpose of considering an obligatory five-day working week. As amended, rule 19 provided that the members practising law in Ennis would close their offices on Saturdays, while members practising elsewhere were at liberty to decide by a majority of solicitors in the locality whether to follow a five-day working week and what day would be the non-working day. The one opposing vote to this amendment was made by plaintiff, and three members abstained.

Plaintiff claimed a declaration from the Court that it was outside the Association's powers to change its rules except by consent of all

R

its members, and that the amendment to rule 19 as adopted was also outside the Association's powers with no binding effect on plaintiff or other members. He also claimed an injunction to restrain the Association and its officers from representing to the public that plaintiff was bound by Association rules and would not open his Ennis office on Saturdays.

Plaintiff argued that by opening his office on Saturdays, he was open to a pecuniary penalty and risk of expulsion from the Association. In response, Teevan J. first noted that since 25 June 1966, Ennis solicitors other than plaintiff kept their offices closed on Saturdays, while plaintiff kept his open, and that plaintiff's personal attendance in his office on Saturday was infrequent, although his staff was there for the convenience of the country people. Teevan J. then held plaintiff was not entitled to ask the courts for a remedy for a grievance of others unless he stands in a legally recognised representative relationship with them, and though he granted that plaintiff was open to a maximum penalty of £25 for each Saturday opening and deprivation of privileges by violating the Association rules, the fact was that:

> So far, no action whatever has been taken against the plaintiff and there is no evidence that any such has been threatened or even contemplated. I accept Mr. Parke's submission that if and when it so should be sought to penalize the plaintiff, the time would then have arrived for challenging in court the validity of the new rule. It is not the new rule, nor the fact of its having been adopted by a majority of members and in spite of the plaintiff's opposition which causes any risk to plaintiff. He has not made out a case of loss or damage in the practice of his profession in consequence of the mere amendment, nor has he shown that to conform to it he would suffer such loss or damage. His colleagues may well continue to ignore the plaintiff's infringement of the new rule . . . the plaintiff's action is premature . . . . The court must not be made a court of appeal from decisions of the association but will intervene if the livelihood or reputation of the complaining member is at stake. I am not concerned with the propriety of closing law offices on Saturdays, or with the question whether it is in, or against the interests of the members, or any of them.

Concerning plaintiff's complaint that publication by the *Clare Champion* newspaper of the decision to observe a five-day week conveyed to the public that his office would not be open for business on Saturdays, and that he was entitled to an injunction restraining the Association from making such representations, Teevan J. held:

> In my opinion it makes not the slightest difference to the issue whether this was a formal decision arrived at in general meeting, or informally decided upon by the defendants after the meeting. The *Clare Champion* must have had its information from some of the defendants ... Even if it were to be approached on its own ground, it is a claim that must fail. What has been published is now irrevocable and beyond the reach of an injunction. The plaintiff reads too much into the publication . . If it could be construed . . as a misrepresentation to the public that the plaintiff's office would not be open for business on Saturdays, the publication of the present proceedings ought to provide him with ample relief in that it will apprise the public that his office remains open for five and a half days each week.

This rejection by Teevan J. of plaintiff's claims for declarations and an injunction again illustrate the doctrine of ripeness for review, for the reasons that there had been no actual or imminent adverse effect upon plaintiff, and the granting of an injunction would have been futile as a remedy.

The Scope of Judicial Review: Comparative Aspects

Assuming that questions of administrative finality, *locus standi*, exhaustion of administrative remedies and ripeness for review have been resolved, the final issue in regard to judicial review of administrative determinations is the scope of that review. This issue goes to the heart of the relationship between administrative agencies and the courts, and their respective roles in the governmental process. Certain cases provide explicit consideration of issues in the scope of judicial review, namely the extent to which the courts should or should not substitute judgment on questions of facts determined by administrative agencies, on mixed questions of fact and law and on questions of law.

The term 'mixed questions of fact and law' epitomises the reality of administrative decision-making since the elements of an administrative determination often do not fall neatly within mutually exclusive questions of fact and questions of law. One of the most cogent statements concerning the problem of distinguishing between these questions, and the basis upon which a resolution may be reached, is that of Louis J. Jaffe, Byrne Professor of Administrative Law at Harvard University:

> How then do we distinguish fact from law? *It will be more meaningful, I think, to put the question: how do we distinguish a finding of fact from a conclusion of law?* In this way we emphasize that we are concerned with the function and the functioning of the decisional process; what is the officer doing, we ask, when he 'finds' a fact and how does this action differ from his making a conclusion of law? ... *A finding of fact is the assertion that a phenomenon has happened or is or will be happening independent of or anterior to any assertation as to its legal effect* ... Thus a statute may provide compensation for injuries arising out of and during the course of employment. It has been found that an employee while at work has been intentionally hit on the head by a fellow employee. This is a finding of fact. . . . If, however, it is asserted that the injury arose out of the employment and is therefore compensable, the assertion is . . . a conclusion of law. . . . It is . . an assertation that the purpose of the statute will be served by awarding compensation.[15]

In the United States, the Administrative Procedures Act 1946, section 10 (e) (60 STAT 237 (1946) 5 USCA section 706, Scope of Review, as amended) provides a statutory frame of reference for judicial review of administrative determinations:

> Scope of review–To the extent necessary to decision and when presented, the reviewing court shall decide all relevant questions of law, interpret constitutional and statutory provisions, and determine the meaning or applicability of the terms of an agency action. The reviewing court shall–(1) compel agency action unlawfully withheld or unreasonably delayed; and (2)

hold unlawful and set aside agency action, findings, and conclusions found to be–(A) arbitrary, capricious, an abuse of discretion, or otherwise not in accordance with law; (B) contrary to constitutional right, power, privilege, or immunity; (C) in excess of statutory jurisdiction, authority, or limitations, or short of statutory right; (D) without observance of procedure required by law; (E) unsupported by substantial evidence in a case subject to sections 556 and 557 of this title or otherwise reviewed on the record of an agency hearing provided by statute; or (F) unwarranted by the facts to the extent that the facts are subject to trial *de novo* by the reviewing court. In making the foregoing determinations, the court shall review the whole record or those parts of it cited by a party, and due account shall be taken of the rule of prejudicial error.

In effect, the Administrative Procedures Act (APA) enacted the substantial evidence rule which had been developed by the American courts in their review of administrative determinations. However, as established in the leading case of *Universal Camera Corporation v. NLRB* 349 US 374 (1951), the APA also broadened the scope of judicial review which previously had been self-limiting to the extent that if there was evidence in the record which viewed by itself would support administrative findings of fact, such findings would receive judicial support. Under the APA, as expressed in *Universal Camera,* the courts must also take into account contrary evidence or evidence from which opposite inferences may be drawn before reaching the conclusion that there is substantial evidence based upon review of the *whole* record to support the agency's decision.

In respect of the law–fact distinction, Davis notes that if American courts choose to substitute their judgment for that of the administrative agency, they may 'convert questions of discretion and of fact into questions of law by making law about them', e.g. holding that discretion must be exercised in a specific manner. If they wish not to substitute judgment, either the application of law to fact is characterised as a 'question of fact' for administrative determination, or the law–fact distinction is ignored and the standard phrase applied that where there 'is warrant in the record and a reasonable basis in law' the administrative decision is final, which Davis calls the 'rational basis' test.[16]

There is greater tolerance of administrative findings of fact and less on questions of law in Britain than in the United States, in the view of Schwartz and Wade, and questions of legal definition and interpretation are treated as questions of law, once the facts of a case are established. This results in a more definite distinction between law and fact, and there is also the doctrine of 'jurisdictional fact' under which English courts may quash an order if they find that the facts, tried *de novo* or the law or legal aspects of a transaction do not provide the basis for a tribunal's jurisdiction. Error on the face of the record, such as misinterpretation of a statute is also a ground for quashing a decision even though the decision may be *intra vires*. Many administrative tribunals' determinations may be appealed under statutory right of appeal to the High Court on a point of law. It is 'a recognised point of law that a finding of fact is supported by no evidence', which means 'an absence of persuasive proof on the evidence as a whole, so that there is little real difference from the American substantial evidence rule'.[17]

Scope of Judicial Review in Ireland

In Ireland, the scope of judicial review of administrative determinations, as in other aspects of Irish administrative law, reflects the strong influence of English and also certain characteristics of American administrative law. The Irish judicial treatment of evidence to sustain an administrative determination has distinct aspects of the American substantial evidence doctrine, although the court opinions do not use that term as such (see chapter 5). On the other hand, as in England, Irish law and judicial review commonly provide for reference of points of law to the High Court by lower tribunals, and reflect other aspects of English judicial review, such as the doctrine of jurisdictional fact.

Questions of Fact

An example of judicial correction of an administrative determination based on a question of fact is provided by *The State (Keller) v. Galway County Council and Another* 1958 IR 143. In the discussion of *Keller* in chapter 5, it was apparent to the Court that Dr McConn, Chief Medical Officer of the Galway County Council, had discounted a certificate of Keller's district dispensary doctor which, in the Court's view, clearly showed Keller was not fit for unskilled labour and at the same time lacked knowledge of any trade, when he made his decision that Keller was not entitled to a maintenance allowance under the Disabled Persons (Maintenance Allowance) Regulations 1954, implementing the Health Act 1953. At the same time, Dr McConn had taken into account an opinion in a report from his assistant, Dr Gallagher, that Keller should have learned some trade that did not require him to stand while working, and that he was fit to contribute to his own maintenance, and Dr McConn had also obtained information on the earnings of Keller's father and brother. Therefore, in the view of the Court, Dr McConn had exceeded his jurisdiction by taking into account matters extraneous to his function and scope of duty under the statute, and since the County Council relied on Dr McConn in reiterating his refusal, the Council had not carried out their duty. A mandamus was issued to Dr McConn and the Council to consider and deal with the facts related to Keller's application according to their proper jurisdiction under law.

The courts will also invalidate an administrative decision when the evidence, as perceived by the court, shows that the decision would be in violation of the governing statute. In *Price v. Leitrim Board of Health* 1941 IR 123 (see chapter 9), the evidence demonstrated that if a compulsory purchase order of the Leitrim Board of Health became effective, the plaintiff's four acres, three roods and ten perches of farm land would be reduced to a low-lying and swampland strip of 72 feet wide and 321 feet long, thus taking the best and largest part of plaintiff's land and leaving him with a completely uneconomic portion of the field. Consequently, Gavan Duffy J. concluded that the proposed compulsory purchase order would violate section 6 of the Labourers (Ireland) Act 1883 providing that the land acquisition must avoid interference with the demesne and amenity of residence of the landowner or any home farm of lands adjoining, and that in selecting land, due regard must be given to the situation and convenience of the property so as to reduce the value as little as possible. The purchase order therefore was quashed.

The absence of sufficient evidence to support a determination (i.e. the 'no evidence' or 'substantial evidence' doctrines summarised earlier) is illustrated by *Hughes v. Wicklow County Council* 90 ILTR 167 (chapter 9). In that case Judge Fawsett's analysis of the evidence offered in support of a demolition order by the Wicklow County Council acting on a determination of the County Manager led him to conclude that the County Manager's notice that the house was unfit was based on only one report on certain aspects of the house which found it was not fit for human habitation but made no findings as to whether the house could be made fit at a reasonable expense. He noted that the subsequent hearing produced contrary opinions between the County Manager, the County Architect and plaintiff's architect which were in no way resolved in the hearing, and a report of the official engineer contained inaccuracies. In Judge Fawsett's opinion:

> I have already stated that the County Manager should have rejected this report, and in so far as he acted upon its contents, he was in error in doing so. No privately owned property should be ordered to be demolished on evidence of this character.

> Finally, I am compelled to find that whilst the County Manager had before him, when making the Demolition Order, an official representation that the plaintiff's house was unfit for human habitation, he had not before him the report of any of the Council's officers, or any other information in his possession known to the Court, on which he, as local authority, could justly be satisfied that the plaintiff's house was not capable at a reasonable expense of being rendered so fit. (page 178)

Furthermore, in a rather unusual form of substitution of judgment by a judge as to facts found by an administrator, Judge Fawsett stated:

> May I add for the information and benefit of the respective parties that I have inspected the house; that I have inspected houses elsewhere with far more sanitary defects; that in my opinion its defects are capable of being repaired and the house thus be made fit for habitation by persons of the working classes. (page 178)

Several grounds for substitution of judgment on questions of fact by the court for that of the administrator are illustrated by *The State (Raftis) v. Leonard: State (Dowling) v. Leonard* 1960 IR 381, 95 ILTR 148. The respondent, Leonard, auditor of the Department of Local

Government, audited the accounts of the County Borough of Waterford, and made a charge and surcharges against Raftis, City Manager of Waterford and Dowling, Finance Officer of Waterford Corporation, for certain losses incurred. Plaintiffs in response sought orders of certiorari to quash the charge and surcharges.

The charge against Raftis was for alleged negligence in hiring haulage lorries for the Corporation at a rate higher than that offered by hauliers who had submitted the lowest tender, despite Raftis's explanation that he had not hired the lowest bidders owing to unsuitability of their lorries and previous unsatisfactory service given to the Corporation. The High Court, per McLoughlin and Murnaghan J.J. (Davitt P. dissenting), held that this charge should be quashed, since grounds given by respondent Leonard were not sufficient to justify his findings that the loss had been incurred by plaintiff Raftis's negligence within the meaning of section 20, Local Government (Ireland) Act 1902. Davitt J. felt Leonard was justified in rejecting Raftis's explanation for want of a more detailed account of his reasons.

Surcharges were also made against Raftis for wages paid to a person for one week's clerical work in a housing scheme and one week's clerical work in the motor tax office of the Corporation, and against Dowling who as interim acting City Manager for two days had authorised the payment (although the work had been done before his two-day term of office). The ground was that the employment of that person was illegal since he had not been chosen after public advertisement and competitive examination or other procedures prescribed by the Local Government (Officers) Regulations 1943, nor appointed as a temporary officer for not more than six months, as allowed by those Regulations. Raftis claimed the person had been employed as a labourer and not as an officer, to which Leonard replied that since the person employed was one of a number of additional persons temporarily employed on clerical work on the Corporation's housing scheme when the number of manual workers employed on that scheme was consistently declining, such employment was unnecessary. A related factor in this situation was that Dowling was not responsible for the original employment of the person nor aware of the surcharge against him or reasons for it until after it had been made.

In respect of the surcharges, the High Court quashed the surcharge relating to the employment of the person in the motor taxation office, since the evidence demonstrated a doubt had arisen whether the employment was done as an officer of the Corporation or as a servant, and such a question was a matter for final decision by the Minister under section 11(1), Local Government Act 1955, and was not within Leonard's jurisdiction. However, the surcharge against Raftis for employment of the person on the housing scheme was upheld, since there was sufficient evidence to support the auditor's conclusion that such employment was unnecessary. Finally, the surcharge against Dowling was quashed since he was not given opportunity to be heard before being surcharged. In conclusion, the Court held that in considering an application for certiorari under section 12, Local Government (Ireland) Act 1871, to quash a charge or surcharge by a local government auditor, the Court is limited to considering only those materials before the auditor. However, based on those materials, the Court is free to come to a different conclusion of fact to that reached by the auditor, as well as a different conclusion of law.

The *Raftis* case thus illustrates several bases for judicial review and substitution of judgment on administrative determinations of fact, including insufficiency of evidence, jurisdiction to determine a factual question, and failure to afford an adversely affected party opportunity to submit evidence on his behalf.

The substitution of judgment as to the facts of a controversy by the courts for that of the administrative authorities in the *Keller, Hughes* and *Raftis* cases involved situations in which the factual evidence pertained to administrative determinations of an adjudicatory or quasi-judicial nature regarding the interests or rights of an individual. However, the courts do not limit their review and evaluation of factual evidence to only those situations involving administrative adjudication, but also engage in such review and evaluation of evidence in instances of administrative rule-making. In *In the Matter of the Fisheries (Consolidation) Act 1959, Dunne and Ors. v. the Minister for Fisheries and Forestry* unreported, High Court, per Costello J., 10 February 1984, the decision of the Court to annul a South Western Fisheries Region Bye-Law No. 629, 1981 (on driftnet salmon fishing) was based on judicial evaluation of the weight of conflicting evidence in support of and contrary to opposing claims that the 1981 bye-law did or did not achieve statutory objectives (see chapter 6). As Costello J. stated:

I do not find the arguments in support of the bye-law to be convincing and as the overwhelming weight of the scientific evidence leads me to conclude that the 1981 bye-law is not expedient for the more effectual government, management, protection and improvement of the fisheries of the State, I must annul it.

Of particular interest in respect of the scope of judicial review as asserted by Costello J. in this case, is his response to the submission on the Minister's behalf that since the ministerial power to make bye-laws under section 9 of the 1959 Act was a delegated power from the Oireachtas to the Minister, the power of the courts in reviewing the Minister's order to make bye-laws is very limited. In support of this argument for the Minister, Craies on *Statute Law* (7th edition) and *Carltona Ltd v. Commissioners of Works* (1943) 2 All ER 560 quoted therein were cited, in which the concept was expressed that the courts have only the power to determine whether the statutory instrument is within the law and exercised in good faith, and may not enquire into the reasonableness, the policy or the means provided in the instrument. In addition, the Canadian case of *Minister of National Revenue v. Wright's Canadian Ropes Ltd* (1947) AC 127 was cited which expressed a similar view that when hearing an appeal from an administrative act, a court is limited to considering whether there was a contravention of some principle of law, since the fact of reasonableness or normalcy is solely a minister's judgment and the court may not substitute its own opinion for that of a minister.

Costello J. pointed out that these references do not take into account the distinction between the exercise by a court of its common law powers of judicial review, and an appellate jurisdiction given by statute, citing Wade, *Administrative Law* (5th edition), page 34. He also noted that the Canadian case was drawn from de Smith, *Judicial Review of Administrative Acts* (4th edition) and that de Smith does call attention to the fact that courts have held that they may not substitute their discretion for that of an administrative authority when exercising common law powers. Following this, however, de Smith also states that in regard to statutory powers of appeal, the extent to which courts may review the exercise of the discretion depends on the provisions of each individual act. Often an aggrieved party's right of appeal is to be construed as empowering the court

to substitute its own opinion for the opinion of the authority if it is
satisfied that the authority's decision was wrong, and power to
entertain an appeal on the merits may give a court much wider
discretionary authority than the inherent jurisdiction of the High
Court over questions of legality and than the statutory power to
entertain appeals on matters of law. Since de Smith refers to the
Canadian case as an illustration of the provision for appeal not
granting power to review an exercise of discretion *de novo*, the
Canadian case in Costello's view lays down no principle of general
application.

Costello J. held therefore, that when a court is granted appellate
jurisdiction by an Act to confirm or annul a bye-law or other
administrative action, it must interpret the words used by the
legislature to determine whether it has the power to substitute its
opinion for that of the administrative authority if the court, based
on the evidence, considers that the administrative action was wrong
on its merits, and not just wrong in law. He noted the precedent of
Dodd v. Minister for Fisheries 1934 IR 291, in which the appellate
provisions of the Fisheries Act 1925 (which were very similar to
those of the 1959 Act) were considered, and in which it was held
that if the material available to the Minister is not made available
to the court, the court may hear the evidence itself and decide the
appeal on that basis. Further, the court is not confined to determining whether the minister acted in violation of a legal principle
but must be satisfied that the bye-law is for the more effective
management of the fisheries.

On this basis, Costello J. said that as he would construe the 1959
Act:

> the Oireachtas must have intended that the Court's jurisdiction
> on an appeal should be wider than its powers when exercising
> its inherent jurisdiction at common law. Secondly, the right of
> an appeal is not expressly limited to an appeal on a point of
> law only as, for example, is to be found in the case of an appeal
> under section 45 of the Social Welfare Act 1952. Thirdly, the
> Court's power to confirm or annul an instrument to which
> the section applies can arise . . . in a number of different
> circumstances in some of which the party aggrieved may have
> had an opportunity to present a case to the Minister before the
> impugned instrument had been made and in some of which he

may not. To be effective, therefore, the Court may well have to allow an appellant to give evidence and then decide the matter on new material not available to the Minister. This would indicate that both in cases where new evidence is given and in cases where the appeal is decided on the same material as was before the Minister, the Court is empowered to annul a bye-law or other 'instrument' if it reaches a decision on the merits different to that of the Minister.

Costello J. concluded that he had jurisdiction to annul the 1981 bye-law if in his opinion it was not expedient for the more effective government, management, protection and improvement of the fisheries of the state. He also stated that it was desirable to hear an appeal from a bye-law based on the evidence given in the public inquiry and the materials the Minister had when making the bye-law, but the Court does have the power to hear additional evidence by affidavit or oral testimony and should exercise this power if the Minister declines (as happened in this case) to make available to the Court the report of the inspector who held the enquiry and other material on which the Minister's opinion was based. In general, however, the Court should be slow to substitute its opinion for the Minister's in cases where departmental experience and knowledge is an important factor in arriving at its policy.

Mixed Questions of Law and Fact
The frequently raised scope of judicial review issue of the application of law to fact also referred to as 'mixed questions of law and fact' is illustrated by *Murren v. Brennan* 1942 IR 466, discussed earlier in conjunction with issues of finality of administrative determinations. After Gavan Duffy J. had analysed the facts concerning the evolution of, and elements in, the arrangements between Brennan and Murren for Murren's support and employment as being eleemosynary on Brennan's part, terminable at any time by either without notice, he concluded as a matter of law that this 'free and easy arrangement' did not constitute a contract of service, and was outside the purview of the Agricultural Wages Act 1936. Gavan Duffy J. also held that although the Minister under the Act could decide whether one man was a farmer and another a farm labourer, he did not have the statutory authority to determine the question of law as to whether

an employment under a contract of service existed.

The opinion of Gavan Duffy J. in *Murren* clearly shows that courts may draw inferences and conclusions from evidence different from those of administrators, and assert their expertness in interpretation of law applied to facts over that of the administrator, particularly in traditional areas of law such as that of contract. In the later case of *Pigs and Bacon Commission v. Monaghan Curing Co Ltd* 1948 Ir. Jur. Rep. 34, Gavan Duffy J. reiterated the authority of the courts as to inferences drawn from facts and interpretation of the meaning of statutory provisions applied to facts. In this instance, two cases sent from the District Court for review by the High Court arose from the District Court's dismissal of two summonses, brought on the instance of the Pigs and Bacon Commission against the Monaghan Curing Company, which was operating under curing and slaughtering licences under the Pigs and Bacon Act 1935. One summons claimed failure by the company to keep records required by the Act, and the other claimed failure by the company to produce certain records of its business to an officer of the Commission. Every licensee is required by section 113(1) of the 1935 Act to keep prescribed records in the required form at the licensed place, and to make specified entries in every record within a certain time. Such records are termed as a 'book or books' under the 1939 regulations implementing the Act, and the entries specified are all transactions related to bacon produce. Section 113(1) distinguishes between keeping prescribed records and making specified entries within a certain time, and section 113(3) of the Act creates offences related to these requirements. There are three offences leading to penalty upon summary conviction of any person who: (1) fails to keep prescribed records; (2) fails to make any entry required in such records within a stated time; and (3) makes a false or misleading entry.

The first summons charged that the company had failed to keep the prescribed records. Gavan Duffy J. noted that the evidence established that the company had not entered in its books certain dealings constituting a small proportion of the entire records. However, it did keep sales books, invoice books and quota books, and no complaint was made by the Pigs and Bacon Commission on the kind of books kept. Moreover, when the Commission initiated their proceedings, the normal six-month time limit for summary offences had expired in respect of a complaint and summons based on the omission of certain entries. Gavan Duffy J. believed that the Commission recognised it had exceeded the time limit for that offence and instead charged the company with the different offence of failure to keep prescribed records or books. Given the evidence and the statutory provisions, he held that the District Justice was correct in law when he interpreted the law as creating two distinct offences, and in dismissing the summons for failure to keep the prescribed books, when the only evidence was that there had been a failure to make the prescribed entries in those books. Regarding the second summons, claiming violation of section 113(2) of the 1935 Act which requires licensees to produce any record kept under the statute and documents needed to verify entries or omissions from such record, Gavan Duffy J. held that the evidence showed that an authorised officer had asked to see the books and certain other documents. However, he did not ask for documents explaining the omission to enter certain transactions, had little information on omitted entries, and the District Court record had an admission by the officer that every document he demanded was produced to him. Consequently the District Court was correct in law in dismissing the second summons.

The *Monaghan* case involved a substitution of judgment by the courts for that of the Commission in regard to interpretation of law as applied to facts, as well as a judicial correction of a charge of violation which was not applicable under the statute. A more complete substitution of judgment based on inferences drawn from a set of facts and the meaning of a statutory provision applied to those facts is illustrated by *Petitions of Lynch and Daly* 1970 IR 1. In this case, Lynch and Daly appealed to the High Court from a decision by the Veterinary Council that they had been guilty of conduct disgraceful to them in a professional respect, arising from the basis for and manner in which they submitted claims for fees to be paid to them by the Minister for Agriculture and Fisheries, and that the registration of their names should be suspended for six months from the Register of Veterinary Surgeons in Ireland. Petitioners had provided their services and claimed payment of veterinary fees according to the Diseases of Animals (Control of Certain Vaccinations and Extension to Brucellosis) Order 1965 (SI No. 111) implementing the Diseases of Animals Act 1894. This order authorises a scheme for vaccinating three- to six-month old calves against brucellosis. The scheme involved a detailed control system of records including a list of veterinarians doing such work, to whom field books and prescribed forms were sent, namely BA 15 forms, for making entries of work done, to be signed by veterinarians and farmers, and BA 17 forms for making claims for payment. Such work was often carried out by veterinarians assisting a principal veterinarian. Calves were to be vaccinated only once, but since ear tattoo marks or blue cards identifying calves already vaccinated were often faded or lost, reliance had to be placed on the farmer's word, short of searching through entries in field books.

Lynch had a large practice and employed Daly who performed many vaccinations including some based on requests of herd owners without checking as to prior vaccinations, and some when the herd owner was not present to sign the BA 15 forms (as had been true in certain instances of vaccinations done by veterinarians previously assisting Lynch). During the period in question, Lynch pressured Daly to complete the BA 15 forms so that BA 17 forms could be submitted to claim payment, which was further complicated by a dispute between them concerning payment due to Daly. This concluded with Lynch telling Daly that he would pay nothing until all the claims were cleared for payment, upon which Daly filled out BA 17 forms based on all the BA 15 forms present in Lynch's office (at times forging herd owner signatures on unsigned BA 15 forms or certifying he had done vaccinations performed by previous veterinarian assistants to Lynch who had neglected to sign the forms–a fact not known or charged prior to the hearing on the charges). Lynch signed the forms without checking field books and sent them to the Department of Agriculture.

The Department's review of these claims against other claims submitted resulted in one summary showing that 8 animals in 27 herds were vaccinated twice, and in a second summary showing 29 additional double-vaccinations, of which most were done by Daly and a few by Lynch. On a report of these facts by the Minister to the Veterinary Council, the Council, under the Veterinary Surgeons Acts 1931 and 1960, charged Lynch with being 'guilty of misconduct disgraceful to you' for claiming fees for vaccinations of previously vaccinated animals, animals over six months old, and failure to supervise his assistant to ensure compliance with regulations and keeping proper records. Daly was charged with disgraceful conduct for the double vaccinations, vaccinating animals over six months old, and failing to take reasonable steps to ensure he was not violating regulations. A special committee appointed by the Council heard evidence from departmental officials and from Lynch and Daly (who were represented by counsel) and reported to the Council they were satisfied that Lynch and Daly were guilty of conduct disgraceful to them, on the grounds specified, largely owing to failure to keep proper records. The committee rejected Daly's argument that his errors were owing to pressure of work and lack of clerical staff in Lynch's office, and Lynch's claim that his error was due to reliance on his assistant. Suspension for six months from the Register of Veterinary Surgeons was recommended and confirmed by the Council.

In the High Court, Kenny J. held that Lynch had made claims contrary to regulations, had not supervised Daly, had signed forms without checking them in his anxiety to get rid of Daly, and lacked clerical staff, thus letting claims be so far in arrears that it was inevitable there would be mistakes when they were submitted. However, many professionals fall behind in clerical and documentary work, and Lynch was justified in relying on Daly to complete the documentary work and forms, and not culpable in not checking the claims against field books. Kenny J. was also satisfied that Lynch did not make the claims fraudulently, and that his vaccination of animals over six months old was inadvertent. Again, Daly's double vaccinations and vaccinations of animals over six months old resulted from not checking against field books, relying on requests by herd owners or their employees, and haste, combined with trying to do as many vaccinations as possible to increase his earnings. He was charged with careless and reckless conduct indicating a disregard for rules, but he was not being fraudulent in terms of acting dishonestly with intent that he or Lynch should get money to which they were not entitled. Even the forgeries of signatures (which Kenny J. thought *was* conduct disgraceful to him but with which he was not charged) was done to get money to which he thought Lynch had legitimate claim. In this regard:

> the conduct must be of a kind which brings disgrace upon the person primarily in the eyes of the members of his profession, but also in those of the public. 'Disgraceful' implies an element of conscious wrong doing or the doing of something which a professional person by reason of his training must have realised would cause him to incur shame in the eyes of his professional

colleagues. The conduct must also be in a professional respect
and so it must relate to something which he does when carrying
on his profession and in the course of the performance of the
duties which it imposes. (page 11)

In the opinion of Kenny J., there was no dishonesty, fraud or moral
turpitude in the acts charged against Lynch and Daly:

nor was there such persistent and reckless disregard of records
which could be regarded as dishonesty. There was carelessness;
there was delay amounting to folly in filling up the forms and
then, when there were considerable arrears, there was a hurried
attempt to complete the forms for payment so that an unhappy
association between them could be ended. I do not think that
this was disgraceful conduct. (page 13)

Kenny J. therefore cancelled the two decisions of the Veterinary
Council but did not award costs, since the Council may well have
considered that gross carelessness was disgraceful. In his opinion,
the lawyers representing the Minister and petitioners should have
used their knowledge of the law to explain what 'disgraceful to him
in a professional respect' means as interpreted by the courts in
specifically referred to cases, in which case the Council would not
have made the decision they did make.

Questions of Law
Although factual elements are always present when a court makes
a ruling in a case on a point of law, there are cases in which the
primary issue to be resolved is the meaning of the statute itself. A
case involving mixed questions of fact and law, and questions of
law as such is *Philip Rahill and Joseph Goode v. Thomas Brady* 1971 IR
69. Defendant Brady held a licence to sell liquor at a hotel and
applied for and obtained an order from the District Court authorising him to sell liquor at a livestock mart, to which no licence was
attached, in Cavan town during the month of April every Tuesday
and Thursday when there were pigs and cattle sales. The order was
made under section 11(1) of the Intoxicating Liquor Act 1962,
which provides that a District Justice may make such an order if
he thinks fit to do so provided he is 'satisfied that a special event'
will be held at a location or premises to which no licence has been
attached. Objectors to the order appealed by way of case stated to

the High Court, claiming that the decision was erroneous on a point of law since the bi-weekly sales of the livestock mart did not constitute 'special events' within the meaning of section 11 of the 1962 Act. On appeal from the High Court to the Supreme Court, Ó Dálaigh C.J., in affirming the High Court order, held that the issue did involve a point of law and the District Justice's decision was open to review by way of case stated. The Supreme Court then held that the interpretation of the phrase 'special event' as contained in section 11(1) of the 1962 Act, was to be determined by application of the ordinary meaning of the word 'special' and not in conjunction with the word 'occasional' employed to categorise the licence mentioned in the Act. Given this interpretation of the word 'special', bi-weekly sales of cattle and pigs in a country town, at premises customarily employed only for that function, did not constitute special events within the meaning of the 1962 Act.

A case which turned more completely on a question of law was that of *Russell v. Minister for Local Government* 1976 IR 185 (see chapter 5 on the issues of official notice and the interrelated roles of the departmental inspector and minister). In this case, the appeal to the Supreme Court was from an order of the High Court quashing a compulsory purchase order by Cobh Urban District Council, as housing authority under the Housing Act 1966, to acquire lands held by plaintiffs. The ground for the High Court order was that since Cobh Urban District Council had no building programme, which they are required to prepare under section 55(1) of the 1966 Act, they could not exercise validly the powers granted by sections 76 and 77 of the Act, under which they had issued the acquisition order.

Walsh J., for the Supreme Court, held that although the Urban District Council did not have a building programme, it nevertheless did have housing needs, and among the purposes of the 1966 Act was the satisfying of such needs. Section 76 enables a housing authority to acquire land compulsorily for purposes of the Act. Furthermore, section 77 provides that a housing authority may also be authorised to acquire compulsorily for those purposes, land which is not immediately required for such purposes. Acquisition for future use is subject to the requirement that the Minister is of the opinion that there is a reasonable expectation that the land will be needed by the authority in the future, in order to achieve any of the multiple and varied objectives to which the housing authority is to have regard under section 55(3), when preparing a building programme.

In the opinion of Walsh J., there is nothing in the Act which restricts a housing authority from carrying out the purposes of the Housing Act until they have drawn up a building programme approved by the Minister. Sections 76 and 77 of the Act cannot be read as being dependent upon the pre-existence of a building programme, since the only criterion of these sections is that such acquisition be for purposes of the Housing Act 1966. Section 76 deals with present needs and section 77 with needs reasonably expected to arise which enables development of 'land banks', and it is section 77 which is dependent on the Minister's approval on the grounds of reasonable expectation of future need for the land. In this case, he felt there was ample evidence on which the Minister could hold that the land sought to be acquired was for the purposes of the Act. Though the Minister would have a clearer picture of the future needs of the housing authority if a building programme had been made and had been approved by him, it does not follow that given proper evidence he could not form an opinion as to reasonable expectations for the future. To sum up:

> The learned trial judge, having come to that opinion in respect of s. 77, formed the view that if a building programme was a necessary condition precedent for the invocation of s. 77, that *a fortiori* it must be a necessary condition precedent for the invocation of section 76. If however, it is not a condition precedent for s. 77, which in my view–it is not–then the reasoning as to s. 76 does not apply. Taking s. 76 independently of section 77, I can find nothing in the section which would import such a condition precedent. (page 189)

The High Court decision was reversed by the Supreme Court based on its interpretation of the 1966 Act and finding that there was ample evidence for the Minister to determine that the land acquisition was for a statutory need.

A case in which the relevant facts were perhaps even less of a consideration in the resolution of the issue based on a point of law as to the meaning of a crucial statutory phrase was *Duffy v. Corporation of Dublin* 1974 IR 33. The Corporation had purchased land and provided a cattle market on that land in 1863, under the Dublin

Improvement Act 1849. It had been the major market in Ireland for sale of cattle for export but fell into great decline in modern times and required an annual subvention from rates increasing to over £33,000 in 1972. Persistent losses were caused in part by the holding of cattle marts throughout Ireland, and since the Corporation was advised that those marts were sufficient to meet the need, it seemed logical to close the Dublin market. However, the plaintiffs, who were members of the Dublin Cattle Salesmasters Association, sought orders in the High Court which would require the market to be kept open and also required defendants to provide an auction. The controversy centred on interpretation of certain sections of the 1849 Act under which the Dublin Cattle Market was established. The 1849 Act incorporated the Markets and Fairs Clauses Act 1847. Section 14 of the 1847 Act provides that after a marketplace is opened for public use, those so opening it shall hold markets on the prescribed days (if any) and on such other days as they appoint from time to time by any bye-law made under this Act or the special Act.

Among the issues raised and grounds argued in this case, the fundamental point upon which the final decision was made in the Supreme Court was the claim by the defendant Corporation that the use of the land for a market is merely a statutory discretion vested in them. Therefore, the Corporation could legally exercise that discretion by deciding not to use that land any more as a market. This argument rested upon section 79 of the Dublin Improvement Act 1849 providing that 'it shall be lawful for the Council, at any time . . as they may think fit, to purchase, rent and provide other lands . . . to be appropriated and used as a market or markets', and section 80 which states that 'it shall be lawful for the Council to build and provide upon the land to be purchased, rented or provided by them . . . and forever afterwards to maintain and improve, one or more market place or market places for the sale of cattle, animals . . . within the limits of this Act . . . as the Council shall think fit'. The defendant Corporation argued that the words 'it shall be lawful' in each section were enabling only, and thus discretionary, rather than mandatory. The plaintiff Association contended that the opposite meaning should be given to these words, i.e. that the words are mandatory.

Henchy J., for the Supreme Court, cited *Julius v. Bishop of Oxford* (1880) 5 App. Cas. 214 as the correct approach to interpretation of

the words 'it shall be lawful', namely that those words were enabling
and empowering words to do a particular thing which otherwise
there would be no authority to do, and that the donee of such a
power may either exercise it or leave it unused. It is true that there
may be an aspect in the nature of the thing empowered to be done,
or the object for which it is to be done, which may couple the power
with a duty to exercise it for those persons for whose benefit the
power was granted. However, the burden lies upon those who claim
a duty exists to exercise that power to show in the circumstances
something which creates the obligation. In the present instance,
Henchy J. stated:

> it must be held that the words 'it shall be lawful' in ss. 79 and
> 80 of the Act of 1849 merely gave the defendants power to
> acquire the site for the market, to build and provide the market
> place, and forever afterwards to maintain and improve it. It is
> for the plaintiffs to show that, having regard to all the relevant
> circumstances, the power to maintain the market for ever
> should be treated as a duty to maintain it for ever. (page 40)

Henchy J. noted that the verbs used in the 1849 Act show that the
legislature was intent upon distinguishing between discretionary
and obligatory provisions, i.e. 'shall', 'may', 'it shall be lawful' and
'it shall not be lawful'. Section 78 provided that 'it shall be lawful'
for the Council to purchase or lease with consent of the owner any
land and premises which shall then be used as a market, and in his
opinion, this power carried no duty. Section 79 of the Act had a
marginal note, providing that 'it is lawful for the Council at any
time and from time to time as they may think fit to purchase, rent
and provide other lands'. If one inserted that it shall be 'obligatory
on' in place of 'lawful for', it becomes clear that the following words
'from time to time as they may think fit' would be inappropriate, if
the intent were to make such purchase and provision mandatory.
Section 80 of the 1849 Act was crucial since regardless of whether
they were obliged to do so, defendants had exercised their powers
by establishing a market, and section 80 states 'it shall be lawful
for the council . . . for ever afterwards to maintain and improve'
that market place. The question as to whether that power is a duty
is answered by the analagous case of *R. v. Great Western Railway Co*

(1893) 62 LJ QB 572, in which the issue was whether a company given power to acquire land compulsorily for a railway and to maintain that railway should be subject to mandamus to force the company to reinstate the railway which had been allowed to fall into disuse. In that case, the Court held:

> If the Act of Parliament intended that it should be maintained for ever by the persons making it, nothing would have been easier than to have said so. Many Acts of Parliament do say so, and if an Act does not say so it is because it was not intended to do so. (IR, page 43)

In the view of Henchy J, this statement showed the way to the correct interpretation of section 80 of the 1849 Act. Had the legislature intended to make the power granted by section 80 a duty, 'then nothing would have been easier to do than to have done so'.

The decision in the *Duffy* case thus rested on analysis by Henchy J. of the internal content and phraseology of the statute and analagous judicial decisions, in which the facts of the case were not the determining factor. Other illustrations of determinations also made on issues of interpretation of law include *Phillips v. Minister for Social Welfare: In the Matter of the Social Welfare Acts 1952 to 1972* unreported, High Court, per Kenny J., 28 February 1974, in which the Court corrected a misinterpretation of the Social Welfare Act 1952 by a social welfare appeals officer. The appeals officer had used as a basis for categorising employees as agricultural workers under the 1952 Act, a test applicable under the Unemployment Insurance Act 1920 as interpreted by the Supreme Court in *Warner v. Minister of Industry and Commerce* (1928) ILTR 121. Since the 1952 Act test was whether the enterprise in which the employee is working is an agricultural enterprise, the 1920 Act test of whether the employee himself or herself is personally doing agricultural work did not apply. Similarly, a misinterpretation of Garda Síochána regulations was rectified in *The State (Sheehan) v. McMahon and Others* unreported, Supreme Court, per Henchy J., 25 October 1977. An appeal from a finding at the first instance of a disciplinary process was made to the Commissioner, who under the regulations chose to refer the appeal to an Appeals Board rather than deciding the matter. The Appeals Board referred the matter back to the Commissioner on the ground that the regulations did not give the

Board jurisdiction over the matter. The Court held that the Board had misconstrued the regulations, that the matter was properly before them for review, and that they also lacked jurisdiction to refer the matter back to the Commissioner.

Finally, an informative discussion of the role of the courts in interpreting law, especially as to what judges may and may not imply from statutory provisions, was provided by Finlay J. in his judgment in *Dublin Corporation v. Smithwick* unreported, High Court, per Finlay J.,12 July 1977. In this case section 55 of the Local Government (Planning and Development) Act 1963 on the right to compensation of a property owner who had been refused planning permission because of an anticipated change in zoning requirements was under consideration. Finlay J. construed this statutory provision in relation to the powers of the Minister for Local Government under section 58(1) of the 1963 Act to make a declaration that the property owners were entitled to compensation. A critical part of this question was whether there was a time limit set on the Minister's making of such a decision. In this latter regard, Finlay J., in a statement typical of other aspects of his opinion on the role of the courts in interpreting the statutes, stated:

> There is no doubt that it would be very desirable that there should be a reasonable time limit upon the Minister in reaching a decision in this case. It is unnecessary for me to emphasise again that it is not my function to legislate and I am not entitled to interpret into an Act something which I consider to be desirable; I must interpret the Act and construe it and I can only interpret it by way of implication if there is something which is absolutely essential for its construction or working. I am not satisfied that the provision of a reasonable time for the making of the Minister's decision under Section 58 comes within that category and this point also fails.

From an overall standpoint, these judicial decisions show that, in regard to the availability of judicial review, the Irish courts in certain instances have upheld finality of administrative determinations in the absence of an *ultra vires* action or violation of procedural aspects of natural justice, thus raising the constitutional question analysed by Barrington J. (pages 426-7). At the same time, the courts have also asserted their power of review in recent instances, despite legislative provisions for administrative finality, thus presenting a mixed picture which is typical in American administrative law. The judicial determinations on standing to sue in Ireland can be characterised as liberal, in terms of applying pragmatic criteria as to what constitutes sufficient interest to enable a person or organisation to be heard in court, rather than strict or narrowly defined tests of legal interest. Concepts of exhaustion of administrative remedies, and ripeness for review, have been applied so that they limit availability of review only in those situations where it is patently obvious that judicial determinations would be contrary to statutory intent or premature from the standpoint of the relative roles of administrative agencies and the courts. The scope of judicial review gives credence to administrative findings of fact under what amounts to a substantial evidence based on the whole record doctrine, while maintaining an activist role for the courts in reviewing and, where it is felt necessary, substituting the judgment of the courts for that of administrators on mixed questions of law and fact, and on questions of law.

Notes to Chapter 10

1. Wade, *Administrative Law* 605, and generally 598-606 (1982)
2. Schwartz and Wade, *Legal Control of Government [Legal Control]* 291-6 (1972)
3. Wade, *Administrative Law* 573
4. Wade, *Administrative Law* 590 and generally 587-90 (1982)
5. Wade, *Administrative Law* 591
6. Schwartz and Wade, *Legal Control* 281
7. Donal Barrington, 'Private Property under the Irish Constitution ['Private Property'], *Irish Jurist* 16 (1973)
8. Donal Barrington, 'Private Property', 16
9. Donal Barrington, 'Private Property', 16
10. *Irish Jurist* 1-17 at 17 (1973)
11. See also O'Sullivan and Shepherd, *A Sourcebook on Planning Law in Ireland [Sourcebook]* 364-6 (1984). Note: footnotes 11-14 refer the reader to extracts from cases discussed in the text.
12. See also O'Sullivan and Shepherd, *Sourcebook* 364-5
13. See also O'Sullivan and Shepherd *Sourcebook* 211-15, 316-21
14. See also O'Sullivan and Shepherd, *Sourcebook* 320
15. Jaffe, *Judicial Control of Administrative Action* 548 (1965)
16. Davis, *Administrative Law Text* 554-6 (1972)
17. Schwartz and Wade, *Legal Control of Government* 238

11   Further Modes of Oversight

Administrative law in Ireland is a well developed and evolving field of law generating issues recognised in legal and governmental publications,[1] in official studies[2] and in legislative enactments. The issues relate in various ways to the central concern of this study as to how existing modes of oversight and review of administrative determinations balance protection of individual rights with administrative effectiveness in advancing the public interest. This concern has also been present in judicial decisions on the constitutionality of delegation of discretionary powers to administrative bodies and the requirements of natural and constitutional justice to be met in the procedures followed in making administrative determinations, as discussed in this study.

Issues and Related Needs for Oversight

The earlier discussion of judicial remedies and the grounds for granting them (see chapter 3) show that the availability and scope of judicial review has broadened to provide greater opportunity for relief. However, the multiple grounds for, and forms of, judicial remedies may result in non-resolution of a controversy because of legal technicalities surrounding the remedies. As the Law Reform Commission stated:

> The present system of remedies . . . is comprehensive in that it is difficult to envisage any justiciable grievance which would not come within the purview of one or other of the present remedies. It is effective because, as experience in France shows, it is essential for the courts to have power to compel or to restrain action by the administration. But there is also a major defect – the line of demarcation between overlapping remedies is uncertain and there is no machinery for claiming such remedies in the alternative.[3]

It is evident from the judicial resolution of issues concerning liability and immunity of Irish central and local government (chapter 4) that judicial doctrine has evolved in the direction of increasing the government's liability to citizen suits in such areas as action against a minister regarding provision of services, or based on contractual relationships with the state or based on torts committed by its agents. This contrasts with the United States where permitting citizen suits in such matters has, until recently, required legislation.

The liability of local authorities in Ireland for damages suffered by citizens under the Malicious Injuries Code has no counterpart in the United States save for statutes on liability for mob violence or riot damages. The problem raised by Kelly concerning compensation costs falling on ratepayers of a local authority for damages done by a non-resident has been ameliorated somewhat by the Malicious Injuries Act 1981 providing that the national government is responsible for anything over 2p in the pound, as well as all claims the Garda Superintendent identifies as arising from the troubles in the North of Ireland. It is, however, something of an anomaly that inaction by local authorities in such matters as road repair constitutes nonfeasance, which does not lead to liability, while action to repair a road may, if a court holds that such action involved negligence, lead to liability for damages for misfeasance.

The most significant issues and developments in Irish administrative law discussed in chapter 5 are those concerning legislative and judicial requirements regarding compliance with natural and constitutional justice in making administrative determinations. These issues are further illustrated in chapters 6 to 9 since the exercise of rule-making, investigating, licensing and directing powers raises such issues. The statutory provisions and judicial decisions discussed illustrate the variety of institutional arrangements and procedures referred to in the Devlin Report, together with increasingly sophisticated analyses by the courts of procedural requirements of natural and constitutional justice in the more complex institutional aspects of administrative decision-making. This is apparent in recent judicial decisions on the interrelated processes and roles of local authorities, inspecting officers, appeals officers, ministers, administrative tribunals and courts in carrying out their respective functions. In addition, the findings made in the Devlin Report are still pertinent in respect of the difference between theory and practice regarding ministers making all decisions pertaining to their departments under the corporation sole concept, and the increasing number of administrative tribunals with varying degrees of independence from ministerial control, which are staffed in different ways and have diverse operating procedures. These factors led to the finding that the time had come:

> to rationalise these tribunals, to standardise so far as possible the procedures in like cases, to clarify relations with Ministers on the one hand and with the Courts on the other, to improve the professionalism of a number of those who discharge such duties, and to make this type of remedy available to as many as possible of those aggrieved by administrative action.[4]

In addition to these issues which apply generally to the exercise of all types of discretionary administrative powers, there are issues peculiar to each of those powers. In regard to rule-making power, the discussion in chapters 3 and 6 reveals that although the breadth of discretion delegated by statute in Ireland equals and at times exceeds that of the United States, Ireland has not been confronted with the issues of constitutionality of such delegation to a degree comparable to the United States. Moreover, Ireland, like England, has not differentiated between legislative and interpretative-type rule-making in its statutes, thus avoiding the extensive litigation prevalent in the United States over distinctions which are difficult to determine in certain instances. The customary grounds for invalidating administrative rules, i.e. unconstitutionality, excess of jurisdiction, unreasonableness and bad faith, and retroactivity do not raise issues which suggest a need for change. However, no Act of general application requires procedures for public participation in rule-making, e.g. giving notice of proposed rules and an opportunity to submit written comment; or to testify at legislative-type hearings held at the discretion of the agency, subject to exceptions for emergencies. In addition to increasing public acceptance as a result of the opportunity to participate in the rule-making process, such procedures could provide administrators (and ultimately the Houses of the Oireachtas when regulations are laid before them) with facts and opinions from interested parties on a systematic basis. No administrative body has a monopoly of information and some sense of interest group reaction to proposed rules may be obtained.

In regard to investigating power, the absence of judicial determinations on the application of the constitutional protection against unreasonable searches and seizures in administrative law cases, and lack of a specific constitutional provision against self-incrimination place a particular responsibility on the legislature to specify such protections in statutes delegating investigating power to agencies. As the judicial determinations in chapter 7 reveal, such protective statutory provisions are applied with rigour by the courts if they exist, but in their absence, those protections might not be provided by judicial interpretation alone. Rather, protection against arbitrary application of investigating power depends upon judicial interpretation as to whether the investigation is *ultra vires* the statute, relevant to the statutory purpose, adjudicatory in nature requiring natural justice, or is an invasion of natural rights.

As the statutory provisions and judicial determinations on licensing power in chapter 8 show, Irish courts have applied the concepts of right versus privilege so as to preserve the requisites of natural and constitutional justice in reviewing the administrative grant, renewal and revocation of licences. Their decisions in most instances affirm concepts of licensing as a preventive rather than a punitive control system to protect the public, and on this basis the fundamental issues in this type of regulatory control have been resolved. However, since licensing is essentially a system of prior consent to operate, with continued administrative supervision to maintain compliance with licence requirements, it seems somewhat anomalous that a number of licensing systems are administered directly by the courts, with the Garda Síochána in certain instances providing what amounts to continuing supervision to determine compliance. The lower courts are thus placed in the role of administrative bodies making initial determinations of fact and law in deciding on the grant of licences subject to appeal to higher courts on mixed questions of law and fact or law alone. It may also lead to varied evidential standards in licensing determinations made by individual judges as against those made by a single administrative body.

In respect of directing power (as indicated in chapters 6 and 9), there is a confusing semantic problem. The terms 'statutory instrument' and 'order' are used in statutes and court judgments to designate both rules and rule-making power and what this study calls 'directions' and 'directing power' also referred to by other terms such as a 'declaration' or a 'warning notice'). Since the courts hold that exercise of directing power must meet procedural due process requirements not normally expected of rule-making, it would seem appropriate to develop a consistent use of these terms.

'Rule' and 'rule-making power' would then refer to the making and promulgation of standards of general application while the terms 'direction' and 'directing power' (or order and ordering power if preferred) would mean the power to take adjudicative decisions leading to commands to stop and/or take corrective actions as specified. In addition, the nature and breadth of discretion given in Acts to administrative bodies to make detailed directions designed to stop or remedy specific actions of persons in individual situations emphasises the need to rationalise and develop uniform procedures and institutional arrangements.

The discussion in chapter 10 of the availability and scope of judicial review reveals that, in general, if a justiciable grievance exists, there is a judicial remedy. Moreover, the judiciary in Ireland have been relatively liberal in their application of concepts of *locus standi,* exhaustion of administrative remedies and ripeness for review, and increasingly so regarding finality of administrative determinations, in relation to the availability of review. The scope of review, while giving weight and support to administrative expertise in findings of fact, also reflects an activist attitude concerning the judicial role in dealing with mixed questions of law and fact and questions of law. Through the case-by-case process of judicial inclusion and exclusion the courts have exercised a major influence in developing general understanding and application of substantive and procedural concepts of natural and constitutional justice in administrative law in Ireland. However, it must be recognised that despite the advantages of incremental development of policy in response to problems as they arise, there are also limitations upon the case-by-case process for development of policy through judicial decisions. Courts are limited to dealing with issues brought to them by the initiative of parties in controversies involving particular situations and they are bound by precedent or *stare decisis,* although at times they do expand issues raised and indicate their views on matters beyond the immediate issue through *obiter dicta,* and may reverse previous decisions. Less obvious is the fact that the initial action or decision of the first level of administration is often final. Through ignorance, lack of financial resources, a feeling of futility, or calculation of time and money expended for an uncertain outcome in making an appeal, the individual often does not appeal to higher administrative authority or tribunal, and is even less inclined to appeal to the courts. Furthermore, courts are not in a position to recommend remedial legislation, except implicitly in their decisions, nor can they provide the continuous oversight across the wide spectrum of administrative agencies necessary to secure greater uniformity of organisation and procedures in administrative law matters. The need for action to respond to these issues would appear to call for a central governmental agency (or agencies) with the following functions:

1. Undertake continuing research and develop recommendations for legislation on issues in administrative law, such as: a single general form of application for judicial review of administrative determinations; amendment of existing Acts and recognition in future Acts so as to provide for definition and differentiation between administrative rule-making power and rules, as against directing power and directions; transferring the jurisdiction over granting of licences by courts to appropriate administrative agencies; general legislation regarding unreasonable searches and self-incrimination in administrative investigatory processes.

2. Undertake continuing research on existing agency procedures for rule-making, and either: (1) recommend legislation requiring, or (2) make rules under a grant of rule-making power providing for, a more uniform mode of rule-making procedure by administrative bodies. Such procedure might include notice to the public of proposed rules or amendments of existing rules and an opportunity to submit written comments, supplemented by agency discretion to hold hearings to receive oral comments on proposed rules. Exceptions to such requirements should be provided to obviate situations where strict adherence to rule-making procedures would be dysfunctional. Establishment of such general rule-making procedures by regulations of the central agency rather than legislation might be preferable so as to allow for change and adjustment.

3. Undertake continuing surveys of existing agency organisational arrangements and administrative procedures for determinations made in conjunction with exercise of investigatory, licensing, directing or other powers such as determining benefits, payments or other government subsidies.

Based upon such surveys, the agency could either: (1) recommend legislation, or (2) under a grant of rule-making power, make rules of general application, with the aim of achieving greater rationality and uniformity in organisational arrangements and administrative procedures. To be considered in this regard are the decentralisation of first-instance decisions from ministers to deciding officers of appropriate rank, provision for administrative tribunals to hear appeals, and procedures designed to conform with judicial expectations as to natural and constitutional justice. Such measures should provide for appropriate interaction with ministers in policy matters. Establishing standards by rule to allow for variations in organisation and procedure to avoid the effects of excessive uniformity is initially preferable to legislation.

4. Provide training, advisory and technical services to departments and agencies since it is unreasonable to expect agencies of varied size, function and degree of administrative maturity to adapt to and conform with changes required by general rule or statute without such supportive advisory and technical assistance.

5. Provide redress without expense to persons aggrieved by adverse action of administrative agencies when initial investigation reveals negligence, an absence of authority or of reasons, discrimination, lack of fairness, inadequacy or unavailability of existing remedies and where there is a grievance which calls for correction and for which there is no judicial remedy.

Modes of Oversight: Applicability to Issues and Needs

In addition to the legislative and judicial controls which exist in Ireland, there are four modes or prototypes for oversight of actions and determinations of administrative agencies exercising discretionary powers. One form of oversight is that of an ombudsman (which became operative in Ireland in 1984) to receive and investigate complaints by citizens against the determinations, undue delay or maladministration of administrative agencies and to seek correction of the cause of complaint through recommendation, negotiation or criticism. According to a survey made in 1979, ombudsman offices such as the British Parliamentary Commissioner for Administration[5] existed in approximately twenty countries with some seven ombudsman offices in their subdivisions,[6] including France which, in addition to its administrative court system, established a Mediateur in 1973. The Mediateur has the investigatory functions of the Scandinavian Ombudsman and is patterned to some degree after the British Parliamentary Commissioner with the brief to inquire into complaints about maladministration or unfairness and to make annual reports.[7]

Another mode is the enactment of an administrative procedures Act of general application to provide for standardisation of administrative processes and institutional arrangements for rule-making, adjudicatory decision-making and appeal to the courts. This is typified by the Administrative Procedures Act 1946 (APA) in the United States and its amendments which include what are commonly designated the Freedom of Information Act 1966 (section 552, APA), the Privacy Act 1974 (section 552(a), APA) and the Government in the Sunshine Act 1976 (section 552(b), APA).[8] The three amendments (broadly speaking) provide for access to governmental data, protection of individual records from unwarranted exposure, and openness of governmental decision-making respectively. A third mode is a central administrative court system for review of appeals from administrative actions and determinations, epitomised by the Conseil d'État in France[9] and to a much lesser (and more restricted in jurisdiction) degree, the recommendation made for an administrative court in the United States in the Ash Council Report.[10]

A fourth mode is the establishment of a central administrative body concerned with achieving more rational and standardised institutional arrangements and processes in administrative bodies involved in administrative law and process, through a composite of investigating, supervising, and advisory powers and functions granted by an Act of the legislature. Proposals for this mode which have been made include the recommendations of the Devlin Report's 'Note on Administrative Law and Procedures' for a Commissioner for Administrative Justice[11] details of which will be discussed later. In addition, the United States Attorney General's Committee on Administrative Procedure Report of 1941 recommended an Office of Federal Administrative Procedure which

s

would examine critically the procedures and practice of agencies, receive suggestions and criticisms, gather and collate information concerning administrative practice and procedures, and appoint or remove members of a corps of independent hearing officers nominated by various departments of government to serve in those departments.[12] In a third study, *Administrative Adjudication in the State of New York* (1942), constituting a report to the governor of that state, and commonly known as the 'Benjamin Report', a recommendation was made for establishment of a division of administrative procedure in the Executive Department of the New York State government.[13] Finally, the Franks Committee Report in Britain led to the Tribunals and Inquiries Act 1958, which created the Council on Tribunals. Operating examples of this form of oversight include the British Council on Tribunals (functioning under the Tribunals and Inquiries Act 1971, a consolidating Act which did not change the substance of the original 1958 Act)[14] and the Administrative Conference of the United States established in 1968, under the Administrative Conference Act 1964.[15] Among the activities of the Council on Tribunals in practice are commenting on bills and on procedural rules, and assisting departments in developing provisions in regard to new tribunals. It has made studies of tribunals, investigated complaints made to it, and in certain instances has achieved reform of tribunals' practices. The Council on Tribunals was not given the power to appoint chairpersons and members of tribunals, as recommended by the Franks Committee, and in Wade's opinion, is limited by its position in relation to Parliament, and thus is essentially an advisory committee.[16]

The Federal Administrative Conference of the United States is composed of members from government services, practising lawyers and law school professors. It is a research and advisory body organised into committees on various aspects of administrative organisations, procedure and processes. It has produced 'three volumes of rich and useful recommendations and reports', according to Davis, who feels that the Conference has had limited success in securing congressional adoption of recommendations, and achieved more through pressure on administrative agencies.[17]

The Ombudsman

Subsequent to the proposal for an Ombudsman in the *Report of the All-Party Informal Committee on Administrative Justice* (1977), the

Ombudsman Act 1980 was enacted by the Oireachtas, brought into effect by order of the government in July 1983, and an Ombudsman was appointed in January 1984. Under section 2 of the Act, the Ombudsman is appointed by the President on resolution of the Dáil and Seanad for a six-year term, is removable only for stated cause by the President on resolution by the Dáil and Seanad, and is disqualified from continuing in office if appointed to any other public office. The Ombudsman shall be independent in the performance of his functions, according to section 4, and on receiving a complaint or on his own motion, he may investigate any action taken by anyone in performance of administrative functions where preliminary examination reveals certain characteristics. These include action adversely affecting a person which is taken without authority, or on irrelevant grounds, negligently or carelessly. Action based on incomplete or erroneous information, involving discrimination or 'undesirable administrative practices' or which is contrary to 'fair or sound administration' is also included. The Ombudsman has discretion to refuse to investigate if preliminary investigation reveals that the complaint is trivial, that the complainant has insufficient interest, or has not taken reasonable steps to seek redress, or has sought redress which has not yet been refused, or the subject of the complaint is being dealt with in another investigation. If the Ombudsman decides not to investigate, reasons must be given in writing to the complainant.

Investigating powers are granted to the Ombudsman by section 7 of the Act to require submission of documents and appearance to testify, backed by contempt of court penalties for non-compliance. Witnesses are given the same privileges and immunities as if appearing in the High Court. Information or documents concerning decisions and proceedings of the government or its committees are exempt from investigation, but the privilege of secrecy under the Official Secrets Act 1963 does not apply unless a minister gives notice in writing that disclosure other than to the Ombudsman would be prejudicial to the public interest. There is also a prohibition against disclosure of preliminary investigations of the Ombudsman (section 9), and investigations are not to be conducted in public.

The powers and procedures to be followed by the Ombudsman require that the Ombudsman will not make a finding of criticism adverse to a person without giving opportunity to that person to consider and make a representation responding to such finding (section 6). The results of the investigation and recommendation related thereto are to be sent to the department involved, and to any person involved in the action in regard to the complaint. A statement of the result of the investigation and recommendation, and responses given by the department are given to the complainant. The Ombudsman may also notify any other person whom he considers appropriate. He may recommend further consideration of the matter at issue by a department or remedial means for mitigating or altering adverse action and may request a department to submit its reasons for taking action. If there is an unsatisfactory response to his recommendations, he may make a special report to the Oireachtas. Beyond the specified procedures in the Act the Ombudsman may establish such procedures (under section 8) for conducting an investigation as he considers appropriate in the circumstances of a case including whether a person may or may not be represented by counsel. The Ombudsman makes annual reports and such other reports as he thinks desirable to each House of the Oireachtas. All publications of the Ombudsman, reports to the Houses of the Oireachtas and statements by parties to a dispute are absolutely privileged against action for defamation.

The Ombudsman's jurisdiction extends to 41 departments of state, commissions, offices, agencies and persons specifically listed in the First Schedule of the 1980 Act. However, matters occurring within such departments and agencies are excluded from his juris-diction (section 5) if legal proceedings have been initiated or a statutory right of appeal to a court or an independent appeals body exists (except for social welfare appeals officers). Also excluded are the government's decisions relating to personnel; security, military and intergovernmental activities; administration of prisons, matters relating to aliens and clemency; and situations where a minister requests in writing with reasons, that there not be an investigation. In addition, section 9 of the Act provides that ministers and the Revenue Commissioners may give written notice that the disclosure of a document, information or a specified item would for stated reasons be prejudicial to the public interest, which precludes the Ombudsman from communicating such data to anyone. Finally, Schedule II of the Act lists 88 bodies or agencies not subject to the Ombudsman's scrutiny. They include state-sponsored bodies, local authorities, bodies set up under the Health Acts and Health (Corporate Bodies) Act, regulatory boards such as the Dental Board, Medical Council and Pigs and Bacon Commission, and specifically named boards or commissions exercising administrative adjudicatory powers attached to the Departments of Justice, Labour, Industry, Trade, Commerce and Tourism, Posts and Telegraphs, and Defence.

It would appear from the provisions of the Ombudsman Act 1980 that the newly established Ombudsman has the potential for meeting the fifth type of need summarised above in respect of providing redress to individuals aggrieved by administrative actions or determinations where a grievance is not being remedied owing to inadequacy or non-existence of meaningful relief. This is especially true regarding grievances which do not necessarily constitute a formal legal cause for appeal, or where the individual lacks knowledge or resources for seeking redress. Moreover, a means for voicing complaint and securing corrective action is provided as a matter of statutory right through an impartial, independent officer, rather than as a matter of privilege or political connection in bringing a complaint to one's legislative representative or a minister. Indirectly there is potential for the Ombudsman, through his special and annual reports, to call the attention of the Oireachtas to organisational and procedural problems in the administrative process which constitute the causes for the individual complaints he receives. This conceivably could form the basis for remedial legislation. However, this last potential line of action is by way of inference rather than any mandate in the 1980 Act; and the focus of the office upon redress of individual complaints and demands on the Ombudsman's time and energies in regard to individual cases mitigates against this office being a major source of systematic studies of administrative organisation and procedure.

The exemptions from the Ombudsman's jurisdiction specified in the Act limit the scope of his functions and potential for suggesting statutory change. The Act in no way suggests that the Ombudsman might provide expert assistance in developing procedures, and in providing training for improved administrative procedures.

Administrative Procedures Act

Adoption of an administrative procedures Act of government-wide application, which includes provisions for freedom of information

and safeguards for privacy of persons whose records might otherwise
be available, would meet certain issues and needs of Irish administrative law, but not others as identified earlier. Such an Act could
meet the needs of defining and differentiating between types of
regulatory powers, providing for more systematic and standardised
notice-and-comment procedures for rule-making, and requiring
more uniform procedures in making adjudicatory determinations
so as to meet the requirements of natural and constitutional justice.
It could also specify generally applicable organisational arrangements for hearing officers and administrative tribunals, and provide
for access to governmental records, i.e. 'freedom of information',
subject to appropriate protection of individual privacy and legit-
imately confidential governmental records. Provision could be made
for a single mode of appeal from administrative determinations
leading to judicial remedies which could vary in accordance with
what was appropriate to the situation and the scope and nature of
judicial review as developed in judicial decisions, such as the nature
of evidence necessary to sustain an administrative determination.
In this regard, the extensive experience of the United States in the
operation and judicial interpretation of its Administrative Procedure Act with its 'freedom of information', 'privacy' and 'government in the sunshine' sections could be profited from so as to avoid
certain problems which have become apparent in its application,
and emphasise the positive gains achieved under those Acts.

However, the issue raised by the Devlin Report in regard to
an administrative procedures Act still remains, namely whether
administrative law in Ireland has evolved to the point where it is
desirable to codify it into an all-encompassing statute. Implicit in
this issue is the difficulty of devising explicit statutory standards to
rationalise and standardise administrative procedures and institutional arrangements which do not impose a rigid uniformity upon
the wide spectrum of agencies with differing programmes, clienteles,
complexity and magnitude of operations and degree of maturity.
On the other hand, broad statutory standards, multiple escape
clauses and exceptions to allow for flexibility encourage frequent
litigation and the courts are then obliged to provide standards
which are not in the statute on a case-by-case basis. Finally, the
implementation of an administrative procedures Act in the absence
of a central agency to oversee and facilitate compliance through

assistance and training, depends upon the degree of maturity and sophistication of the agencies and their co-operation, and their degree of awareness that non-compliance with the requirements of the Act may lead to challenge and reversal in the courts. It also should be recognised that the American Administrative Procedures Act was adopted in relation to a presidential system of government, and in response to strong pressure from external groups such as the American Bar Association seeking codification of standards which up to that point had been developed and applied over time in statutes and judicial decisions pertaining to individual agencies and practices. The need for such an Act may not be perceived as being essential in the Irish parliamentary system among those interest groups in Ireland most concerned with the operation of administrative law in the legal system, particularly at this stage of development of Irish administrative law.

Central Administrative Court

A third mode of oversight, the central administrative court, is typified by the Conseil d'État in France. Many of the functions of the Conseil d'État and its role in the French government would be critical to achieving the full advantage of adopting this mode, subject to modifications essential in the context of Ireland's government. A central administrative court, smaller, but comparable to the Section du Contentieux (the 'contentious' or judicial section) of the Conseil d'État would have to be established. It could exercise controls to achieve greater uniformity in administrative law procedures since it would provide a simple and relatively inexpensive appeals process to one central court devoted to administrative law matters, with power to make final decisions for persons aggrieved by determinations of departments and administrative tribunals (and set precedent for such bodies), in place of the current system of appeals to the courts in Ireland. Its effectiveness would also depend upon applying certain, if not all, concepts and procedures developed by the French administrative court system, some of which differ in various degrees from concepts and procedures typical in common-law, non-administrative court countries. For research and development of legislation or regulations on administrative law and provision of supportive training and advice, modified versions of certain powers of the Conseil d'État would seem to be necessary. In France, bills introduced into Parliament are submitted for advice to the

Conseil d'État, and when the government legislates by decree (which has the force and effect of law), such decrees must also be submitted to the Conseil d'État for its advice. In this regard, the Conseil d'État has the last word through its judicial power to annul a decree which does not conform to the original text or the modifications which the Conseil has suggested. The Conseil d'État must be consulted in respect of the content of administrative regulations made to supplement details of Acts passed by the Parliament. It also acts as general legal adviser to the government and ministers, and carries out a supervisory role over the administration through four sections: finance, home affairs, public works and social matters, with widely defined spheres encompassing the departments and local administration. It submits an annual report to the President of the Republic which contains both a summary of work done and recommendations with respect to administration or legislation.[18]

The status, role and functions of the Conseil d'État are directly related to French government and law and have been a part of that system since the establishment of the Conseil d'État in 1799. The French constitutional, legal and governmental system has elements and characteristics different from those of Ireland. To transplant this institution to Ireland would involve constitutional and legal adjustments which seem excessive in relation to the objectives of dealing with the issues and needs of Irish administrative law identified above. A less far reaching alternative to this type of oversight mode, i.e. adopting a central administrative court along the lines of the Ash Council proposal in the United States (but not restricted in jurisdiction to a limited number of named agencies as in that proposal)[19] would also provide the same advantages of a court specialising and expert in both law and administration. Such a court would exert influence through its review on appeal from administrative actions and determinations for improved organisational arrangements and procedures reflecting concepts of natural and constitutional justice among the various administrative agencies. However, if only a central administrative court is established, certain important needs will not be met such as continuing survey and research on issues in administrative law, providing recommendations for legislative acts related to such issues, and providing support services.

Two basic problems arise in the Conseil d'État or central administrative court mode. There is the constitutional-legal problem of dividing jurisdiction between a central administrative court and the traditional court system, which has been a source of considerable litigation and difficulties in France. A basic conceptual problem involving underlying values is that of losing the viewpoint of judges who are in the traditional court system and thus have the broader perspective of generalists dealing in the various branches of law and cognisant of the common law, in reviewing administrative determinations affecting the rights of individuals. Administrative law is related to constitutional, criminal and various aspects of civil law. Judicial review and resolution of conflict over administrative determinations frequently benefit from several branches of law being brought to bear in the court's judgment.

Central Oversight Agency for Administrative Process and Justice

A central agency to oversee the organisation and processes of public bodies for effecting administrative justice merits the most serious consideration since neither the Ombudsman nor an administrative procedures Act meets the full range of issues and needs of Irish administrative law, and the legal problems in establishing a central administrative court system comparable to the Conseil d'État make its adoption unlikely. In this regard, the recommendations of the working group chaired by Ó Dálaigh C.J. in the 'Note on Administrative Law and Procedure' in the Devlin Report, subject to certain modifications, would seem to have the greatest potential for meeting Irish administrative law issues and needs. It was proposed that ministers should confer by statute to executive agencies powers of decision in the first instance to be made by persons of appropriate rank, such as deciding officers in the Department of Social Welfare. Appeals tribunals should be established in every major executive agency or attached to the parent ministry to serve groups of small agencies with lower volumes of appeals. There should be right of appeal in simple matters to a single appeals officer of the agency with adequate training and independence, while for more complex issues a tribunal composed of three persons combining particular expertise and knowledge of administrative law should be available. If policy matters are involved, a minister's representative should be a member of the tribunal.[20]

To provide centralised oversight of the system of administrative determinations and appeals, an independent Commissioner for Administrative Justice, attached probably to what is now the

Department of Public Service was recommended, with the following powers and functions:

1. Initially preparing legislation for his office, regulating existing tribunals and constituting new ones; expressing principles and general directives to govern the procedures of tribunals and formulating access to judicial review.

2. Arranging to recruit and have trained a necessary corps of tribunal chairmen and appeals officers.

3. Exercising a power of review on questions of fact, discretion and procedure of the working of a tribunal leading to a report and comment on specific decisions, but not including the power to alter a particular decision.

4. On review of questions of law, inviting the High Court to give an interpretation of any point of law developing from a decision of an appeal tribunal, when the Commissioner feels that an important public issue is involved or that the law as interpreted by the appeals body has too harsh an impact on the individual. Such action by the Commissioner should involve no financial risk to the citizen.

5. Advising on aspects of administrative law in relation to existing legislation, and preparation of new legislation as well as in establishment of new tribunals and appointment of their members.

6. Performing the functions of an ombudsman in following up complaints from the public in instances where no tribunal may exist or where there has been an exhaustion of administrative remedies.[21]

Obviously, an accommodation would have to be made to the fact that the last function listed above will be performed by an already established Ombudsman, either by deleting it from the responsibilities and jurisdiction of the Commissioner for Administrative Justice or by making the Ombudsman a part of the overall operation of the Commissioner's office. The latter alternative could facilitate coordination of the Ombudsman's informal investigatory procedures for providing relief where existing remedies are inadequate for correcting grievances, with the Commissioner's responsibilities and powers for improving the formal processes for administrative justice. On the other hand, it can be argued that the Ombudsman should remain an independent operation, reporting directly to the Dáil, thus constituting an independent source of relief from, and critic of, the aspects of the administrative process falling under the Commissioner's jurisdiction. Another modification should be a grant of rule-making power to the Commissioner for Administrative Justice to make regulations of general application to departments and agencies regarding their rule-making and adjudicatory procedures in those instances where it is deemed premature to enact such requirements in legislation passed by the Oireachtas. His office should have adequate staff to provide for research, advice and training. Such a staff need not be of the size necessary to carry out all research and training activities; rather it should be composed of persons qualified to identify research and training needs and then contract for and audit research and training to be done by appropriate public and private institutions and individuals with the demonstrated skills, experience and capability for providing the research and training projects needed.

Given these functions and powers, the office of a Commissioner for Administrative Justice could meet the issues and needs of Irish administrative law regarding systematic research into, and development of, recommendations for legislation on such matters as a single means of application for judicial review of administrative determinations, revision of statutes to differentiate between rules and directions, and other problems previously mentioned requiring legislation. Based on a survey of existing processes, the Commissioner, in consultation with executive agencies and departments, could develop recommendations for legislation on rule-making procedures of general application or, if research indicates that the time is not right for freezing such policy in legislation, the Commissioner's office could develop regulations of general application on rule-making. Alternatively, his office could experiment with pilot programmes to determine the extent to which different forms of consultation with or participation by the public in rule-making are of benefit to the public and the agencies involved before making any particular form generally applicable.

The Commissioner and his staff would be in an equally strong

position to make systematic surveys and exercise oversight of existing institutional arrangements and procedures for making adjudicatory determinations concerning grant of benefits, licences, or the
issue of directions if the proposals of the Devlin Report for deciding
officers and appeals tribunals in the departments and the powers
of the Commissioner regarding recruiting and training a corps of
appeals officers and tribunal chairmen are followed. The powers to
review and comment on individual determinations of tribunals and
to invite the High Court to rule on questions of law are also critical.
If these functions and powers were augmented by authority to
make regulations of general application on procedural standards for
making adjudicatory determinations, it would further the capability
of the Commissioner and his staff to act as a major force for
stimulating or, if necessary, requiring development of more uniform
institutional arrangements and administrative procedures. These
powers would also enable experimentation with pilot programmes
to accumulate experience and knowledge such as where exceptions
must be made for certain types of agencies and programmes, before
crystallising policies on adjudicatory procedure in a generally applicable administrative procedures Act.

Conclusion

It would appear that the establishment of a Commissioner for
Administrative Justice or comparable executive office having the
functions and powers indicated above would be a logical extension
of recent developments and trends in Ireland's administrative law.
In addition to the governmental studies and publications discussed
above, these developments include the creation of An Bord Pleanála,
which may be viewed as a response in one major area to the issues
and needs of administrative law. The Ombudsman Act 1980 further
indicates an increasing awareness of the issues and needs. There
has also been for some time increasing recognition of, and sophistication in, dealing with administrative law and process in legislative
Acts, administrative rule-making and adjudication, and particularly
in the judgments of the courts in response to such issues and needs
in recent years.

   In this context, the concept of a Commissioner for Administrative
Justice or a comparable central agency should be viewed as a
complementary mode of oversight to those already existing, which

would render services to, as well as exercise controls over, departments and administrative bodies which cannot be provided by traditional means of legislative and judicial oversight. It should not be perceived as a substitute for, but rather as a supplement to, improving the balance between administrative effectiveness in advancing the public interest and protecting individual rights in the operation of administrative law.

Notes to Chapter 11

1. See publications dealing with Irish administrative law listed in footnote 4, pages 12-13.
2. See governmental studies dealing with aspects of Irish administrative law listed in footnote 12, pages 13-14.
3. The Law Reform Commission, Working Paper No. 8, *Judicial Review of Administrative Action: The Problem of Remedies* 77 (1979)
4. Report of Public Services Organisations Review Group, 1966-1969 [Devlin Report]. Note on Administrative Law and Procedure 449
5. See Wade, *Administrative Law* 76-90 (1982) for analysis of Parliamentary Commissioner.
6. See Barry and Whitcomb, *The Legal Foundations of Public Administration* 261 (1981) citing International Bar Association Committee and International Ombudsman Institute in 8 *Ombudsman and Other Complaint Handling Systems Survey* 1 July 1978-30 June 1979.
7. Brown and Garner, *French Administrative Law* 19-20 (1983)
8. P.L. 404, 60 Stat. 237 (1946) as amended through 9th Congress, First Session (1979); 5 USCA sections 551-9, 701-706, 1305, 3344, 5362, 7521
9. See Brown and Garner, *French Administrative Law* (1983)
10. See President's Advisory Council on Executive Organization: *A New Regulatory Framework; Report on Selected Independent Agencies* 53-5 (Jan 1971)
11. Devlin Report, Appendix I 'Note on Administrative Law and Procedure' 453-6
12. Attorney General's Committee on Administrative Procedure, *Final Report, Administrative Procedure in Government Agencies* Senate Document No. 8, 77th Congress, 1st Session, 45-53, 123-4 (1941)
13. Benjamin, Commissioner under Section 8 of the Executive Law, Report to the Governor of the State of New York, *Administrative Adjudication in the State of New York* Vol. I, 18-21 (1942)
14. Wade, *Administrative Law* 796 (1982)
15. Administrative Conference Act 1964, 5 USC, sections 571-5
16. Wade, *Administrative Law* pages 794-801 (1982)
17. Davis, *Administrative Law Treatise* Vol. 1, 32-3 (1978)
18. See Brown and Garner, *French Administrative Law* 42-50 and in general (1983).
19. President's Advisory Council on Executive Organization, *A New Regulatory Framework; Report on Selected Independent Agencies* 53-5 and in general (January 1971)
20. Devlin Report, 447, 451-2
21. Devlin Report 452-5

Appendix 1

Indicators of Growth and Extent of Administrative Law

The growth and scope of administrative law in Ireland is demonstrated by such indicators as the increasing number of statutes which delegate discretionary rule-making, investigating, licensing, directing and adjudicatory power to ministers and their departments, to administrative bodies associated with departments, and to certain 'regulatory' types of state-sponsored bodies. Another indicator is the volume of appeals taken to administrative tribunals from decisions of administrative bodies. The examples summarised below are intended to illustrate but not cover comprehensively such statutory delegations and appeals to tribunals in Ireland.

Department of the Environment

The Department of the Environment oversees activities of local authorities in regard to planning and development, environmental services, housing, pollution control, building and maintenance of roads. It exercises certain controls over local authority staff numbers and salaries, and audit of local accounts, and is concerned with road traffic matters (legislation, vehicle testing and registration). (*Administration Yearbook and Diary* 30-32 (1984)) The Minister for the Environment is given extensive powers to make rules and to issue general directives by statutes such as the Local Government Acts, 1941, 1955 and 1960, the Housing Acts 1966, 1979 and 1982, the Local Government (Planning and Development) Acts 1963-83 and the Local Government (Water Pollution) Act 1977. Local authorities and An Bord Pleanála (which now hears planning and water pollution appeals from local authorities formerly heard by the Minister) are required to have regard to his general directives when discharging their functions. The Minister also has functions of an administrative adjudicatory nature in the review and confirmation of compulsory purchase orders by local authorities under the Housing Act 1966 and in revocation of certificates of reasonable value under the Housing Act 1979.

Department of Health

The Department of Health exercises overall control of the services provided by health authorities. (*Administration Yearbook and Diary* 39-42 (1984)) An example of such control and the regulatory powers of the Minister for Health is the Health (Mental Services) Act 1981, under which the Minister may make regulations, and at the request of a Health Board may designate a hospital or unit as a district psychiatric centre to be maintained by the Health Board. After consultation with a Health Board, he may cancel the registration of a psychiatric centre. No person other than a Health Board may operate a psychiatric home within the functional area of the Health Board unless it is approved and registered by the Board in accordance with regulations of the Minister. If a Health Board refuses to register a psychiatric home or cancels its registration, an appeal may be made to the Minister, who may affirm or reverse the decision and if the latter, direct it to register or restore the home to the register. Power to inspect psychiatric facilities is provided in the statute. Safeguards for patients include psychiatric review by boards appointed by the Minister to review detention of any person upon application by the persons specified in the statute. A decision of a review board may be appealed to the Minister, who may refuse the appeal or direct the discharge of the person conditionally or unconditionally.

An example of direct administration of a regulatory scheme by the Minister is the Misuse of Drugs Act 1977, which provides that possession of controlled drugs is prohibited except under regulations made by the Minister authorising their possession in accordance with a licence. The Minister may give a direction to a medical practitioner or pharmacist who has been convicted of an offence, prohibiting him from having in his possession, prescribing, compounding or supplying a controlled drug specified in the direction. In addition, if the Minister considers a practitioner to be prescribing, administering or supplying or authorising supply of a controlled drug in an irresponsible manner so as to merit a 'special direction', he may refer the matter to the appropriate registration committee. That committee must appoint an investigating committee, and, based on its report, recommend for or against issue of a special direction. If the recommendation is against a special direction, the Minister so notifies the practitioner; if the recommendation is for its issue, the Minister may give a special direction to the practitioner prohibiting him from prescribing, administering or supplying any drugs, or such controlled drugs as specified in his direction. After consultation with the registration committee, the Minister may suspend or cancel a special direction. The power to inspect and demand production of drugs, books or documents is also provided in the Act.

The Tobacco Products (Control of Advertising, Sponsorship and Sales Promotion) Act 1978 enables the Minister for Health to make regulations for the control and regulation of advertising, sponsorship, or any other promotional activities for the sale of tobacco products.

Responsibility for An Bord Uchtála (the Adoption Board) was transferred from the Minister for Justice to the Minister for Health from 1 January 1983. The Adoption Board, under the Adoption Act 1952, must follow an administrative adjudicatory process in making adoption orders which place the adopted child in the same position legally as if it has been born to the adopters in lawful wedlock.

Department of Justice

The Department of Justice administers the courts, prisons, and Garda Síochána in maintaining law and order. Its responsibilities include matters concerning censorship of films and publications, and licensing of firearms, explosives, betting, lotteries, money lending, pawnbroking, dance halls, sale of intoxicating liquor and street trading. (*Administration Yearbook and Diary* 43-5 (1984)) The Film Censor's office grants certificates for public showing of films, subject to appeal to the Censorship of Films Appeal Board in the event of refusal of certificate (Censorship of Films Act 1923 and amending Acts of 1925, 1930 and 1970). The Censorship of Publications Board, under the Censorship of Publications Acts 1929, 1946 and 1967, has power to make regulations and to examine books and periodicals referred to them by individuals or custom officials and based on criteria in the authorising Acts may make prohibition orders forbidding sale, distribution or importation of books. Appeals from prohibition orders may be taken to the Censorship of Publications Appeal Board by the author, editor, or publisher or five members of the Dáil or Seanad acting jointly. Investigating powers related to enforcement are granted by the statutes; and the Censorship of Publications Board maintains a register of prohibited publications. In accordance with statutory provisions and procedural rules of the Minister for Justice, the District Courts and Garda Síochána administer licensing systems to regulate possession of firearms (Firearms Acts 1925-71), bookmakers (Betting Act 1931), moneylenders (Moneylenders Act 1933) and dance halls (Public Dance Halls Act 1935). The sale and consumption of intoxicating liquor is subject to an elaborate and complex licensing system also administered by the District Courts and Garda Síochána under the Licensing Acts, 1833-1981 (alternatively referred to as Intoxicating Liquor Acts).

Department of Labour

Among the Department of Labour's responsibilities are manpower policy (schemes for placement, occupational guidance), employment related schemes, industrial relations, and administration of worker protection legislation (terms of employment, occupational health, safety and welfare, non-discrimination, unfair dismissals, employment equality). The Labour Court, established by the Industrial Relations Act 1946, is concerned with resolution of industrial disputes. If an industrial relations officer does not achieve agreement in an industrial dispute, the conflicting parties may request formal investigation and recommendation by the Court. The Court makes employment regulation orders based on proposals from Joint Labour Committees which establish legally enforceable minimum pay rates. Employment agreements registered with the Court on pay or conditions of employment are binding on workers and employers in the category to which they apply.

Under the Industrial Relations Act 1969, Rights Commissioners may investigate trade disputes other than those on rates of pay or hours of work and make a recommendation, which may be appealed to the Labour Court for a binding decision. Claims for redress under the Unfair Dismissals Act 1977, and disputes under the Maternity (Protection of Employees) Act 1981, may also be referred to a Rights Commissioner, whose recommendations under either Act may be appealed to the Employment Appeals Tribunal. Such claims and disputes also may be referred directly to the Employment Appeals Tribunal (established by the Redundancy Payments Act 1967). The

Tribunal also determines disputes arising under the Redundancy Payments Acts and the Minimum Notice and Terms of Employment Act 1973. The Employment Equality Agency, established by the Employment Equality Act 1977, supervises operation of the Anti-Discrimination (Pay) Act 1974 and the Employment Equality Act 1977; after formal investigation it may issue non-discrimination notices requiring that conduct contravening the Acts cease, enforceable by High Court injunction.

The Safety in Industry 1980 empowers the Minister to make regulations for safety and health of workers, to make investigations on the request of employee safety representatives, or in the event of an accident, and to issue prohibition notices (directions) to stop activities contrary to safety in a factory. (*Administration Yearbook and Diary* 45-8 (1984))

Department of Social Welfare

The Social Welfare (Consolidation) Act 1981 provides for a wide range of social insurance and social assistance schemes. The Act gives the Minister extensive powers of investigation by his inspectors into applications for benefit and assistance. Applications are determined, in the case of pensions by the local pensions committee and in regard to other benefit and assistance schemes by deciding officers appointed by the Minister with appeal to appeals officers by dissatisfied clients who have the powers associated with adjudicatory hearings such as administering oaths to witnesses, requiring their attendance and the production of documents. They may decide matters on appeal as if they were being decided for the first time.

Department of Industry, Trade, Commerce and Tourism

Among the administrative bodies of the Department of Industry, Trade, Commerce and Tourism is the Restrictive Practices Commission established by the Restrictive Practices Act 1972. It holds inquiries on the recommendation of the Examiner of Restrictive Practices or at the request of the Minister into the conditions alleged to be in restraint of trade or monopolistic which obtain in regard to the supply and distribution of goods or the provision of services. It has power to summon witnesses and require the production of documents. The Commission reports to the Minister who may then make an order or rules to prevent restrictive practices in an industry.

Under the Mergers, Take-overs and Monopolies (Control) Act 1978, the Minister on written notice of a proposed merger, as required by the Acts, may prohibit the merger absolutely or allow it subject to conditions. Before giving his decision, the Minister may require the Examiner of Restrictive Practices to give an opinion as to whether the proposed merger or take-over is against the common good according to scheduled criteria.

Regulatory-Type State-Sponsored Bodies

In addition to commercial, developmental, and cultural state-sponsored bodies, there are certain regulatory and advisory bodies, in which the regulatory role is a major aspect. The first two of the examples of this type of state-sponsored body are engaged primarily in regulation of economic enterprises; the remaining five are concerned with maintaining standards of professions through rule-making and registration processes (which are essentially licensing systems).

Bord na gCon (Irish Greyhound Board)
The Irish Greyhound Board, established under the Greyhound Industry Act 1958, controls the promotion and operation of greyhound racing and coursing. It also licenses greyhound racing tracks, officials employed at tracks, makes coursing regulations, authorises bookmakers to do business at tracks and collects a levy on course bets. It may conduct investigations and may issue exclusion orders to be enforced by track officials against persons associated with the industry such as greyhound trainers. (*Administration Yearbook and Diary* 118 (1984))

The Nuclear Energy Board (An Bord Fuinnimh Nuicleigh)
The general functions of the Nuclear Energy Board, established under the Nuclear Energy Act 1971, include regulation and control of the use, transportation and disposal of radioactive materials through making safety regulations and monitoring radiation so as to safeguard the public. (*Administration Yearbook and Diary* 138 (1984))

An Bord Altranais (Nursing Board)
The Nursing Board established under the Nurses Acts, 1950 to 1961 approves hospitals as training hospitals, examines and registers

nurses, and acts as the disciplinary body for the nursing profession, with power to make rules, investigate complaints, remove nurses from, and restore them to, the register. (*Administration Yearbook and Diary* 117 (1984))

Bord na Radharcmhastóirí (Opticians Board)
The Opticians Board makes rules with the approval of the Minister for Health in respect of its functions of training and registration of ophthalmic and dispensing opticians and the control of the practice of optics. It is illegal to prescribe spectacles unless a person is a registered medical practitioner or registered ophthalmic optician. (*Administration Yearbook and Diary* 119 (1984); Opticians Act 1956)

Dental Board
The Dental Board, established under the Dentists Act 1928, exercises controls over the dental profession and maintains the register of dentists. (*Administration Yearbook and Diary* 123 (1984))

The Medical Council
The Medical Practitioners Act 1978 established the Medical Council and made it an offence punishable by fine and/or imprisonment falsely to represent oneself as a registered medical practitioner. An unregistered person may not sue for recovery of medical fees or sign various medical certificates. To be registered as a medical practitioner one must meet statutory standards and satisfy the Council that one has been trained and passed examinations specified by Council regulations. The same process applies to qualify for registration in the register of medical specialists maintained by the Council. The Council may refuse to register a person otherwise entitled to be registered, on the grounds of unfitness to practise medicine, or may grant a provisional or temporary registration. The Medical Council may initiate an inquiry to be conducted by its Fitness to Practise Committee into alleged professional misconduct or unfitness, based on findings of the Committee in its report to the Council. The Council may erase a practitioner's name from the register, suspend his or her registration, censure or admonish the practitioner, and later may restore the practitioner to the register. In addition, the Council has duties in relation to education and training, and functions relating to directives of the Council of the European Communities as to education and training.

Veterinary Council
The Veterinary Council, established under the Veterinary Surgeons Act 1931, is charged with the registration and control of veterinary surgeons under the Veterinary Surgeons Acts, 1931, 1952 and 1960 and after investigation of a complaint may suspend or remove a person from the register. (*Administration Yearbook and Diary* 145 (1984))

Administrative Tribunals: Volume and Disposition of Appeals

An Bord Pleanála
An Bord Pleanála is a regulatory-type state-sponsored body, with functions which are essentially those of an administrative tribunal for deciding appeals, under the Local Government (Planning and Development) Acts, 1963 to 1983. The majority of these appeals are from refusals by planning authorities under section 26, 1963 Act of applications by entrepreneurs for permission for development of land. Appeals are also against conditions attached to permissions and by third parties against grant of permission (see Table 1). The aggregate effect of these decisions in regard to degree of reversal, variation or confirmation of the original decision is summarised in Table 2 below. The next highest number of appeals to the Board is on references as to whether what is being done is development or not or is exempted development, and from tree preservation orders (see Table 3).

The Board also hears appeals under the Local Government (Water Pollution) Act 1977, since this function was transferred to the Board by order of the Minister for the Environment in 1978. (For number of appeals see Table 4.) (See An Bord Pleanála, *Annual Report and Accounts* for 1981, 1982, 1983)

Table 1: Appeals under section 26, 1963 Act to An Bord Pleanála

Year	Total appeals	Third party appeals	Invalid appeals	Appeals withdrawn	Appeals determined	Total appeals disposed of	Appeals on hand at start and end of year
1981	4,526	868	381	698	2,980	4,059	1,710/2,177
1982	4,740	1,040	351	733	2,578	3,662	2,177/3,255
1983	3,593	880	305	558	3,484	4,396[a]	3,255/2,452

Source: An Bord Pleanála *Annual Reports and Accounts* 1981, 1982 and 1983.
[a] Includes 49 appeals not considered because the original application for permission was withdrawn by the applicant or the appeal or application was dismissed or declared withdrawn pursuant to section 5 of the Local Government (Planning and Development) Act 1982 or sections 16, 17 or 18 of the Local Government (Planning and Development) Act 1983.

Table 2: Results of appeals to An Bord Pleanála

	Decision of planning authority reversed		Decision of planning authority varied		Decision of planning authority confirmed	
Year	No.	%	No.	%	No.	%
1981	809	27.2	464	15.5	1,707	57.3
1982	718	27.9	380	14.7	1,480	57.4
1983	1,011	29.0	598	17.2	1,875	53.8

Source: An Bord Pleanála, *Annual Reports and Accounts* 1981, 1982 and 1983

Table 3: Summary of Appeals to An Bord Pleanála on References and Tree Preservation Orders

	References[a]				Tree Preservation Orders		
Year	On hand/ received during year	Invalid/ withdrawn	Decided	On hand end of year	On hand/ received during year	Decided	On hand end of year
1981	12/30	0/1	22	1[b]	40/1	4	37[c]
1982	20/46	4/4	21	37	37/6	3	40[c]
1983	37/54	16/6	27	42	40/3	40	3

Source: An Bord Pleanála *Annual Reports and Accounts* 1981, 1982 and 1983.
[a] 'Reference' means a reference under section 5 of the Local Government (Planning and Development) Act 1963.
[b] No statement made on cases on hand at end of year.
[c] Appeals in abeyance pending outcome of discussions at local level.

**Table 4: Summary of Water Pollution (Discharges to Sewers and to Waters)
Appeals to An Bord Pleanála**

Year	On hand start of year	Received during year	Invalid or withdrawn	Decided	On hand end of year
1981	55	43	5	13	80
1982	80	29	13	45	51
1983	51	28	16[a]	24	39

Source: An Bord Pleanála, *Annual Reports and Accounts* 1981, 1982 and 1983.
[a] Of these 16, 2 appeals were late, 14 withdrawn.

Labour Court
With regard to the Labour Court and its functions of dealing with labour disputes through its conciliation service and recommendations issued on cases referred to it, Table 5 indicates the increasing interventions by the Labour Court since 1971.

**Table 5: Disputes dealt with by the Conciliation Service and
Recommendations made by the Labour Court**

Year	Disputes dealt with by Conciliation Service	Recommendations issued by Court
1971	628	162
1973	855	326
1975	1,108	403
1977	1,175 (89,200)[a]	462 (115,600)[a]
1983	2,090 (330,714)[a]	1,045 (226,629)[a]

Source: McDonagh and Casey, *Personnel and Industrial Relations Directory 1979-80* 258, citing *Labour Court 31st Annual Report for 1977* Prl. 7110; *Labour Court Annual Report* (1983).
[a]Figures available from both sources used in compiling this table indicate the numbers of workers involved in disputes dealt with by the Conciliation Service and the recommendations issued by the Labour Court. These figures are given in brackets for 1977 and 1983 in the table.

Employment Appeals Tribunal
The Employment Appeals Tribunal hears appeals and claims under the Redundancy Payments Acts, 1967 to 1974; the Minimum Notice and Terms of Employment Act, 1973; the Unfair Dismissals Act, 1977; and the Maternity (Protection of Employees) Act, 1981, as well as hearing appeals against decisions of Rights Commissioners under the Unfair Dismissals and Maternity Protection Acts (see Table 6).

Table 6: Number and disposition of appeals to Employment Appeals Tribunal

Act and Years	No. of appeals referred	Allowed	Dismissed	Withdrawn during hearing	Appeals disposed of without a hearing	Total no. of appeals disposed
Redundancy Payment						
1981	612	327	143	77	194	741
1982	1,026	455	154	114	165	888
1983	1,173	579	163	99	197	1,038
Minimum Notice and Terms of Employment						
1981	1,313	858	205	96	251	1,410
1982	1,965	1,052	245	109	193	1,599
1983	3,045	2,058	291	140	293	2,782
Maternity (Protection of Employees)						
1981	3	—	—	—	—	—
1982	18	1	4	1	6	12
1983	19	5	9	—	—	14
Unfair Dismissals						
1981	730	254	286	103	159	802
1982	1,020	181	397	131	207	916
1983	1,120	193	372	172	236	973
All four Acts						
1981	2,658	1,439	634	276	604[a]	2,953
1982	4,029	1,689[a]	800[a]	355[a]	571[a]	3,415[a]
1983	5,357	2,835[a]	835[a]	411[a]	726[a]	4,807[a]

Source: Employment Appeals Tribunal, 14th-16th *Annual Reports* Annexes 3(a), 1981-1983.
[a] Some of the appeals heard by the Tribunal in this year were referred in the preceding year.

Department of Social Welfare Appeals Officers
The Department compiles statistics annually of the number of appeals against decisions given by deciding officers in respect of a wide range of schemes (see Table 7).

Table 7: Appeals against decisions given by deciding officers and pension committees

	Awaiting decision at beginning of January	Received	Decided	Withdrawn	Sent on inquiry during the year	Awaiting decision at end of December
1978	2,697	15,915	18,062	77	–	473
1980	438	14,106	12,269	72	1,423	780
1982	457	13,663	12,352	79	1,157	532
1 July 1983–30 June 1984	762	20,753	17,317	85	2,338	1,775

Source: *Department of Social Welfare Annual Reports* 1976-8, 1979-81; *Statistical Information on Social Welfare Services* 1983-4.

Office of the Revenue Commissioners
The Office of the Revenue Commissioners is responsible for the assessment and collection of taxes and duties. The taxpayer has a statutory right of appeal to the Appeals Commissioners against a tax assessment. The number of appeals to the Revenue Commissioners is increasing (see Tables 8 and 9).

To give enough time to lodge appeals before demands are issued by the Collector General, assessments are made some three months before due date. Consequently, virtually all assessments are estimated, and appeals lodged in most instances as a matter of course. If the inspector and taxpayer disagree, an appeal is listed for determination by the Appeals Commissioners. The taxpayer also may request rehearing by the Circuit Court, and both parties may appeal on a point of law to the High Court. These processes (including taxpayer delay in submitting data) lead to an accumulation of appeals awaiting determination. Remedial measures in the Finance Act 1982 were designed to reduce delays in the settlement of appeals and to counteract abuses. (See report of the Comptroller and Auditor General in *Appropriation Accounts 1982* Pl. 1530.)

**Table 8: Ordinary appeals to the Office of the Revenue Commissioners
(1982)**

Type of Tax	Number unsettled at 1 January 1982	Number received in year	Number determined in year	Number unsettled at 31 December 1982
Income Tax (Schedules D & E) and PAYE estimates on employers	92,408	14,761	35,680	71,489
Corporation Tax	19,669	3,974	10,674	12,969
Value Added Tax	568	1,172	1,133	607
Capital Gains Tax	3,053	n.a.	n.a.	3,936

Source: *Report of the Comptroller and Auditor General on the Appropriation Accounts, 1982* Pl.1530.

**Table 9: Ordinary appeals to the Office of the Revenue Commissioners
(1983)**

Type of Tax	Number unsettled at 1 January 1983	Number received in year	Number determined in year	Number unsettled at 31 December 1983
Income Tax (Schedules D & E) excluding PAYE estimates on employers	102,848	14,118	48,538	68,428
Corporation Tax	23,103	5,028	14,452	13,679
Value Added Tax	607	1,321	1,255	673
PAYE estimates on employers	5,691	3,899	4,675	4,915
Capital Gains Tax	3,936	n.a.	n.a.	5,271

Source: Table 9 is compiled from the reply to a Parliamentary Question for Tuesday, 27 November 1984 by Richard Bruton, TD which asked for a written answer from the Minister for Finance 'in respect of each of the past five financial years, the number of ordinary appeals unsettled at the end of the year; number of appeals received in the year; and if he will give the most up-to-date position in relation to 1984'. The Minister for Finance replied to the effect that the Revenue Commissioners had advised that statistics were not recorded in such a manner as to provide the information requested for the years prior to 1982, and to obtain such information would require an enquiry at a disproportionate cost. After referring to the Appropriation Accounts 1982 (Pl.1530) for information for 1982, a schedule of comparable statistics was attached to the Minister's reply.

Index